A
GENEVA
SERIES
COMMENTARY

1 PETER

EXPOSITORY DISCOURSES ON

1 PETER

John Brown D.D.

Volume One

THE BANNER OF TRUTH TRUST

THE BANNER OF TRUTH TRUST
3 Murrayfield Road, Edinburgh EH12 6EL
P.O. Box 652, Carlisle, Pennsylvania 17013, U.S.A.

First published in three volumes 1848
First Banner of Truth Trust edition in two volumes 1975

ISBN for set of 2 volumes 0 85151 204 6
ISBN for this volume 0 85151 205 4—vol. 1

*Printed by offset lithography in Great Britain
by Billing & Sons Limited, Guildford and London*

PREFACE.

THE work now laid before the public is substantially a Commentary, though in a form somewhat peculiar. It is not a continuous comment on words and clauses, nor does it consist of scholia or annotations, nor of lectures in the sense in which that word is ordinarily employed in this country, nor of sermons, either on select passages, or on the successive verses, of the sacred book, which is its subject. The Epistle is divided into paragraphs, according to the sense—of course varying very considerably in length. Each of these paragraphs embodying one leading thought, forms the subject of a separate discourse, in which an attempt is made to explain whatever is difficult in the phraseology, and to illustrate the doctrinal or practical principles which it contains; the object being not to discuss, in a general and abstract manner, the subjects which the text may suggest, but to bring clearly out the Apostle's statements, and their design; and to show how the statements are fitted to gain the objects for which they are made. If the Author has been able, in any good measure, to realise his own idea, the exposition will be found at once exegetical, doctrinal, and practical.

Whatever can be interesting and intelligible only to the scholar, has been thrown into the notes. Had the Author yielded to his own tastes these notes would probably have been more numerous and elaborate than they are. But the recollection of the primary design of the work checked the inclination to indulge in philological remark ; though he trusts that in almost every instance, where the exegesis is difficult or doubtful, the foundation of the interpretation adopted has been indicated with sufficient clearness.

The translation of the Epistle, though prefixed to the Expository Discourses, was written after them, and indeed contains a condensed statement of the result of the Author's investigations. This accounts for the fact that, in an instance or two, the sense given in the translation slightly differs from that commented on in the Exposition.

To prevent disappointment, it is right to state that the object of the Author has been to produce not so much an original work, as a satisfactory exposition. In his estimate of the duties of an interpreter of Scripture, next to the careful study of the original text, ranks the attentive reading of what has been published for its illustration. Under this conviction he has studied the Epistle, not only without note or comment, but with all the notes and comments that were within his reach; and the book he now respectfully lays before the church contains the substance of all that, in his thoughts and reading, seemed best fitted to illustrate the meaning and promote the objects of the inspired writer. Of the helps of which he has availed himself, a list is furnished at the close of these prefatory remarks.

He has distinguished by an asterisk those to which
he has been chiefly indebted.

There is one author to whom his obligations are
peculiarly great—ARCHBISHOP LEIGHTON. The in-
dex bears witness to the number of references to
"The Practical Commentary upon the First Epistle
General of St Peter;" and, in perusing the Discourses, the reader will find many quotations from
its pages. That very remarkable work teaches a
singularly pure and complete theology—a theology
thoroughly evangelical, in the true sense of that
often abused epithet, being equally free from
Legalism on the one hand, and Antinomianism on
the other; in a spirit of enlightened and affectionate
devotion, love to the brotherhood, and charity to all
men; and in a style which, though very unequal,
indicates in its general structure a familiarity with
the classic models of antiquity,—and, in occasional
expressions, is in the highest degree felicitous and
beautiful. As a biblical expositor, LEIGHTON was
above his own age; and, as a theologian and an
experimental and practical writer, few have equalled,
still fewer surpassed him, either before or since his
time.

For these quotations the Author expects thanks
from his readers, most of whom are not likely
to be very familiar with the Archbishop's writings;
and, though not unaware of the hazard to which
he has exposed his own homely manufacture, by
inserting into it—it may be, often somewhat inarti-
ficially—portions from a web of such rich material
and exquisite workmanship, he will greatly rejoice
if these specimens induce his readers to cultivate
a more extensive acquaintance with those truly

precious remains; which, though labouring under more than the ordinary disadvantages of posthumous publications, through the extreme slovenliness with which they, with but few exceptions, were in the first instance edited, are eminently fitted to form the Student of Theology to sound views and a right spirit, and to minister to the instruction and delight of the private Christian; possessing in large measure and rare union, those qualities which must endear them to every christian mind, however uncultured; and those which are fitted to afford high gratification to them in whom the knowledge and love of evangelical truth are connected with literary attainment and polished taste. The experience of Dr Doddridge's correspondent[1] is not singular: " There is a spirit in ARCHBISHOP LEIGHTON I never met with in any human writings, nor can I read many lines in them without being moved." COLERIDGE borrowed his texts from him, in his " Aids to Reflection;" and it is readily acknowledged, that these volumes owe to him their most attractive ornaments.

The Author would probably never have thought of offering these illustrations to the world, had not a number of much respected members of his congregation earnestly solicited him, before increasing age should make it difficult, or approaching death impossible, to furnish them with a permanent memorial of a ministry of considerable length, full of satisfaction to him, and, he trusts, not unproductive of advantage to them. Such an application could not be treated lightly; and, on weighing the

---

[1] Dr Henry Miles.

subject, he found that he durst not refuse to comply with it.

Having arrived at this conviction, it did not appear to him that the object in view could be better gained, than by presenting them with the substance of those illustrations of a very precious portion of the inspired volume, which had already been delivered to them in the ordinary course of pastoral instruction. That this offering, intended for their spiritual improvement and their children's, will be accepted in the spirit in which it is made, he knows them too well to entertain a doubt; and if to them it serve its great objects, he will have an abundant reward. If beyond these limits it should find a favourable reception, and produce salutary effects, this will be an additional subject of agreeable reflection and grateful acknowledgment.

As the copy of the Expository Discourses fell short of filling the number of pages calculated on, room has been found in the third volume for six Sermons; two " on the Son of Man and his Going," and four " on the Duty of Keeping Ourselves in the Love of God," and for the Lecture " on the Ministry of our Lord, and its Results," delivered at the opening of last Session of the Theological Seminary of the United Presbyterian Church; for the publication of all of which a wish had been expressed, by those whose judgment the author respects, and whose wishes he finds it a satisfaction to gratify.

10, GAYFIELD SQUARE, May 1848.

LIST

THE PRINCIPAL AUTHORS CONSULTED

DURING THE COMPOSITION OF

THESE EXPOSITORY DISCOURSES.

Besides the General Commentaries on the whole Scriptures, by *GROTIUS, LE CLERC, POOLE, HENRY, GOADBY, *S. CLARK, SCOTT, A. CLARKE, MANT and D'OYLEY; and on the New Testament, by BEZA, E. SCHMIDT, MARLORATUS, * WOLFIUS, BEAUSOBRE and L'ENFANT, *BENGEL, KUTTNER, ROSENMULLER, HAMMOND, WHITBY, GUYSE, WELLS, DODDRIDGE, and GILPIN, the following works on the Apostolical Epistles, the Catholic Epistles, and the Epistles of Peter, have been consulted :—

1. *JOANNIS CALVINI Commentarii in Epistolas Canonicas Petri, Joannis, Jacobi, et Judæ. Folio, Geneva, 1554.

2. *OIKOYMENIOY Εξηγήσις εις τας επτα καθολικας λεγομενας επιστολας. OECUMENII Expositio in septem illas, quæ Catholicæ dicuntur, Epistolas. Cum interpretatione latina Joannis Hentenii. 4to. Francofurti, 1610.

3. *Paraphrase sur les Epistres Catholiques, par MOYSE AMYRAUT. 8vo. Samur, 1646.

4. An Exposition of all St Paul's Epistles; together with an explanation of those other Epistles of the Apostles St James, Peter, John, and Jude, by DAVID DICKSON, Professor of Divinity in the University of Glasgow. Folio. Lond. 1659.

5. Urim et Thummim seu exegesis Epistolarum Petri et Joannis. Autore D. JOANNE LANGIO, SS. Prof. Theol. in Acad. Hal. 2 vols. folio. Halæ, 1734.

6. * A Paraphrase and Notes on the Seven (commonly called) Catholic Epistles, attempted in imitation of Mr Locke's manner; to which are annexed several Critical Dissertations, by GEORGE BENSON, D.D. 4to. Lond. 1756.

7. Epistolarum Catholicarum Septenarius Græce, cum nova versione

latina ac scholiis grammaticis et criticis. Opera Jo. B. CARP-
ZOVII. 8vo. Halæ, 1790.

8. D. SAM. FRED. NATH. MORI Prælectiones in Jacobi et Petri Epistolas. Edidit Car Aug. Donat. 8vo. Lipsiæ, 1794.

9. A New Literal Translation, from the Original Greek, of all the
Apostolical Epistles; with a Commentary and Notes, philological,
critical, explanatory, and practical, by JAMES MACKNIGHT, D.D.
4 vols. 4to. Edin. 1795.

10. Versio Latina Epistolarum Novi Testamenti, perpetua annotatione
illustrata a GODF. SIGISM. JASPIS. 2 vols. 8vo. Lipsiæ, 1797.

11. *Epistolæ Catholicæ Græce, perpetua annotatione illustratæ a
DAV. JUL. POTT. 2 vols. 8vo. Gotting. 1810.

12. Conciones in Epistolam primam Petri habitæ per D. MEINHAR-
DUM SCHOTANUM, SS. T. P. in Academia Franequerensi. 4to.
Franecker, 1637.

13. Sermons on the First Epistle general of Saint Peter, by NICHOLAS
BYFIELD. Folio. Lond. 1637.

14. S. Apostoli Petri Epistola Catholica prior, perpetuo Commentario
explicata, una cum partitione tum generali totius Epistolæ ac
singulorum capitum, tum speciali singulorum versuum; necnon
cum observatione doctrinarum ex singulis vocibus per JACOBUM
LAURENTIUM, Amstelodamensem. 4to. Campis, 1640.

15. Utriusque Epistolæ Divi Petri Apostoli Explicatio Analytica, docu-
cumentis suis ubique illustrata et usibus ad singularem pietatis
profectum applicata. Authore GULIELMO AMESIO, SS.T.D. 24mo.
Amst. 1650.

16. JONÆ SLICHTINGII A BUKOWIEK Commentarius in priorem Apostoli
Petri Epistolam Catholicam. Bib. Frat. Pol. vol. vii. Folio.
Irenop. 1656.

17. JOANNIS CRELLII Franci Commentarius in prioris Epistolæ Petri
partem. Bib. Frat. Pol. vol. iv. Folio. Eleuther. 1656.

18. *A Brief Exposition of the First and Second Epistle general of
Peter, by ALEXANDER NISBET, Minister at Irwin. 12mo. Lond.
1658.

19. *Commentarius super priorem D. Petri Epistolam, in quo textus
declaratur, quæstiones dubiæ solvuntur, observationes eruuntur, et
loca in speciem pugnantia conciliantur. Opera et studio JOANNIS
GERHARDI, SS. Th. Doc. 4to. Jenæ, 1660.

20. *A Practical Commentary on the First Epistle general of St Peter,
by the Most Reverend Dr ROBERT LEIGHTON, sometime Archbishop of Glasgow. 2 vols. 4to. York and London, 1693, 4.

21. D. Jo. SAL. SEMLERI Paraphrasis in Epistolam I. Petri cum latinæ
translationis varietate et multis notis. 12mo. Halæ, 1783.

22. *Exposition of the First Epistle of Peter, considered in reference to the whole System of Divine Truth. Translated from the German of WILHELM STEIGER, by the Reverend Patrick Fairbairn. 2 vols. 16mo. Edin. 1836.

The ANNOTATA in the CRITICI SACRI, tom. ix. by VALLA, ERASMUS, VATABLUS, CASTALIO, CLARIUS, ZEGERUS, H. STEPHANUS, DRUSIUS, CAMERO, and CAPPELLUS, have been carefully looked at; and also the Notes in CAMERARIUS, RAPHELIUS, ELSNER, KNATCHBULL, KYPKE, PALAIRET, LŒSNER, AL. MORUS, ALBERTI, OTTIUS, KEUCHENIUS, HOMBERGK, BOS, HEINSIUS, BOWYER, and WAKEFIELD.

The Author also gratefully notices the advantages he has derived from FLEETWOOD, STENNET, and JAY, on Relative Duties; from Bishop SANDERSON and JOSEPH FAWCETT on Christian Freedom, and Honouring all Men; from ANDREW FULLER, on the duties of church members to their office-bearers; and from Notes of a Sermon by BINNEY on Christian Courtesy. He has little doubt that there are both thoughts and expressions for which he is indebted to others that are not expressly ascribed to their authors; but his readers will do him but justice in believing, that such obligations are not acknowledged, merely because they have not been observed.

CONTENTS.

I.—PRELIMINARY MATTER.

II.—ORDER AND OUTLINE OF DISCOURSES.

DISCOURSE I.

INTRODUCTORY.

CHAPTER I. 1, 2, pp. 1-24.

Introduction, page 1. PART I. Of the writer of the Epistle; his history, 6; his office, 11. PART II. Of those to whom the Epistle is addressed, 14. PART III. The salutation of the Epistle, 20. NOTES, 22.

DISCOURSE II.

THE CHRISTIAN SALVATION DESCRIBED AND ACKNOW-LEDGED.

CHAPTER I. 3-5, pp. 25-53.

PART I. Of the blessings acknowledged, page 27. § 1. Divine Sonship, 27. § 2. The inheritance provided for them, 30. § 3. The living hope of the inheritance, 36. PART II. Of the acknowledgment of these blessings, 44. § 1. God is the author of these blessings, 44. § 2. It is as the God and Father of our Lord Jesus Christ that God bestows these blessings, 47. § 3. These blessings originate in the abundant mercy of God, 49. § 4. These blessings are of vast magnitude and incalculable value, 51. § 5. The proper method of acknowledging these benefits is to bless their munificent Giver, 51.

DISCOURSE VII.

A FIGURATIVE VIEW OF THE STATE AND CHARACTER OF CHRISTIANS, WITH APPROPRIATE EXHORTATIONS.

CHAPTER II. 1-3. pp. 169-219.

DISCOURSE VIII.

THE PECULIAR PRIVILEGES OF CHRISTIANS, AND HOW THEY OBTAIN THEM.

CHAPTER II. 4-10. pp. 220-321.

DISCOURSE IX.

A SECOND FIGURATIVE VIEW OF THE STATE AND CHARACTER OF CHRISTIANS, WITH APPROPRIATE EXHORTATIONS.

CHAPTER II. 11, 12. pp. 322-340.

DISCOURSE XIII.

DISCOURSE XIV.

III.—TABLE FOR FINDING OUT THE EXPOSITION OF ANY VERSE OR CLAUSE OF THE EPISTLE IN THIS VOLUME.

CHAPTER I.

CHAPTER II.

CHAPTER III.

A TRANSLATION

OF THE

FIRST EPISTLE OF THE APOSTLE PETER.

I. 1. PETER, an Apostle of Jesus Christ, to the elected
sojourners of the dispersion in Pontus, Galatia,

2. Cappadocia, Asia, and Bithynia—*elected* according
to the fore-appointment of God the Father, by a spiritual separation, in order[1] to obedience,[2] and being
sprinkled with the blood of Jesus Christ:[3] May
grace and peace be multiplied to you.

3. Blessed be the God and Father of our Lord
Jesus Christ, who, according to the abundance of
his mercy, has anew made us his children;[4] so as to
give us a living hope[5] through the resurrection of

4. Jesus Christ from the dead; so as to make us heirs
of an inheritance, incorruptible, undefiled, and un-

5. fading, secured in Heaven for you,[6] who are pre-

---

[1] BEZA's theology seems to have mastered his scholarship when he rendered
ιν as = εις by *ad*, and εις as = δια. by *per*. E. α. π. seems = in a state of spiritual
separation, spiritually separated.

[2] Obedience of faith, of the truth, verse 22. Rom. i. 5; xvi. 26; vi. 16, 17.
Acts vi. 7.

[3] Ut obediant, et Jesu Christi sanguine conspergantur.—CASTALIO.

[4] Ch. i. 23. James i. 18. John iii. 3, &c. Fait renaitre, autrement, rege-
nerez.—BEAUSOBRE.

[5] Amat Petrus Epitheton *vivus*.—BENGEL.

[6] Some MSS. of good note read ἡμας us.

served[1] by the power of God through faith, till[2] the salvation prepared to be revealed[3] in the last time;

6. in which time[4] you shall rejoice,[5] who now for a short season (since it is needful), are sorrowful

7. amid manifold trials, that the proof[6] of your faith[7] may be found[8] much more valuable than that of gold (which, even though proved by fire, perisheth), resulting in[9] praise, and honour, and glory, at the

8. revelation of Jesus Christ; whom, though you have not seen him, you love; in whom, though now not looking on him but believing in him, you shall rejoice with an unspeakable and triumphant joy,[10]

9. 10. receiving the end of your faith, soul-salvation;[11] respecting which salvation, prophets who uttered predictions concerning this grace towards you,

11. made inquiry and diligent search, examining what, and what kind, of season,[12] the Spirit of Christ in them did signify, when testifying beforehand of the sufferings in reference to Christ,[13] and the succeeding

---

[1] Guarded. Gal. iii. 23.

[2] Εις, till. Acts iv. 3. Phil. i. 10. Gal. iii. 13, 24. 1 Thess. iv. 15. We have a parallel phrase, 2 Pet. ii. 4, τηρουμινους εις κρισιν.

[3] By being bestowed.

[4] 'Ω cannot grammatically refer to σωτηριαν. Even although it did, as that salvation is future, the rejoicing in it must be future too. HARWOOD takes this view of it.

[5] In quo exultabitis. VULGATE.

[6] Δοκιμιον is not = to δοκιμη, Rom. v. 3; the last is the result of the first; both here and James i. 3, it seems = δοκιμασια.

[7] Explorata vestra fides.—CASTALIO. Your faith once tried.—COVERDALE. MATTHEWS.

[8] STEIGER, i. 136, 137. KNATCHBULL, 292.

[9] ROBINSON. Εις. 3. α.

[10] Exultabitis lætitia inenarrabili et glorificata. VULGATE.

[11] Hoc perinde valet acsi diceretur; " salus æterna." Est enim tacita comparatio vitæ mortalis et caducæ quæ ad corpus pertinet. 1 Cor. v. 5. 'Ινα το πνευμα σωθη.

[12] The period and the circumstances. Quo et quali tempore.—JASPIS. In relation to whom, and what time.—PURVER. Quel tems, et quelle conjuncture. —BEAUSOBRE.

[13] Or the sufferings until Christ, that is, the manifold trials, till the revelation of Jesus Christ, v. 7.

12. glories; to whom it was revealed that, not to themselves, but to us they were ministering those things,
which have now been declared to you by those who,
inspired by the Holy Spirit sent down from Heaven,
have proclaimed to you the good news; into which
things angels earnestly inquire.[1]

13. Seeing these things are so, girding up the loins
of your mind,[2] being watchful,[3] hope[4] steadfastly[5] for
this grace, which is to be brought to you in the

14. revelation[6] of Jesus Christ. As children of obedience, not fashioning yourselves by your former

15. propensities in *your state of* ignorance, but in imitation of the holy one, who has called you,[7] be you

16. also holy in your whole behaviour; because it is

17. written, ' Be ye holy, for I am holy.' And since
you call Father,[8] Him who judges the work of
every man without respect of persons, pass the
time of your sojourning in reverence *of him;*

18. knowing that you have been ransomed from your
foolish[9] hereditary[10] course of behaviour, not by cor-

19. ruptible things—silver or gold—but by precious
blood,[11] as of a lamb, perfect and spotless, *the blood*

20. of Christ;[12] fore-appointed, indeed, before the

[1] James i. 25.

[2] Lumbos succingimus ad iter, ad opus, ad bella, ad ministerium.—C. A.
LAPIDE. Prepared, ready for work or warfare, for toil or travel.

[3] Vigilance, not moderation, seems the idea here. Awake to all events.

[4] Τελιως ελπισατε = κατεχετε την ελπιδα τελιαν; or as the Apostle to the Hebrews
has it, ch. iii. 6. Perfecte sperate.—VULGATE.

[5] Or perseveringly, τελιως.

[6] At his second coming, when He shall be unveiled, manifested to be what he
is. By the revelation.—HAMMOND. By the declaring.—COVERDALE. MAT-
THEWS. CRANMER. The figures here seem borrowed from Luke xii. 35, &c.

[7] Literally " according to." ROM. xv. 5. Κατα Χριστον Ιησουν, rendered in the
margin " after the example of." Ad exemplum illius sancti qui vocavit vos.—
ERAS. SCHMID.

[8] Call on the Father.

[9] Eph. iv. 17.

[10] Handed down from father to son.

[11] 'Ως = ut. ætiologia του precioso.—BENGEL.

[12] For the rendering of this verse, which seems to me to bring out the Apos-

foundation of the world, but manifested in these

21. last times, on account[1] of you, who through him, believe in God who raised him from the dead and gave him glory, so that your faith and hope are in God.

22. Having purified your souls by the obedience of the truth, through the Spirit,[2] so as sincerely from a pure heart, to love the brethren, love one another

23. intensely, being anew made the children *of God*, not of a perishable race,[3] but of an imperishable, through the living word of God, which endureth

24. for ever ; for " all flesh is as grass, and all the glory of it[4] as the flower of grass ; the grass withereth,

25. and its flower falleth off, but the word of the Lord endureth for ever." Now the gospel which has been proclaimed to you is this word.

II. 1. Laying aside then all malice, and all deceit, and simulations, and envyings, and all evil speakings,

2. like new-born babes, desire the unadulterated spiritual milk,[5] that by it you may grow unto salvation ;[6]

---

tle's precise sense very clearly and forcibly, I am indebted to my learned and ingenious colleague and much esteemed friend, the Rev. Dr EADIE.

[1] On behalf of you.

[2] Διὰ πνευματος. The evidence of the genuineness of this clause is so deficient, that MILL, BENGEL, GRIESBACH, and LACHMANN, would omit it. If genuine, its meaning is doubtful. It may qualify υπακον = πνευματικη.

[3] Σπορα, genus. proles. SCAPULA refers to Sophocles and Euripides, in support of this sense. The cognate word σπερμα is often used in this way. John vii. 42; viii. 33, 37. Gal. iii. 16, 19, et al. If λογος Θεου be merely exegetical, would not the same preposition have been connected with it as with the word of which it is the interpretation?

[4] Αυτης is the preferable reading.

[5] Rationale sine dolo lac.—VULGATE. That reasonable milk that is without corruption.—COVERDALE. MATTHEWS. The milk not of the body, but of the soul, which is without deceit.—CRANMER. The reasonable milk of the word, which is without deceit.—BISHOPS' BIBLE. The rational pure milk.—HAMMOND. Le lait spirituel, et tout pur.—MONS VERSION. Λογικον, i. q. πνευματικον. v. 5. —VATER. " Illis temporibus rex Messias apparebit synagogæ Israeliticæ ad quem Israelitæ sic dicent : veni esto frater noster, et profiscamur Hierosolyma et sugemus tecum gustum legis, quemadmodum infans ubera matris suæ sugit. TARGUM in Cant. viii. 1. Apud WETSTEIN.

[6] Εις σωτηριαν is found in a number of the most ancient Codd., and is admitted into the text by the most distinguished critical editors of the New Testament.

3. seeing[1] you have tasted the goodness[2] of the
4. Lord; coming to whom, *the* living stone, by men
disapproved, but by God chosen and honoured,
5. even you[3] as living stones are built up a spiritual
house, a holy priesthood to offer spiritual sacrifices
6. well pleasing to God, by Jesus Christ; according
to what is contained in the Scripture, " Behold, I lay
in Sion, a corner stone, chosen, honoured; and he
7. that believeth on him shall not be ashamed." To
you then who believe there is honour,[4] but to them
who disbelieve *there is dishonour;* the stone which the
builders disallowed, has become the principal corner
8. stone, and a stumbling stone, and a rock of offence,
on which they who believe not the word stumble, to
9. which also they were appointed. But you *are* a
chosen race, a royal priesthood, a holy nation, a
people for a peculiar possession *to God,* that you
may proclaim the excellencies of Him who has
called you out of darkness into his marvellous
10. light; who once were not a people, but now are
the people of God; who once were not the objects of *his* mercy, but now are the objects of *his*
mercy.
11. Beloved, I exhort you, as foreigners and sojourners, to keep yourselves from fleshly lusts, which
12. war against the soul, conducting yourselves honourably among the heathen, that with regard to that in
which they speak evil of you as evil-doers, they may,
from your good works,[5] having observed them, glorify
13. God in the day of visitation. Submit yourselves
therefore, from a regard to the Lord, to every

[1] Quia.—CARPZOV. E*.*—LACHMANN.
[2] Psal. xxxiv. 8.
[3] Parietes spirituales quia homines pii sunt præcipuum templum.—R. AL-
SCHECH in Hag. ii. 10. Ap. WETSTEIN.
[4] Vobis igitur honor credentibus.—VULGATE.
[5] Ex bonis operibus vos considerantes.—VULGATE. May revering *you* (*εκ*
from), by your good works.—HAMMOND.

14. institution of man,[1] for the punishment of evil doers, and the praise of those who do well ; whether it be king as supreme, or governors as commis-
15. sioned by him; for thus, is it the will of God, that doing well you muzzle the ignorance of fool-
16. ish men. As free men, yet not using your liberty as a cloak[2] of wickedness, but as the servants of
17. God, honour all men, love the brotherhood, fear God, honour the King.[3]
18. Servants, submit yourselves, with all reverence, to your masters, not only to the kind and gentle, but
19. also to the perverse ;[4] for this is well pleasing, if any one who suffers unjustly, from religious prin-
20. ciple endure his grievances patiently; for what credit is it if, when you commit a fault, and are chastised, you endure patiently? but if suffering while acting properly, you patiently endure, this
21. is well pleasing to God. For to this were you called ; because even Christ suffered on our account, leaving us foot-prints[5] that we should follow in his
22. steps, who committed no fault, and in whose mouth
23. no deceit was found ; who, being reviled, did not revile in return, suffering did not threaten, but com-
24. mitted himself to the righteous judge ; who himself, in his own body, bore our sins to the cross,[6] that we dying by sins might live by righteousness : by
25. whose weals[7] you are healed ; for you were as stray-

---

[1] Humanæ creaturæ.—VULGATE. Humanæ ordinationi.—BEZA. Creature of man.—WICLIF. Humane creature.—RHEMISTS. HAMMOND.

[2] A covering of, a pretext for. Use it neither for concealing nor for excusing wickedness.

[3] The Roman emperor is termed βασιλευς by the Greek writers. POLYŒNI Strag., p. 1. HEROD, i. 3. The usage of the Jews appears from John xix. 15. Acts xvii. 7.

[4] Cross, ill-conditioned, morose, wayward. Tyrants.—WICLIF.

[5] WAKEFIELD. 1 John ii. 6.

[6] Lit. Stake, timber. Επι. ROBINSON in verb. iii. 6. α and β.

[7] Μωλωψ non est vulnus sed vibex, sive vestigium verberum aut flagellorum Πληγη μαστιγος ποιει μωλωπας. Ecclus. xxviii. 17.—RAPHELIUS.

ing sheep, but you have now returned to the shepherd, and overseer of your souls.

III. 1. Likewise, you wives, submit yourselves to your own husbands; that if some of them are disbelievers in the doctrine, they may, without the doctrine,[1] be
2. won over by contemplating your pious, chaste be-
3. haviour. Let your adorning not be the outward adorning of plaited hair, or of golden ornaments,
4. or of curious dress; but let the hidden man of the heart *be adorned* with the imperishable *ornament* of that meek and quiet spirit, which, in the estimation
5. of God, is of great value.[2] For even thus, of old, the holy women who trusted in God adorned themselves, submitting themselves to their own husbands
6. (as Sarah, whose children you are, obeyed Abraham, calling him Lord[3]), doing what is good, and alarmed by no terrors.
7. Likewise, you husbands, dwell with your wives with a wise consideration of the greater weakness of the female frame; giving them honour as also fellow heirs of the gracious gift of life, that your prayers may not be hindered.
8. Finally, be all of one mind and one heart,[4] love
9. as brethren. Be compassionate, be courteous. Do not render injury for injury, or railing for railing; but, on the contrary, bless, knowing that you are
10. called to this, that you may obtain a blessing: " For as to him, who wishes to enjoy life[5] and to see good days, let him restrain his tongue from mischief, and
11. his lips from speaking deceit; let him depart from

[1] As the article is wanting, α. λ. may not refer to τ. λ., but may mean without discourse or discussion.

[2] Much set by.—COVERDALE. GENEVA. MATTHEWS.

[3] CARPZOV. WAKEFIELD. Gal. iv. 31. Gen. xii. 13, 15; xx. 2; xxvi. 7. Prov. iii. 25.

[4] Be united in judgment and affection. Unanimes, compatientes.—VULGATE. Unanimes, eodem modo affecti.—CASTALIO. Omnes eodem animo, eodem affectu.—CARPZOV.

[5] BENSON. The opposite of αγαπᾶν ζωην is μισειν ζωην. Ecc. ii. 17.

mischief and do good, let him seek peace and pursue
12. it ; for the eyes of the Lord are upon the righteous,
and his ears towards their prayer ; but the face of the
13. Lord is against[1] evil doers." And who shall harm
14. you if you are imitators of Him who is good?[2] But
even if you should suffer for righteousness, you are
blessed. Be not then afraid of their terror, neither
15. be troubled, but sanctify the Lord God in your
hearts. And be always ready to vindicate, with meekness and reverence, your hope to every one who asks
16. of you an account of it, maintaining a good conscience, in order that in the thing regarding which
they speak against you as evil-doers, those who
slander your good Christian behaviour may be put to
17. shame. For it is better that you should suffer, if so
be the will of God, doing good rather than doing evil.[3]
18. For, even Christ, once, on account of sins, suffered, the righteous in the room of the unrighteous,
that he might bring us to God ; having become,
dead, with respect to the flesh, but, quickened, with
19. respect to the Spirit, whereby he went and preached
20. even to the spirits in prison, who were in former
times disbelieving, when the patience of God continued waiting in the days of Noah, while the ark
was preparing, in which few—that is, eight—souls
21. were saved by water, which also now—the anti-type
baptism—saves us, not as the removal of the filth of
the flesh,[4] but as the profession of a good conscience
towards God, through the resurrection of Jesus
22. Christ, who is at the right hand of God, having
passed into heaven, angels and authorities and
powers having been subjected to him.

---

[1] Ἐπι, on.—WICLIF. Beholdeth.—COVERDALE. MATTHEWS. Upon.—GE-
NEVA. RHEMISTS. Mali huic non latent.—CAMERARIUS.

[2] WYNNE.

[3] Melius enim est ut bene agentes, si ita velit Dei voluntas, aliquid patia-
mini, quam male agentes.—BEZA.

[4] Baptismus non ei rei servit, cui balnea sufficiunt.—DEYLINGIUS.

IV. 1.   Christ, then, having suffered for us in the flesh, do you even arm yourselves with this same thought[1] —'that he who hath suffered in the flesh hath been

2. made to rest from sin,'—in order to the living the remainder of the time in the flesh, not according to the lusts of men, but according to the will of God;

3. for the time that is past is enough for us to have wrought the will of the Gentiles, having walked in impurities, in lusts, in intoxication, in revels, in ca-

4. rousings, and lawless idolatrous rites; wherein they think it strange that you run not with them, into the same mire of profligacy, speaking evil of you;

5. these[2] shall render an account to Him who is in

6. readiness[3] to judge[4] the living and the dead; for, for this purpose also was the gospel preached to the dead, that as to man they might be judged in the flesh, but as to God might live in the Spirit.

7.   Now the end of all things is at hand;[5] be, therefore, prudent and watchful with regard to prayers.

8. But, above all things, have a fervent love of each other; for this love will cover a multitude of faults.

9. Be hospitable to each other without grudgings;

10. as good stewards of the manifold kindness of God, let every one employ the gift he has received for

11. mutual service (if any one speak as oracles of God,[6] if any one minister as of the ability God has bestowed[7]), that in all things God may be glorified, through Jesus Christ, whose is the[8] glory and the power for ever and ever, Amen.

---

[1] Cogitatione.—VULGATE.   Armez-vous de cette pensée que, &c.—MONS VERSION.

[2] ROBINSON. ὅς, ἥ, ὅ. 2. a. β.

[3] 2 Cor. x. 6. Εχειν εν ετοιμω,

[4] Inflict righteous judgment on.

[5] James v. 8, 9.

[6] 'Ως veritatis. What are, indeed, divine oracles—speaking as the ἱερμενευς of God.

[7] Of the ability which God has really given him, as a divinely-qualified minister.

[8] Cui est.—VULGATE.

12.   Beloved, be not surprised at the scorching[1] among you which is coming for your trial, as at some strange

13. thing happening to you; but rejoice, inasmuch as you are partakers in the sufferings of Christ, that you may also rejoice with exultation at the reve-

14. lation of his glory. If you suffer reproach in Christ's name, you are blessed, for the Spirit of glory and of power,[2] even the *spirit* of God, resteth on you; with regard to them there is reproach, but

15. with regard to you there is glory.[3] But let none of you suffer as a murderer, or a thief, or an evil-

16. doer, or as an intermeddler;[4] but if *any suffer* as a Christian, let him not be ashamed, but let him

17. glorify God on this account.[5] For it is the time of the commencement of the judgment from the house of God; and if the beginning be from us, what will be the issue[6] with those who disbelieve

18. the gospel of God? And if the righteous scarcely be delivered, where shall the ungodly and sinner

19. appear? Wherefore let even[7] those who suffer, according to the will of God, in well doing commit their souls *to Him*, who is[8] a faithful Creator.

V. 1.   To the elders among you, I who am a fellow elder and a witness of the sufferings of Christ, and a sharer in the glory that is about to be revealed, give this

2. exhortation. Act as shepherds to the flock of

---

[1] Prov. xxvii. 21; lxx. 1 Cor. iii. 13, 14. Apoc. xviii. 19.

[2] Δυνάμεως is introduced into the text by GRIESBACH, MATTHAI, and LACHMANN.

[3] They will reproach, but you will be honoured. This clause is of doubtful authority. GRIESBACH and LACHMANN omit it.

[4] Alienorum appetitor.—VULGATE. Rerum ad se non pertinentium curiosus inspector.—ERASM. SCHMID.

[5] 2 Cor. iii. 10; ix. 3.

[6] Finis *judicii*.—ERAS. SCHMID.

[7] Καὶ *etiam*, concessivé cum participio, idem quod εἰ καὶ *et si* cum verbo: εἰ καὶ πάσχοιτε ch. iii. 14. Non debemus ex passione diffidentiam capere.—BENGEL.

[8] Ὡς ἀληθῶς HESYCHIUS. Revera, vere SCHLEUSNER. Answering to the Heb. *Caph veritatis*. Neh. vii. 2. Hos. v. 10; lxx. John i. 14.

God that is among you,[1] superintending them, not
reluctantly, but willingly; not from a sordid love of

3. gain, but from a spirit of zeal; neither lording it
over the allotted portions,[2] but being patterns for

4. the flock; and[3] when the chief shepherd[4] appears,

5. you shall receive the unfading crown of glory. In
like manner, you juniors, submit yourselves to the
elders,[5] and all of you being subject to each other, be
girdled with humility;[6] for God opposes the haughty,
but to the humble he shows favour.

6. Humble yourselves, then, under the mighty hand
of God, that he may exalt you in due season;[7] casting

7. all your anxiety on Him, for he cares for you.

8. Be sober, be wakeful; your adversary the devil,
like a roaring lion, is going about seeking whom

9. he may devour; Him resist, standing fast in the
faith,[8] knowing that the same kinds of suffering
are accomplished in your brotherhood while in the

10. world. But the God of all grace who has called
you to his eternal glory in Christ Jesus, after you
have suffered a little, shall himself[9] make you perfect,

11. stablish, strengthen, settle you;[10] His *is*[11] the glory
and the power, for ever and ever. Amen.

[1] As much as lieth in you.—CRANMER.

[2] The clergy.—WICLIF. RHEMISTS. The parishes.—COVERDALE. MATTHEWS. CRANMER. Your charges.—HAMMOND.

[3] THEOPHYLACT and ŒCUMENIUS consider και as an αιτιολογικος συνδεσμος.

[4] Prince of shepherds.—WICLIF. Prince of pastors.—RHEMISTS.

[5] The Syriac version has "your elders," which shows us how its author understood νεωτεροι.

[6] Put on humility as your badge.—HAMMOND.

[7] 1 Tim. vi. 15. 2 Cor. vi. 2. Whether here or hereafter, certainly at a seasonable time.—STEIGER.

[8] Erga diffidentes robur habet, erga fideles imbellis est.—BULLINGER.

[9] Phil. i. 6.

[10] The elder English versions—COVERDALE, MATTHEWS, and CRANMER—render this in the future; and the reading on which this rendering rests, that of the vulgate, is recognised by GRIESBACH, SCHOLZ, and LACHMANN, as genuine. Digna Petro oratio: confirmat suos fratres.—BENGEL.

[11] If, as is generally admitted, the verbs in the previous verse be in the future, *is* seems a more suitable supplement than *be*.

12.   By Silvanus, to you a faithful brother, as I judge,
I have briefly written, exhorting *you*, and testifying *to you* that this is the true grace of God, with
13. regard to which do you stand.[1] *The church*[2] in Babylon, chosen as you are, saluteth you; also Marcus, my
14. son.   Salute each other with a kiss of love. Peace
be with you all who are in Christ Jesus. *Amen.*

---

[1] Στητε.—LACHMANN.   See the authorities in GRIESBACH and SCHOLZ.

[2] Literally *she*, that is, either εκκλησια or διασπορα.

EXPOSITORY DISCOURSES.

EXPOSITORY DISCOURSES.

DISCOURSE I.

INTRODUCTORY.

THE AUTHOR—THE ADDRESS—AND THE SALUTATION.

1 Peter i. 1, 2.—Peter, an apostle of Jesus Christ, to the strangers scattered throughout Pontus, Galatia, Cappadocia, Asia, and Bithynia, elect according to the foreknowledge of God the Father, through sanctification of the Spirit, unto obedience and sprinkling of the blood of Jesus Christ: Grace unto you, and peace, be multiplied.

INTRODUCTION.

The Holy Scriptures—the inspired record of the revealed will of God—are not occupied with a systematic view of religious and moral truth and duty, but consist of a great variety of separate treatises, some of them historical, others didactic, others prophetical, most of them written in prose, though some of them in verse, composed at irregular intervals during a period of fifteen hundred years, and generally having a peculiar reference to the circumstances of those to whom they were originally addressed. The miscellaneous and occasional character thus impressed on the sacred writings, like every thing else about them, bears in it indications of their divine origin. It prevents every thing like the appearance of human art or contrivance; proves that the harmony which prevails in them could not be the result of a preconcerted plan; and leads us to inquire for a reason—which can only be found in the admission of their having been given by the inspiration of Him who is "the only wise God"

—why writings, so plainly occasional in their origin, should,
notwithstanding, be so well fitted to serve the purpose of a
universal and permanent rule of religious belief and moral
conduct.

A very considerable part of the second volume of the inspired writings—the Christian Scriptures—consists of letters,
addressed by Apostles of Christ, some of them to individual
Christians, most of them to bodies of Christians resident in
particular cities or districts.   These Epistles form one of the
most valuable portions of the Book of God.   They embody
in them much evidence, in a peculiarly satisfactory form, of
the truth of the Gospel history, and of the divine origin of
Christianity; they contain in them the full development of
the Christian doctrine, given by men on whom, according to
His promise, the exalted Redeemer had conferred the Holy
Spirit, "to guide them into all the truth;" they give us a
striking exhibition of the living spirit of Christianity, and
its influence on the formation of character, both in the writers
of the Epistles and in those to whom they are addressed;
they present us with authentic information in reference to
the constitution, government, and worship of the primitive
Church; and they furnish, in the most useful and impressive
form, a complete code of Christian morals.

Among these apostolical letters, the First Epistle of the
Apostle Peter has always held a very high place in the estimation of the Church.   That opinion cannot be better
expressed than in the words of the heavenly Leighton :
" This excellent epistle, full of evangelical doctrine and
apostolical authority, is a brief and yet very clear summary,
both of the consolations and instructions needful for the
encouragement and direction of a Christian in his journey
to heaven; elevating his thoughts and desires to that happiness, and strengthening him against all opposition in the way,
both that of corruption within, and temptation and afflictions
from without.   The heads of doctrine contained in it are
many; but the main that are most insisted on, are these
three—Faith, Obedience, and Patience—to establish them

in believing, to direct them in doing, and to comfort them in suffering."[1]

The authenticity and genuineness of the Epistle, and its apostolic origin and consequent divine inspiration, rest on the most satisfactory evidence. It is alluded to in the Second Epistle bearing Peter's name; the very great antiquity of which is undoubted, though its canonical authority has been questioned. It is plainly referred to by the earliest Christian writers, as Clement of Rome, Ignatius, Polycarp, and Irenæus; and Eusebius ranks it among the books universally admitted to belong to the sacred canon. The doubts which have been thrown out by certain German critics, in later times, have obviously originated in the very wantonness of scepticism, and but little deserve the grave discussion and elaborate refutation they have received from sounder scholars.

Like the letters of Paul, this composition holds a middle place between the treatise or discourse and the familiar epistle. It is not, like the Epistles to the Romans, Galatians, and Hebrews, principally occupied with one great doctrinal theme. It more resembles the minor Pauline Epistles, with this difference, that the doctrinal and the practical statements are more commingled. There is comparatively little discussion or argument in it. It is—as the author himself describes it (ch. v. 12)—a testimony and an exhortation.[2]

The natural warmth of the author's disposition[3] gives a character of energy approaching to vehemence to the style; and there is to be found just such a familiarity with the Old Testament Scriptures, manifesting itself not only in direct quotations, but in numerous natural allusions, which have all the appearance of having been unconscious, as might be

---

[1] Epistolam profecto dignam apostolorum principe, plenam autoritatis ac majestatis apostolicæ verbis parcam, sententiis differtam.—ERASMUS. Habet hæc epistola τὸ σφοδρὸν conveniens ingenio principis apostolorum.—GROTIUS. Mirabilis est gravitas et alacritas Petrini sermonis, suavissime retinens lectorem.—BENGEL.

[2] Παρακαλων και επιμαρτυρων.

[3] Chrysostom terms him Ο πανταχου Θερμος.

expected in the composition of a pious, though, when compared with Paul, an unlettered Jew.[a]

There are plain traces in the epistle of an intimate acquaintance with the modes of thought and expression characteristic of the writings of Paul, which, even without the references in the second epistle (ch. iii. 14, 15), would have led to the conclusion that the writer had read his epistles.[b] Peter's mode of writing is much less than Paul's that of a scholar; but he has much of the same natural ease of diction, tendency to digression, and use of figurative language.

This Epistle holds an intermediate place between those of the great Apostle of the Gentiles and that of James the Apostle of the Circumcision. It resembles both in a greater degree than they resemble each other.[c]

With respect to the time when this epistle was written, we have not the means of arriving at absolute certainty. The probability seems to be, that its true date is about A.D. 65, the eleventh year of Nero's reign, two or three years before the Apostle's martyrdom, which is generally supposed to have taken place A.D. 67.[1]

It may be proper here to say a word as to the meaning of the epithet General or Catholic, which, since the fourth century, has been given to this epistle, as well as to the Second Epistle of Peter, and the Epistles of James, John, and Jude. It is not a question of vital importance (for the appellation has no claim to divine authority), and it is well it is so, for there seems no means of determining it with any thing like certainty. The term appears originally to have meant an epistle, not directed to one church, but to all, or at any rate to many churches,—a description which belongs to five of the seven epistles so distinguished; the other two being addressed to individuals. In the time of Eusebius, with this sense seems to have been connected the somewhat cognate one, of epistles

---

[1] Hug's Introduction, sect. clxiii.; Steiger's Exposition, i. 33; Kitto's Cyclopædia; Michaelis' Introduction, iv. 325.

[a] See note A.   [b] See note B.   [c] See note C.

publicly read in many or all the churches, on account of the excellence and usefulness of their contents; and, till the writings of the New Testament were collected into one volume, it appears to have been the technical name by which this collection of epistles was distinguished from the Pauline Epistles.[1]

The object of the Apostle in this Epistle is plainly to confirm the disciples in the faith, profession, and obedience of the Gospel, by deepening their conviction, that the source of happiness and the foundation of the everlasting kingdom of God were contained in that faith of the Redeemer which had been announced to them, and received by them into their hearts; that that doctrine was indeed the everlasting unchangeable word of God, and therefore that they ought to aim at appropriating it with childlike simplicity, that so they might continually advance towards " the measure of the stature of the fulness of Christ;" and to exhort them to maintain their steadfastness in the faith under all persecutions, and a corresponding course of conduct, by which they would " shine as lights in the world," and refute the false accusations against Christianity and Christians.[2]

It is my intention, " if the Lord will," to lay before you at irregular intervals, a series of Expository Discourses on this "weighty and powerful" epistle, and the passage which I have read shall form the subject of the first of these discourses.

These verses contain the inscription and the salutation, according to the ordinary usage of the apostolical epistles; and naturally lead us to speak, I. Of the writer of the epistle—" Peter, an apostle of Jesus Christ;" II. Of those to whom the epistle is addressed—" The elect strangers of the dispersion in Pontus, Galatia, Cappadocia, Asia, and Bithynia—elect according to the foreknowledge of God, by a spiritual sanctification, to obedience and to the sprinkling

---

[1] Euseb. H. E. ii. 23; Nœsselti Opuscula, fasc. ii.; Michaelis; Hug; Schott; De Wette.

[2] Neander.

of the blood of Jesus Christ;" and III. of the benevolent wish which he expresses, or the solemn prayer which he presents for them—"Grace unto you, and Peace, be multiplied."

I. OF THE WRITER OF THE EPISTLE.

The writer of this epistle, whose original name was Simon, was a native of Bethsaida, at that time an inconsiderable village on the banks of the sea of Galilee. He was bred to the occupation of a fisherman, which seems to have been the family profession; and at the time of his becoming acquainted with Jesus Christ, he was married, and had removed with his family to Capernaum. His brother Andrew, who was a disciple of John the Baptist, having heard his master pronounce Jesus, whom he had lately baptized, "the Lamb of God," solicited an interview with him, which ended in his conviction that he was indeed the great deliverer, concerning whom the ancient prophets had uttered so many glorious predictions, and whose appearance was at this period generally expected by the Jews without delay. He communicated the joyful intelligence to his brother Simon, whom he introduced to Jesus. He also appears to have become from that day a believer; and in the exercise of that knowledge of the secrets of the heart and of futurity, by which he was distinguished, Jesus, in reference to the dispositions he should discover, and the services he should perform, surnamed him Cephas, or Petros— the one a Chaldee-Syriac, the other a Greek word—both signifying a stone or rock.

For some time after this these two brothers continued to follow their profession, as fishermen. But one day Jesus, after having confirmed their faith by a miraculous draught of fishes, which he intimated was emblematical of the vast multitudes who, through their instrumentality, were to become his followers, required their constant attendance on him; and when he very soon afterwards selected twelve of his disciples, whom he termed apostles, and entrusted with

miraculous powers, we find Peter's name holding the first
place in the list. He obviously from the beginning was
" among the chief of the apostles," and occupied a high
place, comparatively as well as really, in his Master's esteem
and affection. Of this we have satisfactory evidence in his
being, along with John and James, the sons of Zebedee,
honoured as a witness of his glory on the Mount of Transfi-
guration, and of his agony in the garden of Gethsemane.

None of the apostles were more firmly persuaded of the
divinity of Jesus' mission, more affectionately attached to
his person, and more zealously devoted to his cause.
When, on many of his disciples, who had expected from the
Messiah a worldly kingdom, becoming offended with a discourse in which he had intimated that the blessings he came
to procure and bestow were of a heavenly kind, and " going
back, and walking no more with him," Jesus turned to his
little chosen band, and put to them the touching question,
" Will ye also go away?" Peter exclaimed, " To whom can
we go but to thee? thou hast the words of eternal life.
And we know and are sure that thou art the Christ, the
Son of the living God." On another occasion, when our
Lord, having inquired of his disciples what were the
opinions generally entertained of him by his countrymen,
put the question to them, " Who say ye that I am?"
Peter immediately replied, " Thou art the Christ, the Son
of the living God." His warm attachment to his Lord was
equally strongly, though not equally wisely, manifested, in
his dissuading him from submitting to suffering and death,
in his refusing to allow him to wash his feet, in his declaration that though he should die with him he would never
deny him, in his singly drawing his sword against a numerous body of armed men in his defence, and in his persisting
to follow him when the rest of the disciples had forsaken
him and fled.

To teach Peter his own weakness, he was permitted to
fall before the temptations to which he had rashly exposed
himself. Thrice in the course of a very short period he

denied with execrations that he knew *Him* for whom he
had so lately, both by words and deeds, shown that he was
then ready to lay down his life.   The fact is recorded not
for Peter's shame but for our instruction ; and it proclaims,
" Let him who thinketh he standeth take heed lest he fall."
" Be not high-minded, but fear."   " Without Christ ye can
do nothing."

> " Beware of Peter's word,
>   Nor confidently say,
> ' I never will deny my Lord ; '
>   But 'grant I never may.' "

On our Lord's casting on Peter a look of wounded but
unchanging affection, he was stung to the heart.   At the
thought of his base ingratitude, he retired into solitude, and
" wept bitterly."

It is a touching proof of Jesus' peculiar affection to
Peter, that in the message he sent by the angel to his
disciples by Mary Magdalene, to whom he first appeared
after his resurrection, that Peter is particularly mentioned.
" Go tell the disciples, and Peter."   This token of kindness
was not lost on him.   He ran immediately to the sepulchre,
and went into it to ascertain that the body was indeed
removed ; and he had the high honour of being the first
among the apostles who saw his risen Redeemer, though we
have no particular account of the interview.

Some time after the resurrection, our Lord gave Peter a
most overwhelming proof of his regard, and afforded him an
honourable opportunity of manifesting, in the presence of
his brethren, his unabated love for the Saviour, and his
increased distrust of himself.   It would be injustice to tell
the story in other words than those of the inspired historian,
John xxi. 15–19   " So, when they had dined, Jesus saith
to Simon Peter, Simon, *son* of Jonas, lovest thou me more
than these ?   He saith unto him, Yea, Lord ; thou knowest
that I love thee.   He saith unto him, Feed my lambs.   He
saith to him again the second time, Simon, *son* of Jonas,
lovest thou me ?   He saith unto him, Yea, Lord ; thou

knowest that I love thee. He saith unto him, Feed my sheep. He saith unto him the third time, Simon, son of Jonas, lovest thou me? Peter was grieved because he said unto him the third time, Lovest thou me? And he said unto him, Lord, thou knowest all things; thou knowest that I love thee. Jesus saith unto him, Feed my sheep. Verily, verily, I say unto thee, When thou wast young, thou girdedst thyself, and walkedst whither thou wouldest: but when thou shalt be old, thou shalt stretch forth thy hands, and another shall gird thee, and carry thee whither thou wouldest not. This spake he, signifying by what death he should glorify God. And when he had spoken this, he saith unto him, Follow me."

Peter was present with his brethren on that memorable day, when Jesus " led them out as far as to Bethany, and lifted up his hands and blessed them; and while he blessed them, he was parted from them, and carried up into heaven." Not one of them gazed with a more eager eye upward till the form of the Saviour vanished in the cloud of glory, or with a heart more full of solemn gladness returned to Jerusalem.

Immediately after the outpouring of the Holy Ghost, Peter was honoured to open the gates of the kingdom of heaven to the Jews, by preaching the first Gospel sermon properly so called, and his preaching was blessed to the conversion of three thousand souls.

After having, along with John, performed a miracle of healing, he delivered an eloquent and convincing discourse, by means of which multitudes were induced to embrace the Gospel. And when brought before the council, he showed how completely our Lord's promise had been performed, that he would give to his apostles " a spirit and a wisdom which all their adversaries would be unable to resist."

At his reproof Ananias and Sapphira, who had attempted to impose on the apostles, were struck with instantaneous death.

Many of the Samaritans having embraced Christianity in consequence of the preaching of Philip, Peter visited them,

and conferred on them the supernatural gifts of the Holy
Spirit. We find him afterwards at Lydda, healing Eneas,
who had been eight years confined to his bed by palsy; and
at Joppa raising Tabitha from the dead.

He who had opened the gate of the kingdom of heaven
to the Jews, was called on also, in the case of the Centurion
Cornelius and his family, to open the same gate to the Gentiles. In consequence of a divine mission, he preached to
them the Gospel, and while he was preaching it, "the Lord
gave testimony to the word of his grace," and shed forth on
them abundantly the Holy Ghost.

On his return to Jerusalem, he was cast into prison by
order of Herod-Agrippa, with the intention of his being
speedily publicly put to death, but was miraculously delivered by an angel.

At the meeting of what is ordinarily termed the
council or synod of Jerusalem, Peter asserted strongly
the freedom of believing Gentiles from all obligation to
observe the law of Moses, and urged the circumstance of
the conversion of Cornelius and his family, as an irrefragable
proof of the doctrine which he taught. Some time after
this, being at Antioch, he acted on this liberal principle, by
maintaining an unrestricted freedom of intercourse with the
converted Gentiles, till a fear of offending some Jewish
Christians, zealous for the law, induced him, from a mistaken notion of expediency, to "withdraw himself." This
inconsistent rather than unprincipled conduct, drew on him
the honest reproof of the Apostle Paul, who in a very convincing manner shows that he was now contradicting by
action what he had asserted in words, and building up again
what he had destroyed.

We have no further account of the Apostle Peter in the
New Testament. A careful attention to the hints met with
in authentic Church history, has led the best informed
writers to believe, that, having returned to Judea from Antioch, he remained at Jerusalem for some years, and that he
then returned to Antioch or Syria, and from thence visited

those provinces mentioned in the inscription of this Epistle, and formed an acquaintance with those Churches for whose edification his two Epistles were intended. On leaving these parts, he probably went into the Parthian Empire, where he appears to have been labouring when the Epistle was written. The remaining history of the Apostle is involved in obscurity. It is not impossible that he went to Rome after Paul had left it for the last time; and there, now an old man, sealed his testimony with his blood, and obtained the crown of martyrdom, being put to death by the order of the inhuman Nero. It is storied that he was crucified with his head downward—himself observing with characteristic affection and humility, "that he was unworthy of the honour of being crucified in the same way as his Master was." The observation savours so much more of the morbid piety of what is called ancient Christianity, than of simple apostolic humility, as to go far to discredit the story. It seems certain, however, that he was crucified, and that thus was the enigmatic prophecy of our Lord explained by its fulfilment, in which he signified by what death Peter should glorify God —John xxi. 18–19, " Verily, verily, I say unto thee, When thou wast young, thou girdedst thyself, and walkedst whither thou wouldest: but when thou shalt be old, thou shalt stretch forth thy hands, and another shall gird thee, and carry thee whither thou wouldest not. This spake he, signifying by what death he should glorify God. And when he had spoken this, he saith unto him, Follow me."

Such is a short outline of the more important facts known in reference to the venerable writer of this Epistle.[d]

Peter describes himself as an Apostle of Jesus Christ. The word apostle signifies a person sent by another, a messenger. The term is in the New Testament generally employed as the descriptive appellation of a comparatively small class of men, to whom Jesus Christ entrusted the organization of his Church, and the dissemination of his religion among mankind. At an early period of his ministry

d For the authorities of the above statement, see note D.

" he ordained twelve" of his disciples, " that they should be
with him." These he named apostles. Some time afterwards, " he gave to them power against unclean spirits, to
cast them out, and to heal all manner of disease;" and " he
sent them to preach the kingdom of God."[1] To them he
gave "the keys of the kingdom of God," and constituted
them princes over the Spiritual Israel, that people whom
God was to take from among "the Jews and the Gentiles
for his name."[2] Previously to his death he promised them
the Holy Spirit, to fit them to be the founders and governors of the Christian Church.[3] After his resurrection, he
solemnly confirmed their call, saying, " As the Father hath
sent me, so send I you;"[4] and gave them a commission to
" preach the gospel to every creature."[5] After his ascen-
sion, he, on the day of Pentecost, communicated to them
those supernatural gifts which were necessary to the performance of the high functions he had commissioned them
to perform; and in the exercise of these gifts, they, in the
Gospel history, and in their Epistles, with the Apocalypse,
gave a complete view of the will of their Master, in reference
to that new order of things of which he was the author.
They " had the mind of Christ." They spoke " the wisdom
of God in a mystery." That mystery " God revealed to
them by his Spirit," and they spoke it " not in words, which
man's wisdom teacheth, but which the Holy Ghost teacheth."
They were " ambassadors for Christ," and besought men
" in Christ's stead to be reconciled to God." They authoritatively taught the doctrine and law of the Lord; they
organized Churches, and required them to " keep the tradi-
tions," i. e. the doctrine and ordinances "delivered to them."[6]

The characteristic features of the apostles as official men
were, that they had seen the Lord, and been eye and ear

---

[1] Mark iii. 14; Matt. x. 1-5; Mark vi. 7; Luke vi. 13; ix. 1.

[2] Matt. xvi. 19; xviii. 18; xix. 28; Luke xxii. 30.

[3] John xiv. 16, 17, 26; xv. 26, 27; xvi. 7-15.

[4] Καθως απεσταλκε με ὁ Παιηρ, καγω πεμπω υμας.

[5] John xx. 21-23; Matt. xviii. 18-20.

[6] Acts ii.; 1 Cor. ii. 16; ii. 7, 10, 13; 2 Cor. v. 20; 1 Cor. xi.

witnesses of what they testified to the world;[1] that they had been called and chosen *immediately* by Christ;[2] that they were infallibly inspired to declare his doctrine and laws;[3] that they possessed the power of working miracles;[4] and that their commission was strictly speaking catholic, extending to the whole Church,—to the whole world.[5]

It must be obvious, from this scriptural account of the apostolical office, that the apostles had—could have, in the strict sense of the term—no successors. Their qualifications were supernatural, and their work once performed, remains in the infallible record of the New Testament for the advantage of the Church and the world in all future ages. They are the only authoritative teachers of Christian doctrine and law. All official men in Christian Churches can legitimately claim no higher place than that of expounders of the doctrines, and administrators of the laws, found in their writings. Few things have been more injurious to the cause of Christianity, than the assumption, on the part of ordinary office-bearers in the Church, of the peculiar prerogatives of " the holy Apostles of our Lord Jesus." Much that is said of the latter is not at all applicable to the former, and much that admits of being applied, can be so, in accordance with truth, only in a very secondary and extenuated sense.[6]

To this, the highest and holiest office ever held by mere man, the author of this Epistle had been called by his Master; and it would appear that in the exercise of its important functions his labours were chiefly, though not exclusively, devoted to his " brethren, his kinsmen according to the flesh." [7] Though there is no ground for the assertion, that Peter was the Prince of the Apostles, or had even a perma-

---

[1] John xv. 27; Acts i. 21, 22; 1 Cor. xv. 8; ix. 1; Acts xxii. 14, 15.

[2] Luke vi. 13; Gal. i. 1.

[3] John xvi. 13; 1 Cor. ii. 10; Gal. i. 11, 12; John xiv. 26.

[4] Mark xvi. 20; Acts ii. 43; 1 Cor. xii. 8-11; 2 Cor. xii. 12.

[5] 2 Cor. xi. 28; Acts xvi. 4; 1 Cor. v. 3-6; 2 Cor. x. 8; xiii. 10.

[6] *Vide* Campbell's Lectures on Ecclesiastical History, Lect. v.; Kitto's Cyclopædia of Bib. Lit. vol. i. p. 179, &c.

[7] Gal. ii. 8, 9.

nent presidency among them, yet there can be no doubt he
stood very high in the estimation of his brethren—was
among those who " seemed to be pillars,"—" the very
chiefest apostles." [1]

II. OF THOSE TO WHOM THE EPISTLE IS ADDRESSED.

The persons to whom the Epistle is addressed, come
next to be considered. They are described first, generally,
as " elect," or chosen, and then, particularly, both as to their
external circumstances and to their spiritual state and character. With regard to the former, they are " the strangers scattered abroad, throughout Pontus, Galatia, Cappadocia, Asia, and Bithynia." With regard to the latter,
they are " elect, according to the foreknowledge of God,
through sanctification of the Spirit, to obedience and
sprinkling of the blood of Jesus Christ."

It has been, and is, a question among expositors, who are
the class of persons to whom this Epistle is addressed. It
is plainly addressed to Christians, and to Christians resident
in the countries specified ; but, according to one class of interpreters, it is addressed to the Jewish converts resident
in these regions ; by another class, it is considered as addressed to the Gentile converts resident there ; by a third
class, it is considered as addressed to those who are called
" proselytes of the gate,"—persons by birth Gentiles, but
who had embraced Judaism, and had afterwards been converted to Christianity.

We apprehend that the true view of the matter is, that
the Epistle was addressed to the converts generally, whether
Jews or Gentiles, residing in the countries mentioned. As
a majority of these were Jews, this circumstance, along
with the fact that Peter was a Jew, and the Apostle of the
Circumcision, sufficiently accounts for the fact, that the
circumstances and duties of the persons addressed are so
frequently, I had almost said so uniformly, spoken of, in

[1] Gal. ii. 9 ; 2 Cor. xi. 5.

language referring to the peculiarities of the Jewish economy.[1]

The persons are described, first, generally, as "elect," or chosen. It appears to me not only a doctrine very plainly revealed in Scripture, but necessarily resulting from the principles of natural religion, that all who enjoy the blessings of Christianity, the saving benefits of pardon, sanctification, and eternal life, do so in consequence of the sovereign free love of God, which, like himself, is necessarily eternal; or, in other words, were elected from unbeginning ages to the happiness bestowed on them. This doctrine is taught with peculiar plainness in the 1st chapter of the Epistle to the Ephesians, i. 3–5 : " Blessed be the God and Father of our Lord Jesus Christ, who hath blessed us with all spiritual blessings in heavenly places in Christ ; according as he hath chosen us in him before the foundation of the world, that we should be holy and without blame before him in love : having predestinated us unto the adoption of children by Jesus Christ to himself, according to the good pleasure of his will."

At the same time, I apprehend, the word " elect" here, and in a number of other places in the New Testament, does not refer directly to what has been termed the electing decree,[2] but to the manifestation of it in the actually *selecting* certain individuals from amidst a world lying in wickedness, that they may be set apart to God, and become his peculiar people. The remark of Leighton appears to me very judicious: " Election here means the selecting them out of the world and joining them to the fellowship of the people of God." This is the election which our Lord speaks of when he says, " Because ye are not of the world, but I have chosen[3]—elected—you out of the world, therefore the world hateth you;"[e] and the Apostle

---

[1] *Vide* Michaelis' Introduction, by Marsh, vol. iv. 315-325 ; Schott Isagoge in lib. N. F. Sac. p. 403. For a particular account of the countries here referred to, *vide* Steiger Exp. of the First Ep. of Peter, Introd. sec. 6, vol. i. pp. 14-19.

[2] 'Η κατ' εκλογην προθεσις.—Rom. ix. 11.   [3] John xv. 19.

[e] See note E.

Paul plainly speaks of the election and the vocation of the Corinthians, as the same thing. "Ye see your calling—for God hath chosen the foolish things of the world to confound the wise; and God hath chosen the weak things of the world to confound the things which are mighty; and base things of the world, and things which are despised, hath God chosen, yea, and things which are not, to bring to nought things that are: that no flesh should glory in his presence."[1]　As Israel, as a nation, were selected to be a peculiar people to Jehovah, so true Christians are as individuals selected to be a part of God's spiritual "purchased inheritance," or peculiar people.

These selected or chosen persons are described, first, as to their external condition. They are represented as "strangers[2] scattered abroad." The appellation is borrowed from the term generally given to Jews dwelling in Gentile lands.[3]　The situation of Christians while on earth does not resemble that of Israel dwelling in peace and security in Canaan, but that of Israelites sojourning among strangers and enemies. The selected people of God, while here below, are not gathered into one place, assembled together as citizens of the same city—children of the same family. They will be so by and by, but now they are "strangers," "pilgrims," "sojourners," being a small minority among a people whose habits of thought and feeling, whose pursuits and whose pleasures, are altogether alien from theirs; and "scattered" strangers, as being not merely far from home, but often far from each other, and but imperfectly enjoying the comfort and support arising from intimate communion with persons of kindred sentiments and affections. Such was the external state of the Christians to whom this epistle was addressed—such is the external state of true Christians still.

The particular description of the spiritual state of these selected and dispersed strangers now requires our attention.

---

[1] 1 Cor. i. 26-29.

[2] Παρεπιδημοις. The word expresses two ideas: not natives of the country in which they are; not settled residents in that foreign country.

[3] Ἡ διασπορα.—John vii. 35.

They are " chosen according to the foreknowledge of God"
—they are " chosen by sanctification of the Spirit"—
they are " chosen to obedience and sprinkling of the blood
of Jesus."

They are " chosen according to the foreknowledge of
God."[f] Here is the doctrine of election very plainly stated.
They were selected from the rest of mankind, not because
they were better than others. They were selected in accordance with the sovereign will of Him " to whom all his
works are known from the beginning of the world." They
are the " called" or chosen " according to his purpose ;" and
the purpose in reference to his choice of them stands, " not of
works, but of him that calleth." No cause can be assigned
for them being selected rather than others, but the sovereign free love of God. " He hath mercy on whom he
will have mercy; he hath compassion on whom he will
have compassion." When the Lord set his love on Israel,
and chose them to be his peculiar people, the cause was not
in them, but in himself; it was just because he loved
them—" because he had a delight in them to love them ;"
and it is equally true that the selection of certain individuals
to enjoy the better blessings of the better economy, can be
traced by us to nothing but the sovereign kindness of Him
who " worketh all things according to the counsel of his own
will."[1]

They are " elect through sanctification of the Spirit."
Sanctification means here, as usually in the New Testament, separation—setting apart; and sanctification of the
Spirit[2] means spiritual separation, as opposed to external or
bodily separation.[g] When Israel was chosen to be God's
peculiar people, in being separated from all nations they
were marked by a great variety of external distinctions.
They lived in a country of their own, and were distinguished by peculiar civil laws and customs, and were

---

[1] Rom. ix. 11, 15; Deut. x. 15; Eph. i. 11.

[2] Εν αγιασμω πνευμαΊος, not τυ ΠνευμαΊος.

[f] See note F.   [g] See note G.

warned to abstain from all intimate intercourse of any kind with the surrounding nations. The peculiar people of God, under the new dispensation, are also separated from the rest of mankind : but their separation is of a spiritual kind. They are separated from them not civilly, but religiously— separated from them in their sentiments and affections. Spiritually they " come out from the world, and are separate ;" but in reference to the affairs of this world they are not a separate society.

They are " elected according to the divine foreknowledge, and by this spiritual separation to obedience." [h] The full expression is the obedience of faith, or the obedience of the truth; and to obey the faith or the truth, is just to believe the gospel and live under its influence. That the New Testament writers use the word " obedience" simply, when they mean the obedience of faith, is evident from the following passage in the epistle to the Romans. ch. vi. 16, 17 : " Know ye not, that to whom ye yield yourselves servants to obey, his servants ye are to whom ye obey; whether of sin unto death, or of obedience unto righteousness ? But God be thanked, that ye were the servants of sin ; but ye have obeyed from the heart that form of doctrine which was delivered you." When Israel became the peculiar people of God, by his selecting them according to his sovereign good pleasure, and externally separating them to himself, it was that they might be subject to his laws. In like manner, when individuals are selected by God to form a part of his peculiar people under the better economy, according to his foreknowledge, and are spiritually separated and set apart, it is that they may obey its law—that they may believe the gospel, and give up their whole inner and outer man to be regulated by its influence—it is that, taught by " the grace of God, which brings salvation," they may " deny ungodliness and worldly lusts, and live soberly, righteously, and godly, in this present world ; looking for that blessed hope,

[h] See note H.

and the glorious appearing of the great God and our Saviour Jesus Christ: who gave himself for us, that he might redeem us from all iniquity, and purify unto himself a peculiar people, zealous of good works." [1]

Still farther, they are " selected to the sprinkling of the blood of Jesus Christ." When Israel were chosen to be God's people, and externally set apart for this purpose, it was not only that they might be subject to his law, but that they might share in the effects of that law's expiatory offerings—that, being sprinkled with the blood of the sacrifices by which that covenant was ratified, their ceremonial guilt might be pardoned, their ceremonial pollution removed, and that they might be fitted for external fellowship with Jehovah as their God and King. When God, in accordance with his sovereign purpose of mercy, selects individuals, and sets them spiritually apart for his people, it is that, through the faith of the gospel, they may be personally interested in the blessings procured by the death of Jesus Christ as a propitiatory sacrifice for the sins of men—that their sins may be forgiven them, that the jealousies of guilt may be removed, that they may be enabled and disposed with a true heart to approach to God, as rich in mercy, ready to forgive, " God in Christ reconciling the world to himself;" and in spiritual fellowship with him, with minds conformed to his mind, and wills conformed to his will, serve him with their souls and bodies, which are his, not only because they are made by him, but because they have been " redeemed" to him, " not by such corruptible things as silver and gold, but by the precious blood of Christ, as of a lamb without blemish and without spot." [2]

Such is the apostle's description of the spiritual state, character, and circumstances of those whom he addresses. They are selected by God according to his own sovereign purpose, and spiritually set apart for him, that, believing the gospel, they may enjoy all the blissful results of the

---

[1] Tit. ii. 11-14.   [2] 1 Pet. i. 18, 19.

death of Jesus Christ the just one, in the room of the unjust.[i]

III.—THE SALUTATION OF THE EPISTLE.

The benevolent wish or solemn prayer which the apostle presents for those to whom he writes, now calls for our consideration : " Grace unto you, and peace, be multiplied."

" Grace" is free favour—sovereign kindness—the principle in the divine mind from which all blessings to sinful men flow. It is often used as a general name for those blessings which flow from this sovereign kindness. Grace here plainly is the grace of God. The prayer, " Grace be multiplied unto you," implied that they were already objects of the grace of God, and is equivalent to—' God loves you, and has given you proofs of his love. Had he not loved you, would he have selected you—would he have spiritually set you apart for himself—would he have brought you to the obedience of the truth—would he have sprinkled you with the blood of Jesus? May you have continued, increasing, and multiplied proofs that God loves you, in the continuance, and increase, and multiplication of all heavenly and spiritual blessings !'

" Peace" is not so much a different thing from " grace," as a different view of the same thing. We call blessings " grace," as springing from God's sovereign kindness. We call them " peace," as calculated to tranquillize our minds and make us happy. The prayer, " Peace be multiplied to you," is equivalent to—' You already enjoy peace and happiness.' For " they who believe, do enter into rest." May your happiness be continued—may it increase! May " the peace of God, which passeth all understanding, keep your hearts and minds in Christ Jesus !"

Having, thus, very cursorily considered the interesting

[i] See note I.

topics suggested by this passage of scripture, let us, my brethren, endeavour to turn them to practical account. A great majority of us are professors of Christianity. Does the description given in the text suit us? Have we any satisfactory evidence that we have been selected by God—called by his grace—spiritually separated to his service—that we have believed the truth, and are enjoying the happy consequence of the belief of the truth, in having the heart sprinkled from an evil conscience by the blood of Christ? Do we feel that *here* we are "strangers of the dispersion," and are waiting for "the gathering together," for the period when all the citizens of heaven shall be assembled in the New Jerusalem, when all the children of God shall be brought home to their Father's house? If this is the case with you, brethren, then let your conduct correspond with your privileges; and "may grace and peace be multiplied to you, and to all the Israel of God."

If it be otherwise, now obey the truth, and, through the obedience of the truth, submit your hearts and consciences to the pacifying and purifying influence of the atoning blood of Jesus. We know nothing about the purpose of God in reference to individuals till that purpose is manifested in its execution; but we do know the purpose of God in reference to lost men generally, and we proclaim it as the appointed means of gathering from among men the elect of God. "God so loved the world, that he gave his only begotten Son, that whosoever believeth in him should not perish, but have everlasting life. God sent not his Son into the world to condemn the world, but that the world through him might be saved." "Be it known unto you, men and brethren, that through this man is preached unto you the forgiveness of sins: and by him all who believe are justified from all things, from which they could not have been justified by the law of Moses."[1]

---

[1] John iii. 16, 17; Acts xiii. 38, 39.

Note A.

The following are the principal references to the Old Testament in the Epistle :—Ch. i. 16 ; Lev. xi. 44. Ch. i. 24, 25 ; Isa. xl. 6, &c. Ch. ii. 3 ; Psal. xxxiv. 9. Ch. ii. 4 ; Psal cxviii. 16. Ch. ii. 6 ; Isa. xxviii. 16. Chap. ii. 7 ; Psal. cxviii. 22. Ch. ii. 9 ; Exod. xix. 5, 6 ; Isa. xliii. 20, 21. Ch. ii. 10 ; Hos. ii. 23 ; Ch. ii. 17 ; Prov. xxiv. 21. Ch. ii. 22 ; Isa. liii. 4, 6, 7, 9. Ch. iii. 6 ; Gen. xviii. 12. Ch. iii. 10-12 ; Psal. xxxiv. 13, &c. Ch. iii. 14, 15 ; Isa. viii. 12, &c. Ch. iii. 20 ; Gen. vi. 3, 12. Ch. iv. 8 ; Prov. x. 12 ; comp. xvii. 9. Ch. iv. 18 ; Prov. xi. 31. Chap. v. 5 ; Prov. v. 34. Ch. v. 7 ; Psal. lv. 23.

Note B.

Of the assertion in the text the reader will be furnished with ample evidence, in comparing the passages here noted :—1 Pet. i. 3. Eph. i. 3. 1 Pet. i. 20. Rom. iv. 24 ; xvi. 25. Col. i. 26. 1 Pet. ii. 13. Rom. xiii. 1-5. 1 Pet. ii. 16, &c. Gal. v. 13. 1 Pet. ii. 18 ; iii. 1. Eph. vi. 5. Col. iii. 18. 1 Pet. iii. 3, 4. 1 Tim. ii. 9. 1 Pet. iii. 22. Eph. i. 20, &c. 1 Pet. iv. 10. Rom. xii. 6, &c. 1 Pet. v. 1. Rom. viii. 18. 1 Pet. v. 8. 1 Thess. v. 6. 1 Pet. v. 14. 1 Cor. xvi. 20. Rom. xvi. 16. 1 Thess. v. 26. Wetstein notices a very remarkable character of style which Peter has, in common with Paul. " Ita sermonem suum ordinat ut membrum sequens ex precedentis fine inchoet et cum eo connectat. I. 4.—εἰς ὑμας. 5.—φρουρουμενους—εν καιρω εσχατω. 6.—εν ὡ. 7.—Ιησου Χριστου. 8.—ὁν ειδοτες. 9. —σωτηριαν ψυχων. 10.—περι ἡς σωτηριας—προφητευσαντες. 11. ερευνωντες. The same peculiarity strongly marks the first paragraphs of Rom. v. and Eph. i., and also the proem of the Gospel of John.

Note C.

The following similarities between Peter and James are remarkable :—1 Pet. i. 6, 7 ; James i. 2, 3. 1 Pet. i. 24 ; James i. 10, 11. 1 Pet. i. 3, 23 ; James i. 18. 1 Pet. ii. 1, 2 ; James i. 21. 1 Pet. iv. 8 ; James v. 20. " Videtur omnino vel Jacobo Petri prior vel Petro Jacobi Epistola ob oculos versata fuisse ; maxime si utraque Epistola ad easdem ecclesias pertinuerit."— Storr, *Opuscula*, ii. 52.

Note D.

Matt. iv. 18, 19. Luke v. 3-11. John i. 40-42. Mark v. 37. Matt. xvi. 16-23 ; xiv. 28-31 ; xvii. 1-4, 24-27 ; xiii.

3, 4.   Luke xxii. 8.   John xiii. 6.   Matt. xxvi. 36, 37.   John
xviii. 10, 11.   Matt. xxvi. 31-35, 69-75.   John xx. 2-7.
Mark xvi. 7.   John xxi.   Acts i. ; xii. 17 ; xv. 6-11, 14.   Gal.
i. 18 ; ii. 7-9, 11-14.   *Vide* Neander's Planting and Training
of the Christian Church.—Vol. ii. p. 23-41.

Note E.

"There is an election to sanctification, as performed by the
power of the Gospel, separating the fore-ordained from the mass
of forlorn men unto holiness of life.   There is nothing else than
effectual vocation."—BYFIELD.   "Hic non proprie æterna electio
significatur, sed electio in tempore e communi turba hominum ac
imprimis Judæorum, quæ electio in Scriptura, alio modo, etiam
vocatio, sive vocatio secundum Dei propositum appellatur."—
BELG. ANNOT.

Note F.

I think it right to mention that Œcumenius and a number
both of ancient and modern interpreters, have connected κατα
προγνωτιν κ. τ. λ. with Αποστολος, and not with εκλεκτοις,—referring to Rom. i. 1, and especially to Acts xv. 7.   The exegesis
is so unnatural as not to require to be refuted.   "Προγνωσις hic
non præscientiam, sed antecedens decretum significat ut et Act.
ii. 23 : idem sensus qui Eph. i. 4."—GROTIUS.   There is no exegetical ground for explaining προγιγνοσκειν, and its derivatives of
"love," as has often been done to serve a purpose.

Note G.

Ἁγιασμος segregatio illa sive credentium consecratio, separatio
a reliquis hominibus extra Christum perituris.—BEZA.   "Il
vous a séparés effectivement d'avec eux, non pas en vous sancti-
fiant comme il fit le peuple d'Israël au désert, d'une sanctification externe et corporelle seulement, lorsqu'il le fit arrouser du
sang de la victime, qui ratifia par sa mort l'alliance de la loy ;
mais en vous consacrant d'une sanctification intérieure et spiri-
tuelle lorsque par la vertu de sa vocation il vous a amenés à
l'obéissance de son Evangile et à recevoir l'aspersion du sang
de Jesus Christ épandu pour l'établissement de l'alliance de
grâce en rémission des pêchés."—AMYRAUT.   Semler, no safe
guide, seems right here ; he considers the phrase as equivalent
to εν αγιασμω πνευματικω.

Note H.

It would be difficult to find an instance in which attachment
to an artificial system of Christian doctrine has been carried far-

ther into the interpretation of Scripture, than the explaining, as Nisbet does, "election into obedience, and sprinkling of the blood of Jesus Christ," of election to a participation in the active and passive righteousness of Christ,—obedience standing for the first, and blood for the second.

Note I.

The exposition given of this passage is that which the principles of a strict exegesis require ; and it is free from many difficulties which attend interpreting the passage according to our received translation. " Elect," in the sense of eternally chosen " according to the foreknowledge of God," is language which seems to suit a conditional better than a sovereign choice: " Elect, according to the foreknowledge of God through sanctification of the Spirit," presents a very strange arrangement of ideas. Is " the foreknowledge of God," or " election" according to that foreknowledge, *through* sanctification of the Spirit ? Surely " sanctification of the Spirit," meaning by that, sanctification by the Spirit, is the result of the divine decree,—the object of the divine foreknowledge,—the cause or means of neither. Then, what is to be made of " obedience," as placed before " sprinkling of the blood of Jesus ? " Is not all obedience which deserves the name, the consequence of being justified through the sprinkling of the blood of Jesus, and being sanctified by the Spirit ? and does the Spirit sanctify any who are not sprinkled with the blood of Jesus ? All these difficulties, which I confess I cannot solve, are got rid of in the exegesis proposed. " Selected according to the divine foreknowledge," which is just equivalent to the divine purpose (Acts ii. 23 ; 1 Pet. i. 20), " by a spiritual separation unto obedience," that they might obey the truth," *i. e.* believe the Gospel—" and," through that " obedience" to the truth, " be sprinkled with the blood of Jesus,"—enjoy all the saving results of the death of Christ—in pardon, sanctification, and eternal life. The only other passage (2 Thess. ii. 13) where the phrase αγιασμος πνευματος occurs, is to be interpreted in the same way. The choice there seems plainly selection ; by a. π. spiritual separation and " belief of the truth."

DISCOURSE II.

THE CHRISTIAN SALVATION DESCRIBED AND ACKNOWLEDGED.

1 PET. i. 3-5.—Blessed be the God and Father of our Lord Jesus Christ, which, according to his abundant mercy, hath begotten us again unto a lively hope, by the resurrection of Jesus Christ from the dead, to an inheritance incorruptible, and undefiled, and that fadeth not away, reserved in heaven for you, who are kept by the power of God through faith unto salvation, ready to be revealed in the last time.

IT has been finely remarked by a pious writer, that " it is a cold and lifeless thing to speak of spiritual things on mere report : but when men can speak of them as their own—as having share and interest in them, and some experience of their sweetness—their discourse of them is enlivened with firm belief and ardent affection : they cannot mention them, but straight their hearts are taken with such gladness as they are forced to vent in praises." [1]

Thus the Apostle Paul, in his Epistle to the Ephesian Church, when about to unfold the numerous, and varied, and invaluable benefits of the Christian's salvation, instead of commencing with a mere formal statement of them, bursts forth into a hymn of thanksgiving, " Blessed be the God and Father of our Lord Jesus Christ, who hath blessed us with all spiritual blessings in heavenly places in Christ ; according as he hath chosen us in him before the foundation of the world, that we should be holy and without blame

[1] Leighton.

before him in love : having predestinated us unto the adoption of children by Jesus Christ to himself, according to the good pleasure of his will, to the praise of the glory of his grace, wherein he hath made us accepted in the Beloved : In whom we have redemption through his blood, the forgiveness of sins, according to the riches of his grace; wherein he hath abounded toward us in all wisdom and prudence ; having made known unto us the mystery of his will, according to his good pleasure, which he hath purposed in himself : That in the dispensation of the fulness of times, he might gather together in one all things in Christ, both which are in heaven, and which are on earth, even in him ; in whom also WE have obtained an inheritance, being predestinated according to the purpose of him who worketh all things after the counsel of his own will; that we should be to the praise of his glory, who first trusted in Christ. In whom YE also *trusted* (or rather *have obtained an inheritance*), after that ye heard the word of truth, the gospel of your salvation : in whom also, after that ye believed, ye were sealed with that Holy Spirit of promise, which is the earnest of our inheritance, until the redemption of the purchased possession, unto the praise of his glory." [1]

And in the Epistle before us, the Apostle Peter, whose object plainly is to confirm the converts to whom he wrote in the faith and practice and profession of Christianity, notwithstanding all the difficulties and trials to which they were exposed, in bringing forward the vast magnitude and the absolute security of the happiness which the Gospel reveals and secures as one of the most powerful motives to perseverance, presents it in the impressive and animating form of devout ascription of praise to a redeeming God, in the name of himself and his believing brethren : "Blessed be the God and Father of our Lord Jesus Christ, which, according to his abundant mercy, hath begotten us again unto a lively hope, by the resurrection of Christ from the dead, to an inheritance incorruptible, undefiled, and that fadeth not

[1] Eph. i. 3-14.

away, reserved in heaven for you, who are kept by the power of God through faith unto salvation, ready to be revealed in the last time."

In illustrating this very interesting passage of Scripture, our attention must be directed, I. To the blessings acknowledged; and II. To the acknowledgment of these blessings.

The blessings acknowledged are these: (1.) the privilege of being the children of God—God, even the Father of our Lord Jesus Christ, hath begotten us again; (2.) an inheritance corresponding with this privilege—the salvation ready to be revealed in the last time, which is an inheritance incorruptible, undefiled, and unfading, reserved in heaven, and for which Christians are kept by the power of God through faith; and (3.) a present well-grounded and joyful hope of this inheritance.

The acknowledgment of these blessings naturally turns our attention, (1.) to the author of those blessings—God; (2.) to the character in which he bestows them—the God and Father of our Lord and Saviour Jesus Christ; (3.) to the principle from which they flow—his abundant mercy; (4.) to their vast magnitude and incalculable value; and (5.) to the proper method of Christians expressing their sense of their magnitude and value, by blessing their Divine Author. Such is the outline which I shall endeavour to fill up in the remaining part of this discourse.

1. OF THE BLESSINGS ACKNOWLEDGED.

Let us then, according to this plan, consider, in the first place, the blessings which the Apostle here so gratefully acknowledges.

§ 1.—*Divine Sonship.*

The first of these is the privilege of being children of God, "God, even the God and Father of our Lord Jesus Christ, hath begotten us again." When it is said, God hath "begotten us," the meaning is, "God hath made us his children:" and when it is said that God hath "again," anew, a second time, "begotten us," the meaning is, 'we were his children in one sense before, but in another, a higher, a better sense, a sense in which we were not his children, he has now made us his children.'

As his rational creatures, the objects of his kind providential care, all men are the children of God. "Have we not one Father? Hath not one God created us?" He is "the Father of the spirits of all flesh." "We are all his offspring." [1] But, as Christians, we have become the children of God in a sense in which all men are not his children. The appellation, children of God, as applied to true Christians in a mystical spiritual sense, like most of their peculiar appellations, is borrowed from one of the titles bestowed on the peculiar people of God under the former economy: "Israel," said Jehovah, "is my son, my first-born." "Ye are the children of the Lord your God," says Moses. Jehovah is spoken of as "the Rock that begat them." [2]

When Christians are represented as the children of God, there are two ideas suggested by the appellation. They are brought by him into the relation of children—and they are formed by him to the character of children.

The relation in which every human being stands to God in the present state, previously to his being personally connected with Jesus Christ as the Saviour, is that in which a violator of the law, convicted and condemned, stands to his sovereign. He is the appropriate object of Divine displeasure; in the language of Scripture, "The wrath of God abideth on him." [3] His ultimate happiness, if he remains in this state, is incompatible with the honour of God, the good order of his moral administration, and the well-being of his rational and accountable subjects.

But in the case of genuine Christians, a change of state takes place. The obedience to the death of God's incarnate

---

[1] Mal. ii. 10. Acts xvii. 26-28.   [2] Exod. iv. 22. Deut. xiv. 1; xxxii. 18
[3] John iii. 36.

Son, makes the salvation of sinners consistent with the illustration of the perfections of the Divine character, and subservient to the interests of the Divine government. Faith in Christ is that which, according to the Divine constitution, interests the individual sinner in the "obedience to death" of God's Son. On believing the truth, then, the individual who was condemned is no longer condemned—he is forgiven ; he who was a sentenced criminal, is now a beloved child. The relation in which he now stands to God, is that of a son to a father. God no longer frowns on him—he smiles on him. He no longer curses him—he blesses him. He was " angry with him, but he now comforts him."[1]

But when God makes men his children, he not only brings them into the relation of children, but he forms them to the character of children. When he gives men the privilege of being his children, he "sends forth into their hearts the Spirit of his Son," who forms in them a habitual temper and disposition, which may be termed " the spirit of adoption."[2] Our sentiments in reference to God, while in our natural condition, are not child-like. Our state is that of condemned criminals, and our character corresponds with our state. The leading feelings of the unrenewed man towards God, are dislike, and jealousy, and fear—"the fear that hath torment." But when God makes us his children, he forms us to the affectionate, confiding character of children. While he leads us to " sanctify him in our hearts," and to fear him without being afraid of him, he disposes us to love him as infinitely amiable and infinitely kind ; and to trust in him, as perfectly knowing what is good for us— perfectly able to secure our welfare—perfectly disposed to make us happy.

To be thus brought into the state and formed to the character of God's children, form the two great elements of true happiness, as they form the two grand fundamental blessings of the Christian salvation. They are most intimately connected together. The being brought into the

<hr />

[1] Isa. xii. 1.   [2] Gal. iv. 4-7. Rom. viii. 15.

state of children is absolutely necessary to the being formed
to the character of children. It is impossible to form a
slave to the character of a freeman, without making him
free. And the formation of us to the character of children,
is the great design of God in bringing us into the state of
children. He regards and treats us as his children, that we
may regard him and treat him as our Father.

We become the children of God—both in reference to state
and character, to condition and disposition—through the
belief of the truth; and this belief of the truth is produced
and maintained by the influence of the Holy Spirit. We
are "the children of God by faith in Christ Jesus." We
are "begotten" or "born" again, "not of corruptible seed,
but of incorruptible, by the word of God, which liveth and
abideth for ever." It is through the faith of the truth that
the condemned sinner is forgiven and justified: "He that believeth is not condemned, and can never come into condemnation;" while on him that believeth not, "the wrath of
God abideth." And it is through the faith of the truth that
the unholy sinner is sanctified. The heart is "purified by the
faith." It is through the knowledge and belief of the truth,
with regard to God's character as a Father, that we are
formed to the disposition and feelings of children. And this
faith of the truth is the result of the influence of the Divine
Spirit; so that, when born again—born from above—we are
"born of the Spirit." [1] So much for this first blessing, for
which the Apostle presents his acknowledgments.

§ 2.—*The inheritance provided for them.*

The second blessing is the future inheritance which God
has provided for us as his children. He has "begotten us again
to an inheritance,"—*i. e.,* that we may obtain an inheritance,
&c. "If children," says the Apostle, "then heirs," [2] *i. e.,* if
he bring us into the relation and form us to the character of
children, he will give us the treatment of children.

When God made ancient Israel his children—brought

---

[1] Gal. iii. 26. 1 Pet. i. 23. John iii. 18. Acts xv. 9.   [2] Rom. viii. 17.

them into a covenant relation with him—he assigned to them an inheritance. That inheritance was, like the economy to which it belonged, material and temporal. It was the large and fertile land of Canaan which they were to possess in security and peace, but into which they were not to enter immediately—nor till after a long course of wandering in the wilderness.

When God brings men into the relation of children under the new and spiritual and eternal economy, he assigns to them an inheritance which corresponds with the character of that new dispensation—an inheritance of which they are not to obtain the full possession, till "the times of the restitution of all things." The inheritance here is obviously the celestial blessedness, properly so called—the final state of good men—that state which, commencing with the general resurrection, is to be continued unchanged, except by indefinite progress, for ever and ever. What is figuratively termed "the inheritance," v. 4, is literally described, v. 5, as "the salvation ready or prepared to be revealed in the last time."

Of that state we can form but very inadequate conceptions, for it has not yet been "revealed." "It does not yet appear what we shall be;"[1] it will be fully unveiled by and by, but not till "the last time"—the period of "the glorious appearing of our Lord Jesus Christ." But we may form correct conceptions, so far as they go; and it is of the greatest importance that we should do so. It is a state of complete freedom from evil, both moral and physical, in all its forms and in all its degrees; and it is a state of perfect holy happiness, suited to a spiritual nature, endowed with intellect and affection and active power, united to a material frame, every way suited to minister to its progressive improvement and enjoyment; a state in which every capacity of blessedness shall be filled to overflowing, and in which the growing capacity shall never outrun the increasing blessedness.

Knowledge and holiness are the two great elements of

---

[1] 1 John iii. 2.

the celestial happiness. The holy spirits of the just made perfect, clothed upon with their house from heaven—the immortal, incorruptible, powerful, glorious resurrection body, shall be perfectly conformed to God, so far as their limited capacities admit, in knowledge and purity and happiness. God's mind shall be their mind—God's will, their will—God's happiness, their happiness. They shall "know Him as he is—and they shall be like him."[1] This is, I am persuaded, the justest view we can take of the celestial happiness. This is "the inheritance."

The celestial blessedness receives here, and in many other passages of Scripture, the appellation of "the inheritance" for two reasons—to mark the gratuitousness of its nature, and to mark the security of its tenure.

An inheritance is something that is not obtained by the individual's own exertions, but by the free gift or bequest of another. The earthly inheritance of the external people of God, was not given them because they were greater or better than the other nations of the earth. It was "because the Lord had a delight in them to love them." "They got not the land in possession by their own sword, neither did their own right hand save them; but thy right hand, and thine arm, and the light of thy countenance, for thou hadst a favour unto them."[2] And the heavenly inheritance of the spiritual people of God is entirely the gift of sovereign kindness. "By grace are we saved;" "eternal life is the gift of God through Jesus Christ our Lord."[3]

A second idea suggested by the figurative expression, "the inheritance," when used in reference to the celestial blessedness, is the security of the tenure by which it is held. No right is more indefeasible than the right of inheritance. If the right of the giver or bequeather be good, all is secure. The heavenly happiness, whether viewed as the gift of the Divine Father, or the bequest of the Divine Son, is "sure to all the seed." If the title of the claimant be but as valid as

---

[1] 1 John iii. 2.   [2] Psal. xliv. 3.   [3] Eph. ii. 5. Rom. vi. 23.

the right of the original proprietor, their tenure must be as secure as the throne of God and his Son.

The idea of the security of this happiness is brought forward, however, more distinctly in the description of the inheritance, which immediately follows. It is described as "incorruptible, undefiled, and unfading—reserved in heaven" for Christians, while they are kept "by the power of God through faith."

In this description of the inheritance, there are two things which require consideration—the excellence of the inheritance itself; and the security that the Christian shall in due time enjoy it.

As to the excellence of the inheritance itself, it is "incorruptible, undefiled, and unfading."[1] These epithets may seem in a great degree synonymous, and there is no doubt that permanent, unchanging excellence is the leading idea in them all. Yet, on looking a little more closely at them, we will find that each of them presents that general idea in an instructive and pleasing peculiarity of aspect.

The celestial happiness viewed as an inheritance, is "incorruptible." There is nothing in its own nature which can lead to its dissolution. It is not material, but spiritual. It is not composed of "such corruptible things as silver and gold," but of knowledge and of holiness. It is not "meat and drink,"—it is not costly and splendid apparel—it is not stately buildings, nor extensive estates. It is "joy and peace" and happiness arising from sources which, from their very nature, are inexhaustible,—possession of the Divine favour—conformity to the Divine image—intercourse and fellowship with God.

It is not only incorruptible, and therefore everlasting, but it is "undefiled." It is debased by no extrinsic, heterogeneous ingredient. In all our enjoyments on earth, however pure and exalted in themselves, there is a mixture. There is

---

[1] Αφθαρτος æternum durans. Αμιαντος purum—cui nihil mali, nihil vitii est ad mixtum—ut purum gaudium—gaudium cui nihil tristitiæ admiscetur. Αμαραντος non marcescens.—MORUS.

always something wanting—something wrong; and sin, that vilest of all things, taints and pollutes them all. But into heaven there enters "nothing that defileth." There is knowledge, without any mixture of error—holiness, without any mixture of sin—love, without any mixture of malignity; the highest dignities excite there no pride—the richest possessions, no covetousness. The inheritance is undefiled.

Still further—the heavenly inheritance is " unfading!" It "fadeth not away."[1] The garland worn by the blessed is of amaranth—it never withers. The idea here seems to be, It not only is everlasting in its own nature, but it will never cease to give happiness to the possessor. How often do worldly possessions wither,—cease to give the happiness they once gave to those who continue to hold rather than to enjoy them! It has been beautifully remarked, that " the sweetest earthly music, if heard but for one day, would weary those who are most delighted with it. But the song of Heaven, though for ever the same, shall be for ever new."[2] Here we are often sated, but never satisfied—there, there is constant satisfaction, but there never will be satiety. Such is the excellence of the celestial inheritance.

But may the Christian say, the inheritance is indeed inestimably precious; but will it ever be mine? It is as secure as it is precious, says the apostle. It is " reserved in heaven for you," and ye are " kept for it by the power of God through faith."

This inheritance is " reserved in heaven" for Christians—i. e., it is secured beyond the reach of violence or fraud. Many a person, born to a rich inheritance, has never obtained possession of it, but has lived and died in poverty; but this inheritance is liable to none of the accidents of earth and time. It is " in heaven," under the immediate guardianship of divine power, wisdom, and love.

But the inheritance may itself be secure, but not secure for me. There may be perfect happiness in heaven, but

---

[1] ἀμάραντον.   [2] Leighton.

I may never reach it there. To meet this suggestion the apostle adds, " Ye are kept by the mighty power of God through faith." The apostle's doctrine is, and it is quite accordant with the doctrine of his Master and the other apostles, that all who are begotten again by God shall be preserved to the enjoyment of the inheritance. None of them shall fall in the wilderness. " I give unto my sheep eternal life," says Jesus Christ ; " and they shall never perish, neither shall any one pluck them out of my hand. My Father, who gave them me, is greater than all ; and none can pluck them out of my father's hand."[1] " Who shall separate us from the love of Christ ? shall tribulation, or distress, or persecution, or famine, or nakedness, or peril, or sword ? Nay, in all these things we are more than conquerors, through him that loved us. For I am persuaded, that neither death, nor life, nor angels, nor principalities, nor powers, nor things present, nor things to come, nor height, nor depth, nor any other creature, shall be able to separate us from the love of God, which is in Christ Jesus our Lord."[2]

They are " kept"—preserved safe—amid the many dangers to which they are exposed, " by the power of God." The expression, " power of God," may here refer to the divine power both as exercised in reference to the enemies of the Christian, controlling their malignant purposes, and as exercised in the form of spiritual influence on the mind of the Christian himself, keeping him in the faith of the truth, in the love of God, and in the patient waiting for our Lord Jesus Christ. It is probably to the last that the apostle principally alludes, for he adds " by faith." It is through the persevering faith of the truth that the Christian is by divine influence preserved from falling, and kept in possession both of that state and character which are absolutely necessary to the enjoyment of the heavenly inheritance.[3]

---

[1] John x. 28.   [2] Rom. viii. 35-39.

[3] " When εν and διὰ are connected in one sentence, διὰ refers to external means, whilst εν relates to that which is effected in or on a person, as if adhering to him. Eph. i. 7.—εν ὦ ὦ (χϱ) εχομεν την απολυτϱωσιν διὰ του ἁιματος αυτου. Even when impersonal things are spoken of, the distinction between εν (of an internal

The perseverance thus secured to the true Christian is perseverance in faith and holiness, and nothing can be more grossly absurd than for a person living in unbelief and sin, to suppose that he can be in the way of obtaining celestial blessedness.

So much for the illustration of the second blessing for which the apostle gives thanks—the future inheritance which God has provided for his children.

§ 3. *The living hope of the inheritance.*

Let us now proceed to consider the third of these blessings: The living or lively hope of the inheritance, through the resurrection of Christ Jesus from the dead. God hath " begotten us again to a lively hope"—*i. e.,* in making us his children, he has excited in us an influential and enduring hope of final and complete happiness.

Mankind in their natural state are said to "have no hope"[1] —*i. e.,* they are without any well-grounded rational hope of final happiness. This is true of all men without exception, of the elect of God as well as of others. They have broken the divine law, they have incurred the divine displeasure. They are guilty, and depraved, and miserable. They deserve everlasting destruction; and if mercy interpose not, they must meet with their desert.

It is an inquiry of very deep moment, then, how is the well-grounded hope of final happiness excited and maintained in the human mind? Now there are two questions which must be resolved, in order to our distinctly apprehending the truth on this subject; the first, what is the ground of the hope referred to in our text? and the second is, how is an individual brought to cherish the hope of final happiness on this ground?

With reference to the former of these questions, it is obvious that the ground of hope is not any thing in the sinner himself. It is not that he is innocent. It is not

psychological state or power), and διά, of means, is apparent: as 1 Pet. i. 5.— τους εν δυναμει θεου φρουρουμενους δια πιστεως; and v. 22.— εν τη υπακοη της αληθειας, δια πνευματος.—WINER, Part iii. sec. 52, p. 312.   [1] Eph. ii. 12.

that he is less guilty than others. It is not that a great change has been produced, or is to be produced on him. When he looks at himself in the light of the divine law, a sinner may well perceive abundant reason for fear, abundant reason for despair; but he can never perceive any sufficient reason for hope.

The ground of hope is not in us, but in God. The ground of the sinner's hope—(and the ground of the saint's hope is just the ground of the sinner's hope; for what is a saint but a saved sinner?)—is sometimes represented as the sovereign benignity of God; sometimes as the obedience to death, the finished work, the perfect atonement of Christ; and sometimes as the free untrammelled revelation of mercy in the word of the truth of the gospel. These are all but different aspects of the same thing, and the truth on this subject may be thus stated. The ground—the sole ground of a sinner's hope—is the sovereign mercy of God, manifested in consistency with, in glorious illustration of, his righteousness, in the obedience to death of his Son Jesus Christ the just one, in the room of the unjust, of which we have a plain and well accredited account " in the word of the truth of the gospel." The ground of hope is exhibited in such passages of Scripture as the following :—" God so loved the world, that he gave his only begotten Son, that whosoever believeth in him might not perish, but have everlasting life." " The righteousness of God without the law is manifested, being witnessed by the law and the prophets; even the righteousness of God, which is by the faith of Christ unto all and upon all them that believe; for there is no difference: for all have sinned, and come short of the glory of God; being justified freely by God's grace, through the redemption that is in Christ Jesus; whom God hath set forth as a propitiation through faith in his blood." " It is a faithful saying, and worthy of all acceptation, that Christ Jesus came into the world to save sinners; of whom I am chief." " God is in Christ, reconciling the world to himself, not imputing their trespasses to them; for he hath made him to be sin

for us, who knew no sin, that we might be made the righteousness of God in him."　"The blood of Jesus Christ, his
Son, cleanseth us from all sin.　He is able to save to the
uttermost them that come unto God by him, seeing he ever
liveth to make intercession for them."[1]

The second question is, how is the sinner brought to
cherish the hope of eternal life on this ground?　Now, if
the preceding remarks have been understood, there can be
no difficulty in answering this question.　The free sovereign
mercy of God, manifested in a consistency with his righteousness, is revealed in the gospel; and it can only be by that
gospel being understood and believed, that the individual
sinner can obtain the hope of eternal life.　If I believe this
revelation, I hope for eternal life, and I hope for eternal life
on this ground.　If I do not believe this revelation, I either
have no hope of eternal life, or, if I have, it is a hope
built on another and a false foundation.　It is in the
faith of the truth that the sinner finds hope.　Not that the
sinner's faith is the ground of his hope, but that it is through
believing alone that he can discover the ground on which
his hope must rest.　When Elisha's servant was over-
whelmed with fears lest his master should fall into the
hands of the Syrians, his fears were turned into assured
hope, when, with enlightened eyes, he beheld the heavenly
host with which they were surrounded.　His hope rested,
not on his seeing that host, but on their being there; but
still his seeing them there was in the nature of things necessary to his hope.[2]　In like manner the sinner's hope
rests entirely on God's free sovereign kindness, manifested
in harmony with his righteousness; but it is only in the
belief of the truth that this sovereign kindness can be apprehended as a ground of hope.

The ground of hope never varies.　The ground of the
hope of eternal life to an aged and accomplished saint, just
about to enter Paradise, is the very same as that of the most

---

[1] John iii. 16.　Rom. iii. 21-25.　1 Tim. i. 15.　2 Cor. v. 19, 21.　Heb. vii. 25.
[2] 2 Kings vi. 15-17.

guilty and depraved of men who has just been brought to
the knowledge and faith of the truth.   The beginning of
our confidence is the end of our confidence.   Our first hope
is our last hope.

It follows, of course, that the great means of maintaining
and strengthening hope, is just the continued and the increasing faith of the truth; at the same time it is plain from
Scripture, that as the faith of the truth uniformly produces
holiness as well as hope, unholy tempers are in their own
nature calculated to cloud our hope; and holy tempers and
conduct to strengthen it, not by adding to its foundation,
but by affording evidence that we have built on that foundation.

There are two other questions respecting this hope,
which, though not of such vital importance as those which
I have now endeavoured briefly and plainly to answer, are
yet of very considerable interest at all times, and particularly at present, when much darkening of counsel by words,
without knowledge on this subject, seems to me to prevail.[1]
Is the hope of eternal life connected with the faith of the
gospel?   And does every believer enjoy an unclouded hope
of eternal life?

With regard to the first question, I would unhesitatingly
reply in the affirmative.   The gospel cannot be believed
without, in the degree in which it is believed, producing the
hope of eternal life.   It is not only not necessary that a
sinner should wait till the faith of the gospel has proved its
efficacy in a moral transformation of his nature, before he
begin to cherish the hope of salvation, but he cannot believe
the gospel without cherishing that hope; and it is through
means of this hope that the gospel believed, in a great
measure, works that moral change.   To believe the gospel,
and to despair of salvation, are two utterly incompatible
states of mind.   We hold, then, that every believer, ac-

---

[1] The reference here is to the speculations about Universal Pardon, which,
at the time this discourse was delivered, December 1830, were very prevalent
in this country.

cording to the measure of his faith, has the hope of eternal life.

And in this principle we also find the true answer to the second question : 'Does every believer enjoy the unclouded hope of eternal life?' He does enjoy that hope according to the measure of his faith. If he is strong in faith, he abounds in hope. But as every believer in the present state has but an imperfect apprehension both of the truth and its evidence, and is still to a certain extent under the influence of false views, every believer, while in the present state, is imperfect both in holiness and in hope. At the same time, his imperfection in both is not more his misfortune than his fault. A perfect faith of a completely understood gospel would produce unshaken, unclouded hope, and enable the Christian at all times, in all circumstances, to " rejoice in hope of the glory of God."

This hope of eternal life, grounded on the sovereign mercy of God manifested in harmony with his holiness and righteousness, through the mediation of Christ revealed in the gospel ; and excited, and maintained, and strengthened by the faith of the gospel, is described here as " a lively," or rather " a living hope." [1] The hope of the Christian is a " living" hope, in opposition both to a dead and a dying hope—in opposition to the dead hope of the hypocrite, and the dying hope of the self-deceiver.

The apostle James speaks of " a dead faith," which, on examination, turns out to be no faith at all, but merely a man's saying he has faith.[2] There is also a dead hope, which is in reality no hope at all, but merely a profession of it. A mere professed hope, founded on a mere professed faith, is a dead thing—it can neither make a man holy nor happy—it cannot animate to duty—it cannot support under suffering. But the hope of the Christian is a living hope. It fills him with joy and peace in the degree in which it prevails ; and it leads him to purify himself, even as he in whom he

---

[1] ελπιδα ζωσαν.   [2] James ii. 17.

places his confidence is pure. The hope of eternal life is
the well-grounded expectation of perfect holy happiness.
Now, is it not perfectly plain, so plain as to need no illustration, that this must be a living operative hope, and that, just
in the degree in which it exists, it must make him in whom
it dwells both holy and happy? It will induce a man to
submit to the greatest evils rather than renounce the faith of
Christ; and it will keep him cheerful and happy under all
the sacrifices which he may be called on to make in the
cause of his Saviour.

This hope is termed a living hope, not only in opposition
to a dead hope, but also in opposition to dying hopes.
There are many hopes which are not merely professed, but
really entertained, that will never be realised. This is true
both as to worldly hopes and as to religious hopes. With
regard to worldly hopes, have we not all from experience
discovered the truth of the remark,—" They are not living,
but lying, dying hopes. They often die before us, and we
live to bury them, and see our own folly and simplicity in
trusting to them, and at the utmost they die with us when
we die, and can accompany us no farther." [1] With regard
to religious hopes, it is a happy thing when all of them, not
founded on the faith of the truth, die before we die; for till
these dying hopes expire, the living hope cannot exist. All
hopes of eternal life, excepting that which we have been
endeavouring to describe, will most assuredly expire when
we expire, and make those who relied on them ashamed and
confounded world without end. But this hope lives in
death. This hope remains unshaken by all the calamities
which can befall the believer here; for he knows nothing can
separate him from the love of God. Death and judgment
and eternity do not destroy, they fulfil this hope; and as the
object of the hope is ever-enduring holy happiness, it is
plain that hope as well as enjoyment must continue for ever.

This " hope makes not ashamed," *i. e.* it never disappoints;

[1] Leighton.

and, if you would know the reason, you will find the
apostle Paul assigning it, from the 5th to the 10th verse of
the 5th chapter of the epistle to the Romans : " Hope
maketh not ashamed; because the love of God is shed
abroad in our hearts by the Holy Ghost, which is given
unto us. For when we were yet without strength, in due
time Christ died for the ungodly. For scarcely for a righteous man will one die ; yet peradventure for a good man
some would even dare to die. But God commendeth his
love toward us, in that, while we were yet sinners, Christ
died for us. Much more then, being now justified by his
blood, we shall be saved from wrath through him. For if,
when we were enemies, we were reconciled to God by the
death of his Son ; much more, being reconciled, we shall be
saved by his life."[1]

This living hope is produced "by" means of "the resurrection of Christ Jesus from the dead." The resurrection of
our Lord Jesus Christ is one of the most striking and satisfactory proofs of the divinity of his mission, and, of course, of
the truth of all his doctrines, and, among the rest, of that
grand characteristic doctrine of his gospel on which the
hope of eternal life is founded. It is, indeed, not so much
one evidence as " a cloud of witnesses." It is the fulfilment of
Old Testament prediction respecting the Messiah, and thus
proves him to be the Messiah—it is the fulfilment of his own
prediction, and therefore proves him to be a true prophet.
It is God determining the controversy between him and his
unbelieving countrymen. He declared himself to be the
Son of God, and they put him to death because he declared
himself to be the Son of God; and God interposed, and by
doing for him what none but God could have done, proved
that He was right, and they were wrong. Most powerfully
was Jesus Christ demonstrated to be the Son of God by the
resurrection from the dead.[2]

---

[1] The above remarks, somewhat amplified, have been repeatedly published,
under the title of " Hints on Hope."

[2] Rom. i. 4.

But there is a more intimate connexion than this between the resurrection of Christ from the dead, and the hope of eternal life. Christ's resurrection from the dead is a clear proof of the reality and efficacy of His atoning sacrifice. He " who was given for our offences, has been raised again for our justification." [1] When God " brought again from the dead our Lord Jesus, that great Shepherd of the sheep, by the blood of the everlasting covenant," he manifested himself to be " the God of peace," the pacified divinity. He " raised him from the dead, and gave him glory, that our faith and hope might be in himself." Had Jesus not risen, " our faith had been vain ; we should have been still in our sin," [2] and without hope. But now that He has risen—

> " Our surety freed, declares us free,
>   For whose offences He was seized ;
> In His release our own we see,
>   And joy to view Jehovah pleased."

But even this is not all. Our Lord's resurrection is to be viewed not only in connexion with his death, but with the following glory. Raised from the dead, he has received all power in heaven and on earth, that he may give eternal life to as many as the Father had given him. How this is calculated to encourage hope, may be readily apprehended. " Because he lives, we shall live also." Having the keys of death and the unseen world, he can and will raise us from the dead, and give us eternal life. He sits at the right hand of God. " Our life is hid with him in God ; and when he who is our life shall appear, we shall appear with him in glory." We are not yet in possession of the inheritance; but he, our head and representative, is. " We see not yet all things put under us ; but we see Him," the Captain of our salvation, " for the suffering of death crowned with glory and honour. [3]" The resurrection of Christ, when con-

---

[1] Rom. iv. 25.   [2] Heb. xiii. 20.   1 Pet. i. 21.   1 Cor. xv. 17.
[3] John xiv. 19.   Rev. i. 18.   Col. iii. 3.   Heb. ii. 9.

sidered in reference to the death which preceded, and the glory which followed it, is the grand means of producing and strengthening the hope of eternal life.

Let us all beware of false hopes. Let him who never hoped, now receive the truth in the love of it, and begin to hope. Let those who have believed abound in hope. There is, there can be, no danger of hoping too confidently, if the hope be but placed on the right foundation. " We desire that every one of you do show the same diligence, to the full assurance of hope unto the end ; [1] that ye be not slothful, but followers of them who through faith and patience inherit the promises."

II.—OF THE ACKNOWLEDGMENT OF THESE BLESSINGS.

The devout acknowledgment of these blessings comes now to be considered : " Blessed be the God and Father of our Lord and Saviour Jesus Christ, which, according to his abundant mercy, hath begotten us again unto a lively hope, by the resurrection of Jesus Christ from the dead, to an inheritance incorruptible, and undefiled, and that fadeth not away, reserved in heaven for you, who are kept by the power of God through faith unto salvation, ready to be revealed in the last time." This devout acknowledgment naturally leads the mind to reflect on God as the author of these blessings — on the character in which he bestows them, " the God and Father of our Lord and Saviour Jesus Christ"—on the principle in which the bestowal of these blessings originates, " abundant mercy"—on their vast magnitude and inestimable value—and on the proper manner of Christians expressing their sense of this magnitude and value.

§ 1. *God is the author of these blessings.*

The first remark suggested by this devout acknowledgment is, that God is the author of the blessings acknow-

[1] ἵνα. Heb. vi. 11, 12.

ledged. This is not only implied in making the acknowledgment—for when we return thanks for a favour, to whom
do we offer our acknowledgment but to him who has bestowed it?—but it is distinctly expressed: God has begotten
us again. God has provided us an inheritance. God
has given us a living hope.

God is the author of all good. All the holiness and all the
happiness in the universe come from him. " Every good gift
and every perfect gift cometh down from above, from the
Father of lights." In the new creation, " All things are of
God."[1] The blessings enjoyed are all the free gifts of his
sovereign goodness. HE makes us his children. HE brings
us into the relation of children. HE forms us to the character
of children. When we are brought into the relation of
children our sins are forgiven, and we are justified freely by
God's grace. But "who can forgive sins, but GOD only?"
" It is GOD that justifieth."[2] The sentence of the law can
be remitted only by the great Lawgiver. The privilege of
being the sons of God can be conferred by none but God.
As it is God who brings us into the relation of children, it
is God who forms us to the character of children. " For
we are HIS workmanship, created anew in Christ Jesus." It
is God, by the agency of his own Spirit, through the instrumentality of his own word understood and believed, who
transforms the character of a condemned felonious slave
into that of a beloved and dutiful child. It is HE who
takes "the hard and the stony heart out of our flesh, and
gives us a heart of flesh." It is HE who disposes us to
venerate, and esteem, and love, and trust him. It is HE
who enables us cheerfully to obey his commandments, and
submit to his appointments. It is HE who sends forth
his Spirit into our hearts, teaching us to cry, " Abba,
Father."[3]

As it is God who makes us his children, bringing us into
the filial relation, forming us to the filial character, so it is

---

[1] James i. 17. 2 Cor. v. 18.   [2] Mark ii. 7. Rom. viii. 33.
[3] Eph. ii. 10. Ezek. xi. 19. Gal. iv. 6.

God who has provided, and who will bestow on his people the inheritance, corresponding to the relation into which he has brought them, and the character to which he has formed them. "It is the FATHER's good pleasure to give them the kingdom." The final happiness of the saints is entirely the result of divine love, and wisdom, and power. "Eternal life is the gift of God." [1]   God himself is, indeed, if I may use the expression, the very substance of the celestial blessedness. To know him—to see him as he is—to find in him the adequate object of all our unbounded capacities of knowledge, and affection, and enjoyment—to love him, and to be loved by him, and to know that we are loved by him —to be like him, having no mind different from his, no will opposed to his—to enter into his joy, and thus to have our joy made full—this is the inheritance ; and who can thus give us God, but God himself?

And all that was necessary, in order to make the communication of such a happiness to such creatures as we are— guilty, righteously condemned—consistent with the honour of the divine character ; and all that is as necessary to make such depraved creatures as we are capable of such a happiness—all is the work, not of men or of angels, but of God. His love originated the purpose—his wisdom formed the plan—his power will work out the accomplishment of his people's salvation.

As the inheritance is his gift, so also is the hope of the inheritance. It is God who gave us the living hope. The ground of that hope is HIS sovereign kindness—that kindness is displayed in harmony with righteousness, in HIS giving HIS Son to be the propitiation for the sins of men. This display of his sovereign kindness is made in HIS revelation of HIS will by " holy men, who spoke as they were moved by HIS Spirit ;" and this revelation, in the belief of which alone the condemned sinner can find hope, is understood and believed by the individual sinner, in consequence of the

---

[1] Luke xii. 32.   Rom. vi. 23.

effectual working of HIS Spirit. It was HE who "delivered his Son for our offences." It was HE who "raised him again for our justification." It is HE who disposes us to believe this revelation of mercy. It is HE who thus gives us "good hope through grace." Every measure of the living hope, from the faint dawn which opens on the mind of the sinner coming to the knowledge of the truth, to the clear unclouded radiance which enlightens the mind of him who has received "the full assurance of understanding," every measure of this living hope is the gift of God; and we end as we began the illustration of this particular with the sublime declaration of the apostle respecting the new creation, "All things are of God." "Of HIM, and through him, and to him, are all things." "God is all in all."[1]

§ 2. *It is as the God and Father of our Lord Jesus Christ, that God bestows these blessings.*

The second remark suggested by this devout acknowledgment is, that in bestowing the favours here acknowledged, God acts in the character of "the God and Father of our Lord Jesus Christ." God is infinitely holy, and cannot but disapprove of sin—cannot but loathe and abhor it in a degree of which we can form no adequate conception. God is inflexibly just, and can "by no means clear the guilty." He is "not a God that hath pleasure in wickedness, neither shall evil dwell with him. The foolish shall not stand in his sight; and he hates the workers of iniquity." "Snares, fire and brimstone, and a furious tempest, will he rain on the wicked; this pertains to them as the portion of their cup."[2] How is it, then, that this holy and righteous God blesses sinful men with all heavenly and spiritual blessings? how is it that he makes them his children; gives them a heavenly inheritance, and cheers them with a living hope?

It is as "the God and Father of our Lord Jesus Christ," that he does all this. In the riches of his sovereign mercy

---

[1] Rom. iv. 25. 2 Thess. ii. 16. 2 Cor. v. 18. Rom. xi. 36. 1 Cor. xv. 28.
[2] Exod. xxxiv. 7. Psal. v. 4, 5; xi. 6.

he determined to save an innumerable multitude of sinful men, and in the depth of his wisdom he formed a plan for realizing the determination of his mercy, not merely in consistency with, but in glorious illustration of, his holiness and justice. The leading feature in that plan is, the appointment of his only begotten Son to be the representative of those who were to be saved, to be dealt with as they deserved to be dealt with, that they might be dealt with as he deserved to be dealt with. The second person of the glorious Trinity is essentially his Father's equal—possessed of the same divine essence and perfections; but in this assumed character he is the Father's inferior; he acts a subordinate part in the economy of salvation. God essentially considered, in the person of the Father, is the God of " the Mediator between God and man;" and he is his Father not merely essentially, as he is the second person of the Trinity, but also economically, as he is the head of the chosen family—" the first born among many brethren."

The great truth intended to be taught us by God being represented as the author of spiritual blessings to men, in the character of the God and Father of our Lord Jesus Christ, is this—that it is only as viewed in connexion with him; or, as the inspired writers usually express it, as " in him," that we sinners can obtain any saving blessing from God. The order is, " all things are ours, we are Christ's, Christ is God's." He is our God because he is his God, our Father because he is his Father.[1] Take the blessings mentioned in the text as an illustration. God makes us his children—*i. e.*, he pardons our sins, he receives us into his favour, he conforms us to his image. Now, how does he do this? He gives " us redemption in Christ, the forgiveness of sins." He makes us " accepted in the beloved." " We are his workmanship, created anew in Christ Jesus unto good works." He gives us an inheritance. How? in

---

[1] 1 Cor. iii. 22, 23. John xx. 17.

Christ. "In him," says the apostle, " we have obtained an inheritance." He makes us to " sit in heavenly places in him." [1] He gives us a living hope. How? While " without Christ," viewed as unconnected with Christ, there is no hope for man; all his well-grounded expectations of happiness must be founded on what Christ has done, and is doing, as the representative of his people. While in the new creation, all things are of God, all things are through Christ Jesus. It is as well pleased with Him, that God is well pleased with us; and it is as his God and Father, that he blesses us with all heavenly and spiritual blessings in him.

§ 3. *These blessings originate in the " abundant mercy" of God.*

The third remark suggested by this devout acknowledgment is, that in the bestowment of these blessings by God, there is a remarkable display of the divine benignity. It is " according to his abundant mercy, that he begets us again unto a lively hope, by the resurrection of Jesus Christ from the dead, to an inheritance incorruptible, and undefiled, and that fadeth not away, reserved in heaven for you, who are kept by the power of God through faith unto salvation, ready to be revealed in the last time." This remark invites us into a very wide field of most interesting and improving illustration; but I must satisfy myself with merely opening to you a few tracks of thought, which you will do well to pursue in private meditation.

Think on the character of him who bestows these blessings. The absolute, independent Jehovah, perfectly, infinitely, unchangeably happy in himself. How could the self-incurred ruin of guilty mankind affect his interest? It might illustrate his holiness, his righteousness, his faithfulness, but how could it disturb his peace, or lessen his blessedness? It is impossible to conceive the communication of

[1] Eph. i. 3-13.

saving blessings to man, to originate in any principle in the divine mind but sovereign benignity. It was "only because he had a delight in man to love him."

Think on the nature of the blessings. The very highest which can be conferred on us creatures, the noblest in their own nature, and in their measure limited by nothing but the capacity of their recipient. "Behold, what manner of love" is this,[1] to be God's sons, to see him as he is, to be like him, and all this for ever and ever!

Think on the character of those on whom they are bestowed;—sinners, guilty, depraved, righteously condemned; deserving everlasting destruction; naturally forgetters, haters, contemners of God. Surely the mercy which confers such blessings on such sinners is abundant mercy, and the Apostle may well say, "Behold what manner of love the Father hath bestowed on *us*, that *we* should be called the sons of God."

Think of the number of those on whom these blessings are bestowed. "The nations of the saved" are a numerous host.[2] The sons who are to be brought to glory are "many sons." They are "a great multitude, an innumerable company, out of every kindred, and people, and tongue, and nation:" and all these are blessed up to their largest capacity of enjoyment, during the whole eternity of their being. Is not this abundant mercy?

Once more think of the means through which the blessings are communicated. The incarnation, the sacrifice of God's own Son. He did not spare him, he delivered him up for us all, that he with him might freely give us all things. "Herein surely is love, not that we loved God but that God hath loved us, and gave his Son to be the propitiation for our sins." "God so loved the world, that he gave his only begotten Son, that whosoever believeth in him might not perish, but have everlasting life."[3]

Surely it is in his "abundant mercy" that "God, even

---

[1] 1 John iii. i.   [2] Rev. xxi. 24; vii. 9.   [3] 1 John iv. 10. John iii. 16.

the Father of our Lord Jesus Christ, has blessed us with all
heavenly and spiritual blessings."

§ 4. *These blessings are of vast magnitude and incalculable
value.*

The fourth remark suggested by this devout acknowledgment is, that the blessings acknowledged are of vast magnitude and of incalculable value.   The plain meaning of the
acknowledgment is this : for conferring these blessings on
us, God richly deserves to be thanked and praised uninter-
ruptedly, everlastingly.   For every blessing, even for a breath
of air, a crust of bread, a draught of water, a moment of
ease, we ought to give thanks ; for we are unworthy of any
favour.   Every thing in the shape of blessing coming to us
from God should excite our gratitude.   But the blessings
mentioned in the text are obviously peculiarly valuable.
They are not " such corruptible things as silver and gold."
They include in them deliverance from guilt, depravity, degradation, death, everlasting misery ; the enjoyment of the
favour of God, tranquillity of conscience, ever growing conformity to the divine image in holiness and happiness,
throughout eternity.   Just look at them as here described,
and say if they are not unspeakably great, incalculably
valuable.   What is said of the love in which they originate
may be equally applied to them : They have " a height
and a depth, a length and a breadth, which pass knowledge." [1]

§ 5. *The proper method of acknowledging these benefits is, to
" bless" their munificent giver.*

The fifth and last remark suggested by this devout acknowledgment is, that the appropriate manner of expressing
our sense of the magnitude and value of these blessings is,
to bless their munificent author.   When God blesses men
he confers on them blessings, he makes them blessed ; when

[1] Eph. iii. 18, 19.

men bless God, they merely declare that he is infinitely excellent and blessed in himself—that he deserves to have his infinite excellencies acknowledged and celebrated—that they recognize this obligation as lying on them—and that they wish to express in every proper method their sense of the infinite praiseworthiness of the divinity.

Nothing surely can be more reasonable than that those who have received such blessings as are here acknowledged, should bless Him who has bestowed them. This is one of the purposes for which they are begotten again. "This people," may Jehovah say of them, "I have formed for myself, that they may shew forth my praise." "Ye are a chosen generation," says the Apostle, "a royal priesthood, a holy nation, a peculiar people; that ye should shew forth the praises of him who hath called you out of darkness into his marvellous light."[1] Christians ought to cultivate the feelings of gratitude for the blessings they have received, and which they hope to receive, and often to express their feelings in thanksgiving and praise. Indeed their whole lives should be a hymn of praise to the God of their salvation. The habitual language of their heart should be, "What shall I render to the Lord for all his benefits!" "Bless the Lord, O my soul, and never be forgetful of his benefits: who forgiveth all thine iniquities; who healeth all thy diseases; who redeemeth thy life from destruction; who crowneth thee with loving-kindness and tender mercies." "I will praise thee, O Lord my God, with all my heart; and I will glorify thy name for evermore. For great is thy mercy toward me; and thou hast delivered my soul from the lowest hell."[2]

If we really feel gratitude to God for his abundant goodness, we will express it not merely by our lips, but by our lives. Constrained by "the mercy of God, we will present our bodies, ourselves, living sacrifices, holy, and acceptable, which is our reasonable service." While we through

---

[1] Isa. xliii. 21; 1 Pet. ii. 9.   [2] Psal. ciii. 1-4; lxxxvi. 12, 13.

Christ "offer to him continually the sacrifice of praise, the fruit of our lips, giving thanks to his name;" we will also, "do good and communicate," knowing that "with such sacrifices God is well pleased;" and while we feel ashamed of the coldness of our feelings of gratitude, and the imperfection of our services of acknowledgment, we will look forward with earnest longings to that happy period, when, having been made partakers of the inheritance, we shall, under the influence of the gratitude which "the salvation which is in Christ, with eternal glory," fully possessed, is fitted to exert over a thoroughly sanctified human heart, join in the rapturous anthem of eternity: "Blessing, and honour, and glory, and power, be to him that sitteth on the throne, and to the Lamb for ever and ever."[1]

[1] Rom. xii. 1. Heb. xiii. 15, 16. Rev. v. 13.

DISCOURSE III.

THE PRESENT AND FUTURE STATE OF THE CHRISTIAN CONTRASTED.

1 PET. i. 6-9.—Wherein ye greatly rejoice, though now for a season (if need be) ye are in heaviness through manifold temptations; that the trial of your faith, being much more precious than of gold that perisheth, though it be tried with fire, might be found unto praise, and honour, and glory, at the appearing of Jesus Christ: Whom having not seen, ye love; in whom, though now ye see him not, yet believing, ye rejoice with joy unspeakable, and full of glory: Receiving the end of your faith, even the salvation of your souls.

THE first step towards the satisfactory interpretation of a long, complicated, parenthetical sentence, like that just now read, is to analyze it. The sentence consists of a direct assertion, with a long parenthesis interposed. The direct assertion is, " In that time, the last time, ye greatly rejoice; ye rejoice with a joy unspeakable and full of glory, receiving the end of your faith, even the salvation of your soul." The parenthetical statement is, "though *now* for a season, if need be"—or, " since there is need, ye are in heaviness through manifold temptations, that the trial of your faith, being more precious than that of gold which perisheth, though it be tried with fire, might be found unto praise, and honour, and glory, at the appearing of Jesus Christ, whom, though you have not seen, ye love, not seeing him, but believing in him."

With respect to the direct assertion, a careful reader will easily perceive, that though expressed in the present time, it refers to the future.

The time of the Christian's joy unspeakable and full of glory, is the last time, contrasted with the time of his trial—"now;"[1] when he shall receive the end of his faith, even the salvation of his soul—the same period which is described as that of the appearing or manifestation of Jesus Christ. Instances of an assertion made in the present tense, when it plainly refers to the future, are not unfrequent. "Yet a little while I am (*i. e.*, I shall be) with you, and then I (*i. e.*, I shall) go unto him that sent me. Ye shall seek me, and shall not find me : and where I am (*i. e.*, shall be), thither ye cannot (*i. e.*, ye shall not be able to) come." "How are (*i. e.*, shall be) the dead raised, and with what bodies do (*i. e.*, shall) they come?" "And if any man will hurt them, fire proceedeth (*i. e.*, shall proceed) out of their mouth, and devoureth (*i. e.*, shall devour) their enemies."[2]

The phrases, "a joy unspeakable and full of glory," are too strong to describe the Christian's habitual feelings in the present state ; and we find the very same words employed, in reference to the happiness of the final state, in an after part of the Epistle. "But rejoice, inasmuch as ye are made partakers of Christ's sufferings ; that, when his glory shall be revealed, ye may be glad also with exceeding joy."[3]

The meaning of the Apostle would have been more evident to an English reader, had the assertion been rendered in the future time; "in which time," *i. e.*, in the last time, ye shall greatly rejoice—(though now for a season, since it is needful, ye are in heaviness through manifold temptations; that the trial of your faith, which is more precious than that of gold which perisheth, though it be tried with fire, might be found to praise, and honour, and glory, at the appearing of Jesus Christ: whom, not seeing him, but believing on him,

---

[1] It is rendered in the future in the Latin Vulgate, and versions made from it.

[2] John vii. 33, 34. 1 Cor. xv. 35. Rev. xi. 5.

[3] Ch. iv. 13. The parallelism of the two passages is striking :—Ch. i. 6, 8.— ἐν ᾧ (*i. e.* ἐσχάτῳ καιρῷ) ἀγαλλιᾶσθε χαρᾳ ἀνεκλαλήτῳ και δεδοξασμενη. Ch. iv. 13.—ἐν τῃ ἀποκαλυψει της δοξης αὐτου, χαρητε ἀγαλλιωμενοι.

ye love, though ye have not seen him)—" ye shall rejoice with joy unspeakable, and full of glory: receiving the end of your faith, the salvation of your soul."[1]

The passage thus interpreted, contains in it a beautiful and instructive comparison, or rather contrast of the state of Christians in the present and in the last time, on earth and in heaven. The points of comparison or contrast are the following :—I. Now and here, Christ, the great object of their affection, is not bodily present with them, is but imperfectly known by them, and all their knowledge of, and intercourse with him, is by means of faith—Then and there, he will be bodily present with them, intimately known by them, and their knowledge and intercourse will be direct and immediate. II. Now and here, they are exposed to manifold trials—Then and there, they will enjoy the glorious results of these trials. III. Now and here, complete salvation is a subject of faith and hope—Then and there, it shall be the subject of enjoyment. IV. Now and here, they are for a season in heaviness—Then and there, they greatly rejoice ; they rejoice with a joy unspeakable and full of glory. In the remaining part of the discourse I shall endeavour shortly to illustrate this contrasted view of the present and the future state of the true Christian.

I. CHRIST ABSENT AND BELIEVED ON, CONTRASTED WITH CHRIST PRESENT AND SEEN.

The first point of contrast is, that now and here, Christ, the great object of their affection, is bodily absent from them—is but imperfectly known by them—and all their knowledge of him is by means of faith; then and there, Christ will be revealed—manifested : he will be bodily

---

[1] The interpretation we have been led to prefer, is that supported by Œcumenius and Theophylact among the Greek Fathers; by the translators of the Vulgate; by Luther, Vatablus, Clarius, Benson, Pott, and others. Τὸ Ἀγαλλιασθε ἀντι μελλοντος ειληται.—ŒCUMENIUS.

present with them; he will be intimately known by them, and their knowledge and intercourse will be direct and immediate.

Christ is the great object of his people's affection; he is, by way of eminence, HE whom they love. This is an essential element of the Christian character. When a person is brought under divine influence to understand and believe the Gospel, he perceives that in Christ Jesus centres every amiable excellence in absolute perfection; and that the benefits which he has obtained for us, are infinite in number, value, and duration. He appears at once infinitely lovely and infinitely kind. Contemplating his glory, " the glory as of the only begotten of the Father, full of grace and of truth," the believer says in his heart, " He is the chiefest among ten thousand, and altogether lovely." " This is my beloved, and this is my friend."[1] Reflecting on what he has done and what he has suffered; what he has given, and what he has promised—the believer says in his heart, " I love him, because he first loved me." I love him who " loved not his life to the death," for my salvation. I love him who hath " washed me from my sins in his own blood, and made me a king and a priest to God, even his Father."[2] The Christian has other objects of affection as well as his Saviour; but HE is the object of his supreme affection. In comparison of HIM, " he hates even his father and mother."[3]

It is of the very essence of love to seek union with its object. We naturally wish to be present with, to become intimately acquainted with, to have frequent intimate intercourse with, the object of our affection. These wishes of the Christian, in reference to the great object of his affection, are—can be, but very imperfectly gratified in the present state. He whom we love was once a man among men. Yes, " the word was made flesh, and dwelt

---

[1] John i. 14. Cant. v. 10, 16.   [2] John iv. 19. Rev. i. 5.
[3] Luke xiv. 26.

among men." "Inasmuch as the children were partakers of flesh and blood, he also took part of the same." [1] There was a time when it was possible to have become, in the ordinary sense of the term, familiarly acquainted with Jesus Christ; and I believe very few Christians, not naturally deficient in the imaginative and affectionate parts of our nature, have ever read the history of his going out and in among his chosen followers, without in some measure envying their enjoyment. Who has not occasionally felt a wish rising in his heart that he had come into existence eighteen centuries sooner, and that he had had his lot cast in that land gladdened and dignified above all lands by the presence of the incarnate Divinity—that so he might have contemplated the humble shrine of the divine glory, and seen its radiance bursting through in miracles of power and mercy—that he might have gazed on that countenance which beamed with divine intelligence and benignity, and listened to that voice which poured forth a stream of divine wisdom, and truth, and kindness? Who has not sometimes said in his heart, O happy family of Bethany, all whose members were the objects of Jesus' peculiar love, and under whose hospitable roof he spent so many of his hours! O that, like the three favoured disciples, we had been admitted to witness the glory on "the Holy Mount," and to watch and weep with him amid his agony in the garden of Gethsemane! O that we had seen him displaying at once the tokens of his unexampled love, and the proofs of the reality of his resurrection! O that we had been with the two disciples when he so opened the Scriptures about himself, as to make their hearts burn within them! O that we had heard the cheering salutation, "Peace be unto you," and felt his warm breath when he said, "Receive ye the Holy Ghost." Such wishes are natural, I believe, to the renewed mind; and though they belong, it may be, to the weakness of regenerated humanity, I do not think they will be severely

---

[1] John i. 14.   Heb. ii. 14.

judged by Him " who knows our frame, and remembers we are dust."

But in the present state these longings cannot be gratified. On the day on which he " led out his disciples as far as to Bethany, and lifted up his hands, and blessed them," " the heavens received him," and they must " retain him till the times of the restitution of all things."[1] And with this arrangement we have good reason to be satisfied, both for his sake and our own. For his sake : for what has earth to offer in the shape of dignity and enjoyment, in comparison of that " name above every name," which he bears in the heaven of heavens, or of that " river of pleasures" that are at his Father's right hand? " If we loved him, we would rejoice that he is gone to the Father." For our own : for " it was expedient for us that he should go away ; for if he had not gone away, the Comforter would not have come ; but having gone, he has sent him to us." Yet still, though we know and believe all this, we feel that our happiness would be increased were we allowed to see his face, and to hear his voice ; for we are sure " his voice is sweet, and his countenance is comely." [2]

But not merely is Jesus Christ, the great object of his people's love, bodily absent from them in the present state ; but they are while here but very imperfectly acquainted with him. They *are* acquainted with him, and they would not part with their knowledge of him for all the stores of human science. They feel that " it is life eternal to know him ;" and they " count all things but loss for the excellent knowledge of Christ Jesus our Lord." [3] They know, and they are following on to know him. They are studying his word, and they are studying his providence, which are both manifestations of Him, and they are gradually becoming better acquainted with him. But there is much in his word that they but imperfectly comprehend. There is much in his

[1] Luke xxiv. 20, 21. Acts. iii. 21.
[2] Phil. ii. 9. Psal. xvi. 11. John xiv. 28; xvi. 7.
[3] John xvii. 3. Phil. iii. 8.

providence which perplexes and confounds them. If it were not their own fault, they might know much more of him than they do; for he is not backward to manifest himself to his people in another way than he does to the world. A more careful study of the Bible, and a more careful study of providential dispensations in the light of the Bible, would be found exhaustless sources of satisfactory information about Him whom we love, affording most amazing displays of his wisdom and power, and faithfulness and kindness. Yet, however carefully these means might be improved, still would it be true that here " we see through a glass darkly ; we know but in part," [1] in reference to him whom we love.

While in the present state, our knowledge of him, and our intercourse with him, is through the medium of faith. " We do not see him—we believe in him." His mind and his heart are made known to us in his word. It is only so far as we understand this word that we know him ; and it is only as far as we can believe it that we have intercourse with him ; his mind then becoming our mind, and his will our will. It is true that we have " the Spirit whom he hath given us ;" [2] but that Holy Spirit does not directly give us information about Christ ; he only, by his enlightening influence, enables us to understand and believe the information contained in the scriptures ; and while, if we are Christians, we are " joined to the Lord," [3] and are " one Spirit" with him we love, the intercourse of holy desire and affection is carried on entirely by means of clear and impressive views of revealed truth. Such is the Christian's situation while here below, in reference to the object of his supreme love. He is not bodily present with us—he is but imperfectly known by us ; and all our knowledge of him, and intercourse with him, are through the medium of faith.

It will be otherwise by and by. In " the last time" there will be " a revelation of Jesus Christ." At the appointed season He will bodily return to earth for the entire salva-

---

[1] 1 Cor. xiii. 12.   [2] 1 John iii. 24.   [3] 1 Cor. vi. 17.

tion of his chosen ones—shall deliver them completely from "the last enemy" by raising them from the dead ; and shall in his glorified body for ever dwell in the midst of his people, all of them possessed of bodies "fashioned like unto his glorious body." "Ye men of Galilee," said the angels to the disciples who stood gazing up to heaven, after the cloud had received the ascending Saviour out of their sight—"Ye men of Galilee, why stand ye here gazing up to heaven? this same Jesus, which is taken up from you into heaven, shall so come in like manner as ye have seen him go into heaven." "Behold," says John the divine, hurried forward by the inspiring Spirit to "the last time," even "the time of the revelation of Jesus Christ, "—"Behold, he cometh in clouds, and every eye shall see him." The man Christ Jesus, ordained to be the judge of the world, shall descend from heaven, and having raised the dead, and pronounced and executed righteous judgment on all the living and the dead, shall return to heaven, and spend the endless years of eternity amid his reanimated and completely redeemed people, a glorified man amid glorified men, their Lord and yet their brother, the visible Head of his visible body the Church— "the fulness of him who filleth all in all." [1]

That the happiness of the saints will be greatly increased by the bodily presence of their Lord and Saviour and Brother, there can be no doubt ; but "the revelation of Jesus Christ" seems to me to import something more than this—something still more closely connected with the happiness of his people. He will not only be bodily present with them, but he will be much more extensively known by them. A much more complete manifestation will be made of his excellence and kindness, and they will be rendered much more capable of comprehending this manifestation. Every obscurity in his word will then be removed. Every dark dispensation will be explained. "In his light they shall see light clearly." [2] The excellencies of his personal charac-

[1] Acts i. 11. Rev. i. 3. 1 Cor. xv. 26, 42-55. 1 Thes. iii. 15-17. Phil. iii. 20, 21. Eph. i. 23.   [2] Psal. xxxvi. 9.

ter, the wisdom and benignity of his mediatorial administration, and the nature and transcendent dignity of his mediatorial honours, will all be apprehended to an extent, and with a clearness, of which at present we have no conception. The meaning of the scriptural description of his excellencies will then be distinctly understood; and they will find that he is excellent and amiable above all that they have thought. The whole of his varied dispensations in the administration of universal government, will appear a consistent display of infinite wisdom, righteousness, and benignity; and the glories of that higher order of administration which is to characterise the celestial state, shall be as fully displayed to them as the limited faculties of their glorified nature admit.

The only other idea which I wish to bring before your minds just now, in illustration of this point of contrast between the present and the future state of the Christian, is, that whereas now, all our knowledge of, and all our intercourse with, Christ is through the medium of faith, then it will be direct and immediate. How knowledge is then to be communicated to us by him, how our intercourse with him is to be carried on, we cannot distinctly say, we cannot clearly conceive. We know it will be as different from our present mode of obtaining knowledge and maintaining intercourse, as seeing a thing is from merely crediting a report about it. We shall live, not by faith, but by sight. We shall see no longer as "by means of a mirror,[1] but face to face; we shall know no longer in part; we shall know as we are known." Our knowledge will not be infinite, but it will be very extensive and perfectly clear, altogether unmixed with error or doubt. So much for the illustration of the first point of contrast.

II. THE TRIALS OF CHRISTIANS IN THE PRESENT STATE CONTRASTED WITH THEIR RESULTS IN THE FUTURE STATE.

The second point of contrast between the present and

---

[1] Δι' ἐσόπτρου, ἐν αἰνίγματι.—1 Cor. xiii. 12.

future state of Christians is, that now and here, Christians are exposed to numerous and varied trials; then and there, they will enjoy the glorious results of their trials. Christians in the present state are exposed to " temptations," to " manifold"—*i. e.*, numerous and varied " temptations." Temptation is ordinarily used to signify enticement to sin; but in the New Testament it very frequently signifies afflictions generally, viewed as trials, and this is obviously its meaning in the passage before us. The apostolical assertion then is, Christians are exposed in the present state to numerous and varied afflictions, and these numerous and varied afflictions are trials of the reality and strength of their faith, and hope, and love and patience, and other Christian graces.

An abstract consideration of the divine character, and of the relation in which true Christians stand to God, would lead us to expect that they should be completely exempted from affliction. He is infinitely powerful, and wise, and good. They are the objects of his peculiar love. Is it not natural, then, to conclude, that from the moment they are brought into the relation of children to him by faith in Christ Jesus, they should be freed from evil in all its forms and degrees, and made happy up to their largest capacity of happiness? But " his ways are not our ways; nor are his thoughts our thoughts. As the heavens are high above the earth; so are his thoughts above our thoughts, and his ways above our ways." [1]

Christians are not exempted from the ordinary evils of life. It is true of them, as of mankind generally, that they are " born to trouble as the sparks fly upward." They are " of few days and full of trouble." Poverty, reproach, sickness, disappointment, sorrow, pain, and death, are the lot of the saint as well as the sinner. Many who are " rich in faith," are " poor in this world," strangers to the comforts and conveniences, and but scantily furnished with even the

---

[1] Isa. lv. 8, 9.

necessaries of life. They may be, they often are, the subjects of the most painful and loathsome diseases, and the general law of mortality holds in their case equally as in that of their irreligious neighbours, " Dust thou art, and unto dust thou must return." Indeed, in very many cases a larger proportion of suffering than ordinary seems to fall to the lot of the children of God. " Whom the Lord loveth he chasteneth, and he scourgeth every son whom he receiveth."[1]

Besides the afflictions which are common to the saint as a man, there are others which are peculiar to him as a Christian. He is exposed to sufferings from the world "lying under the wicked one," and he is exposed to suffering from the wicked one himself. " In the world," said our Lord to his followers, " ye shall have tribulation," and the faithful witness did not lie. All who have lived godly in this world have suffered; " all who will live godly must suffer persecution." Some of them have " had trials" of cruel mockings and scourgings; yea, moreover, of bonds and imprisonments. They were stoned, they were sawn asunder, they were tempted, they were slain by the sword, they wandered about in sheeps' skins and goats' skins—destitute, afflicted, tormented, they wandered in deserts and in mountains, in dens and in caves of the earth.[2] And even where they are not exposed to open violence, they find that " this world is not their friend, nor this world's law;" that the world which hated their Lord and Master does not love them; and that a malignant influence in reference to their best interests is constantly proceeding forth from " the present evil world."

In addition to trials from the world, the Christian is exposed to affliction from the assaults of his unseen enemies. He has to strive, not only " with flesh and blood, but with principalities and powers, with the rulers of the darkness of this world, with spiritual wickednesses in high places."

---

[1] Job v. 7; xiv. 1.   James ii. 5.   Gen. iii. 19.   Heb. xii. 6.
[2] John xvi. 33.   2 Tim. iii. 12.   Heb. xi. 36-38.

" His enemy, the devil, goeth about like a roaring lion, seeking whom he may devour."[1] His fiery darts, when not warded off by the shield of faith, sink deep into the heart, and inflict, though not a deadly, yet a most painful wound; and the buffetings of some of his messengers are all but intolerable.

All these afflictions, from whatever quarter they come, are " trials." They are intended to prove and to improve the Christian, to try at once the reality and the vigour of his gracious principles; and not only to try them, but to strengthen them. This, then, is the state of the Christian; while here, he is exposed to numerous and varied afflictions, by means of which he is tried and improved.

But in the state of final happiness there will be no affliction. The trial, having served its purpose, shall cease, and nothing but the glorious result of the trial will remain. " The trial of the Christian's faith," by means of these manifold afflictions, " is more precious than the trial of gold." The apostle does not here directly contrast faith and gold, but the trial of faith and the trial of gold.[2] Trial by fire improves gold; it frees it from all debasing alloy, but it does not render it indestructible. Refine gold as you will, it is, after all, a perishing thing. But the trial of the faith of the Christian has a nobler result. Purified and strengthened by the trials it is exposed to under the influence of the Holy Spirit, faith, with all the graces which grow out of it, survives the wreck of all material things, and " at the revelation of Jesus Christ, is found to praise, and honour, and glory." The results of all the trials to which they have been exposed in the present state, will be found in that character of perfect conformity to the image of God, in which consists at once their perfect holiness and their perfect happiness.

" Praise, honour, and glory," are synonymous expressions, and are equivalent to a very strong superlative. The praise,

---

[1] Eph. vi. 12. 1 Pet. v. 8.

[2] πολυ τιμιωτερον χρυσιου—i. e. του δοκιμιου του χρυσιου.—GROTIUS.

glory, and honour, may be referred either to the saints
themselves or to their Lord and Saviour. To the saints
themselves, for we know that "praise, and honour, and
glory," shall be to every saint "in the day when Jesus
Christ shall judge the secrets of all hearts;" to their Lord
and Saviour, for we know that "he shall be glorified in his
saints, and admired in all them that believe." [1] It has
been beautifully remarked, " These two will well agree together; that it be both to their praise and to the praise of
Christ; for certainly all their praise and glory will end in
the praise and glory of their head, Christ, who is God over
all, blessed for ever. They have each their crown, but their
honour is to cast them all down before HIS throne." [2]

III. THE CHRISTIAN'S PRESENT STATE A STATE OF
EXPECTATION—HIS FUTURE STATE A STATE OF EN-
JOYMENT.

The third point of comparison or contrast between the
present and future state of Christians is, that now and here
complete salvation is the object of faith and hope; then
and there it shall be the object of enjoyment.

Saints in the present state are made partakers of many of
the blessings of the Christian salvation. So far as the purchase of salvation is concerned, immediately on believing the
truth they are interested indefeasibly in that all perfect work
of Christ which secures their everlasting happiness. They
obtain the forgiveness of all their sins. " In him they have
redemption through his blood—the forgiveness of sins."
They obtain deliverance from the prevailing power of sin.
" Sin shall not have dominion over them." [3] They obtain a
joy, and peace, and satisfaction, to which, till they believed,
they were strangers. But still they are but very imperfectly
possessed of the Christian salvation—complete deliverance
from evil in all its forms and all its degrees.

[1] Rom. ii. 10.   2 Thess. i. 10.   [2] Leighton.   [3] Eph. i. 7.   Rom. vi. 14.

We have seen, that they are still exposed to the ordinary calamities of life, to the persecution of the world, and to the temptations of Satan. They are still but imperfectly delivered from their innate depravity. Sin, though it no longer reigns, yet it dwells in them. There is still much darkness in the understanding, much disorder in the affections, much perversity in the will. They are far, very far, from being " holy as God is holy, perfect as he is perfect." This mortal has not yet put on immortality. This corruption has not yet put on incorruption. In one word, perfect holy happiness—complete salvation, is in the present state the object, not of enjoyment, but of faith and hope. " We ourselves," says the Apostle, " who have the first fruits of the Spirit, even we ourselves groan within ourselves, waiting for the adoption, to wit, the redemption of our body"—the final deliverance on the day of the resurrection ; " for we are saved by hope"—*i. e.*, our salvation at present is not in possession, but in expectation : we are not so much saved as we hope to be saved. " For hope that is seen is not hope; for what a man seeth, why doth he yet hope for ? " [1]

In the future state, however, they shall obtain, in all its extent and perfection, " the salvation that is in Christ with eternal glory." They shall receive " the end of their faith, even the salvation of their soul."

The final salvation is termed the salvation of " the soul," not to exclude the salvation of the body; " for we look for the Saviour from heaven, the Lord Jesus Christ, who shall change these vile bodies, and fashion them like unto his own glorious body;" but because the soul in itself, immaterial and immortal, is both the noblest part of human nature, and the immediate seat of that holy happiness in which the Christian salvation essentially consists.[a]

This salvation is said to be " the end of their faith"—*i. e.*, I apprehend, the termination of their faith.[2] The attain-

[1] Rom. viii. 23-25.   [a] Phil. iii. 20, 21. See note A.

[2] Heb. xi. 39.—Υποστολη tends to, ends in Απωλεια. Πιστις tends to, ends in Περιποιησις ψυχης—the same thing as σωληρια ψυχων.

ment of complete salvation shall no more be a matter of
faith; it shall be a matter of experience. They shall no
more believe that they shall be saved; they shall know that
they are saved. We are persuaded that faith will continue for ever in heaven; but the object of faith will then
be, not the attainment of a complete salvation, but the eternal continuance of the enjoyment of a complete salvation
already attained. In one word—here Christians believe
they shall be saved, here they hope to be saved; there they
are saved.

IV. THE SORROWS OF THE CHRISTIAN'S PRESENT STATE CONTRASTED WITH THE JOYS OF HIS FUTURE STATE.

The fourth point of contrast is, Now, and Here, the
Christians are " for a season in heaviness" on all these accounts; Then, and There, they will " rejoice, greatly rejoice,
rejoice with a joy that is unspeakable and full of glory."
The bodily absence of Jesus Christ, their imperfect knowledge
of him, their indirect and interrupted intercourse with him,
their manifold trials, their imperfect enjoyment of the blessings
of the Christian salvation—all these naturally produce, to a
certain degree, a depression of spirit. The Christian is " in
heaviness." He mourns the absence of his Lord, and says
in his heart, " Oh! that I knew where I could find him,
that I might come even to his seat." Under the pressure
of bodily affliction or mental distress, he is constrained to
cry out, " I am oppressed—undertake for me." Harassed
with the movements of remaining corruption, he groans
out, " Wretched man that I am; who will deliver me?"
And feeling that he is saved but in hope, he sighs out,
" How long, O Lord, how long?" " When shall I come
and appear before God?"[1]

This heaviness of heart is but for a season—it is, at least
in an oppressive degree, not constant, but only occasional,

---

[1] Job xxiii. 3. Isa. xxxviii. 14. Rom. vii. 24. Rev. vi. 10. Psal. xlii. 2.

and at any rate it is only for the season, the short season of mortal life. And what should still farther prevent Christians from murmuring, is the thought that, if they are in heaviness even for a season for these causes, it is " since there is need for it."[1] All is ordered, and all is well ordered. He does not " afflict willingly, nor grieve without a cause."[2] Every thing in the saint's lot is arranged in the way best suited to promote his true, his everlasting welfare.

But in the future state there will be no heaviness, no, not even " for a season." It will no more be needful. Affliction will have served its purpose, and will for ever cease. There, then, will be nothing but unmingled happiness and unending rejoicing. " They shall rejoice ; they shall rejoice with a joy which is unspeakable," which cannot be adequately expressed, " and full of glory"—i. e., either in the highest degree glorious and excellent, or full of gloriation or triumph. It is needless for us to attempt to illustrate this subject ; we can do nothing but quote a few passages of Scripture, which, in all their extent of meaning, seem applicable only to this final state of happiness. " The ransomed of the Lord shall return and come to Zion, with songs, and with everlasting joy on their head ; they shall obtain joy and gladness, and sorrow and sighing shall flee away." " Thy sun shall no more go down, neither shall thy moon withdraw her shining ; for the Lord God shall be thy everlasting light, and the days of thy mourning shall be ended." " God himself shall be with them, and be their God ; and there shall be no more death, neither sorrow, nor crying ; neither shall there be any more pain, for the former things are passed away. The Lamb who is in the midst of the throne shall feed them, and lead them to fountains of living waters ; and God shall wipe away all tears from their eyes."[3]

Thus have I shortly considered the beautiful and instructive contrast contained in the text between the saint's condi-

---

[1] εἰ δέον ἐστι.   [2] Lam. iii. 33.   [3] Isa. xxxv. 10. Isa. lx. 19, 20. Rev. xxi. 3, 4.

tion on earth and in heaven. And now, in conclusion, ought
not all Christians, with the Apostle, to " reckon," judge, conclude on the most satisfactory premises, " that the sufferings
of the present time are not worthy to be compared with the
glory that shall be revealed in them"—and that, however
heavy and long continued, that " affliction" is but "light,"
and " for a moment," which "worketh out for them such a
far more exceeding and eternal weight of glory." [1]

Who would not be a Christian ? For ah! how different
are the prospects of the unbeliever ? He, too, must see
Christ Jesus, whom he does not love, but it will be as a
righteous judge, coming " in flaming fire to take vengeance" on him as an adversary of God. His afflictions
here will prove to have been but " the beginning of sorrows ;" what he now fears he will then feel, and feel to
be far worse than he feared ; and, instead of joy unspeakable
and full of glory, there will be woe unutterable, but in
" weeping, and wailing, and gnashing of teeth." [2]

Let Christians live like those who have such prospects.
Let them " be stedfast, immoveable, always abounding in
the work of the Lord, inasmuch as they know their labour
is not in vain in the Lord ;" and, " having such promises,
let " them cleanse themselves from all filthiness of the flesh
and spirit, and perfect holiness in the fear of God."

[1] Rom. viii. 18.   2 Cor. iv. 17.   [2] 2 Thess. i. 8.   Matt. viii. 12.

NOTE A.

Perhaps there is in the expression σωτηριαν ψυχων, a reference to the scriptural trichotomy of human nature.—1 Thess. v. 23. Heb. iv. 12. Phil. i. 27. Luke i. 47. 1 Cor. xv. 44. Exod. xxxv. 21. Ψυχη is that to which moral corruption and consequent misery cleave. In the present state it is but partially subjected to the πνευμα, which is "life because of righteousness ;" but, at the revelation of Jesus Christ, σωμα, ψυχη, and πνευμα, shall all equally, according to their nature, enjoy the σωτηρια. Rom. viii. 10, 11. Bengel considers ψυχη as used generally of the spiritual part of man. His note is, as usual, brief but significant. "Anima precipue salvatur : corpus in resurrectione participat." It has been thought by some, that there is here a tacit reference to the Jewish hope of external bodily deliverance, from slavery and oppression, by the Messiah. The Christian's hope is, "the salvation of the soul."

DISCOURSE IV.

THE FINAL HAPPINESS OF CHRISTIANS THE SUBJECT OF OLD TESTAMENT PREDICTION, NEW TESTAMENT REVELATION, AND ANGELIC STUDY.

1 Pet. i. 10-12.—Of which salvation the prophets have inquired and searched diligently, who prophesied of the grace that should come unto you: searching what, or what manner of time, the Spirit of Christ which was in them did signify, when it testified beforehand the sufferings of Christ, and the glory that should follow. Unto whom it was revealed, that not only unto themselves, but unto us, they did minister the things which are now reported unto you by them that have preached the gospel unto you with the Holy Ghost sent down from heaven; which things the angels desire to look into.

IF we would satisfactorily understand any book or any passage in a book, there are two points which we must distinctly apprehend, and never lose sight of. These are, what is the subject of which the author treats, and what is the object which he has in view in treating it. Let us endeavour to ascertain those two points with regard to that paragraph which I have just read, and which I intend to make the subject of the following discourse.

The subject of the Apostle is, plainly, the final deliverance and complete happiness which Christians are to obtain at the second coming of Jesus Christ. This is spoken of as "the inheritance incorruptible, undefiled, and that fadeth not away, reserved in heaven;" as "the salvation prepared to be revealed in the last times;" as " the grace which is to be brought to Christians at the revelation of Jesus Christ." This is plainly the subject of the paragraph.

With regard to the object of the Apostle in treating this subject, it is obviously to sustain the minds of the Christians to whom he wrote, amid the manifold trials to which they were exposed—to enable them to remain "stedfast and immoveable" in the profession of the faith, and in the practice of the duties of their high and holy calling. He states the truth with regard to the immeasurable grandeur, and absolute certainty of this final salvation, that they might be induced to "gird up the loins of their mind, be sober, and hope to the end," that they might "fashion themselves as obedient children," and "be holy in all manner of conversation, as he who had called them is holy."

No means could be better fitted to gain the end proposed, than that adopted by the Apostle ; for if they firmly believed that such a salvation most certainly awaited every one who "held fast the beginning of their confidence steadfast to the end," [1] it is obvious that the smiles and the frowns, the allurements and the terrors of the world, would be equally incapable of shaking their attachment to their Lord, who should in due time so munificently reward all his faithful followers.

The manner in which the Apostle brings the magnitude and certainty of this salvation before their minds, shows that he, as well as his "beloved brother Paul," speaks "according to the wisdom given to him." [2] He first describes it generally, as "an inheritance incorruptible, undefiled, and that fadeth not away, reserved in heaven for them, while they are kept to it by the power of God through faith." Then he brings out more prominently its characteristic excellencies, by describing it in contrast with the present state of the people of God. In opposition to a state in which Jesus Christ, the object of the Christian's supreme affection, is bodily absent from him, in which his knowledge of him is

---

[1] Heb. iii. 14.   [2] 2 Pet. iii. 15.

limited and obscure, and his intercourse with him carried on entirely through the medium of believing—it is exhibited as a state in which Christ is bodily present with his people, in which their knowledge of him is extensive and distinct, and their communion with him direct and immediate; in opposition to a state in which they are exposed to numerous and varied trials—it is exhibited as a state in which, freed from all trials, they shall enjoy the glorious results of these trials to which in a previous state they had been subjected; in opposition to a state in which complete deliverance and happiness are merely objects of faith and hope—it is exhibited as a state in which they are the objects of enjoyment; and, in fine, in opposition to a state in which they are " for a season, since it is needful, in heaviness"—it is exhibited as a state in which they shall for ever " greatly rejoice ; rejoice with a joy which is unspeakable, and full of glory."

In the paragraph which forms our text, he takes another and an equally efficient method of bringing before the minds of his readers, the greatness and the certainty of this final salvation, by representing it as one great or leading subject of Old Testament prophecy, apostolic preaching, and angelic study. " Of this salvation the prophets prophesied"—of this salvation " they who preached the gospel with the Holy Ghost sent down from heaven made a report"—and " into this salvation the angels desire to look." In the remaining part of this discourse, then, I shall turn your attention to the view which the Apostle gives us of the final salvation of Christians, first as the subject of Old Testament prophecy; secondly, as the subject of apostolical preaching; and, thirdly, as the subject of angelic study.

I. THE FINAL HAPPINESS OF CHRISTIANS THE SUBJECT OF OLD TESTAMENT PROPHECY.

Let us first, then, attend to the statement which the Apostle makes as to this final salvation being the subject of Old Testament prophecy.

" Of, or concerning, this salvation the prophets inquired and searched diligently, who prophesied of the grace that should come unto you : searching what, or what manner of time, the Spirit of Christ which was in them did signify, when it testified beforehand the sufferings of Christ, and the glory which should follow. Unto whom it was revealed, that not to themselves, but to us, they did minister."

The truths taught us in these words are the following :— The ancient prophets, inspired by the Spirit of Christ, predicted that final salvation which remains for the people of God ; they diligently inquired into the meaning of their own prediction ; and they obtained information that these predictions referred to blessings not to be conferred during the economy under which they were placed, but during that higher one which was to supersede it. The first of these truths is taught us in these words, " The prophets prophesied of the grace which should come to you "—" The Spirit of Christ which was in them did testify beforehand of the sufferings of Christ, and the glory that should follow." The second of these truths is taught us in these words—" concerning this salvation the prophets enquired and searched diligently, searching what, or what manner of time the Spirit of Christ which was in them did signify." And the third truth is taught in these words—" To them it was revealed, that not to themselves, but to us, they did minister." [1]

The ancient prophets predicted that final salvation which will be bestowed on the people of God at the coming of Jesus Christ. They " prophesied of the grace which should come to us." " The grace which should come to us" has often been considered as a general expression for the blessings of the New Testament economy, on earth as well as in heaven—" the grace which came by Jesus Christ ;" but if we look closely at the passage, we will find the sole subject to be the final and complete salvation

[1] John i. 17.

awaiting Christians, or, as it is expressed more fully, "the grace that is to be brought to Christians at the revelation of Jesus Christ." The words, "they prophesied of the grace which should come to us," is just then equivalent to, 'they predicted the final salvation which awaits the people of God.'

The same sentiment is, I apprehend, repeated in another form of words, when it is said, "the Spirit of Christ which was in them did testify beforehand of the sufferings of Christ, and the glory which should follow."

"All Scripture is given by divine inspiration." "Prophecy came not in old time by the will of man, but holy men of God spake as they were moved by the Holy Ghost."[1] The Holy Ghost is termed "the Spirit of Christ," inasmuch as he is essentially related to the second person of the Trinity, who is Christ, as well as to the Father; and inasmuch as previously, as well as subsequently to his incarnation, all communications of the divine will were made by the Son through the Spirit. Never was there a time when the Father immediately revealed himself. "The only begotten Son, who is in his bosom, he declared him"—declared him by the Spirit. This divine person, inspiring the prophets, taught them what things to reveal and in what words to reveal them. To use the language of one of themselves, "He spake by them, and his word was on their tongue."[2]

This Spirit of Christ, then, "testified of the sufferings of Christ and the glory which should follow them." These words naturally suggest, and have been ordinarily understood of, the personal sufferings and glories of Jesus Christ, the degradation and sorrows to which the incarnate Son was exposed, when, "being found in fashion as a man, he humbled himself, and became obedient unto death, even the death of the cross;" and the high dignity and inconceivable

---

[1] 2 Tim. iii. 16.   2 Pet. i. 21.   A valuable dissertation on the last of these passages is to be found in "Knappii Scripta Varii Argumenti."
[2] 2 Sam. xxiii. 2.

happiness to which he was raised when "God highly exalted him, and gave him a name which is above every name," "angels, and authorities, and powers, being made subject to him."[1] I am persuaded, however, that if we attend to the connexion of the words, and to the words themselves, we will find they do not refer to the personal sufferings and glories of Christ, but to the sufferings of his people during the present state, and the glories which are to follow "in the last time," "at the revelation of Jesus Christ." It is not the sufferings of Christ personally, and the subsequent glories, which are the subject of the Apostle's discussion, but the manifold trials to which Christians are exposed for a season, and the glory which is to be theirs in the last time. Looking at the construction of the passage we naturally conclude that the clauses, "the prophets prophesied of the grace which is to be brought to us," and, "the Spirit of Christ testified beforehand of the sufferings of Christ, and the glory which should follow," are parallel—that the prophecy of the prophets, and the testimony of the Spirit of Christ, refer to the same thing.

Besides, the original expression is quite peculiar, and is altogether different from that ordinarily rendered the sufferings of Christ. It is literally—the sufferings in reference to Christ, *i. e.*, on Christ's account, in Christ's cause—or the sufferings till Christ, *i. e.*, the sufferings to be undergone by his body the Church, and by every member in particular, till he come "the second time, not as a sin-offering, but for their salvation." The sufferings till Christ,[a] and the subsequent glories, are then just "the afflictions of the present time, and the glory which shall be revealed in us,"[2] and the Apostle's statement is, the 'prophets, under the influence of the Spirit of Christ, predicted the sufferings to which Christians are to be exposed in the present state, and the glories which are to be bestowed on them at the second coming of their Lord.'

[1] Phil. ii. 8, 9.   1 Pet. iii. 22.   [a] See note A.   [2] Rom. viii. 18.

Let us then show, by the quotation of particular passages from the Jewish Scriptures, that the final salvation of the people of God was indeed the subject of Old Testament prediction. Before commencing these quotations, however, let us recollect that we are not in the Old Testament declarations to expect what, for perspicuity and distinctness, can compare with the declarations " which they who have preached the gospel with the Holy Ghost sent down from heaven," have made to us. It is enough that we meet with declarations of a completeness of deliverance and a perfection of happiness, far surpassing any thing ever yet enjoyed by the Church on earth—far surpassing any thing the New Testament warrants her to expect till her Lord return. I also think it right to add, that I am not prepared to assert that all the passages which I quote have a *direct* reference to a *heavenly* state, though it is only in that state that the blessings predicted will be enjoyed in that perfection which will completely exhaust the meaning of the prophetic oracles.

The first prediction I quote, of the final and complete salvation of the people of God, is the prophecy of Enoch, "Behold the Lord cometh with ten thousand of his saints."[1] This may seem a prophecy rather of the destruction of God's enemies than of the salvation of his people ; but the two events are closely connected, and it seems to me probable that the Apostle refers to this prophecy when he says, " Them who sleep in Jesus God will bring with him." [2]

The next prediction that I shall refer to, is that wonderful passage in the 19th chapter of Job, " Oh that my words were now written! Oh that they were printed in a book— that they were graven with an iron pen, and with lead in the rock for ever : For I know that my Redeemer liveth, and that he shall stand at the latter day upon the earth ; and though, after my skin, worms destroy this body, yet in my flesh shall I see God, whom I shall see for myself, and

[1] Jude, 14.   [2] 1 Thess. iv. 14.

mine eyes shall behold, and not another, though my reins be consumed within me."[1]

I now turn your attention to a passage in the 8th Psalm, "What is man, that thou art mindful of him? and the son of man, that thou visitest him? for thou hast (after he had been in a state equal to the angels as to immortality) made him a little (rather for a short season) lower than the angels; and (then, afterwards) hast crowned him with glory and honour; thou hast made him to have dominion over the works of thy hand—thou hast put all things under his feet."[2] That this refers to the final salvation of the redeemed from among men, is plain from the Apostle's commentary on it in the Epistle to the Hebrews. He plainly applies it to redeemed man, "For unto the angels hath he not put in subjection the world to come, whereof we speak? But one in a certain place testified, saying, What is man, that thou art mindful of him? or the son of man, that thou visitest him? Thou madest him a little lower than the angels; thou crownedst him with glory and honour, and didst set him over the works of thy hands: thou hast put all things in subjection under his feet. For in that he put all things in subjection under him, he left nothing that is not put under him. But we see not yet all things put under him (redeemed man): But we see Jesus (who was a man—the head of the ransomed race), who was made a little (for a season) lower than the angels, for the suffering of death, crowned with glory and honour; that he by the grace of God might taste death for every man." He suffered, and then was glorified, and so shall all his people.[3]

There are other quotations from the Psalms that deserve notice: "As for me, I shall behold thy face in righteousness: I shall be satisfied, when I awake in thy likeness." "Surely goodness and mercy shall follow me all the days of my life, and I shall dwell in the house of the Lord for ever." "How excellent is thy loving-kindness, O God! therefore the chil-

---

[1] Job xix. 23-27   [2] Psal. viii. 4-6.   [3] Heb. ii. 5-9.

dren of men put their trust under the shadow of thy wings. They shall be abundantly satisfied with the fulness of thy house; and thou shalt make them drink of the river of thy pleasures. For with thee is the fountain of life; in thy light shall we see light." [1]

The following quotations from the prophets Isaiah, Daniel, Hosea, and Malachi, will serve as further specimens of the manner in which the prophets prophesied of the grace which is to be brought to us, and in which the Spirit of Christ, which was in them, testified beforehand of the glories which were to follow the sufferings till Christ: "Then the moon shall be confounded and the sun ashamed, when the Lord of hosts shall reign in Mount Zion, and before his ancients gloriously." " He shall swallow up death in victory, and the Lord God shall wipe away tears from off all faces, and the rebuke of his people shall he take away from off all the earth, for the Lord hath spoken it." " Thy dead men shall live; together with my dead body shall they arise: Awake and sing, ye that dwell in dust; for thy dew is as the dew of herbs, and the earth shall cast out the dead." " The sun shall be no more thy light by day, neither for brightness shall the moon give light unto thee: but the Lord shall be thy everlasting light, and the days of thy mourning shall be ended." "And many of them who sleep in the dust of the earth shall awake, some to everlasting life, and some to shame and everlasting contempt." " I will ransom them from the power of the grave: I will redeem them from death: O death! I will be thy plague: O grave! I will be thy destruction; repentance shall be hid from mine eyes." " They shall be mine, saith the Lord of hosts, in that day when I make up my jewels; and I will spare them as a man spareth his own son that serveth him. Then shall ye return and discern between the righteous and the wicked, between him that serveth God and him that serveth him not." [2] All these oracles speak

[1] Psal. xvii. 15; xxiii. 6; xxxvi. 7-9.

[2] Isa. xxiv. 23; xxv. 8; xxvi. 19; lx. 19, 20. Dan. xii. 2. Hos. xiii. 14. Mal. iii. 18, 19.

of "suffering" as the lot of a peculiar people down to a particular period, and of "glory that is to follow" that period.

These prophetic oracles were but imperfectly understood
by those who uttered them. We are not to suppose, however, that in uttering them, their minds were entirely passive,
and that the Holy Spirit only employed their organs of
speech to express words to which they attached no idea.
They understood the meaning of the words; they were the
expression of thoughts communicated to their minds. They
knew that they referred to great blessings to be bestowed
on the Church; but as to the precise nature and extent of
these blessings, and as to the period when, and the manner
in which they were to be bestowed, they were much in the
dark. "The prophecy came not by their own will." It was
"not of *self-interpretation*."[1] Either the event referred to,
or another explicatory revelation, was necessary to unfold
fully its meaning.

These holy men were desirous of knowing all that could
be known on the subject. They "inquired and searched
diligently" concerning the salvation—the grace which was
to come to us; " they searched what, or what manner of
time, the Spirit of Christ did signify, when he testified beforehand the glory which was to follow the sufferings until
Christ." They wished to know when, and in what circumstances, these glorious predictions were to be fulfilled; and
the means they employed for that purpose were the study
of the Scriptures—comparing one passage with another, and
fervent supplication to God. We have an example of this in
the case of Daniel, in reference to another class of prophecies:
" I Daniel understood by books the number of the years;
and I set my face unto the Lord God, to seek" (further
insight as to what and what manner of time) " by prayer
and supplications, with fasting, and sackcloth, and ashes."[2]

The prophets did not obtain all the information they desired; but it was revealed to them, that "not to themselves,

---

[1] Ἰδιας επιλυσεως ου γινεlαι.—2 Pet. i. 20.   [2] Dan. ix. 2, 3.

but to us, they did minister those things which have been reported to us by those who preached the gospel with the Holy Ghost sent down from heaven." Those things which have been reported, &c.—are, I apprehend, the statements made by the Apostles with regard to the final salvation of the people of God. It was revealed to the ancient prophets, that this glorious salvation was not to be enjoyed under the Jewish economy—that it was to take place "in the latter days"—" in the last times"—in the days of the Messiah. They were made to perceive that their predictions would be better understood, and therefore would be more useful to those who lived under the Messiah, than they were to themselves. "They ministered not to themselves, but to us;" that is, these predictions, uttered by them, though not useless to them, for they, like Abraham, wished to see the day of Christ, and saw it afar off, and were glad, are still more useful to us who have had them explained by a further revelation. The Apostle's idea has been very finely illustrated by the following beautiful figure :—" The sweet stream of their doctrine made its own banks fertile and pleasant, as it ran by and flowed still forwards to after ages, and, by the confluence of more such prophecies, grew larger as it proceeded, till it fell in with the main current of the gospel revelation ; and thus united into one river clear as crystal, this doctrine of salvation hath still refreshed the city of God, and shall continue to do so till it empty itself into the ocean of eternity."[1]

How strikingly does the fact, that the *final* salvation was the subject of prophetic testimony from the beginning, illustrate at once the grandeur of this salvation, and the certainty that it will in the appointed season be conferred on the people of God! That must be a glorious object to which God, by his Spirit, directed the admiring eyes of inspired prophets while at the distance of so many thousand years. The highest conceptions we can form of it must come inconceivably short of the truth, when we think of it as the

[1] Leighton.

glorious termination of the whole wondrous systems of nature, and providence, and grace, which have been in operation for nearly six thousand years.

And the fact that it is the subject of Old Testament prophecies, proves not only its grandeur, but its security. We have " the word of prophecy more confirmed "[1] than the Old Testament believers. They had enough to make it most reasonable in them to believe, that whatever was predicted in the Scriptures should be fulfilled; but we have far more evidence than they had for the second coming of the Lord, and the complete salvation that is to accompany it. We have the fulfilment of the predictions as to the first coming, and of many succeeding events, to confirm our faith. The final salvation of believers, at the second coming of the Lord, is one of those things which ought to be " most surely believed among us." If we do not believe, it is not for want of evidence. " He will come the second time; and to all who look for him, he will come unto salvation."

If it was the duty of the ancient prophets to inquire into the meaning of the oracles revealed by them, respecting the great salvation of the people of God at the coming of the Lord, it certainly must be our duty to do so. Every part of divine revelation deserves and requires study; and, surely, those portions of it which have a reference to the coming of Christ, and the complete salvation of his people, have a peculiar claim on our attention. The extravagancies into which some students of prophecy have run, ought not to prevent us from imitating the ancient prophets in "inquiring and searching diligently concerning this salvation," knowing that a blessing is pronounced on him " that readeth, and on them that hear the words of that prophetic book which is the revelation of Jesus Christ."[2] " Were the prophets not exempted from the pains of search and inquiry, that had the Spirit of God not only in a high degree, but after a singular manner—how unbecoming, then, is slothfulness and idleness

---

[1] εχομεν βεβαιοτερον τον προφητικον λογον.—2 Pet. i. 19.   [2] Rev. i. 3.

in us! Whether is it, that we judge ourselves advantaged
with more of the Spirit than these holy men, or that we
esteem the doctrines and mysteries of salvation, on which
they bestowed so much of their labour, unworthy of ours?
We do ourselves much injury if we bar ourselves from
sharing in our measure of the search of these same things
that were the study of the prophets, and which, by their
studying and publishing them, are made more accessible
and easy to us. These are the golden mines in which the
abiding treasures of eternity are to be found, and therefore
worthy of all the digging and pains we can bestow upon
them." [1]

II.—THE FINAL HAPPINESS OF CHRISTIANS THE SUBJECT OF APOSTOLICAL PREACHING.

The final salvation of the people of God, at the second
coming of Jesus Christ, is the subject of apostolical preaching. Things in reference to that salvation, concerning which
the prophets prophesied and made inquiry, " have been reported to us by those who preached the gospel with the
Holy Ghost sent down from heaven."

" Those who preached the gospel with the Holy Ghost
sent down from heaven," are, we apprehend, the apostles
and other miraculously gifted teachers of the primitive age.
They " preached the gospel;" *i. e.,* they published the glad
tidings of a full, and a free, and an everlasting deliverance
from sin and all its dreadful consequences, through the
mediation of the incarnate Son of God, who having expiated
sin by the shedding of his own precious blood, which cleanses
from all sin, has been raised from the dust of death, and invested with all power in heaven and earth, that he may be
able to save to the uttermost all coming to God by him.

They preached this gospel " with the Holy Ghost sent
down from heaven." These words intimate, either that their

---

[1] Leighton.

preaching the gospel was accompanied by miraculous works, proving the truth and the divinity of what they taught,—works which they were enabled to perform by the Holy Ghost, whose miraculous influence was "sent down from heaven;" *i. e.,* communicated to them by God;—or that their preaching was accompanied by the influence of the divine Spirit on the minds and hearts of those to whom it was addressed, leading them to attend to, to understand, and to believe it; "opening their understandings" to understand the truth, and "their hearts to receive the love of the truth, so as to be saved by it." Both these statements are true, and I think it not improbable that the words of the Apostle were meant to include both. "The Lord the Spirit" "bore testimony to the word of grace" in both ways. "The great salvation was begun to be spoken by the Lord, and was confirmed unto us by them who heard him; and God bore witness by signs and wonders, and divers miracles, and gifts of the Holy Ghost, according to his will."[1] When Peter was preaching the gospel to Cornelius and his friends, "the Holy Ghost fell on all them which heard the word." When Paul preached to the Thessalonians, "Our gospel," says he, *i. e.,* the gospel as preached by us, "came not to you in word only, but in power, and with the Holy Ghost, and with much assurance;"[2]—with abundant evidence given by him, and apprehended by them.

These holy Apostles of our Lord Jesus, who, in words not taught by men but by the Holy Ghost, preached the gospel with evidence and with efficacy both derived from the divine Spirit, "made a report" concerning the things of which the prophets had prophesied, and into which they had inquired; *i. e.,* they made a report concerning the final salvation which is to be bestowed on believers at the second coming of their Lord. Much of their preaching was occupied in telling us what is the nature of that salvation; what Jesus Christ had done and suffered in order to procure that

---

[1] Heb. ii. 3, 4.   [2] Acts x. 44.   1 Thess. i. 5.

salvation; how the individual sinner is to become a partaker of its blessings; and in showing that there is a present salvation from guilt and the dominion of sin, and the tormenting fear of divine displeasure and everlasting misery.   But it also included in it a plain statement of the fact, that the full salvation of the Christian is not to be bestowed on him till the second coming of his Lord, and a description more or less particular of the varied and complete blessedness which was then to become his portion.

They "reported" these things.   In making these declarations, they did not utter the dreams of their own imagination, or the deductions of their own reason.   They merely "spoke the things which they had heard."   They made known to others what had been made known to themselves.   This was true of all they said; and, in particular, in reference to things which they reported concerning the final salvation of the people of God.   They " did not follow cunningly devised fables when they made known the power and coming of our Lord Jesus."   " The things which God had laid up for them who love him, were things which eye had not seen, which ear had not heard, and which it never could have entered into the mind of man to conceive; but God revealed them to them by his Spirit;"[1] and of this revelation they made a faithful report.

Let us attend, then, to the report which these men, who preached the gospel with the Holy Ghost sent down from heaven, have made respecting this salvation, which is to be brought to Christians at the revelation of Jesus Christ.   Their report refers both to what their Lord and Master revealed on this subject when he was on earth, and to what was revealed to them by that Holy Spirit whom he promised to send to them, to " lead them into all the truth."

Let us attend first, then, to the report they gave us of what our Lord when on earth revealed respecting this salvation.   The following passages of Scripture contain that

---

[1] 2 Pet. i. 16.   1 Cor. ii. 7-10.

report:—" Verily I say unto you, that ye which have followed me in the regeneration, when the Son of man shall sit in the throne of his glory, ye also shall sit upon twelve thrones, judging the twelve tribes of Israel. And every one that hath forsaken houses, or brethren, or sisters, or father, or mother, or wife, or children, or lands, for my name's sake, shall receive an hundred-fold, and shall inherit everlasting life." " When the Son of man shall come in his glory, and all the holy angels with him, then shall he sit upon the throne of his glory; and before him shall be gathered all nations; and he shall separate them one from another, as a shepherd divideth his sheep from the goats: And he shall set the sheep on his right hand, but the goats on the left. Then shall the King say unto them on his right hand, Come, ye blessed of my Father, inherit the kingdom prepared for you from the foundation of the world: For I was an hungered, and ye gave me meat: I was thirsty, and ye gave me drink: I was a stranger, and ye took me in: Naked, and ye clothed me: I was sick, and ye visited me: I was in prison, and ye came unto me. Then shall the righteous answer him, saying, Lord, when saw we thee an hungered, and fed thee? or thirsty, and gave thee drink? When saw we thee a stranger, and took thee in? or naked, and clothed thee? Or when saw we thee sick, or in prison, and came unto thee? And the King shall answer and say unto them, Verily I say unto you, Inasmuch as ye have done it unto one of the least of these my brethren, ye have done it unto me; and the righteous shall go away into life eternal." " In the end of the world the Son of man shall send forth his angels, and they shall gather out of his kingdom all things that offend, and them who do iniquity. And cast them into a furnace of fire: there shall be weeping and gnashing of teeth. Then shall the righteous shine forth as the sun in the kingdom of their Father." " God so loved the world, that he gave his only begotten Son, that whosoever believed on him might not perish, but have everlasting life." " He that believeth my word, and believeth on him who sent me, hath everlasting life, and shall not come into condemnation ; but is passed from death to life. The hour is coming when all that are in their graves shall hear the voice of the Son of God, and come forth ; they who have done good to the resurrection of life." "This is the will of him that sent me, that every one which seeth the Son, and believeth on him, may have everlasting life ; and I will raise him up at the last day." " In my Father's house are many mansions : if it were not so, I would have told you. I go to prepare a place for you. And if I go and prepare a place for you, I will come again, and receive you unto myself; that where I am, there ye may be also. And whither I go ye know, and the way ye know." [1]

The following passages embody revelations made directly to the Apostles by the Holy Ghost sent down from heaven :—" God will render to every man according to his deeds—to them who, by patient continuance in well-doing, seek for glory, and honour, and immortality, eternal life. Glory, honour, and peace shall be to every man that worketh good, in the day when God shall judge the secrets of men by Jesus Christ." " The sufferings of this present time are not worthy to be compared with the glory which shall be revealed in us. For the earnest expectation of the creature waiteth for the manifestation of the sons of God. For the creature was made subject to vanity, not willingly, but by reason of him who hath subjected the same, in hope that the creature itself also shall be delivered from the bondage of corruption into the glorious liberty of the children of God. For we know that the whole creation groaneth and travaileth in pain together until now: And not only they, but ourselves also, which have the first-fruits of the Spirit, even we ourselves groan within ourselves, waiting for the adoption, the redemption of our body." " Christ is risen from the dead,

---

[1] Matt. xix. 27-29; xxv. 31-40, 46; xiii. 41, 43.   John iii. 16; v. 24, 26, 29 vi. 38, 40; xiv. 2-4.

and become the first-fruits of them that slept. For since by man came death, by man came also the resurrection of the dead; for as in Adam all die, so in Christ shall all be made alive. The last enemy death shall be destroyed. It is sown in corruption, it is raised in incorruption: it is sown in dishonour, it is raised in glory: it is sown in weakness, it is raised in power: it is sown a natural body, it is raised a spiritual body. This corruptible must put on incorruption, and this mortal must put on immortality. The saying that is written shall be brought to pass, Death is swallowed up in victory." " We know that if your earthly house of this tabernacle were dissolved, we have a building of God, a house not made with hands, eternal in the heavens." " Your life is hid with Christ in God. When Christ, who is our life, shall appear, we also shall appear with him in glory." " The Lord shall descend with a shout, with the voice of the archangel, and with the trump of God; and the dead in Christ shall first arise. Then we which are alive, and remain, shall be caught up together with them in the clouds to meet the Lord in the air, and so shall we be for ever with the Lord." " It is a righteous thing with God to recompense to you who are troubled rest with us, when the Lord Jesus shall be revealed from heaven." " An entrance shall be ministered unto us abundantly into the everlasting kingdom of our Lord and Saviour Jesus Christ." " We, according to his promise, look for a new heaven and a new earth, wherein dwelleth righteousness." " To him that overcometh will I give to eat of the tree of life in the midst of the paradise of God. I will give him a crown of life. He shall not be hurt with the second death. I will give him to eat of the hidden manna, and will give him a white stone, and in the stone a new name, which no man knoweth save he who receiveth it; and I will give him the morning star. He shall be clothed in white raiment, and I will not blot his name out of the book of life; but will confess his name before my Father, and before his angels. I will make him a pillar in the temple of my God, and he shall no more go

out. I will grant him to sit with me on my throne, even as
I also overcame, and am set down with my Father on his
throne." "And God shall wipe away all tears from their
eyes; and there shall be no more death, neither sorrow nor
crying, neither shall there be any more pain; for the former
things are passed away." "And there shall be no more
curse; and there shall be no night there; and they shall
reign for ever and ever."[1]

These are "the things which have been reported to us by
them who have preached the gospel with the Holy Ghost
sent down from heaven." There is a good deal in those descriptions which is dark through excessive brightness,—
imperfectly intelligible by us, because descriptive of a state
more pure, and felicitous, and glorious, than our limited,
obtuse, sensualised faculties can distinctly apprehend; but
what is clear and what is dark equally prove, that this happiness, with the love in which it originates, has a height and
a depth, a length and a breadth, that pass knowledge.
And O, delightful, solemnizing thought! this is no airy
dream. These are the true and faithful sayings of God.
The period referred to is hastening on apace; and all this
happiness must either be gained or lost by every one of us
—gained or lost for ever.

III.—THE FINAL HAPPINESS OF CHRISTIANS THE SUBJECT OF ANGELIC STUDY.

It only remains that I turn your attention to the last view
which the Apostle gives us of the final salvation of Christians,
—as the subject of angelic study: "Into these things the
angels desire to look."

Into what things? Obviously into the things "of which
the prophets prophesied, and into which they inquired"—
into the things "reported to us by them who preached the

---

[1] Rom. ii. 6, &c.; Rom. viii. 18-25. 1 Cor. xv. 20, &c. 2 Cor. v. 2, 3. Col.
iii. 3, 4. 1 Thess. iv. 13. 2 Thess. i. 6, &c. 2 Pet. i. 11. Rev. ii. passim; iii.
passim; xxi. 4; xxii. 1-5.

gospel with the Holy Ghost sent down from heaven," *i. e.*, into the things respecting " the salvation prepared to be revealed in the last time"—into the things respecting " the grace to be brought to Christians at the revelation of Jesus Christ"—into those things the angels desire to look. The meaning of these words is obviously, the angels have an intense desire to understand the whole truth in reference to the final salvation of the people of God.

The angels here spoken of are, without doubt, " the elect angels,"—those holy, happy, unembodied spirits who retain their original integrity, who, infinitely beneath God, are yet far superior to men in the scale of being, who excel in wisdom and strength, and who find their happiness in contemplating the divine excellencies and in doing the divine will.

These exalted spiritual beings are represented as " desirous to look" into the things which respect the final salvation of the redeemed from among men. The original expression is very beautiful. They are with earnest desire bending down, fixing their intensest gaze on these things.[1] The peculiar mode of expression probably alludes to the figures of the cherubim above the mercy-seat, who with downcast eyes were represented as looking on the mercy-seat, as if seeking to penetrate the mystery of wisdom and kindness which the fiery law covered by the blood-sprinkled golden propitiatory, embodied.

We have no reason to think that the angels directly know any thing more about the final salvation of the redeemed among men than we do. It is " by the Church," *i. e.*, by the dispensations of God to the Church, that " the principalities and powers in the heavenly places" become acquainted with that revelation of " the manifold wisdom of God" [2] contained in the plan of human redemption. We have no doubt that they know all that is revealed in the Bible on this subject ; and from their higher faculties, and their more diligent study, and their juster and more extended views of the

---

[1] ἃ ἐπιθυμοῦσιν ἀγγελοι παρακύψαι.   [2] Eph. iii. 10.

divine perfections, and of what constitutes the happiness of intelligent creatures, they understand what is revealed there much better than we do. But still they are not satisfied— they are desirous to understand these wondrous divine declarations more completely, and they are looking forward with intense desire to the period when fulfilment shall develope the full extent of their meaning.

Nor is it at all difficult to divine what are the principles in the minds of angels which make them thus desire to look into these things. Enlightened curiosity, piety, and benevolence, all combine in turning their attention with unwearied interest towards this subject. Enlightened curiosity, or the desire of useful knowledge, is one of the characteristic features, we have reason to believe, of angelic as well as human minds. They know far more than we do, but there is much they do not know; and it is probable their thirst for knowledge exceeds ours just in a similar proportion to their possession of knowledge. It is easy to conceive how desirous they must be of knowing what it is for " corruption to put on incorruption," what it is for "mortality to be swallowed up of life." Enlightened philosophers have great pleasure in the witnessing, and in anticipating the witnessing, of experiments tending to throw light on the processes of nature. A world in flames, the elements melting with fervent heat, and the heavens flying away like a scroll, and a new heaven and a new earth rising out of the fiery chaos, are spectacles which it is not wonderful the angels should look forward to with eager desire and almost holy impatience.

Their piety interests them still more deeply in the subject. This salvation is to be the full manifestation of the divine excellencies, as displayed in the whole of that wonderful economy which shall then be completed. Angels will then see more of the power, and wisdom, and holiness, and benignity of God than they had ever seen, than they had ever conjectured; and then, in the final pulling down of every thing which opposes his will or obscures his glory, they will obtain the fullest gratification of the strongest wish of a loyal creature's heart—that God should be "all in all."

Their benevolence, too, keeps their minds fixed on the subject. " They are all ministering spirits, sent forth to minister to those who shall be heirs of salvation." They " encamp round about them that fear God, and deliver them."[1] They have a kind interest in, a tender affection for, those committed to their care. They regard their manifold trials with a benignant pity, though themselves strangers to pain; and they take a generous interest in those events which are to consummate their blessedness. They wonder at the height of glory reserved for the redeemed among men ; and, completely free from envy, they desire to understand what is meant by " all things being put under their feet," and by men who have overcome through the blood of the Lamb, sitting down with him on his throne, as he, when he overcame, sat down on his Father's throne.

The practical use to be made of these truths is not difficult to discover. If these things have been reported to us by men who preached the gospel with the Holy Ghost sent down from heaven, surely we should believe them. And if we believed them—if we really believed them—O what an influence would they have on our temper and conduct ! A faith of this truth would induce the man, who is yet uninterested in the Christian salvation, immediately to seek a share in its heavenly and spiritual blessings, and would make those who are interested in it very holy, very happy, very active, and perfectly contented amid all the calamities and trials of life.

What is the subject of the constant, intense contemplation of angels, surely deserves our most careful study. We are far more closely connected with, far more deeply interested in, the subject of study than they. The salvation they desire to look into will promote, but it will but indi-

[1] Heb. i. 14. Psal. xxxiv. 7.

rectly promote their happiness. Their happiness may be secure without reference to it. But as to us, this salvation must be ours, or we are undone for ever and ever. It is *now* that an interest is to be obtained in it, if obtained at all. It is only by knowing and believing the truth about this salvation, that an interest in it is to be obtained. Oh, then, let us, with intensest ardour, seek the knowledge of this salvation! If we die unacquainted with it, we die uninterested in it; and if we die uninterested in it, it never, never can become ours. "Now is the accepted time, now is the day of salvation."

Note A.

Τα εις Χριστον παθηματα—the *till Christ* sufferings.—Gal. iii. 24. Εις Χριστον=εις ἡμεραν Χριστου.—Phil. i. 10. The view we have taken of the expression τ. ε. Χ. π. κ. τ. μ. τ. δ. is substantially that taken both by Luther and Calvin. Calvin's remark savours of his ordinary exegetical sagacity : " Non tractat Petrus quid Christo sit proprium sed de universali ecclesiæ statu disserit." Le Clerc's note is good : " Τα εις Χριστον παθηματα intellexerit de piorum perpessionibus, Christi causa exantlandis : quas previderant obscurius Prophetæ, et gloriam fidelium post sequuturum ; sed quarum nescierunt tempora nisi quod revelatum eis est, ipsorum ævo eas non eventuras. Hæc egregie consentiunt cum serie orationis Petri qui loquitur de malis quibus religionis causa afficiebantur Christiani." Winer, though he does not adopt our exegesis, distinctly says that the expression before us is incorrectly taken for Τα Χριστου παθηματα.—Gram. Part iii. sec. 30, p. 157.

DISCOURSE V.

CHRISTIAN DUTY—MEANS OF, AND MOTIVES TO, ITS PERFORMANCE.

1 PET. i. 13-21.—Wherefore gird up the loins of your mind, be sober, and hope to the end, for the grace that is to be brought unto you at the revelation of Jesus Christ: as obedient children, not fashioning yourselves according to the former lusts in your ignorance: but as he which hath called you is holy, so be ye holy in all manner of conversation; because it is written, Be ye holy; for I am holy. And if ye call on the Father, who without respect of persons judgeth according to every man's work, pass the time of your sojourning here in fear: forasmuch as ye know that ye were not redeemed with corruptible things, as silver and gold, from your vain conversation received by tradition from your fathers; but with the precious blood of Christ, as of a lamb without blemish and without spot: who verily was fore-ordained before the foundation of the world, but was manifest in these last times for you, who by him do believe in God, that raised him up from the dead, and gave him glory; that your faith and hope might be in God.

AMONG the numerous mistaken notions of Christianity which prevail among its professors, few are more common, and none more fatal, than that in which it is viewed merely as a theory—a system of abstract principles, which, however true, are but remotely connected with human interests; and which, therefore, can but feebly influence human character and conduct. It is but too evident that the grand characteristic doctrines of Christianity, such as the trinity, the incarnation, the atonement, justification by faith, sanctification by divine influence, are, with many who readily admit their truth, and who would indeed be shocked at having their orthodoxy called in question, mere inoperative opinions, which exercise no more practical influence over their temper and conduct than the philosophical doctrines respecting the nature of space and time, or the size and distance of the celestial bodies, or the historical facts respecting the victories of Alexander or the discoveries of Columbus.

It is painful to think that it is no uncommon thing for a person to be able to talk plausibly about these principles of Christianity, to reason conclusively in their support, and to be zealous even to rancour against those who deny, or even doubt their truth; while he yet continues a total stranger to their transforming efficacy, the slave of selfishness, malignity, and worldliness. And, what is the most lamentable part of this sad history, the infatuated man seems in a great measure unaware of the shocking inconsistency he is exhibiting, in displaying the most unchristian tempers in defence of Christian truth. He mistakes his knowledge and zeal about certain propositions—which, it may be, embody Christian truth—for Christianity itself; and looking, it would seem, on orthodoxy of opinion as the sum and substance of religious duty, wraps himself up in an overweening conception of his own attainments, and resigns himself to the pleasing dreams of a fancied security, from which but too frequently he is first and for ever awakened by the awful mandate, " Depart from me, I never knew you;" and finding his place assigned him with the hypocrites, in the regions of hopeless misery.

It is an interesting inquiry, and, if properly conducted, would certainly elicit some important results—How comes it that men, with the Bible in their hands, can practise such fatal impositions on themselves? How comes it that the mere speculator should so readily conclude himself a sound believer? How comes it that the truth of doctrines should not only be readily admitted, but zealously maintained, while their appropriate influence is altogether unfelt, and, indeed, steadily resisted? It would lead me too far out of our way just now to engage in such an inquiry; but I must be permitted to observe, that whatever influence deficient human representations of divine truth may have had in producing so mischievous and lamentable a result (and I believe that influence has been extensive and powerful), the truths of the Gospel themselves, and the scriptural representation of them, cannot be justly charged as in any degree the cause of this evil. The doctrines of the Gospel are of such a nature, that, if apprehended in their meaning and evidence, if understood and believed, they must, from the constitution of the mind of man, have a commanding influence over its principles of action; and these doctrines, as taught in the Bible, are not exhibited as mere abstract propositions, but are stated in such a manner as distinctly to show, how closely the belief of them is connected with every thing that is good in disposition, and right in conduct. The speculatist in religion must not seek, for he will not find, in the Bible, an apology for his infatuation and inconsistency. On the contrary, he will meet with much to prove him altogether inexcusable.

The principles of Christianity are never in the New Testament exhibited in an abstract systematic form. They are interwoven with the injunctions to the cultivation of right dispositions, and to the practice of commanded duties, to which in truth they form the most powerful motives. The Author of Revelation, who is also the Author of our nature, and who is intimately acquainted with all its intellectual and moral obliquities in its present fallen state, has mercifully and wisely led those " holy men who spoke as they were moved by his Spirit," to guard their readers against that tendency to consider the doctrines of Christianity as mere matters of speculation, to which we have been adverting, by almost invariably following a statement of doctrine, with a statement of the practical consequences, which that doctrine, understood and believed, is at once calculated and intended to produce.

Of this we have a very striking and instructive exemplification in the passage which we have here chosen as the subject of this discourse. In the preceding paragraph we have a statement of some of the most sublime and delightful peculiarities of Christian doctrine. We are instructed respecting that state of ineffable purity, dignity, and happiness, to which it is the purpose of God ultimately to raise men, through the mediation of his incarnate only begotten. This state is described as " salvation"—deliverance from evil, in all its forms and degrees, for ever—a holy happiness, filling to an overflow all the capacities of enjoyment during the entire eternity of man's being—as " an *inheritance*," intimating at once the gratuitousness of the nature, and the security of the tenure of this happiness—" an inheritance incorruptible," having nothing in its own nature which can lead to decay or termination—" undefiled," its pure elements unmingled with any inferior or heterogeneous ingredients— " unfading," retaining unimpaired its power to communicate happiness—" laid up in heaven," pure and ethereal in its nature, and secured beyond the reach of fraud or of violence; while those for whom it is destined, those who, according to the divine fore-knowledge, have been selected by a spiritual separation from the world lying under the wicked one, that they may obey the truth, and be sprinkled by the blood of Jesus—*i. e.*, possess the blessings secured by his atoning sacrifice—are preserved for its enjoyment amid all the dangers they are exposed to, by the power of God and through the instrumentality of believing.

Still further to illustrate the glories of this salvation, this final state of blessedness, we are told, that unlike the present state, in which Jesus Christ is bodily absent from his chosen ones, and in which the imperfect knowledge they have of him is obtained entirely through the medium of believing, in which they are exposed to numerous and severe trials, in which complete deliverance from evil is the object of faith and hope, and in which, owing to these causes, they are often in heaviness—the future state of Christians is a state in which Christ Jesus is bodily present with them, and maintains intimate and uninterrupted intercourse with them—a state in which nothing of their trials but their blissful and glorious results remain—a state in which complete deliverance is the object of enjoyment—a state in which, in consequence of all these things, they "rejoice with a joy which is unspeakable and full of glory;" and, as if even all this were not enough to give us just ideas of the glories and felicities "which God has laid up for those who love him," we are told, that this state of final happiness is a leading subject of Old Testament prophecy, apostolical preaching, and angelical study.

These delightful and wonderful announcements are not brought forward as abstract principles—things to speculate and to talk about. They are no sooner stated than the apostle proceeds to urge them on Christians as most powerful motives to the duties of their high and holy calling, and equally powerful supports and consolations under the afflictions to which the discharge of these duties might expose them. "Wherefore," for these reasons, since these things are so—" Wherefore gird up the loins of your mind, be sober, and hope to the end, for the grace that is to be brought unto you at the revelation of Jesus Christ: As obedient children, not fashioning yourselves according to the former lusts in your ignorance: But as he which hath called you is holy, so be ye holy in all manner of conversation; because it is written, Be ye holy; for I am holy. And if ye call on the Father, who without respect of persons judgeth according to every man's work, pass the time of your sojourning here in fear. Forasmuch as ye know that ye were not redeemed with corruptible things, as silver and gold, from your vain conversation received by tradition from your fathers; but with the precious blood of Christ, as of a lamb without blemish and without spot: Who verily was fore-ordained before the foundation of the world, but was manifest in these last times for you, who by him do believe in God, that raised him from the dead, and gave him glory; that your faith and hope might be in God." In this admirable paragraph we have a most instructive view—I. Of Christian duty; II. Of the means of performing it; and III. Of the motives to its performance. Of CHRISTIAN DUTY—described, first, generally as obedience, Christians being expected to act " as obedient children," *i. e.*, rather children of obedience; and then described more particularly—first negatively, " Not fashioning yourselves according to your former lusts in your ignorance;" and then positively—" Be holy in all manner of conversation." Of the MEANS OF PERFORMING CHRISTIAN DUTY; first, determined resolution—" Gird up the loins of your mind;" secondly, moderation in all our estimates, and desires, and pursuit of worldly objects—" Be sober;" thirdly, hope—" Hope to the end," hope perfectly; fourthly, fear—" Pass the time of your sojourning here in fear." Of THE MOTIVES TO THE PERFORMANCE OF CHRISTIAN DUTY. First, the grandeur and excellence and security of the Christian inheritance, the full possession of which we can attain only by Christian obedience. " Wherefore," referring to the whole of the preceding description of the final state of happiness which awaits the saints; secondly, the holiness of God—" Be ye holy, for I am holy;" thirdly, the equity of God—" The Father on whom we call, without respect of persons, judgeth every man according to his works;" and fourthly, the wonderful provision which had been made for securing this holiness, in their having been redeemed, or bought back to God, by the blood of his own Son—" Forasmuch as ye know that ye were not redeemed with corruptible things, *as* silver and gold, from your vain conversation received by tradition from your fathers; but with the precious blood of Christ, as of a lamb without blemish and without spot: Who verily was fore-ordained before the foundation of the world, but was manifest in these last times for you, who by him do believe in God, that raised him up from the dead, and gave him glory; that your faith and hope might be in God."

Such is the outline which I shall attempt to fill up in the subsequent illustrations.

I. CHRISTIAN DUTY.

§ 1. *General view—obedience.*

According to the plan which has just been sketched, our attention must be first directed to the view of Christian duty with which we are presented in the passage before us.

Christian duty is in this paragraph represented generally as obedience. The apostle calls on Christians to conduct themselves " as obedient children," or rather children of obedience, which is the literal reading of the original terms. The apostle's meaning does not seem to be, " Behave yourselves towards God as obedient children do towards their father," but act the part not of children of disobedience —a strong idiomatic phrase for disobedient persons; but of children of obedience—a strong idiomatic phrase for obedient persons.[1] Obedience, then, is the great duty of the Christian. Obedience has always a reference to a law to be obeyed. Christians are often, in the epistolary part of the New Testament, represented as not only completely delivered from subjection to the law of Moses; but the state into which they are brought by the faith of the gospel is described as a being " not under law, but under grace."[2] Their pardon and salvation are not to be procured by their own obedience to any law, but to be received as the " gift of God, through Jesus Christ our Lord." But though delivered from the Mosaic law, and though " not under *law*," in the sense of their final salvation being the stipulated reward of stipulated labour, they are " not without law to God; they are under the law to Christ."[3]

The law to which the Christian owes obedience is the revelation of the divine will contained in the Holy Scriptures. This law, is like its Author, " spiritual" and " holy," both " just and good."[4] It reaches not merely to action, but

[1] Τεκνα υπακοης is a Hebraism of the same kind as τεκνα φωτος, υιοι ημερας, υιος απωλειας, υιοι απειθειας, τεκνα οργης, τεκνα καταρας.
[2] Rom. vi. 14.   [3] 1 Cor. ix. 21.   [4] Rom. vii. 12, 14.

to the principles of action, and requires obedience of *mind*, obedience of *heart*, and obedience of *life*.

Obedience of mind consists in the implicit belief of whatever is revealed in the Holy Scriptures. It is counting true whatever God has said, just because God has said it. A Christian is not left to think as he pleases. The command of God is, " Let the mind be in you which was also in Christ Jesus." [1] We must think in conformity to the mind of God, as made known in his word. We must receive what is written there, " not as the word of man, but as it is in truth the word of the living God." [2]

This submission of mind to the authority of God is the fundamental part of Christian obedience, and naturally leads to that obedience of heart which is equally required by that law, which is exceeding broad. By obedience of heart, I understand a state of the affections corresponding to the character of God as revealed in the manifestation he has made of his will. He appears in that manifestation infinitely venerable and estimable, and amiable and trustworthy; and reverence and esteem, and love and confidence, are the dispositions which these excellencies ought to excite in our minds. To " sanctify the Lord God in our hearts," to " make him our fear and dread," to " love him with our heart, and our soul, and our strength, and our mind," and " to trust in him at all times." [3]—this is the obedience of the heart.

As the obedience of the mind naturally leads to the obedience of the heart, as it is impossible to venerate and esteem, and love and trust God, without knowing and believing that he is venerable and excellent, and amiable and trustworthy, and impossible to believe him possessed of those excellencies without exercising those dispositions, so the obedience of the mind and of the heart naturally express themselves in the obedience of the life.

The obedience of the life is twofold—active and passive :

---

[1] Phil. ii. 5.   [2] 1 Thess. ii. 13.
[3] 1 Pet. iii. 15.   Isa. viii. 13.   Matt. xxii. 37.   Psal. lxii. 8.

the one consisting in conscientiously doing whatever God commands; and the other consisting in cheerfully submitting to whatever God appoints. It is the duty of the Christian to " walk in all God's commandments and ordinances blameless," to be " patient in tribulation," and even to " count it all joy when brought into manifold trials."[1] Such is the general idea of obedience as the duty of the Christian. A conformity of mind and heart and conduct to the revealed will of God.

There are certain general characters which belong to this obedience when it is genuine, and which distinguish it from all counterfeits. It is *implicit* obedience. The Christian not only believes what God reveals, but he believes it because God has revealed it; he not only does what God commands, but he does it because God has commanded it; he not only submits to what God appoints, but he submits to it because God has appointed it. It is obviously just so far as the faith and conduct of a Christian have this character, that they deserve the name of obedience at all.

The obedience which forms the sum and substance of Christian duty, is *impartial* and *universal* obedience. If it is implicit, it will be impartial and universal. If I really regard the will of God at all, I will regard it whenever I see it clearly manifested. I will not, among equally clearly commanded duties, choose which I will perform, and which I will neglect. I will " esteem all his precepts concerning all things to be right," and I will " hate every wicked way."[2]

Cheerfulness is another essential character of Christian obedience. External obedience may often be constrained and mercenary; but the obedience of the life, which proceeds from, and is the expression of, the obedience of the mind and heart, cannot be either. In obeying, the Christian is doing what he knows to be right; and what he feels to be good. He " consents to the law that it is good." He " delights in the law after the inward man." When his

[1] Luke i. 6.   Rom. xii. 12.   James i. 2.   [2] Psal. cxix. 128.

heart is enlarged by just and impressive views of the reasonableness and excellence of the divine laws, he runs in the
ways of God's commandments, and finds that " in keeping
them there is great reward."[1]

The obedience which is the sum of the Christian's duty,
in fine, is not an occasional and temporary, but a *habitual*
and a *persevering* obedience. It is the business of his life :
" Whatsoever he does, whether in word or in deed," ought
to be done " in the name of the Lord Jesus, giving thanks to
God the Father by him." " Whether he eats, or drinks, or
whatsoever he does," he ought to do " all to the glory of
God." His obedience ought to be " a patient continuance
in well-doing," " a stedfast, immoveable, constant abounding in the work of the Lord," " a forgetting the things
which are behind, a reaching forth to those which are before,
a pressing to the mark for the prize of the high calling of
God in Christ Jesus."[2]

§ 2.—*Particular view of Christian duty.* (1.) *Negative.*
(2.) *Positive.*

The duty of the Christian is not only generally described
as obedience, but more particularly, first, negatively, as a
" not fashioning themselves according to the former lusts in
their ignorance," and then, positively, as a " being holy in
all manner of conversation." Let us shortly attend to these
very instructive descriptions of Christian duty.

(1.) The Apostle's negative statement is, that Christians
ought not to fashion themselves " according to the former
lusts in their ignorance." While a man continues unacquainted with the meaning and evidences of the revelation
which God has made of himself in his word—and this is the
case with every unbeliever,—he is in a state of ignorance
respecting the most important of all subjects, the character
and will of God—the duty and happiness of man. While
in that state he does not " fashion himself," *i. e.,* regulate

---

[1] Rom. vii. 16, 22.   Psal. xix. 11.
[2] Col. iii. 17.   1 Cor. x. 31.   Rom. ii. 7.   1 Cor. xv. 58.   Phil. iii. 13, 14.

his conduct—form his character, "according to the will of God," but according to his "lusts," *i. e.*, his desires. The desires which are natural to men while they are unrenewed, are the principles which regulate their conduct and form their character. One man loves pleasure, another loves money, another loves power, another loves fame. The ruling desire, or lust, is the principle which forms the character and guides the conduct.

Now the Christian, being no longer in ignorance, but knowing and believing the revelation God has made of his will, must no longer permit his character to be fashioned by those desires, to the guidance of which, when in a state of ignorance, he delivered himself up. All these desires, so far as they are sinful, must be mortified, and, even so far as they are innocent, they must cease to be governing principles, and must be subordinated to a higher principle—the principle of submission of mind and heart to the will of God.

The objects of these desires are sensible and present things—things which are "in the world;" so that the not fashioning ourselves according to our former lusts in our ignorance, and our not being "conformed to this world," are but two different modes of expressing the same thing. An unregenerated man's character is entirely formed by the desires of his fallen nature, excited by their appropriate objects in the present world. It was once so with the Christian, but it must be so with him no longer. On the contrary, "as he who has called him is holy, so must he be holy in all manner of conversation."

(2.) This is the Apostle's positive statement with respect to Christian duty. There is no word, I apprehend, to which more indistinct ideas are generally attached, than holiness; yet, surely, there is no word of the meaning of which it is of more importance we should have a clear and accurate conception; for "without holiness no man shall see the Lord."[1] The clearest and the justest idea we can form of holiness, as

---

[1] Heb. xii. 14.

a quality of an intelligent being, is conformity of mind and will with the Supreme Being, who alone is, in all the extent of meaning belonging to the word, holy. Holiness does not consist in mystic speculations, enthusiastic fervours, or uncommanded austerities; it consists in thinking as God thinks, and willing as God wills. God's mind and will are to be known from his word; and, so far as I really understand and believe God's word, God's mind becomes my mind, God's will becomes my will, and, according to the measure of my faith, I become holy.

And this conformity of mind and will to God—this holiness, is to be manifested " in all manner of conversation." " Conversation " here, as usually in the New Testament, signifies not colloquial intercourse, but general conduct.[1] In every part of your character and conduct let it appear that the ruling principles of your conduct, the forming principles of your character, are no longer what they once were—your lusts, your natural desires, but the mind and the will of him who has called you, even God, who is holy; his mind and will having become your mind and will, through the knowledge and belief of the truth; that these are now the principles by which your character is formed and your life governed. In every thing show that you think as God thinks, that you will as God wills, that you love what God loves, that you hate what he hates, that you choose what he chooses, that you seek enjoyment in what he finds enjoyment. Such is a short account of the Christian's duty.

There are two conclusions to which these observations necessarily conduct us, highly worthy of considerate reflection. First, that there are many who call themselves Christians who have no title to that name, habitually violators of God's law, strangers to the very principle of obedience, still " walking according to the course of this world, serving divers lusts and pleasures." [2] How vain—how much worse

---

[1] The only exception is Phil. iii. 20, where the word in the original is not·ανα-στροφη, but πολιτευμα—citizenship.

[2] Eph. ii. 2, 3.   Tit. iii. 3.

than vain is their profession—how dangerous their circumstances—how awful, if they continue in their present state, their final doom ! The second conclusion is, that those who are really Christians are still very far, indeed, from being what they ought to be—from being what they might be. The best Christians, then, need to have such exhortations addressed to them as these : " Follow holiness," seek growing conformity of mind and heart to God, and recollect this can only be obtained by growing knowledge and faith of the truth. Though already not of the world, even as their Lord is not of the world, they need the great Intercessor continually to pray for them, " Sanctify them through thy truth, thy word is truth." [1]

II. MEANS FOR THE PERFORMANCE OF CHRISTIAN DUTY.

We now proceed to direct your minds to the view here given us of the means of performing this duty. If we would be children of obedience, not fashioning ourselves after our former lusts in our ignorance—if we would be holy in all manner of conversation, it is necessary that we should "gird up the loins of our mind"—that we should be "sober" —that we should " hope to the end "—and that we should " pass the time of our sojourning here in fear." Determined resolution, moderation, hope, and fear, are the means here prescribed for our realizing, in our own character and conduct, those views of Christian duty presented to us by the Apostle. Let us shortly attend to them in their order.

§ 1.—*Determined Resolution a means of Christian Obedience.*

Determined resolution is one of the instrumental means which we ought to employ, in order to our complying with the Apostle's exhortation. "Gird up," says he, "the loins of your mind." The ancients were accustomed to wear loose, flowing garments, which, though graceful and agreeable on

<hr>

[1] John xvii. 17.

ordinary occasions, were found inconvenient when strenuous
and long-continued exertion was necessary. In such cases
it was usual to gather together the folds of the flowing
drapery, and, having wrapped them round the waist, to confine them by a belt or girdle. This was termed girding up
the loins.

The phrase is here plainly used figuratively. To inquire,
as some have done, what are meant by the loins of the
mind, and to reply—the sensual affections and appetites, the
lower propensities of human nature ; and to inquire what is
meant by girding up the loins of the mind, and to reply—
the restraint and mortification of these debasing propensities, is rather ingeniously to play with, than satisfactorily to
explain, the phraseology of the sacred writer. " To gird up
the loins of the mind " is to gird up the loins mentally ;
that is, to cultivate that state of mind of which the girding
up the loins is the natural emblem. When a man has got
nothing to do, or nothing which requires any thing like
exertion, he permits his robes to flow in graceful negligence
around him ; or, even if called on to a sudden, transient,
though vigorous effort, he may not think it worth his while
to make any change in his dress ; but if he has a work to
perform, which requires at once strenuous and continued
exertion—if he is about, not to take a walk for pleasure,
but to undertake a journey on business, then he girds up his
loins. The action is naturally emblematical of that state of
mind in which a person contemplates a course of conduct,
which, while he considers it as highly eligible and indispens-
ably obligatory, he plainly perceives to involve in it serious
difficulty, and to demand the persevering putting forth of all
his active energies.[1]

The apostolical command, " Gird up the loins of your
mind," is equivalent to ' Set yourselves with resolute determination to the performance of these duties. Impress on your
minds a sense of their importance, obligation, advantages, and

---

[1] Exod. xii. 11.   1 Kings xviii. 46.   Job xxxviii. 3 ; xl. 7.   Luke xii. 35.

necessity. Let there be no halting between two opinions. Considering Christian obedience as the business of life; a business, the right discharge of which will require all the care you can devote to it; a business, in the prosecution of which no exertion must be spared, no sacrifice grudged; enter on it with a determination, that whatever may be neglected this shall be attended to; and with a distinct understanding, that this is not to be an occasional employment for your by-hours, but the habitual occupation to which all your time and all your faculties are to be devoted.'

Such a spirit of determined resolution is absolutely necessary to the proper performance of the duties involved in a life of Christian obedience. These duties are numerous, varied, and laborious. They are all in the highest degree reasonable, and to a being whose moral constitution was in a completely sound state, none of them would be in the slightest degree grievous. The yoke of Christian duty should be very easy—the burden of Christian duty should be very light. But who that believes the declarations of Scripture—who that is in any degree conversant with the realities of Christian experience, needs to be told that the remains of native depravity, acted on by the temptations of Satan, and by the influence of a world lying under his power, often make irksome what ought to be delightful, difficult what should be easy, laborious what should be spontaneous? How endless, varied, and diversified are the circumstances which have a tendency to induce spiritual sloth, and make us become "weary in well-doing!" How apt are we to turn out of the way, instead of proceeding right onwards; to loiter, when we should quicken our pace; to think we have "attained, and are already perfect," when we have little more than entered on our Christian course! How often, when the spirit is willing, is the flesh weak! Oh, how does "the flesh war against the spirit, so that we cannot do the things that we would!" [1]

---

[1] Gal. v. 17.

To meet this state of things, nothing is more necessary than that resolute determination here recommended by the Apostle. Without it we will make but little progress in our Christian course, and the little progress we make, will be productive of but little comfort to ourselves—little glory to our Lord; every thing will be a difficulty; we will be constantly stumbling, and but too often falling. But with it, our progress will be steady and rapid, delightful to ourselves, comfortable to our brethren, honourable to our Lord; we will "forget the things which are behind, reach forward to those which are before, and press toward the mark for the prize of the high calling of God in Christ Jesus."[1]

This resolute determination must not rest on the mistaken opinion of our possessing in ourselves all the energies, which are necessary for the successful performance of all the duties implied in Christian obedience, but on an humble yet confident reliance on the promises of God, securing for us all those supplies of Divine influence which are requisite for this purpose. It is the faith of the truth, and that alone, that can brace the mind for spiritual work and warfare. It is this which makes us "strong in the Lord, and in the power of his might."[2]

Let us, then, like the Israelites when leaving Egypt, gird up our loins, resolved to prosecute our journey, undeterred by the fury of our spiritual enemies, endeavouring to bring us again into bondage by the billows of the Red Sea of persecution, or by the endless toils and troubles of the wilderness of this world; till, having passed the Jordan of death, we shall lay by the staff and the sword for the palm and the harp, and exchange the humble garb of the pilgrim for the flowing robes of the victor. Meanwhile, to use the language of the heavenly Leighton, "Let us remember our way, and where we are, and keep our robes girt up, for we walk among briars and thorns, which, if we let them down, will entangle and stop us, and possibly tear our gar-

---

[1] Phil. iii. 13.   [2] Eph. vi. 10.

ments; we walk through a world where there is a great mire of sinful pollutions, and therefore cannot but defile them: and the crowd we are among will be ready to tread on them; yea, our own feet may be entangled in them, and so make us stumble and possibly fall." Our only safety is in girding up the loins of our mind.

§ 2.—*Moderation a means of Christian Obedience.*

Moderation is another of the instrumental means which the Apostle recommends for the performance of the duty of Christian obedience. "Be sober." To be sober, in ordinary language, is descriptive of that particular variety of the duty of temperance, which is opposed to the undue use of intoxicating liquors. But the word used by the Apostle has a much more extensive meaning. The sobriety or temperance of the Apostle is another word for moderation, and is descriptive of that state of mind, and affections, and behaviour, in reference to "things seen and temporal," "the present world," by which a Christian should be distinguished.

The foundation of true Christian sobriety or moderation lies in a just estimate of the intrinsic and comparative value of "all that is in the world, the lust of the flesh, the lust of the eye, and the pride of life,"[1]—all that the eye or the flesh desires—all of which living men are apt to be proud. He does not consider the wealth, and the honour, and the pleasures of this world, as without their value; but he sees that that value is by no means what the deluded worshippers of Mammon suppose it to be. He sees that the possession of them cannot make him happy, nor the want of them make him miserable. They cannot obtain for him the pardon of his sin, they cannot pacify his conscience, they cannot transform his character, they cannot give him life in death, they cannot give him happiness for ever. They appear to him polluted with sin, replete with temptation, full of danger.

[1] 1 John ii. 6.

With these views, he is moderate in his desires for them, moderate in his pursuit of them, moderate in his attachment to them, while he enjoys them; moderate in his regrets for them, when he is deprived of them. This is Christian sobriety. It is for those who have earthly relatives to be as if they had them not; for "those who weep to be as though they wept not; for those who rejoice to be as though they rejoiced not; for those who use this world to use it as not abusing it, knowing that the fashion of this world passeth away."[1]

The cultivation of this sobriety is of the utmost importance to the proper performance of the duties of Christian obedience. The supreme love of the world is inconsistent with Christian obedience altogether. "No man can serve two masters: for either he will hate the one, and love the other; or else he will hold to the one, and despise the other; ye cannot serve God and mammon."[2] And, as the supreme love of the world necessarily makes and keeps men "children of disobedience," so the undue love of the world prevents even those who are "the children of God, through faith in Christ Jesus," from being, in the degree to which they ought, "the children of obedience." What is it that makes obedience so often feel a tiresome task, but the undue love of the world; and how do the commandments of our Lord become to us not grievous, but by our victorious faith overcoming the world?[3] It has been finely said, that "the same eye cannot both look up to heaven and down to earth at the same time." And the heart must be emptied of the love of the world, that it may be filled with that love of God, which is at once the seminal principle and the concentrated essence of all Christian obedience. Those who are quite engrossed with earth's business and pleasure cannot be "seeking a country —a better country, i. e., an heavenly." They who, by their immoderate attachment to earth, show they are at home, cannot be "strangers and sojourners." The Captain of the

[1] 1 Cor. vii. 29-31.   [2] Matt. vi. 24.   [3] 1 John v. 4.

Lord's host, our New Testament Gideon, will not own as his soldiers those who lie down to drink of the streams of earth's delight, but only those who, in passing, drink of them with their hand, as of the brook in the way.[1]

It were much to be desired that professors of Christianity were more deeply impressed with this truth, that the supreme love of the world is utterly inconsistent with the very existence of Christianity; and that real Christians were more deeply impressed with the kindred truth, of the utter inconsistency of an undue love of the world with a healthy thriving Christianity, a Christianity bringing forth the fruits of true holiness and true happiness, fruits which are to the glory of God, and to the happiness of the believer. It is, my brethren, this worldliness, this want of Christian sobriety, which spreads such a withering blight over the blossoms of fair profession, and prevents their ever ripening into fruit. To quote again the spiritual commentator already referred to : "All immoderate use of the world and its delights injures the soul in its spiritual condition, makes it sickly and feeble, full of spiritual distempers and inactivity, benumbs the graces of the Spirit, and fills the soul with sleepy vapours, makes it grow secure and heavy in spiritual exercises, and obstructs the way and motion of the Spirit of God in the soul."[2]   If we would then be children of obedience, if we would not fashion ourselves according to the former lusts, if we would be holy in all manner of conversation, let us " be sober."

Let each of us, ere we proceed farther, examine himself. Am I girding up the loins of my mind? Am I, in a dependence on the promised aids of divine influence, honestly, heartily determined to make the service of God, through Christ Jesus, my great business, and to make the life I live in the flesh a life of subjection to his will, and obedience to his law, by making it a life of faith in his Son? Am I sober, temperate, moderate in all things, in my estimates, my

---

[1] Leighton.   Heb. xi. 13, 14.   Judges vii. 4-7.   [2] Leighton.

desires, my pursuits, my enjoyments, my sorrows? If we are not girding up the loins of our minds, if we are not sober, we are not Christians. We may be calling Christ Lord, Lord; but we are not doing the things which he says to us; and unless a thorough change take place, to us, at last, must be addressed these heart-withering words— "Depart from me, I never knew you, ye workers of iniquity."

§ 3. *Hope a means of Christian Obedience.*

We proceed now to observe, that Hope is the third means recommended by the Apostle for securing the proper performance of the duty of Christian obedience. If ye would be " children of obedience," if ye would " not fashion yourselves according to your former lusts in your ignorance," if ye would " be holy in all manner of conversation," ye must " hope to the end; for the grace which is to be brought to you at the revelation of our Lord Jesus Christ."

" The grace," or favour, " which is to be brought to Christians at the revelation of Christ Jesus," *i. e.,* when Christ Jesus is revealed, is plainly that perfection of holy happiness to which they are to be raised at the close of the present state of things—" the salvation that is ready," prepared, " to be revealed in the last time"—" the inheritance incorruptible, undefiled, and that fadeth not away, reserved in heaven for them"—" the glory that is to follow" the second coming of the Lord.

For this grace, this manifestation of his sovereign favour, —for the salvation of Christ from the beginning to the end is of grace—the Apostle exhorts Christians to " hope," and to " hope to the end."

He exhorts them to hope for it, to expect it, to consider it as something that is absolutely secure, something that in due season they shall certainly enjoy; and he exhorts them to " hope to the end,"[1] *i. e.,* either to hope perfectly, to cherish

---

[1] Τελείως.

an undoubting confidence, or to persevere in hoping to the very close of life, " not casting away our confidence," but " holding it fast to the end," knowing that " we have need of patience," *i. e.*, " the patience of hope ;" in other words, knowing that we must persevere in hoping, in order that we may do the will of God, and that " we may obtain the promise," *i. e.*, the promised blessing.[1]

The practical truths here taught by the Apostle are plainly these—that it is the duty of Christians to cultivate a persevering confident hope of final salvation ; and that the cultivation of this persevering confident hope of final salvation, is a necessary and important means of enabling them to perform the duties of Christian obedience.

(1.) That it is the duty of Christians, believers of the truth as it is in Jesus, to cherish the hope of eternal happiness, is exceedingly plain. God has very distinctly stated, that " whosoever believeth on Christ Jesus shall not perish, but shall have everlasting life ;" and surely it must be the duty of the Christian to believe what God says, and to expect what God has promised.[2] For an unbelieving and impenitent person, continuing in unbelief and impenitence, to hope for eternal life is the extreme of presumption. That were to believe something which God has never said—that were to expect something which God has never promised. Nay, that were to believe the very reverse of what God says— to expect the very reverse of what God has declared. His declarations are, " Except ye repent, ye shall perish." " He that believeth not, shall be damned."[3] The unbeliever is trusting to a hope which will make him " ashamed and confounded world without end," who is cherishing the hope of " *grace* to be brought" to him, continuing an unbeliever " at the revelation of Jesus Christ." For He will be " revealed then in flaming fire, to take vengeance on such as know not God, and obey not the gospel of his Son."[4]

---

[1] Heb. x. 35, 36.   [2] John iii. 16.   [3] Mark xvi. 16.   [4] 2 Thess. i. 7, 8.

But let this impenitent man change his mind; let this unbeliever but credit the testimony of God, counting it a faithful saying, that " God is in Christ, reconciling the world to himself, not imputing to men their trespasses; seeing he hath made him who knew no sin to be sin in our room, that we may be made the righteousness of God in him," [1]—and immediately that hope which, in his previous state, it would have been absurdity and error, folly and presumption, in him to cherish, naturally grows up in his mind; its enjoyment is one of his highest privileges, and its cultivation one of his most important duties.

When we call on Christians to cultivate hope, we would press upon their attention the importance of three things. First, let them endeavour to obtain clear and ever extending views of that holy happiness which is the object of their hope, of that " grace which is to be brought to them at the coming of our Lord Jesus." Let them not rest satisfied with some indistinct general notion of it as a state of deliverance from all suffering, and of the enjoyment of every species of blessedness; but let its character as a state of holy happiness be familiar to their minds; a state of endearing and transforming communion with the Holy, Holy, Holy One, a seeing Him as he is; a being like him, a beholding his face in righteousness, a being satisfied with his likeness, a being holy as he is holy, perfect as he is perfect.

Secondly, let them never forget that the only ground on which their hope of obtaining this blessedness rests, is the sovereign mercy of Him whose nature as well as name is love, exercised in perfect consistency with, in glorious illustration of, his righteousness, through the obedience to death of his only begotten Son, made known to them in the word of the truth of the gospel. That appeared to them the only ground of hope, when, in the hour of conviction, every refuge of lies was swept away, and they were made to see that, so far as depended on themselves, so far as depended on the universe of creatures, there was no hope for them. They were then absolutely "without hope" till "the hope set before them in the gospel" was disclosed to their mind. There is no other ground of hope. Never, Christians, shift from this foundation—never attempt to add to this foundation. " Hold fast the beginning of your confidence, stedfast to the end." Let your hope of eternal life be that of a sinner who knows that eternal death is his merited portion, but who believing, because God has said it, that " eternal life is the gift of God through Jesus Christ our Lord," gladly and gratefully receives what is freely given him of God, and setting to his seal that God is true, confidently trusts, humbly expects, that he will do as he has said.

Thirdly, in hoping for this holy happiness entirely on the ground of sovereign mercy, let Christians expect to obtain it only in the way in which God has promised to bestow it on them. To expect eternal life in a course of thoughtlessness and sin, is to expect what God has never promised. It is "through faith and patience" that the promised blessing is to be inherited. It is " in a patient continuance in welldoing," that " glory, honour, and immortality" are to be expected. It is " after doing the will of God that we are to receive the promise." Let Christians, keeping these three things in view, expect only what God has promised—expect this only on the ground that He who is infinite in kindness, and wisdom, and power, and faithfulness, has promised it—and expect it only in the way and by the means which he has appointed for obtaining it; and it is impossible for them to be too confident in that " hope for the grace which is to be brought to them at the revelation of our Lord Jesus Christ."

(2.) This confident persevering hope of final salvation, is one of the most necessary and important means for enabling a Christian to perform the duties of Christian obedience. There are some theologians who would represent the performance of the duties of Christian obedience as the ground of the hope of eternal life. These are not wise builders.

They turn things upside down, and place the superstructure in the room of the foundation. Till a man has, through the faith of the gospel, obtained the hope of eternal life, he will never take a step in that path of filial obedience which is the only road to heaven ; and the more he has of a well-grounded hope of eternal life, the more rapidly will he run along that road, the more easily will he master the difficulties, and surmount the obstacles which threaten to prevent his progress. When by a lively hope the Christian is enabled, as it were, to feast on the clusters of the grapes of the promised land, which faith has furnished him with in the wilderness, he is disposed to say with Caleb, 'It must be a good land; and, seeing it is a good land, let us go up and possess it. What though hosts of spiritual enemies oppose our progress; what though the Jordan of death, that river over which there is no bridge, roll his waters deep and dark between us and the Canaan above, He, who is infinite in power and in faithfulness, hath promised to make us "more than conquerors," und to bring us to, and make us reside for ever in, that good land.'

" It is," to borrow the well-considered language of Leighton, " a foolish misgrounded fear, and such as argues inexperience of the nature and workings of divine grace, to imagine that the assured hope of salvation will beget unholiness and presumptuous boldness in sin. Our Apostle is not so sharp-sighted as these men think themselves : he apprehends no such matter : he, indeed, supposes the contrary as unquestionable : he takes not assured hope and holiness as enemies, but joins them as honest friends. Hope perfectly, in order to your being holy in all manner of conversation. The more assurance of salvation, the more holiness—the more delight in it, the more study of it, as the only way to that end; and as labour is then most pleasant when we are made surest that it shall not be lost, nothing doth make the soul so nimble and active in obedience as this oil of gladness, this assured hope of glory." Accordingly, the Apostle John says, " It does not yet appear what we shall be ; but when he shall appear we shall be like him, for we shall see him as he is. Every man that hath this hope in him purifieth himself, even as he is pure." In perfect accordance with these two apostles, their beloved brother Paul, in his Epistle to the Hebrews, declares his desire "that every one of them would give all diligence to the full assurance of hope to the end;" would sedulously cultivate an unshaken, confident, persevering hope of eternal life, in order that they might not be " slothful, but followers of them who, through faith and patience, are now inheriting the promises." [1]

This is, I am persuaded, the only way of securing habitual Christian obedience. Let Christians, then, learn to say with the Psalmist, "But I will hope continually ; and I will go in the strength of the Lord, making mention of his righteousness, even of his only." [2]

It may be proper, before leaving this part of the subject, to remark, that as the hope of eternal life has a powerful influence on Christian obedience, so Christian obedience has a powerful influence on the hope of eternal life. We have seen that Christian obedience is not the ground of the hope of eternal life, but it is its evidence. It is in the nature of things impossible that a Christian, while negligent about the duty of obedience, should enjoy in any high degree the privilege of hope. It is the same truth which inspires hope and stimulates to obedience ; and if it is not present to the mind doing the last, it cannot be present doing the first. It has been finely said, " The greatest affliction does not damp the hope of eternal life, as the smallest sin; affliction often renders hope more vigorous, sin uniformly weakens it." [3] If Christians would be " obedient children," they must "hope to the end;" and if they would "hope to the end," they must be "obedient children." These two things are linked together by divine appointment; and "what God has thus joined, let no man attempt to put asunder."

[1] Heb. vi. 11, 12.   [2] Psal. lxxi. 14-16.   [3] Leighton.

§ 4. *Fear a means of Christian Obedience.*

Fear is the fourth and last instrumental means which the Apostle prescribes for securing the performance of the duties of Christian obedience. If we would be " children of obedience," if we would not " fashion ourselves according to the former lusts in our ignorance," if we would " be holy in all manner of conversation," then must we " pass the time of our sojourning here in fear."

This injunction may not at first view appear to harmonize very well with that which we have just been illustrating. It may be said, does not perfect love cast out fear?"[1] and must not " the full assurance of hope," which the Apostle has been recommending, cast it out also? The discrepancy is apparent only, not real. The fear which the Apostle recommends, so far from being inconsistent with love and hope, and destructive of that comfort and happiness to which they give origin, naturally grows out of those views of the divine character which excite love and hope, and acts the part of guardian to the comfort and happiness which they produce on the mind.

The fear recommended by the Apostle is beyond doubt the fear of offending God, and of the consequences of offending God. Such a fear is not only consistent with love and hope, but is their inseparable companion. The more highly I value the favour of God, the more must I fear that, which, in the degree in which it prevails, deprives me of the sense of this favour. The more I delight in the anticipation of the holy happiness of heaven, the more must I be afraid of that, the direct and certain effect of which is, to deprive me of this delight. The happiness of Christians is in the love of God, and the light of his countenance is the life of their life. It matters little to them if the world frowns on them, if he smiles; and it matters little to them that the world smiles, if he frowns. Nothing in the world

---

[1] 1 John iv. 18.

can deprive them of the token of their Father's love but
sin; and, therefore, they consider it as of all things the most
terrible. "By this fear of the Lord they are made to
depart from evil." It is implanted in their hearts by God
for this express purpose, "I will put my fear in their hearts,
and they shall not depart from me."[1] It naturally leads
them to keep at a distance from sin; to guard against
temptation, to beware of what may lead to the interruption
of their delightful communion with their reconciled Father;
and involve in clouds of perplexity and doubt the prospect
of future blessedness. "Happy is the man who *thus* feareth
always."[2] When a Christian believer thinks of the remains
of corrupt principle within, and the number and force of
temptations without; when he sees how many fall before
these temptations, and make shipwreck of faith and a good
conscience, surely it must be good for him to "be not high-
minded, but fear."[3]

There is a system which passes with many for a peculiarly pure Christianity, the object of which seems to be to
set believers free from every species of fear as inconsistent
with faith, which, according to them, consists in believing that, at all events, the individual shall be saved.
Every species of fear is run down under the name of
unbelief. Now, it is quite plain the Apostles had a very
different view of the subject, since Paul exhorts the
Hebrew Christians to "fear, lest, a promise of entering into
God's rest being left to them, any of them should seem to
come short of it,"[4] and since Peter, in the words of our
text, exhorts Christians to "pass the time of their sojourning here in fear." They inculcate fear as a means of
preventing unbelief and its consequences.

It is justly remarked by a judicious divine,[5] that both

---

[1] Prov. xvi. 6.   Jer. xxxii. 40.   [2] Prov. xxviii. 14.
[3] Rom. xi. 20.   [4] Heb. iv. 1.

[5] The late Archibald M'Lean, from whose writings I have derived much advantage. It may be worth stating, that when introduced to the late Robert
Hall, one of the first things he said to me was, "Sir, you have found me read-

" believers and unbelievers have their fears, but they arise
from very different sources, and have quite opposite effects.
The fears of unbelievers arise from unworthy thoughts of
God; a distrust of his power, faithfulness, and goodness;
and, also, from a prevailing love of the present world and
its enjoyments, which makes them more afraid of worldly
losses and sufferings for righteousness sake, than of forfeit-
ing the divine favour," or incurring the divine displeasure.
" Such fears not only indispose the mind to obedience, but
lead directly to sin. But that godly fear which is proper to
believers, arises from a just view, reverence, and esteem of
the character of God, and a supreme desire of his favour, as
their chief happiness; and is a fear lest they offend him and
incur his just displeasure. Such a fear outweighs all the
allurements of sin on the one hand, and all the terrors of
present sufferings on the other."

Such is the fear inculcated by the prophet when he says,
" Sanctify the Lord God in your heart, and let him be your
fear · and your dread, and he shall be for a sanctuary."
Such is the fear enjoined by our Lord on his disciples:
" Fear not him who, after he has killed the body, hath no
more that he can do; but fear him who, after he hath killed
the body, can cast both soul and body into hell fire; yea, I
say unto you, fear him." Such is the fear prescribed by
the Apostle in the passage before us, as an instrumental
means for securing Christian obedience: " Pass the time of
your sojourning here in fear." [1]

This fear must be habitually exercised during the whole
continuance of our mortal life. None are so highly advanced in grace here below, as to be out of the need of this
principle; but when their pilgrimage is finished, and they
are come home to their Father's house above, there shall be
no more fearing. There are no dangers there, and therefore no fear. They shall indeed have, in a higher degree

ing your countryman, Archibald M'Lean. He was a man mighty in the Scriptures, sir; mighty in the Scriptures."

[1] Isa. viii. 13. Matt. x. 28.

than ever, a holy reverence of the Divine Majesty, but the fear of offending God will pass away with the possibility of offending him. In that blessed world there is neither sin, nor temptation to sin; no more conflict, no more danger; the victory is complete, the peace secure, the triumph eternal.[1]

These observations have been addressed exclusively to Christians. But I am afraid there are persons now hearing me who are not Christians. I call on them to fear: they have good reason; I dare not call on them to hope, while they continue in unbelief and impenitence. "There is no peace to the wicked, saith my God."[2] No hope for the unbelieving. But I present to them "the hope set before us" in the gospel. I tell them, Christ Jesus died for sinners; for the chief of sinners. I assure them that "eternal life is the gift of God, through Jesus Christ our Lord." I put them in mind of the solemn oath of God, that he has no pleasure in their death; I put them in mind of the most condescending expostulation, "Why, why, will ye die?" I beseech them to despair of salvation in themselves; I assure them that Jesus is "able to save them to the uttermost," and as willing as able.[3] Oh, if they would but believe "these true and faithful sayings of God," a hope that will never make them ashamed would spring up in their hearts; and, along with that fear of the Lord by which men depart from evil, a fear in which there is sweet awful pleasure, not torment, in delightful harmonious operation, would induce them, from "children of disobedience," to become children of obedience; and, instead of continuing to "fashion themselves according to their lusts in their ignorance," would lead them to "be holy in all manner of conversation."

III. MOTIVES TO THE PERFORMANCE OF CHRISTIAN DUTY.

Let us now illustrate the motives to Christian duty, which are unfolded in the paragraph under consideration.

---

[1] Leighton. [2] Isa. lvii. 21. [3] Rom. vi. 23. Ezek. xxxiii. 11.

These are four in number. (1.) The grandeur, excellence, and security of that inheritance, the full possession of which can be attained only in a course of Christian duty: "Wherefore," says the Apostle, referring to the whole of the preceding description of the final happiness which awaits Christians at the second coming of their Lord. (2.) The holiness of God: "Be ye holy, for I am holy." (3.) The equity of God: "The Father on whom ye call, or he whom ye call Father, judgeth every man according to his works." And, (4.) The provision made for sanctification, by the sacrifice of the Son of God: "Ye are redeemed, not with such corruptible things as silver and gold, from your vain conversation received by tradition from your fathers; but with the precious blood of Christ, as of a lamb without blemish and without spot; who verily was fore-ordained before the foundation of the world, but was manifest in these last times for you, who by him do believe in God, that raised him from the dead, and gave him glory; that your faith and hope might be in God." Let me turn your attention to these most powerful motives in their order.

§ 1. *The grandeur, excellence, and security of the Christian salvation, a motive to Christian duty.*

The grandeur, excellence, and security of the inheritance, the full possession of which can be attained only in a course of Christian duty, is a most powerful motive to obedience, and to the employment of all the means which are fitted to secure it. When the Apostle says, "Wherefore," for these reasons, we naturally ask, for what reasons? and we readily find an answer. The preceding context is principally occupied with a description of the final happiness, the eternity of holy blessedness, which awaits the genuine followers of Jesus Christ in the last time, at the revelation of the Saviour.

Now, is not the attainment of this eternity of holy happiness well worthy of every exertion that man is capable of?—will it not infinitely more than compensate for privations however great, sacrifices however costly, sufferings however severe, that may be required in pursuing it? When we look around us, and see "all things so full of labour, that man cannot utter it;" when we see men, in order to obtain some worldly advantage, the value of which is in a great measure imaginary, and the possession of which must be insecure and short-lived, rising early, sitting late, eating the bread of carefulness, compassing sea and land, straining to the utmost every faculty of exertion, and taxing to the utmost every power of endurance, we cannot help being painfully struck at the disproportion between the worthlessness of the object, and the multitude and mightiness of the means. It "resembles ocean into tempest tost, to waft a feather or to drown a fly." We feel disposed to ask the infatuated labourer, "Wilt thou set thine heart on things which are not?" "Why do you spend your money for that which is not bread, and your labour for that which satisfieth not?"[1]

But there is no such disproportion here. "The crown of righteousness," "the crown of life," is an adequate, ay, infinitely more than an adequate reward, for all the toils, and privations, and fatigues, and agonies, of the Christian race and warfare; and all the sufferings of the present state, to which a Christian may be exposed in the cause of his religion, are not "worthy to be compared with the glory which is to be revealed in us;" the afflictions of the present state, however numerous and severe, are lighter than dust in the balance, when weighed against that "far more exceeding and eternal weight of glory."[2]

Is not this calculated to arouse to active exertion, to prepare for patient suffering? Is it not most reasonable, that, in prosecuting such a pursuit, our determination to do nothing that can hazard failure, every thing that can promote success, should be most resolute, and that we should

---

[1] Prov. xxiii. 5. Isa. lv. 2.   [2] Rom. viii. 18. 2 Cor. iv. 17.

look away from every thing, however otherwise attractive, which is calculated to divert our attention or divide our affections. Is not the attainment of such a blessing a fit object of hope? Is not the loss of such a blessing a fit object of fear?

But it may be said, Is not the "salvation which is in Christ, with eternal glory," "the gift of God," and is it not "sure to all the seed?" Is it not "laid up for *them* in heaven?" and are *they* not kept for it by the mighty power of God?[1] What need, then, of all this obedience and submission? What need of all this determined resolution, and self-denied moderation, and animating hope, and cautious fear? The answer to those questions is at hand, and it is brief and satisfactory. The final salvation is the gift of God, and the objects of his love shall, assuredly, not come short of it. But there is a divinely appointed method for obtaining that eternal life, which is the gift of God; and none can enjoy the well-grounded hope of possessing it, who do not seek it in this divinely appointed method. Nothing is more distinctly stated in Scripture, than that it is only in the way of persevering faith and holiness that heaven is to be expected; and that, in the way of persevering faith and holiness, heaven cannot be too confidently expected. It is in the way of persevering faith and holiness alone that we can reach heaven. "We have need of patience," *i. e.*, we must persevere, "that, by the will of God, we may obtain the promised blessing." "Without holiness no man can see the Lord."[2] Unbelief and disobedience are the road to hell; and even a true Christian, when, under the influence of the evil heart of unbelief, he falls into backsliding, may be justly said to be in the road to hell, though, blessed be God, it is certain he will never reach the termination of that road; for the prayer of his Redeemer, who is mighty, will prevent his faith from utterly failing, and his backslidings will be healed, and he will be made to retrace his

1 Rom. vi. 23; iv. 16.   2 Heb. x. 36; xii. 14.

steps, and walk onward in faith and holiness towards heaven.

Still it is a general truth which all should attend to, "He that lives after the flesh shall die." "He that sows to the flesh, shall of the flesh reap corruption." He that turns back, "turns back towards perdition."[1] On the other hand, nothing is more certain than that, in a persevering course of Christian faith and obedience, the celestial blessedness in all its grandeur and excellence will be realized. "He who, through the Spirit, mortifies the deeds of the body, shall live." He who, "through a constant continuance in well-doing, seeks for glory, honour, and immortality, shall obtain eternal life." He who "endureth to the end, shall be saved." He who perseveres in believing, shall obtain "the salvation of the soul." He who "adds to his faith virtue, and to virtue knowledge, and to knowledge temperance, and to temperance patience, and to patience godliness, and to godliness brotherly kindness, and to brotherly kindness charity;" he who doeth these things, "shall never fall, but thus an entrance shall be ministered to him abundantly, into the everlasting kingdom of our Lord and Saviour Jesus Christ."[2] The attainment of the celestial blessedness in this way, is not merely a high probability: even in this case the motive would be a powerful one: it is an absolute certainty. It is as secure as the word and oath, the perfections and being of God, can make it.

How well fitted are such considerations to repress weariness, to rekindle ardour in the Christian race! "I run not as uncertainly," I keep along the marked course race, and I am sure of "the prize of the high calling of God in Christ Jesus." How admirably calculated to revive fainting courage in the Christian conflict! "I fight not as one that beateth the air." I know that, "waxing valiant in fight, I shall put to flight all the armies of the aliens." "I

[1] Rom. viii. 13. Gal. vi. 8. Heb. x. 39. Εἰς απωλειαν.
[2] Rom. viii. 13; ii. 7. Matt. x. 22. Heb. x. 39. 2 Pet. i. 5-11.

know in whom I have believed."[1] Continuing to "fight the good fight of faith," I shall be "more than a conqueror through him that loved me." The men of the world, in prosecution of their fancied good, spare no pains, shrink from no difficulty, decline no hazard, though they have nothing but probability, often a very weak probability, to excite and encourage them. How unnatural, how inexcusable, on the part of those professing to believe the gospel revelation, to be careless and inactive in the pursuit of a happiness which "eye hath not seen, ear hath not heard, and which it hath never entered into the heart of man to conceive;" and of the attainment of which, in the appointed manner, we may be, we ought to be as certain, as we are of our own existence! Well might the Apostle, when his mind was warmed and elevated by the contemplation of the glories of the final deliverance, say, " *Wherefore* gird up the loins of your mind, be sober, and hope to the end ; and be obedient children, not fashioning yourselves according to your former lusts in your ignorance; but being holy in all manner of conversation."

This is the effect which the believing contemplation of the heavenly blessedness is calculated and intended to have on the mind. It is not intended to afford an indolent delight, but a powerful excitement, and to induce Christians to be " stedfast and unmoveable, always abounding in the work of the Lord; for as much as they know their labour shall not be in vain in the Lord."

§ 2. *The holiness of God, a motive to Christian duty.*

The second motive which the Apostle presents to the mind as urging to Christian obedience, is the holiness of the Divine Being—" Be holy in all manner of conversation, as he who has called you is holy; as it is written, Be ye holy, for I am holy."

There is none holy as Jehovah. He is "glorious in

---

[1] 1 Cor. ix. 36. Phil. iii. 14. 2 Tim. i. 12.

holiness." " He" only " is holy"—" holy and reverend" is HIS name.[1] And these intelligent beings, who are capable of apprehending most of the perfections and beauties of his uncreated nature, have their attention chiefly fixed by this lovely attribute, and "day without night" hymn his praises as the "holy, holy, holy" One.[2] The holiness of God is just another word for the moral perfection of his nature. It is not something different from justice and benignity. It is the absolute perfection and the harmonious union of justice and benignity.

The sum of the Christian's duty is to be holy ; that is, to be conformed to God ; to have the same views, and judgments, and sentiments with him ; to approve what he approves ; to disapprove what he disapproves ; and the strongest and best reason why the Christian should have these views, and judgments, and sentiments, and likings and dislikings, is just because God has them. The strongest and best reason why he should thus think and thus will, is just that God thus thinks and thus wills. To be holy, is to be conformed to God; and to be conformed to God, is at once man's highest honour, duty, and happiness ; and what more cogent reason can be given for following any tenor of disposition and conduct than that it is " the whole of man,"[3] the whole of his honour, his duty, and his happiness ?

The divine being is the most glorious and venerable being in the universe; and it is his holiness far more than his power or his wisdom, far more than his eternity or his immensity or his immutability, that makes him so. His other perfections, separate from this, would make him an object of terror rather than of veneration. He is emphatically " glorious in holiness ;" and it is this perfection which clothes all the others with moral attractive influence, and makes their possessor at once infinitely estimable and infinitely lovely. When there is no resemblance to God in moral

---

[1] 1 Sam. ii. 2.   Exod. xv. 21.   Psal. xcix. 5; cxi. 9.
[2] Isa. vi. 3.   [3] Eccles. xii. 13.

excellence in an intelligent being, there is nothing really dignified and honourable; no proper cause of moral respect or approbation; and just in the degree in which there is a resemblance, is that intelligent being a fit object of moral esteem; honourable, and honoured by God and all right-thinking angels and men. This, then, is one portion of the force of the motive, " Be holy, for I am holy." Be holy, for to be holy is to be conformed to God, and to be conformed to God is true honour.

But there is more in it than this. To be conformed to God is man's highest duty. To think in opposition to God, to will in opposition to God, must surely be the most un-natural and wicked of all things in beings capable of think-ing and willing; and to think along with him, to will along with him, must, from the very nature of things, be their first and highest duty. To have the mind and will and active faculties in perfect accordance with the mind and will and command of God, is the clearest conception we can form of the moral perfection of an intelligent creature.

But even this is not all. To be conformed to God is man's truest, highest happiness. God is the happiest being in the universe; and the true reason is, he is the holiest being in the universe. He is perfectly happy, for he is perfectly holy. Men cannot participate in the happiness of God, but by becoming "partakers of his holiness." God him-self cannot make a being like man really, permanently happy in any other way than by making him holy. "They who are far from him must perish;" and there is nothing so good for man in all the extent and emphasis of mean-ing, which belongs to the word good, as the being " near to God."[1]   The force of this motive, then, briefly expressed, is this : to perform Christian duty, to be obedient children, is to be holy; and to be holy is to be like God; and to be like God is man's highest honour, duty, and happiness. Surely he must be an obtuse-minded, he must be an obdurate-

---

[1] Psal. lxxiii. 27, 28.

hearted, man who does not perceive, who does not feel, the overwhelming force of such a motive.

There is a superadded force in the motive, as urged in the passage before us. There is an additional power of persuasion in the descriptive appellation, by which, instead of one of his proper names, the Divine Being is in this passage spoken of: As " he that has called you is holy, so be ye holy in all manner of conversation." When they were running the mad career of error and folly and sin, God's powerful voice reached their hearts, and " called them out of darkness into his marvellous light." When that holy One called you, it was for a purpose consonant with his character. That calling was " a holy calling;" he called you, " not to uncleanness, but to holiness." He has chosen you, " that you might be holy, and without blame before him in love."[1] To use the words of holy Leighton, " He hath severed you from the mass of the profane world, and picked you out to be jewels for himself; he hath set you apart for the end that you may be holy to him. It is sacrilege for you to dispose of yourselves after the impure manner of the world, and to apply to any profane use those whom God has consecrated to himself. He who hath called you is holy; and therefore, when he called you, it must have been that ye should be holy. Therefore ' Be ye holy.' "

§ 3. *The strict equity of God, a motive to Christian duty.*

The strict equity of God is the third motive brought forward by the apostle for urging Christians to obedience, and to the use of the means calculated to facilitate and secure obedience. " Be obedient children; fashion not yourselves according to the former lusts in your ignorance; be holy in all manner of conversation; gird up the loins of your mind; be sober; hope to the end; pass the time of your sojourning here in fear;" " since the Father on whom ye call," or rather, " since he whom ye call Father,

---

[1] 1 Pet. ii. 9.   2 Tim. i. 9.   1 Thess. iv. 7.   Eph. i. 4.

without respect of persons, judgeth according to every man's work."[1]

The primary idea here plainly is, that the strict impartiality of God, as the moral governor of the world, should be felt as a powerful motive to Christian duty. This consideration is urged as a motive to that holy fear, which we have seen to be one of the great means of Christian obedience; but it is also a powerful, direct motive to Christian duty in general. God is the moral governor of the world. " The Lord hath prepared his throne for judgment, and he shall judge the world in righteousness." " The Lord hath prepared his throne in the heavens, and his kingdom ruleth over all." Every human being is the subject of this government. All must stand before his tribunal. He judgeth every man, and every work of every man; for God will bring every work into judgment, whether it be good, or whether it be evil.[2]

In the administration of his moral government, he is regulated by the principles of the strictest impartiality and righteousness. " He judgeth every man's work without respect of persons." " To have respect of persons" is a Hebrew mode of expression, descriptive of that most iniquitous and mischievous abuse of the judicial function, when accidental circumstances, not fixed principles, guide the decision ; when men are rewarded or punished, not according to the desert of their conduct; when they gain or lose their cause, not according to its merits and demerits, but according to the personal partialities of the judge, from arbitrary caprice, or from his regard to the wealth, or rank, or power, or influence of the parties. The divine administration, from the absolute independence and moral perfection of the judge, is completely free from this fault. " The Lord your God," says Moses, " is a God of gods, and Lord of lords, a great God,

---

[1] " Particula *u* non est conditionalis sed assertiva, non dubitantis, sed rem notam presupponentis—quia patrem invocatis."—CALVIN. Others render it " quandoquidem," or " quoniam."—HOTTINGER. ROSENMULLER.

[2] Psal. ix. 7; ciii. 19. Eccles. xi. 9.

a mighty and a terrible one, who regardeth not persons, nor taketh reward." " Let the fear of the Lord be upon you," says Jehoshaphat to the judges whom he had appointed; " for there is no iniquity with the Lord our God, nor respect of persons, nor taking of gifts." " Far be it from God," says Elihu, " that he should do wickedly; from the Almighty, that he should commit iniquity. For the work of a man will he render unto him, and cause him to receive according to his ways. Yea, surely God will not do wickedly, neither will the Almighty pervert judgment. He accepteth not the persons of princes, nor regardeth the rich more than the poor, for they are all the work of his hands." " Of a truth," says Peter, " I perceive that God is no respecter of persons: but in every nation he that feareth God, and worketh righteousness, is accepted of him." " In the day of the revelation of his righteous judgment," says Paul, " God will render to every man according to his deeds: to them who, by patient continuance in well-doing seek for glory, honour, and immortality, eternal life ; but unto them who are contentious, and do not obey the truth, but obey unrighteousness, indignation and wrath, tribulation and anguish to every soul of man that doeth evil; to the Jew first, and also to the Greek: for there is no respect of persons with God. For as many as have sinned without law, shall perish without law; and as many as have sinned in the law, shall be judged by the law." " God," says he in another passage, " accepteth no man's person." " There is no respect of persons with him."[1]

This strict impartiality of the divine Being, as the righteous judge, is a very powerful motive to the duties enjoined, whether the injunction be considered as addressed to professed Christians or to real Christians. Let us endeavour to unfold its force, as bearing respectively on these two classes.

Viewed as addressed to professors of Christianity, it is as

[1] Deut. x. 17.   2 Chron. xix. 7.   Job xxxiv. 10-12, 19.   Acts x. 34, 35.   Rom. ii. 5-12.   Gal. ii. 6.   Eph. vi. 9.   Col. iii. 25.

if the apostle had said, " A mere profession of Christianity
will avail you nothing. It is to no purpose that ye have been
baptized in the name of Christ, that ye have a place in his
church, that ye sit down at his table, that ye perform the
external acts of worship which he requires, if ye are not
' obedient children.' If ye are not ' renewed in the spirit
of your mind,' if ye are ' not transformed by the renewing
of your mind,' so as not ' to be conformed to the world,' if
ye are not ' holy in all manner of conversation,' if ye are
not perseveringly active in the performance of Christian
duty, if ye are not moderate in all things, if ye have not
the hope of eternal life, and are not in the fear of the Lord
all the day long, it is madness in you to think that you are
in the way of obtaining ' the inheritance incorruptible and
undefiled.' Remember with whom you have to do. He is
not capable of being imposed on by external appearances.
He is not capable of being biassed by weak partialities. He
will judge you, and judge you according to your works.
You will find that the principle on which his decisions go is
the plain one : ' He that doth righteousness is righteous.
He that doth not righteousness is not righteous.' You will
find that within the gates of the heavenly Jerusalem there
is room only for those who do his commandments; and that
' without, in outer darkness,' is the allotted everlasting habitation of ' the hypocrite' as well as ' the unbeliever,' of
the unprofitable and unfaithful servant. ' Not every one
that calleth Jesus Christ, Lord, Lord, shall enter into the
kingdom of heaven; but he that doeth the will of his Father,
who is in heaven.' " [1]

The ultimate destiny of the worldly immoral professor of
Christianity will be more dreadful than that of the heathens
or the open infidel. Oh! that sinners in Zion were but
afraid that fearfulness might surprise the hypocrites. The
God, of whom ye say that he is your God, is no respecter of
persons ; he will judge you according to your works.

[1] 1 John iii. 7, 10.   Matt. xxiv. 51; vii. 21.

" Know ye not that the unrighteous shall not inherit the kingdom of God ? Be not deceived : neither fornicators nor idolaters, nor adulterers, nor effeminate, nor thieves, nor covetous, nor drunkards, nor revilers, nor extortioners, shall inherit the kingdom of God." " Be not deceived ; God is not mocked. Whatsoever a man soweth, that shall he also reap ; for if ye sow to the flesh, of the flesh ye shall reap corruption ; but if ye sow to the Spirit, ye shall of the Spirit reap life everlasting." " If ye live after the flesh, ye shall die ; but if ye through the Spirit do mortify the deeds of the body, ye shall live."[1] " You profess the true religion, and call him Father ; but if you live devoid of his fear, and be disobedient children, he will not spare you on account of that relation, but rather punish you more severely, because you pretended to be his children, and yet were not."[2] Beware of supposing that a life of irreligion and immorality, or even a life of indolence, or of worldliness, under a Christian profession, can have any end but one—redoubled damnation. How can it be otherwise, if he with whom you have to do, without respect of persons, judgeth according to every man's work? How fearful is the situation of that man who can only hope for impunity and salvation if the righteous Lord shall cease to judge righteously ! Such is the force of the motive viewed as addressed to professors of Christianity—who may be, many of whom are, false professors.

Let us now look at the motive as it bears on those who are really Christians. While " eternal life is the gift of God through Jesus Christ our Lord," while " the salvation which is in Christ Jesus with eternal glory," is freely bestowed on, not purchased by, those who obtain it ; yet it is plainly the doctrine of Scripture, as it appears to me, that the degrees of happiness in a future world will be proportioned to the degrees of holiness in the present world. In judging of the works of the redeemed, strict impartiality will be main-

[1] 1 Cor. vi. 9, 10.   Gal. vi. 7, 8.   Rom. viii. 13.   [2] Leighton.

tained. To use the figurative language of our Lord, one shall be made ruler of ten cities, and another shall be made a ruler of five; or, to adopt the plainer terms of his apostle, " Let every man prove his own work, for every man must bear his own burden." The apostle, as a motive to Christian duty, assures the Hebrews that " God is not unrighteous to forget the works of faith and labour of love of Christians ;" and the righteous Judge, who will give the crown of righteousness to all who love his appearing, proclaims : " Behold ! I come quickly, and my reward is with me, to give every man according as his work shall be." When Christians stand before the judgment seat of Christ, they will " receive the things done in the body, according to what they have done." If any man's work, any Christian man's, abides the great trial which it must then undergo, he will obtain a reward. If any man's work will " not abide the trial, he shall suffer comparative loss," though he himself " be saved." There will be a difference, ay, and an important one, between those Christians who have added to their " faith, virtue; and to virtue, knowledge; and to knowledge, temperance; and to temperance, patience; and to patience, godliness ; and to godliness, brotherly kindness; and to brotherly kindness, charity; who have had these things in them, and so abounded in them, that they were neither barren nor unfruitful in the knowledge of our Lord Jesus Christ ;" and those who, though true Christians, in consequence of indulged indolence and worldliness, have done but little to honour their Lord, and advance his cause. To the former, " an abundant entrance shall be ministered into the everlasting kingdom ;"[1] they shall enter with full spread sail and with a favourable wind the harbour of eternal rest; while of the latter it may be said, that " some of them on boards, and some on broken pieces of the ship, escape safe to land." It is a general principle of the divine government of his people, extending to other cases

---

[1] 2 Pet. i. 11. Ὀυτω πλουσιως επιχορηγηθησεται ὑμιν ἡ εισοδος εις την αιωνιον βασιλειαν.

than that of ministers receiving a recompense according to
their respective services to the church of God : " Every
man shall receive his own reward, according to his own
labour." [1]

In this point of light the force of the motive may be thus
expressed : ' Be holy,—for in proportion to your attainments in holiness here, will be your measure of enjoyment
hereafter.' Such seems to me the force of this motive,
viewed as addressed respectively to professed Christians and
to real Christians.

Like the preceding motive, this receives additional force
from the peculiarity of the phraseology in which it is
clothed. It is not, since God, or the righteous Judge ; but it
is, since " the Father on whom ye call"—or " he whom ye
call Father—judgeth every man according to his work." If
we consider the rendering given by our translators as the
just one, then the force of the descriptive appellation in increasing the force of the motive, may be thus expressed: ' It
is not wonderful that your heathen neighbours should be
characterised by injustice and inhumanity; it is not wonderful that they should fashion themselves according to
their lusts in their ignorance. He whom they call on as
father,—Jupiter, their father of gods and men,—is a being
actuated by human passions, liable to human vices, arbitrary in his dealings, and capricious in his acquittals and
condemnations, in his rewards and punishments. An unholy life is just what you might expect in them from the
character of the object of their worship. But it should be
otherwise with you. He on whom you call, whom you
worship, is the Father—the Creator, Preserver, Benefactor, Saviour of men. He is " holy in all his ways, and
just in all his doings." How incongruous, then, were you
not obedient and holy, would the character of the worshipper
be with the character of the Deity !'

If we prefer the rendering, "since he whom ye call Father,

---

[1] Luke xix. 13.   Gal. vi. 4, 5.   Heb. vi. 10.   Rev. xxii. 12.   2 Cor. v. 10.
1 Cor. iii. 13-15.   Acts xxvii. 44.   1 Cor. iii. 8.

judgeth every man according to his work," which we are
rather disposed to do, then the manner in which the peculiar phraseology modifies the motive, may be thus unfolded.   'You stand in the relation of children to a father,
to the great object of religious and moral duty.   He has
acknowledged you as his "children through faith in Christ
Jesus;" and you, by his Spirit sent forth into your hearts,
have called him Father.   May he not then say to you, "a
son honoureth his father; if I be a Father, where is my
honour" if ye are not children of obedience?   Surely, if
you have cried to him "My Father," you should permit
him to be your guide.   Surely, when you have called him
Father, you should not turn away from him.[1]

And beware of presuming on this endearing relation, as
if it would secure his winking at your negligence and disobedience.   His very love as a Father would prevent this;
but this is not all.   The kind Father is the righteous and
impartial Judge.   He whom you call Father, without respect of persons, judgeth every man's works.   Again to
quote Leighton: "The true Christian reasons thus, 'I will
not sin, for my Father is the just Judge; but for my frailties
I will hope for mercy, for the Judge is my Father.'"

§ 4.—*The provision made for sanctification in the sacrifice
of Christ, a motive to Christian duty.*

The fourth motive urged by the Apostle for the discharge
of Christian duty, and the employment of the means calculated and intended to secure and facilitate its performance,
is drawn from the wonderful plan which God has formed and
executed for making men holy, even the death of his own
Son as a sacrifice for sin.   "Be obedient children; fashion not
yourselves according to your lusts in your ignorance; be
holy in all manner of conversation ; and in order to this,
be resolutely determined, be moderate, hope to the end,
and pass the time of your sojourning here in fear: foras-

---

[1] Gal. iii. 26.   Mal. i. 6.   Jer. iii. 4, 19.

much as ye know that ye were not redeemed with corruptible things, as silver and gold, from your vain conversation received by tradition from your fathers; but with the precious blood of Christ, as of a lamb without blemish and without spot: who verily was fore-ordained before the foundation of the world, but was manifest in these last times for you, who by him do believe in God, that raised him from the dead, and gave him glory; that your faith and hope might be in God."

In pressing home a motive adduced by an inspired writer, the Christian expositor has two things to do: first, distinctly to exhibit the meaning of the statement made, and then to show how that statement is fitted to serve the purpose for which it is made. In a complicated sentence, like that which is now the subject of consideration, it is of importance clearly to apprehend what is the primary sentiment, and what are the secondary and subsidiary ideas which are introduced for the purpose of its more impressive exhibition. Happily in the case before us, the leading idea is so prominent as to be easily recognised. It is obviously this: 'Jesus Christ died as a sacrificial victim, in order that men might be made holy;' and the secondary and subservient ideas, all calculated to give additional force to this wonderful statement as a motive to Christian duty, are the following:—the intrinsic value of the sacrifice; its divine appointment; its having been actually offered; and the abundant evidence that it has not been offered in vain.

The primary idea is, Jesus Christ died as a sacrifice for sin, in order to make men holy; the most animating of all encouragements, the most powerful of all motives to Christian duty. Christ Jesus shed his blood as a sacrificial victim, to redeem or deliver men from "the vain conversation received by tradition from their fathers."

"Conversation" here, as in a previous part of the paragraph, and as indeed in almost every place in the New Testament, signifies character and conduct, habitual temper and behaviour. The expression, "conversation received by

tradition from your fathers," [1] has by many, by most interpreters, been considered as referring principally, if not solely,
to what may be called the hereditary Jewish religious and
moral character and habits, the mode of thinking and
feeling and acting formed in the natural mind under the
influence of the peculiarities of the Jewish dispensation, and
handed down from generation to generation. This appears
to me to limit unduly the meaning of the very expressive
phrase now before us. The "conversation" here mentioned is
not any thing peculiar to Jews, it is something common to
man; it is the character and conduct formed by men
"fashioning themselves according to their lusts in their
ignorance;" the character and conduct which result from
the influence of present things on the depraved principles of
our fallen nature; what the Apostle Paul calls "the flesh"
and "the old man," in its members and operations, in
his desires and deeds; the hereditary character of fallen
man, received by tradition, i. e., handed down from father
to son, from generation to generation. This conversation is
termed "vain,"—foolish,[2] useless conversation. This character and conduct in some of its variations, "has a show
of wisdom," but in every case it is really foolish. They who
are distinguished by it, even when they profess to be wise—
boast of their wisdom, show themselves to be fools.[3] It
serves no good purpose. It does not, it cannot, lead to solid
satisfaction, to permanent happiness. It may well be asked,
"what fruit had ye," what fruit can ye have, "in these
things?"[4]

To be "redeemed" is to be delivered, and the word
"redeem"[5] is employed rather than another, because the deliverance referred to is deliverance through the payment of
a ransom. To be delivered from this character and conduct,
this mode of thinking, feeling, and acting, which is natural,
hereditary to man, and which is foolish, because vain, is
just to be delivered from depravity, to be made holy, to

---

[1] πατροπαραδότου. [2] ματαίας. [3] Rom. i. 21. [4] Rom. vi. 21. [5] ἐλυτρώ θητε.

be "delivered from this present evil world," to be redeemed from all iniquity, to be rescued from the slavery of sin.[1]

Having thus shortly illustrated what is peculiar or difficult in the phraseology, let us proceed with equal briefness to elucidate the statement, which plainly consists of two parts—Jesus Christ died as a sacrifice for sin, and Jesus Christ died as a sacrifice for sin to deliver men from depravity, to make them holy.

Jesus Christ died as a sacrifice for sin. This is the only satisfactory account which can be given of that most wonderful of all events—the death, the violent death, the shameful, painful, accursed death of the innocent, the perfect, incarnate, only-begotten of God. This event would have been utterly inexplicable, had we not been informed in a plain, well-accredited divine revelation, that this immaculately holy, this absolutely perfect, this infinitely dignified person, by divine appointment, and to gain the most important and otherwise unattainable objects in the moral government of the universe, occupied the place of guilty men; and, occupying their place, met with their desert, did what they were bound to do, suffered what they deserved to suffer, did and suffered all that was necessary, in the estimation of infinite wisdom and righteousness, to lay a foundation for their pardon and salvation. "We all, like sheep, had gone astray; we had turned every one to his own way; and the Lord made to meet on *him*," as the destined victim, "the iniquities of us all." The consequence was, "exaction was made, and he became answerable." "It pleased the Lord to bruise him," instead of destroying us; and "he was wounded for our transgressions, and bruised for our iniquities, and the chastisement of our peace was on him, and by his stripes we are healed." "He bare our sins in his own body on the tree," was "made sin in our room," died as "the just one, in the stead of the unjust," "redeemed

---

[1] Gal. i. 4. Tit. ii. 14.

us from the curse by becoming a curse in our room." [1]   The direct and primary end of this sacrifice, so far as man is concerned, was to effect a change in his relation to God —to lay a foundation for an alteration in our state—to secure pardon, and restoration to the enjoyment of the divine favour.   But the ultimate and most important end of this sacrifice in reference to man was, through this change of relation to effect a change of disposition; through this alteration of state to secure a transformation of character.

This is the second part of the Apostle's statement. When the blood of Christ was shed as a victim for sin, it was to deliver men from "the vain conversation received by tradition from their fathers."   Deliverance from depravity is an essential part, in some points of view the most important part, of the Christian salvation; and deliverance from guilt, and that sacrifice which was necessary, and is sufficient to secure deliverance from guilt, are the grand means of securing this deliverance from depravity.   The connexion of the atonement with sanctification is frequently stated in Scripture, and is one of the most peculiar and important principles of the Christian faith.   "Christ gave himself for us, that he might redeem us from all iniquity, and purify unto himself a peculiar people, zealous of good works."   "Christ gave himself for us, that he might redeem us from this present evil world."   Christ "sanctified himself, devoted himself to suffer as a sacrificial victim, that his people might be sanctified through the truth."   "When he died for all, all died in him; and he died for them, that they might not live to themselves, but to him who died and rose again."   "Christ hath redeemed us from the curse of the law, having become a curse in our room, not only that the blessing of Abraham," i. e., a full and free justification, "should come upon us Gentiles, but that we also might obtain the promised Spirit," the source of all true holiness, "by believing." [2]

---

[1] Isa. liii. 5, 6, 10.   1 Pet. ii. 24.   2 Cor. v. 21.   1 Pet. iii. 18.   Gal. iii. 13.
[2] Tit. ii. 13, 14.   Gal. i. 4.   John xvii. 19.   Gal. iii. 13, 14.   2 Cor. v. 14, 15.

The manner in which the shedding of the blood of Jesus Christ, as the great sacrificial victim, secures the holiness of all who believe in him, may be stated in a few words, though fully and satisfactorily to illustrate it, would require more space than we can here devote to it.

The atonement, by making it consistent with the divine justice to confer spiritual blessings on sinners, removes out of the way of their sanctification obstacles otherwise unsurmountable ; by procuring for the Saviour, as one part of the reward of his generous labours in the cause of God's glory, the power of dispensing divine influence, it secures what is at once absolutely necessary and completely sufficient for making men holy; and, finally, the statement of the truth about Christ, the Son of God, suffering and dying in the room of sinners, contained in the Scriptures, when understood and believed, is, under divine influence, the grand means of destroying in the sinner's mind that enmity against God which is the elementary principle of all depravity, and of kindling up in them the love of God, which is the elementary principle of all holiness ; of delivering the man from the demoralizing influence of " the present evil world," " things seen and temporal," and bringing him under the sanctifying influence of " things unseen and eternal." This, then, is the apostle's statement, ' The blood of Christ has been shed to redeem you from your vain conversation received by tradition from your fathers. The Son of God has died as a sacrifice for sin, in order to secure your holiness.'

Surely it does not require many words to show that this is a motive, an all-powerful motive to the Christian to avoid sin, and practise duty. Has deliverance from depravity been secured at such a cost, and shall I pour contempt on the divine generosity ? Shall I counteract the great design of the death of Christ ? Though he shed his blood that I might be redeemed from my vain conversation, shall I still fashion myself according to my former lusts in my ignorance ? Shall I still hug the chains, to break asunder which the Lord of glory toiled, and bled, and died? How can I, in whose room Christ died for sin—how can I any longer live in sin? Reckoning myself as, if I believe the truth I well may, to have died by sin in Christ Jesus, and to be alive in Christ Jesus by God, surely it is the most unnatural and incongruous of all things in me to allow sin to " reign in my mortal body, so that I should obey it by its desires." Surely I should not " yield my members to sin as instruments of unrighteousness ; but I should yield myself to God, as one alive from the dead, and my members to Him as instruments of righteousness ;" surely I should be a child of obedience, surely I should " be holy in all manner of conversation."[1] To use the words of Archbishop Leighton : " This is an answer for all the enticements of sin and of the world,—' Except you can offer my soul something beyond the price that was given for it on the cross, I cannot hearken to you. Far be it from me that I should prefer a base lust, or any thing in this world, or it all, to him who gave himself to death for me, and paid my ransom with his blood. His matchless love has freed me from the miserable captivity of sin, and hath for ever fastened me to the sweet yoke of obedience. Let him alone to dwell and rule in me, and let him never go forth from my heart, who, for my sake, refused to come down from the cross.'"

The motive, even when presented in this simple unadorned form, is surely one of transcendent power; but it derives additional force from the circumstances with which the inspired writer, with obvious intention, surrounds it in the passage before us. He fixes our mind on a variety of circumstances respecting that sacrifice for sin, by means of which we are emancipated from depravity, all of which are plainly calculated to make the consideration, that such a sacrifice had been offered for such a purpose, tell more powerfully on the understanding, on the conscience, and on the heart.

---

[1] Rom. vi. 8-13.   1 Pet. iv. 1-6.

And, first, there is the intrinsic worth of the sacrifice. This is brought before the mind in two ways. It was "not silver and gold, those corruptible things;" it was "the blood of Christ, as of a lamb without blemish and without spot." The value of what was given to secure our emancipation from depravity, cannot be estimated by any created mind. All the gold and silver in the world, the universe of created things, are as nothing and vanity, when compared to the life-blood of the only begotten of God. The blessing to be obtained was too valuable to be procured by such means. "It could not be gotten for gold, neither could silver be weighed for the price thereof. It could not be valued with the gold of Ophir, with the precious onyx, or the sapphire. The gold and the crystal could not equal it; and the exchange of it could not be for jewels of fine gold. No mention need be made of coral, or of pearls; for the price of it was above rubies. The topaz of Ethiopia could not equal it, neither could it be valued with pure gold."[1] What must be the value of holiness, when, to secure it, such a price was paid; and what must be the folly of him who contemns so valuable a possession, secured for him at so inestimable a cost!

A second way in which the value of the sacrifice is brought before the mind, is by describing it "as the sacrifice of a lamb without blemish and without spot."[2] In plain language, it was an all-perfect sacrifice. The death of Jesus Christ, viewed as the crowning act of a course of perfect obedience to the precept, and of perfect submission to the sanction, of the divine law, on the part of the most exalted being, both as to essential dignity and moral worth, "magnifies the law and makes it honourable," in a degree which the perfect obedience of a universe of unerring creatures, or the everlasting torments of a universe of sinning creatures, could not have done; and sweeps away, as with the force of ocean

---

[1] Job xxviii. 15, &c.

[2] Αμωμου. Jesus Christus *in se* non habuit labem. Ασπιλου neque *extrinsecus* maculam contraxit.—BENGEL.

bursting from her bed, all the obstructions which human guilt had placed in the way of human holiness. And shall I, in opposing the ultimate design of this all-perfect sacrifice in reference to myself, show my contempt of it?

The second circumstance respecting this sacrifice, the grand means of holiness, which the Apostle notices, is, that it was the subject of divine appointment; Jesus as the victim of the sins of men, and thus the author of holiness to men, was "fore-ordained before the foundation of the world." He was a voluntary but not self-appointed victim. He was "set forth," *i. e.*,[1] fore-appointed "a propitiation in his blood." When "Herod and Pontius Pilate, with the Gentiles, and the people of Israel, were gathered together against God's holy child Jesus, they but did what his hand and counsel had before determined to be done." He was "set up from everlasting."[2] And shall we, by disregarding or counteracting the design of Christ's death as a sacrifice for sin, to secure holiness, show that we lightly esteem what has employed the thoughts of the uncreated mind from all eternity?

The third circumstance noticed by the Apostle is, that this sacrifice has been actually offered. This wondrous scheme is not now mere plan. The spotless inestimable price has been paid; the amazing expiation has been made; the Lamb of God has been manifested in these last times, bearing, and bearing away, the sins of the world. And shall all this have been done in vain, so far as we are concerned? for it is done in vain if we continue still in our sins.

The fourth and last circumstance noticed by the Apostle, respecting the death of Christ as a sacrifice for sin, designed for securing holiness to man, calculated to increase its efficacy as a motive to avoid sin and perform duty, is the abundant evidence that it has answered the purpose for

---

[1] Rom. iii. 25. Προεθετο.—There is no doubt of the fact; but it may be doubted whether προεθετο refers to appointment or to exhibition.

[2] Acts iv. 27, 28.　Prov. viii. 23.

which it was intended.   The sacrifice has been offered, and
it has not been offered in vain.   Had not the death of
Christ served its purpose, it could not have been followed
by his resurrection.   If he had not risen again, then would
we have had reason to conclude, "we are yet in our sins,"
guilt is unexpiated, and the fetters of depravity are unbroken.   But we have abundant ground for concluding that
"Messiah, cut off, but not for himself," has "finished transgression, made an end of sin."   If he died "for our offences,"
he has been "raised again for our justification."[1]   "God
has raised him from the dead, and given him glory."   "It is
finished," said the dying Saviour on the cross; and from the
throne of his glory, when he broke the bands of death, the
Father responded, It is finished.   In the resurrection and
exaltation of Jesus, we have a sure foundation laid for our
"faith and hope in God," as "the God of peace," the pacified divinity, "who brought again from the dead our Lord
Jesus, that great Shepherd of the sheep, through the blood
of the everlasting covenant."[2]   In this we have a proof that
he is well pleased with Christ, well pleased with sinners in
Christ, and disposed, as "the God of peace, to sanctify
them wholly, and preserve their whole spirit, soul and body,
blameless, unto the coming of our Lord Jesus Christ."[3]
And shall we, notwithstanding these proofs of God's approbation of the sacrifice of his Son—shall we, by not improving
it for the purpose of our own sanctification, treat this
"blood of the covenant, by which alone men can be sanctified, as if it were a common thing," destitute of all power to
"purge the conscience from dead works, to serve the living
God?"[4]

Such, then, is the Christian's duty, such are the means of
performing it, and such are the motives to its performance.

The whole of this discourse has been practical, and stands

---

[1] Rom. iv. 25.   [2] Heb. xiii. 20.
[3] 1 Thess. v. 23.   [4] Heb. x. 29. Εν ὡ ηγιασϑη.   Heb. ix. 14.

little in need of what is ordinarily termed application or improvement. May the Holy Spirit give efficacy to the word of his grace, and may we all learn habitually, through the truth by the Spirit, to " cleanse ourselves from all filthiness of the flesh and the spirit, and perfect holiness in the fear of God;" " denying ungodliness and worldly lusts, living soberly, righteously, and godly, in this world; and looking for that blessed hope, the glorious appearing of the great God and our Saviour Jesus Christ; who gave himself for us, that he might redeem us from all iniquity, and purify unto himself a peculiar people, zealous of good works ! "

DISCOURSE VI.

CHRISTIAN BROTHERLY LOVE, ILLUSTRATED AND RECOMMENDED.

1 Pet. i. 22-25.—Seeing ye have purified your souls in obeying the truth through the Spirit unto unfeigned love of the brethren, see that ye love one another with a pure heart fervently: being born again, not of corruptible seed, but of incorruptible, by the word of God, which liveth and abideth for ever. For all flesh is as grass, and all the glory of man as the flower of grass. The grass withereth, and the flower thereof falleth away: but the word of the Lord endureth for ever. And this is the word which by the gospel is preached unto you.

THE sentence now read as the theme of discourse, though long and somewhat complicated, will be found, when carefully examined, to be entirely occupied with one subject,— the great Christian duty of brotherly love. That duty is at once very explicitly enjoined, and very powerfully recommended. The injunction is contained in these words, " See that ye love one another with a pure heart fervently." The motives by which compliance with this injunction is enforced, are brought forward in the clauses which precede and follow this injunction : " Seeing ye have purified your souls in obeying the truth through the Spirit unto unfeigned love of the brethren," and " being born again, not of corruptible seed, but of incorruptible, by the word of God, which liveth and abideth for ever. For all flesh is as grass, and all the glory of man as the flower of grass. The grass withereth, and the flower thereof falleth away: but the word of the Lord endureth for ever. And this is the word which by the gospel is preached unto you."

The duty enjoined, then, and the motives which urge to its performance, are the two great topics to which our attention must be successively directed in the illustration of this passage. The duty is brought before our minds in its nature,—mutual love, " love one another," " the love of the brethren ;" and in two of its distinctive characters,—love " with a pure heart," " fervent love." The motives to the cultivation and expression of this Christian affection are two, which we will find it convenient to consider in an order the reverse of that in which they are stated in the text. *First,* Christians are distinguished by a mutual relation extremely intimate and altogether indissoluble. By their " being born again," they are all of them " the children of God through faith in Christ Jesus," and therefore brethren ; and the tie of that brotherhood is not, like that of all natural relations, liable to dissolution, its bond being the infallibly true word of the ever-living, immutable God, lodged, by being understood and believed, in the mind of immortal man, v. 23. And *secondly,* Christians are possessed of a common character corresponding to this relation, to which they have been formed by the Holy Spirit, through the operation of truth believed under his influence, v. 22. This mutual relation, and this common character, equally call on Christians to cultivate and exercise brotherly love. Such, then, is the outline of thought which I shall endeavour to fill up in the remaining part of the discourse.

I. BROTHERLY LOVE ILLUSTRATED.

§ 1. *The objects and elements of this love.*

The duty enjoined is LOVE. There is a love which every man owes to every other man, without reference to his spiritual state or character, merely because he is a man, —a sincere desire to promote his true welfare. This is the love which the Apostle, with obvious propriety, represents as "the fulfilling of the law,"[1] so far as it refers to our duties to our fellow-men ; for he who is under its influence can "do no ill" to any man ; he cannot intentionally injure his person, property, or reputation ; but, on the contrary, must, "as he has opportunity, do good to all men." Good-will is the essence, the sole component element, of this love. The love enjoined in our text is obviously much more limited in its range, and much more comprehensive in its elementary principles.

(1.) It is called "the love of the brethren," "brotherly kindness," as contradistinguished from that "charity" which has for its objects the whole race of man ; who, though all brethren, inasmuch as "they have one Father, one God has created them," are not all brethren in the sense in which this appellation is here used. This appellation is limited to what was then, to what is still, a comparatively small class of mankind,—genuine Christians. It can only be exercised by them ; it can only be exercised to them. A man who is *un*christian, who is *anti*christian in his opinions and temper and conduct, may highly esteem, may tenderly love a true Christian, but he cannot cherish towards him "brotherly kindness ;" he loves him not because, but notwithstanding, he is a Christian. A Christian man may, he does, cordially love all mankind ; he desires the happiness of every being capable of happiness ; he esteems what is estimable ; he loves what is amiable ; he admires what is admirable ; he pities what is suffering, wherever he meets with it ; but he cannot regard with "brotherly kindness" any one but a Christian brother. None but a Christian can either be the object or the subject of this benevolent affection. None but a Christian can either be the agent or the recipient of the kind offices in which it finds expression.

This limitation is a matter not of choice, but of necessity. Most gladly would the Christian regard all his fellow-men as fellow-Christians, if they would let him, by becoming

---

[1] Rom. xiii. 8-10.

Christians; but till they do so, it is in the nature of things impossible that he should feel towards them as if they were what they are not. This affection originates in the possession of a peculiar mode of thinking and feeling produced in the mind by the Holy Spirit, through the knowledge and belief of Christian truth, which naturally leads those who are thus distinguished to a sympathy of mind and feeling, of thought and affection, with all who, under the same influence, have been led to entertain the same views, and to cherish the same dispositions. They love one another " in the truth; for the truth's sake, that dwelleth in them, and shall be with them for ever." [1]

(2.) This circumstance, which necessarily limits this principle as to its range, gives it greater comprehension of elementary principles, and greater intensity of influence and activity of operation. It includes good-will in its highest degree; but to this it adds moral esteem, complacential delight, tender sympathy. This it does in every instance; but the degree in which these elementary principles are to be found in individual cases of Christian brotherly kindness, depends on a variety of circumstances, and chiefly on the approach that is made to completeness and perfection in the Christian character, on the part of him who exercises it, and of him towards whom it is exercised. Every Christian loves every other Christian when he knows him; but the more accomplished the Christian is, whether the subject or object of Christian love, the more does he put forth, or draw forth, its holy benignant influence.

The end of all love is the good or the happiness of its object, as that happiness is conceived of by its subject. The great end which Christian brotherly love contemplates, is the happiness of its object, viewed as a Christian man; his deliverance from ignorance and error and sin, in all their forms and in all their degrees; his progressive, and ultimately his complete happiness, in entire conformity to

---

[1] 2 John i. 2.

the mind and will of God; the unclouded sense of the divine favour, the uninterrupted enjoyment of the divine fellowship, the being like the ever-blessed "holy, holy, holy One." It does not overlook any of the interests of its object, but it views them all in reference to, in subordination to, the enjoyment of "the salvation that is in Christ, with eternal glory." Such is the general nature of the brotherly love here enjoined.

§ 2.—*The distinctive characters of Christian love.*

Let us now look a little at the characters by which it is required to be distinguished. (1.) Christians are required to love one another "with a pure heart." The leading idea here has generally been supposed to be genuineness—sincerity. It must be real love, not affected or put on. It must be what the apostle Paul calls, "love without dissimulation;"[1] what the apostle John calls, "loving not in word, neither in tongue, but in deed and in truth."[2] It is an affection, of which the internal feeling and the practical effects fully correspond to, rather outrun than fall short of, the verbal expression. While the "law of kindness is on the lips," kindness itself is in the heart, and the fruits of kindness, substantial benefits, make their appearance in the conduct.

But while there can be no doubt that hypocrisy is one species of "filthiness of the spirit," of the impurity of the heart, it is not the only species which opposes the exercise of Christian love. The "pure heart" includes more than sincerity; it includes freedom from all low, selfish motives and ends. "Love with a pure heart" signifies the benevolent affection that naturally flows from a sanctified heart, and which can issue from no other fountain; which loves chiefly for such causes as can excite affection only in a sanctified heart; and which seeks for its objects such a happiness as only a sanctified heart can desire; and which seeks it by

---

[1] Rom. xii. 9. [2] 1 John iii. 18.

means which only a sanctified heart can dispose, or enable a man to employ.

(2.) But Christians are required to "love one another," not only "with a pure heart," but "fervently." The term rendered "fervently" is a very expressive one, and I do not know any one English word which fully brings out its meaning.[1] It conveys the idea of constancy. It is the word used in the Acts of the Apostles, where it is said— Prayer was made by the church for Peter when in prison, "without ceasing."[2] Brotherly kindness must be constant, not fitful. Its causes are permanent and constant in their operation, and so should it be. It should be such love as will prevent "weariness in well-doing." A Christian brother, when he acts like himself, "loves at all times." No change of circumstances, especially to the worse on the part of its object, should affect it except in the way of increasing it.

But besides the idea of constancy, the word conveys the idea of intensity and power. It is the term employed where it is said that our Lord, "being in an agony, prayed more EARNESTLY."[3] Our Christian love should be strong as well as genuine, such as slight causes would not be able to destroy, or even materially to affect, and such as shall be capable of producing great effects, making us willing to make strenuous exertions and costly sacrifices for its objects, when these are necessary to gain its ends. It should be so fervent as that "many waters" of neglect, infirmities, offences, petty injuries, "should not quench it," or even damp its ardour. It has been happily, though in homely phrase, said, "It should be like the sacred fire which descended on Elijah's sacrifice, which licked up the water and mud in the surrounding ditch; it should absorb a whole trenchful of such stuff, and still retain strength enough to send up to heaven the grateful fumes of the sacrifices with which God is well pleased." And it should manifest its strength, not merely by overcoming opposing obstacles, but by making exertions and

---

Ἐκτενῶς.   [2] Acts xii. 5.   [3] Luke xxii. 44.

sacrifices.　It should be such as would lead us even "to lay down our lives for the brethren,"[1] if so costly a sacrifice were required of us.

This love is to be manifested in choosing for our friends and associates our Christian brethren, joining ourselves to the brotherhood, casting in our lot with them, "walking with them in all the ordinances and commandments of the Lord blameless," sympathizing with them in their grief, rejoicing with them in their joys, communicating to them in their necessities, assisting them in their labours, bearing with their infirmities, ay, bearing their infirmities; admonishing them, and reproving them, it may be sharply, when they are to be blamed, yet all in kindness, loving them too well to suffer sin upon them; delighting in their Christian attainments and triumphs as if they were our own; never ashamed of them however low their place in society, and however frowned on and persecuted by the world—never "ashamed to call them brethren."

And it must manifest itself, not only in what we do, but in the manner in which we do it.　To relieve a poor brother, it should not be necessary that he implore our help. If " we see him have need," that should be enough to secure our assistance.　We should be " GIVEN," disposed " to hospitality;" " READY to distribute;" " WILLING," inclined " to communicate."　Instead of waiting for the call of a distressed brother, we should run to his help.　We should feel one another's crosses, bear one another's burdens, allay the sorrows, supply the wants, sympathize with the wrongs, espouse the cause, protect the persons, and relieve the necessities of our brethren in Christ.

(3.) There is one character which it is of peculiar importance that our mutual affection as Christians should be distinguished by.　It should be love like Christ's.　" Little children," said he who " is not ashamed to call us brethren,"— " Little children, a new commandment I give unto you,

---

[1] 1 John iii. 16.

That ye love one another; as I have loved you, that ye like-wise should love one another."[1]   And how did he love his people?   His love was free and ready, considerate and wise, laborious and expensive, generous and self-sacrificing; look-ing to all their interests, but chiefly to their highest interests; not forgetting that they had bodies, but chiefly concerned about their souls : and such should be our brotherly love. He took an interest in every thing that concerned them; he instructed, and counselled, and comforted them; he prayed with them, and for them; he vindicated them when they were accused, apologised for them when their conduct admitted of apology; reproved them, but in love, when they deserved it; bore with their infirmities, made much of what was good in them, and publicly owned them to be dearer to him than sister, brother, or mother: and thus should we manifest our love to the brethren.[2]

Like all the commands of our divine Lord, this injunction is characterised by benignant wisdom.   It is by loving one another that the highest interest of the whole Christian family is promoted.   Every thing thus becomes common property.   I have the advantage of all that any of my Christian brethren possesses.   Under the influence of this principle, the wise direct the strong, and the strong protect the wise; the zealous stimulate the considerate, and the considerate restrain the zealous.   The means of promoting holy happiness are thus prodigiously enlarged; every one employing his peculiar gift and opportunities for the good of every other, and thus advancing the common benefit of all. Thus it is that Christians (αληθευοντες), " sincere, truthful in love, grow up into all things to him who is the head, even Christ: from whom the whole body fitly joined toge-ther and compacted by that which every joint supplieth, ac-cording to the effectual working in the measure of every part, maketh increase of the body, unto the edifying of itself in love."[3]

---

[1] John xiii. 34.   [2] Henry *in loc.*   [3] Eph. iv. 15,16.

(4.) This love is obviously not to be confined—when it is enlightened and genuine it cannot be confined—within the pale of any particular sect or denomination of Christians. The members of individual churches, and of bodies of associated churches, have no doubt opportunities of cultivating this affection towards each other, which they do not enjoy in an equal degree in reference to Christians of equal, it may be of higher, spiritual excellence, with whom they have not the same means of becoming acquainted. But wherever I recognise the character, I should cherish and manifest the love, of a brother. These are well-considered words of the compilers of the Westminster Confession : " All saints that are united to Jesus Christ their head, being united to one another in love, have communion in each other's gifts and graces, and are obliged to the performance of such duties, public and private, as conduce to their mutual good, both in the inward and outward man. Saints by profession are bound to entertain a holy fellowship and communion in the worship of God, and in performing such other spiritual services as tend to their mutual edification, as also in relieving each other in outward things according to their several abilities and necessities, which communion, as God offereth opportunity, should be extended to ' all those who in every place call on the name of the Lord Jesus.' "[1]

" There is something inexpressibly awful"—I use the words of " a brother beloved"—" to a believer's mind, in the idea that his Christian affections should be confined within narrower limits than the love of Jesus ; that he should harbour in his heart any feeling inconsistent with love towards one whom Christ died to redeem ; that any should be excluded from his prayer for the household of faith, that have a part in the Saviour's intercession. Pitiably dreary must be the mind of that man who can look around on the wide world, and count his dozen or his score whom alone he can salute as brethren, or expect to accompany to heaven. Far from

---

[1] Westminst. Conf. xxvi. 1, 2.

me, and from you, my Christian friends, be such self-sufficient bigotry, which freezes the fountain of love, and keeps
the heart cold under the melting beams of ' the Sun of
righteousness.' " [1]

To the cultivation and exercise of this love, the fundamental requisite is, the being a genuine Christian. The
love of God is the elementary principle of the believer's
character; and as no man loves him who begat who does
not love them who are begotten of him, no man can love
those who are begotten who does not love him who begat
them. We must love God, in order to our loving his children. We must be in the family, in order to our having
the family spirit. No man who has not been born of God
can love those who are born of him, as HIS children; and all
who are " born of God" are " taught of God to love one
another." [2] It is a divinely implanted instinct, as well as a
divinely commanded duty, to love one another.

But this gift needs to be stirred up; and the two grand
means of stimulating it are, under divine influence, first, the
cultivating of an intimate acquaintance, the maintaining of a
holy fellowship with our Christian brethren. We cannot
love those whom we do not know; for it is the manifestations
of the character of our common Lord, which our brethren,
who have contemplated him " with open face," like so many
mirrors make, that endear them to us, and draw out our
affection to them; and second, the keeping habitually
before the mind the truths stated in the divine word respecting the spiritual relation and character of the objects of
our Christian affection, which are calculated to excite and
strengthen it.

In the passage before us, the Apostle employs the last of
these means for urging on those to whom he was writing,
the duty of Christian love. He brings before their minds
the intimate mutual relation, and the common spiritual character, of true Christians. The consideration of these, as

---

[1] Wardlaw.   [2] 1 Thes. iv. 9. Θεοδίδακτοι.

motives to Christian brotherly love, shall form the second part of the discourse.

II. BROTHERLY LOVE RECOMMENDED.

In the words in the first part of the twenty-second verse, and in the twenty-third, twenty-fourth, and twenty-fifth verses, the motives to Christian brotherly love are urged. Though the motive from common character, in this passage, precedes that drawn from mutual relation; yet, as relation is the basis of character, we apprehend some advantages may be derived from reversing the order. In the sequel, then, I shall shortly illustrate these two remarks :—The intimate and indissoluble mutual relation among Christians, as brethren, rising out of their common, spiritual, and indissoluble relation to God as their Father, is a strong motive to the cultivation and display of brotherly kindness ;—and the common character to which they have been all formed by the agency of the same Spirit, and the instrumentality of the same truth, is another powerful motive to cherish and exercise this Christian grace. Let us illustrate these two principles, or rather let us attend to the Apostle's illustration of them.

§ 1.—*The mutual relation of Christians a motive to brotherly love.*

The intimate and indissoluble mutual relation between Christians as brethren, rising out of their intimate and indissoluble common relation to God as their Father, is a strong motive to the cultivation and exercise of Christian brotherly kindness. "See that ye love one another with a pure heart fervently: being "—*i. e.,* since ye are—all of you "born again," become the children of God by a new, a spiritual, a heavenly birth,[1] "not of corruptible seed, but of incorruptible, by the word of God, which liveth and abideth

---

[1] " Nova cognatio novum desiderat affectum."—ERASMUS.

for ever. For all flesh is as grass, and all the glory of man as the flower of grass. The grass withereth, and the flower thereof falleth away: but the word of the Lord endureth for ever. And this is the word which by the gospel is preached unto you."

These words were originally addressed to churches, most of the members of which were converted Jews. These had, by their first and natural birth, been related mutually as members of the external holy family, by their common relation to Jehovah, the God of Israel, through the link of their natural descent from Abraham. That relation, however, as belonging to the "flesh," to things seen and temporal, was liable to dissolution,—in the case of the individual at death, in the case of the nation when the new and better economy was introduced, when the substance took the place of the shadow, and the spirit of the letter. They were now, by a spiritual change termed the new or second birth, become mutually related as brethren, by becoming in common related to God as their spiritual Father. This relation was far superior to the former. It bound them together as spiritual beings to God, as " the Father of their spirits;" and it was effected in a manner corresponding to its nature. It was formed by truth being introduced into their minds—"by the word of God," "the word preached in the gospel," being understood and believed by them.[1] They were all ONE, inasmuch as they were "all the children of God, through faith in Christ Jesus."[2] That faith bound them to God, and to one another, and formed a bond suited to their natures as rational beings.

The intimate relation thus formed was a permanent one. The seed was "incorruptible." The phrase, "the word of God," is explanatory of the figurative expression—"the

---

[1] Few things could more strikingly show the power of preconceived opinion to produce misinterpretation than the fact, that "the word" has been here explained of the personal word, to support a particular metaphysical theory respecting the nature of regeneration.

[2] Gal. iii. 26.

seed not corruptible, but incorruptible." The words, "which liveth and abideth for ever," viewed by themselves, might refer to God, who alone hath immortality, who is the living One, inhabiting eternity; but when, in the passage quoted from the prophet Isaiah,[1] apparently for the purpose of illustrating this phrase, we find the terms, "the word of the Lord endureth for ever," we cannot doubt that the epithets, "living and abiding for ever," are intended to be descriptive of "the word of the Lord," the grand link of the common connexion of Christians with their heavenly Father, and of their mutual relation to each other.

That word is eternal truth. That truth, introduced into the heart through divine influence, by being understood and believed, becomes a "living," active, operative principle there, producing holiness and joy. And it "abideth for ever:" it dwells an ever-living principle in an indestructible shrine— the never-dying human spirit; and dwelling for ever there, in the case of all the holy family it forms an everlasting link of connexion with their common Father, and with each other.

This relation far surpasses all other relations. There is no brotherhood like this, none so intimate, none so lasting. The relation of a Jew to a fellow Jew was very intimate. It was the relation of man to man, of kinsman to kinsman, of common heirs of the privileges of the first covenant to one another; but that relation, fruitful as it was of advantages (for the Jew, during the preparatory economy, had much and manifold advantage),[2] had the taint of mortality. It belonged to "the flesh," to what was carnal and outward, not to what was spiritual and inward. It was perishable. But this relation, as it is spiritual in its nature, is unending in its duration. Till mind ceases to be mind, truth to be truth, God to be God, it must continue, binding believers in a holy, happy relation to God as their Father, and to one another as brethren, to all eternity. Was it not reasonable and right, then, that *they* should "love one

---

[1] Isaiah xl. 6, 7.　　　　　[2] Rom. iii. 1, 2; ix. 4, 5.

another with a pure heart fervently?" If he is rightly considered as a monster who refuses to cherish and manifest peculiar regard to those who are connected with him by the ties of a natural relationship, which may in a moment, which must in a few years, be dissolved for ever, what name is to be given to a man calling himself a Christian, who does not regard and treat as brethren those who, if his profession be a sincere one, stand to him in a relation, of the intimacy of which the nearest earthly relation is but a feeble figure, and the duration of which can be measured only by the years of the Eternal?

§ 2.—*The common character of Christians a motive to brotherly love.*

The common character to which all Christians have been formed by the agency of the same Spirit, and the instrumentality of the same word, is a strong motive to the cultivation and exercise of Christian brotherly kindness: "Seeing ye have purified your souls in obeying the truth through the Spirit to the unfeigned love of the brethren, see that ye love one another with a pure heart fervently." The force of this motive is, Ye are now in a *moral capacity* for loving the brethren constantly and fervently; exert and manifest your moral power.

It was once otherwise. The unpurified soul, overrun with the loathsome leprosy of ungodliness, worldliness, selfishness, and malignity, was morally incapable of the healthy functions of its affectionate nature. It could not love Christ, Christianity, or Christians. But "old things are passed away;" there has been a radical cure effected; divine truth, under divine influence, has put forth its healing power over the diseased mind; the moral capacity of loving what is really lovely, has been called into being;— and now what remains but that it should be improved by being exercised?

The human heart is naturally a very impure place. It is "a habitation of devils, the hold of every foul spirit, the cage of every unclean and hateful bird." "He who searches the heart," and is "the true and faithful witness," declares, that "out of it proceed evil thoughts, murders, adulteries, and false witness."[1] Every thing that defiles the man originates there.

While the heart remains unpurified, the love of Christians, as Christians, cannot dwell there. There is no harmony, there is direct powerful antagonism, between the modes of thinking and feeling which characterise the natural, the unrenewed,—and the spiritual, the renewed, the Christian mind. But in the case of those whom the Apostle was addressing, this impurity of soul was cleansed. "They had purified their souls in obeying the truth."

"The truth" is the revelation of the character of God, the great reality in the person and work of his Son, contained in the gospel; "the word of the truth of the gospel," a well-accredited declaration of the mind and will of Him who cannot be deceived, and who cannot deceive; the very truth most sure. To obey that truth is to yield to its influence, and that from the constitution of man can only be done by understanding and believing it. He who refuses to attend to, to consider, to believe, the truth, rebels against it—cannot submit to its influence. He, on the other hand, who attends to, considers, and believes it, cannot but yield to its influence.

The persons referred to had believed the gospel. They had received the grace of God not in vain, and they had done this " by the Spirit;" that is, under the influence of the Holy Spirit. It is the Spirit who fixes the mind on the truth and its evidence, so as to lead to the belief of the truth. It is the man in the exercise of his rational faculties who believes; but he exercises these faculties under a divine influence. It is the man, not the Holy Spirit, who believes; but the man who believes, acts as he is influenced by the Holy Ghost.

[1] Matt. xv. 19.

The consequence of this faith, produced by divine influence, is such a purification of the soul as leads to the " unfeigned love of the brethren." " Ye have purified your souls to the unfeigned love of the brethren ;" that is, ' Ye have so purified your souls, as that ye have now an unfeigned love of the brethren.' While the soul remains unpurified, if love to the brethren be expressed, it must be feigned, hypocritical; but when the soul is purified, the love of the brethren is a natural, spontaneous feeling. In the degree in which the truth is obeyed, the soul is purified ; and in the degree in which the soul is purified, the brethren are loved.

Now, says the Apostle, the Holy Spirit, through the faith of the truth, has bestowed on you the good gift of the love of the brethren. " Neglect not the gift that is in you." Cultivate the lovely plant. " Quench not the Spirit."[1] " Grieve not the Spirit."[2] Allow the truth, under his influence, " to dwell in you richly," " to reign in your minds and hearts," and fill them to an overflow with the love of the brethren.

A question naturally rises out of these discussions, which well deserves the serious consideration of each of us. Do we love the brethren with a pure heart fervently ? Do we love the brethren *as* brethren ? Do we love Christians *as* Christians ? Do we love them on account of their relation to God and Christ, on account of their attachment to both, and on account of their resemblance to both ? Do we cordially esteem them ? Do we affectionately love them ? Is our " delight" in them, as " the excellent ones of the earth ?"[3] as the Psalmist phrases it. Have we complacency in them ? Do we make them " the men of our counsel ?" Have we pleasure in their society, and are we endeavouring, by every means in our power, to promote their welfare ? If we can answer these questions in the affirmative,

---

[1] 1 Thess. v. 19.   [2] Eph. iv. 30.   [3] Psal. xvi. 3.

the Apostle John authorizes us to consider this as evidence of our having undergone a saving change of character. Hereby do " we know that we are passed from death to life, because we love the brethren."[1] Happy are we if we indeed habitually cherish this holy affection ; but let us remember, that it is at once our duty and our interest to abound in this affection and its fruits more and more. Let us remember, that the love of the brethren is the evidence that " we are in the light," and the continuance of it is the evidence that we are " abiding in the light"—that we are continuing to believe the truth, and are " rooted, grounded, and built up" in it.

Let us manifest our love in deeds of Christian kindness, and remember that that only is the love of the brethren, which is " not in word and tongue only, but in deed and in truth." Let us show our love by " walking in all lowliness, esteeming each other better than ourselves ; forbearing one another in love ; endeavouring to keep the unity of the Spirit in the bond of peace ; putting away all bitterness, and anger, and wrath, and clamour, and evil-speaking ; being kind to one another, tender-hearted, forgiving one another, even as God for Christ's sake hath forgiven us. Let us put on, as the elect of God, holy and beloved, bowels of mercies, kindness, humbleness of mind, meekness, and long-suffering; and, above all, let us put on charity, which is the bond of perfectness. Let us do good, and communicate, especially to the household of faith. If a brother or sister be naked, and destitute of daily food, let us not be content with saying, Depart in peace, be ye fed, be ye clothed ; but let us give them the things which are needful for the body: for whoso hath this world's goods, and seeth his brother have need, and shutteth up his bowels of compassion from him, how dwelleth either the love of God, or of the brethren in him ?"[2]

[1] 1 John iii. 14.
[2] Eph. iv. 2, 3, 31. Col. iii. 14. Heb. xiii. 16. James ii. 15, 16. 1 John iii. 17.

If we would have this affection, so closely connecting us with God, for "he who dwelleth in love, dwelleth in God, and God in him," and never are we surer of having "our fellowship truly with the Father and his Son Jesus Christ," than when we love the brethren—if we would have this godlike affection strong within us, constantly, powerfully operative, we must continue "purifying our souls by obeying the truth by the Spirit." "Whence come wars and fightings among Christians? Come they not from hence, even of our lusts which war in our members?"[1] And how are these selfish desires to be mortified, weakened, destroyed, but by the growing faith and influence of the truth as it is in Jesus? If we would have our hearts warm with the love of the saints, we must seek to have them warm with the love of the Saviour; and if we would have our hearts warmed with his love, we must keep near him, in the believing study of his word, and in affectionate intercourse with him, in all the offices of Christian devotion. "Let us then abide in *Him*," and he will abide in *us;* and thus shall we "bring forth much fruit"[2] in works and labours of love. The mind that was in him will be thus in us; we will be "in the world as HE was in the world," and "walk as he also walked." May He whose name and nature is love, bind us as a Christian church more and more in the bonds of a sincere, enlightened, holy love; and, as "the God of patience and consolation, grant us to be like minded one towards another, according to Christ Jesus; that we may walk together in love, even as Christ has loved us; and that we with one mind and one mouth may glorify God, even the Father of our Lord Jesus Christ!"[3]

If there be in this audience—as I know there may be—as I fear there are—some, whether with or without a profession of religion, whose hearts tell them that they do not love the brethren, that they have no complacency in Christian excellence, no relish for Christian society, I affectionately

---

[1] James iv. 1   [2] John xv. 4.   [3] Rom. xv. 5, 6.

beseech them to consider what awfully important facts are necessarily connected with that fact, to which their consciences now give testimony, that they do not love the brethren. It is a proof, my friends, that you have "not passed from death to life;" that you have no part nor lot as yet in the Christian salvation; that you do not love God, that you do not love Christ; that you are not God's children, not Christ's brethren; that you are utterly unfit for heaven, where none of the human race but *the brethren* dwell. You have no relish for their society here, you would have still less there; for the peculiarities of character which make them disagreeable to you on earth, will be greatly heightened in heaven. What a deplorable state is that man in, who, even if he could get into heaven, the abode of perfect happiness, the only place where happiness is to be found at all, could not be happy!

But into heaven, continuing unprepared, you cannot be admitted. If you do not love Christians, you do not love Christ; and "if any man love not our Lord Jesus Christ, he will be anathema maranatha,"[1] accursed at his coming. Oh, my friends, "ye must be born again, not of corruptible seed, but of incorruptible, even the word of God, which liveth and endureth for ever," else "ye cannot enter into the kingdom of God." Ye must "purify your souls in obeying the truth by the Spirit to the unfeigned love of the brethren," else you can never "sit down with Abraham, Isaac, and Jacob, in the kingdom of our Father." No, you must be "shut out in utter darkness, where there is weeping and wailing and gnashing of teeth."[2] What a dreadful prospect to every one who loves not the brethren, especially who calling himself a brother loves not the brethren! He that loves not his brother, hates him; and "he that hateth his brother is in darkness, walketh in darkness;"[3] and though he may not know whither he is going, "for darkness hath blinded his eyes," "his feet go down to death, his steps take hold of

---

[1] 1 Cor. xvi. 22.　　[2] Matt. viii. 11, 12.　　[3] 1 John ii. 11.

hell," and he is moving onward to the blackness of darkness for ever.

Oh that he would but open his eyes to "the light of life!" Oh that he would but look at the glory of God, as it irradiates the countenance of his incarnate Son! Then would he learn to love God; "the love of God would be shed abroad in his heart by the Holy Ghost given to him;" and, learning to love God, he would learn to love all his children, all his children of mankind, especially all his children by "faith in Chris. Jesus." In the mutual kind offices of Christian friendship, he would enjoy a satisfaction which worldly fellowship never can bestow; and in due time join the general assembly on high, where love has its triumphs; where "all the wise, the holy, and the just, who ever existed in the universe of God, shall be associated without any distress to trouble their mutual bliss, or any source of disagreement, either from within or without, to interrupt their harmony; where the voice of discord never rises, the whisper of suspicion never circulates; where each, happy in himself, participates in the happiness of all the rest, and by reciprocal communications of love and friendship, at once receives from, and adds to, the sum of general felicity."[1] Who would not wish to belong to this happy society, this goodly fellowship, this glorious company! The door stands open: "Obey the truth by the Spirit." The road lies plainly before you: "Purify yourselves by this obedience." Thus will you come immediately into the enjoyment of the fellowship of the saints on earth, and "being made meet for," will erelong be made partakers of, the "inheritance of the saints" in heaven.

[1] Blair.

DISCOURSE VII.

A FIGURATIVE VIEW OF THE STATE AND CHARACTER OF CHRISTIANS, WITH APPROPRIATE EXHORTATIONS.

1 PET. ii. 1-3.—Wherefore, laying aside all malice, and all guile, and hypo-crisies, and envies, and all evil speakings, as new-born babes, desire the sincere milk of the word, that ye may grow thereby; If so be ye have tasted that the Lord is gracious.

ON no subject is it of more importance that mankind should entertain correct views, than on the nature and extent of that inward change, that moral revolution, in which genuine personal Christianity originates, and which, according to the different aspects in which it is viewed, is termed effectual calling, conversion, repentance or a change of mind, regeneration or the new birth. This, if any thing is, is a matter of fundamental, vital, practical, import-ance. Error here cannot be innocent in either sense of the word. It can neither exist without fault, nor be held with-out danger. Mistakes on such a subject must be hazardous, may be fatal.

Yet on few points do even that part, that small part of mankind, who have made it in some degree a subject of thought, err more seriously, and in opposite directions, than on this. By a large portion of men, very low, narrow views are entertained respecting the extent of the change, and the agency necessary in order to effect it. In their estimation, there is nothing radically wrong with human nature. Man has no doubt fallen into errors which need to be corrected;

he has formed bad habits which require to be changed; but in order to effect such an alteration in human character and conduct, nothing more is necessary than to awaken into action the sleeping energies of his intellectual and moral nature, and direct them steadily towards the desired object; and education and self-discipline are held quite sufficient to answer this purpose.

On the other hand, not a few seem to think that the change is so entirely supernatural as to preclude the necessity and propriety of the employment of human agency as the means either of originating or advancing it. They seem to think, that it is so God's work, as that in no way is it, or can it be, man's work; that men have nothing to do in the matter, but to wait till God has made them new creatures, and that, after God has made them new creatures, they need give themselves no concern—God will look after his own work; and they, being quite sure of final salvation, have only to guard against unbelief, which, in their way of viewing it, means, entertaining doubts with regard to the safety of their spiritual state, and the certainty of their ultimate happiness.

The passage of Scripture which I have just read, especially in connexion with that which precedes it, cuts up both these soul-ruining errors by the root. On the one hand, it teaches us plainly that the change is no superficial one. It is a new birth; there is a new moral nature produced, of which the ever-enduring, ever-living word of God is the seminal principle. It is a change produced by the Spirit; and the soul, the heart, the inner man, is the subject of this change. It is no such surface change as the progress of civilisation, the authority of law, the influence of education, the force of self-discipline, can effect. It is a permanent, divinely effected, change in the deepest springs of human action, the understanding, the conscience, and the affections.

But, on the other hand, it teaches us as plainly, that this change is effected through the knowledge and belief of the truth, in a manner quite consistent with man's rational, moral nature, with that freedom of choice which is essential to his being a responsible agent; that the change, though reaching every part of man's nature, is in no part of that nature complete or perfect; that though a new creature, he is but as a new-born babe, and needs to grow, and must use the appointed means of growth; that though he has "put on the new man," he needs more and more to "put off the old man, who is corrupt in his deeds," and more and more to "put on the new man, who, after God, is renewed in righteousness and true holiness;" that though he is made a "partaker of the divine nature, and has escaped the corruption that is in the world through lust," he must "give all diligence to add to his faith virtue, and to virtue knowledge, and to knowledge temperance, and to temperance patience, and to patience godliness, and to godliness brotherly kindness, and to brotherly kindness charity," knowing that, "if these things be in him and abound, he is not barren or unfruitful in the knowledge of our Lord Jesus Christ;" and that "in doing these things," for doing which "the divine power has given to him all things that pertain to life and godliness," "he shall never fall, but so an entrance shall at last be ministered to him into the everlasting kingdom of our Lord and Saviour Jesus Christ." [1]

These are the views given us in the context, and confirmed by many other passages of Scripture, in reference to that great change by which a natural man becomes a spiritual man; and in perfect accordance with them we find the Apostle exhorting those who had by the Spirit been born again, to get rid, with all possible speed, of all the characteristics of their unregenerate state, and to seek, with untiring eagerness, progress and perfection in all the characteristics of their new state; and, for this purpose, constantly to employ the means in their own nature calculated, and by

---

[1] Eph. iv. 24. Col. iii. 10. 2 Pet. i. 3-11.

divine statute appointed, to gain these ends; accompanying his exhortation with powerful motives, suited to the nature of the duties enjoined, and the character and circumstances of those to whom the exhortation is addressed.

To this exhortation it is my purpose at present to turn your minds, and that it may have an appropriate effect on our understandings, consciences, and hearts, let us briefly consider, I. Who the persons are to whom the exhortation is addressed; II. What are the duties to which the exhortation urges; and, III. What are the motives by which the exhortation is enforced.

I. THE PERSONS TO WHOM THE EXHORTATION IS ADDRESSED.

§ 1. *General view of their state and character.*

The persons to whom the exhortation was primarily addressed were the Christians, chiefly recently converted Jews, scattered abroad through the regions of Asia Minor. They were a part of the mystical Israel, the spiritual people of God. They are described in the preceding chapter as " elected," chosen, selected from the rest of their brethren and from the world lying under the wicked one, like ancient Israel, not on the ground of their being better than others, but on the ground of the divine foreknowledge or appointment, the gracious sovereign decree of God ; and, unlike their fore-fathers, they were by their selection separated or sanctified, not by an external, but by a spiritual separation from the unbelieving part of mankind ; and the object of this spiritual separation, originating entirely in sovereign mercy, was not, that, like their forefathers, they might obey the law of Moses, and, being sprinkled with the blood of the victims by which the first covenant was ratified, might enjoy the external privileges of that covenant, but that they might obey the truth, believe the gospel, and, being sprinkled with the blood of Jesus Christ—that is, being personally interested in the sav-ing results of his atoning sacrifice—they might enjoy the heavenly and spiritual blessings of the second covenant, of which the shedding of the blood of Christ, as an expiatory victim, was the effectual ratification. They were persons, who, through the resurrection of Christ—as the seal of the divine acceptance of his atoning sacrifice, and as one grand source of that evidence on which rests the faith which interests men personally in Christ and in his salvation—had been brought into the state, and formed to the character, of the children of God, secured of ultimate complete salvation as their inheritance, and blessed with a present living hope of that complete salvation. They were the sincere lovers of an unseen Saviour; they were devout worshippers of the Father. Their faith and their hope were in God, who had raised Christ Jesus from the dead, and given him glory. They had purified their souls in obeying the truth, so as to love the brethren unfeignedly ; and the new relation into which they had been brought, both to God and to one another, by their regeneration, through the eternal Spirit and the ever-living word, was a permanent and indissoluble one.

Such are the statements respecting them in the former chapter; and in the passage before us, they are brought before our minds as, though regenerate, by no means perfect; really, but far from being completely, holy; having much to part with, and much to attain to, before reaching "the measure of the stature of perfect men in Christ Jesus." They have need to "lay aside malice, and guile, and hypocrisies, and envyings, and evil-speakings." These words plainly imply, that the old man, though mortified, is not dead ; that, though crucified, he has not yet expired; that there still clings to them, as the fatal robe to the fabled hero, a corrupted nature. The putrifying dead body is still attached to the living man, which draws out the deep groan, "Who will deliver me from the body of this death?" There is still flesh as well as spirit, though in them the Spirit not only struggles, but prevails; but in their flesh dwells nothing that is good; dwells all that is evil. Of course, they need constant vigilance and energetic effort to prevent the encroachments, and to effect the eradication, of this evil principle.

§ 2. *Particular, figurative view of their state and character, as " new-born babes."*

But it is chiefly on the figurative representation in the passage, " new-born babes," that I wish to fix your attention. The ideas suggested by these words, respecting those whom they describe, are, I apprehend, principally these three : They have undergone, lately undergone, an important and very beneficial change ; they are possessed of characters, of which some of the distinctive properties of infants are suitable emblems ; and while they are not what they once were, they also are not what they shall be,—they are but " new-born babes ;" they are far from being men in stature, and vigour, and understanding, and acquirement, and enjoyment.

(1.) They have undergone a great and salutary change of state. They have been brought out of a state of darkness, and pollution, and confinement, into a state of light, and purity, and glorious liberty. They are in a new, a better, a higher state of spiritual and moral being. New spiritual faculties are developed. They are in a new world. The Jewish doctors were accustomed to call their proselytes little children. The change from Paganism to Judaism was very great, very beneficial ; but it was a very imperfect figure of the magnitude and blessedness of the change from nature to grace.

(2.) The term " new-born babes" seems intended to indicate character and disposition, as well as state and condition. To mark the distinctive character of his genuine disciples, our great Master states that they must become as " little children." When his disciples came to him, saying, Who is the greatest in the kingdom of heaven ? He " called a little child to him, and set him in the midst of them, and said, Verily I say unto you, Except ye be converted, and become as little children, ye shall not enter into the kingdom of heaven.

Whosoever shall humble himself as this little child, the same is greatest in the kingdom of heaven." And on another occasion, when "they brought young children to him that he should touch them, and his disciples rebuked those that brought them, Jesus, on seeing this, was much displeased, and said unto them, Suffer the little children to come to me, and forbid them not ; for of such is the kingdom of God. Verily I say unto you, whosoever shall not receive the kingdom of God as a little child, he shall not enter therein."[1] It has been common to find the points of analogy between Christians, especially young Christians—new converts, and little children, in comparative innocence and gentleness. But this I apprehend is to mistake our Lord's meaning. It is their conscious helplessness, their entire confiding dependence on others, their ready belief, as their faculties expand, of every thing told them, till the falsehood of men teaches them distrust, that make infants fit emblems of the disciples of Christ. They "renounce themselves." They believe what he says to them, because he says it. They do what he bids them, because he bids them. They feel that they are entirely dependent on *Him*, and they are well pleased that it should be so. They confide in Him, in his wisdom, in his power, in his grace, just as an affectionate child feels safe and happy in his father's house, or in his mother's arms, and takes no thought for himself, because he knows they will take thought for him; and never doubts either their affection for him, or their following out the dictates of that affection in protecting him from evil, and obtaining for him every thing he needs.

As the reference here is to "new-born" infants, a leading idea intended to be conveyed to the mind seems to be, that, like new-born infants, the Christian has a kind of instinctive, unquenchable desire, after the suitable, spiritual aliment of his new nature. He loves the truth as it is in Jesus; he is restless when it is out of the

[1] Matt. xviii. 3 ; xix. 13, 14.

view of the mind. The whole world without this cannot make him happy; and he never enjoys himself more, than when clearly apprehending the meaning and evidence of these " exceeding great and precious promises" by which his new nature is sustained; like the healthy infant on its mother's bosom, " he sucks, and is satisfied with these breasts of consolation; he milks out, and is delighted with the abundance of their glory."[1]

(3.) There is yet another idea which we conceive the figurative appellation is calculated and intended to bring before our minds. Young Christians are very far from being what they are yet to be even on earth; and all Christians are very far from being what they are to be in heaven.

The young convert is to grow in all Christian excellence— to "grow up in all things to him who is the head."[2] Paul was a very different person when it was at first said of him, "Behold he prayeth"—a poor helpless sinner falling into the arms of the Saviour; and when he said, "I can do all things through Christ who strengthens me." "I am now ready to be offered, and the time of my departure is at hand. I have fought a good fight, I have finished my course, I have kept the faith : Henceforth there is laid up for me a crown of righteousness, which the Lord, the righteous Judge, will give to me; and not to me only, but to all that love his appearing."[3] And Paul even then was but a child in comparison of what Paul is now; the "spirit of a just man made perfect" "with the Lord," and fully, so far as his capacities admit, conformed to his mind and will, "like him, seeing him as he is."

This view of the subject is so beautifully illustrated by that heavenly man Leighton, that I can make no apology for the length of the following quotation :—"The whole estate and course of the Christian's spiritual life here is called their infancy, not only as opposed to the corruption and wickedness of their previous state, but likewise as signi-

[1] Isaiah lxvi. 11.   [2] Eph. iv. 15.
[3] Acts ix. 11.   Phil. iv. 13.   2 Tim. iv. 6-8.

fying the weakness and imperfection of it at the best in this life, compared with the perfection of the life to come; for the weakest beginnings of grace are by no means so far below the highest degree of it possible in this life, as the highest degree falls short of the state of glory: so that, if one measure of grace is called infancy in respect of another, much more is all grace infancy in respect of glory. And sure as for duration, the time of our present life is far less to eternity than the time of our natural infancy is to the rest of our life; so that we may still be called but new or lately born. Our best pace and strongest walking in obedience here, is but the stepping of children when they begin to go by hold, in comparison of the perfect obedience in glory, the stately, graceful steps with which, on the heights of Zion, we shall walk in the light of the Lord; when 'we shall follow the Lamb whithersoever he goeth.' All our knowledge here is but the ignorance of infants, and all our expressions of God and of his praises, are but as the first stammerings of children (which are, however, very pleasant both to child and parent), in comparison of the knowledge we shall have of him hereafter, ' when we shall know as we are known;' and of those praises we shall offer him, when that new song shall be taught us," which is sung before the throne, and before the four living creatures, and which none can learn but those who are redeemed from the earth.[1] "A child hath in it a reasonable soul; and yet, by the indisposedness of the body, and abundance of moisture, it is so bound up, that its difference from the beasts, and its partaking of a rational nature, is not so apparent as afterwards; and thus the spiritual life that is from above infused into a Christian, though it doth act and work in some degree, yet it is so clogged with natural corruption still remaining in him, that the excellency of it is much clouded and obscured: but in the life to come it shall have nothing at all encumbering and indisposing it. And this is the

---

[1] Rev. xiv. 3.

Apostle Paul's doctrine: 'For we know in part, and we
prophesy in part. But when that which is perfect is come,
then that which is in part shall be done away. When
I was a child I spoke as a child, I understood as a child, I
thought as a child; but when I became a man, I put away
childish things. For now we see through a glass, darkly;
but then face to face : now I know in part; but then shall
I know even as I am known.'[1]

" And this is the wonder of divine grace, that brings so
small beginnings to that height of perfection that we are not
able to conceive of; that a little spark of true grace, that is
not only indiscernible to others, but often to the Christian
himself, should   yet be the beginning of that condition
wherein they shall shine brighter than the sun in the firmament. The difference is great in our natural life, in some
persons especially, that they who in infancy were so feeble
and wrapped up like others in swaddling clothes, yet afterwards come to excel in wisdom and in the knowledge of the
sciences, to be commanders of great armies, or to be kings :
but the distance is far greater and more admirable, between
the weakness of these new-born babes, the small beginnings
of grace, and their after perfection, that fulness of knowledge
that we look for, and that crown of immortality that all are
born to who are born of God. But as in the faces and
actions of some children, characters and presages of their
after greatness have appeared, as a singular beauty in
Moses' countenance, as they write of him, and as Cyrus
was made king among the shepherd's children, with whom
he was brought up, so also certainly in these children of
God there be some characters and evidences that they are
born for heaven by their new birth. That holiness and
meekness, that patience and faith, that shine in the actions
and sufferings of the saints, are characters of their Father's
image, and show their high original, and foretell their
glory to come; such a glory as doth not only surpass the

[1] 1 Cor. xiii. 9-12.

world's thoughts, but the thoughts of the children of God themselves. 'It doth not yet appear what we shall be; but we know that, when He shall appear, we shall be like him; for we shall see him as he is.' "[1]

Before proceeding further in the exposition, let me urge the importance of putting this question seriously to ourselves, What part or lot have I in this matter? What is my state before God? What is my spiritual character? Have I been born again? Do I possess the instincts and dispositions of the new creature? The question is a serious one; for if I have not been born again, I am a stranger to true wisdom, worth, and happiness; and should I die, not having been born again, it had been better for me never to have been born. For, "except a man be born again, he cannot enter into the kingdom of heaven."[2] He can neither enjoy the peculiar blessings of Christianity here nor hereafter. The question is one which should not be difficult to answer; for the characteristic qualities of the new creature are sufficiently palpable. There is one in particular, with regard to which no one can mistake without absolute wilfulness: "Whatsoever is born of God, overcometh the world."[3] He lives above the world, through the power of faith. The terrors of the world cannot drive him, the blandishments of the world cannot allure him, from the course on which he has entered. When he became a new creature, he came into a new creation; and "the world to come," in its power, opening on his mind, delivered him from the dominant influence of "the present evil world." Are you looking at things seen and temporal? Are present and sensible things the chief subjects of your thoughts, the chief objects of your affections? Then you have been born only of the flesh. "Ye must be born again." You must be thoroughly changed, for if you are not so, you are quite unfit for heaven; and heaven would be no heaven to you even were you placed in it. You must *repent*, that is, change

----

[1] 1 John iii. 2.   [2] John iii. 3.   [3] 1 John v. 4.

your mind, for " except ye repent, ye *must* perish." There is no preventing it. The nature of things, the nature of God, requires that it be so. But what hinders you changing your mind? You are most assuredly wrong. Why should you not believe the truth clearly stated, abundantly accredited? " Repent, and believe the gospel." And in repenting, and believing the gospel, ye will be " born again," " transformed by the renewing of your minds;" and " being born again not of corruptible seed, but of incorruptible by the word of the Lord, which liveth and endureth for ever," you will become as " new-born babes," and will feel, what you cannot now do, how reasonable and right it is that ye should " desire the sincere milk of the word, that ye may grow thereby;" and " growing up into him in all things who is the Head," shall become every day while in the world more like him while he was in the world—in it—not of it; and at the appointed season, along with all the brethren, when he appears, shall be made, so far as the difference of your natures admits, like him, " seeing him as he is."

And you who through the agency of the Spirit, and the instrumentality of the word, have been born again, and become as little children, cultivate the childlike character. Confide in your heavenly Father's wisdom, power, grace, and faithfulness; trust not to your own understanding; implicitly believe his declaration, unhesitatingly comply with his injunctions; " be anxious about nothing;" your heavenly Father knows what you need, and can deliver you out of every trial. But while you cultivate the childlike character, seek in connexion with it the vigour and activity of mature manhood. " In malice " be always " children, but in understanding be men." Seek to have your spiritual " senses exercised, to discern truth and falsehood, good and evil." With the simplicity of childhood join the sagacity of age; and while in one sense ye always are children, become more and more children; in another, " be no more children, tossed to and fro, and carried about with every word of doctrine, by the sleight of men, and cunning craftiness, whereby they lie in wait to deceive;" but seek to arrive at "the unity of the faith and knowledge of the Son of God, at perfect manhood, at the measure of the stature of the fulness of Christ."[1] Brethren, we are glad when ye are "strong, through the word of God abiding in you," and enabling you to overcome the wicked one; and "this also we wish even your perfection;" and this we pray, that "your love may abound yet more and more in knowledge and in all judgment, that ye may approve the things which are excellent; that ye may be sincere and without offence till the day of Christ: being filled with the fruits of righteousness, which are by Jesus Christ unto the glory and praise of God."[2]

So much for answer to the first question proposed, Who are the persons to whom the exhortation in the text is addressed?

II.—THE EXHORTATION.

Let us now attend to the exhortation itself: "Laying aside all malice, and all guile, and hypocrisies, and envyings, and evil speakings, as new-born babes, desire the sincere milk of the word, that ye may grow thereby." The exhortation is twofold, first dissuasive, and then persuasive. The dissuasive exhortation is in these words: "Lay aside all malice, and all guile, and hypocrisy, and envy, and evil speaking,"—an exhortation to seek complete freedom from sin in all its forms and in all its degrees, and particularly in those forms which interfere with the great Christian duty of brotherly love, which the Apostle had just been enjoining and recommending. The persuasive part of the exhortation is in these words: "Desire the sincere milk of the word, that ye may grow thereby." This exhortation resolves itself into two parts: (1.) Seek spiritual growth; seek to grow wiser, better, happier; seek wider, more accurate, more influential views of divine truth; a firmer faith;

[1] Heb. v. 14. Eph. iv. 14, 15.
[2] 1 John ii. 14. 2 Cor. xiii. 9. Phil. i. 9-11.

deeper humility; a more assured hope; a warmer zeal; a more expanded operative benevolence; in one word, "the measure of the stature of the fulness of Christ;" and (2.) Seek spiritual growth by appropriate means; desire the sincere, the uncorrupted, and undeceiving appropriate nutriment of the new man, the milk of the word, or the rational milk; the nutriment suited to a rational immortal being in the season of the development of its faculties. There is a connexion, too, between the dissuasive and persuasive parts of the exhortation, which will require to be noticed, to prevent mistakes, and to secure all the advantages which the inspired counsel is calculated to communicate. Such is the outline I mean to fill up in the succeeding illustrations.

§ 1. *The Dissuasive Exhortation.*

Let us attend then, in the first place, to the dissuasive part of the exhortation. " Lay aside all malice, and all guile, and hypocrisies, and all evil speakings."

(1.) The first evil habit against which the Apostle warns is, " malice."[1] It is the same word which is frequently in the New Testament rendered " wickedness," and sometimes stands for moral evil in all its forms and degrees, as in Acts viii. 22, " Repent of thy wickedness," and at verse 16 of this chapter, where Balaam is said to have been reproved for his "iniquity;" and some interpreters have understood it so here, as if the Apostle had said, lay aside every form of evil, all error, all impiety, all malignity, every form of improper desire or pursuit; and, as if the other terms mentioned were merely explanatory of this general one, different forms of wickedness. At the same time the word is often in the New Testament used to describe a particular form of moral evil, and is not unfrequently employed as one of a number of words all expressive of different modifications of sinful principle and conduct.[2] I have no doubt that here it is equivalent to malignity, or ill-will, or malevolent disposition.

---

[1] Κακία.   [2] Rom. i. 29. Eph. iv. 31. Col. iii. 8. Tit. iii. 3. James i. 21.

Self-love is a leading principle in human nature. In depraved human nature this useful, necessary principle is in excess,—supreme instead of subordinate. Self-love thus becomes selfishness, and being connected with false views of our own interest, which we are led to think inconsistent with that of others, takes the form of malignity, ill-will towards others whose interests seem to stand in the way of our own. This disposition is the very reverse of the love which leads to the fulfilling of the law in reference to our fellow-men. If that is " the fulfilling," this is " the violation" of the law; for if love doeth, can do, no injury to a brother, malice, ill-will, can do him no good, and will do him all the harm which it finds necessary to gain its mere selfish objects.

(2.) The objects malice seeks are not such as can creditably be avowed and prosecuted. Malice, therefore, naturally leads to " guile" or deceit, the second of the evil habits denounced by the Apostle. The word is descriptive of all fraudulent, deceitful means for gaining an end; it is a general name for all untruthfulness and dishonesty, from their most refined to their grossest forms. To manage these deceits with any probability of success, a man must not appear to be what he is; he must act a part, he must be a hypocrite, a stage-player. The known open liar, the notoriously dishonest person, has little power to deceive. When Satan would deceive he assumes the appearance of an angel of light. When our Lord's enemies sought to entrap him, they " sent forth spies, which should feign themselves just men, that they might take hold of his words, that so they might deliver him to the power and authority of the governor."[1] Here you see malice leading to deceit, and deceit to " hypocrisy."

(3.) The " hypocrisy" here forbidden is the pretending to be what we are not; to have excellences, or degrees of excellence, of which we are destitute ; to have respect or affec-

[1] Luke xx. 20.

tion, when we have it not, or to have it in a degree far beyond what we really feel. As the opposite of malice is love, and of deceit, uprightness; so the opposite of hypocrisy is sincerity, the speaking the truth as it is in the heart, the expressing in language and conduct our real sentiments and feelings, the being in appearance what we are in reality.

(4.) " Envy" is the fourth evil disposition which the Apostle requires to be laid beside. It is the natural effect of malice, or ill-will. The word properly signifies the uneasiness which a malignant man feels in the happiness of the object of his ill-will, and the restless, painful desire he has to deprive him of his advantages, especially of those which he possesses in larger measure than the malevolent person himself. It is the corruption of the natural principle of emulation, or the desire to excel, which seeks its gratification fully as much in bringing its object below our level, as in raising ourselves honourably to his level, or above it; and one of the most ordinary methods which it employs, in order to gain this unworthy end, is the fifth and last bad habit from which the Apostle here dissuades,

(5.) " Evil speakings." Calumnious slander is the worst form of this evil; but all whisperings and backbitings, all sly insinuations, hinting at faults and hesitating dislike, every species of statement having for its object the lowering the reputation of another, which justice does not require, as well as truth warrant, are included.[1] The mouth is as it were the vent through which the smoke and flames of the infernal fire of malice and envy, which rages as in a furnace within, escape, polluting and withering all around.

Such are the evil tempers and habits which the Apostle dissuades from. You see how closely they are connected, how naturally the one produces the other; and you must observe how all of them are directly opposed to that "sincere

---

[1] Πασας καταλαλιας. Multis modis committitur detractio, aut bonum negando, aut obfuscando, aut diminuendo, aut malum ascribendo, aut intentionem in bono opere pervertendo.—Jo. Hus.

fervent love" which he had been, and still is, inculcating as one of the Christian's first duties.

The exhortation of the Apostle is, " lay aside these evil tempers and habits." This exhortation strongly implies that those addressed had been originally depraved, wholly depraved beings, and that they were still partially under the influence of depravity. The exhortation is not, beware of putting these on, but put them off. Every renewed man has in his flesh his unrenewed nature,—the evil heart,—the seminal principle of every species of moral evil; and I do not know what is the sin which he, if unwatchful, unprayerful, exposed to temptation, and unrestrained by divine influence, may not commit. Such exhortations to regenerate persons loudly proclaim, " Be vigilant;" repress the first movements of evil; shun even its appearance: " Let him who thinketh he standeth, take heed lest he fall." [1]

The exhortation of the Apostle, is not to cover these unsightly deformities of the old man with the veil of an assumed courteousness and politeness, or sanctimony. In his estimation, and in that of his Master, these were, however admired by men, abominable in God's sight, being but forms of that hypocrisy which he so pointedly condemns. To do this were to add iniquity to iniquity. The exhortation is to " lay them aside." The object of Christianity is not to conceal the evil which still exists, and exists it may be but in the greater force, acts but with the greater virulence, because it is concealed; but it is to destroy it, so that there may be no need of concealment, because there is nothing to conceal.

The Apostle does not require the modification, but the extinction of those evil principles. The filthy rags must not be mended, and in some measure purified; they are to be put off, and cast away. Christian morality is very uncompromising. Those polluted vestments, fast as they may cling to the diseased mind, must be torn off. Every one of them; *all* malice, *all* guile, hypocrisies, and envies, and *all*

[1] 1 Peter i. 8.   1 Cor. x. 12.

evil speakings, must be put off. There is no exception; all sin, in all its forms and in all its degrees, must be abandoned, abandoned for ever. It is impossible to read this passage without being impressed with the inward, thorough character of the Christian morality, the spirituality of "the royal law," "the law of Christ." Malice and envy are forbidden, as well as deceit, and hypocrisies, and evil speakings.

And you will notice, too, the order in which the prohibition stands. In the world's morality, they set about pruning the branches while the root is undisturbed; and the evil tree is often rather strengthened than weakened by the process; but here "the axe is laid to the root of the tree." Lay aside *malice*. If that is laid aside, deceit and hypocrisy will soon disappear, and never re-appear. Destroy the root, the leaves and even the stem will soon wither and die. Lay aside envies, and there will be no evil speakings. Such is the import of the dissuasive part of the exhortation.

And now, my brethren, let us open our hearts to the word of exhortation here addressed to us. Let us not turn aside from these statements, as too plain and common-place to deserve much consideration. Do some say, we know all this already? I answer with my Master, " If ye know these things, happy are ye if ye do them;" but if ye do them not, it had been better for you that you had not known them. The preaching of Christian doctrine and law is intended for some other, some nobler purpose, than to add to the stock of what has been termed "men's speculative discoursing knowledge." There is something wrong, either with the minister or the people, it may be with both, when plain Christianly moral discourses are not delivered, or not relished. It was a proof of any thing but growth in spiritual strength, when the Israelites loathed the daily manna, called it dry food, and required flesh to satisfy their lust. It is a very bad sign of a man if he does not like a plain practical sermon. " There is," as one well remarks, " an intemperance of the mind as well as the mouth. You would think, and may be not spare to call it a poor cold sermon, that was made up of such plain precepts as those which have been the subject of discourse. And yet this is the language of God; it is his way, this foolish despicable way, by which he guides and brings to heaven them that believe." [1]

Let us never forget that Christianity is the religion of love and the religion of truth. The spirit which the Father hath given us is the spirit of meekness and charity. That dovelike spirit dwelt without measure in our Head, and by him is communicated in various degrees to all his members. "If we have not the spirit of Christ, we are none of his." [2] Let us remember that the true way to put off malice is to put on charity; and the true way to put on charity is to put on Christ: so as that the mind which was in him may be in us.

Let us then "walk in love," and in truth as well as in love. Let us put off all deceits and hypocrisies. There is a meanness in hypocrisy which should make us despise it, a folly in it which should make us ashamed of it, as well as impiety in it which should make us abhor it. Oh, "what is the hope of the hypocrite, when he has gained the whole world, when God taketh away his soul?" [3] "What avails it to wear this mask?" A man may indeed, in the sight of men, act his part handsomely under it; but know we not, that there is an eye that sees through it, and a hand which, if we will not put off this mask, will pull it off to our shame, either here in the sight of men, or if we should escape all our life, and go fair off the stage under it, yet there is a day appointed when all hypocrites will be unveiled, and appear what they are indeed, before men and angels ? It is a poor thing to be approved or even applauded by men, while God condemns, by whose sentence all must stand or fall. "Let us seek to be approved and justified by him, and then who shall condemn ? It does not matter who do. Oh, how lightly may the contempt and reproaches of men lie on us, if we are but secure of his approbation ! It is a small thing to be judged

[1] Leighton.   [2] Rom. viii. 9.   [3] Job xxvii. 8.

of man's judgment; there is one that judgeth me, that is the Lord."[1]

There is a common, and I am afraid by no means unfounded, complaint, that many hearers of the word are wholly unfruitful, and that others are little edified. Our text furnishes us with the true account of this melancholy fact. They do not "lay aside malice, and guile, and hypocrisies, and envyings, and evil speakings." Till they do so, though they were under the ministry of an angel, they would never receive the sincere milk of the word, that they might grow thereby. Those who wish to get good from the word of God, must guard against all those tempers which war with truth and love.

There is no keeping out of controversy at all times in our world, without sacrificing truth; but controversy is full of hazards. Oh, how seldom is it conducted, even on substantially the right side, without "malice, and guile, and hypocrisies, and envyings, and evil speakings!" And so strangely deluded are men, that they often seem to think that the more they are under the influence of those unchristian principles, while professedly, and it may be really, contending for Christian truth, so much the better Christians are they. They seem to measure their love for the truth, by their hatred of those who they suppose are opposing it. I trust we, my brethren, have not so learned Christ; but that "having heard him, and been taught of him the truth as it is in Jesus: we are putting off, concerning the former conversation, the old man, who is corrupt according to the deceitful lusts; and are renewed in the spirit of our minds; putting on the new man, who after God is created in righteousness and true holiness: and putting away all bitterness, and wrath, and anger, and clamour, and evil speaking, with all malice." Then will "the word of Christ dwell in us richly," and then will the light of God, shine in our minds, and "the peace of God rule in our hearts."[2]

---

[1] Leighton.   [2] Eph. iv. 20-24, 31.   Col. iii. 15, 16.

§ 2. *The Persuasive Exhortation.*

The persuasive part of the exhortation comes now before us for consideration : " Desire the sincere milk of the word, that ye may grow thereby."[1] This exhortation refers both to an end, and to the means by which this end is to be accomplished. The end is the attainment of spiritual growth, and the means, the taking spiritual nourishment. Thus the exhortation naturally divides itself into two parts. (1.) Seek spiritual growth, that is the end ; and (2.) " Desire the sincere milk of the word," that is the means ; for it is by the right use of this appropriate nourishment that spiritual growth is to be attained. Let us look at these two exhortations first separately, and then in their relation to each other.

(1.) The first exhortation is, seek spiritual growth. The figurative view of the state and character of the persons addressed, " new-born babes," and the corresponding view of their daily " growth," suggest the ideas of life, of faculty, and of imperfection. What is dead cannot grow, what is perfect does not need to grow. Life is necessary to growth, vegetable life to vegetable growth, animal life to animal growth, rational life to rational growth, spiritual life to spiritual growth. The still-born babe never grows. It is the living new-born babe that grows. Till a man is " born again, not of corruptible seed, but of incorruptible," even of that word which in the gospel is preached to us, he is destitute of spiritual life, and therefore he is incapable of spiritual growth. On all such men the declaration of our Lord must be urged : " Ye must be born again,

---

[1] It is right to notice that the words εις σωτηριαν—"unto salvation"—follow ινα εν αυτω αυξηθητε—" that ye may grow thereby," in most of the Codd. and old translations, and that all the great critical editors of the New Testament, with the exception of Mill, consider them as entitled to a place in the text. They do not materially change the sense. They mark salvation—complete deliverance from evil in every form and degree—as the end of spiritual growth, and spiritual growth through the use of the γαλα λογικον, as the appointed means of salvation. The phrase εις σωτηριαν may be thus resolved—εις το τυγχανειν υμας της σωτηριας, " that you may thus obtain salvation."—Eph. iv. 13.

ye must repent and be converted." The persons addressed
here are plainly persons who, under the influence of the Holy
Spirit, having been brought to believe the saving truth,
have undergone a radical change of mind and heart, of
sentiment and disposition. They are spiritually alive, they
can perform the functions of spiritual living beings, they
are capable of spiritual growth.

But the idea of imperfection is just as plainly suggested
by the figurative language of the text as that of capacity.
They are living beings; but the principle of life, though
unextinguishable, is as yet feeble. They need to grow.
They have not been all at once brought into a state of spiritual perfection. Their emblem is not Adam, proceeding
from the hand of God in all the completeness of manhood;
it is the new-born babe. And they need not only to grow,
but to grow a great deal. They are not represented as
youths just approaching manhood, they are "new-born
babes." They have entered on their course, but only entered.
Even in the case of those who have proceeded farthest,
what is behind is as nothing in comparison of what is
before them. They have "not attained." This is the testimony respecting himself of one who had made more progress perhaps than any other. "Not as though I had
already attained, either were already perfect."[1]

But we have said enough of what is presupposed in the
injunction, to "grow as new-born babes." Let us now
enquire into its meaning. What is it then to grow? For
the natural new-born babe to grow, is to increase in size,
and strength, and beauty, and intelligence, and active, graceful use of all its various faculties. For the spiritual new-born
babe to grow, is to increase in the knowledge of the only
true God and his Son Jesus, which is eternal life, obtaining
more extensive, more accurate, more influential views, on
this boundlessly extensive and infinitely important subject;
in the faith of the truth as it is in Jesus; in the love of God,

1 Phil. iii. 12.

of Christ, of the brethren, of all mankind; in reliance on the free grace of the Father, the finished work of the Son, the promised aids of the Spirit; in knowledge and heartfelt conviction of his own worthlessness and helplessness, weakness and folly; in deep humility; in hatred of sin; in vigilance against temptation; in love of holiness; in zeal for the divine honour; in growing delight in God as the portion of the soul; in weanedness from the world; in a spirit of self-sacrifice for God's glory and man's salvation; in desire for the pure peace, the holy happiness of heaven; and by the growth of these principles, "being strengthened with all might in the inner man," to become more alert, and constant, and persevering in performing all the functions of the new life, both inward and outward; doing and suffering the will of God; "walking in all the commandments and ordinances of the Lord blameless;" "denying ungodliness and worldly lusts, and living soberly, righteously, and godly in this present world;" walking at liberty, keeping God's commandments, "fighting the good fight of faith," running "the race that is set before him."

Growth in the knowledge of Christian truth, is that on which spiritual growth, generally, depends. The great influential principles of saving truth are few and simple, and some are apt to think that they are easily, and soon, fully learned; but this is a dangerous mistake. The oldest and most intelligent Christian may grow in the knowledge of these truths. It is a very important remark, that after a man is really converted, growth in knowledge consists chiefly in knowing better the very truths by which conversion has been produced. He may see more deeply into the meaning of what he had only a general notion of; he may see additional evidence of their truth; he may see more of their mutual connexion and dependence; he may see more of the uses they are intended to serve; he may obtain more skill in turning them to their proper use, both to himself and others; he may obtain a more deep and extensive experimental acquaintance with them, and he may rise to a

much higher esteem for, and love of them. The most
important kind of growth in knowledge to a true Christian,
is to grow in the knowledge of what he does know, rather
than to grow in knowledge by acquiring an acquaintance
with something that he does not know. The addition of some
degrees to the more needful parts of knowledge which we
already possess, will go farther to promote spiritual growth,
than the acquisition of knowledge respecting less necessary
things, of which we are ignorant. Every Christian knows
the doctrine of Christ crucified; but many a Christian
knows little about scholastic questions respecting the decrees
of God, and the subjects of baptism and the government of
the church. His spiritual growth will be more impeded by
imperfection in the knowledge of the former, than by absolute ignorance of the latter; and his spiritual growth will be
more advanced by knowing a little more of that which he
already knows, than by obtaining even the most accurate
information on the points of which he is ignorant. It is an
admirable observation of an old divine, " There is enough
in one of the articles of our faith, in one of God's attributes,
in one of Christ's benefits, in one of the Spirit's graces, to
hold you in study all your lives, and afford you still an
increase of knowledge. To know God, the Father, Son,
and Spirit, and their relations to you, and operations for
you, and your duties to them, and the way of communion
with them, is a knowledge in which we may, we must be,
still growing, till it be perfected by the celestial beatifical
vision."[1]

It is difficult to conceive a finer or more complete description of what spiritual growth is, than that embodied in
a prayer by the Apostle Paul for the Philippian Christians.
"And this I pray, that your love may abound more and more
in knowledge and in all judgment; that ye may approve the
things that are excellent; that ye may be sincere, and without offence, till the day of Christ; being filled with the fruits

[1] Baxter.

of righteousness, which are by Jesus Christ, unto the glory and praise of God."[1] To use the words of one far advanced towards "the measure of the stature of the fulness of Christ," "That Christian is a growing Christian, who abounds more and more in the varied exercises of that holy love which is the fulfilment of this royal law; whose love is directed and regulated by increasing knowledge, wisdom, and judgment; who acquires by exercise, under the teaching of the Holy Spirit, the habit of prudently examining, and accurately distinguishing, between the things that differ, abhorring the evil, and cleaving to the good more entirely and heartily from day to day; who grows more known and approved for sincerity and integrity in all his professions and engagements, and more singly devoted to God as he advances in years; who becomes more and more circumspect in his words and works, that he may neither inadvertently fall himself, nor cause others to stumble; and becomes more fervent in prayer, to be preserved from bringing any reproach on the gospel to the end of his course; who becomes more abundantly fruitful in the works of righteousness, while at the same time he lies lower before God in deep humility, and is more willing than ever to be abased among men; who acts more and more habitually with the invisible God and the eternal world before his mind, and relies more entirely on the mercy and grace of the Lord Jesus, who thus becomes more precious to his soul; whose dependence on the providence of God becomes more uniform, and accompanied with greater composure, submission, and constancy in the path of duty. This is the growing Christian. Nothing material to the Christian character seems wanting. The various holy dispositions and affections, resulting from regeneration, are advancing to maturity in just proportion and coincidence, and he is evidently ripening for the work, worship, and joy of heaven."[2] Take another representation of spiritual growth by our Apostle himself. He grows spiritually, who having

---

[1] Phil. i. 9-11.   [2] Scott.

been called to glory and virtue, and made a partaker of a
divine nature, through the exceeding great and precious
promises of the gospel understood and believed by him,
" adds to his faith, virtue ; and to virtue, knowledge ; and
to knowledge, temperance ; and to temperance, patience ;
and to patience, godliness ; and to godliness, brotherly kindness ; and to brotherly kindness, charity ; who has these
things in him, and abounding in him, and is not idle nor
unfruitful in the knowledge of our Lord Jesus Christ."[1]

We have now got the general idea of spiritual growth ; it
is just progressive sanctification. Grow spiritually, is in
plain terms, become more and more holy. But we will
fail of getting all the instruction which the inspired writer's
words are intended and fitted to convey, if we do not enquire
whether there are not some important truths, in reference to
progressive holiness, suggested by the figurative view here
given of it. Are there not certain points of resemblance between natural growth and progressive holiness, which deserve
notice ? We apprehend there are, and, principally, the following. Both are, in the sense proper to them, natural ;
both are gradual, and upon the whole constant ; both are
universal and generally simultaneous ; and both of them are
perceptible, and sometimes more perceptible to others than
to their subject. A word or two of illustration on these
instructive points of resemblance, is all that is necessary.

1. It is the order of the natural world for the child to
grow. It is the order of the spiritual world for the saint to
improve. An infant not growing, but wasting away, is an
unnatural and melancholy object ; and still more unnatural,
still more melancholy, is it for one who seems to be a saint,
to be seen becoming no wiser, no better, or, more deplorable
still, becoming worse. There is want of nourishment, or
disease in both cases, where there is not growth. Truth, it
has been said, does not lie in the heart as a stone on the
earth, but as seed in the earth, which naturally germinates.

[1] 2 Pet. i. 5-7.

2. Growth is gradual—very gradual, and so is Christian improvement. No infant becomes a man at once, but every day sees him nearer manhood; and so is it in the spiritual world. The saint becomes gradually wiser and better. Like the child, he makes more progress at some times than others; yet in all cases the progress is gentle, not sudden. And as, when in health, the child is always growing, so, when the Christian is not labouring under spiritual disease, he is always making progress.

3. When the child grows, the whole of its body and mind grows. Swelling, which is a diseased unnatural affection, may be confined to a part of the body, but natural growth extends to the whole of it. And so it is with the spiritual new-born babe. He grows in knowledge, and faith, and holiness, and comfort at the same time. And the growth in both cases, where things are as they ought to be, is proportional. It also deserves notice, that though there be general growth, if any part of the system be preternaturally active, if any member of the body is preternaturally enlarged, any faculty of the mind preternaturally developed, there is disease and disorder. And so it is in the spiritual world. If the understanding be enlightened while the affections are not proportionally affected, or if the affections are strongly excited while the understanding is not proportionally enlightened, there is no healthy growth, no satisfactory progress. Healthy nourishment in a healthy constitution, whether bodily or mental, natural or spiritual, produces both universal and simultaneous growth.

4. Where there is real growth, it will be perceptible; not perceptible in its progress, but perceptible in its effects. In the case of a healthy child, he who sees it when new-born, and when it is a twelvemonth old, distinctly perceives that there has been growth. In the same way, a person who sees a young convert, if he meets with him months or years after, will perceive progress both in knowledge and in holiness. The child is seldom sensible of growth. It requires to look back, and compare what it is now with

what it recollects itself to have been, to convince it of its
having grown. And so it is with the spiritual babe. It is
only by comparing what he now is with what he was at
some previous period, that he can be convinced that he is
making progress. Indeed, not unfrequently, from the increase both of spiritual sensibility and spiritual perspicacity,
he feels as if, instead of becoming better, he was becoming
worse. He is, in his own feelings, less conformed to the
divine law as he now sees it, than he was, it may be years
ago, as he then saw it. And yet this may be, indeed is,
one of the best proofs that there is progress in knowledge,
both of God's law and of himself; and in a corresponding
humility and growing dependence on the atonement as the
ground of acceptance, and on the Spirit as the fountain of
holiness. The sight Christians have of their defects in
grace, and their thirst after greater measures of grace,
makes them think that they do not grow when they do.[1]

A healthy child grows without thinking much about its
growth. It takes its food and its exercise, and finds that it
is growing in the increase of its strength and its capacity for
exertion. And an analogous state is, I believe, the healthiest
state of the spiritual new-born babe. While self-examination,
rightly managed, is very useful, a morbid desire of the satisfaction of knowing that we are improving, is in danger of
drawing the mind away from the constant employment of the
means of spiritual nourishment and health. The best state
of things is, when, in the healthy vigorous state of the spiritual constitution, ready for every good work, we have the
evidence in ourselves that we are growing; and when that is
wanting, application to the sincere milk of the word will do a
great deal more good than poring into ourselves, to find either
proof that we are growing or not growing. So much for the
first part of the persuasive exhortation, Seek spiritual growth.

(2.) The second part of the exhortation refers to the means

---

[1] Watson.

for gaining this end of spiritual growth. "Desire the sincere milk of the word, that ye may grow thereby." There are here three things which we must attend to—1. What is this sincere milk of the word? 2. How is it that we grow by it? 3. And what is it to desire this sincere milk of the word?"

1. The phrase "milk of the word" is singular, and a variety of opinions have been entertained both as to its reference and meaning. If we can certainly fix the first, there will be comparatively little difficulty in apprehending the second. Some, among whom we are surprised to find the judicious Calvin, have supposed that the reference is to those Christian virtues which stand in direct opposition to the vices which are condemned in the previous verse; but these cannot well be represented as the spiritual food of the spiritual new-born babe. They are rather the symptoms that the food has produced its proper effect in the bloom and vigour of a healthful frame. The inspired writer furnishes us with the means of determining the reference. Whatever the milk of the word be, it is that by which spiritual new-born babes are nourished; in plainer words, it is that by which the sanctification and holy happiness of the regenerate soul are promoted. Now there can be no doubt, that that is divine truth understood and believed. It is "by this that men live; in this is the life of our souls." "Sanctify them through the truth; thy word is truth," says our Lord. "Purifying their hearts by faith," says the Apostle Peter. "Grace, mercy, and peace is multiplied through the knowledge of this truth." "It is by unity of the faith, and knowledge of the Son of God, that we come to the measure of the stature of the fulness of Christ," says the Apostle Paul."[1]

The reference then, without doubt, is to the truth respecting the divine character revealed in the Holy Scriptures; but what is the precise meaning of the phrase, "the milk of the word?" The milk is plainly equivalent to the appropriate nourishment; what serves the same purpose to

---

[1] John xvii. 17.   Acts xv. 9.   2 Pet. i. 2.   Eph. iv. 13.

Christians, especially new converts, that the mother's milk does to the new-born babe. The " milk of the word" may either mean the spiritual nourishment which is contained in that word spoken of in the previous context, " the word of the Lord which liveth and abideth for ever, the word of the gospel preached to us ;" or it may mean rational nourishment, nourishment suited to the rational spiritual nature of man, as milk is to his physical or animal nature ;[1] just as the same word is employed in Rom. xiii., " reasonable service,"[2] rather rational worship ; the presenting our bodies living sacrifices, being contrasted with the animal sacrifices under the Old Testament dispensation. It does not matter which interpretation we prefer, both bringing out a truth, and an important and appropriate one.

Spiritual truth is compared to milk ; to intimate its simplicity, its pleasantness to the unsophisticated spiritual palate, and its tendency to produce spiritual growth.

This milk of the word is described by the Apostle as "sincere." The application of the term seems strange, sincerity being with us always considered as a moral, not a physical attribute, a quality not of things, but of persons. It is one of the comparatively rare instances of the use of a word in an obsolete sense in our translation. The original word, when applied to persons, or figuratively to things, means undeceiving; when applied to things in a proper sense, it means pure, unmixed, unadulterated. In either sense it is very applicable. The word of God is pure truth, without the slightest admixture of error; it is only in the degree in which this pure truth is contained in any statement, that that statement is spiritually nourishing; and this pure word is undeceiving: it does what it professes to do, it really nourishes. " It converts the soul, it makes wise the simple, it rejoices the heart, it enlightens the eyes." It " is able to build us up ; to save the soul."[2]

---

[1] Λογικον in contrast with φυσικον. " Το λογικον id est μυστικον, το νοητον."—-Rom. xii. 1.   Spirituale bene vertit Syrus.—GROTIUS.   Geistlech.—LUTHER.

[2] Λογικην λατρειαν.   [3] Psal. xix. 7.   James i. 21.

2. These remarks may suffice to give us a distinct apprehension of the meaning of the terms; but it is required that we look a little deeper into the subject, and inquire how it is that the spiritual new-born babe grows by this pure, undeceiving milk of the word; how divine truth produces spiritual growth. It does not operate as a charm. The power of truth to sanctify the believer is just as much a part of the order of the spiritual world, as the power of milk to nourish the new-born babe is of the order of the natural world. It is easy to see that spiritual knowledge can be increased just as it was originally obtained, only by means of the only revelation of spiritual truth being apprehended by the mind; how faith can grow only by a growing apprehension of the truth which is the object of faith, and of the evidence which is the ground of faith. It is the representation of the loveliness and amiableness of God contained in the word, understood and believed, that produces love and confidence in him. It is the representation of his awful majesty and infinite holiness which produces reverence. It is the view it gives us of sin and of ourselves that produces humility and watchfulness. The precepts show us what to be and to do; and the promises and warnings furnish us with powerful motives to comply with the precepts, and thus make us both in character and conduct what God would have us to be. Every portion of divine truth is intended and calculated to tell on the growth of some portion of the new man; on the development of some of his faculties; the strengthening of some of his energies; the beautifying of some of his features. To borrow a figure from the Apostle Paul, Divine truth or doctrine is the mould in which the new creature is cast,[1] and every portion of it leaves a corresponding impression. "Truths are the seal, the soul is the wax, and holiness is the impression made by the seal on the wax." [2]

3. Now, the exhortation of the Apostle to those whom he addresses is, that they should "desire" this unadulterated,

---

[1] Τυτον διδαχης εις ον παρεδοθητε.—Rom. vi. 17. [2] Baxter.

undeceiving nourishment, in order to their growth. The
force of the exhortation, "desire" the sincere milk of the word,
is, see that ye feel and act in reference to that truth which is
the nourishment of your souls, as new-born infants do in
reference to that which is the appropriate nutriment of their
bodies. Desire it as new-born babes; show that you cannot do without it; that you must have it; that nothing will
do as a substitute; that you relish it; that you are satisfied
with it; that you never weary of it; that you return to it
again and again, with unabated, with ever increasing delight.[1] The temper enjoined is that which is so beautifully
embodied in the "burning words" of David, "O how love I
thy law! it is my meditation all the day. I will meditate in
thy precepts. I will delight myself in thy statutes. I will
never forget thy word. My soul breaketh for the longing it
hath at all times unto thy judgments. Grant me thy law.
graciously. I have stuck to thy testimonies. I have longed
after thy precepts. I will delight myself in thy commandments, which I love. Thy statutes have been my
songs in the house of my pilgrimage. The law of thy
mouth is better to me than thousands of gold and silver. I
will never forget thy precepts; for by them hast thou
quickened me. How sweet are thy words to my taste; yea,
sweeter than honey to my mouth! Thy word is a lamp to
my feet, and a light to my path. Thy testimonies have I
taken as a heritage for ever; for they are the rejoicing of
my heart. I love thy commandments above gold, yea,
above fine gold. Thy word is very pure; therefore thy
servant loveth it. The righteousness of thy testimonies is
everlasting. Give me understanding, and I shall live.
Consider how I love thy precepts: quicken me, O Lord!
according to thy loving-kindness. Give me understanding
according to thy word. My lips shall utter praise when

---

[1] Ὡς ἀρτιγέννητα. Ut modogeniti qui nihil aliud agunt; tantum appetunt.
—BENGEL. Ὥσπερ γαρ τα ἀρτιτοκα των βρεφων ουδεις διδασκει την τροφην, αυτοματα δε
εκμανθανει και οιδεν εν τοις μαζοις ουσαν αυτοις την τραπεζαν—Achilles Tatius, l. i. cit.
ab Elsnero.

thou hast taught me thy statutes. My tongue shall speak
of thy word; for all thy commandments are righteousness. I
have longed for thy salvation, O Lord! and thy law is my
delight. More to be desired are the judgments of God than
gold, yea, than much fine gold; sweeter also than honey,
and the honeycomb. Moreover, by them is thy servant warned, and in keeping of them there is great reward." I think
no one now can have any difficulty in understanding what
it is to desire the sincere milk of the word as new-born
babes. O that we all knew more of it by our own personal
experience! In this case we should be both better and
happier men.

Fully to apprehend the force of the Apostle's exhortation,
we must connect the exercise enjoined with the end for
which it is enjoined. Desire the sincere milk of the word,
that ye may grow thereby. "Desire the word," says the
pious Leighton, "not that you may only hear it; that is to
fall very short of its true end. Yea, it is to take the beginning of the work for the end of it. The ear is indeed the
mouth of the mind, by which it receives the word, as Elihu
compares it. 'The ear heareth words as the mouth tasteth
meat:' but meat that goes no farther than the mouth cannot nourish. Neither ought this desire of the word to be
only to satisfy a custom; it were an exceeding folly to make
so superficial a thing the end of so serious a work. Again,
to hear is only to stop the mouth of conscience, that it may
not clamour more for the gross impiety of contemning it:
this is not to hear it out of desire, but out of fear. To desire it only for some present pleasure and delight that a
man may find in it, is not the due use and end of it: that
there is delight in it, may commend to those who find it so,
and so be a means to advance the end; but the end it is
not. To seek no more but a present delight, that vanisheth
with the sound by the words that die in the air, is not to
desire the word as meat, but as music. To desire the word
for the mere increase of spiritual knowledge, or for the
venting of that knowledge in speech, and frequent dis-

courses, is still to miss the true end. If any one's head or tongue should grow apace, while all the rest of the body stand at a stay, it would certainly make him a monster: and they are no other, that are knowing and discoursing Christians, and grow daily in that, but not at all in holiness of heart and life, which is the proper growth of the children of God." Our object in desiring the sincere milk of the word, in studying with intense interest the truth as revealed in the word of God, is, that we may, as men of God, be "thoroughly furnished for every good work."[1]

The dissuasive and the persuasive parts of the exhortation, are closely connected. "Laying aside all malice, and all guile, and hypocrisies, and envies, and all evil speakings, as new-born babes, desire the sincere milk of the word, that ye may grow thereby." The idea intended to be conveyed by thus connecting the two exhortations, is not, that the one must be fully complied with before we can obey the other, that we must get rid of all malice, and all guile, and hypocrisies, and envies, and all evil-speakings, before we at all "desire the sincere milk of the word, that we may grow thereby." The true view of the matter is, that the two parts of the exhortation must be obeyed at the same time. A man full of "malice, and all guile, and hypocrisies, and envies, and all evil-speakings," cannot "desire the sincere milk of the word, that he may grow thereby." A man who "desires the sincere milk of the word, that he may grow thereby," cannot be clothed in malice, and other evil habits. The two exercises mutually influence each other. Nothing can displace "malice, and guile, and hypocrisies, and evil-speakings," but truth believed. But the putting off of malice, and the other evil habits, greatly promotes desire of the sincere milk of the word; while, just as we yield to this desire, "malice, and guile, and hypocrisies, and envies, and evil-speakings," and all other evils habits are put off. The body cannot grow in a fever, the soul cannot thrive where sinful

[1] 2 Tim. iii. 17.

dispositions are cherished : yet it is returning health which expels disease. It is just like some other scriptural injunctions, " Cease to do evil, learn to do well;" we cannot cease to do evil but in the degree in which we learn to do well ; and in the degree in which we cease to do evil, do we learn to do well. " Repent, and believe the gospel." It is the gospel, coming into the mind in its meaning and evidence, that changes the mind ; and it is in that change of mind that we believe the gospel.

If you have listened attentively, I think you can scarcely have failed to gain a distinct apprehension of the meaning of the exhortation which has been the subject of discourse. The important question is, have ye complied; are ye complying with the exhortation ?

I turn, first, to those who have been " born again, not of corruptible seed, but of incorruptible," and I ask them, have ye not much need to grow ? Are you not yet very infantine, babes when you ought to have been young men, if not fathers ? Have you not much need to grow in knowledge ? Are you able " to give an answer to every one that asketh you a reason of the faith and hope that is in you?" Does " the word of Christ dwell in you in all wisdom ?" Have you clear satisfactory views of the economy of mercy, of the system of divine truth ? Can you " discern the things that differ, so as to approve the things which are excellent?" Have not too many of us reason to say, when " for the time we ought to have been teachers, we have need that some one teach us again what be the first principles of the oracles of God; and are become such as have need of milk, and not of strong meat." [1]

Have you not need to grow in holiness ? Is there not much wanting, much wrong ? Have you no corrupt propensities to resist and subdue ? Are you " strong in faith?" Do you " abound in hope ?" Does " the love of God reign in your hearts ?" Have you " overcome the

---

[1] 1 Pet. iii. 15.　Col. iii. 16.　Heb. v. 12-14.

world?" Are you "clothed with humility?" Is your
worship always spiritual, and your obedience impartial,
habitual, universal, cheerful? Have you not cause to
say, "my leanness, my leanness; my soul cleaveth to the
dust."[1]

Have you not need to grow in holy happiness? Have
you, "believing, entered into rest?" Are you "anxious
for nothing?" Do you habitually "joy in God, through
our Lord Jesus Christ, by whom we have received the
atonement?" Are you able to "glory in tribulation?" to
"rejoice in hope of the glory of God?" Do you "walk in
the light of God's countenance, rejoice in his name all the
day, and are you exalted in his righteousness?" or are you
not beset with doubts and perplexities, walking in darkness,[2]
and having but little light. It is intended that you should
grow. An infant is not born to continue an infant, for that
were to be a monster, but to grow up to manhood. If you
do not grow, it is not because growth is unnecessary. There
are labours and trials before you, which will require the
vigour and intelligence of manhood. To perform these
labours aright, to endure these trials aright, you must "quit
yourselves like *men*, and be strong."

Now on all who feel that they need to grow, and are sensible of the importance of growth, I would press the exhortation of the Apostle, "Desire the sincere milk of the
word." Alas, what a multitude of dwarfs, as Richard Baxter
says, has Christ, that are but like infants, though they have
numbered ten, twenty, thirty, forty, fifty, or even sixty
years of spiritual life. Go not to yourselves, go not to your
fellows; go to God in his word for his Spirit, and seek
growth there. That is the only way to grow. True holiness, true happiness, can be obtained in no other way.
Various methods may be employed, various methods have
been employed, to produce the feeling and the appearance of

[1] Rom. iv. 19; xv. 13. 1 John v. 4. 1 Pet. v. 5. Isa. xxiv. 16. Psal.
cxix. 25.

[2] Heb. iv. 3. Phil. iv. 6. Rom. v. 3, 11. Isa. l. 10.

spiritual health and growth. But in vain. Men may by
other methods be bolstered up in vain confidence, amused
with delusive joys; but they cannot be made really happy.
They may be brought to make a fair show in the flesh; but
they cannot be made really holy. The milk of the word,
the unadulterated milk of the word, is the only wholesome
nourishment of the new-born soul. Divine truth lodged in
the mind and heart, by the influence of the good Spirit, is
the only well of living water which will spring up unto
eternal life. Seek, then, to " grow in the knowledge of our
Lord and Saviour." " Let his word dwell in you richly, in
all wisdom;" and under its influence, " walk worthy of the
Lord unto all pleasing, being fruitful in every good work,
and increasing in the knowledge of God."[1]

We your ministers have a very subordinate yet an important part to perform, in promoting your growth in grace.
It consists chiefly in " holding forth to you the word of
life," in bringing before your mind, and keeping before your
mind, " the truth as it is in Jesus;" and it is our earnest
desire not to handle this word of the Lord deceitfully, but,
" in the manifestation of the truth, to commend ourselves to
every man's conscience in the sight of God;" for we trust,
"we are not as many which corrupt the word of God," adul-
terate the sincere milk of the word, "but as of sincerity, but
as of God, in the sight of God, speak we in Christ."
" Teaching every man in all wisdom, we would fain present
every man perfect in Christ Jesus." May our wishes be
realised; may our labours not be in vain! " May the God
of peace, who brought again from the dead our Lord Jesus,
that great Shepherd of the sheep, make you perfect in every
good work, working in you that which is well-pleasing in his
sight, through Jesus Christ; to whom be glory for ever and
ever."[2]

But there are those here, I am afraid, whom I cannot call
on to *grow*, for they are dead; nay, I am afraid, there may

[1] 2 Pet. iii. 18.   Col. i. 10.
[2] Phil. ii. 16.   2 Cor. iv. 2; ii. 17.   Col. i. 28.   Heb. xiii. 20, 21.

be some here who are "twice dead, plucked up by the roots." I cannot call on you to come to the word that ye may grow, but I do call on you to come to the word that ye may live; for that word of Christ is "spirit and life," living and life-giving. "He that believes" it, "though he were dead, yet shall he live." "Awake, then, ye that sleep, and arise from the dead, and Christ shall give you light." "Repent, and believe the gospel." "Be transformed by the renewing of your minds." "Repent and be converted, every one of you, and ye shall receive the two inestimable gifts, both the immediate and irrevocable remission of sins, and the habitual purifying and sanctifying influence of the Holy Ghost." Receive the truth in the love of it, and you shall be saved. Born of the word and of the Spirit, you will learn from experience what it is to purify your hearts, through the truth, by the Spirit. "Born again, not of corruptible seed, but of incorruptible," the exhortation will be addressed to you, and, by the grace of God, not in vain, "to lay aside all malice, and guile, and hypocrisies, and envyings, and evil-speakings, and, as new-born babes, to desire the sincere milk of the word, that ye may grow thereby;" for then ye shall have tasted that the Lord is gracious. Oh, that even now the Lord may give testimony to the word of his grace, and that in the annals of heaven it may be recorded, that this man and that man was born, now and here, and that many who entered within these walls "dead in trespasses and sins," may depart "written among the living in Jerusalem." [1]

III.—MOTIVES ENFORCING THE EXHORTATION.

§ 1. *Motives from the State and Character of Christians.*

I come now to the third question, What are the motives by which this exhortation is enforced? These are presented in two different forms? They are either folded up in the con-

---

[1] John vi. 63; xi. 25. Eph. v. 14. Mark i. 15. Acts iii. 19. 2 Thess. ii. 10. Rom. xii. 2. Isa. iv. 3.

nective particle "Wherefore," or lie unfolded in the statement, "Ye have tasted that the Lord is gracious." Let us
look at them in their order, and not merely open our minds to
apprehend their meaning, but our hearts to feel their force.

Let us then inquire, What are the motives to "lay aside
all malice, and guile, and hypocrisies, and envies, and all
evil-speakings," and to "desire the sincere milk of the
word, that they may grow thereby," that are folded up
in the connective particle Wherefore? This word looks
backward to the statements in the 22d and 23d verses of the
last chapter: "Ye have purified your souls in obeying the
truth through the Spirit unto unfeigned love of the brethren,"
and "Ye have been born again, not of corruptible seed,
but of incorruptible, by the word of the Lord, which liveth
and abideth for ever;" and forward to the clause, "As new-
born babes," which is equivalent to 'being new-born babes.'
The meaning of these statements has already been explained.
It is their force as motives to the duties here enjoined that
we are now to illustrate. The general statement is, "Ye
have lately become the children of God both as to state and
character, by the belief of the truth, under the influence of
the Holy Spirit." The force of the statements as a source
of motives will be plainer by resolving it into its elements:
Ye are as new-born babes; ye are the children of God;
ye are brethren as being the children of God, members of
the same family; ye became so by obedience to the truth;
ye became so under the influence of the Spirit. Every one
of these propositions, all of them, evidently included in the
statements referred to in the connective term "Wherefore,"
is instinct with impulsive energy, replete with powerful
motives.

(1.) Ye are little children, lay then aside malignity and
craft. These, hateful wherever they appear, are monstrous
in an infant. They are quite incongruous with the childlike character that belongs to genuine Christians. Like
little children, too, desire growth, and for this purpose desire
your appropriate nourishment. It is natural for a child to

grow, and to wish to grow.   It is unnatural for a child to be
stationary, and to have no desire for growth; and so it is
with the spiritual babe.   The child is born to grow, and has
an instinctive desire to grow.   A Christian not making progress, not desiring to make progress, is something quite out
of the natural course of the spiritual world.   And as the
mother's milk is the natural, the needful, means of nutriment
to the infant, so is the pure truth the natural and needful
means of progressive holiness to the regenerate soul.

(2.) Ye are the children of God; ye should then be like
your Father in heaven, who is infinitely benignant and
truthful.   If you were malicious, guileful, and envious,
would you not falsify your profession of divine sonship?
Would you not prove yourself the children of a very different father, even of him who was a murderer and a liar
from the beginning?   It is the same argument which the
Apostle Paul puts so strongly in his Epistle to the Philippians: " Do all things without murmurings and disputings;
that ye may be blameless and harmless as the sons of God,
without rebuke,"[1] and which our Lord urges in a still more
forcible form in the Sermon on the Mount: " Love your
enemies, bless them that curse you, do good to them that
hate you, and pray for them that despitefully use you, and
persecute you; that ye may be the children of your Father
who is in heaven: for he maketh his sun to rise on the evil
and the good, and sendeth rain on the just and the unjust.
Be ye therefore perfect, as your Father in heaven is perfect."[2] It is the same principle of motive as in these words:
" Be ye holy, for I am holy;" " Be followers of God as
dear children."[3]   And if ye are the children of God, ye
should desire to grow, for it is thus, thus only, you can
honour your Father: "Herein is my Father glorified, in that
ye bring forth much fruit"[4]—that is, grow, make rapid progress in holy attainment.   And ye should desire the sincere
milk of the word, ye should seek to understand and practically

---

[1] Phil. ii. 15.   [2] Matt. v. 44-48.
[3] Eph. v. i.   [4] John xv. 8.

to improve divine truth, for it is the revelation of the mind of your Father. "As obedient children," you should seek to know the will of your Father, that ye may do the will of your Father. He is an unnatural, undutiful, child who acts otherwise.

(3.) Then you are all the children of God by faith in Christ Jesus, and of course form one spiritual brotherhood. This is a new aspect of the statement, full of additional motive to the duties enjoined. There can be no doubt that Christians are not permitted to indulge in "malice, guile, cursing, or evil-speaking," in reference to any class of men; but there can be as little, that in the passage before us, there is a direct reference to the conduct of Christians to each other, and that those evil tempers and habits are condemned as opposed to that pure fervent love of the brethren, which had been enjoined in the close of the preceding chapter. The bearing of this consideration, that they are all brethren, on the *dissuasive* exhortation, is direct and powerful. Brothers should treat one another with an ingenuous openness. If there is to be malice and deceit in the family circle, where is true sincerity to dwell? Love one another. Surely malice, deceit, hypocrisies, envyings, and evil speakings, are peculiarly out of place among those who have *all* been " born again, not of corruptible seed, but of incorruptible ;" who have been bound by ties of a brotherhood that neither time nor eternity can dissolve, and who have "purified their souls, through the truth by the Spirit, to the unfeigned love of the brethren." It is substantially the same motive that is brought forward in these exhortations : " Love as brethren. Put off anger, wrath, malice, blasphemy, which is the same thing as evil speaking; lie not one to another, seeing that ye have put off the old man, who is corrupt in his deeds; and put on the new man, which is renewed in knowledge after the image of him who created him." " Putting away lying, speak every man truth with his neighbour : for ye are members one of another."[1]   Con-

---

[1] 1 Pet. iii. 8.   Col. iii. 9.   Eph. iv. 25.

fraternity, in its very nature, and especially such a confraternity, implies an obligation to kindness and sincerity on the part of the members. This motive also strongly urges to compliance with the *persuasive* exhortation ; for spiritual growth is not only necessary to individual happiness, but to the prosperity of the body. The same idea that is expressed by Christians being represented as brethren, is still more strikingly expressed by their being represented as mutually connected as members of one body. The growth of every member is necessary to the welfare of the whole body. The more individual growth, the more general prosperity. It is by every member growing up to him that is the Head, that "the whole body fitly joined maketh increase."[1] It is by becoming wiser, better, and happier myself, that I increase the wisdom, and holiness, and peace, of the body to which I belong.

(4.) Then still farther, you became the children of God, and were formed into a spiritual brotherhood, "by obeying the truth." Wherefore, put away all those evil habits, which can be retained only by disobeying, resisting, the influence of the truth. Every evil temper or action is a practical lie ; an implied denial of, and opposition to, the truth ; and thus is very inconsistent in those who profess to have submitted to the truth, to have received it into their hearts as the animating, regulating principle of their souls. And as it was by the influence of the truth ye were made holy, so it is by the continued, increased, influence of the truth, that you are to continue holy, to become more and more holy. Therefore, "desire the sincere milk of the word, that ye may grow thereby."

(5.) Finally, here you become the children of God under the influence of the Spirit; therefore, you should put off "malice, and guile, and hypocrisies, and envies, and evil speakings," and all those other evil tempers and habits; for these are the fruits, not of the Spirit, but of the flesh. The

[1] Eph. iv. 16.

fruit of the Spirit is in all "goodness"—benignity, "righteousness, and truth." You would "grieve the holy Spirit of God, whereby ye are sealed unto the day of redemption," if ye "put not away from you all bitterness, and wrath, and clamour, and evil speaking, with all malice." "If ye live in the Spirit, see that ye walk in the Spirit." And therefore, too, should you desire the sincere milk of the word; for it is by the word, understood and believed, that the Spirit carries on his sanctifying work. It is presumptuous folly to expect to be sanctified or guided by the Spirit, without the word. The Spirit leads to the word; and it is through the word that he enables us to "put off the old man who is corrupt in his deeds, and put on the new man, who, after God, is created in righteousness and true holiness."[1] Such is the variety and force of appropriate motive which is folded up in the connected particle "wherefore," with which our text commences.

§ 2.—*Motives from having tasted that the Lord is gracious.*

Let us now examine the motive which is unfolded in the statement with which our text closes. "If so be," or rather, seeing "ye have tasted that the Lord is gracious." There can be no doubt that the ordinary usage of the language favours the rendering of our version, "If so be." If it be admitted, the meaning is, If you have indeed tasted that the Lord is gracious, you are peculiarly bound to "lay aside those evil habits," and to "desire the sincere milk of the word;" and if you do not lay them aside, and desire the sincere milk, then it is a plain proof that, whatever profession you make, you have not "tasted that the Lord is gracious." The particle, however, admits of being rendered "since," taking for granted, not throwing into doubt, their having "tasted that the Lord is gracious." It is the same word that in 2 Thess. i. 6, is rendered, and obviously rightly, "seeing." "We glory in you, for your patience and

---

[1] Eph. v. 9; iv. 30, 31. Gal. v. 25.

faith in all your persecutions and tribulations which you
endure; a manifest token of the righteous judgment of God,
that ye may be accounted worthy of the kingdom of God,
for which ye also suffer: *seeing* it is a righteous thing with
God to recompense tribulation to them who trouble you; and
to you who are troubled rest with us."[1]   This mode of rendering the particle here, better accords with the whole strain
of the epistle, in which the persons addressed are always
spoken of as Christians, and gives greater point and direct-
ness to the motives, " Lay aside all malice, and guile, and
hypocrisies, and envies, and evil speakings," and " desire
the sincere milk of the word, since ye have " tasted that the
Lord is gracious."

To bring out the force of the motive, it is necessary to
inquire who is meant by " the Lord?"   What is meant by
his being gracious?   What is meant by tasting that he is
gracious?   And then, how the having tasted that the Lord
is gracious, affords grounds for the exhortations, " Lay aside
all malice, and guile, and hypocrisies, and envies, and evil
speakings," and " desire the sincere milk of the word ? "

(1.) " The Lord" here is plainly the Lord Jesus.   This is
evident from what follows: for without doubt he is " the
living stone" on whom, as a foundation, Christians, " as
living stones, are builded into a holy temple."   It is to Him
that the passage cited from the prophet Isaiah certainly
refers.

(2.) Our Lord Jesus is " gracious," is kind.   Benignity,
holy love, is his leading moral attribute.   His kindness is
manifested in what he does, and in what he gives.   " The
grace" or kindness " of our Lord Jesus" is shown in that,
"though he was rich, yet for our sakes he became poor, that
we through his poverty might be rich."[2]   He bestows on

---

[1] This seems also the force of ειπερ in Rom. viii. 9.   Such a use of ειπερ can
be supported by classical usage.   Το τυπτεσθαι αλγεινον, ειπερ σαρκινοι.   " To be
struck is painful" *to men,* "*since* they are made of flesh;" *i. e.* not of dead matter.—Aristot. Eth. Nic. iii. 9.

[2] 2 Cor. viii. 9.

men, utterly undeserving of any thing but punishment, true knowledge, pardon, restoration to the divine favour, peace, holiness, abundant consolation, good hope, eternal life; in one word, happiness, perfection, suited to all the capacities of his nature, during the eternity of his being. And that he might do this, He who was in the form of God assumed the nature of man, the form of a servant, the likeness of a sinner; bore our sins, carried our sorrows; became obedient to death, even the death of the cross. "Herein is love." This is kindness. Verily, the Lord is gracious.[1]

(3.) To "taste" that the Lord is gracious is a figurative expression. It seems borrowed from the words of the Psalmist, "O taste and see that God is good,"[2] where two of the bodily senses are employed to denote clear mental apprehension, along with appropriate mental affection. To taste that the Lord is gracious, is to know that the Lord is gracious; and to know this, not from the report of others, but from our own experience. This knowledge is derived primarily from the faith of the truth as to what the Lord is, and has proved himself to be, by his gifts; and secondarily, from the enjoyment of these gifts of his, on the possession of which we enter by the belief of this truth; and the measure of which enjoyment corresponds with the measure of our faith. He tastes that the Lord is gracious, who believes the love which the Lord has to sinful men; who counts it a faithful saying, and worthy of all acceptation, that he came not to be ministered to, but to minister, and to give his life a ransom for many; to save sinners, even the chief; and he tastes the graciousness, the kindness of our Lord, who, in the faith of this truth, has peace with God; has access to him; holy love; fervent gratitude; good hope; joy in God, through our Lord Jesus Christ, by whom he has received the reconciliation.[3] Every believer of the truth thus tastes that the Lord is gracious; and he

---

[1] Phil. ii. 6-8.   [2] Psal. xxxiv. 8.
[3] 1 John iv. 16.   John i. 16.   1 Tim. i. 15.   Rom. v. 1-11.

does so just in the measure of his faith. The man who does not know Christ to be kind, and his benefits to be precious, is not a believer; and he who does so, cannot, but in the degree in which he is a believer, trust in Christ as his Saviour, and rejoice in the benefits of his salvation. "That is to taste," says Luther, "when I with the heart believe that Christ has been sent for me, and is become mine own; that my miseries are his and his life mine; when this truth enters into the heart, then it is tasted."[1]

It has been supposed by some, that the term is intended to intimate, not only that they had a true personal knowledge of Christ's kindness, but that that knowledge was as yet but very imperfect. They had tasted, but only *tasted*. They know, but they know but little, of that love that passeth knowledge. No doubt this is a truth; but we should hesitate to say it was in the Apostle's mind when he used the words now before us.

(4.) It only remains that I endeavour to bring out the force of the motive to "lay aside all malice, and guile, and hypocrisies, and envies, and evil speakings," and to "desire the sincere milk of the word;" which is afforded by the fact, that Christians have "tasted that the Lord is gracious." The love of God in Christ Jesus, reconciling the world to himself, known and believed, is the grand source of motive to holy obedience in all its forms. "The grace of God," of which the kindness of the Lord is an expression, "which brings salvation to all," when the divine testimony regarding it is understood and believed, "teaches us to deny ungodliness and worldly lusts, and to live soberly, righteously, and godly in this present world; looking for that blessed hope, the glorious appearing of our Lord Jesus Christ; who gave himself for us, that he might redeem us from all iniquity, and purify unto himself a peculiar people, zealous of good works." "When the kindness and love of

---

[1] Χριστος ὁ Κυριος. Dulcis est Dominus in contemplatione, ad meditandum, Cant. ii. 3; in aure spirituali ad audiendum, Cant. v. 13; in ore ad loquendum, Psal. cxix. 39; in prospectu ad videndum, Sir. xxiii. 37.—Jo. Hus.

God our Saviour towards man (his philanthropy) appeared, not by works of righteousness which we have done, but according to his mercy he saved us, by the washing of regeneration, and renewing of the Holy Ghost; which he shed on us abundantly through Jesus Christ our Saviour; that, being justified by his grace, we should be made heirs according to the hope of eternal life." It is this faithful saying respecting the kindness of the Lord, firmly believed, that makes men, " careful to maintain good works." It is "the mercies of God" through Christ, known and believed, that induce men to " present their bodies living sacrifices, holy and acceptable unto God: rational worship;" and to be "not conformed to this present world; but to be transformed by the renewing of their minds, so as to prove what is that good, and acceptable, and perfect will of God."[1]

1. If you have tasted that the Lord is gracious, "Lay aside all malice, and all guile, and hypocrisies, and envies, and all evil speakings." " Sure if you have tasted of that kindness and sweetness of God in Christ, it will compose your spirits and conform you to him; it will diffuse such a sweetness through your soul, that there will be no place for malice and guile. There will be nothing but love, and meekness, and singleness of heart. They that have bitter malicious spirits, evidence that they have not tasted that the Lord is gracious; for they who have done so, cannot but, in the degree in which they have done so, 'be kind, one to another, tender-hearted, forgiving one another, even as God, for Christ's sake, has forgiven them.' "[2]

2. If you have tasted that the Lord is gracious, " desire the sincere milk of the word, that ye may grow thereby." It was in the word that you tasted the Lord was gracious. And is not this a powerful motive to go back to the word, that again, and again, and again, you may "taste and see that God is good;" and thus grow holier and happier,

---

[1] Tit. ii. 12-14; iii. 4-8. Rom. xii. 1-3.   [2] Eph. iv. 32. Leighton.

"keeping yourselves in the love of God, building yourselves up in your most holy faith, and looking for the mercy of the Lord Jesus, unto eternal life."[1]

I cannot conclude the illustration of this point in more appropriate words than in those of the pious Archbishop, a man who always makes it evident that " he spoke what he knew, and testified what he had seen and tasted," when he spoke on such themes as these: " This is the sweetness of the word, that it has the Lord's graciousness in it; it gives us the knowledge of his love. This they find who have spiritual life and senses exercised to discern good and evil; and this engages a Christian to a further desire of the word. They are fantastical, delusive tastes, that draw men from the written word, and make them expect other revelations. This graciousness is first conveyed to us by the word when we taste it, and therefore there still we are to seek it; to hang upon those breasts which cannot be drawn dry. There, the love of God in Christ, springs forth in the several promises. The heart that cleaves to the word of God, and delights in it, cannot but find in it daily new tastes of his goodness. There it reads true love, and by that stirs up its own to him, and so grows and loves every day more than the former, and thus is tending from tastes to fulness. It is but little we can receive here—some drops of joy that enter into us; but there we shall enter into joy as vessels put into a sea of happiness."

There is a question which here presses for an answer from the conscience of every individual who now hears me. Have I tasted that the Lord is gracious? Do I know, experimentally " know, the grace of the Lord Jesus?" You have all often heard of his grace; but have you tasted it? Have you believed his kindness? Have you enjoyed his benefits? The most satisfying evidence of this is, the laying aside all malice and similar tempers, and

[1] Jude 20, 21.

the desiring the sincere milk of the word. This indeed is the only permanently satisfactory evidence; for there is a dead faith, a presumptuous hope, a false peace. If you really have believed the love of Christ to you, that faith will " work by love" to God, to Christ, to the brethren, to all mankind, and it will " overcome the world." If the hope you cherish be founded on that faith, it will lead you to " purify yourselves as he is pure." If your peace rest on his finished work, it will keep your mind, and fortify it against the assaults of your spiritual enemies.

I trust not a few of this audience have tasted, are tasting, that the Lord is gracious. Let them bless the sovereign grace that made them partakers of this distinguishing blessing, opening their blinded eyes, and restoring soundness to their diseased taste. Let them seek new and more abundant discoveries of the graciousness of the Lord, and let them seek these in his word, and by his word. In his word let them seek discoveries of his kindness; by his word let them seek the enjoyment of his benefits. Let them open their mouths wide, and he will fill them " with the finest of the wheat," " angel's food," " meat which the world knoweth not of; " " the flesh and blood of the Son of man, who came down from heaven that he might give life to the world, meat indeed, drink indeed." And let them look forward with earnest expectation and humble hope to the manifestation of his grace, to the communication of his benefits, which is to be made " at his appearing and glory," when they shall be abundantly satisfied with the fatness of HIS house, and shall be made to drink of the river of his pleasures, " with whom is the fountain of life," and " in whose light they shall see light clearly."[1] Thus shall " they know," and ever "follow on to know, the loving-kindness of the Lord."

But what shall I say to what I am afraid is not a small class in the audience,—to those who have never tasted that the Lord is gracious? I might express wonder at their infa-

[1] Psal. xxxvi. 8, 9.

tuation, blame their pertinacity, pity their folly, and bewail their misery. I might ask how is it, when the Lord is gracious, so gracious, and when the revelation made of his grace is so plain and so well accredited, and when the blessings of his salvation are so suited to your circumstances, and so kindly urged on your acceptance, that you remain experimentally strangers to a sense of his kindness, and to the value of his salvation, as if he were not gracious, or as if you did not need, or were excluded from tasting, his grace? But I choose rather to content myself with proclaiming with the Psalmist, "O taste and see that the Lord is good." The Lord is good and gracious, long suffering, and abundant in mercy, rich in grace, ready to pardon, mighty to save. "Behold HIM, behold HIM." Look, look to Jesus, obeying, suffering, dying, the just in the room of the unjust, rising, ascending, sitting down on the right hand of the Majesty on high, giving gifts, the gifts of pardon and peace, and holiness and salvation to men, even to the rebellious, to you, and then say if the Lord is not gracious. "Herein is LOVE, not that you loved him, but that he loved you;" loved you, so as to "give himself" for you on the cross; loved you, so as to give himself to you in the gospel. And is all this love to be slighted and despised? Ah! if you *will* not taste his grace, you *must* feel his wrath. "Be wise, be instructed; kiss the Son, lest he be angry, and you perish from the way, if his wrath be kindled but a little. Blessed," only blessed, truly blessed, eternally blessed, "are they who trust in him."[1]

Thus have we filled up the outline sketched on our entering on the consideration of the subject. Our labour and your time have been lost, more than lost, if they do not lead to practical results. It is to worse than no purpose that we better understand the meaning, that we more clearly perceive the obligation, of the divine exhortation, if we do not set about complying with it. It increases responsibility

---

[1] 1 John iv. 10.   Psal. ii. 10-12.

and deepens guilt. If henceforth we cherish malignant feeling, and neglect the study of divine truth as the great means of spiritual improvement, we do so at an increased peril. Oh that the divine energy may accompany these statements ; so that, laying aside all malice, and all guile, and hypocrisies, and envies, and all evil speakings, all of us may desire the sincere milk of the word, and thus give satisfactory evidence that we have indeed tasted that " the Lord is gracious !"   Amen and Amen.

DISCOURSE VIII.

THE PECULIAR PRIVILEGES OF CHRISTIANS, AND HOW THEY OBTAIN THEM.

1 Pet. ii. 4-10.—To whom coming, as unto a living stone, disallowed indeed of men, but chosen of God, and precious, ye also, as lively stones, are built up a spiritual house, an holy priesthood, to offer up spiritual sacrifices, acceptable to God by Jesus Christ. Wherefore also it is contained in the scripture, Behold, I lay in Zion a chief corner-stone, elect, precious: and he that believeth on him shall not be confounded. Unto you therefore which believe he is precious: but unto them which be disobedient, the stone which the builders disallowed, the same is made the head of the corner, and a stone of stumbling, and a rock of offence, even to them which stumble at the word, being disobedient; whereunto also they were appointed. But ye are a chosen generation, a royal priesthood, an holy nation, a peculiar people; that ye should show forth the praises of him who hath called you out of darkness into his marvellous light: which in time past were not a people, but are now the people of God: which had not obtained mercy, but now have obtained mercy.

To unfold the nature and illustrate the value of the numerous "exceeding great and precious" privileges, which the peculiar people of God have in present possession, and in certain expectation, is one of the most important, as it is one of the most delightful, duties of the public Christian instructor. Such illustrations are calculated to serve many valuable purposes. They honour the Saviour, from whom all these privileges are derived, by displaying the ardour and tenderness of his love, the efficacy and value of his sacrifice, the prevalence of his intercession, and the munificence of his liberality. They tend to the conversion of sinners, by showing them that it is their obvious interest, as well as their undoubted duty, to yield to the claims of the Saviour's authority and love; and they greatly conduce to the consolation and joy of the saints, by fixing their attention on the number, and variety, and value, and security, of their distinguishing blessings; and to their holiness, by calling forth into vigorous, sustained exercise, that gratitude for these unspeakable gifts, which is the most powerful stimulant to Christian obedience. The more accurately the Christian apprehends the intrinsic excellence, the more fully he appreciates the inestimable worth, of his privileges, the more deeply must he feel his obligations to him, to whose sovereign love he is indebted for them all; and the more readily will he embrace every opportunity of manifesting his sense of this kindness, by actively doing, and patiently suffering, his will.

From these remarks it is obvious, on the one hand, that an enlightened preacher of Christian privilege is one of the best friends of practical religion; and, on the other, that the public Christian instructor who confines himself exclusively to what may be termed the moral part of Christianity, neglects the principal means with which that divine system furnishes us, for reclaiming the vicious and improving the pious, for converting the sinner and edifying the saint, for making the bad good, and the good better.

Such plainly were the views of the Apostle Peter, who in that Epistle, of which our text forms a part, insists largely on the peculiar privileges of Christians, representing them as at once a perennial, exuberant source of abundant consolation and good hope, amid all the trials and afflictions of the present state, and an inexhaustible store of (to a Christian mind) irresistible motive to perseverance and activity in the discharge of all the varied obligations of religious and moral duty. One of those exhibitions of Christian privilege, obviously brought forward as intended and calculated to serve these practical purposes, lies before us in the interesting and beautiful, though highly figurative and somewhat complicated paragraph which we have chosen as the subject of this discourse.

At first view, the paragraph may appear, to a considerable degree, disjointed, and on that account obscure; but on a narrower inspection we will find it to be just a beautiful expansion and illustration of the sentiment stated in the words which immediately precede it, and which embodies one of the Apostle's powerful enforcements of the duties, with the affectionate injunction of which this chapter of the Epistle commences : " Ye," Christians, " have tasted that the Lord," that is, your Lord Jesus Christ, " is gracious," kind. You have obtained, you enjoy, important, invaluable, blessings in consequence of your connexion with him. What these are the Apostle states in our text.

In consequence of coming to him, they had been brought by him to God, his Father and their Father. From a state of alienation from God, a state necessarily of deep degradation and misery, they had been brought into a state of most intimate relation to God, a state necessarily of the highest honour and the richest felicity. This is the leading idea; but it is brought out by a variety of figures borrowed from the facts of the Jewish economy, peculiarly calculated to be interesting and instructive to those to whom the Epistle was originally addressed.

By becoming connected with him, they had become in one point of view constituent parts of a great spiritual temple, infinitely more glorious than the temple at Jerusalem ; and in another point of view, ministering priests in that temple, possessed of a more dignified office, and engaged in holier services, than Aaron or any of his sons. They had become the true circumcision, the spiritual Israel, the possessors of those spiritual privileges of which the external advantages of Israel, according to the flesh, were but the imperfect figures ; they had become in a sense far superior to that in which their fathers had ever been, " a chosen generation, a royal priesthood, a holy nation, a peculiar people, the people of God," the objects of his distinguishing love, his sovereign choice, his most complacential delight. Having come to Christ, the living stone, the divinely appointed and the divinely qualified foundation of the great spiritual temple, they had, from union to him, become living stones, fit materials for the sacred spiritual edifice; and on him they had been built up, made a part of this mystical building, become devoted to the rational service of the great Father of Spirits; a sentiment repeated under the plainer figure of their having been constituted "a holy priesthood, to offer up spiritual sacrifices, acceptable to God by Christ Jesus."

The Apostle, according to his manner, seeks in the writings of the Old Testament, illustration both of the privileges, in the enjoyment of which those to whom he wrote had the evidence in themselves that the Lord is gracious, and of the manner in which they had obtained this spiritual connexion with him, arising out of faith in him. The prophet Isaiah, in the 28th chapter of his prophecies, in an oracle plainly belonging to the time of the Messiah, uses these words; "Therefore thus saith the Lord God, Behold, I lay in Zion for a foundation a stone, a tried stone, a precious corner-stone, a sure foundation; he that believeth shall not make haste." The Apostle quotes this passage apparently from memory, as his citation does not verbally correspond either with the Hebrew text or the Greek translation, though it accurately enough expresses the common meaning of both. 'In your experience,' as if the Apostle had said, 'this glorious prediction has been fulfilled, "He that believeth shall not be ashamed," that is, he shall have no reason to be ashamed. Not shame, but honour shall be his portion. He who, by believing in the sure foundation, is built up on him, shall not be ashamed, he shall be honoured. "To you, then, who believe, there is," according to this ancient oracle, "honour" (for this is the literal meaning of the words rendered, not very happily, "To you who believe he is precious;" a very delightful truth, no doubt, but a truth which the words do not naturally signify, and which have no direct bearing on the obvious object of the whole paragraph). " To you, then, who believe, there is honour, but to them who believe not, or are disobedient," there is shame and ruin ; for " the stone which they as builders reject, is," notwithstanding their rejection, " made the head of the corner."[1] And more than this, " this stone," which to them who build on it is honour and security, to them rejecting it " is a stone of stumbling, a rock of offence," an occasion of their stumbling and falling, and being broken to pieces, a doom long ago denounced against them, appointed for them, as disobedient, as appears from the ancient oracle referred to in the 8th chapter of the prophecy of Isaiah, verses 14, 15. But while thus, to these unbelieving disobedient ones, not building on, but stumbling at, this foundation, there is shame and ruin, to you who by believing build on it, there is honour; for, in consequence of your connexion with this living stone, ye are " a chosen generation, a royal priesthood, an holy nation, a peculiar people ; that ye may show forth the praises of him who hath called you out of darkness into his marvellous light : who in time past were not a people, but are now the people of God ; who had not obtained mercy, but now have obtained mercy."

The coherence of the passage is now, I trust, quite evident, as well as the bearing of every part of it, on the illustration of the general thesis, " Ye have tasted that the Lord is gracious." In the privileges which ye possess, so inestimably valuable and dignifying, ye have abundant experimental proof that the Lord is kind.

We are prepared now for entering on a somewhat more particular consideration of this view of the peculiar privileges of Christians, as a manifestation of the Lord's kindness to them ; and I do not know that the whole truth can be brought before our minds more fully and impressively, than by attending in succession, I. To the view which the

---

[1] The construction is ανακολουθον. It is equivalent to λιθος ουτος ον απεδοκιμασαν οι οικοδομουντες, ουτος εγενηθη εις κεφαλην γωνιας—just as 1 Cor. x. 16. Τον αρτον ον κλωμεν ουχι κοινωνια. κ τ. λ. for ουχι ο αρτος, ον κλωμεν κ. τ. λ.

text gives us of their degraded and unhappy state previously to their obtaining these privileges. II. To the manner in which they obtained them ; by coming to Christ as the divinely laid foundation. III. To the dignified and happy state in which, as Christians, they are placed. And, IV. To the disgrace and ruin of those who refuse these privileges, by neglecting the only way in which they can be obtained. This will bring before our minds all the truth contained in the passage, and will bring it before our minds as all intended to bear on this one point,—the manifestation of the Saviour's kindness, which his people possess in the distinguishing privileges which he bestows on them.

I. THE DEGRADED AND MISERABLE CONDITION OF CHRIS
   TIANS PREVIOUSLY TO THEIR OBTAINING THEIR PECU
   LIAR PRIVILEGES.

Let us first, then, attend to the view which the text gives us of the state of Christians previously to their connexion with Christ, as a means of throwing light on the statement, "Ye have tasted that the Lord is gracious." The degree of kindness manifested in conferring certain privileges, is materially affected by the state in which the object of kindness and the subject of privilege was, previously to the bestowment. The bestowal of a higher degree of nobility on one already noble, is a very different favour, a very different manifestation of kindness, on the part of a prince, from the bestowal of the same, or even an inferior degree of honour, on a peasant or a slave. To form a just idea of the graciousness of the Lord towards his peculiar people, we must keep steadily in view the state in which his grace finds them. That state is here presented to our minds, in contrast with the state into which that grace has brought them. It has made them " living stones" who were " dead stones." It has brought them into marvellous light who were in darkness. It has made those the people of God who were not a people, not the people of God. It has bestowed

mercy on those who had not obtained mercy. Dead stones ;
in darkness; not a people; not the people of God; not
having obtained mercy ;—these are the images under which
the inspired writer describes the original state of those who
now have tasted that the Lord is gracious. Let us inquire
into their meaning.

§ 1.—*They were " dead stones."*

They were not lively, or rather living stones; they were
" dead stones." The language here is so boldly metaphorical,
that, to our cold occidental imaginations, it is apt to appear
harsh and unnatural. Yet it is not obscure, and is a very
striking expression of a very important truth. The Christian
church is represented under the figure of a temple, an edifice
intended to indicate the presence and promote the glory of
the divinity. This is a spiritual, living temple, far more
worthy of the spiritual living God than any material building. Of this living temple, Jesus Christ is the living foundation. That a body of men are fitted for indicating the
presence, and promoting the honour of the only living and
true God, is entirely owing to their relation to Jesus Christ,
to their personal interest in the saving efficacy of his mediation ; and all who, through this personal interest in these saving effects, are transformed by the renewing of their minds,
are living stones, fit materials for forming part of such a
spiritual edifice.

But this is not a natural, it is a supernatural state. The
living stones were once " dead stones." That is, they were
utterly unfit for forming a part of the living temple ; of the
true Church of God. They were "without God" in the
world, " alienated from the life of God." " They did not like
to retain him in their knowledge." " He was not in all their
thoughts." God was not in them by his sanctifying Spirit.
The language of their hearts was, " Depart from us, we desire
not the knowledge of thy ways."

Looking at such a man, or at a collection of such men,

surveying their habitual character and conduct, the heaven-enlightened observer says, No, this is not the living temple of the living God. This is not " the house of God," this is not " the gate of heaven." This is " the habitation of devils, the hold of every foul spirit." And as they give no indication of God's presence in them, they are quite unfit for promoting his honour. Such men, such bodies of men, while they continue unchanged, cannot worship or glorify God. They are little disposed usually to engage in acts of worship; and when they do engage in them, to employ the prophet's phraseology, it is rather " howling" than " praying," a dead oblation, not a living sacrifice.[1]

Such were some, such were all, who have tasted that the Lord was gracious. To them all, it may be said, though in a different sense from that in which the prophet uses the words, "Look unto the rock whence ye were hewn, and to the hole of the pit whence ye were digged," or, in the words of the Apostle, " Remember, that ye were in times past in the flesh; without Christ, aliens from the commonwealth of Israel, strangers to the covenant of promise, having no hope, and without God in the world :" utterly unqualified, utterly indisposed for intercourse and fellowship with God; not knowing God, not wishing to know him; altogether unfit for making him known.[2]

§ 2.—*They were in " darkness."*

A second view of the original state of those who have tasted that the Lord is gracious is, that they " were in darkness." Darkness is an emblem of ignorance, error, depravity, and misery; and in all the extent of significance which belongs to the emblem, the persons here referred to were in darkness. All men by nature are under the influence of ignorance and misapprehension of the true character of God, and this necessarily involves ignorance and misapprehension of every subject which it is of most importance

[1] Hos. vii. 17   [2] Isa. li. 1   Eph. ii. 11, 12.

for man to be rightly and thoroughly informed on. " They
know not, neither do they understand; they go on in darkness." [1]

This ignorance and error is naturally connected with
moral depravity. As truth and holiness, so ignorance, error,
and depravity go together. Men are " alienated from the
life of God, by the ignorance that is in them." Instead of
serving the God who is light, they serve the prince of darkness. Their works are " the unfruitful works of darkness." [2]

And as their state was one of ignorance, error, and sin, it
was also one of misery. They were strangers to " the light
of life." The light of God's countenance did not shine on
them. They were destitute of " his favour, which is life; of
his loving-kindness, which is better than life." [3]

§ 3. *They were " not the people of God."*

A third view given of the previous state of those who had
tasted that the Lord was gracious is, that " they were not a
people," " not the people of God." The former views
respect Christians in their previous state individually, this
seems rather to refer to them as a body.

They were not " the people of God." They did not belong to the holy society. They were " aliens from the commonwealth of " the spiritual " Israel." They were equally
destitute of the character and the privileges of God's peculiar people. Instead of sitting with Abraham, Isaac, and
Jacob, in the kingdom of God, they were " without, in outer
darkness," lying under the power of the wicked one, the
prince of darkness.

They were not, properly speaking, at all " a people;"
they were so base and miserable as not to deserve the name
of " a people." Men in their natural state are incapable
of the highest form of social relation, that of being members
of the holy commonwealth, subjects of the heavenly king-

---

[1] Psal. lxxxii. 5.   [2] Eph. iv. 18; v. 11.   [3] John viii. 12. Psal. lxiii. 3.

dom.   They are rather a herd of outlaws, a band of rebels,
than a properly organized " people."

§ 4. *They had " not obtained mercy."*

The last view given us of the previous state of Christians
is, that they " had not obtained mercy."   The meaning of
that is not, that they were not the objects of the benevolence
or of the saving purpose of God.   " The tender mercy of
God is over all his works."[1] God has a love to *man*,[2] guilty,
depraved, righteously condemned, self-ruined man, and this
love to man appears, not first, when man by believing the
truth, and being transformed in the renewing of his mind,
becomes, in the degree in which he is so, the proper object
of the divine moral approbation and complacential delight ;
but " herein God manifested and commended his love to us,
in that, while we were yet sinners, enemies, Christ died for
us ;" and as to all who ever taste that the Lord is gracious,
there can be no doubt that he " loved them with an everlasting love, *therefore* with loving-kindness does he draw them"
to himself.   Yes, when God " blesses them with heavenly
and spiritual blessings in Christ," it is in accordance with,
and in consequence of, his having " chosen them in him before the foundation of the world, having in love predestinated them unto the adoption of children by Jesus Christ, to
himself, according to the good pleasure of his will, and to
the praise of the glory of his grace."[3]

The meaning is not, that they were not the objects of
divine love, but that they were not the subjects of divine
saving benefits.   They were the objects equally of his judicial displeasure, and of his moral disapprobation.   They
were not blessed by him with any heavenly blessing.   They
were unpardoned, unjustified, unsanctified.   They were
" poor and miserable, blind and naked."   They were in a
state, in which, if they had continued, they must have
been miserable for ever.   For such persons to be made to

Psal. cxlv. 9.   [2] 'H φιλανθρωπια. Tit. iii. 4.   [3] Rom. v. 8. Eph. i. 3-6.

taste that the Lord was gracious, was mercy indeed, mercy which should have a constraining power to make them most dutiful subjects of their gracious Lord.

II. THE MANNER IN WHICH CHRISTIANS OBTAIN THEIR PECULIAR PRIVILEGES; BY FAITH OF THE TRUTH, AND RELIANCE ON THE SAVIOUR.

Let us now turn our attention, for a little, to the view the text gives us of the manner in which those miserable beings became possessed of their peculiar privileges, to the immediate cause of so favourable a change in their state and circumstances. It was by " coming to Christ as a living stone, disallowed indeed of men, but chosen of God, and precious;" it was by " believing on Him," as " the chief corner-stone, elect, precious, which God had laid in Sion."

To believe on Christ as the chief corner-stone, and to come to him as the living stone, have generally been understood as synonymous expressions, and both have been viewed as significant of that faith which, by the constitution of the new covenant, is necessarily connected with the enjoyment of the blessings of the Christian salvation ; and the passage, " He that cometh to me shall never hunger, he that believeth on me shall never thirst,"[1] has often been quoted as clearly proving this. I apprehend that that passage merely proves, that " he that cometh to Christ," and " he that believeth on him," are two descriptions of the same person, not that they are expressions entirely synonymous in meaning. The following passage seems, indeed, clearly to distinguish between believing on and coming to, and to represent the latter as the consequence of the former, the former as the means of the latter, " He that cometh to God, must believe that he is, and that he is the rewarder of all who diligently seek him."[2]   To believe, is to count a proposition true on the ground of what appears satisfactory testimony; to believe *on*, or *in* a person, is a Hebraistic mode of expression, and signifies to count a testimony, given either by or respecting that person, to be true; to believe in Christ, is to count true what Christ says, or what is said about Christ; to know and be sure of it, to reckon it a faithful saying, and worthy of all acceptation.[1] To come to Christ is a figurative expression, denoting those mental exercises which may be termed the movement of the mind and heart towards Christ, in the various characters in which the divine testimony represents him, and which equally, by the constitution of human nature and of the new covenant, grow out of the faith of the truth respecting him, of which the bodily movement of coming is a natural figurative representation. The peculiar character of the mental movement, depends on the view at the time before the mind respecting Christ. Believing the truth respecting him as the great Prophet, I come to him seeking the knowledge of his will, with a determination to receive any doctrine, every doctrine, which he delivers, just because he delivers it. Believing the truth with respect to him as a Priest, I come to him relying with undivided, unshaken confidence on his atonement and intercession. Believing the truth with respect to him as a King, I come to him in a cheerful, unquestioning obedience to his commands and appointments, just because they are his. This exactly accords with the view given in our excellent Shorter Catechism, which teaches us not that faith is resting and relying on Jesus Christ for salvation, but " that it is by faith that we rest and rely on Christ;" and in the Confession of Faith, which teaches us, " that it is by faith that we accept and rest on Christ, yield obedience to the commands, tremble at the threatenings, and embrace the promises of God."[2]

It was, then, by believing the truth about Christ, and by those outgoings of the mind and heart to him that neces-

---

[1] *Vide* " Hints on Faith and Hope."
[2] Westminster Short. Cat. Q. 86.　Confession of Faith, Ch. xiv. sec. 2.

sarily grow out of this faith, that the Christians to whom Peter wrote obtained and retained possession of the high honours and privileges which are here enumerated. It was thus that not shame but honour was their portion, that they became living stones, that they were built up, on him the living foundation, a spiritual house, that they became a royal priesthood, a chosen generation, a holy nation, partakers of the inheritance of the saints in light, a people, the people of God, partakers of distinguishing saving blessings. This is just the fundamenal doctrine of the gospel, which meets us every where in the Bible; that it is by the faith of the truth as it is in Jesus, that individuals obtain personal possession of the blessings of the Christian salvation.

Let us look a little more closely at this interesting view of the faith of the gospel, and its immediate and necessary effects. Those to whom Peter wrote had believed on, and come to the Lord. What they believed, and how they came to him, will appear very plain on examining the passage before us. What they believed was, that Jesus Christ was indeed " a living stone, disallowed indeed of men, but chosen of God, and precious; the chief corner-stone laid by God in Sion, elect, precious;" and that every man thus believing may rest satisfied that he shall not be ashamed by the disappointment of his hopes. And, believing this, they had come to him as the divinely appointed and divinely qualified foundation; they had exercised hope and confidence in him; they had built their creed on him; they had rested their expectations of eternal life on him; they had submitted to him as their only Lord and King.

There is some difficulty in forming a clear, distinct idea of the principal figurative representation here used, in which Christ is compared to a stone, a living stone, a chief corner-stone, elect, precious. There can be no doubt that the Apostle had before his mind the following passages of Scripture: "The stone which the builders rejected is become the head of the corner; this is the doing of the Lord, and it is marvellous in our eyes;" "He shall be for a sanctuary; but for a stone of stumbling, and for a rock of offence to both the houses of Israel; for a gin and a snare to the inhabitants of Jerusalem. And many among them shall stumble, and fall, and be broken, and be snared, and taken;" and, "Therefore thus saith the Lord God, Behold, I lay in Zion a foundation stone, a tried stone, a precious corner-stone, a sure foundation : he that believeth shall not make haste." [1]

It is sufficiently obvious that the general representation is, Jesus Christ is the foundation of a spiritual temple, of which believers in him form the superstructure. He is the foundation, they are stones built on the foundation. Whatever the meaning of this may be, so far the figurative expression is distinct enough; but what are we to make of the epithet, " living," applied both to the foundation and to the superstructure? He is the "living stone," they are "living stones." It seems impossible satisfactorily to account for our translators having rendered the same word living in the first instance, and lively in the second. Some have supposed that, in these expressions, there is an allusion to the undoubted fact, that the ancients were in the habit of speaking of stone in its native state, lying compact, unbroken in its original place in the earth, as the living rock.[a] Jesus Christ, according to this view of the matter, is compared to a mighty rock, resting in the place where the omnipotent hand of God placed it, when "by his power he set fast the mountains, being girded with power," affording an immoveable foundation, very different from any stone, however large, which the hand of man could lay; and when it is said that believers are built upon him as living stones, the idea intended to be conveyed is the closeness and indissolubleness of their connexion with him; they form as it were a part of the living rock; so intimately connected are they, that they cannot be disjoined either from the foundation, or from one another.

This is certainly ingenious, but we doubt if it be the Apostle's reference. The epithet " living," in reference to the

[1] Psal. cxviii. 22. Isa. viii. 14; xxviii. 16.   [a] See note A.

foundation, and the stones built on it, like the epithet
"spiritual," in reference to the house or temple, seems to belong not to the figurative representation, but to the exposition of it, just as in the 12th chapter of the Epistle to the
Romans, the epithet "living" is connected with sacrifice;
and " reasonable" or rational with " worship," religious service. The epithets are intended to indicate that the temple
spoken of, is a temple worthy of him who cannot " dwell in
temples made with hands ;" a living temple for the living
God : a spiritual temple for God who is a spirit. Its foundation
is a living foundation; the stones of which it is composed are
living stones. Considering this as the true interpretation
of the phraseology, let us now enquire what are the great
truths respecting Christ contained in this figurative phraseology, the belief of which is represented as that by which
the Christians, whom Peter was addressing, had obtained possession of their high and distinguishing privileges.

The great principle is, Jesus Christ is the foundation of
the spiritual temple of God; this is the central statement :
Then, this foundation has been laid by God; it is a chief
corner-stone ; it is elect or chosen ; it is precious ; it was disallowed of men, but by God it is made to serve the purpose
for which it was intended; and this foundation is a living
stone;—these are the subsidiary statements which cluster
round that central one. Let us endeavour to ascertain their
meaning, and, if I mistake not, we will find that they contain
a very full and striking statement of the gospel of our salvation.

Jesus Christ is the foundation, the sole foundation, of the
spiritual temple of God.[1] What that temple is, there is no
room to doubt. It is true Christians, viewed as connected
with Christ, and with each other, through their common connexion with him. It is this holy society, viewed as the residence of God, and as the grand means of promoting his
glory in the world. These are the purposes of a temple. It is
the Deity's house; and it is the medium by which he is

---

[1] " Christus est vera et prima Ecclesiæ petra ; a quo Petrus, et ceteri fideles
fiunt petræ.—Cornelius a Lapide.

known and honoured among men. Now, keeping this in
view, it will not be difficult to see what is meant by Christ's
being the foundation of this spiritual temple. It is just this,
that it is by connexion with him that Christians, either individually or collectively, are fitted to serve the purposes of a
temple; to be a residence for God, and the means of showing
forth his glory among mankind. In his original state, man
was fitted and designed to be a temple of God ; and the race,
had man retained his primeval innocence, would have been,
as it were, one magnificent temple, " formed for himself to
show forth his praise." This was the pre-eminent glory of
man among all terrestrial creatures, that he was "formed for
God's self;" " capable of and full of God;" sacred in a peculiar way to divinity; his chosen habitation, the mansion and
residence of his indwelling glory. But by sin man individually and collectively has become unfit for the purpose of a
temple. He has brought on himself the divine curse; the
necessary effect of which is the withdrawing of the divine
gracious presence. He has become unworthy of, in a moral
sense unfit for, being the seat of the divine residence.

The consequences of sin in unfitting human nature to be a
temple for God, have been so strikingly described by one of
the greatest of our divines, that I gladly borrow his language : " What could be expected on all this, but that man
should be forsaken of God; that the blessed presence should
be withdrawn that had been so spitefully slighted, to return
no more ? No more until, at least, a recompense should be
made him for the wrong done, and a capacity be recovered
for his future converse : namely, till both his honour should
be repaired and his temple; until he might again honourably return, and be fitly received. But who could have
thought in what way these things should ever be brought to
pass ? that is, neither could his departure be but expected,
nor his return but be above all expectation. To depart was
what became him; a thing, as the case was, most godlike
or worthy of God, and what he owed to himself. It was
meet, so great a Majesty, having been so condescendingly

gracious, should not be also cheap, or appear inapprehensive of being neglected and set at nought. It became him, as the self-sufficient Being, to let it be seen that he designed not man his temple for want of a house; that having of old inhabited his own eternity, and having now "the heavens for his throne, the earth his footstool," he could dwell alone, or where he pleased else, in all his great creation, and did not need, where he was not desired. It was becoming of his pure and glorious holiness not to dwell amidst impurities, or let it be thought that he was a God who took pleasure in wickedness: and most suitable to his equal justice to let them who said to him 'Depart from us,' feel they spake that word against their own life and soul; and that what was their rash and wilful choice, is their heaviest doom and punishment. It was only strange that when he left his temple he did not consume it; and that, not leaving it without being basely expelled, he had thought of returning without being invited back again."[1]

Of this new and more glorious restored temple, formed of human beings, in which Jehovah is to dwell for ever, Jesus Christ, the only begotten of God, is the foundation and chief corner-stone. It required such a foundation. "The indignity offered to the majesty of the Most High God, in his most ignominious expulsion from his own temple, was to be recompensed; and the ruin must be repaired which had befallen the temple itself. In reference to both these performances, it was determined that Immanuel, that is, his own Son, his substantial image, the brightness of his glory, the eternal word, should become incarnate; and being so, should undertake several parts, and in distinct capacities, and be at once a single temple himself; and that this temple should also be a sacrifice, and thereby give rise to a manifold temple, conformed to that original one, of each whereof, in the virtue of his sacrifice, he was himself to be the glorious

---

[1] Howe. The best thoughts in these paragraphs are borrowed from that wonderful book "The Living Temple."

pattern, the firm foundation, the magnificent founder, and the most curious architect and framer, by his own various and most peculiar influence." [1]

It is Jesus Christ who, by his sacrifice, and intercession, and Spirit, and word, and providence, makes individual men fit residences for the Holy Divinity: and it is Jesus Christ also who renders these men united into a holy society, the effectual means of promoting his glory. It is IN HIM, that is, united to him, as the great corner-stone of the foundation, that " all the building fitly framed together, groweth into a holy temple in the Lord." It is as united to him, that the individual members of the church " are builded together for a habitation of God in the Spirit." Or, to vary the figure, " HE is the head, from whom the whole body fitly joined together and compacted by that which every joint supplieth, according to the effectual working in every part, maketh increase of the body, unto the edifying of itself in love." [2]

This, then, is the great central truth. Jesus Christ is the foundation of the spiritual temple. Through him, we are reconciled to God; through him, we are conformed to God. It becomes, through his atonement, congruous, that God should dwell in us, as his temple; and, by his Spirit, we are fitted to be the means of proclaiming his name, and manifesting his glory, to men and to angels; for " by the church is made known, to principalities and powers, the manifold wisdom of God." [3] He is " the author of salvation," THE SAVIOUR.

How different is the religion of the New Testament from the religion of many who profess to believe it! In the religion of many self-called Christians, there is but a very unfrequent and indirect reference to Christ. While they profess to believe all the doctrines of the New Testament relative to his person and mission, and would be shocked to be considered as enemies to his divinity or atonement, they

---

[1] Howe.   [2] Eph. i. 20-22; iv. 15, 16.   [3] Eph. iii. 10.

have no deep abiding views of the importance of these
truths to their own hope, holiness, comfort, and salvation.
They have no habitual sense of the absolute necessity of
his mediation, no habitual trust in his sacrifice, no habitual
dependence on his spirit. Their professed belief of the peculiar principles of the gospel seems to exert no influence
over their religious and moral dispositions, and conduct.
They think and feel much as if there never had been such
a person as Jesus Christ; their life is any thing but a life
" by the faith of the Son of God."

The religion taught in the New Testament, of which our
text is a fair specimen, is Christianity in the most emphatic
and peculiar sense of the term, " Christ is all in all." It is his
religion. It is all *by* him; it is all *about* him; he is its author,
he is its substance; he is the sun of this system, the soul
of this body. Every thing is viewed in its connexion with
him. Every doctrine and every precept, every privilege
and every duty, every promise and every threatening. The
ground of acceptance is his sacrifice; the source of light and
life, holiness and peace, his spirit; the rule of duty, his law;
the pattern for imitation, his example ; the motives to duty, his
authority and grace; the great end of all, his glory, God's glory
in him. He is considered as the great reservoir of spiritual
blessing, filled by the grace of God, ever full, ever flowing to
our needy race. " Of God, Christ is made to men, wisdom,
righteousness, sanctification, and redemption." Every devout
feeling, every religious duty, takes a peculiar flavour and co-
lour from its reference to his mediation. He, he alone, is the
foundation : " other foundation can no man lay."[1] Let us
seek that Christ may be in us what he is in our Bibles !
Let us see to it that he be not only admitted by us to be
the foundation, but that he be *our* foundation ; and let us every
day, every hour be, in the faith of the truth, coming to him
as the divinely-appointed foundation. Let us seek to be
more and more " grounded on him in love," and let the lan-

---

[1] 1 Cor. i. 30; iii. 11.

guage of our hearts be that of the dying martyr: " None but Christ, none but Christ."

The truths now stated cast also a steady and pleasing light on a subject of deep interest at all times, of peculiarly deep interest in the times that are passing over us; the true nature of the union of the church, and the true means of promoting it. It is the union of "living stones," and that is to be promoted by "coming to *the* living stone." No union of dead stones can ever form a "spiritual house." There is no becoming living stones, but by coming to *the* living stone; no coming closely together among the living stones, but by coming individually closer to the living stone; no coming closer to the living stone, without coming closer to one another. No combination of worldly men can form or promote the union of the church. That union is union in truth and love; and this can have place only among those who " have received out of his fulness," who, according to the benignant good pleasure of the Father, is "full of truth and grace." And it will take place just in proportion to the degree in which these communications are received. Oh, when the church, the visible assembly of the professed people of God, becomes, as we trust it one day shall, obviously a well-compacted building of living stones, closely cemented to one another, by all being firmly attached to the great living foundation, what a spectacle will the Zion of the Lord, all radiant with divine light, then exhibit? Then will be accomplished the promise which has cheered the heart of her genuine children in the seasons of her desolation: "O thou afflicted, tossed with tempest, and not comforted! behold, I will lay thy stones with fair colours, and thy foundations with sapphires. And I will make thy windows of agates, and thy gates of carbuncles, and all thy borders of pleasant stones. In righteousness shalt thou be established: thou shalt be far from oppression; for thou shalt not fear: and from terror; for it shall not come near thee. The glory of Lebanon shall come to thee, the fir-tree, the pine-tree, and the box together, to beautify the place of my sanctuary; and I will make the place of my feet glorious." Then, then, will the palace of the great King, the Lord of Hosts, the temple of the God of heaven and earth, be "established on the top of the mountains, and be exalted above the hills; and all nations shall flow into it." And should the kings of the earth, as they have often done, assemble against it, "they will pass by together; they will see it, and marvel; they will be troubled, and pass away." And a great voice shall be heard in heaven: "Behold, the tabernacle of God;" the spiritual house, formed of the living stones on the living foundation; all shining with living light and holy beauty: "Behold, the tabernacle of God is with men, and he will dwell with them, and they shall be his people, and God himself shall be with them, and be their God." Who, that has any part in the faith and feeling of a Christian, can help saying in his heart, "Hasten it, O Lord, in its time. How long, O Lord, how long?" "He that testifieth these things saith, and he is faithful who has promised, Behold, I come quickly. Amen. Even so come, Lord Jesus."[1]

I proceed now to call your attention shortly to the subsidiary statements, which all as it were cluster around this great central one, which is, indeed, the sum and substance of "the gospel of our salvation."

The first of these is, Jesus Christ, as the foundation of the spiritual temple, is "laid by God." "Behold," saith Jehovah by the prophet, "I lay in Sion a sure foundation." The phrase "in Sion" seems intended to mark that the foundation was the foundation of a temple, a palace for himself. "Mount Sion beautiful for situation, the joy of the whole land," was "the mountain of God's holiness," the mountain set apart for himself. "He chose the Mount Zion, which he loved." While "he was known in Judah, and his name was great in Israel, in Salem was his tabernacle, and his dwelling-place in Zion."[2] To lay a foundation, then, "in

---

[1] Isa. liv. 11-14; lx. 13. Micah iv. 1. Rev. xxi. 3; xxii. 20.
[2] Psal. xlviii. 1, 2; lxxviii. 68; lxxvi. 1, 2.

Zion" is to lay the foundation of a temple, and of a temple to Jehovah.

We have already seen what is signified by Jesus Christ being this foundation. Our inquiry now is, what is meant by this foundation being laid by Jehovah. It indicates that the whole arrangement is not the result of human, of created wisdom or power, but of divine. No man, no angel, laid this foundation. "I lay it," says Jehovah. It is equivalent to,—I appoint him to the character emblematised by the foundation of the spiritual temple. I invest him with it. I qualify him for it. I accredit him in it. Jesus Christ is the divinely appointed, the divinely qualified, the divinely raised up, the divinely accredited Saviour of men; "fore-ordained before the foundation of the world;" at the appointed period "sent forth;" possessed of every necessary qualification, and bringing along with him every necessary credential; and "all" these "things are of God." His destination, his constitution, his qualifications, his attestation, are all divine. There seems to be a peculiar reference to the manifestation of this glorious truth, when "God raised Jesus from the dead, and set him at his own right hand." Then was "the stone set at nought of the builders" made to appear to be indeed "the head stone," the principal stone "of the corner." Then was it proclaimed as from heaven, "Let all the house of Israel," let all the family of man, "know asssuredly, that God has made that same Jesus, whom men crucified, both Lord and Christ." [1]

The second subsidiary statement is, this foundation is "a chief," or the chief "corner stone." The stone on which the angle of a building rests, gives not only support, but connexion, to the different parts of the building. It joins the different walls and stones into one building. The idea intended to be conveyed seems to be this, that the union of Christians as a body fitted for enjoying the divine presence and promoting the divine honour, depends on their

[1] 1 Pet. i. 20.　Gal. iv. 4.　Psal. cxviii. 22.　Acts iv. 10-12; ii. 36.

individually being connected with Jesus Christ, as the divinely appointed, qualified, constituted, accredited Saviour. It is this common connexion with him which is the basis of their connexion with each other. "In him," united to him, "they are builded together, a habitation of God through the Spirit," a spiritual habitation of God. It is thus that they are "knit together;" thus that they are "fitly joined and compacted."

The third subsidiary statement is, that this foundation is "chosen or elect." These words seem intended as a translation of the Hebrew phrase translated a "tried stone," proved and approved, and therefore chosen, selected, appointed, and employed to serve an important purpose. When God from eternity appointed his Son to be the Saviour of men, the foundation of the spiritual temple, the Father knew the Son; he knew his capacities, he knew he could bear all that was to be laid on him, both the weight of suffering, and "the exceeding great and eternal weight of glory;" and previously to his actually constituting him and holding him forth to men in these characters, he had been exposed to every species of trial competent to him, and had stood the trial. Every test applied but brought out more fully his complete fitness for the mighty work to which he was appointed.

The fourth subsidiary statement is, that this foundation is "precious," i. e., highly valuable, as possessed of every quality necessary in a foundation, and as alone being possessed of the qualities necessary in the foundation of such a building; for "other foundation can no man lay save that which is laid, Christ Jesus." The idea is, Jesus Christ is a precious, an all-accomplished Saviour, a perfect Redeemer, having all the knowledge, all the wisdom, all the power, all the merit, all the compassion arising from himself having "suffered, being tried," which are necessary to fit him for accomplishing the work of salvation in the best possible way. And he is precious, too, as the only Saviour. He is not one among many saviours; not the best among them, but he is the only Saviour. He can, and he only can, save from evils; he, and he only, can raise to blessings; deliverance from the first, and possession of the second of which, are absolutely necessary and completely sufficient to secure us from being miserable, and for making us happy, without measure and without end, up to the largest capacity of our nature for suffering or enjoyment, and during the whole eternity of our being. " The Deity filling his human nature, with all manner of grace in its highest perfection, made him infinitely precious and excellent; and not only was he thus excellent in himself, but he is of precious virtue, which he lets forth and imparts to others, of such a virtue that a touch of him is the only cure of spiritual diseases. Men tell of strange virtues of some stones; but it is certain that this precious stone hath not only virtue to heal the sick, but even to raise the dead. Dead bodies he raised in the days of his abode on earth, and dead souls he doth still raise by the power of his word."[1]

The fifth subsidiary statement is, this foundation-stone was " disallowed and rejected of men;" but, notwithstanding, made by God to answer all the purposes for which it was intended. The direct reference is to the rejection of Jesus Christ as the Saviour promised to the Fathers by the Jewish nation. When the word made flesh, of the seed of David according to the promise, " came to his own, his own received him not."[2] Instead of honouring him as the sent of God, the divinely destined, qualified, accredited Saviour, they regarded him with contempt and abhorrence as a low-born impostor, and put him to the death of a blasphemer and a traitor. But while this is the direct reference, the statement is meant to embrace a wider range of facts. The Jews were just a specimen of our race, and acted as the race would have done in similar circumstances; and men generally, universally till they are taught of God, disallow and reject Jesus Christ as the foundation; and though they do

---

[1] Leighton.   [2] John i. 11.

not do this exactly in the same way as the Jews did, for this is impossible, they manifest the same spirit, they do substantially the same thing.   Jesus Christ, made known in the word of the truth of the gospel as the only and all-sufficient Saviour, is by the great body of mankind not acknowledged.   They do not own his authority, trust in his atonement, imbibe his spirit, obey his laws.   But though men reject him, God owns him: he shows that in his estimation he is proved, approved, excellent, invaluable.   The stone which the " Jewish builders rejected," he made " the chief stone of the corner."   He raised him to his own right hand, and gave him all the authority and power, as Mediator, which were necessary to carry forward to accomplishment the benignant purposes of those severe trials by which his excellence had been so fully proved.   And still, though mankind very generally reject the Saviour, and so, refusing to build on him the only foundation, perish, yet this foundation of God standeth sure.   " Jesus Christ" remains " the same yesterday, to-day, and for ever;" and while he is to multitudes, to all who reject him, " a stumbling-block and foolishness," by divine power and grace he is " the wisdom of God, and the power of God to salvation, to all who believe;" " made of God to them wisdom, righteousness, and sanctification, and redemption."[1]   Men may stumble at the foundation so as to fall, but they cannot move it, or render it, in any degree, unfit for the great purpose for which it is laid, the sure support of that edifice of mercy and holiness, of which Jehovah has said, " It shall be built for ever."

The last subsidiary statement is, that this foundation is a " living stone."   The general meaning of this, at first sight paradoxical, declaration, is abundantly obvious.   He is a suitable foundation for a spiritual temple, formed not of dead matter, but of intelligent beings.   But while this is its meaning, this does not exhaust its meaning.   The epithet " living" is, I apprehend, intended to

---

[1] Heb. xiii. 8.   1 Cor. i. 23, 24, 30.

express those qualities in Christ Jesus which make him a fit foundation of a spiritual temple. He is so a living stone, as that dead stones, when laid on him, become living stones. He has in himself, and has the capacity of communicating to others, all that is necessary to make them fit recipients of the divine presence, fit instruments for promoting the divine glory. He is the living and life-giving foundation. He is full of spiritual life, grace, and truth ; and so full, that no man can be brought near him, but straightway he fills him with grace and truth too. It is well said by an old interpreter, " He is called the living stone, as he is called the living bread and the living water, not only because he has life in himself, but also because he gives life to the dead. He lives, and because he lives, they who eat him as the living bread, they who drink him as the living water, they who come to him and build on him as the living stone, live also." In the words of the good archbishop, " He is here called a living stone, not only because of his immortality and glorious resurrection, being a lamb that was slain, and is alive for ever and ever, but because he is the principle of spiritual and eternal life to us," a living foundation that transfuses its life into the whole building, and every stone of it, "in whom," united to whom, " all the building is fully framed." It is the spirit that flows from him which enlivens it, and knits it together, not as a dead mass, but as " a living body." This foundation, from the peculiarity of the case, does for its living superstructure what the root does in the vegetable world to the trunk, the branches, and the leaves, and what the head or the heart in the animal body does to all the members.

Such, then, is the truth about Christ, which the converted strangers scattered abroad believed, that Jesus Christ, though rejected by the great body of mankind, is the divinely chosen, the divinely qualified, the divinely proved, the divinely approved, the divinely constituted, the divinely accredited, Saviour of man,—possessed of every necessary excellence for making man truly and eternally happy, by making him the fit recipient of the divine presence and benefits, and the fit instrument for declaring the divine excellence,—showing forth the divine praise. This they believed, for they had heard it "in the word of the truth of the gospel"—a word to which "God bore witness by signs and wonders, and divers miracles and gifts of the Holy Ghost," and which was confirmed by the testimony of the law and the prophets. And believing this, they had come to him as the sure foundation laid by God, and built themselves on him. Believing the truth about him, they had acted towards him according to their faith, implicitly submitting to his teaching as their great prophet, relying on his atonement as their only priest, obeying his commandments as their Sovereign Lord and King. This is the way in which they ceased to be dead stones, and became living stones, came out of darkness into light ; and from not being a people became God's people, and from not having found mercy became the happy possessors of the peculiar favour of Jehovah, and of all its glorious results.

There is a peculiarity in the phraseology which deserves attention before we close our remarks on this part of the subject. The word is in the present, not in the past tense. It is not "having come," but " coming;" not "he who has believed," but "he that believeth." This intimates, that to the continued enjoyment of the peculiar privileges of Christians, there must be continued faith in him, continued coming to him. In order to a life of Christian enjoyment, there must be " a life of faith on the Son of God, who loved us, and gave himself for us."[1]

III.—THE PECULIAR PRIVILEGES OF CHRISTIANS.

§ 1. *General Statement.*

It is now time that we proceed, To consider the view which the text gives us of the dignified and happy state into which Christians are brought by their believing on, and coming to, Christ. That state is a state of nearness to God, of reconciliation to him, of resemblance to him, of fellowship with him,—a state of dignity and happiness, just because it is a state of nearness to the infinitely great and glorious and ever blessed God,—a state which strongly contrasts with their previous condition, which was one of distance from God, a state of enmity and alienation; and which, just because it was a state of distance from the source and sum of true glory and happiness, was a state of degradation and misery.

Their happy state, as well as the means by which they reach it, is stated generally in the words, "To you then who believe there is honour:"[1] for this is the literal and natural rendering of the words in the beginning of the seventh verse, which in our version runs thus: "Unto you who believe he is precious." He that believeth on the foundation laid in Zion by Jehovah, that is, as we have shown, he who believes the truth respecting Jesus Christ as the divinely laid foundation, shall not be ashamed or confounded. The faith of the truth naturally, necessarily gives origin to hope or expectation of certain blessings; and this hope, founded on this faith, "maketh not ashamed," does not disappoint. He who cherishes it shall certainly obtain the blessings he expects: and he shall as certainly find in these blessings that satisfying portion of the heart which he had anticipated. Not shame, but honour, shall be to him. The privileges which, as a believer in Christ, a comer to Christ, a builder on Christ, he enjoys, are of the most dignifying nature. He is brought into a near and most honourable relation to the greatest and best being in the universe. Coming to Christ, he comes to God through him. He becomes "an heir of God," by becoming "a joint heir in Christ Jesus." The general statement is expanded in a great variety of expressions, some of them highly figurative, but all of them full of meaning, rich in instruction and consolation. They

---

[1] Ὑμῖν οὖν ἡ τιμὴ τοῖς πιστεύουσιν, "Cedit honori et commodo vestro, quod in Christo creditis.—GERHARD. "Vobis, igitur honos, credentibus, ille nimirum honos ut non confundamini ab eo in adventu ejus, sed sicut ipse ait siquis mihi ministraverit, honorificabit eum pater meus." John xii. 26. BEDA.

become living stones; they are built up a spiritual house; they are a holy priesthood, to offer up spiritual sacrifices, acceptable to God by Jesus Christ; they are a chosen generation; a royal priesthood; a holy nation; a peculiar people, that they might show forth the praises of him who called them from darkness to light; the people of God, objects of his peculiar complacency, the subjects of his saving blessings. Let us very shortly enquire into the import of these descriptions of the Christian's peculiar privileges.

§ 2.—*Particular Statement.*

(1.) *Christians are " living stones," built up into a temple.*

First of all, they are described as becoming "living stones," by coming to Christ as the living stone. We have already seen they were "dead stones," entirely unfit for forming a part of a spiritual temple. But having believed in, and come to "the living stone," they become "living stones." From that connexion with Christ, which is necessarily implied in believing the truth respecting him, a change, both of state and character, takes place, which makes it becoming in Jehovah to employ them as materials in the erection of his spiritual temple, and which fits them for answering the great end of a temple, in doing honour to the divinity who dwells in it. Naturally "far off," they are "brought nigh by the blood of Christ," which is sprinkled on them in the faith of the truth. Alienated from God, they are "reconciled in Christ." Clothed with his righteousness, they are objects of complacent regard to the Holy and Just One; and animated by his Spirit, they are "to the praise of the glory of His grace, by which he has made them accepted in the beloved." Quickened by their connexion to him who, "the second Adam, the Lord from heaven, is a quickening Spirit," they are made fit for serving the living God; fit for yielding spiritual, true worship to Him who is a Spirit, and who must be worshipped in Spirit and in truth.

But they not only become living stones, but as living

stones they are "built up a spiritual house."[1] They are not only honoured and happy as individuals, but they are formed into a holy, honourable, blessed fellowship. They, in consequence of their common connexion with Christ, have a mutual connexion with each other, and form a living spiritual temple, blessed with the presence, devoted to the worship and honour, of Jehovah, the fountain of life, the Father of Spirits. They become members of the most honourable of all societies ; the "family in heaven, and on earth called by the one name ;" "the name above every name." They are enrolled among the brethren, "to whom the perfected Redeemer declares his Father's name."   They are members of the church, "in the midst of which he celebrates his praise." It is the same idea, though under a different image, which the Apostle so beautifully expresses in the Epistle to the Hebrews: "Ye are come to Mount Zion, and unto the city of the living God, the heavenly Jerusalem, and to an innumerable company of angels, the general assembly and the church of the first-born, which are written in heaven, and to God the Judge of all, and to the spirits of the just made perfect, and to Jesus the mediator of the new covenant, and to the blood of sprinkling, which speaketh better things than that of Abel."[2]

(2.) *Christians are "a holy priesthood."*

In the next branch of the inspired account of the Christians' privileges, the figure varies ; and they who were represented under the figure of a spiritual temple, are represented under the figure of "a holy priesthood," set apart "to offer up spiritual sacrifices to God, acceptable to God by Jesus Christ." Under the New Testament economy, there is but one priest, in the

---

[1] Secundum sapientiores Judæos Messias non debet templum tertium materiale ædificare sed בית רוחנית domum spiritualem, cum secundum illos sub Messia omnia debeant esse spiritualia. Ad istam sententiam videtur alludere Petrus Apostolus, qui epistola sua, Cap. ii. 3, dicit nos esse lapides ἐμψύχους et ζῶντας et πνευματικον οικον.—LE MOYNE, Not. et Obs. ad Barnab. Epist. Varia Sacra, vol. ii. p. 914.

[2] Heb. xii. 22-24.

strict meaning of that word as defined by the Apostle Paul: "One taken from among men, ordained for men in things pertaining to God, that he may offer both gifts and sacrifices for sins."[1] Our great High Priest, of whom all the priests under the Mosaic dispensation were but figures, is "the one Mediator between God and man."[2] He presents the only effectual atoning sacrifice. He, on the ground of that sacrifice, makes intercession for those who come to God through him, and obtains acceptance both for them and their services, and authoritatively blesses his people. Whoever professes to be a priest under the new economy, invades the prerogative of Him, who is "a priest for ever, after the order of Melchezidec," and is guilty of presumption, as far exceeding that of Korah and his company, as the ministry which Jesus hath received is "a more excellent ministry" than that of Aaron or any of his sons.

It is common enough, however, in the New Testament, to represent all Christians as figurative priests, in the sense of persons solemnly consecrated to and habitually engaged in the divine service.[3] These two views are given us in the passage before us. Ye are "a holy priesthood," and ye are a priesthood engaged in presenting to God "spiritual sacrifices, which are acceptable to God by Christ Jesus." Ye belong to a higher and holier fellowship than that of the Aaronical priesthood.

Christians are a "holy," a consecrated priesthood. You are aware that the priests under the Old Testament, were separated from among their brethren. They were so by their birth, and by their consecration. As sons of Aaron, they belonged to the priestly order. In like manner, all Christians, by their being born again, are set apart to the service of God. And as Aaron's sons were consecrated by the sprinkling of blood and the washing of water; so Christians

---

[1] Heb. v. 1.   [2] 1 Tim. ii. 5.
[3] Est autem illud non temere factum, ut Spiritus Sanctus nunquam in N. Testamento sacerdotis vel sacerdotii nomen ad evangelii ministros accommodârit.
   BEZA.

have their conscience sprinkled by the blood of Him, " who, by the eternal Spirit, offered himself a sacrifice to God without spot," and are purified " by the washing of regeneration, and the renewing of the Holy Ghost."[1]

As they resemble the priests in their consecration, so they resemble them also in their work. They " offer up spiritual sacrifices." The sacrifices they present are not expiatory, but eucharistic sacrifices. The only effectual expiatory sacrifice ever offered was that offered on Calvary, and that so completely answered its purpose, that it put an end to all such oblations. It " perfected for ever all those who were sanctified;" secured complete reconciliation; full, free, everlasting pardon; eternal redemption; salvation with eternal glory; so that there was no more room for sacrifices for sin. No; it is an undoubted truth, one equally delightful to those who trust in, and dreadful to those who reject, this atoning oblation : " There remaineth no more sacrifice for sin."[2] The eucharistic sacrifices presented by " the spiritual priesthood" are not material, but spiritual; not literal, but figurative sacrifices. The leading idea is, that Christians are brought into a very near relation to God ; and that the whole of their lives should be devoted to his spiritual service.[3] They are to " offer the sacrifice of praise to God continually, that is, the fruit of the lips," " the calves of the lips," as Hosea has it—not literal calves—" giving thanks to his name." " To do good and communicate they are not to forget, for with such sacrifices God is well pleased." They are to " present their bodies"—themselves, embodied living beings, not the dead bodies of slain beasts—" a living sacrifice." " Whether they eat, or drink, or whatsoever they do, they are to do all to the glory of God ;" and " whatsoever they do

---

[1] Heb. ix. 14. Tit. iii. 5.   [2] Heb. x. 26.

[3] Inter hostias spirituales primum locum obtinet generalis NOSTRI oblatio de qua Paulus.—Rom. xii. 1. Neque enim offerre quicquam possumus Deo, donec illi nos ipsos in sacrificium obtulerimus : quod sit nostri abnegatione. Sequuntur postea preces et gratiarum actiones, eleemosynæ et omnia pietatis exercitia.—CALVIN.

in word or in deed, they are to do it in the name of the Lord Jesus, giving thanks to God the Father by him."[1]

External services are only spiritual sacrifices when they embody a right state of mind and heart,—an enlightened mind, a pure devout heart. It is the gift of the heart which makes all other gifts easy to ourselves, acceptable to our God. " My son," says God, " give me thine heart;" and what follows? " let thine eyes observe my ways."[2] " This makes the eyes and ears, and tongue and hands, to be holy as God's peculiar property; and being once given and consecrated to Him, it is sacrilege to turn them to any unholy use."[3]

Such services of the spiritual priesthood, so reasonable, so dignifying, are said to be " acceptable to God by Christ Jesus." These services are in themselves very undeserving of acceptance ; for in the best of them, while we are here below, there is much wanting, and something wrong. But if they are the sincere expression of trust in God's mercy, love to his law, zeal for his glory, with all their imperfections they are acceptable. Like a kind father, he loves to hear even the lisping accents of affectionate confidence from his child ; and a very trifle, presented as a token of loyal submission, is in his eyes of great value. Even under the law, he who had not a lamb was welcome with his pigeon ; and under the better economy, none need forbear sacrifices for poverty. What God desires is the heart, and there is none so poor but he has a heart to give him. Alas ! that so many should want the heart to give the heart they have to give. It is not, however, so much the meanness of the gift offered, as the guiltiness of the offerer, that fills us with anxiety as to the acceptance of our services. Our foul hands pollute the best sacrifices ; but where the sacrifice has not the character of insincerity—a character which will certainly secure rejection, for, " if we regard iniquity in our hearts, God will not hear us,"—notwithstanding all their faults, the

---

[1] Heb. xiii. 15, 16.   Hos. xiv. 2.   Rom. xii. 1.   1 Cor. x. 31.   Col. iii. 17.
[2] Prov. xxiii. 26. תרצנה rendered by Symmachus θελησατωσαν.
[3] Leighton.

services of the Christian are acceptable, "acceptable by or through Jesus Christ." The spiritual priest is clothed with the robe of the Redeemer's righteousness, and in his clothing we are like Jacob in his brother's garments. There is "the smell of a field which the Lord hath blessed." If we offer our sacrifices by him, if we put them into his hands to offer to the Father, we need not doubt that they will be accepted for his sake.

The phrase, "by Christ Jesus," may be considered as qualifying both the phrase "to offer," and the expression "acceptable." We ought not to offer any thing but by him, trusting in his mediation, depending on his Spirit; and in doing so we are sure to be accepted, for he is God's beloved Son, in whom his soul is delighted; not only delighted and pleased with himself, but in him, with all things and persons that appear in him, and are presented by him. "This alone answers all our doubts; for we ourselves, for as little as we see in that way, may yet see so much in our best services, so many wanderings, so much deadness to prayer, as would make us still doubtful of acceptance, and might say with Job, 'Although he had answered me, yet would I not believe that he had hearkened to me,' were it not this, that our prayers and our sacrifices pass through Christ's hands. He is that angel that hath much sweet odour to mingle with the prayers of the saints. He purifies them with his own merits and intercessions, and so makes them pleasing unto the Father. Oh, how ought our hearts to be knit to him, by whom we are brought into favour with God, and kept in favour with him, in whom we obtain all the good we receive, and in whom all we offer is accepted. In him are all our supplies of grace, and our hopes of glory."[1]

(3.) *Christians are a "chosen generation."*

Let us now look at the next representation of the Christians' privileges. They are "a chosen generation." This, like the

[1] Leighton.

other appellations here given to Christians, is borrowed from the descriptive names given to the Israelitish people under a former dispensation. They are spoken of as "a generation," a race or family, the descendants of one father, standing to each other in the relation of brethren. Sometimes they are represented as the race or family of Abraham and of Israel, and sometimes they are represented as the family or the children of God. "Seek the Lord, and his strength," says the Psalmist; "seek him for evermore. Remember his marvellous works which he hath done; his wonders, and the judgment of his mouth; O ye, the seed of Abraham his servant, ye children of Israel his chosen." And they are very frequently termed the house or family of Israel. "Ye are the children of the Lord your God," says Moses; "Israel," says Jehovah, by Moses, to Pharaoh, "is my son, my first-born; let my son go, that he may serve me;" "Out of Egypt," says he by the prophet Hosea, "Out of Egypt have I called my son."[1]

And as the Israelites are often spoken of as a race or generation, the family of Abraham, the family of God, so they are spoken of as "a chosen generation," a selected family: "The Lord," says Moses, "loved thy fathers, therefore he chose their seed after them. The heaven, and the heaven of heavens, is the Lord thy God's, the earth also, and all that is therein; only the Lord had a delight in thy fathers to love them, and he chose their seed after them, even you above all people, as it is at this day."[2] "I give water in the wilderness," says Jehovah, "and rivers in the desert, to give drink to my people, my chosen."

Now this descriptive appellation, a chosen generation, originally given to the people of Israel, belongs to the people of God, under the new economy, in a far higher sense, with a much greater depth of meaning: "They that are Christ's are Abraham's seed, and heirs according to the

[1] Psal. cv. 4, 5, 6.   Deut. xiv. 1.   Exod. iv. 22.   Hos. xi. 1.
[2] Deut. iv. 37; vii. 6; x. 15.   Isa. xliii. 20.

promises." Though originally aliens from the commonwealth of Israel, they have been brought near, and, having
believed, "they are blessed with believing Abraham." They
all are, like him, justified freely by God's grace. They all,
like him, have Jehovah for their God, according to the
promise, "I will be a God to thee, and to thy seed after
thee." They all, like him, have "the inheritance of the
world" secured to them; a holier, happier, securer possession than Canaan, is their common property; "the inheritance incorruptible, undefiled, and that fadeth not away,
laid up in heaven for them, and to which they are kept by
the power of God, through faith, unto the salvation ready to
be revealed in the last time."[1]

But the appellation, generation or race, leads us to think
of them, not only as the spiritual family of Abraham, but as
the spiritual family of God. They are "all the children of
God through faith in Christ Jesus." They are the family
of God in a far higher sense than ancient Israel: "For to
as many as receive Christ, to them gives he the privilege[2] of
being the sons of God; and they are born, not of blood, nor
of the will of the flesh, nor of the will of man, but of God."
"They are born, not of corruptible seed, but of incorruptible,
even of the word of the Lord, which liveth and abideth for
ever." "Of his own will begat he them by the word of
truth, that they might be a kind of first-fruits among his
creatures." They are brought into the relation, formed to the
character, of "sons and daughters of the Lord God Almighty." "To them pertains the adoption," in a far more
exalted sense than it ever belonged to Israel after the flesh:
"God hath sent forth his Son, made of a woman, made
under the law, to redeem them who were under the law,
that we" all believers "might receive the adoption of sons;"
and, because they are sons, he sends the Spirit of his Son into
their hearts, the spirit not of bondage, but of adoption,
teaching them to cry Abba, Father. And "since they are

---

[1] Gal. iii. 29, 9. Eph. ii. 12, 13. 1 Cor. iii. 23. Rom. iv. 13. 1 Pet. i. 4, 6.
[2] Εξουσια.

now sons, they are heirs; heirs of God, and joint heirs with Christ Jesus." What the crowning dignity and happiness included in this sonship is, we cannot tell, we cannot adequately conceive. Well might the Apostle say of this race, this generation, "Behold what manner of love the Father hath bestowed on us, that we should be called the sons of God! Beloved, now are we the sons of God; and it doth not yet appear what we shall be: but we know that, when he shall appear, we shall be like him; for we shall see him as he is."[1]

This view of the state of Christians as a race, brings before our minds two ideas, disconnexion from the rest of mankind, and intimate union among themselves. "Israel, as a people, dwelt alone, and was not numbered with the nations."[2] Christians "come out from the world, and are separate." They are in the world, not of it. They have "saved themselves from the untoward generation," who are of their father, the devil, and do his works.

Israel was not only a separate body from the rest of mankind, but a brotherhood. "Moses, when he would have set at one two Israelites who strove, said, Sirs, ye are brethren; why do ye wrong one to another?" Christians have one Father, one Elder Brother; they have a common faith and hope, common interests and enemies, common duties and dangers, common joys and sorrows, one mind, one heart, one inheritance. These are the leading ideas suggested by Christians being called a race, a generation, or family.[3]

But they are not only addressed as a generation, but as "a chosen generation." The choice here referred to may either be their eternal sovereign election of God, to the enjoyment of eternal life through the mediation of Jesus Christ, or what is the result and manifestation of this, their actual selection from the body of mankind, in what we are accus-

---

[1] Gal. iii. 26. John i. 12, 13. 1 Pet. i. 23. James i. 18. 2 Cor. vi. 18. Gal. iv. 4-7. Rom. viii. 17. 1 John iii. 1, 2.

[2] Numb. xxiii. 9. 1 Cor. vi. 16. Acts ii. 40.

[3] Acts vii. 26. John xx. 17. Heb. ii. 11.

tomed to denominate effectual calling. In both respects they are a chosen generation. There is an important difference between the sense in which Israel after the flesh, and the spiritual Israel have the appellation "chosen generation" given to them, which deserves to be noticed. Israel, as a race or family, was selected from other races and families. It was the race, not the individuals, that was the direct object of choice. In the case of the spiritual Israel, the individuals are elected; and it is the aggregate of the elected individuals that forms "the chosen generation."

With regard to the first kind of election, the Apostle Paul tells us that "God hath chosen them in Christ before the foundation of the world," that he "predestinated them unto the adoption of children by Jesus Christ to himself, according to the good pleasure of his will."[1] With regard to the second kind of election, David speaks of them as "set apart by God for himself;" our Saviour says, "I have chosen you out of the world;" James represents Christians as "a people for his name taken out by God from among the Gentiles;" and our Apostle describes them as "elected, or rather selected, according to the foreknowledge, the pre-ordination of God, by a spiritual consecration, to obedience, the obedience of the truth, the faith of the gospel, and to the sprinkling of the blood of Jesus," the enjoyment of the saving effects of the shedding of his blood in expiating sin, opening up a channel for the Spirit, and securing all the blessings of eternal life, the salvation that is in Christ, with eternal glory.[2]

It seems to be the latter of these elections which is the fruit of the former, to which here, as well as in the passage just quoted, the Apostle refers; for as Leighton justly remarks, "this descriptive appellation, like the others along with which it stands, is plainly designed to describe their present state as different from what it had been," whereas their personal election was, like him who made it, strictly

---

[1] Eph. i. 4-6.
[2] Psal. iv. 3. John xv. 19. Acts. xv. 14. 1 Pet. i. 2.

eternal and unchangeable. No change had taken place, could take place with regard to it.

The privilege involved in being thus a chosen generation is one of inappreciable value; and being enjoyed by Christians entirely in consequence of their connexion with Christ Jesus, its possession is a striking personal demonstration to every one of them of the grace of the Lord. In the enjoyment of this privilege they "have tasted that the Lord is gracious." This will appear, if we attend for a moment to the state of those from among whom they were selected, to the purposes for which they were selected, to him who has selected them, and to the cause in which their selection originated.

The original state of this chosen generation was not better than that of other men. It was a state of ignorance and error, and guilt and depravity, of degradation and wretchedness, of condemnation and death. To use the expressive language of the Apostle : They were "dead in trespasses and in sins; wherein in time past they walked according to the course of this world, according to the prince of the power of the air, the spirit that now worketh in the children of disobedience : among whom they had their conversation in the lusts of the flesh, fulfilling the desires of the flesh and of the mind; and were by nature the children of wrath, even as others : without Christ, aliens from the commonwealth of Israel, strangers to the covenant of promise, without God and without hope in the world."[1] What a blessing to be selected from among these victims of error, these slaves of corruption, these heirs of destruction!

And then how does our sense of the value of the blessing rise, when we think of the purpose for which they have been selected, selected to be "heirs of God, and joint heirs" with his only begotten Son; to be justified, sanctified, glorified, conformed both in holiness and happiness to the image of God's own Son; to be blessed with all heavenly and spiritual

[1] Eph. ii. 1-3, 11, 12.

blessings in Christ Jesus; to possess an inheritance, incorruptible, undefiled, and that fadeth not away, reserved for them in heaven, while they are kept for it by the power of God through faith unto the salvation ready to be revealed in the last time; to be the means of manifesting to the whole intelligent universe of God, how holy, how happy the omnipotent, all-wise, infinitely holy, infinitely benignant Jehovah can make those who are the objects of his peculiar love!

For to judge aright of the value of this privilege we must never forget that it is HE who makes both the election and the selection. The value of choice depends on the qualities of the chooser. It is a disgrace not an honour, an evil not a benefit, to be the object of the choice of the unprincipled and foolish. The value of being the object of the choice of an individual is in proportion to his intellect and moral worth, his wise benignity, and his power to gratify it. What is the value, then, of election by the all-perfect One? There is prodigious emphasis on the word God, in these two sayings of the Apostle: "Knowing, brethren beloved, your election of God;" "Who shall lay any thing to the charge of God's elect?" [1]   Whom he chooses he chooses for ever. He rests in his love. His "purpose, according to election, must stand; and the gifts and the callings which originate in it, are without repentance." [2]

But to raise our ideas still higher, if possible, of the value of this choice or selection, as a proof of the grace of the Lord, let us think once more on the causes in which it originates. It has no cause in the selected ones; the cause is in the selector himself, and that cause is, can be, nothing but grace, sovereign kindness. The cause of God's selection of ancient Israel was not in them but in him: "The Lord did not set his love on you," says Moses, " nor choose you, because ye were more in number than any people; (for ye were the fewest of all people;) but because the Lord loved

---

[1] 1 Thess. i. 4. Rom. viii. 23.   [2] Rom. ix. 11; xi. 29.

you, and because he would keep the oath which he had sworn unto your fathers, hath the Lord brought you with a mighty hand, and redeemed you out of the house of bondmen, from the hand of Pharaoh king of Egypt." What is said of their entrance into Canaan, is equally true of their choice: " Speak not in thy heart, For my righteousness the Lord hath chosen me ; for the wickedness of these nations the Lord hath rejected them, and drove them out. But not for thy righteousness, or the uprightness of thy heart, art thou chosen, and brought in, but that the Lord may perform the word which he spake unto thy fathers, Abraham, Isaac, and Jacob. Understand therefore, that the Lord thy God giveth thee not this good land to possess it for thy righteousness ; for thou art a stiff-necked people." [1]

In like manner, the election of those who form the chosen generation under the new economy, is not owing to any previous good quality in them. They are not selected for their worldly wisdom, power, or dignity: "Ye see your calling, brethren, how that not many wise men after the flesh, not many mighty, not many noble, are called: but God hath chosen the foolish things of this world to confound the wise; and God hath chosen the weak things of this world to confound the mighty; and base things of the world, and things which are despised, hath God chosen, yea, and things which are not, to bring to nought things that are: that no flesh should glory in his presence. But that, according as it is written, He that glorieth, let him glory in the Lord. For it is written, I will destroy the wisdom of the wise, and will bring to nothing the understanding of the prudent. Where is the wise ? where is the scribe ? where is the disputer of this world ? hath not God made foolish the wisdom of this world ?" [2]

They are not selected for their previous moral worth: " Know ye not that the unrighteous shall not inherit the kingdom of God? Be not deceived; neither fornicators, nor

---

[1] Deut. vii. 7; ix. 4-6.   [2] 1 Cor. i. 26-31, 19.

nor idolaters, adulterers, nor thieves, no: covetous, nor drunkards, nor revilers, nor extortioners, shall inherit the kingdom of God; yet such were some of you,"—now the "sanctified of Christ Jesus, called to be saints." And even in the case of those who were not remarkable for depravity and guilt, the cause of their being selected cannot be found in their moral worth. In man, in every man born merely of the flesh, "dwelleth no good thing." The only account why any of the human family are selected, and the only account why one rather than another is selected, is, "Even so, Father; for so it seemed good in thy sight." "He has mercy because he wills to have mercy, he has compassion because he wills to have compassion."[1] The cause of his own selection appears to every one of the chosen generation "a mystery hid in God;" and, when he thinks of it, his heart overflows equally with gratitude and amazement, "What am I, and what is the house of my father, that I should be brought hitherto? Is this the manner of man, O Lord?"

> " Why was I made to hear thy voice,
>   And enter while there's room;
> While thousands make a wretched choice,
>   And rather starve than come?
> 'Twas the same grace that spread the feast,
>   That sweetly forc'd me in;
> Else I had still refus'd to taste,
>   And perish'd in my sin."[2]

So rich is the display of the grace of the Lord to those who, out of many a kindred, and people, and tongue, and nation, have been selected to form the chosen generation, of which Israel's race was the type and emblem.

(4.) *Christians are a " royal priesthood."*

Let us now turn our attention to the next descriptive appellation given to Christians: "Ye are a royal priesthood." In the preceding part of this paragraph, Christians are represented as " a holy priesthood, to offer up spiritual sacrifices

---

[1] 1 Cor. vi. 9-11.   Matt. xi. 26.   Rom. ix. 15.   [2] Watts.

acceptable to God by Jesus Christ;" that is, in other words, consecrated to, qualified for, engaged in, the spiritual and acceptable service of God, as God in Christ reconciling the world to himself, in the discharge of all religious and moral duties. Here they are represented as "a royal priesthood."

These words admit of, and have received, various interpretations. By many they have been considered as equivalent to the declarations in the Apocalypse, that Jesus Christ makes his people "kings and priests unto God, even his Father." " The glory which thou hast given me, I have given them whom thou hast given me," says our Lord, in that wonderful prayer recorded in the 17th chapter of the gospel by John. The glory the Father gave him was, that he should be the great Priest and King of his ransomed people; "a priest upon his throne," according to the ancient oracles: " I have set my King upon my holy hill of Zion." " The Lord hath sworn, and will not repent, Thou art a priest for ever after the order of Melchizedec."[1] Of these glories, strictly speaking, no created being can share. But so far as the thing is possible, he makes his people possessors of priestly and regal honours. We have already seen how he makes them priests; and he makes them kings in giving them even now a noble superiority to things seen and temporal, in enabling them to trample under foot those spiritual enemies, the powers of darkness, and the lusts of their own hearts, which once reigned over them. He will at a future period, in a manner of which we can form only an indistinct conception, the obscurity of unfulfilled prediction resting on it, enable his saints to "take the kingdom," and "reign on the earth."[2] In the great day of final retribution, they, along with him, shall "judge angels;" and to them all, as overcomers, made more than conquerors through him that loved them, will it be given in that day to "sit with him on his throne, even as he also having overcome, sat down with his Father on his throne."[3]

---

[1] Rev. i. 6; v. 10. John xvii. 22. Zech. vi. 13. Psal. ii. 6; cx. 4.
[2] Dan. vii. 18. Rev. v. 10.   [3] 1 Cor. vi. 3. Rev. iii. 21.

By others the expression has been considered as indicating the exalted nature of the priesthood to which they are raised, or the noble and dignified temper in which they discharge its functions. Their priesthood is not a *plebeian*, but a *royal* priesthood, as far exalted in dignity above the Levitical priesthood as royalty is above the level of ordinary life; and they perform their priestly functions not in the servile spirit of bondage, but in the noble kingly spirit of the adopted sons of the great King, to whom they minister, " the spirit of glory," as the Apostle calls it. Their mien and deportment are " like the children of a king," doing the will of their royal father. Freed from all degrading submission to human authority, they are sovereign in spiritual things; because, as kings, they own in them no authority but that to which kings are subject, the authority of " the King of kings, and Lord of lords." Viewed in these lights, the expression suggests true and important thoughts, thoughts well fitted to elevate and stimulate the Christian mind.

But I cannot help thinking, that as the phrase is certainly borrowed from a passage in the Old Testament Scripture, that the first thing to be done to ascertain its meaning, is to refer to that passage. It is to be found in the book of Exodus, " And ye shall be to me a kingdom of priests, and a holy nation."[1] The words are quoted from the translation in common use when the Apostle wrote, of which our version is a literal rendering, but we cannot doubt he means to express the meaning of the inspired text.

The meaning of the words " ye are a kingdom," as addressed to the Israelites, is by no means obscure. The word kingdom plainly signifies, not the territory, but the subjects. You are not a confused mass, a fortuitous assemblage— you are an organized political body; and you are not a republic, a self-governing body—you are a kingdom, the subjects of a sovereign; and you are a kingdom of priests—you

---

[1] Exod. xix. 6.

have no human supreme magistrate; Jehovah, the object
of your worship, is your King, so that the discharge of all
your civil duties has a religious character, all being done
to God.

Such is plainly the meaning of the language in its original application. Now what is its meaning, as applied by
the Apostle to Christians as a body? " To you who believe
there is honour." All the honours of the ancient people of
God are yours, and yours in a far higher sense than ever
they were theirs. They were a chosen generation, so are you.
They were a kingdom of priests, and so are you. You are
"a kingdom;" you form a regular social body. Christians are
not a collection of isolated individuals; they are " the body
of Christ, and members in particular." They are " one
body in Christ, and every one members one of another."[1]
And they are not a republic, they are not a self-governing
body; they are " a kingdom," they are the subjects of a sovereign. They have *one* King, Jesus. They should " call no
man master on earth," for they have no master on earth ;
" their Master is in heaven."[2] In every thing connected
with religion, they must be regulated by his will; they
must believe no doctrine but what he has revealed; observe
no ordinances but what he has appointed; and they must
believe every doctrine he has revealed, and observe every
ordinance he has appointed, and believe the doctrine because
he has revealed it, and observe the ordinance because he
has appointed it. For them to follow on these points the
guidance of their own reason or caprice, is to usurp their
Sovereign's place. For them to follow on these points the
guidance of other men, is to exalt them into his throne. So
far as men are concerned, they have a right to think and act
for themselves in religion, but, so far as their rightful Sovereign is concerned, they have no such right. They are to
think as he directs them, they are to do as he bids them.
This would be a hard arrangement if their King were a

---

[1] 1 Cor. xii. 27. Eph. iv. 12.   [2] Matt. xxiii. 8.

fallible creature, though the best of men, the wisest of angels; but instead of there being hardship or degradation in the case, this arrangement is full of honour and blessedness. Their Sovereign is the infinitely wise, righteous, holy Jehovah.

They are a kingdom, but they are " a kingdom of priests." They belong to, complexly taken they form, the kingdom that is not of this world. They belong to a spiritual monarchy, at the head of which is Jehovah, in the person of the only begotten Son. They are his subjects; and, being his subjects, all their duties are religious duties, all exercises of the priestly function. " Whatsoever they do," in the way of duty, they are required to " do it as to the Lord." " They serve the Lord Christ." " Whatsoever they do, whether in word or deed, they do all in the name of the Lord Jesus, giving thanks to God the Father by him." And " whether they eat, or drink, or whatsoever they do, they do all to his glory." [1]

Who can contemplate such holy dignities without a disposition to felicitate their possessors? " Holy brethren, partakers of the heavenly calling," allow me to congratulate you on the dignity and blessedness of belonging to a society so illustrious as this chosen family, this priestly kingdom; for if you really are what your profession declares you to be, you do belong to it. " Happy are ye, O people saved by the Lord! who is like unto you?" " The lines have fallen to you in pleasant places, and ye have a goodly heritage." " Children of Abraham." " Children of God." Brethren of him who is " the first-born among many brethren." " Sons and daughters of the Lord God Almighty." " Heirs of God." " Joint heirs with Christ." " Priests of the Lord." " Ministers of your God." Ever dwelling in his sanctuary, ever engaged in his service, gratefully acknowledge that grace of the Lord to which you are indebted for all this honour, security, and happiness. It is all the

---

[1] Col. iii. 23, 24. 1 Cor. x. 31. Col. iii. 17.

gift of rich sovereign mercy. Not to you, not to you, but to him is due all the glory.

I trust you are saying in your hearts, "Who is a God like unto our God," "rich in mercy," "mighty to save?" "There is none like the God of Jeshurun." "What shall we render to the Lord for all his benefits?"[1] The best way of showing your gratitude is, by acting in a manner corresponding to the high and holy dignity to which you are raised. Conduct yourselves like members of the chosen family, denizens of the priestly kingdom. Be affectionate children; give your Father the veneration, the esteem, the love, the confidence, he so well deserves. Be obedient children. "Submit to the Father of spirits." Give due honour to Him, your elder brother, who has been appointed "as a son over the whole family;" and remember, that it is the Father's will, "that all should honour the Son as they honour himself." Seek to know and do all his will. "Observe all things whatsoever he has commanded you," and "walk in all his ordinances and commandments blameless." Cherish an enlightened, warm, influential affection for all the members of the chosen generation. "Love as brethren," and "walk in love," even as our Father and elder Brother have loved us. Be jealous of the honour of the family, be active in promoting the interests of the family, seek to be instrumental in increasing the number of the family. Are you a chosen generation, a selected race? See that you "make your calling and election sure, by adding to your faith virtue; and to virtue, knowledge; and to knowledge, temperance; and to temperance, patience; and to patience, godliness; and to godliness, brotherly-kindness; and to brotherly-kindness, charity."[2] Remember the great object for which you were chosen: both elected and selected, that ye might be conformed to the image of God's Son; that ye should be holy, and without blame before God in love; that

---

[1] Micah vii. 18.   Eph. ii. 4.   Isa. lxiii. 1.   Deut. xxxiii. 26.
[2] John v. 23.   Matt. xxviii. 20.   Eph. v. 2.   2 Pet. i. 5-7.

ye should be zealous of good works; and, in one word, "as he whom we call Father is holy, so be ye holy in all manner of conversation; for it is written, Be ye holy for I am holy." And remember, that ye are not only children of your Father in heaven, but that ye are subjects of your Sovereign in heaven; and as Israel, "rejoice in him who made you" a kingdom of priests; as "children of Zion, be joyful in your king." "Remember that he is your Lord, and worship him." You are not to be regulated, either as to faith or practice, by your own will, or by the reason or will of other men, but by his mind as made known in his word. Seek entire subjugation of mind and will to him. Have no mind but his mind, no will but his will.[1]

And beware of invading his prerogative, in trampling on one another's rights. It is God alone who has a right to dictate to his own subjects. Let us remember, that "for this cause Christ both died, and rose, and revived, that he should be the Lord of the dead and of the living," of his own people, in life and in death. Beware of attempting to lord it over one another's consciences. "Why, then, dost thou judge thy brother, or why dost thou set at nought thy brother; for we shall all stand before the judgment seat of God," "the great God our Saviour, Jesus Christ?" "For it is written, As I live, saith the Lord, every knee shall bow to me, and every tongue shall confess to God. So then every one of us shall give account of *himself*, not of his brother, to God."

Finally, never forget the sacred character of your relation as subjects, that ye are sacerdotal subjects, ministering to a Divine Sovereign. Always think, and feel, and act, as in the holy place, in the immediate presence of "the Holy, Holy, Holy One;" let your whole lives be an act of worship, as well as an act of allegiance: "offer the sacrifice of praise to God continually, that is, the fruit of your lips, giving thanks to his name; and to do good, and to commu-

---

[1] Psal. cxlix. 2; xlv. 11.

nicate, forget not, for with such sacrifices God is well
pleased." [1]

(5.) *Christians are a " holy nation."*

The next descriptive appellation of Christians, which our
text brings before us for consideration is, "A holy nation."
This, like those which precede it, is borrowed from the language of the Old Testament in reference to the ancient people
of God: "Ye shall be to me a holy nation," said Jehovah to
Israel, by Moses, at Sinai, immediately before giving the law.
"Thou art a holy people unto the Lord thy God," said Moses
to his countrymen, when just about to cross the Jordan.
And in the promulgation of the various laws given to
them, we often meet with these words: "Ye shall be holy,
or be ye holy, for I am holy." [1] Israel was "a nation," a large
body of men, residing in the same neighbourhood, subject
to the same government, regulated by the same laws; distinguished by the same customs, having common rights, interests,
and enemies. Previously to the giving of the law, Israel was
"a generation," a race, a family, a chosen generation; but it
was at Sinai that they became a "kingdom, a nation; a kingdom of priests, a holy nation." Then began to be fulfilled the
promises made to Abrahâm, "I am God Almighty: be
fruitful and multiply: a nation, and a company of nations,
shall be of thee." [2] Israel was "a holy nation." There can
be no reasonable doubt, that by far the greater part of those
individuals who were really morally holy in the world, at
that time belonged to this nation; but when, as a nation,
they are called "holy," the meaning obviously is, separated
from the nations who were devoted to idolatry, and consecrated to the service of Jehovah, the only living and true
God. Such is the import of the expression, "a holy nation,"
as applied to ancient Israel.

We are now prepared to answer the more important and
interesting question, What are the truths respecting the

---

[1] Exod. xix. 6. Deut. vii. 6. Lev. xix. 2; xx. 7, &c. &c.
[2] Gen. xii. 2.

situation and character of Christians, which the appellation, as addressed to them, is intended to suggest? Like the denomination, generation or race, kingdom and people, it indicates that they are, properly speaking, not a number of unconnected individuals, but a society; not disjointed members, but a "body fitly joined and compacted by that which every joint supplieth." They do not indeed reside all in the same geographical district. Even those of them who are more immediately addressed in the text, were "strangers," scattered over a wide region, residing in the midst of various nations. At that time, members of the society, the spiritual nation, were to be found throughout every part of the Roman empire, and even beyond its bounds, "in every nation under heaven;" and since that time, "the holy nation" has still more fully realised the description given of it, as "a people redeemed from among men, out of every kindred, and tongue, and people, and nation."[1]

Yet, in a sense suitable to the spiritual nature of the society, they all dwell together: they are all "a people near to Jehovah," and therefore near to one another. They all dwell in the spiritual Canaan; in the "Jerusalem, which is the mother of them all." They all "dwell in the secret place of the Most High, and abide under the shadow of the Almighty." The whole of the tribes of the spiritual Israel encamp around "the ark of testimony," "the true tabernacle, which God pitched, and not man." The ordinary limitations of time and place do not indeed affect this society. This nation is identical with the chosen generation; the family in heaven, and on earth, called by one name. This accounts for their being called a nation, which always suggests the idea of great numbers. A family may be few, but a nation must be numerous. He who joins the society here referred to, obtains a citizenship more honourable, and connecting him with a wider field of association, than the citizenship of ancient Rome in all its glory; he joins a com-

[1] Rev. v. 9.

monwealth, of which the commonwealth of Israel, even in
its most flourishing state, was but an imperfect figure. He
"sits down with Abraham, and Isaac, and Jacob, in the
kingdom of their Father." He joins "the church of the
living God;" a society which, even as now existing on
earth, is "a multitude," which could not easily be numbered;
and he "comes also to the general assembly and church of
the first-born, whose names are written in heaven; an
innumerable company of angels, and of the spirits of just
men made perfect."[1]

But a nation is not merely a numerous body of men. It
is a numerous body of men, subject to the same government,
regulated by the same laws; a government and laws which
distinguish it from other nations. In this sense, the appellation is strikingly descriptive of true Christians. The
whole race of men, with the exception of true Christians, are
the subjects of " the god of this world," the Prince of darkness. They " lie under the" dominion of that " wicked
one ;" they " serve divers lusts and pleasures ;" they "yield
themselves the servants of sin; and they yield their members," the various faculties and capacities of their nature,
" to sin, as the instruments of unrighteousness."[2] Christians
have been " turned" from the service of the God of this
world, " to the service of the living and true God," " the
God and Father of our Lord Jesus Christ." To his sove-
reignty, as administered by his Son, to whom he has given
all power in heaven and earth, they have submitted their
minds, their hearts, their consciences, their conduct. " Jehovah is their Judge; Jehovah is their Lawgiver; Jehovah
is their King." " They serve the Lord Christ;" subject to
his authority, they are regulated by his law. Other men
regulate themselves by various principles, to which they
give the authority of law; the law of interest; the law of
custom ; the law of honour; the law of caprice. Christians

[1] Psal. cxlviii. 14. Gal. iv. 26. Psal. xci. 1. Eph. iii. 15. Matt. viii. 11.
Heb. xii. 22, 23.
[2] 1 John v. 19. Rom. vi. 13.

regulate themselves by the law of God. The Bible is their statute book. They are cheerfully subject to all lawful ordinances of man; but it is "for the Lord's sake;" because the Lord commands them to be so. But when the law of man is opposed to the law of God, the principle upon which they act is, "We must obey God rather than man." They are persuaded of the principle, and act on it, "No man can serve two masters; we cannot serve God and mammon." The description which Haman gave of the Jews, slightly altered, is very applicable to "the true circumcision:" They are "a people scattered abroad, and dispersed among the nations, and their laws are diverse from all people; neither keep they the laws" of man, when these are opposed to the law of their Sovereign in heaven.[1]

Christians, also, are with propriety termed "a nation;" for they are distinguished by the same customs; and their customs are different from, and opposed to, the customs which generally prevail among men. They all seek often to be alone; they all are given to prayer; they all "lay up treasures in heaven;" they all "deny themselves;" they all look not only not chiefly at their own things, but at the things of Christ, and of others. They all forgive, instead of avenging injuries.[2] These are but a specimen of their peculiar customs. Their whole mode of thinking, feeling, speaking, and acting, is decidedly different from that of other men. They are in the world, but not of it.

Further, Christians, like a nation, have common and peculiar immunities and privileges. They are all made free by the Son; made "free indeed;" "free with the liberty of the children of God;" they are all "blessed with heavenly and spiritual blessings;" all "rich in faith, and heirs of the kingdom;" all secured of the guidance of the good Spirit, and the guardianship of angels.[3] By these, and a variety of other privileges, which belong to none but themselves, they are distinguished from all other bodies of men.

[1] Matt. vi. 24. Est. iii. 8. [2] Matt. v. 20. Phil. ii. 4.
[3] John viii. 36. Eph. i. 3. James ii. 5.

Like a nation, Christians have a common cause, the cause of their common Lord; common interests, the interests of truth, and holiness, and peace, of God's glory, and man's salvation. They are engaged in a war with common enemies, ignorance, error, superstition, sin in all its forms, and the powerful being of whom all these are the works. They "wrestle not with flesh and blood, but with principalities and powers; with the rulers of the darkness of this world; with spiritual wickednesses in high places." And they carry on the war in the same way. "The weapons of their warfare are not carnal, but mighty, through God," for the accomplishment of their purpose.[1]

But Christians are not only a nation—they are " a holy nation." The term holy, or sacred, properly signifies separated from other persons or things, and dedicated to a sacred purpose. The Babylonian armies are termed by Isaiah God's " sanctified or holy ones,"[2] because selected by God as the instruments of his righteous judgment against Israel. The Sabbath is called holy, because set apart from secular to religious purposes; the vessels of the Tabernacle and Temple are called holy for a similar reason; and the Israelites are very often represented as holy, because separated from the rest of mankind to be the depositories of religious truth and worship, " till the seed should come, in reference to whom the promises were made."[3]

When the word is applied to Christians either as individuals or as a body, it is employed in the same general sense, but with a higher reference. The Christian church, though figuratively a nation, has nothing secular in its constitution or object. It is completely separated, completely distinct, from all worldly societies. It is not political, it is not commercial, it is not philosophical; it is religious. If it is a kingdom, it is " a kingdom not of this world;"[4] if it is a nation, it is " a holy" sacred " nation." And its genuine

---

[1] Eph. vi. 12.   2 Cor. x. 4.   [2] Isa. xiii. 3.
[3] Exod. xvi. 23; xxv. 2.   Deut. vii. 6.   Dan. viii. 24.   Lev. viii. 9; xvi. 4. 33.
[4] John xviii. 36.

members are all holy, taken out from among the world lying under the wicked one; dedicated to the service of God and his Son, by the sprinkling of the blood of atonement, by the washing of the water of regeneration, and by their own inward consent and outward profession. They are all sanctified ones; " chosen in Christ before the foundation of the world, that they might be holy, and without blame before God in love." In consequence of the Saviour sanctifying himself, setting apart himself to save them, they are set apart, sanctified by the truth to serve him: for " Christ loved the church, and gave himself for it; that he might sanctify and cleanse it with the washing of water by the word; that he might present it to God a glorious church, not having spot, or wrinkle, or any such thing; but that it should be holy, and without blemish." " That he might sanctify the people;" that he might constitute the chosen ones a holy nation " by his own blood, he suffered without the gate." He went out of " the Jerusalem" that then was the type of all that is corrupt both in secular and ecclesiastical association, and his saved people are to " go forth to him without the camp, bearing his reproach," devoted to God as he was devoted to God; determined to do and suffer the will of God as he did, apart from the world lying in wickedness.[1]

They are a people *entirely* devoted or sacred; their faculties, their property, their time, their opportunities, their bodies, their spirits, are all HIS, and they cannot devote them to purposes different from his without being guilty of desecration and sacrilege. It is to this state of things that the prophet Isaiah looks forward when he says, " Go through, go through the gates; prepare ye the way of the people; cast up, cast up the highway; gather out the stones; lift up a standard for the people. Behold, the Lord hath proclaimed unto the end of the world, Say ye to the daughter of Zion, Behold, thy salvation cometh;

---

[1] Eph. v. 25-27. Heb. xiii. 12, 13.

behold, his reward is with him, and his work before him. And they shall call them, The holy people, The redeemed of the Lord : and thou shalt be called, Sought out, A city not forsaken ;" and Zechariah, when he says, " In that day shall there be on the bells of the horses, HOLINESS UNTO THE LORD ; and the pots in the Lord's house shall be like the bowls before the altar. Yea, every pot in Jerusalem and in Judah shall be holiness unto the Lord of hosts ; and all they that sacrifice shall come and take of them, and seethe therein : and in that day there shall be no more the Canaanite in the house of the Lord of hosts." Every day is, or ought to be, a Sabbath-day ; every meal a sacrament; for whether they eat or drink, or whatsoever they do, they should do all to the glory of God ; " and whatsoever they do in word or in deed, they should do it in the name of the Lord Jesus, giving thanks to God, even the Father, by him." Among them " no man liveth to himself, and no man dieth to himself; but whether he lives, he lives to the Lord ; whether he dies, he dies to the Lord. In life and in death he is the Lord's."[1]

I think it not improbable that the Apostle had a particular object in giving Christians, as a body, the designation, " a holy *nation*," rather than the more ordinary phrase in the Old Testament, " a holy *people*."[2] It is not without a purpose that he quotes Exodus xix. 6, rather than Isaiah lxii. 11. The very name nations,[3] or Gentiles, was hateful to the Jews. They were " the people ;"[4] all the rest of the world were the nations : the people were holy and beloved ; the nations profane and abominable in the sight of God. But under the new economy, the chosen name of the people of God is " nation," there being now no distinction between Jew and Gentile, but all are one in Christ. As the Apostle Paul says, " There is neither Jew nor Greek, there is neither bond nor free, there is neither male nor female ;" but

---

[1] Isa. lxii. 10-12.   Zech. xiv. 20, 21.   Col. iii. 17.   Rom. xiv. 7, 8.
[2] Εθνος rather than λαος.   [3] ‫גוי‬.   [4] ‫העם‬.

all " believers are one" nation " in Christ Jesus." And " if ye be Christ's, then are ye Abraham's seed, and heirs according to the promises." The holy nation is " God's workmanship, created in Christ Jesus unto good works, which God had before ordained that we should walk in them." " Wherefore remember, that ye being in time past Gentiles in the flesh, who are called Uncircumcision by that which is called the Circumcision in the flesh made by hands ; that at that time ye were without Christ, being aliens from the commonwealth of Israel, and strangers from the covenants of promise, having no hope, and without God in the world : but now, in Christ Jesus, ye who sometimes were far off are made nigh by the blood of Christ. For he is our peace, who hath made both one, and hath broken down the middle wall of partition between us ; having abolished in his flesh the enmity, even the law of commandments contained in ordinances ; for to make in himself of twain one new man, so making peace ; and that he might reconcile both unto God in one body by the cross, having slain the enmity thereby ; and came and preached peace to you which were afar off, and to them that were nigh. For through him we both have access by one Spirit unto the Father. Now therefore ye are no more strangers and foreigners, but fellow-citizens with the saints, and of the household of God ;"—" A holy nation."[1]

(6.) *Christians are " a peculiar people."*

The next appellation that calls for our consideration is, " a peculiar people." To a mere English reader, these words convey the idea, a perfectly just one, that they are a people, a collection of men, who have many peculiarities about them, many things which distinguish them from other men, and other bodies of men ; they are peculiar in their origin, their principles, their dispositions, their habits and customs ; their hopes, their fears, their pursuits, their privi-

<hr />

[1] Gal. iii. 28, 29. Eph. ii. 10-19.

leges. In this case the designation would include all that is expressed in all the other designations, and perhaps something more.

But the truth is, the English expression conveys very imperfectly the meaning of the original term. It is literally " a people for a purchased possession," or for a treasure; [1] for the word employed is used in both senses: in the first, in the Epistle to the Ephesians, " Until the redemption of the purchased possession;" [2] in the second, in the passage of the book of Exodus, from which this is quoted, " Ye shall be a peculiar treasure to me." [3] In Malachi it is rendered "jewels," and on the margin, " special treasure." [4] The significancy here does not lie chiefly, if at all, in the word people, which does not, like generation or race, kingdom and nation, suggest any important idea; though people does seem to be used as distinctive of a respectable assembly, in opposition to an illiterate and vulgar rabble. " No doubt ye are the *people*." [5] It lies in what is said about this people. They are a people " for a purchased possession," for a special treasure. The sentiments which the appellation seems intended to convey are these two : That they are the subjects of the divine peculiar property, and the objects of the divine peculiar regard.

They are God's " purchased possession," his " special treasure." Like the preceding appellation, this was originally employed as descriptive of the Israelitish people. " Ye shall be a peculiar treasure to me above all people; for all the earth is mine." " The Lord thy God hath chosen thee to be a special people to himself, above all people that are on the face of the earth." " The Lord hath avouched thee to be his peculiar people, as he hath promised to thee." [6] The whole universe is God's inalienable property. " The earth is the Lord's, and the fulness thereof; the world, and they that dwell in it." [7] All the nations were God's pro-

---

[1] Λαος εις περιποιησιν.   [2] Eph. i. 14.   [3] Exod. xix. 5.   [4] Mal. iii. 16.
[5] Job xii. 2.   [6] Exod. xix. 5.   Deut. vii. 6; xiv. 2; xxvi. 18.
[7] Psal. xxiv. 1.

perty; but, so far as the thing was possible, they had alienated themselves as divine property. They had given themselves up into the hands of God's enemy, to be used by him as his property. But Jehovah, while allowing the other nations to remain in the hands of him to whom they had sold themselves, rescued Israel out of the hands of Pharaoh, and out of the hand of him of whom Pharaoh was but a type and instrument, and he became, as it were, doubly his property, and he treated them as an object of "peculiar favour." "When the most High divided to the nations their inheritance, when he separated the sons of Adam, he set the bounds of the people according to the number of the children of Israel: for the Lord's *portion* was his people; Israel was the lot of his inheritance. He found him in a desert land, and in the waste howling wilderness; he led him about, he instructed him, he kept him as the apple of his eye. As an eagle stirreth up her nest, fluttereth over her young, spreadeth abroad her wings, taketh them, beareth them on her wings; so the Lord alone did lead him, and there was no strange god with him. He made him to ride on the high places of the earth, that he might eat the increase of the fields; and he made him to suck honey out of the rock, and oil of the flinty rock; butter of kine, and milk of sheep, with fat of lambs, and rams of the breed of Bashan, and goats, with the fat of kidneys of wheat: and thou didst drink the pure blood of the grape." "He showed his word to Jacob, his statutes and his judgments to Israel." "In Judah was he known; his name was great in Israel. In Salem also was his tabernacle, and his dwelling-place in Zion." And "many times did he deliver them." "He gave Egypt for their ransom, Ethiopia and Seba for them." "He suffered no man to do them wrong with impunity; he reproved kings for their sake." "What nation was there so great, who had Jehovah so nigh to them, as the Lord their God was in all things that they called on him for?" "What nation was there so great, that had statutes and judgments so righteous as all the law, which he set before them?"[1] Thus was ancient Israel, a people for a purchased possession, for a special treasure to Jehovah, the subjects of his peculiar property, the objects of his peculiar regard.

But these glorious appellations are applicable in a far higher sense to the spiritual Israel. They are God's peculiar property. They are his in a sense different from, higher than, that in which they originally and all other human beings were his. It is difficult to find in human affairs any thing that so corresponds to the important facts referred to, as to illustrate them; but we shall attempt it. Let us conceive what we know is not possible, that a wealthy man should have righteous property in a great multitude of his fellow men, and let us conceive of him as just and kind in his dealings with them; but they commit crimes which expose them to the vengeance of the law, and they at the same time renounce subjection to him, and become the willing slaves of his worst enemy. Having a great regard for them, he buys them off from the law's vengeance; and he at the same time prevails on them to wish to return to his service; and by superior force obliges his powerful enemy, however reluctantly, to quit his hold of them; and, having got them again back to his own estate, he bestows on them peculiar marks of his kindness. Would not such redeemed criminals, such ransomed slaves, though his property originally, be now doubly his—his purchased possession; and might they not well be called his special treasure? The figure is imperfect, but it may assist your minds in forming distinct and accurate conceptions of the case before us. Christians have been "redeemed by the blood of Christ, as of a lamb without blemish and spot," from guilt, the judicial displeasure of God, and everlasting destruction. They have been "bought with a price." "Redeemed to God by the blood of his Son; delivered from the wrath to come." And they have also

[1] Deut. xxxii. 8-14. Psal. cxlvii. 19; lxxvi. 1, 2; cvi. 43. Isa. xliii. 3. Psal. cv. 14, 15. Deut. iv. 7, 8.

been, " through the redemption that is in Christ Jesus,"
delivered from sin and Satan, and the present evil world ;
" redeemed from all iniquity, that they may be a peculiar
people, zealous of good works." By the effectual working
of the good Spirit through the instrumentality of the word,
they are freed from the degrading bondage of sin, and made
to " walk at liberty, keeping God's commandments ;" feeling,
and delighting to feel, that they are " not their own," but
wholly and for ever his, who has bought them by " a price
all price beyond;" redeemed them by an arm so " full of
power " and of mercy.[1]

And as they are the subjects of his peculiar property, so
are they objects of his peculiar regard. They are his special
treasure, his jewels; he heaps on them tokens of his regard.
They are his vineyard; of which he says, " I the Lord do
keep it. I will water it every moment. I will keep it
night and day." He " blesses them with all heavenly and
spiritual blessings;" so that they may well say, " Who is
a God like unto our God, who pardoneth iniquity, and passeth by the transgression of the remnant of his heritage? he
retaineth not his anger for ever, because he delighteth in
mercy. He will turn again, he will have compassion on us;
he will subdue our iniquities; and he will cast all our sins
into the depths of the sea." " The Lord their God, in the
midst of them, is mighty; he will save, he will rejoice over
them with joy; he will rest in his love; he will joy over them
with singing." " He giveth unto them eternal life : and
they shall never perish, neither shall any pluck them out of
his hand." He gives many distinct proofs, both to others
and to themselves, that they are the objects of his peculiar
regard. " All things are theirs, whether Paul, or Apollos, or
Cephas, or the world, whether in life, or death ; all is theirs ;
for they are Christ's; and Christ is God's." Even in the
present state, he makes it evident that the Lord hath set apart
the godly man for himself, and " in the day that he shall

[1] 1 Cor. vi. 20.   1 Pet. i. 18, 19.   Rev. v. 9.   1 Thess. i. 10.   Tit. ii. 14.

make up his jewels," collect his treasure, he will bestow on
them such " an exceeding and eternal weight of glory," as
shall make all the intelligent universe see and acknowledge
that they are HIS : in a peculiar sense his property, his portion ; those whom he is determined to honour and bless, to
the greatest degree in which created beings can be made possessors of dignity and blessedness.[1]

And all the glory, all the felicity, included in God having
them a people for a purchased possession, a peculiar treasure,
is obtained by connexion with Christ, and is a farther demonstration of his grace to those on whom it is bestowed. In
coming to Christ ye were made such a people, and in this
surely " ye have tasted that the Lord was gracious."

Is it possible to estimate too highly these honours, and
advantages, and delights, to which Christians are, by the
grace of their Lord, raised ?   Is it not obviously and unde-
niably true, that " the things which God laid up for those
who love him," under the new economy, and which he has
made known to us by his Holy Spirit, are what " eye had
not seen, what ear has not heard, and what it had never
entered," it could never have entered, " into the heart of
man to conceive ?"[2]   How glorious is the society they are
connected with, embracing in it all the true excellence in
the universe.   They are, indeed, associates of no ignoble
confraternity, citizens of no mean city ; and how rich, how
varied, how invaluable, are the privileges which, as members of the holy nation, of the peculiar people, they
enjoy !

How strong a motive to gratitude, and obedience, and
submission !   Well does it become every Christian, " gathered from among the heathen," and " made to inherit
the throne of glory," to say with David, " Who am I, and
what is my Father's house, that thou hast brought me
hitherto ?"   " What shall I render to the Lord for all his

---

[1] Isa. xxvii. 2, 3. Eph. i. 3. Micah vii. 18, 19. Zeph. iii. 17. John x. 28.
1 Cor. iii. 21-23. Mal. iii. 17, 18.
[2] 1 Cor. ii. 9, 10.

benefits. Truly, O Lord, I am thy servant, the son of thine handmaid : thou hast loosed my bonds. I will take the cup of salvation. I will call on the name of the Lord. I will pay my vows to the Lord in the presence of all his people." Redeemed by the precious blood of Christ from my vain conversation, I will no longer fashion myself according to my former lusts in my ignorance ; but as he who has called me is holy, I will be holy in all manner of conversation. Bought with a price, I am not my own, and will glorify him who redeemed me, in my body, and in my spirit, which are HIS.[1]

What an abundant source of consolation and support under evil, of every kind, does this view of the Christian's situation afford to him ! Jehovah will take care of his own, of what is committed to him, of what has been redeemed by the blood of his Son, rescued by the power of his Spirit, blessed with the tokens of his peculiar regard. Fear not, Christian, whatever may be the number and amount of thy experienced or anticipated perplexities and trials, and bereavements and sorrows. Listen to his voice, whose thou art, and whom thou servest : " Fear thou not ; for I am with thee : be not dismayed ; for I am thy God : I will strengthen thee ; yea, I will help thee ; yea, I will uphold thee with the right hand of my righteousness. Fear not, for I have redeemed thee ; I have called thee by thy name, thou art mine. When thou passest through the waters, I will be with thee ; and through the rivers, they shall not overflow thee : when thou walkest through the fire, thou shalt not be burned ; neither the flame kindle on thee. For I am Jehovah thy God, the Holy One of Israel, thy Saviour." And when HE thus says, " I will never leave thee, I will never forsake thee ; surely WE may boldly say, The Lord is my helper, and I will not fear what either man or devil can do to me."[2]

---

[1] 2 Sam. vii. 18. Psal. cxvi. 12-14. 1 Cor. vi. 20.
[2] Isa. xli. 10 ; xliii. 2. Heb. xiii. 5, 6.

What a powerful incentive is here offered, to seek " part and lot " in this holy nation, among this peculiar people! All who belong to it were once " aliens from the commonwealth of the spiritual Israel, strangers to the covenant of promise." They were " as sheep going astray; but they have returned to the Shepherd and Bishop of souls." And how were they brought near? By the blood of the cross, by the power of the Spirit, by the faith of the truth. They believed on Christ, they came to him, and thus " they tasted that the Lord is gracious." Does not their happiness proclaim, louder than any language, " O, taste and see that the Lord is good?" The way, though alas an unfrequented one, is an open one. The grace of the Lord is not " a well shut up, a fountain sealed." " Return ye backsliding children; I have redeemed you." " I, even I, am he who blotteth out transgression, for my own sake." " I will heal your backsliding, I will love you freely." Believe the truth as it is in Jesus, come to HIM, and all the blessings of salvation are yours. " He that hath the Son hath life, he that hath not the Son shall never see life." " Eternal life is the gift of God, through Jesus Christ our Lord." It may, it must be yours, if you do not obstinately refuse to receive what is freely given us of God;[1] refuse, neglect to receive it, and you are undone for ever, and must receive what you have earned; " the wages of sin—*death :*"

> " Future death,
> And death still future. Not a hasty stroke,
> Like that which sends us to the dusty grave;
> But unrepealable, enduring death—
> Ages of future misery."[2]

Escape, then, from the city of destruction; break off all connexion with " the sinful nation," " the people of God's curse." " Escape for thy life; look not behind thee, neither stay thou in all the plain : escape to the mountain," to the

[1] 1 Pet. ii. 25.   Jer. iii. 14, 22.   Isa. xliii. 25.   Rom. vi. 23.   1 John v. 12.
[2] Cowper.

city of refuge, the mystical Jerusalem, whose name is Jehovah-Tzidkenu, "the Lord our righteousness." Escape lest thou be consumed; delay is madness, may be ruin: "Now is the accepted time, now is the day of salvation." [1]

The statements now made, have not produced their proper effect if they have not excited in our bosoms an earnest desire, which finds its appropriate utterance in these beautiful words of the Psalmist, "Remember me, O Lord, with the favour which thou bearest unto thy people: O visit me with thy salvation; that I may see the good of thy chosen, the chosen generation; that I may rejoice in the gladness of thy nation, the holy nation; that I may glory with thine inheritance," "the peculiar people, the purchased possession, the special treasure." [2]   That prayer, offered in faith, is sure to be answered; and that prayer offered and answered, we are made up for eternity; "we have all and abound." Our need is supplied according to God's glorious riches. We have "exceedingly abundantly above all that we can ask or think." Our joy is full, full for ever.

(7.)—*Christians are "called to show forth the praises of God."*

The next appellation applied to Christians is, "Called to show forth the praises of him who has called them out of darkness into his marvellous light." To the consideration of this let us now proceed.

The allusion to ancient Israel, which pervades the previous part of the verse, and attention to which we have found of so much use to bring out its meaning, is to be recognised here also. Jehovah called Israel out of Egypt, a state of slavery and degradation, figuratively termed by the Psalmist "a state of darkness and the shadow of death," into a state of liberty and dignity, figuratively described as "the light of the countenance of Jehovah," probably with a

[1] Gen. xix. 17.   Jer. xxxiii. 16.   Isa. xlix. 8.   2 Cor. vi. 2.
[2] Psal. cvi. 4, 5.

reference to that supernatural bright cloud, the emblem of the divine presence, to be to himself a chosen generation, a kingdom of priests, a holy nation, a peculiar people, in order to manifest by them his own infinite excellencies, his power, his wisdom, his righteousness, his benignity, his faithfulness. When God " went to redeem Israel for a people to himself, it was to make to himself a name."[1] When " he brought them up out of the sea," to use the sublime language of Isaiah, " with Moses, the shepherd of his flock, when he put his Holy Spirit within him, and led them by his right hand, dividing the waters before him, it was to make to himself an everlasting, a glorious name."[2] And of Israel, thus called and redeemed by him, he says, " I have created him for my glory, I have formed him ; yea, I have made him." I have caused to cleave to me, says Jehovah by the prophet Jeremiah, " I have caused to cleave to me the whole house of Israel and the whole house of Judah ; that they may be to me for a people, and for a name, and for a praise, and for a glory."[3]

The whole of the great economies of Providence and Redemption form one system of divine manifestation ; a connected series of revelations of the eternal power and godhead; the infinite wisdom, righteousness, and benignity of Him, " of whom, and through whom, and to whom, are all things." The Mosaic economy, the history of the Israelitish people, is a very interesting chapter in this book, in which God manifested his character. All that God did for Israel in making them a nation ; all the privileges he bestowed on them as a nation ; all the deliverances he vouchsafed them, and all the judgments he inflicted on them : all that he did to them, and all that he did by them, was intended for the revelation of his character, for the manifestation of his glory.

---

[1] 2 Sam. vii. 23.

[2] Isa. lxiii. 11-14; xliii. 7. " Respectus habetur ad caput xv. Exodi, in quo describitur canticum laudis quod Israelitæ post eductionem ex Egypto per mare rubrum, in gloriam DEI liberatoris composuerunt."—BEDA.

[3] Jer. xiii. 11.

Israel became to him a chosen generation; a kingdom of priests; a holy nation; a peculiar people; to show forth his praise. His dispensations to Israel manifested his character, not only to them, but to the surrounding nations. He made "his wrath and his power," his wisdom and his mercy, known in the redemption of Israel, and in the destruction of their proud oppressors. "He saved them for his name's sake, that he might make his mighty power to be known, and that men might know that he was Jehovah." And this was not only their design and tendency, it was to some extent their effect. Jethro was not at all singular in the sentiments he avowed in his address to his son-in-law : "Now know I that Jehovah is greater than all gods ; for in the thing wherein they dealt proudly he was above them." [1]

Israel was intended, not merely passively, but also actively, to declare the character, to show forth the praises, of Jehovah. While the nations around them were " worshipping and serving the creature more than the Creator ; having changed the truth of God into a lie, and his glory into an image made like unto corruptible man, and to birds, and to four-footed beasts, and to creeping things," [2] throughout the land of Israel was proclaimed the sublime truth, " Jehovah is our God, Jehovah is one." They were his " witnesses ;" and in the holy oracles, which they preserved most faithfully; in the ordinances of worship, which they maintained; and in the degree in which their characters were moulded by that revelation, and those ordinances, did they shine as the lights of a darkened world, and hold forth to their benighted fellow-men the truth respecting the Supreme Being.

These observations respecting the manner in which ancient Israel, after the flesh, was called by Jehovah out of darkness into light, to be a chosen generation, a kingdom of priests, a holy nation, a peculiar people, in order to show forth his praise, will be found of material use to us in

---

[1] Exod. xviii. 11.   [2] Rom. i. 21-25.

our inquiry into the higher sense, the deeper meaning, in which these statements are applicable to the spiritual Israel.

Taking them as our key, let us now proceed to ask, What is this calling here spoken of? Who is its author? What is its object? And how does such a call from such a being, for such an object, afford illustration of the graciousness of the Lord to those who receive it?

To the first of these questions the answer is short and easy. As the calling of ancient Israel was the divine command and invitation, by Moses, to leave Egypt, and enter on the privileges and duties of God's peculiar people, first in the wilderness, and then in Canaan, a calling made effectual by a series of divine interpositions; so the calling of the spiritual Israel, is the divine call and invitation to enter, through the belief of the truth, on the privileges and duties of his spiritual, peculiar people, first on earth, then in heaven. It is this invitation, rendered effectual by the operation of the good Spirit leading them to comply with it, which the Apostle calls the Christian's " high " and " heavenly," " holy " and " hopeful " " calling, not according to our works, but according to his own purpose and grace, given us in Christ Jesus before the world began;" "a calling into the fellowship of God's Son," whereby we, who were the children of the devil, become, like Him, the children of God; we, who were vile and debased, "without God," "far from God," become, like Him, "kings and priests to God;" we, who were profane and of the world, become in our measure, like Him, the Holy One of God; we, who had denied God's property in us, and who were the fit objects of his judicial displeasure, and moral disapprobation, become, like Him, the subjects of his peculiar property, the objects of his special love. This is the effectual calling, so well described in our Shorter Catechism, as "the work of the Holy Spirit, whereby, convincing us of our sin and misery, enlightening our minds in the knowledge of Christ, and renewing our wills, he doth persuade and enable us to embrace Jesus Christ, as he is offered to us in the gospel," and thus enter on the enjoyment of all the blessings of the "redemption that is in him."[1]

It is equally easy to answer the question, Who is the author of this calling? There is no mistaking who He is, who is described as "He who called Christians out of darkness into his marvellous light." At first sight we might perhaps suppose, that this is a descriptive appellation of our Lord Jesus Christ. But when we look at the passages of Scripture where this calling is mentioned, and they are numerous, we will come to the conclusion that it is God the Father, who, in the whole restorative economy, sustains the majesty of the Divinity. In the new creation, "all things are of God, through Christ Jesus,"[2] by the Spirit. The call to ancient Israel, was the call of Jehovah by Moses. The call to the spiritual Israel, is the call of Jehovah by Jesus, speaking in his word, working in his Spirit. His call alone is effectual. His word is the word that "leaps forth at once into effect; that calls for things that be not, and they are;" the word, that makes men what it calls them to be.

The third question, What is the design of this calling? will require a somewhat more detailed reply. They are called to "show forth the praises of him, who hath called them out of darkness into his marvellous light." The word "praises" is more literally rendered in the margin, as you will observe, "virtues."[3] It is a general name for the excellencies of the Divine Being. His power, and wisdom, and holiness, and benignity, especially as displayed in calling them, and in the privileges, honours, and blessings, to which they are called. The design, then, of calling Christians to the enjoyment of their peculiar privileges, was, that the excellencies of the Divine Author of their calling might be displayed. This is the great ultimate end of God in every thing: the manifestation of his own excellence. "The

[1] Phil. iii. 14. Heb. iii. 1. 2 Tim. i. 9. Eph. i. 18: iv. 4. Short. Cat. Q. 31.
[2] 2 Cor. v. 18.
[3] Αρεταζ.

Lord hath made all things for himself."[1]   To him, as well
as of him, and through him, are all things.   For him, as
well as by him, are all things.[2]

There is no other end so grand, so comprehensive of all
other desirable ends, so worthy of the all-perfect Being, as
this.   "The highest agent cannot work but for the highest
end; so that, as the Apostle speaks, when God would confirm his covenant by an oath, he swears by himself, because
he could swear by no greater; so in all, he must be the end
of his own actions, because there is no greater nor better
end; yea, none by infinite odds, so great or good."[3]   It is
plain, that just in the degree that God manifests his power,
and wisdom, and goodness, must the order and happiness of
the inanimate and sensitive creation be promoted; and just
in the degree in which his moral excellencies are displayed
to rightly constituted, intelligent beings, must their happiness be increased.   The more they know of God, the more
they love God, as known; the more they are conformed to
God, the holier and the happier are they.

Christians, as the called of God, are intended to show
forth the excellencies of God, both passively and actively.
Those wonderful dispensations of power, and righteousness,
and benignity, the incarnation and sacrifice of the divine
Son, and the regenerating and sanctifying influences of the
divine Spirit, are the most remarkable displays which probably ever have been, or ever will be, made to the intelligent universe of the virtues, the powers, the excellencies, of
the divine character.   Every thing else, when compared
with these, may be termed, to use the prophet Habakkuk's
expression, "the hiding" rather than the manifestation of his
excellencies.   If a man wishes to know the true character
of God, let him study it as embodied in these dispensations;
let him look at God in Christ; "the glory of God in the
face of Christ Jesus."[4]   We know that they were intended

---

[1] Prov. xvi. 4.   [2] Rom. xi. 36.   Heb. ii. 10.
[3] Leighton.   [4] 2 Cor. v. 19; iv. 6.

to serve this purpose, not only to men, but to higher orders of intelligent beings. We know that such things took place, " to the intent, that unto the principalities and powers in the heavenly places, might be made known by," through means of, " the church," the called ones, the chosen generation, the kingdom of priests, the holy nation, the peculiar people, not only "the manifold wisdom of God," [1] but the riches of his grace, the exceeding greatness of his power, the unfathomable depth of his knowledge, the immutability of his purpose, the energy of his wrath, the omnipotence of his love.

And we know, too, they answer this purpose. They awaken the holy curiosity of these exalted holy spirits; and, though they feel their highest powers overtasked in the study, " into these things they desire to look." [2]   They discover in Jehovah a depth of excellence, which, though they believed it to exist, they had never seen before exhibited, and they had never distinctly before conceived of.   Forms of moral loveliness present themselves to their minds, more beautiful than any they had ever imagined; they burn with a more intense devotion; they are penetrated with a higher sense of entire confidence in the All-excellent One; the salvation of man thus adding to the happiness of angels.   So glorious is the illustration that is given of the Divine character in these dispensations, that the inspired prophet, when contemplating it, breaks out into those rapturous strains,—" I have blotted out," says Jehovah to the spiritual Israel, " I have blotted out, as a thick cloud, thy transgressions, and, as a cloud, thy sins: return to me; for I have redeemed thee. Sing," exclaims the prophet, " O ye heavens; for the Lord hath done it; shout, ye lower parts of the earth; break forth into singing, ye mountains, O forest, and every tree therein: for the Lord hath redeemed Jacob, and glorified himself in Israel." [3]   And this is true, not only with regard to the grand dispensations in which all the called ones are equally interested; but the individual history of each of them

<hr/>

[1] Eph. iii. 10.   [2] 1 Pet. i. 12.   [3] Isa. xliv. 22, 23.

is a mirror, in which "the ministering spirits who minister to them, as heirs of salvation," see reflected the excellencies of Him who works all for them, in them, and by them.

But the called ones are not merely passive instruments; they are agents in showing forth Jehovah's praise. The manifestation of God made to them in their calling, and the privileges into which it conducts them, produce on their minds just views of the Divine character, and a corresponding mode of thinking and feeling, and speaking and acting, so that they cannot but show forth the praises of Him who has called them. This is the great design of God in giving them the privilege. If they are " predestinated to the adoption of children by Jesus Christ to himself, according to the good pleasure of his will," it is " that they might be to the praise of the glory of his grace."[1] If they are planted by Him as " trees of righteousness," it is " that He might be glorified."[2] If they are " bought with a price," it is that they may " glorify Him with their souls, and with their bodies, which are his."[3] If they are " filled with the fruits of righteousness," it is " to the praise and glory of God."[4] If they " obtain the inheritance," it is " to the praise of His glory." If " the purchased possession" at last is redeemed completely and for ever from all evil, still it is " to the praise of His glory."[5]

How the holy, heavenly temper and conduct of the called ones answer the great purpose of their calling, is very beautifully described by Archbishop Leighton :—" The virtues that are in them tell us of His virtues, as brooks lead us to their springs. When a Christian can quietly repose and trust on God in a matter of very great difficulty, wherein there is no other thing to stay him but God alone: this declares plainer than words that there is strength enough in God that bears him up; that there must be in him that real abundance of goodness and truth that the word speaks

---

[1] Eph. i. 5.   [2] Isa. lxi. 3.   [3] 1 Cor. vi. 20.
[4] Phil. i. 11.   [5] Eph. i. 11-14.

of him. Abraham believed and gave glory to God: this is what every believer can do to declare the truth of God. He can rely, and show that he relies, on it, and thus set to his seal that God is true. Men hear that there is a God who is infinitely holy, but they can neither see him nor his holiness; but when they perceive some lineaments of it in the faces of his children which are in none others, this may convince them that its perfection, which must be somewhere, can be nowhere else but in their heavenly Father. When those that are his peculiar plants bring forth the fruits of holiness, which naturally they yielded not, it testifies a supernatural work of his hand that planted them, and the more fruitful they are, the greater his praise: ' Herein is my Father glorified,' says our Saviour, ' that ye bring forth much fruit.' " [1] Their hymn on earth should be a hymn of praise to him who called them; and we know that in heaven, throughout eternity, they rest not day nor night; but, in a manner suited to their enlarged capacities and exalted station, without interruption " show forth the praises of Him who has called them out of darkness into marvellous light:" " Holy, holy, holy, Lord God Almighty, who wast, and art, and art to come. Thou art worthy, O Lord, to receive glory, and honour, and power : for thou hast created all things, and for thy pleasure they are and were created." [2]

It only remains that we say a word or two on the manifestation of the graciousness of the Lord to Christians, afforded by their being called to show forth the praises of him who called them. To be made capable of, disposed to, and actually to be employed in, showing forth the praises of Jehovah, is the highest dignity and happiness which can be conferred on created intelligent beings. This was the happiness of man in Paradise ; this is the essence of the happiness of the blessed in heaven. " It is," indeed, to refer to the description of man's original state by a master mind,[3] equally applicable to man's restored state,—" It is a most delectable

[1] John xv. 8.   [2] Rev. iv. 8, 11.   [3] Howe.

and pleasant state to be separated to the entertainment of the divine presence, and the manifestation of the divine glory: ' Thou art mine, and for me thou livest. Thee, above all my works, I choose out for myself. Thine employment shall be no laborious, painful drudgery, unless it can be painful to receive the large communications of immense goodness, light, life, and love, that shall of their own accord be perpetually flowing in upon thee, and to express in thy whole character and conduct thy sense of my infinite greatness and goodness!' Surely this is a high privilege; and as, like all the privileges of Christians, it is enjoyed only in Christ Jesus in consequence of believing on him, coming to him, building on him; as it not more certainly comes from God than it comes by Christ; as but for his mediation, this honour, this blessedness, could never have found its way to one of our fallen race; we may well say, that in enjoying it, Christians " taste that the Lord is gracious."

It becomes the called of the Lord to avail themselves of the privileges, and to perform the duties, of their high, and holy, and heavenly calling. By your lips, by your lives, " holy brethren, partakers of the heavenly calling," honour Him who has called you, Him into whose fellowship you have been called. " God's dear Son" did so. Yes, " he glorified his Father on the earth; he finished the work he gave him to do." His most ardent prayer was, " Father, glorify thy Son, that thy Son also may glorify thee." Nothing could shake his determination as to this: " Now is my soul troubled; and what shall I say?" Shall I say, "Father, save me from this hour?" No; "for this cause I came to this hour." I will say, "Father, glorify thy name."[1] And now in heaven he declares his Father's name to his brethren, and in the great congregation he shows forth his praise.[2]

" Let the mind be in you that was in him." " Praise the name of the Lord; for his name alone is excellent: his glory is above the earth and heaven. He exalteth the horn

---

[1] John xvii. 1, 4; xii. 27, 28.   [2] Psal. xxii. 22. Heb. ii. 12.

of his people, the praise of all his saints; even of the children of Israel, a people near to him." " Praise ye the Lord, for he is good; sing praises to his name, for it is pleasant. For the Lord hath chosen Jacob unto himself, and Israel for his peculiar treasure." " Bless the Lord, O house of Israel: bless the Lord, O house of Aaron: bless the Lord, O house of Levi: ye that fear the Lord, bless the Lord." " Praise the Lord, call on his name, declare his doings among the people, make mention that his name is exalted. Sing unto the Lord; for he hath done excellent things: this is known in all the earth. Cry out and shout, O inhabitant of Zion: for great is the Holy One of Israel in the midst of thee." " Publish with the voice of thanksgiving, tell of all his wondrous works." Let every called, redeemed one, adopt the Psalmist's resolution: " I will praise thee, even thy truth, O my God: unto thee will I sing, O thou Holy One of Israel. My lips shall greatly rejoice when I sing unto thee; and my soul, which thou hast redeemed." " I will praise thee, O Lord my God, with all my heart; and I will glorify thy name for evermore. For great is thy mercy towards me; and thou hast delivered my soul from the lowest hell." " I will sing unto the Lord as long as I live; I will sing praise to my God while I have any being. My meditation of him shall be sweet; I will be glad in the Lord."[1] O what a heaven on earth might, would, Christians have, were they acting worthy of their high and holy calling, as a holy priesthood, " offering the sacrifice of praise to God continually, that is the fruits of their lips, giving thanks to his name."

But are all here among " the called, and chosen, and faithful?"[2] Would God it were so. But I more than fear that there are persons here, who, though called, often called, affectionately, earnestly called, have never been effectually called; who are yet without the pale of the chosen race, the king-

[1] Psal. cxlviii. 13, 14; cxxxv. 3, 4, 19, 20.   Isa. xii. 4-6.   Psal. xxvi. 7; lxxi. 22, 23; lxxxvi. 12, 13; civ. 33, 34.
[2] Rev. xvii. 14.

dom of priests, the holy nation, the peculiar people, having no part nor lot in their peculiar privileges. For this class we ought to feel the deepest commiseration, the tenderest pity; and the best way of showing this is to endeavour to make them understand their real position. My dear fellow immortals, there can be no doubt your duty is to show forth the praises of God. That is the first duty of every intelligent creature, and nothing can release you from its obligation. God will be glorified in you whether you will or not. If you will not give him glory, he will make your rebellion and its fearful consequence praise him. How loud is the acclaim which rises among the holy part of God's intelligent creation, " when the smoke of the torment," of the irreclaimably wicked, " ascendeth up for ever and ever!" " Alleluia; and again they cry, Alleluia." " Great and marvellous are thy works, Lord God Almighty; just and true are all thy ways, O King of Saints!" " Righteous is Jehovah, and righteous are his judgments."[1] In your present state you are morally incapable of praising God or glorifying his name. You never will do any thing really glorifying to God, till, casting down the weapons of rebellion against him, you, in the faith of the truth, " kiss the Son," whom he has " set as his King on his holy hill of Zion."[2] Listen to the call, come to Jesus, glorify God by crediting the testimony he has given of a free and full salvation in his Son for the chief of sinners; and then, then, not till then, " tasting that the Lord is gracious," will you find yourselves sweetly constrained to devote yourselves entirely to the honour of Him, whom you will then see and feel to be infinitely excellent, amiable, and kind, the Saviour, your Saviour. You will no longer be able to " live to yourselves," to make self your great object. GOD will appear to be what he is—" all in all;" and this will be your resolution, and your rejoicing, " Whether I live, I live to the Lord; whether I die, I die to the Lord: living and dying I am the Lord's. Whether I eat, or drink,

---

[1] Rev. xix. 3; xv. 3; xix. 2.   [2] Psal. ii. 6, 12.

or whatsoever I do, I will do all to the glory of God. Whatever I do, whether in word or deed, I will do it in the name of the Lord Jesus, giving thanks to God the Father." " My mouth shall speak the praises of the Lord: and let *all flesh* bless his holy name for ever and ever." " Oh that there were in you such a heart to honour God, that it might be well with you for ever."[1] It cannot be well with you otherwise, either in time or eternity.

(8.) *Christians are " called out of darkness into God's marvellous light."*

The next descriptive designation of true Christians which presents itself to our consideration is, "Called out of darkness into God's marvellous light." The language is obviously figurative; and here, as in every similar case, the first thing to be done is to endeavour to obtain a distinct idea of the figure employed. This is obviously necessary in order to our satisfactorily arriving at the thought it is intended to convey. The general meaning of the expression is plain. The appellation describes Christians as brought by divine agency from a very miserable into a very desirable state. But to ascertain the nature of the wretchedness of the one state, and the happiness of the other, it is requisite that we know something as to the darkness to which the one, and the light to which the other, is compared.

It has been supposed by some that the figure here is that which is employed by the Psalmist to describe one class of the deliverances which the redeemed of the Lord are called on to acknowledge as a proof that he is good, that his mercy endureth for ever; deliverance from the darkness of a dungeon, and restoration to the healthful air and the blessed light of heaven.[2] And in this view it would afford a very instructive view of the state of Christians, both before and after their believing on, coming to, building on Christ.

I cannot help thinking, however, that, as in all the other

---

[1] Rom. xiv. 8. 1 Cor. x. 31. Col. iii. 17. Psal. cxlv. 22. Deut. v. 29.
[2] Psal. cvii. 10-14.

descriptive designations of Christians in this beautiful passage, there is a reference to something in the history or situation of the ancient people of God; the figure here, too, is drawn from the same prolific source of illustrations of Christian truth. I apprehend it refers to the remarkable event, their deliverance from Egypt, which led to their becoming the select race, the kingdom of priests, the holy nation, the peculiar people. God " called Israel out of Egypt,"[1] and called them out of Egypt to make them a peculiar people to himself. But how should the call out of Egypt be represented as a call " out of darkness into light," "God's light," "God's marvellous light?" A slight attention to the circumstances of the deliverance from Egypt, will enable us to answer this question.

Egypt was enveloped in midnight darkness, made tenfold more terrible by the last and severest of all its plagues, the death of the first-born of man and beast, when Israel was called by God to leave that scene of his degradation and suffering. On the evening of the tenth day of the month Abib, the Israelites having by divine command made preparations for departure, in each of their families slew a lamb, and sprinkled its blood on the posts and lintels of the doors of their dwellings. They ate the lamb hastily roasted, with their loins girt, their shoes on their feet, and their staves in their hands. At the dark hour of midnight the destroying angel accomplished at one stroke his awful work. " From the first-born of Pharaoh that sat on the throne, unto the first-born of the captive who was in the dungeon," all—all became his victims. Nor was even the brute creation exempted from the general plague. " There was a great cry in Egypt;" for there was not a house, except the blood-sprinkled habitations of Israel, where there was not one dead. It was the voice of Jehovah, though uttered by the mouth of Pharaoh, that proclaimed, amid the darkness and death of that night, " Rise up, and get you forth!"

[1] Hos. xi. 11.

From amidst this fearful darkness, meet emblem of the miseries they had endured, "Jehovah called his people."[1]

And as he "called them out of darkness," so he "called them into his marvellous light." That was a night much to be remembered; for when God called his people from Egypt, "he went before them by night as a pillar of fire, to give them light, to lead them in the way." Thus "he sent darkness, and made it dark. He smote also all the first-born in their land, the chief of their strength. He brought forth his people with silver and gold. Egypt was glad when they departed. He spread a cloud for a covering, and fire to give light in the night."[2] Thus did God call his ancient people "out of darkness into his marvellous light."

Such, we apprehend, is the figure; now for its interpretation. What is the darkness out of which the spiritual Israel is delivered? What the marvellous light, into the midst of which they are brought to dwell? It has often been said that the one is the emblem of the absolute darkness of Heathenism, or the comparative darkness of Judaism, and the other of the pure light of the gospel dispensation. There can be no doubt that the persons directly addressed were delivered out of the former, and were introduced into the latter; but we mistake much, if both the darkness and the light here be not rather subjective than objective, rather that which reigns within than that which prevails without. Like the parallel expression, "Once were ye darkness, but now are ye light in the Lord," the expression in the text refers to the darkness of the unregenerate state, and the light of the renewed mind. It describes what the New Testament represents as so important, "repentance towards God," a change of mind.

The darkness out of which Christians are brought at their conversion, is a state in which the sun of the intelligent world, GOD, who is "light, and in whom there is no darkness at all," "the Father of lights," the Author of true

---

[1] Exod. xii. *passim.*   [2] Psal. cv. 28, 36-39.

knowledge, holiness, and happiness, does not shine; in
other words, where ignorance and error with regard to
God, and therefore with regard to every thing of importance
in a religious and moral point of view, prevails; and in which,
of consequence, there is, there can be no true holiness; in
which there is, and must be, depravity; and in which, in
consequence of this error, and ignorance, and depravity,
there is, there can be, no true solid happiness; where there
is, and must be *misery*, in the highest sense in which that
word can be applied to a being like man.   This is the darkness in which Christians, in common with the rest of the
race, are naturally involved; and this is the darkness out
of which they are called by God.   There is the less necessity
of our dwelling on this part of the subject, as I have already
had occasion, when describing the various aspects of the
state of Christians, previously to their connexion with Christ,
exhibited in the text, to illustrate their state of moral darkness,
in its threefold phases of ignorance, depravity, and misery.[1]

Let us rather turn our attention to the more grateful
object of contemplation, that state of light, divine light,
marvellous divine light, into which Christians are called by
God : " The light of the knowledge of the glory of God,
in the face of Christ Jesus," is made to " shine in the
mind;"[2] that is, in plain words, the individual, by being
brought, under divine influence, to understand and believe
the revelation of the holy and benignant character of God,
contained in that gospel which contains an account of the
person and work of him, the only-begotten of God, who is
the revealer of the Father, attains just views of God,
which necessarily lead to just views on all other subjects,
specially interesting to man as a religious and moral
being.   He no longer " walks in darkness, but has the light
of life."   He knows and is sure " that God is, and that he
is the rewarder of them who diligently seek him."   He
knows, and is sure, that he is " glorious in holiness, and rich

---

[1] *Vide* Part I. § 2.   [2] 2 Cor. iv. 6.

in mercy;" that he is "the just God and the Saviour;" "just and the justifier of the ungodly believing in Jesus;" "God in Christ, reconciling the world to himself; not imputing to men their trespasses, seeing he has made him who knew no sin, to be sin for us; that we might be made the righteousness of God in him." He "knows the only true God, and Jesus Christ whom he has sent."[1] And this glorious light dispels the surrounding darkness, it corrects a thousand mistakes, clears up a thousand difficulties; as the sun not only enables us to see itself, but every thing else.

This light of knowledge is also the light of purity. It is a light which has heat with it, producing the blossoms of holy affection, the fruits of holy conduct. When God is truly known, sanctifying virtue comes forth from him. The love of God, the seminal principle, the concentrated essence of holiness in intelligent creatures, is the natural result of this knowledge of God. What is the knowledge we have been describing, but such an apprehension of the Divine mind and will as makes it our mind and will; and what is this but holiness, for what is holiness in an intelligent creature, but conformity of mind and will to the Holy, Holy, Holy One? This is very beautifully illustrated by the Apostle: "Ye were sometimes darkness, but now are ye light in the Lord: walk as the children of light; for the fruit of the light (for such is the true reading), the fruit of the light is in all goodness and righteousness, and truth."[2] In another passage, he employs another and still more striking image: We all, with unveiled faces, like mirrors, exposed to the glory of the Lord, are made glorious by that which is glorious, the glory of God in the face of his Son; we reflect his light, and thus ourselves become luminous. Through his shining on us, we ourselves shine.[3]

---

[1] John viii. 12. Heb. xi. 6. Exod. xv. 11. Eph. ii. 4. Isa. xlv. 21. Rom. iii. 26. 2 Cor. v. 19-21. John xvii. 3.

[2] Eph. v. 8. Ὡς τεκνα φωτος περιπατειτε, ὁ γαρ καρπος φωτος (not πνευματος as in the textus receptus) εν πασῃ αγαθωσυνη. κ. τ. λ.

[3] 2 Cor. iii. 18.

This light is productive of rational joy, permanent happiness, as well as of knowledge and of holiness. The truth respecting the Divine character cannot be known by man without producing happiness : " It is life eternal to know the only true God, and Jesus Christ whom he has sent:" " Blessed are the people who know that joyful sound, 'Justice and judgment are the habitation of thy throne : mercy and truth go before thy face.' Blessed are the people who know this joyful sound : they shall walk, O Lord, in the light of thy countenance. In thy name shall they rejoice all the day; and in thy righteousness shall they be exalted." All the holy affections which naturally grow out of the knowledge and faith of the truth, are so many wells of living water, springing up to eternal life. " Light is sown," shed forth, its rays scattered, like the seed from the hand of the sower, " on .the righteous, and gladness on the upright in heart." [1] To love God, to fear God, to trust in God, are most delightful exercises. [2]

Such is, I apprehend, in its great leading lineaments, that state of light into which Christians are called by God, a state of knowledge, holiness, and happiness. This light is not perfect in this present world, but it is real, and it is progressive and inextinguishable. It is not like " the light of the wicked," the blaze of thorns, or the deceitful wild-fire, which " shall be darkened;" it is like " the shining light," the sun in the heavens, " which shines more and more unto the perfect day." [3] As the pious Archbishop says, " There is a bright morning, without cloud, which will arise. The saints have not only light to lead them in their journey, but much purer light at home, an inheritance in light. The land where their inheritance lieth is full of light, and their inheritance itself is light. The vision of God, the seeing him as he is, and the being like him, in consequence of seeing him as he is ; that inheritance, the celestial city, has no need of

---

[1] Psal. xcvii. 7.   [2] John xvii. 3.   Psal. lxxxix. 14-16.
[3] Prov. iv. 18.

the sun or moon to shine on it, for the glory of the Lord doth lighten it, and the Lamb is the light of it. That un-created light is the happiness of our soul; the beginnings of it are our begun happiness. They are beams of it sent from above to lead us to the fountain and fulness of it. 'With thee,' says David, 'is the fountain of life; and in thy light shall we see light.'"[1]

This "light," this state of knowledge, holiness, and happi-ness, into which Christians are called, is termed "God's light." "Called out of darkness into his light." It is his; for he is its Author. He is "the Father of lights; from whom cometh down every good and every perfect gift."[2] This is not a light produced by a fire of man's own kindling. It is not knowledge, moral improvement, and happiness, obtained by the exercise of his natural faculties of intelligence and action. It is the work, it is the gift of God. "It is God the Lord who hath showed us light," and who, too, hath opened our blind eyes to "give us the light of the know-ledge of his glory in the face of his Son."[3] HE did the great works in which his holiness and grace were made known; HE made the revelation in which these glorious deeds are recorded; and HE opens the understanding to un-derstand this revelation; HE opens the heart to love it, so that we are enlightened, and purified, and blessed by it. It is thus HIS, as he is the author of it; and it is HIS, too, as he is the subject of it. Yes, God is "all in all" of this light. It is God known that makes us wise; God conformed to that make us holy; God enjoyed that makes us happy. Jehovah is the light of his people, not only the author, but the essence, of their happiness.

This light, this state of knowledge, purity, and happiness, is also termed marvellous, "God's marvellous," strange, won-derful, "light." The light which emblematised it, the pillar of fire, was a marvellous light. It was supernatural, and so is this light. "It is the doing of the Lord, and it is mar-

[1] Psal. xxxvi. 9. [2] James i. 17. [3] Psal. cxviii. 27. 2 Cor. iv. 6.

vellous " in the eyes of all who behold it.   It produces marvellous effects, enabling us to see things invisible and eternal; and by its brightness, casting into the shade things seen
and temporal, it enables us to " see the King in his
beauty, and to behold the land which is afar off." It enables us to penetrate into the true characters of objects, and
to distinguish shadows from realities, and realities from
shadows.   It converts a spiritual waste into the garden of
the Lord, blooming with beauty, rich in the fruits of righteousness :

> " Struck by that light, the human heart—
> A barren soil no more—
> Sends the sweet smell of grace abroad,
> Where serpents lurk'd before.
> The soul—a dreary province once
> Of Satan's dark domain—
> Feels a new empire form'd within,
> And owns a heavenly reign."

(9.) *Christians are " the people of God."*

The next appellation to which our attention must be
turned is, " the people of God."   " Who were not a people,"
but now are " the people of God."   In these words there is
an obvious reference to the following remarkable passages in
the book of the prophet Hosea : " In the place where it was
said to them, Ye are not my people, there it shall be said unto
them, Ye are the sons of the living God."   " I will have
mercy on her who had not obtained mercy ; and I will say
to them which were not my people, Thou art my people ;
and they shall say, Thou art my God." [1]   These words, as
they occur in the Old Testament Scriptures, plainly refer to
the ten tribes, who, in consequence of their idolatries, were to
be delivered up to a long captivity ; and not only deprived
of all external marks of the Divine peculiar favour, but
visited with very distinct evidences of the Divine judicial
displeasure; driven from their own land ; " abiding for
many days without a king, and without a prince, and with-

---

[1] Hos. i. 10; ii. 23.

out a sacrifice, and without an image, and without an ephod, and without teraphim." At a period, which we believe still to be future, these outcasts are to " return, and seek the Lord their God, and David their king; and shall fear the Lord and his goodness in the latter days." [1] Then they who have long not been a people, but a collection of wanderers among the nations, shall become, and be made to appear to be as a nation, the peculiar objects of the Divine favour, the people of the Lord.

The general meaning of the statement in the text is, that the previous state of Christians resembled that of the outcast remnant of Israel; that they were not a people, and that their present state embraces in it all the dignities and advantages of which the dignities and advantages of Israel, the ancient people of God, were a type and emblem. Previously to their coming to Christ, they were "not a people." It is not as bodies of men, still less as political bodies of men, but as individuals, that men are made Christians. There is no such thing as wholesale conversions. It is seldom that a whole family is converted at once; and even when this takes place, as in the case of the family of the jailer of Philippi, they are converted as individuals; and when "a nation shall be born at once," [2] as we hope and believe will one day happen, even then the change will be a personal change in every individual. They who form the true Church of God were previously " not a people;" they were unconverted individuals; " one of a city, two of a family." [3] God does not take the inhabitants of the Roman empire and constitute them his church. He " takes out of the Gentiles a people for his name." His church is a body formed of individuals " redeemed from among men, out of every kindred, and people, and nation." [4]

But though they were previously not a people, but a set of unconnected individuals, generally no way distinguished

<hr>

[1] Hos. iii. 4, 5.
[2] Acts xvi. 34.   Isa. lxvi. 8.
[3] Jer. iii. 14.
[4] Acts xv. 14.   Rev. xiv. 4; vii. 9.

for their worldly respectability, for the most part belonging
to the lower classes, "the foolish, the despised, the weak, the
base things of this world;"[1] yet now they are not only a
people, a regularly organized body, but "the people of God."
The "people of God" is here, I apprehend, just another term
for "the spiritual Israel," "the true circumcision." You are
the people of God, is equivalent to, You are not only a society,
but the most illustrious of all societies; having Jehovah for
your king; standing to him in a peculiar relation, suited to
the genius of the new, and spiritual, and heavenly economy,
analogous to that in which Israel stood to him under the
former external and temporary dispensation. You have the
substance of all the typical and emblematical privileges
which Israel, the people of God under that order of things,
enjoyed. Of these the Apostle gives a comprehensive cata-
logue : " To them pertained the adoption," or the sonship,
" and the glory, and the covenants, and the giving of the
law, and the service of God, and the promises; theirs were
the fathers, and of them, as concerning the flesh, Christ
came."[2]

Now, to Christians pertain a higher species of Divine Sonship than ever did, than ever could, belong to Israel according to the flesh,—a nearer relation, a spiritual conformity;
higher honours; a more valuable and enduring inheritance.
Instead of the Shekinah, or visible glory, they have the
manifestation of God in the person and work of his Son,
contained in his word, and rendered influential by his Spirit,
to guard them from danger, and guide them through the perplexities of the wilderness to the heavenly Canaan. Instead
of the external covenants, they have that covenant which
refers to "the sure mercies of" the mystical "David;" "the
covenant well ordered and sure,"[3] which secures not the
possession of Canaan for many ages, but the enjoyment of
heaven for ever. Instead of "the law which was given by
Moses," and which, in the existing state of the world, was a

---

[1] 1 Cor. i. 26-29.   [2] Rom. ix. 4.   [3] Isa. lv. 3.   2 Sam. xxiii. 5.

"grace," a privilege, the value of which could not easily be estimated, they have what is a far more precious favour, "the grace and the truth which came by Jesus Christ."[1]

Instead of the imposing solemnities of legal worship, they have the simple and spiritual institutions of the gospel of Christ. Instead of the promises of the earthly Canaan and temporal prosperity, they have "the exceeding great and precious promises" of "spiritual and heavenly blessings," and which "are all yea and Amen, in Christ Jesus, to the glory of God by them,"[2] and shall all be completely fulfilled in the Canaan above. They are "Abraham's seed, according to the promise;" "walking in the steps of his faith," and blessed with the highest blessing he enjoyed, justification by believing.[3] And they are connected with the Messiah by a relation far more intimate in its nature, far more important in its results, than that which distinguished the Israelites as his brethren, his kinsmen according to the flesh. "Who is my mother? and who are my brethren?" said the Messiah, "Whosoever shall do the will of my Father who is in heaven, the same is my brother, and sister, and mother."[4] They are connected with him by a relation more intimate in its nature, and more blissful in its effects, than that which bound to him, as mother, the most blessed and honoured of women. "Blessed," said a woman from the midst of a crowd, with which, on one occasion, he was surrounded, "Blessed is the womb that bare thee, and the breasts which thou hast sucked." "Yea, rather," said He in reply, "Yea, rather, blessed are those who hear the word of God, and do it."[5] Thus have true Christians, "who were not a people," become "the people of God," the spiritual Israel, the true circumcision.

(10.) *Christians "have obtained mercy."*

The only remaining designation of Christians, indicative

---

[1] John i. 17. [2] 2 Pet. i. 4. Eph. i. 3. 2 Cor. i. 20.
[3] Gal. iii. 29. Rom. iv. 12. Gal. iii. 14. [4] Matt. xii. 48, 50.
[5] Luke xi. 27, 28.

of their having tasted that the Lord is gracious, that still requires illustration, is, that once they " had not obtained mercy, but now have obtained mercy." The language here, as in the case of the former designation, " who were not a people, but are now the people of God," is borrowed from a statement originally made with reference to the ten tribes, a promise of their restoration from their long captivity.   " I will have mercy upon her who had not obtained mercy."[1] The ten tribes, even in the period of their abandonment by God, are the objects of his peculiar care. They are " beloved for the Father's sake."[2] Yet still there is a sense, and an important one, in which, while in this state, they do " not obtain mercy." They are destitute of all clear manifestations of Divine peculiar regard towards them, and are, indeed, plainly marked as objects of the Divine judicial displeasure. But at the time of their restoration they shall find mercy. They shall obtain very palpable manifestations of the Divine peculiar favour.   " I will make a covenant for them," says Jehovah, " with the beasts of the field, and with the fowls of heaven, and with the creeping things of the ground : and I will break the bow, and the sword, and the battle, out of the earth," or the land, " and will make them to lie down safely. And I will betroth them to me for ever ; yea, I will betroth them to me in righteousness, and in judgment, and in loving-kindness, and in mercies : I will even betroth them to me in faithfulness ; and they shall know the Lord. And it shall come to pass in that day, saith the Lord : I will hear the heavens, and they shall hear the earth ; and the earth shall hear the corn, and the wine, and the oil ; and they shall hear Jezreel. And I will sow her to me in the earth ; and I will have mercy on her that had not obtained mercy."[3]

The general truth, with respect to Christians, indicated by the language borrowed from the Divine dispensation to the ten tribes is this : That from a state in which they were the

[1] Hos. ii. 23.   [2] Rom. xi. 28.   [3] Hos. ii. 18-23.

objects of the Divine judicial displeasure and moral disapprobation, they are brought into a state in which they enjoy the
most abundant evidence of his peculiar favour and complacential delight.   In their original state, as fallen creatures,
ignorant, in error, guilty, depraved, they " had not obtained
mercy." God pitied them, and gave them many proofs of
his forbearance, and patience, and providential munificence.
Nay, more than this, God was determined to save them:
they were the objects of his eternal, electing, sovereign
love.   But they were not, they could not be, the objects
either of his judicial approbation or of his complacential delight.   Oh, no! they were " condemned already;" they
were " children of wrath, even as others." They were
" wicked," and as wicked " God was angry with them every
day."   " Enemies of God" by ignorance of mind, alienation
of heart, and wicked works ;[1] objects of his holy displeasure
and righteous condemnatory sentence ; hopelessly, because
wilfully, enslaved to Satan and to sin ; mortal, with nothing
to sweeten the bitterness of death, or lighten the darkness of
the grave ; immortal, yet destitute of all prospect of an
eternity of blessedness.   Such was their situation, in common with every individual of the fallen race to which they
belong.   Above them was an angry divinity ; around them
were the instruments of his vengeance ; and beneath them
was the pit of perdition yawning wide to receive them.
They " had not obtained mercy."

Such were they once ; but what are they now? They
" have obtained mercy."   In consequence of believing in
Christ, coming to him, they have received in rich abundance
manifestations of the Divine saving grace, of distinguishing
mercy.   " In Christ they have redemption through his
blood, the forgiveness of sins, according to the riches of
divine grace."   God is " merciful to their unrighteousness ;
their sins and their iniquities he remembers no more." They
are " made accepted in the beloved ;" and " in him they ob-

[1] John iii. 18.   Eph. ii. 3.   Psal. vii. 11.   Col. i. 21.   Eph. iv. 18.

tain an everlasting inheritance." " Justified by faith, they have peace with God, through our Lord Jesus Christ: by whom also they have access by faith into this grace wherein they stand, and rejoice in hope of the glory of God," a hope that shall never make them ashamed. And " not only so, but they joy in God through our Lord Jesus Christ, by whom they have received the reconciliation." " Created anew in Christ Jesus unto good works," " God, even the Father of our Lord Jesus Christ, loves them, and blesses them with all heavenly and spiritual blessings." They are " made partakers of a divine nature," and " the Spirit of God and of glory rests on them, and dwells in them." " They are heirs of God, joint-heirs with Christ Jesus." God " makes all things to work together for their good." " None can separate them from the love of God." " None can pluck them out of his hand." " Now are they the sons of God; and it doth not yet appear what they shall be: but when he who is their life shall appear, they shall appear with him in glory; and they shall be like him, seeing him as he is." " Goodness and mercy follow them all their days." " All the ways of the Lord to them," even the most perplexing and mysterious, " are mercy and truth to them;" " they shall find mercy of him on that day;" and throughout eternity will find how true is that declaration so often repeated in Scripture, " The mercy of the Lord endureth for ever." [1] Thus have we completed our illustration of the third great branch of our subject: the numerous and varied dignities and blessings enjoyed by Christians, in consequence of their connexion with Christ, viewed as manifestations of the Lord's graciousness to them.

And here let us pause and inquire, whether we have satisfactory evidence that we are personally interested in these exceeding great and precious privileges; whether we,

---

[1] Eph. i. 3, 7, 8, 11.   Heb. viii. 12.   Rom. v. 1-11.   Eph. ii. 10.   2 Pet. i. 4. 1 Pet. iv. 14.   Rom. viii. 17, 28, 35-39.   John x. 28, 29.   1 John iii. 1-3.   Psal. xxiii. 6; xxv. 10.   2 Tim. i. 18.   Psal. cxxxvi. passim.

as the elect race, the holy nation, the peculiar people, have been effectually called out of darkness into God's marvellous light; that we, from being aliens and outcasts, have really been admitted among the people of God; that we, who were once objects of the Divine judicial displeasure and moral disapprobation, have now obtained mercy? The characteristic marks of a state of unregeneracy and of a state of regeneracy, are so palpable, that no man need, no man can, remain ignorant of which is his own state, without the grossest inattention.

Let those who have good ground to conclude that the great change has taken place in their case, that they have been turned from darkness to light, that they are a portion of that people which God has taken from among the Gentiles to himself, that they are the recipients of those saving blessings which are the manifestation of the love which God has to his own, cherish a grateful sense of the Divine, sovereign kindness. Let them never forget, that it is all grace and mercy, sovereign grace, unmerited mercy. Not to them, not to them, but to Him who loved them because he wills to love them, be all the glory. Let them walk like the children of the light and of the day. Let them make their light shine before men. Let them prove that they are the people of God, by being zealous of good works, by coming out from among the wicked world, and being separate, not touching the unclean thing. Let them show that they are indeed the recipients of divine mercy, by manifesting the effects which the reception of saving benefits uniformly have on the tempers and conduct. Let the grace of God, enjoyed by them, teach them to deny ungodliness and worldly lusts, and to live soberly, righteously, and godly, in this world; while they look for, haste to, the blessed hope, the glorious appearing of our Lord Jesus Christ, who gave himself for them, that he might redeem them from all iniquity, and purify unto himself a peculiar people, zealous of good works.

And O! let those who, if they think at all, must know,

that they are in the darkness of ignorance and sin, that
they are not among the peculiar people, that they have
not obtained mercy, consider what the end must be if they
continue in their present condition. Pass that boundary
which separates time from eternity, and you know that
boundary must be past soon by all of you, how soon, how
suddenly, you do not, you cannot know; pass that boundary,
and the darkness of a natural state will settle down into the
blackness of darkness for ever ; they who are not God's
people, never can become God's people; those who have not
obtained mercy, never can obtain mercy. The change so
absolutely necessary to your happiness, must take place in
time, it cannot take place in eternity ; it must take place on
earth, it cannot take place in hell. Have you made up
your mind that it is never to take place ? If you have not,
why should it not take place now? Till this change take
place, you cannot be secure or happy. Can you be safe and
happy too soon ? All who are dwelling amid the glorious
light of God, were once, like you, in darkness. Those who
are God's people, were once not his people. Those who
have obtained mercy, had not obtained mercy. The grace
which saved them is able to save you ; is willing, is ready to
save you. " Turn ye, turn ye, why will ye die ? " The light
shines around you. Why shut your eyes to it ? The door
of admission to the fellowship of God's people stands open.
Why will ye not enter in ? The blessings of Divine mercy
are held out to you. Why turn away from the proffered
treasure, which gladly, gratefully received, would make you
rich toward God, rich for ever. Why madly strike back
the hand which is stretched out to rescue you from destruction. Now, now, is the accepted time. Yet a little while,
and the voice of invitation and warning will sink into
silence; and instead of it be heard, the voice of generous
regret, " Oh ! that they had known !" They might, they
would not, they shall not. No. No more for ever !

IV. THE MISERY AND RUIN OF THOSE WHO, BY REFUSING
TO "COME TO CHRIST," REMAIN DESTITUTE OF THESE
PRIVILEGES.

The only other branch of the subject which remains to be
considered is, the misery and ruin of those who persist in
unbelief and disobedience, rejecting Christ as the divinely
laid foundation, viewed as an illustration by contrast of the
graciousness of the Lord to those who believe in, come to,
and build on Jesus Christ, as the foundation. This is stated
in the following words, in the 7th and 8th verses: " To
them who are disobedient, the stone which the builders disallowed, the same is made the head of the corner, and a
stone of stumbling, and a rock of offence, even to them
which stumble at the word, being disobedient; whereunto
also they were appointed."

The language is plainly elliptical, and the manner in
which the ellipsis is to be supplied, depends on the manner
in which you render and explain the clause which immediately precedes, rendered in our version, " He is precious."
" To you who believe he," that is, Jesus Christ, " is precious ;"
He is highly valued by you. Supposing this to be true rendering, the ellipsis must be thus supplied, ' To them who
are disobedient, he is contemptible ; by them he is under-
valued and despised ;' and what follows should be the illustration of this. I have already stated to you the reason why
I cannot consider these words, " To you who believe he is
precious,"—though embodying in them a truth very precious
to the heart of every Christian, expressed in words very delightful to the ears of every Christian—as giving the meaning of the inspired writer. They are not the natural meaning of the original words. The statement they contain does
not well accord either with what goes before, or with what
follows them. It is plainly a conclusion or inference from the
prophet's declaration, " He who believeth" on Christ, as the
foundation, " shall not be ashamed." Now, that Christ is

precious to believers, is no inference from this declaration; and the words that follow are plainly meant to be a contrast; but what contrast is there between these statements? Christ, as the foundation, is precious to believers; but unbelievers stumble over him so as to fall, and to be broken, and perish. The natural contrast is, Christ is precious to believers; he is little prized by unbelievers.

On the supposition, that the true rendering of the words is, 'to you who believe there is honour,' a rendering warranted, if not absolutely required, by the original terms, and giving exactly the inference warranted by the prophet's declaration, " he that believeth on him shall not be confounded;" 'to you, then, that believe, there is, according to the prophet's declaration, not shame, but honour;'—on the supposition that this is the true rendering, the ellipsis must be thus supplied, ' To you, then, who believe, there is honour, but to those who are disobedient, there is shame.' What follows is the illustration of this. The stone which they, like the builders, disallowed, is, in spite of their disallowance, made the head stone of the corner. This must cover them with shame and confusion. Nor is this all; they stumble over the stone which they refuse to build on, and are, in consequence, broken in pieces.

There is a reference to two passages of Old Testament prediction : " The stone which the builders rejected is become the head stone of the corner;" " and he shall be for a sanctuary; but for a stone of stumbling, and for a rock of offence, to both the houses of Israel; for a gin and for a snare to the inhabitants of Jerusalem. And many among them shall stumble, and fall, and be broken, and snared, and taken."[1] The figure seems to be this : ' You, the unbelieving and disobedient, rejected the stone laid by God in Zion, and would not build on it; yet, in spite of your rejection, this stone is made the head stone, that is, the chief stone of the corner; and multitudes build on it, and grow up into a holy

[1] Psal. cxviii. 22. Isa. viii. 14, &c.

temple in the Lord.' The word "head stone," does not refer to its being the topmost, but the principal stone of the corner. Indeed, it seems plain, the stone referred to is a foundation stone, not a cope stone, and this explains what follows. Not only will the stone you reject be made the chief stone of the corner; but as foundation corner stones often projected, it will become to you " a stone of stumbling, a rock of offence," two expressions of exactly parallel meaning; a stone, a rock, over which you shall stumble so as to be greatly injured, indeed destroyed; stumble so, to use the prophet's words, as to " fall, and be broken."

The words " whereunto also they were appointed," which have occasioned much controversy among critics and commentators, refer to the word " stumble," not to the word " disobedient." [b] Its reference would have been more obvious had it been rendered, " who, being disobedient, stumble at the word," or rather, " who, being disobedient to the word, stumble." Stumbling is at once the consequence and the punishment of unbelief and disobedience. Sin is never represented as appointed by God; punishment is. God permits men to be sinners—that is, he does not hinder them from sinning; he appoints them, if they sin, to be punished. The reference here, however, does not seem to be to the Divine decree, so much as to the revelation of the Divine decree in the Divine prediction. The apostle refers to the passage quoted, and his words are equivalent to,—' to which stumbling, it appears, from the saying of the prophet, those who are disobedient are appointed.' God has connected this stumbling with unbelief as its natural effect, and in his word has said so.

The word rendered " disobedient," [1] signifies unbelieving as well as disobedient, intimating to us the important truth, that faith and obedience, and unbelief and disobedience, are indissolubly connected; unbelief being disobedience to the great commandment, and the root of disobe-

---

b See note B.   1 απειθουσι.

dience to all the commandments. The unbelieving and disobedient are represented as discrediting and disobeying the gospel revelation; but there seems to be a peculiar reference to "the word"[1] or discourse, the prophetic declaration which the inspired writer is immediately referring to.[2] The direct reference in the term disobedient is, no doubt, to the unbelieving Jews. When God proclaimed to them, " Behold, I lay in Zion for a foundation a stone, a tried stone, a precious corner-stone, a sure foundation; he that believeth shall not make haste,"—they disbelieved the declaration. They disobeyed the command. They rejected the stone. They would not build on it. They would not receive Jesus as the Messiah; on the contrary, they " took him, and with wicked hands they crucified and slew him."

But what was the consequence? Was the stone laid by Jehovah in Zion prevented from becoming the great foundation it was intended for, " the chief stone of the corner?" Oh no ; hear what Peter said on a memorable occasion, and what I have little doubt was in his mind when he wrote the passage now before us—" Jesus Christ of Nazareth, whom ye crucified, God raised from the dead. This is the stone which was set at nought of you builders, which is become the head of the corner."[3] Disappointment and shame was their portion. In all their attempts to prevent the foundation being securely laid in its place, they had been furthering it; and when they " gathered together against the Lord and his Christ," they had done but " what his hand and counsel aforetime determined to be done."[4]

But this disappointment was not their only punishment. "The stone laid in Zion," which they rejected, on which they would not build, " was to them a stone of stumbling, and a rock of offence." Their opposition to the declared purpose of God brought on them severe inflictions of the Divine wrath. " Wrath to the uttermost," as the apostle

---

[1] τω λογω απειθουντες.   [2] Isa. xxviii 16.
[3] Acts iv. 10, 11.   [4] Acts iv. 27, 28.

speaks, " came on them." They " fell, and were broken."
The awful prediction in the book of the prophet Isaiah,
connected with the passage quoted, was fulfilled : " Judgment
also will I lay to the line, and righteousness to the plummet ;
and the hail shall sweep away the refuge of lies, and the
waters shall overflow the hiding-place. And your covenant
with death shall be disannulled, and your agreement with
hell shall not stand ; when the overflowing scourge shall
pass through, then ye shall be trodden down by it. For
the Lord shall rise up as in mount Perazim, he shall be
wroth as in the valley of Gibeon, that he may do his work, his
strange work ; and bring to pass his act, his strange act." [1]

These awful predictions found their accomplishment in
the siege and sack of Jerusalem, in the destruction of the
temple, the dissolution of the polity, the dispersion of the
nation of the Jews. To these unbelieving, these disobedient ones, in consequence of their unbelief, their not
coming to Christ, their not believing in him, there was not
honour, but shame ; they were confounded. Their emblem
is not the temple, to whose stately buildings our Lord directed the attention of his disciples, but its scattered ruins,
when one stone was not to be found upon another. Instead
of " the chosen generation," they became " a rejected race."
Instead of " a royal priesthood," Jehovah proclaims to
them, " He that killeth an ox, is as if he slew a man ; he
that sacrificeth a lamb, as if he cut off a dog's neck. Bring
no more vain oblations." Instead of a holy nation, they
have left " their name as a curse to God's chosen ; for the
Lord God has slain them, and called his people by another
name." [2] Instead of being called out of darkness into God's
glorious light, their light is turned into darkness ; they are
" cast into outer darkness." [3] They who were the people of
God are not the people of God, not even a people ; they
who had found mercy, do not obtain mercy ; " they were a
people of no understanding : therefore he that made them will

---

[1] Isa. xxviii. 17-21.   [2] Isa. lxvi. 3 ; lxv. 15.   [3] Matt. viii. 12.

not have mercy on them, and he that formed them will show them no favour.'[1] Their privileges are taken from them, and heavy judgment inflicted on them.

While I cannot doubt that the primary reference of these words is to the unbelieving Jews, both as individuals and as a nation in the primitive ages, it is plain that the statement here is substantially true of all who are unbelieving and disobedient, of every country and in every age. All who being " disobedient to the word," " disallow the stone laid in Zion," must be disappointed. " He must reign."[1] It is easier to pull the sun from the firmament than to remove the Saviour from his throne ; easier to arrest the course of that sun than to arrest the progress of his gospel. Those who reject him show their wish that all should reject him, and that his religion should be extinguished; and sometimes they are mad enough to think, as the Jews no doubt did, when they had brought him to the cross and laid him in the grave, that they will be successful. Voltaire proudly boasted, that one wise man would undo what twelve fools had done. Hume said, that Christianity could not survive the nineteenth century ; and in the insane impieties of revolutionized France, many of their disciples fancied they saw the token of the accomplishment of these anticipations—

> " Fond impious man ! think'st thou yon sanguine cloud
>   Rais'd by thy breath has quench'd the orb of day ?
> To-morrow He repairs the golden flood,
>   And warms the nations with redoubled ray."[3]

Oh, how will confusion of face cover all unbelievers, when on the great day they find him whom they rejected on the throne of universal judgment, and themselves trembling before his bar. Their miscalculations will make them the objects of " shame and contempt " to the whole intelligent creation of God to all eternity.

But this is not all. They shall stumble so as to fall—fall

---

[1] Isa. xxvii. 11.   [3] 1 Cor. xv. 25.   [3] Gray.

into hell. It is a serious matter to reject the Saviour. He is the only Saviour. " There is no other name given under heaven among men whereby we must be saved." " There remaineth no more sacrifice for sin." He who will not be saved by him cannot be saved at all. He who rejects his sacrifice must bear the weight of unexpiated sin for ever. " There remaineth for such, nothing but a certain fearful looking for of judgment and fiery indignation, to destroy them as the adversaries of God."[1]

To many " this is a hard saying," and they refuse to hear it. They cannot think that there is such a difference, in a moral point of view, between faith and unbelief, that their consequences should be more distant from each other than the poles of the earth, as distant as the heights of heaven are from the depths of hell. But steadily look at this unbelief, and you will cease to wonder. What is it, but to trample at once on all that is great, and all that is gracious, in the Divine character ; to call the God of truth a liar, and the God of wisdom a fool; to trample on his proffered gifts, and defy his threatened vengeance? If there be power in the arm of omnipotent justice, against whom can it be more worthily put forth than against the impenitent unbeliever? And, let it never be forgotten, the unbeliever is the destroyer of his own soul. He refuses to build on the foundation Jehovah has laid. This is folly and sin enough. But this is not all : he madly dashes himself against the chief foundation corner-stone, and breaks himself in pieces.

Oh, how different the state of the believer and the unbeliever ; how happy the one, how miserable the other ! Look at the two, and say if he who has secured the former has not reason to say, that the Lord has been gracious to *him*, for there was no alternative. If he had not obtained the honour and happiness of the believer, the shame and ruin of the unbeliever must have been his. And then let him

---

[1] Acts iv. 12. Heb. x. 26, 27.

further think, who made him to differ ? 'I was an unbeliever and a disobedient one, and, left to myself, I should have been an unbeliever and disobedient one still. In that state I should have lived and died, and entered into eternity. What has made me to differ? Sovereign kindness. Whence came my faith, and all its blessed consequences, in time and in eternity? It is not of myself, "it is the gift of God." It was given me "on behalf of Christ to believe on his name." Surely, surely the Lord has been gracious to *me.*'

I have thus brought before your minds the four great sources of illustrative proof, that the Lord is gracious to Christians. Their natural condition, the manner in which that condition was changed, the blessings of their new condition, and the final state of those who obstinately continue in their natural condition; all these, rightly considered, are fitted to deepen this conviction on a Christian's mind,—verily the Lord is gracious, and I have tasted of his grace.

It is of importance to inquire, what is the practical end which the Apostle seeks to gain by pressing on the attention of Christians these proofs that the Lord is gracious? That end is easily discovered. This was his wish, as it was his Master's will, even their sanctification; and he was fully persuaded that men will never be holy, but in the degree in which they believe that God is good, good to them. "When the love of God our Saviour toward man appeared, not by works of righteousness which we have done, but according to his mercy he saved us, by the washing of regeneration, and the renewing of the Holy Ghost; which he shed on us abundantly through Jesus Christ our Saviour; that we, being justified by his grace, might be made heirs according to the hope of eternal life." "This is a faithful saying, and these things I will that thou affirm constantly, that they who believe in God may be careful to maintain good works."

The Apostle Peter does not leave us to find out his object by such a reference as we have now made to general principles. He distinctly shows us why he appeals to the graciousness of the Lord: " Love one another with a pure heart fervently. Lay aside all malice, and guile, and hypocrisies, and envies, and all evil-speakings," " As new-born babes, desire the sincere milk of the word, that ye may grow thereby," " *Seeing* ye have tasted that the Lord is gracious." He plainly acts on the same principle as his beloved brother Paul, when he says, " I beseech you, brethren, by the mercies of God," manifested in the divine method of justification, " I beseech you, by the mercies of God, that ye present yourselves as living sacrifices, holy and acceptable to God, by Christ Jesus, which is your rational ministry as spiritual priests ; and be not conformed to this world, but be transformed by the renewing of your minds, that ye may prove what is the good, and perfect, and acceptable will of God."[1]

I cannot conclude these illustrations without dropping a word of warning to those to whom this word of salvation has come, but as yet come in vain ; to whom God has long been proclaiming, " Behold, I have laid in Zion as a foundation, a stone, a tried stone, a precious corner-stone, a sure foundation," but who, instead of believing on it, coming to it, building on it, have been, like the Jewish builders, rejecting it, disallowing it. Your situation, " men and brethren," is awfully perilous. If you will not build on that stone, you must stumble over it, and fall, and be broken. As to present privileges, you are in far better circumstances than the heathen, who never heard of the way of salvation ; but as to future destiny, if you do not enter on the way of salvation opened before you, you will be in far worse circumstances than they. Yes, in the day of judgment, " it will be more tolerable for the inhabitants of Tyre and Sidon, of Sodom and Gomorrah, than for you." All the happiness of the highest heavens is freely offered you, if you will accept of it in the only way God can give it, or you receive it ; but if you contemptuously put it away from you, you not only must lose it, but you

[1] Rom. xii. 1, 3.

must sink yourselves into the very lowest depths of hopeless misery.

If you perish—and you cannot perish but by your own obstinate refusal of a salvation, ready to be bestowed on you if you will but accept of it—your perdition will be no ordinary perdition. The awful declarations of the Apocalypse will be realized in your experience : " The same shall drink of the wine of the wrath of God, which is poured out without mixture into the cup of his indignation; and he shall be tormented with fire and brimstone in the presence of the holy angels, and in the presence of the Lamb : and the smoke of their torment ascendeth up for ever and ever : and they have no rest day nor night."[1]

But, oh, why should it be so ?   God has no " pleasure in your death;" he swears by his life that he has not.   He wills you to turn from your evil ways, and live.   If you perish, you must be self-destroyers.   " Turn ye, turn ye, why will ye die ? "   Be no longer disobedient to the word of mercy. Receive it gladly, gratefully; and in receiving it you will receive the Saviour and his salvation.   The feast of gospel grace is set before you, and urged on your acceptance : " O taste and see that the Lord is good."   May the good Spirit render effectual the invitation of the word, and induce you all to take of the bread and the water of life freely, that, eating and drinking, you may live for ever.

---

[1] Rev. xiv. 10, 11.

Note A.

Saxo quod adhuc vivum radice tenetur.—Ovid. Met. xiv. 714.
——— vivoque sedilia saxo.—Virg. Æn. i. 171.   Alex. Morus'
note is curious :—" Apud Ethnicos quoque lapidum vivorum
reperies mentionem, λιθους εμψυχους.   Plutarchus *de fluminibus*
non semel vocat lapides vivos, inter quos θρασυδειλον Eurotæ proprium lapidem nominat, qui tuba sonante, prosilebat, ad ripam
scilicet; Atheniensium autem audito nomine, mergebatur in pro-
fundum. Nec minus fabulosa quæ Suidas habet de Heraisco
Ægyptio Philosopho qui rite dignoscere calleret αγαλματα τα ζωντα,
και μη ζωντα vel αψυχα και αμοιρα θειας επιπνοιας. Contra Petrus
fideles vere lapides vivos vere spirantes ac loquentes, Dei statuas
spirituales et participes θειας επιπνοιας hic dixit." Notæ ad
quædam loca N. F. p. 210.

Note B.

Προσκοπτουσι. Απειθουντες. Horum autem verborum prius de-
signat proprie *pœnam,* posterius *culpam;* pronomen autem *ad quod*
refertur ad prius, non ad posterius. Improbos destinavit Deus
ad pœnam non ad culpam. Cappellus.—" Προσκοπτουσι—
Απειθουντες :" the former of these words designates punishment;
the latter, sin. The pronoun ὁ—εις ὁ refers to the former, not to
the latter. God appoints the wicked to punishment, not to sin.
Some anti-Calvinists have found in these words a proof, that even
they who perish through unbelief were appointed to salvation.
They refer ὁ, in the teeth of grammar, to λογος; and try to bring
out, or rather put in, the sense, to use the words of one of them, a
very worthy Lutheran, Hemmingius : " Etsi illis destinata erat
salutis promissio, tamen non crediderunt." It is sad when the
love of system leads good men thus to " pervert" the word of
God. "Mens Petri est: Hoc infidelium præsertim Judæorum
scandalum et προσκομμα, ad Christum lapidem angularem dudum
a prophetis, Christo, aliisque assertum et prædictum esse."—Jer.
viii. 14, 15. Matt. xxi. 42, 44. Luke ii. 34. Rom. ix. 32,
33.—Kypke, ii. 430.

DISCOURSE IX.

A SECOND FIGURATIVE VIEW OF THE STATE AND CHA-
RACTER OF CHRISTIANS, WITH APPROPRIATE EXHOR-
TATIONS.

1 Pet. ii. 11, 12.—Dearly beloved, I beseech you, as strangers and pilgrims,
abstain from fleshly lusts, which war against the soul; having your conversation honest among the Gentiles; that, whereas they speak against you as evil-
doers, they may, by your good works, which they shall behold, glorify God in
the day of visitation.

THESE two verses, which form one sentence, bring before
our minds a very important department of Christian duty;
to the illustration and enforcement of which it is our intention to devote this discourse. The subject naturally
divides itself into two parts; an injunction of duty, and
a statement of the motives which urge compliance with
that injunction. The duty enjoined is twofold: abstinence
from fleshly lusts, and having their conversation honest
among the Gentiles. The motives are these: "Ye are
strangers and pilgrims." "These lusts war against the
soul;" and abstinence from them, and the maintenance of
an "honest conversation among the Gentiles," have a tendency to overcome their prejudices against both you and
your religion, and to lead them to "glorify God in the
day of visitation." To unfold, then, the meaning of these

injunctions, and to point out the force of these motives, are the two objects which I have in view in the following remarks.

I.—THE DUTIES ENJOINED.

§ 1.—*Abstinence from "fleshly lusts."*

The first duty enjoined in the text is, "Abstinence from fleshly lusts." Lusts, in the New Testament use of that word, signify desires; strong desires; usually, inordinate, unduly strong desires. The phrase "fleshly lusts" is often considered as meaning, desires for sensual enjoyment; desires which obtain their gratification by means of bodily organs. This is, however, very unduly to limit the signification of the term. Among the "works of the flesh," which are just the lusts of the flesh embodied, we find enumerated, "hatred, variance, emulations, wrath, strife, seditions, heresies," as well as "adultery, fornication, uncleanness, and lasciviousness."[1]

Flesh is the principal constituent of the human body, and the body is the visible part of the compound being, man. Hence flesh comes to be used for human nature, or mankind.[2] All mankind, since the fall, are depraved beings; and hence flesh is often, especially in the epistolary part of the New Testament, used to signify fallen human nature, or mankind as depraved.[3] Agreeably to this use of the term flesh, fleshly desires signify those desires which characterise mankind as depraved, which belong to, and are distinctive of, fallen human nature, what are elsewhere termed "worldly lusts."[4]

The desires, including under that name the appetites and the passions, as well as those principles of which the word desires is the appropriate technical name, form a very important part of our active nature, and are fitted to serve

[1] Gal. v. 19-21.
[2] Gen. vi. 13.   Psal. lvi. 4.   Matt. xxiv. 22.   Rom. iii. 20.   John i. 14.
[3] Rom. vii. 18; viii. 5.   Gal. v. 13.   [4] Tit. ii. 12.

numerous useful and benevolent purposes. The desire of
meat and of drink; the desire of knowledge; the desire of
esteem; the desire of power; the desire of property, and
other desires of a similar kind, belong essentially to human
nature, and are as much the gifts of God as reason or conscience; and, like these higher faculties, are plainly intended
and calculated to minister to man's improvement and happiness.

Some of these desires, as belonging to man as an embodied
being, may be termed fleshly, as they cannot exist in purely
spiritual beings; but these are not the desires here referred
to. God never requires impossibilities; and to abstain from
the desires we have mentioned is an impossibility. Those
desires are neither virtuous nor vicious. They are parts of
our constitution, which ought to be regulated and restrained
when they come in competition with more important principles, which, in a perfect state of human nature, they never
would. To eradicate them, if the thing were possible, which
I believe it is not, would not be to improve, but to mutilate
human nature. The amputation of arms and legs would
not at all add to the beauty and usefulness of the human
body; and just such an improvement on the mind, would
be the depriving it of any of those active powers with
which its infinitely wise and benignant Author has endowed
it. That were to make us "new creatures," in a sense very
different indeed from that in which the Apostle uses the
term.

In no part of our nature has the malignant influence of
the fall been more apparent, than in our moral or active
faculties; and in none of these active powers do we discern
clearer marks of degeneration than in our desires. Our
desires, in very many instances, seek their gratification in
objects, the pursuit of which is proscribed by God, as his
will is indicated by reason, by conscience, or by an express
revelation; and where the object of desire is not in itself
improper, the desire itself is often foolish, in consequence of
its being disproportioned to the real or comparative value of

the object; and criminal, because unsubordinated to the will of God.

These are the desires which are here termed "fleshly lusts;" such desires as Adam was a stranger to while he continued innocent; such desires as are now characteristic of the whole of his degenerate offspring. These desires, unlike the original principles referred to above, are not to be regulated, but destroyed. They are right hands that are to be cut off; right eyes that are to be plucked out. As members of the old man, they are to be mortified; as affections and lusts of the flesh, they are to be crucified.

To "abstain from fleshly lusts," then, is to refrain from doing that which is forbidden. It is, in other words, to yield obedience to the tenth commandment, "Thou shalt not covet;" thou shalt not desire that which God says thou shouldst not seek to obtain. Every desire of what is forbidden, what is criminal in itself, or criminal to us in our circumstances, is a "fleshly desire," a desire which marks the being who indulges it as morally depraved, and is not to be indulged, even in the slightest degree, is not to be tampered with, but destroyed, strangled in its birth, repressed on its first rising.

But this is not all : To "abstain from fleshly lusts," is to refrain from all inordinate or excessive desire, even of what is in itself lawful. It is in this form of the evil that Christians chiefly need to be warned against fleshly or worldly lusts. It is a sad mistake to suppose that our desires are lawful, because the objects of our desire are not forbidden. It may be that they are so far from being forbidden, that we would sin if we did not desire them, and yet in desiring them inordinately we may sin. Our desires may be "fleshly desires," that is, desires rising out of the depravity of our nature, and at once exercising and increasing that depravity.

To desire any thing seen and temporal, be it pleasure, knowledge, power, fame, money, or any thing else, as absolutely necessary to, and sufficient for, our happiness, is a fleshly desire. That is, in other words, to make that thing our God, and is in direct opposition to the commandment, " Thou shalt have no other God before me :" to the breathing of the Spirit, " Whom have I in heaven but thee ? and there is none in all the earth whom I desire beside thee." [1] He who cherishes any desire unsubordinated to the will of God, cherishes a fleshly desire ; and from this form of fleshly desire, as well as the former, Christians are commanded to " abstain."   " They are to " flee from idolatry ;" to " keep themselves from idols ;" and " covetousness," that is, the inordinate desire of any created good, " is idolatry." [2]

These, then, are the two branches of the great law, "Abstain from fleshly lusts." Refrain from desiring whatever is forbidden. Refrain from inordinately desiring any thing seen and temporal, however innocent in itself.

This, like every one of God's laws, is " holy, just, and good." It leaves abundant room for the healthy operation of natural desires. It allows us to desire every thing that is really desirable, in the degree in which it is desirable. It only forbids us to indulge a desire which, whether gratified or not, must end in disappointment and ruin. The language is, " Wilt thou set thine eyes upon that which is not?" [3] Surely it is impossible not to recognise the Divine wisdom and kindness in this spiritual commandment. It puts the check in the right place. It seeks to prevent the works of the flesh, by prohibiting the lusts of the flesh. Human laws seek to dam up or divert the stream ; the Divine law seeks to dry up the fountain.

From these few plain remarks, every person who wishes to understand the subject, may easily perceive what it is to abstain from fleshly lusts—a much more extensive and difficult duty than many are aware of : but it may serve a good purpose, before closing this part of the discussion, to say a word or two on the way in which we are to yield obedience

[1] Psal. lxxiii. 25, 26.   [2] 1 Cor. x. 14.   1 John v. 21.   Col. iii. 5.
[3] Prov. xxiii. 5.

to this most reasonable command, " Abstain from fleshly lusts."

The first remark to be made here is, that, in order to abstain from fleshly lusts, we must carefully guard against temptation. There is continual danger; there are always objects at hand fitted to provoke sinful desires in some of its forms; and a busy, crafty adversary is ever ready to take advantage of any opportunity that offers against us. We must therefore avoid placing ourselves in circumstances in which such desires are likely to be excited; and when, by the providence of God, we are placed in such circumstances, we are to " keep our hearts with all diligence;" and, sensible that all our keeping will not serve the purpose, we must give our hearts to God to keep them. We must " watch and be sober;" " be sober and watch;" " watch and pray;" and this should be our prayer : " Incline my heart to thy testimonies, and not to covetousness," the general name of fleshly, worldly desires. " Turn away mine eyes from beholding vanity."[1]

We must recollect that nothing can overcome the world, and the things that are in the world—the lust of the flesh, and the lust of the eye, and the pride of life, and the god of this world, who by these subjugates us, and makes us his slaves—but the word of God dwelling in us. It is " our faith" of that word; in other words, that word believed, that " overcometh the world." It brings us under " the powers of the world to come," and thus " delivers us from this present evil world." Were the realities of eternity habitually before the mind, fleshly lusts could no more take root and flourish there, than " perishable materials be reared into structures amid the fires of the last day."[2]

The grand preservation against " fleshly lusts" is to have the mind pre-occupied with spiritual and heavenly affections; and to have the heart so full of holy happiness in the enjoyment of God, as that there is neither room in it nor relish for low-born, earthly, sensual, sinful enjoyments. The

[1] Prov. iv. 23. 1 Tim. v. 6. 1 Pet. iv. 7; v. 8. Psal. cxix. 36, 37.
[2] Robert Hall.

strong man can be put out of the house, and kept out of it, only by the stronger than he getting possession, and keeping possession of it. The true way of emptying a vessel of atmospheric air, and keeping that from re-occupying its place, is to fill it with some heavier fluid.

It is finely said by the good Archbishop I have so often quoted to you : " The happiness and pleasantness of the Christian's estate sets him above the need of the pleasures of sin. The Apostle has said before : since ye have tasted that the Lord is gracious, desire the sincere milk of the word ; desire that word, wherein ye may taste more of his graciousness ; and as that fitly urgeth the appetites' desire of the word, so it is strong to persuade this abstinence from fleshly lusts ; yea, the disdain and loathing of them. If you have the least experience of the sweetness of his love, if ye have but tasted of the crystal river of his pleasures, the muddy polluted pleasures of sin will be hateful and loathsome to you ; yea, the best earthly delights that are, will be disrelished and unsavoury to your tastes. The embittering of the breasts of the world to the godly, by afflictions, doth something, indeed, to their weaning from them ; but the breasts of consolation that are given them in their stead, wean them much more effectually.

" The true reason why we remain servants to these lusts, some to one, some to another, is because we are still strangers to the love of God, and those pure pleasures which are in him. Though the pleasures of this world be poor and low, and most unworthy of our pursuit, yet so long as men know no better, they will stick by those they have, such as they are. It is too often in vain to speak to men on this, to follow them with the Apostle's entreaty, I beseech you, abstain from fleshly lusts, unless they that are spoke to be, such as he speaks of in the former words, such as have obtained mercy, and have tasted of the graciousness and love of Him whose loves are better than wine. O that we would but seek the knowledge of this love ; for, seeking it, we would find it ; and, finding it, no force would be needful to pull the delights of sin out of our

hands; we should throw them away of our own accord."
This is the true secret of yielding obedience to the commandment in the text, abstain from fleshly lusts. O that
we all were experimentally acquainted with it! How
happy, how holy, would we be!

§ 2.—" *Having a conversation honest among the Gentiles.*"

The second duty enjoined in the text is: "Have your
conversation honest among the Gentiles." "Conversation"
here, and in many other places in the New Testament, does
not mean colloquial intercourse, but conduct, general behaviour; as, "Only let your conversation be such as
becomes the gospel of Christ;" "Be holy in all manner of
conversation."[1]

The term "honest"[2] here, as in some other parts of the
New Testament, is used in a somewhat obsolete sense; as
equivalent to honourable, respectable, morally beautiful and
lovely; what commands esteem and reverence. Have your
conversation honest among the Gentiles, means, Let your
conduct be such as will meet the approbation of God and
good men, and as even the heathen shall be obliged to venerate. It is materially the same exhortation as that given
by the Apostle Paul to the Philippians: "Whatsoever
things are true, whatsoever things are honest," venerable,
"whatsoever things are just, whatsoever things are pure,
whatsoever things are lovely, whatsoever things are of good
report; if there be any virtue, if there be any praise, think
on these things, do these things."[3]

The heathens were poor judges of Christian doctrine:
there was much, too, in the Christian character, the excellencies of which they could not at all appreciate. But
when they saw Christians making it plain that no temptation could induce them to deviate from the straight path
prescribed by the laws of temperance, and chastity, and
justice, and love; rendering no man evil for evil; meekly

---

[1] Phil. i. 27. 1 Pet. i. 15.   [2] Καλὴν.   [3] Phil. iv. 8.

suffering many injuries, but inflicting none; denying themselves the comforts of life, to supply those who were destitute
of its necessaries; sacrificing and suffering every thing,
rather than violate conscience: they could not help feeling how beautiful and how awful goodness is; and a testimony was silently lodged in their hearts, in behalf of the
religion of Christ, which no reasoning could have placed there.
"There is a majesty in strict, serious, consistent goodness, that
commands esteem and reverence from the worst of men."

The positive command includes the negative: Beware of
every thing in your conduct which might shock the moral
feelings of a heathen; beware of any thing which might lead
him in any way to form an opinion dishonourable to "the
worthy name by which ye are called," or open his mouth in
blasphemy against Him to whom it belongs. It is a most
important duty on Christians, in all countries and ages,
living among the men of the world, remembering that,
among other proofs of their Lord's graciousness to them, he
has made them the guardians of his honour among men, to
act a part which shall command the respect and esteem of
those around them, and to be cautious lest they let "their
good be evil spoken of."[1]

It deserves notice, that the two duties enjoined are represented as very closely connected. It is by abstaining from
fleshly lusts that their conversation was to be honest among
the Gentiles. If they did not abstain from fleshly lusts,
their conversation would be dishonourable, both to themselves and to their religion. If they did abstain from
fleshly lusts, an honest, honourable behaviour was a matter
of course. The heart must be kept with all diligence, if
we would wish the issues of life which flow from it to be
satisfactory. Let the heart be rightly regulated; the tongue,
the eyes, the hands, the feet, will all be properly employed.
Let the thoughts and the desires be as they ought to be, and
the actions will be unblameable. If the corrupt spring is

not cleansed, the stream cannot be pure : if it is, the stream cannot but be pure.

It is a sad mistake to think, that the conduct will ever be what God would have it be, till the heart is changed; that the conversation will ever be really comely, while men do not abstain from fleshly lusts. The heart must be "purified by the Spirit through the word," in order to man's being "holy in all manner of life and conversation." And it is not less true, and not less important, that the want of a comely conversation, of a holy behaviour, is a proof, whatever profession men make, that fleshly lusts still hold dominion within. As the fruit cannot be good if the tree is not good, so neither can the tree be good if the fruit is not good. The goodness of the tree is the necessary cause of the goodness of the fruit, and the goodness of the fruit is the only satisfactory evidence of the goodness of the tree.

So much for the illustration of this branch of our subject : The injunction of duty, " Abstain from fleshly lusts, having your conversation honest among the Gentiles." Refrain from desiring what is forbidden; refrain from inordinately desiring any thing that is seen and temporal; and thus maintain a habitual behaviour so morally lovely and venerable, that even your heathen neighbours shall be constrained to take notice of you, and trace the obvious effect to the hidden cause; the goodness of your conduct to the goodness of your principles.

II.—MOTIVES TO THE DISCHARGE OF THESE DUTIES.

Let us now turn our attention to the second branch of the subject : A statement of the motives which urge to compliance with this injunction of duty. The motives are drawn from the character and circumstances of Christians, and from the tendency and consequences, both of the course from which they are dissuaded, and of that to which they are urged. The motive deduced from the character and conduct of Christians, is contained in these words : Ye are "pilgrims and strangers." The motive drawn from the tendency and consequences of the course dissuaded from is: These fleshly lusts war against the soul; and that drawn from the tendency and consequences of the course recommended is: "That the Gentiles, who spoke against them as evil-doers, might, by their good works which they beheld, glorify God in the day of visitation." Let us attend to these motives in their order, and endeavour to show their appropriateness and their power.

§ 1. *Motive from the condition and character of Christians as "pilgrims and strangers."*

The first motive is drawn from the condition and character of Christians as "pilgrims and strangers." In the literal meaning of the words, those to whom they were originally addressed were pilgrims and strangers. They were chiefly Jews and proselytes, living among the heathen inhabitants of the regions of Asia Minor. Viewed even in this way, there is force in the statement, considered as a motive to the duty enjoined. The great body of them among whom you live are serving fleshly lusts; you are constantly exposed to the powerful influence of all but universally prevalent custom. Beware lest "evil communication corrupt good manners."

There can, however, be no reasonable doubt, that the words pilgrim and stranger are used figuratively, and in a sense equally applicable to all Christians, in all countries and ages, as to those to whom they were originally addressed.[1] In a figurative sense all men may be said to be pilgrims and sojourners on earth. They are to continue here but for a short season; they are, as it were, on a journey to their long home; and a consideration of this, places in a strong point of view the folly of men, in allowing their

---

[1] The respective force of the two words παροίκους and παρεπιδήμους is well given by Bengel:—"Gradatio, non tantum ut in aliena domo—sed etiam ut in aliena civitate." Not only away from their own house, but from their own country, —in the fullest sense from home. Neither of the words express what is peculiar in the signification of the English word "pilgrim."

minds to be chiefly occupied with objects and pursuits belonging exclusively to a scene from which they must soon,
and may suddenly, depart for ever; and which are in no
degree fitted to prepare them for that permanent state on
which, on leaving the present, they are to enter.

But the Christian is, in a sense peculiar to himself, a pilgrim and stranger. He is a child of God, living among the
children of the wicked one. He is a citizen of heaven, sojourning for a season on the earth. Heaven is his home.
There is his treasure, and there is his heart also. His great
object here is to promote the interests of the kingdom that
is not of this world; to pass through this land of strangers
and enemies with as little injury as possible; to get safe to
the better land, and take as many as he can along with him.

For such a person to indulge in fleshly lusts is in the
highest degree incongruous. "There is," as Leighton remarks, "a diligence in his calling, and prudent regard of
his affairs, not only permitted to a Christian, but required
of him; but yet in comparison of his great and 'high calling,' as the Apostle terms it, he follows all his other
businesses with a kind of coldness and indifferency, as not
accounting very much how they go: his heart is elsewhere.
The traveller provides himself as he can of entertainment
and lodging, where he comes. If it be commodious, it is
well; but if not, it is no great matter. If he can find but
necessaries, he can abate delicacies very well; for where he
finds them in his way he neither can, nor, if he could, would
he choose to stay there. Though his inn were dressed with
the richest hangings and furniture, yet it is not his home;
he must, and he would leave it. It is not for those born
from above to *mind* earthly things. If Christians would
but consider how little, and for how little a time, they are
concerned in any thing here, they would go through any
estate, and any changes of estate, either to the better or the
worse, with very composed, equal minds, always moderate
in their necessary cares, and never taking any care at all for
the flesh, to fulfil the lusts of it. Let them that have no

better home than this world to lay claim to, live here as at
home, and serve their lusts.   Let them who have all their
portion in this life, who have no more good to look for than
what they can catch here, let them take their time of the
poor profits and pleasures that are here.   But you that have
your whole estate, all your riches and pleasures laid up in
heaven, and reserved there for you, let your lusts, your intense desire, not be fleshly, but spiritual; not earthly, but
heavenly; let the spirit out-lust the flesh; let your hearts be
there, and your conversation there.   This is not the place of
your rest, nor of your delights : unless you be willing to
change, and to have your good things here, as some foolish
travellers, that spend the estate they should live on at home
in a little while, leaving it abroad among strangers.   Will
you, with profane Esau, sell your birthright for a mess of
pottage; sell eternity, for a moment; and such pleasures, as
a moment of them is more worth than an eternity of the
other ?"

§ 2. *Motive from the tendency of the course proscribed—* *" It wars against the soul."*

The second motive is drawn from the tendency and consequences of the course dissuaded from.   These fleshly lusts,
from which Christians are required to abstain, are said " to
war against the soul."[1]   They are injurious to our highest
interests, the interests of the soul; they are inconsistent
with the peace of the soul; they are hostile to the improvement of the soul; they are, if indulged in, fatal to the final
happiness of the soul.

They are inconsistent with the peace of the soul.   The
Christian poet speaks the words of truth and soberness, when
he says,—

> " God is the source and centre of all minds—
> Their only point of rest——
> From Him departing they are lost, and rove
> At random, without honour, hope, or peace."[2]

---

[1] Στρατευονται. Non modo impediunt sed oppugnant."—BENGEL.   They not
only hinder, they oppose.   [2] Cowper.

God is a suitable and a sufficient portion for man; and he, and he only, who takes up with him as a portion, has, or can have, solid rest. He is kept in perfect peace while he trusts in God. Even a single fleshly lust destroys rest; for it takes the soul away from God, the only true rest. But this is not all; "fleshly lusts," though all opposed to that desire after happiness in God which should be the master active principle in our minds, are by no means harmonious among themselves. They "war" with each other "in our members,"[1] and tear their unhappy victim as it were in pieces. The lovers of sinful pleasure, of power, of fame and gain, know well that the way in which these lusts drag or drive him along, is any thing but the way of peace.

They are hostile to the improvement of the soul. The improvement of the soul consists in growth in the knowledge of God, and in true holiness; in increasing conformity to His image. Fleshly lusts are plainly inconsistent with this. They destroy that calm, collected state of mind, which is necessary to progress in knowledge and holiness; they occupy the time which ought to be devoted to the pursuits which conduce to spiritual improvement; and they utterly indispose to, they morally incapacitate the mind for, such pursuits. " The carnal mind is enmity against God; for it is not subject to the law of God, neither indeed can be."[2] " They do not," as has been justly said, " only divert from spiritual things for the time, but they habitually indispose it to every spiritual work, and make it earthly and sensual, and so unfit for heavenly things. Where these lusts, or any one of them, have dominion, the soul cannot at all perform any spiritual duty; can neither pray, nor hear, nor read the word aright; and, in as far as any of them prevail upon the soul of a child of God, they do disjoint and disable it from holy things."[3]

Finally, if indulged, these fleshly lusts will be fatal to the ultimate happiness of the soul. This is equally plain

---

[1] James iv. 1.   [2] Rom. viii. 7.   [3] Leighton.

from the nature of things, and the express declarations of the word of God. A man under the influence of fleshly lusts, even if taken to heaven, could not be happy, must be miserable. Heaven is a prepared place for a prepared people. The declarations of the word of God on the subject are most explicit: The end of a life in the flesh is death, eternal death. "We are not debtors to the flesh, to live after the flesh. For if ye live after the flesh, ye shall die : but if ye through the Spirit do mortify the deeds of the body, ye shall live." "Be not deceived; God is not mocked : whatsoever a man soweth, that shall he also reap. For he that soweth to the flesh, shall of the flesh reap corruption; but he that soweth to the Spirit, shall of the Spirit reap life everlasting." [1]

§ 3. *Motive from the tendency of the course recommended.*

The third motive is drawn from the tendency and probable consequences of the course recommended. The tendency and probable result of their "having their conversation honest among the Gentiles," in consequence of their abstaining from fleshly lusts, is stated to be this: " The Gentiles, who spoke against them as evil-doers, by their good works which they beheld, would be led to glorify God in the day of visitation." The Gentiles, amid whom the Christians addressed by Peter lived, spoke against them as evil-doers. The primitive Christians were very generally represented as monsters of wickedness, as guilty of the most unnatural and atrocious crimes, as atheists and haters of mankind.[2] Even in that circumstance a reason might be found for Christians being peculiarly careful to indulge no disposition, and to follow no course of conduct, which could give even the slightest probability to these calumnious misrepresentations. It was of great importance that, when spoken

---

[1] Rom. vi. 21; viii. 12, 13.   Gal. vi. 7, 8.

[2] They were represented as cannibals, magicians, infanticides; and as indulging in the most shocking impurities at their nocturnal assemblies.—Just. Apolog. i. Œcumen. in loc.   Euseb. iv. 7; v. 1.   August. de Civ. Dei, xviii. 53.

evil of, it should be falsely, obviously, demonstratively falsely.

But this is not the motive here employed by the Apostle. He counts on the natural effect of uniform good behaviour on the minds of the observers; and looking forward to a period, which he calls "the day of visitation," he encourages Christians by the hope that their "honest conversation" might be the means of bringing their heathen neighbours to a better mind, "to repentance, to the acknowledging of the truth;" and lead them, instead of calumniating and cursing *them*, to glorify *God*.

"The day of visitation" is plainly the day of God's visitation. God is said to visit men when he gives very decided proofs of his presence and power, either in works of judgment or of mercy. The phrase is used in the first sense in the following passage in the prophecy of Isaiah: "What will ye do in the day of visitation, and in the desolation that shall come from far? to whom will ye flee for help? and where will ye leave your glory?"[1] It is used in the second sense, when God is said to have "visited Israel" in Egypt, and to have "visited and redeemed his people," when he "raised up for them a horn of salvation in the house of his servant David;" and when God is said to have "visited the Gentiles to take from among them a people to his name;" and probably when Jerusalem is said "not to have known the time of her visitation, the day in which she might have known the things which belonged to her peace."[2]

If the phrase be understood in the first sense, the meaning is, that the good behaviour of the Christians would, when Divine judgments came either on the Jewish or the Pagan opposers of Christianity, induce even those who had formerly spoken evil of them, to admit the righteousness of the Divine judgments, and glorify God by acknowledging how unfounded had been the reproaches they had cast on his people.

---

[1] Isa. x. 3. [2] Exod. xiii. 19. Acts xv. 14. Luke i. 68.

If the phrase be understood in the second sense, then the meaning is, in the day when God visits these poor benighted Gentiles with his grace, your consistent, holy conduct, witnessed by them, will be one of the means employed by him in leading them to glorify him in embracing the gospel and devoting themselves to his service.

This latter view of the words seems, on the whole, best to harmonize with the scope and design of the whole passage. The consistent, holy conduct of Christians, has often been the means of promoting the conversion of unbelievers; and few considerations are more likely to weigh with a true Christian, as to the adoption or rejection of a particular course of conduct, than this. By such a course I may harden men in unbelief, embolden them in sin, smooth their path to perdition, and obstruct their way to the Saviour; by such another course I may rouse them to consideration, I may lead them to inquiry, I may soften prejudice, I may " convert the sinner from the error of his ways, save a soul from death, and hide a multitude of sins." [1]

The great ultimate object which every Christian should, which every genuine Christian does, contemplate, is the promotion of the glory of God. In his estimation, every desirable end is included in God's being glorified. This should be, this is, when he acts in character, his predominant design and thought, that in all things God may be glorified. " In what way shall I most advance the glory of my God? How shall I, who am engaged more than them all, set in with the heavens and the earth, and the other creatures, to declare his excellence, his greatness, and his goodness ?" [2]

What formidable obstacles have the earthly-mindedness and the unlovely temper and behaviour of professed Christians, thrown in the way of the glory of God being displayed in the progress and triumph of the religion of Christ among mankind! How have their envyings, and strifes, and divisions—all, as Paul says, the manifestation of carnality or

---

[1] James v. 20.   [2] Leighton.

fleshliness—how have these impeded, and all but "destroyed, the work of God!" Never can we reasonably hope for a better state of things till those who bear the name of Christ, abstaining from fleshly lusts, have their conversation more honest, more lovely, more venerable, among the Gentiles. When Zion, enlightened by the heavenly beams of sanctifying truth, arises and shines, then, not till then, will "the Gentiles come to her light, and kings to the brightness of her rising."[1]

Such, then, are the motives by which the Apostle enforces his injunction on Christians to abstain from fleshly lusts, and to have their conversation honest among the Gentiles.

Brethren, this is our duty, as well as that of those to whom these words were originally addressed; and the motives presented are such as should influence us as well as them. Abstinence from all that is forbidden or even doubtful, and the having a consistent, uniform, ornamental Christian behaviour, are duties incumbent on Christians in all countries, and in all ages—duties so important and essential, that, if they be neglected, we can have no just claim to "the worthy name" which we bear. And are not we "pilgrims and sojourners before God, as were all our fathers?" Are we not by our profession "plainly declaring, that we are seeking a country, a better country, that is an heavenly?" Do we not feel that the indulgence of inordinate desire for any earthly good disturbs our peace, and impedes our progress, and endangers our salvation? Ought we not to be desirous to be instrumental in advancing the glory of God by promoting the conversion of men? Then let us, as pilgrims on earth, and citizens of heaven, "set our affections on things above, and not on the things which are on the earth; let us seek the things that are above, at the right hand of God; let us mortify our members that are on the earth;" let us "crucify the flesh with its

[1] Isa. lx. 1, 2.

affections and lusts;" let us repress all the desires " which war against the soul;" let us not degrade the souls which God breathed into us, which Christ died to save, which the Holy Spirit is willing to make his dwelling-place, into slaves to those vile subordinate agents of the Prince of Darkness, which seek their destruction. Let us cherish all those desires and affections which give peace and health, and vigour and activity to the hidden man of the heart; let us war with those fleshly lusts which war against our souls ; let us " not be conformed to this world," so full of, so domineered over by, " the lusts of the flesh, the lusts of the eye, and the pride of life ;" but let us be " transformed by the renewing of our minds," and "prove what is that good and perfect and accept-able will of God ;" and, pitying a world lying in wickedness and hurrying to hell, let us do all we can to save them. If we can do little in any other way, let us at least, by a holy, consistent conduct, by exemplifying the purity and the peace of the religion of Christ, proclaim to all around us, " We are journeying towards the land, of which the Lord hath said, I will give it you : come with us, and we will do you good ; for the Lord hath spoken good concern-ing Israel." " Let your light, then, so shine before men, that they, seeing your good works, may glorify your Father who is in heaven." [1]

[1] Col. iii. 1-5.   Num. x. 29.   Matt. v. 16.

DISCOURSE X.

THE NATURE AND DESIGN OF CIVIL GOVERNMENT, AND THE CHRISTIAN'S DUTY IN REFERENCE TO IT.

1 Pet. ii. 13-15.—Submit yourselves to every ordinance of man for the Lord's sake : whether it be to the king, as supreme ; or unto governors, as unto them that are sent by him for the punishment of evil-doers, and for the praise of them that do well. For so is the will of God, that with well-doing ye may put to silence the ignorance of foolish men.

It has been remarked, that the moral precepts of Christianity are highly valuable, not only when viewed in their primary and direct object, the direction and guidance of the movements of the inner and outer man, the regulation of the temper and conduct, the dispositions and actions, but also when considered in their subsidiary and indirect references, particularly in their bearing on the evidence of the Divine origin of that system of revelation of which they form so important a part. That bearing is manifold. Let us look at it in its various phases. Were a book, consisting partly of doctrinal statements and partly of moral precepts, claiming a Divine origin, put into our hands ; and were we finding on perusal the moral part of it fantastic and trifling, inconsistent with the principles of man's constitution, unsuitable to the circumstances in which he is placed, and incompatible with the great laws of justice and benevolence, we should enter on the examination of the evidence appealed to, in support of its high pretensions, under the influence of a strong and justifiable suspicion. The study, for example, of the morality of the Talmud, or of the Koran, would go far, before commencing an investigation of evidence, to satisfy an enlightened enquirer that their claims to a Divine authority could not be satisfactorily supported.

On the other hand, when, in the New Testament, we find a moral code requiring all that is, and nothing that is not, "true, and honest, and just, and pure, and lovely," we cannot but be impressed with the conviction, that the system of which this forms a constituent part is worthy of being carefully inquired into ; and we enter on the inquiry not merely with excited attention, but with a disposition to weigh candidly the evidence that can be brought forward of a supernatural origin.   A man well acquainted with the preceptive parts of the New Testament, cannot help, unless he is completely devoid of candour, regarding the question as a grave and interesting one. He must feel in reference to its claims, not as he would in reference to the claims of a mere stranger, far less of one whom he knows to be a fool, and suspects to be a knave, but as he would in reference to the claims of a person of whose wisdom and worth he had reason to think highly.   The claims are of such a kind, and the consequences of admitting them are so momentous, that even, with all these favourable presumptions, they are not to be admitted without satisfactory evidence; but they obviously deserve to be examined, and respectfully and diligently examined.

But this is not all.   A person in a great measure ignorant of what true Christianity is, as a moral as well as a doctrinal system, may, without much difficulty, be persuaded by an ingenious sceptic or unbeliever, that that religion, like so many others, has originated in imposture or delusion, or in a mixture of both.   It is to ignorance of Christianity, as its principal intellectual cause, that we are disposed to trace the fearfully extensive success of infidel philosophy among the nominal Christians of the continent of Europe, in the period immediately preceding the French Revolution. But on a person well informed as to the moral part of Christianity, all such ingenious sophistry will be thrown away. He is in possession of information which satisfies him that all those hypotheses, on one or other of which the denial of the truth and divinity of Christianity must proceed, are altogether untenable. There is a character of uniform, sober, practical good sense, belonging to the morality of the New Testament, which makes it one of the most improbable of all things, that its writers should have been the dupes either of their own imagination or of a designing impostor : and there is a sustained and apparently altogether unassumed and natural air of " simplicity and godly sincerity," which forbids us, except on the most satisfactory evidence, to admit that they who wore it were other than what they seem to be, honest men.   To the question, were the men who delivered these moral maxims, fools or knaves, or a mixture of both, were they stupid dupes or wicked impostors, the only reasonable answer is, the thing is barely possible, it is in the very highest degree improbable. Evidence tenfold more strong than infidel philosophy has ever dreamed of, would be necessary to give any thing like versimilitude to any of these hypotheses, on one or other of which must be built the disproof of the claims of Christianity, on the attention, and faith, and obedience of mankind.

There is still another aspect in which the morality of Christianity may be considered, in reference to the evidence of the Divine origin of that religion. Viewed in all its bearings, it seems to be of the nature of a moral miracle.   Compare the morality of the New Testament with the morality of ancient philosophy; compare Jesus with Socrates; and Paul, and Peter, and James, and John, with Epictetus, or Plato, or Seneca, or Marcus Antoninus. The difference is prodigious; the superiority is immeasurable. Now, how are we to account for this difference, this superiority ?   On the supposition that the writers of the New Testament were uninspired men, we apprehend it is utterly unaccountable. Nothing but the admission, that they were men who spoke and wrote as they were moved by the Spirit of God, can enable us satisfactorily to explain the undoubted fact, that the purest and most perfect system of morality which the world has ever seen; the system that discovers the justest and widest views of the Divine character and government, and the deepest insight into the recesses of human nature, proceeded not from the philosophers of Egypt or of India, of Greece or of Rome, but from the carpenter of Nazareth and his uneducated disciples.[1]

Such thoughts naturally rise in the mind of every reflecting man, on reading such a passage as that of which our text forms a part, and are well fitted to strengthen our conviction, that we have not followed " cunningly devised fables," when we have yielded credence to the claims and doctrines of Jesus Christ and his apostles. It is, however, full time that we set ourselves to the consideration of the words which are to form the subject of our present discourse : " Submit yourselves to every ordinance of man for the Lord's sake : whether it be to the king, as supreme; or unto governors, as unto them that are sent by him for the punishment of evil-doers, and for the praise of them that do well. For so is the will of God, that with well-doing ye may put to silence the ignorance of foolish men."

The duty here enjoined, and the motive by which it is enforced, are obviously the two topics to which our attention must be successively directed in the sequel; but to illustrate either with advantage, it will be necessary to make a few remarks, having for their object to explain something that is obscure in the phraseology, and to disentangle something that is involved in the construction of the sentence which lies before us.

---

[1] A fuller illustration of these remarks on the bearing of Christian morality on Christian evidence, will be found in the author's Introductory Essay to Collins' edition of Venn's " Complete Duty of Man."

I.—INTRODUCTORY EXPLICATORY OBSERVATIONS.

The word rendered "ordinance,"[1] is the term which is usually and properly rendered "creature." It is the word that occurs when the gospel is commanded to be "preached to every creature," and is said to have been "preached to every creature under heaven;" when the "whole creation," or "every creature," is said to "groan and travail in pain;" and when every one who is in Christ is said to be "a new creature."[2] The literal rendering is, "Submit yourselves to every human creature." Some interpreters, most unsuccessfully, have attempted to explain the passage on the principle that this is its meaning.[3] Our translators, perceiving that the nature of things, equally with the scope of the passage, made such a version inadmissible, have given to the word a figurative meaning. They consider it as equivalent to ordinance, or institution, or appointment, all of which are, as it were, the creatures of those who ordain, institute, or appoint them.[4]

Still, however, it seems a strange injunction, "Submit yourselves to every human institution." Surely there are many human institutions or ordinances to which a Christian is not bound to submit; surely there are not a few human institutions or ordinances to which a Christian is bound not to submit. The injunction plainly requires limitation; and we apprehend it receives it.

The concluding phrase of the 13th verse, "for the punishment of evil-doers, and for the praise of them who do well," is commonly connected with the words which immediately

---

[1] Κτισις.　　[2] Mark xvi. 14.　Col. i. 23.　Rom. viii. 19-22.　2 Cor. v. 17.

[3] Sherlock. Grotius conjectures that the original reading may have been κρισει. The conjecture is ingenious, but entirely unsupported. It is a most instructive fact, that, so far as I know, no mere conjecture as to the original text of the New Testament has ever been confirmed by subsequent examination of Codices.

[4] Κτισιν ανθρωπινην τας αρχας λεγει τας χειροποιητας υπο των βασιλεων, η και αυτους τους βασιλεις καθοτι και αυτοι υπο των ανθρωπων εταχθησαν ητοι ετεθησαν, οιδε γαρ η γραφη και την θεσιν, κτισιν καλειν.— OECUMENIUS.

precede it, as if it were intended to express the object which the king, or supreme magistrate, has in view in appointing deputies. It appears to us far more natural to connect it with the word " ordinance ;" and to view it as intended to define the particular class of human ordinances which the Apostle refers to, when he commands Christians to be subject to every one of them. It is more than doubtful whether kings have always, or usually, had this as their object in appointing governors; and there can be no doubt this is the end of civil government, and is the reason why men are bound to submit to it. " Submit yourselves to every human ordinance, for the punishment of evil-doers, and for the praise of them that do well." This does not require any change in the translation, it only requires you to place a comma after the words, " sent by him."

This command, " Submit yourselves to every human ordinance, for the punishment of evil-doers, and for the praise of them who do well," is, as it were, the trunk of the injunction : the phrases, for the Lord's sake, and whether to the king, as supreme, and to governors, as those sent by him, are, as it were, branches that spring out of it. According to the genius of the English language, the precept would run thus : 'Submit yourselves, for the Lord's sake, to every ordinance of man, for the punishment of evil-doers, and the praise of them who do well, whether to the king, as supreme, or to governors, as to them who are sent by him.'

This mode of construing the passage, not only gives a definite reference to the very general term, ordinance, or institution ; it also enables us to account for the Apostle using the somewhat strange expression in reference to civil government, "ordinance *of man*, or *human* institution, for the punishment of evil-doers, and the praise of them who do well." The persons immediately addressed by the Apostle were Jews, or proselytes who had imbibed Jewish modes of thought. Jews held themselves bound to be subject to the Divine ordinance of civil magistracy, as laid down in their Scriptures. That ordinance, whether embodied in Moses, or in the Judges, or in the Davidical Kings, they regarded as entitled to obedience; but as to human institutions for this purpose, they seem very generally to have doubted, and many of them to have explicitly denied, that they were obligatory on the chosen people of God. If they yielded obedience, it was rather as a matter of expediency than of obligation: they submitted for wrath's sake, that is, to avoid punishment, rather than for conscience sake, because God had so willed it. These views were very likely carried by many of the Jewish converts into their new profession; and there seems to be a peculiar propriety in the Apostle, after having described their privileges and immunities as Christians in such lofty language, borrowed from the peculiarities of the Jewish people under the former economy; after having represented them as "the chosen race, the kingdom of priests, the holy nation, the peculiar people, the people of God;" putting them in mind that these privileges were all of a spiritual nature, and that with regard to human institutions, and especially with regard to human institutions for the purposes of civil government, they were just on a level with the rest of mankind; with the rest of their fellow-citizens, possessed of the same rights, liable to the same obligations.

II.—THE DUTY ENJOINED: SUBJECTION TO THE CIVIL GOVERNMENT, IN THE PERSONS OF ALL ITS LEGAL ADMINISTRATORS.

We are now prepared to proceed to consider the duty here enjoined on Christians: Subjection to the civil government of the country where they reside, in the persons of all its legal administrators. "Submit yourselves to every ordinance of man, for the punishment of evil-doers, and for the praise of them who do well: whether to the king, as supreme; or to governors, as those sent by him."

The description of civil government here given, first calls for consideration. It is described as "an ordinance or in-

stitution for the punishment of evil-doers, and the praise of
them who do well." The great design of civil government is, to protect the liberties, properties, and lives
of mankind, living together in society. For this purpose,
laws with suitable sanctions are enacted and executed, and
officers are created for the enactment, promulgation, and execution of these laws. With reference to civil government,
he and he only is an evil-doer who violates the law; and it is
enough to entitle a man, in the estimation of the magistrate,
to the appellation of one who does well, if he but obey the
law. With sin, as sin, the magistrate has nothing to do.
It is only when sin becomes crime, a violation of law, an in-
fringement of civil order, that it comes under his cogni-
zance. The design, then, of magistracy is " for the punishment of evil-doers," who break the laws enacted for the protection of liberty, property, reputation, and life; and " for the
praise," that is, for the reward of those "who do well" by keeping these laws; giving them that protection and encouragement which, as has been very justly remarked, are the only
rewards which good subjects can expect from their civil
governors.

Civil government is farther described as " an ordinance of
man," or " a human institution," for this purpose. It is, indeed, the doctrine of the New Testament, that civil government in one sense, and that an important one, is a Divine
institution, an ordinance of God; but that doctrine, rightly
understood, is in no way inconsistent with the doctrine, that
in another sense it is a human institution, the ordinance of
man. Civil government is so of God, as to lay a foundation
for a Divine moral obligation on those subject to it to yield
obedience. Some have held that magistracy is of God
merely as all things are of God, as the famine and the pesti-
lence, as slavery and war are of him. Those who take this
view err by defect; for this could lay no foundation for a
claim on obedience. Others err by excess, who hold that
magistracy is a direct, express, Divine institution. It does not
stand on the same foundation as the priesthood under the

law, or the Christian ministry under the gospel. The magistracy of the Jews under the law was the result of a direct divine appointment; but not the magistracy of any other people. It does not stand even on the same ground as marriage, which was formally instituted. It occupies similar ground with the social state, agriculture or commerce. It naturally rises out of the constitution of men's minds, which is God's work, and the circumstances of their situation, which are the result of his providence; and it is highly conducive to the security and well-being of mankind, which we know must be agreeable to the will of Him whose nature, as well as name, is love, and whose tender mercies are over all his works.

All this is perfectly consistent with civil government being a human ordinance or institution. It is the work of man's faculties, called forth by the circumstances in which he is placed, out of which arises the variety of form which the general institution bears in different countries and in different ages: thus far it is the work of man; and it is the work of God, just in as much as he endows man with these faculties, and places him in the circumstances which call them forth to exertion. To borrow the illustration of one of the greatest of our writers on the subject of government: "To say, because civil magistracy is ordained of God, therefore it cannot be the ordinance of man, is as if you said, 'God ordained the temple, therefore it was not built by masons; he ordained the snuffers, therefore they were not made by a smith.'"[1]

Now, the duty of Christians to this "human ordinance" of civil magistracy, is to "submit themselves" to it, practically to acknowledge its authority. It is the duty of a Christian to yield obedience to all laws of the government under which he lives, that are not inconsistent with the law of God. When the human ordinance contradicts the Divine ordinance, requiring us to do what God forbids, or forbidding

[1] Harrington.

us to do what God requires, the rule is plain : " We ought
to obey God rather than man."[1]

Nothing short of this, however, can warrant a Christian
to withhold obedience from a law of the government under
which, in the providence of God, he is placed ; and even
when conscience may compel him to non-obedience, he is
quietly and patiently to suffer the penalty which the law
imposes on his non-obedience. While obliged by the law of
God in such a case not to obey the law of man, he is equally
obliged, while the government continues acknowledged by
the community of which he forms a part, not to resist it.
He may, he ought to, use every means which the constitution of his country puts in his power to have the law improved ; but while it continues in force, however unwise and
iniquitous, if it does not require him to sin, he must obey it ;
and even where it does require him to sin, while he must
by no means obey it, he must submit to the punishment,
however unjust, which the law denounces against him.

One of the most important modes of submission to civil
government is the payment of tribute ; and this, like all the
other duties we owe to our rulers, is to be regulated by the
principle already laid down. We must not refuse, we must
not seek to evade, the payment of a tax, merely because we
think it unwise or unequal. It is only in the case of government requiring us to pay a tax for what we consider as a
sinful object, that we are entitled to refuse compliance, and
even in that case we are bound to submit to the penalty
which the law appoints for our non-compliance.

Under the general name of submission are included also
that respect and reverence with which the institution of civil
government should be regarded by all subjects. " To
despise government, and to speak evil of dignities," are sins
most decidedly condemned in the law of Christ ; and the
Christian Apostle has given his sanction to the command of
the Jewish lawgiver : " Thou shalt not speak evil of the

rulers of the people." Words are the signs of thought: the expressions of sentiment and feeling. They are therefore far from being harmless in themselves, and they are very far from being harmless in their consequences. The man who indulges his tongue in contumelious revilings against the authorities of the land, using language fitted to bring government itself into contempt, is a dangerous enemy of his country's weal, as well as a direct and open violator of the express command of God.[1]

It is highly desirable that the personal character of the magistrate should give additional lustre to his official dignity; while it is deeply to be regretted that the follies and faults of those who fill public stations have so often excited a most pernicious influence, in diminishing the authority of the laws, by making it impossible personally to respect their administrators. It is well remarked by Hooker, that "great caution must be used, that we neither be emboldened to follow them in evil, whom, for authority's sake, we must honour, nor inclined in authority to dishonour them whom, as examples, we must not follow."

To prevent misapprehensions, it is needful to remark here, that particular civil governments may be so faulty in their constitution, or so corrupt in their administration, that it may not only be lawful, but obligatory, on the subjects to seek improvement by thorough change, by depriving of power those who abuse it, and organising a new form of civil rule which will answer its objects; and that there is certainly nothing in the law of Christ which exempts his followers from an obligation to act the part of good citizens in such circumstances; but it is also of importance to add, that nothing short of the demonstrated impracticability of the improvement of a government by constitutional measures, and of the moral certainty of the great body of the citizens being really desirous of a change, can warrant individuals to refuse submission to the form of civil rule under which they

---

[1] 2 Pet. ii. 10.   Exod. xxii. 28.   Acts xxiii. 5.   James iii. 1-6.

live, whatever may be the imperfections and faults by which
it is characterised.

It deserves notice, also, before we close our observations on
this head, that the Apostle's command is, " Submit yourselves *to every* ordinance of man for the punishment of evil-
doers, and the praise of them who do well." These words,
taken by themselves, might mean,—Submit yourselves to
civil government, whatever form it may wear; monarchy,
aristocracy, democracy, or any conceivable combination of
these elements; and there can be no question that in this
sense the words would express the Christian's duty. It is
equally the duty of the Christian, if he live in Austria, to
submit to monarchy; if he live in America, to submit to
democracy; if he live in Great Britain, to submit to our
mixed government of king, lords, and commons; but from
the context it is plain that the reference is not to different
forms of civil rule in different countries, but to the different
organs of civil rule in the same country. " Whether to the
king," that is, to the Roman emperor, within the limits of
whose wide dominions those addressed by the Apostle lived,
" or to governors sent by him," that is, to the proconsuls, or
procurators, deputed by the emperor to perform the offices of
government in the distant parts of the empire. To all the
officers by whom the law is administered, Christians are to
render obedience. Whether they be persons in a higher
station or in a lower; whatever be the nature or the denomination of their office; whether their jurisdiction extend
over the whole land, or be limited to a county or to a parish;
to every one of the persons appointed to execute the laws,
we are bound to render obedience in all those particulars in
which he is authorized to demand it. So much for the
illustration of the duty enjoined by the Apostle.

III. THE MOTIVE TO THE DUTY OF CIVIL OBEDIENCE: " FOR THE LORD'S SAKE."

Let us now turn our attention to the motives by which

the Apostle enforces this duty. That is unfolded in the words, " For the Lord's sake ; for so is the will of God, that with well-doing ye may put to silence the ignorance of foolish men." " The Lord" is here, as generally in the New Testament, our Lord Jesus Christ. Christians are to yield obedience to the civil government under which they live, " for *his* sake ;" for the sake of his commandment ; for the sake of his example ; for the sake of his cause.

First, Christians are to obey the civil government under which they live, for the sake of Christ's commandment. Now, what is his commandment ? This was his commandment when he was on earth, " Render to Cæsar the things which are Cæsar's," that is, give to the civil government its due ; and, if you look into the writings of the Apostles, you will find that the due of civil government is obedience, tribute, and honour. These Apostles had the mind of Christ, and they thus express it : " Let every soul be subject to the higher powers. For there is no power but of God : the powers that be are ordained of God. Whosoever therefore resisteth the power, resisteth the ordinance of God ; and they that resist shall receive to themselves damnation. For rulers are not a terror to good works, but to the evil. Wilt thou then not be afraid of the power ? Do that which is good, and thou shalt have praise of the same : for he is the minister of God to thee for good. But if thou do that which is evil, be afraid ; for he beareth not the sword in vain : for he is the minister of God, a revenger to execute wrath on him that doth evil. Wherefore ye must needs be subject, not only for wrath, but for conscience sake. For, for this cause pay you tribute also : for they are God's ministers, attending continually on this very thing. Render therefore to them all their dues : tribute to whom tribute is due ; custom to whom custom ; fear to whom fear ; honour to whom honour." " Put them in mind," says Paul to Titus, "to be subject to principalities and powers ; to obey magistrates." They who " despise government," who are " presumptuous, self-willed," and " not afraid to speak evil of dignities," are among "the unjust whom the Lord knows how to reserve unto the day of judgment to be punished."[1]

It may be said "the commandment of the Lord," in these words, "is pure,"[2] clear as crystal; but how are we to know what is that civil government to which they refer? We know that the civil government established among the Jews was God's ordinance to them. We know that the Roman government was God's ordinance to the primitive Christians; but how are we to know what civil government is God's ordinance to us? The true answer to that is given by Dr Paley: "It is the will of God that the happiness of human life be promoted. Civil society conduces to that end. Civil societies cannot be upholden, unless in each the interest of the whole society be binding on every part and member of it. So long as the established government cannot be resisted or changed without public inconveniency, it is the will of God that the established government be obeyed." We have not the same means of judging of any particular government that it is God's ordinance to us, as those had to whom the Apostles Paul and Peter plainly told, that the Roman government was the ordinance of God to them; but we have sufficient means of ascertaining that point; and when, by their use, we have come to the conclusion, that the government under which we live is so, then the obligation to obedience, rising out of the commandment of our Lord, binds us as strongly as it bound them.

Happily for us, my brethren, there is no difficulty in coming to a determination. On the one hand, our civil constitution is based on so many just principles—is upon the whole, compared to most other governments, so well administered, and contains within itself such a deep-seated and powerful spring of improvement, that we can have no reasonable doubt that, though an ordinance of man, it is the ordinance of God to us; while, on the other hand, the ruling power in this

---

[1] Matt. xxii. 21.   Rom. xiii. 1-7.   Tit. iii. 1.   2 Pet. ii. 9, 10.
[2] Psal. xix. 8.

country, supported as it is by the approbation of the principles
on which it is founded, by the great body of the subjects, is
so powerful, that to think of resisting it would not only be
highly criminal, but folly almost amounting to madness.
For the Lord's sake, then, let us submit ourselves to this
ordinance of man, whether to the queen, as supreme, or to
inferior magistrates, as commissioned by her.

Secondly, Christians are to obey the civil government
under which they live, for the sake of the example of the
Lord. We are distinctly informed by our Apostle in the
context, that " Christ has left us an example, that we should
walk in his steps."[1] It is the duty of his followers " to be
in the world as he was in the world," and to " walk even as he
also walked." " The life of our Lord Jesus should be manifested in our mortal bodies ;" our lives should be the counter-
part of his. There is caution, however, no doubt necessary,
in applying the example of Christ as a rule of conduct. We
ought always to act on the principles on which he acted ;
and, when our circumstances coincide with his, we cannot
too exactly copy his conduct. But his circumstances and
ours are often very different ; so that an action which was
right in him would be wrong in us. Knowing the hearts
of men, for example, he spoke to hypocrites in a way that it
would be presumptuous in us to speak to any man. His
situation, in reference to the civil government under which
he was placed, was so very different from that in which we
stand to the civil government under which we are placed,
that we need caution in reasoning from the manner in which
he acted to the manner in which we ought to act ; yet still
his example here, and in every other instance, is replete
with instruction. He made it plain that he would not permit political connexions to turn him aside from his great
work. The political state of the world very much needed
improvement ; but his directly interfering in it would have
thrown obstacles in the way of gaining his great object—an

[1] 1 Pet. ii. 21.

object which, when gained, will ultimately put every thing right. He did not " cry nor strive." He took no part in the political controversies of his times. " He did no violence ;" he stirred up no seditions.[1] He rendered to Cæsar the things that were Cæsar's. We should err if we were to draw the conclusion, that we ought to have as little to do with politics as Jesus Christ had ; for our place, as citizens of a free commonwealth, is very different from his, who had no political standing at all in the existing forms of rule, whether Jewish or Roman ; but we are taught, that as Christians we are to place the religious above the political ; the kingdom not of this world, above every worldly kingdom ; that the citizen of heaven must not be sunk either in the citizen of Britain or the citizen of the world ; that where there is no prospect of our improving political institutions, it is wisest to let them alone ; and if he was uniformly obedient and submissive to one of the worst of human governments, it ill becomes us to be factious and seditious and disobedient under a system of civil rule, which, though far, very far indeed from being perfect, is yet among the best which the world has yet witnessed.

It is however chiefly, we apprehend, to the bearing which their submission to the civil government was likely to have on the cause of Christ, that the Apostle refers in the words before us. I therefore go on to remark, in the third place, that Christians are bound to obey the civil government under which they are placed, for the sake of the cause of the Lord. Among the false charges brought against the primitive Christians, this was one, that they were bad subjects ; and their refusal to join in the rites of the idolatrous religion, sanctioned by public authority, seemed to give plausibility to the charge. It deserves notice, that this is a charge which, in all ages, has been brought against the people of God by their enemies. The adversaries of Judah and Benjamin, when God turned again the captivity of his

[2] Isa. xlii. 2 ; liii. 9.

people, branded Jerusalem as " the rebellious and the bad
city—a city hurtful unto kings and provinces, whose inhabitants had moved sedition of old time ; " and Haman,
that wicked adversary and enemy, described the Jews as
" a certain people scattered abroad, and dispersed among the
people in all the provinces of the kingdom ; whose laws were
diverse from all people, and who keep not the king's laws :
whom it was therefore not for the king's profit to suffer." [1]
" There was a strong report," says one of the fathers of the
church,[2] commenting on the parallel passage in the Epistle
to the Romans, " that the apostles were seditious and inno-
vators, and that their principles and practices tended to the
subversion of the common laws." So far as this report was
credited, it was plainly calculated, in a variety of ways, to
impede the progress of Christianity ; and nothing was so
much fitted to give currency and credit to the calumny, as a
neglect or violation on the part of Christians of the injunction contained in the text. This was sure to expose them
to the vengeance of the laws, and so deprive them of the
power of extending Christianity ; while discredit was cast
on the Christian cause as hostile to the order of civil society.
On the contrary, nothing was better fitted to live down the
calumny, than a scrupulous and conscientious compliance with
the injunction. When it was found that no class of subjects so
readily obeyed all the laws of the empire, except those which
required compliance inconsistent with the laws of Christ,
while even in this case they meekly submitted to the consequences of non-compliance, though this often was torture
and death ; that while they refused to give their property
for the support of idolatry, they patiently took the spoiling
of their goods, and readily rendered " tribute to whom tribute
was due, custom to whom custom was due," the conclusion
must have forced itself on every reflecting mind : ' These
are peaceable, orderly men, and there is nothing in their
religion inconsistent with the welfare of the state.' In this

[1] Ezra iv. 12. Esth. iii. 8. [2] Chrysostom.

way their well-doing was fitted to " put to silence"[1] the ignorant and malignant calumnies of their foolish and unprincipled accusers. Such an even tenor of good conduct, such an onward course of well-doing, was better fitted to silence adversaries than the most elaborate apologies and defences.

The principle on which the apostolic injunction proceeds, is one applicable to all countries and ages. If Christians wish to recommend the religion they profess, they must be exemplary in the discharge of all the duties of domestic and social relative life; and few things are more fitted to prejudice worldly men against religion generally, or against particular forms of religion, than the manifestation on the part of their professors of a disposition to evade the laws, or violate the order, or disorganize the constitution of civil society.

At the same time it must not be forgotten, that the interests of genuine Christianity may be as really injured by the maintenance and exemplification of slavish principles as by the maintenance and exemplification of revolutionary principles; and that the true medium is that so happily described in the verse which follows our text, the thinking, and feeling, and acting as free men, guarding against making our liberty a cloak of wickedness, conducting ourselves always as the servants of God, honouring all men, loving the brotherhood, fearing God, honouring the king. Thus have I briefly illustrated the apostolic injunction, " Submit yourselves to every human ordinance for the punishment of evil-doers, and the praise of them that do well;" and the powerful motive by which he enforces it, " for the Lord's sake," from a regard to the law, the example, and the cause of him who is Lord of all; and, with a peculiar emphasis, our Lord Jesus.

---

[1] The word φιμουν, rendered *put to silence*, properly signifies *to muzzle;* which, in one expressive word, shows the Apostle's opinion of these adversaries of Christianity. They belonged to the κυνις, of which Paul warns the Philippians. —Ch. iii. 2.

The discourse has been throughout practical, so that it stands in little need of what is ordinarily called improvement. Almost all that requires to be said in this way is, " If ye know these things, happy are ye if ye do them." It is an easy matter for us to do them, when compared with those to whom they were originally addressed ; and of course, if we fail, our conduct is doubly criminal.

I conclude with a reflection which, I am sure, must have already suggested itself to your minds. If we should submit ourselves to " every ordinance of man for the punishment of evil-doers, and the praise of them that do well," should we not much more submit ourselves to every ordinance, every institution, every appointment of God, all of which have for their object the glory of his great name and the happiness of his intelligent creatures ? If we ought to be obedient to human governments, though necessarily imperfect, faulty both in their constitution and administration, how readily should we yield obedience to the Divine government, which both in principle and administration is absolutely perfect, being formed and conducted by him who is infinite in knowledge and wisdom, and power, and righteousness, and benignity. If we have human governors to whom our bodies are subject, should we not, much rather in our spirits, be subject to the King of souls ? " He is a Rock, his work is perfect ; all his ways are judgment : a God of truth, and without iniquity ; just and right is he." " His work" as a legislator, governor, or judge, " is most honourable and glorious, and his righteousness endureth for ever."[1] How high a privilege should we account it to be the subjects of such a government ! What folly and wickedness must it be to neglect or violate any of its laws ! What madness to expose ourselves to the consequences of such violation ! If, then, every soul should be subject to the powers that be, though they once were not, and may very likely, erelong, cease to be ; should not every soul be subject to that power

[1] Deut. xxxii. 4. Psal. cxi. 11.

which was, and is, and ever shall be? Is it not of supreme importance that we should be loyal subjects of the King of the universe, the immortal, invisible, only wise God?

Oh, let all of us see that our relations to him are in a safe and satisfactory state! Have we acquainted ourselves with Him as he has manifested himself " in the face" of his only Begotten, his visible image, the great revealer of the unseen, the invisible One, and are we at peace with him? It once was otherwise; we were at war with him. Mad, impious rebellion! Has the manifestation of his authority and grace quelled the rebel principles within, brought every high thing down into subjection to him, and sweetly constrained us to cast from us the weapons we had so foolishly, so wickedly, wielded against him? If not, the sooner such a change takes place, the better; for " HE beareth not the sword in vain."

If this all-important change has taken place, let us prove that it has taken place by submitting cordially to his authority, as administered by HIM whom he has " set on his holy hill of Zion." Let us " serve him without fear, in righteousness and holiness, all the days of our lives." Let us " walk in all his ordinances and commandments blameless;" let us " count his precepts concerning all things to be right; let us hate every false way;"[1] and let us show our supreme regard to his authority, by cheerfully doing every thing which our civil rulers require of us, however disagreeable to us, which is not inconsistent with his law, because he has commanded it; and obstinately refusing to do any thing which they command us, however deeply it may involve our worldly interests, which is inconsistent with his law, because he has forbidden it.

It is, indeed, inward subjection to HIS authority, that alone can secure high principled and duly regulated subjection to every lawful inferior authority. It has been justly remarked, that when the spirit of the high-minded sinner has

---

[1] Luke i. 6, 74, 75. Psal. cxix. 128.

been brought down by the gospel, and he has bowed with a broken and contrite heart to the sceptre of the Saviour's grace, the humble subjection of his conscience, which then takes place, involves in it a meek and humble spirit of submission to all the authority which that God has vested in any of his creatures. The obedience which he yields as a child, as a servant, as a subject, being yielded from religious principles, becomes obedience to God; and " whatsoever he does" henceforward, " he does it heartily to the Lord, and not to man."[1]   And hence it is that the Christian minister feels that he never acts more the part of a good citizen, never employs means more fitted for improving the whole scene of domestic and social and political life, than when he urges on men, " repentance towards God, and faith towards our Lord Jesus Christ;" and beseeches them, on the ground of the great atonement, to be reconciled to God.[2]

[1] Col. iii. 23.

[2] The whole subject of this discourse is more fully discussed by the author, in his treatise entitled " The Law of Christ respecting Civil Obedience, especially in the Payment of Tribute."

DISCOURSE XI.

THE CONDITION AND DUTY OF CHRISTIANS "AS FREE," YET "AS THE SERVANTS OF GOD."

1 PET. ii. 16.—As free, and not using your liberty for a cloak of maliciousness, but as the servants of God. [a]

THESE words contain in them a very instructive view of the
condition and duty of Christians, to the illustration and
improvement of which I design to devote the following discourse. The CONDITION of Christians is described as at
once a condition of liberty and subjection. They are "free,"
and yet servants, "the servants of God." The DUTY of Christians is stated with a reference to their condition : they are
to conduct themselves agreeably to their condition, as free,
and as the servants of God; they are to assert and use their
liberty; they are not to abuse their liberty; they are to exemplify or act out their subjection. Such is the outline
which I shall attempt to fill up in the sequel.

I. THE CONDITION OF CHRISTIANS.

§ 1. *They are free.*

Let us then, in the first place, attend to the account contained in the text of the condition of Christians. They are
"free," yet "the servants of God." Christians are a peculiar
people. They are freemen among slaves, the servants of
God among the servants of the wicked one. This was not

always the case. The common condition of the race was originally theirs. They were slaves both in condition and in character. But the Son has made them free, and they are free indeed. The determined rebel has become a loyal subject. " If any man be in Christ Jesus he is a new creature," and to him there is a new creation. " Old things have passed away, and all things have become new." Christians are free: free in reference to God; free in reference to man; free in reference to the powers and principles of evil.

Let us shortly attend to these various aspects of the Christian's freedom.

(1.) *Free in reference to God.*

First, they are free in reference to God. They are "the Lord's freemen." [1] By this we do not mean that they are not under the strongest obligations to conform their minds and wills to the mind and will of God, and to regulate the whole of their temper and conduct according to the revelation of that mind and will contained in his word. They are not free in the sense of being "without law to God;" to be so would be the reverse of a privilege; they "are under the law to Christ." [2] Yet still in a very important sense they are free, both as to condition and character, in reference to God; and these two forms or species of freedom are closely connected, the latter being the result and manifestation of the former.

The relation in which a Christian naturally stood to God in consequence of sin, was that of a condemned criminal; and the character by which he was distinguished was that of a sullen slave, conscious of having exposed himself to punishment for his indolence and unfaithfulness, and equally hating his Master and his work. "All have sinned, all have lost the approbation of God," [3] all have incurred the condemning sentence of the divine law; and

> " Chains are the portion of revolted man—
> 　　Stripes and a dungeon." [4]

[1] 1 Cor. vii. 22.

[2] 1 Cor. ix. 21.

[3] Rom. iii. 23. Δοξα.—John v. 41-44.

[4] Cowper.

They are, as it were, shut up in prison, reserved for punishment, and bound by the fetters of guilt, which no created power can break, no created ingenuity unlock.

In this state, of which no sinner is entirely unconscious, the disposition towards God is, must be, not that of an affectionate child or a loyal subject, but that of a slave punished for disobedience, cherishing a grudge toward his master, as if the unreasonableness of the task assigned him, rather than his own wilful neglect and disobedience, were the true cause of the evils he feels or fears. He is an entire stranger to the love of God, so that free voluntary obedience is a moral impossibility; and if at any time he assume the appearance of submission, and do those actions which the law requires, such conduct springs entirely from the principles of servile fear or mercenary expectation. This is the natural condition and character of all men in reference to God. This was once the condition and character of every Christian.

But the condemned criminal has become a pardoned, accepted child; the slave has obtained both the state and the disposition of a freeman. The prison doors have been thrown open, the fetters of guilt have been unloosed, the prisoner has gone forth. Love has taken the place of dislike, confidence of jealousy, joyful hope of " the fear that had torment;" and while the pardoned, renewed sinner, " keeps God's precepts," " he walks at liberty."

The manner in which this change is produced, must be familiar to the mind of every one who properly understands even " the principles of the doctrines of Christ," " the first principles of the oracles of God."[1] It is by the faith of the truth as it is in Jesus, that man, the criminal and slave, is introduced into the state and formed to the character of a spiritual freeman. Christ Jesus, the only begotten of God, has by the appointment of his Father, moved by sovereign love, done and suffered, as the substitute of man, all that was necessary to make the salvation of sinners perfectly con-

---

[1] Heb. vi. 1; v. 12.

sistent with, gloriously illustrative of, the holiness and justice, as well as the pity and benignity of the Divine character. That wondrous work of "God manifest in the flesh," is made the subject of a plain, well-accredited revelation. In the case of all the saved, by a sovereign Divine influence the mind is so fixed on this revelation, in its meaning and evidence, as to understand and believe it. This is the faith of the gospel.

This faith, by Divine appointment, brings the sinner within the saving power of the atonement. He is redeemed from the curse of the law through him who became a curse in his stead; the blessing of Abraham, even a free and full justification, by believing, comes on him; and he obtains larger and larger measures of the promised Spirit, by believing. "Being justified by faith, he has peace with God, through our Lord Jesus Christ, and has access to God," as his father and friend, "by this faith, in reference to the grace of God;" and he "stands" in this state of reconciliation and favourable fellowship, "rejoicing in hope of the glory of God." "There is no more condemnation to him, being in Christ Jesus; and he walks no more after the flesh, but after the Spirit." The Spirit of Christ the Lord dwells in him, and "where the Spirit of the Lord," which is a free spirit, is, "there is liberty." The love of God is shed abroad in his heart by the Holy Ghost, given to him, and he loves him who has first, and so, loved him. And his love finds its natural expression in conformity to God's mind and will, and in obedience to his commandments. It is no longer the slave, toiling at intervals at a task which he abhors, to secure the morsel or to escape the lash; it is an enlightened, renewed creature, embracing what he sees to be true, and doing what he knows to be right, following out the impulses of his new nature; and doing all this the more readily, because he knows that in doing so he walks in the light of his heavenly Father's countenance, enjoying an elevating consciousness of fellowship of mind and heart with the only wise, the immaculately holy, the infinitely benignant, the ever-blessed God; and because he has learned, by painful experience, that "the way of the transgressor," even of "the backslider in heart," "is hard," and that holiness and happiness are in the nature of things, as well as by the express Divine appointment, so closely conjoined, as to be all but identified with each other. He "knows the truth, and the truth makes him free."[1]

The whole of the Christian's obedience, when he acts like himself, has this character of true-hearted freedom. With regard to a very large portion of his duties, he so distinctly sees their reasonableness and excellence, and the important and blissful purposes which obedience is fitted to secure, that he considers the having this peaceful, joyful path, through a world full of sin and misery, so clearly pointed out in the law of the Lord, as one of the greatest proofs of the kindness of his God and Father. He sees and feels that God has "granted him his law graciously." The language of his heart is, " O ! how love I thy law, it is my meditation all the day :" "Great peace have they who love thy law, nothing can offend them : " " I will run in the way of thy commandments, when thou hast enlarged my heart ; " " I will delight myself in thy commandments, which I love : " "I will keep thy laws continually for ever and ever, and I will walk at liberty; for I seek thy precepts."[2] And if in some cases he may feel a difficulty in perceiving the reason of a particular piece of dutiful exertion, or suffering, or sacrifice, required of him, the deep-seated conviction which the manifestation of God, in the person and work of his Son, has lodged in his mind of the infinite wisdom and power of Jehovah, constantly influenced by holy love, makes him cheerfully comply with the requisition, just because it is HIS.

The measure of this spiritual liberty obviously depends on the measure of faith. In proportion to the clearness of our apprehensions, and the firmness of our persuasion of " the

---

[1] Rom. v. 1, 2 ; viii. 1.   2 Cor. iii. 17.
[2] Psal. cxix. 29, 163, 32, 16, 44, 45.

truth as it is in Jesus," will be the alacrity and delight with which, " delivered out of the hands of our " spiritual " enemies, we serve him without fear, in righteousness and holiness." [1] The spirit of bondage, which leads Christians again to fear, with the fear which hath torment, which fetters their minds and hearts, grows powerful just as saving truth is overlooked or misapprehended; and can be cast out of the heart only by that " perfect love," which grows out of our knowing and believing the love which God has for us, and which he has manifested in giving his Son to be the propitiation for our sins.

The character of manly, Christian, affectionate freedom, which the knowledge and faith of the truth as it is in Jesus, under Divine influence, produces, renders unnecessary and unsuitable such an institution as the Mosaic law, an institution suited to the Church in its infant state. That institution, having served its purpose, has been abrogated; and all attempts, and they have been numerous, to introduce into the Christian Church any system of a similar character, are foolish and criminal; an invasion equally of the prerogative of Christ, and of the privileges of his people. So much for the Christian's freedom in reference to God.

(2.)—*Free in reference to Man.*

Let us now look at the second aspect of the Christian's freedom : He is free in reference to man.

When we say that the Christian is free in reference to man, we do not mean to deny that he is under obligation to seek the happiness of his fellow men, and especially of his fellow Christians ; and that, in prosecuting this end, he is to imitate the conduct of his Lord, who " came not to be ministered to, but to minister." Christians are to " submit themselves one to another, in the fear of God;" they are all of them to be " subject one to another," and " by love to serve one another." The Apostle's being " free from all men,"

---

[1] Luke i. 71.

was not at all inconsistent with his being "the servant of all." "He who would be chief among his brethren, must be the *servant* of all." "He that is greatest among you," says our Lord, "shall be your servant."[1]

We do not mean that the Christian is emancipated from civil authority, and is not bound to "be subject to the powers that be," or that he cannot fill the place of a domestic servant, or discharge its duties. His relations and duties, as a member of civil or domestic society, are in no degree changed by his becoming a Christian. Nor do we mean that the Christian may not be subjected to the most degrading servitude, being treated by a fellow man as if he was as completely his property as his estate or his cattle. This has actually been the situation of multitudes of Christians. It is the situation of not a few at this moment; and Oh, shame! the slaveholder, as well as the slave, bears the worthy name, Christian.

But we mean, that the mind and conscience of the Christian are emancipated from human authority : we mean, that no human power has any right to dictate to him what he is to believe, and what he is to do in matters of religious and moral duty: and that, in the degree in which he is an enlightened Christian, he acts on the principle, that he ought to "call no man on earth master;" but in the exercise of his own faculties, aided by the promised Spirit, to endeavour to ascertain what is the mind and will of the "One Master, who is in heaven."

There is a natural tendency in man to usurp spiritual authority over man; and there is a natural tendency, too, to submit to this usurpation. By far the greater part of mankind have no better reason for their religious opinions, ordinances, and usages, than that they have "received them by tradition from their fathers."[2] What is taught and received, as religious truth and duty, is nothing more than

[1] Eph. v. 21.   1 Pet. v. 5.   Gal. v. 13.   Matt. xx. 28.   1 Cor. ix. 19.   Luke xxii. 26.
[2] 1 Pet. i. 18.   Matt. xv. 9.

"the commandments of men." The great body even of those who assume to themselves the honourable appellation, free-thinkers, are nothing less than what that appellation expresses. They are, almost universally, the blind followers of their blind, self-chosen guides; the veriest slaves of human authority, in one of its least creditable forms.

When a man becomes a Christian, in the recognition of the supreme and sole authority, in all matters of religious truth and duty, of God, and of Jesus Christ whom he has sent, there is necessarily implied the renunciation of all human authority. If the one Master be in heaven, there can be no master on earth. A Christian, acting worthy of the liberty wherewith Christ has made him free, believes no doctrine but what he is persuaded Christ has taught; observes no ordinance but what he believes Christ has appointed; performs nothing as a duty but what he is convinced Christ has enjoined. Helpers of his faith, he gratefully acknowledges in all who will assist him in obtaining wider, clearer, more impressive views, of the mind and will of the supreme Teacher and Sovereign; such he counts his greatest benefactors : but lords of his faith he will not recognise, even in the wisest and best of men. He feels that there is but one with whom he has to do, as authority, in religion ; "one lawgiver, who can save and who can destroy;"[1] and that he must stand before HIS judgment-seat, and give an account of himself to Him. The answer to the questions, What say the fathers? what say the reformers? what say the symbolical books? the answer to any or all of these questions, does not determine his faith : it is the question, What saith the Lord? "What is written in the law? how readest thou?"[2] This is the touchstone by which he examines all religious doctrines and institutions. "To the law, and to the testimony : if men speak not according to this word, it is because there is no light in them."[3] It is unworthy of the condition and character of spiritual

---

[1] James iv. 12.   [2] Luke x. 26.   [3] Isa. viii. 20.

freemen, to which Christ by his Spirit, through the faith of the truth, hath raised them, to be the servants of men. Their judgments must not be guided, when they act like themselves they will not be guided, by the writings of Luther or Calvin, nor based on the decisions of councils, however venerable. They will honour their fellow disciples, especially such of them as have obviously profited by the teaching of their common Master; but they will sit only at his feet, and take the law only from his mouth.

There is another aspect of the Christian's freedom, in reference to his fellow men, that deserves to be cursorily noticed before leaving this part of our subject. Human approbation, in some form or other, is a leading object with the great body of mankind, and exercises a powerful influence over their conduct. They seek the praise, they fear the censure, and reproach, and revilings of men; and they fashion their conduct so as to secure the one and avoid the other. With the Christian, Divine approbation is the great object. He seeks the honour which comes down from above; and, in doing this, he is set free from the enslaving influence of the hopes and fears which spring out of an exaggerated estimate of the value of the good opinion of men. With him, "it is a very small thing to be judged of man's judgment; for he believes that there is one that judgeth him, that is the Lord."[1]

(3.)—*Free in reference to the Power and Principles of Evil.*

Let us now look at the third aspect of the Christian's condition as *free*. He is free in reference to the powers and principles of evil. By the powers of evil, I understand the devil, that crafty, and powerful, and active spiritual being, of whom we read so often in Scripture, and of whose personal existence I think no unprejudiced reader of the Sacred Volume can entertain a doubt; who introduced moral evil into our world in the beginning of the history of our

[1] 1 Cor. iv. 3.

race, and has been ceaselessly endeavouring, with but too much success, to uphold and extend its influence; and his subordinate agents, " the evil angels." By the principles of evil, I understand the various depraved propensities of our fallen nature, acted on by the present world, "things seen and temporal."

By these powers and principles all men are naturally enslaved. The evil spirit is "the god of this world;" he "worketh in the hearts of the children of disobedience;" he "leads them captive at his will." They "are of their father the devil, and the lusts of their father;" the things which he desires and delights in, "they will do," they choose to "do."[1] Though to a great degree the unconscious, they are not the less the devoted, servants of the wicked one.

When a man becomes a Christian, he is delivered from the power of Satan. "The prey is taken from the mighty, and the captive of the terrible one is delivered." He by no means ceases to be the object of the malignant attempts of his great enemy. "Like a roaring lion, he goes about seeking to devour"[2] him. Like a cunning serpent, he lies in wait to dart into his soul the poison and pollution of sin. But he ceases to be his slave. His new state of favour with God, secures for him the protection of a power, compared with which diabolical power is weakness; and the guidance of a wisdom, compared with which diabolical craft is folly: so that he can "tread upon the lion and the adder; the young lion and the dragon he can trample under foot:" and the good Spirit, by the instrumentality of his word, furnishes him with principles which enable him to baffle his devices, and frustrate all his attempts to regain his lost dominion.

Men are by nature not only the slaves of Satan, but they are represented as serving divers lusts and pleasures as the servants of sin: "Whosoever committeth sin is the servant," the slave, "of sin." The Apostle represents them as so: " the servants, the slaves of sin;" as to be "freemen [b] so far as righteousness is concerned," that is, to be entirely unin-

[1] Cor. iv. 4.   2 Tim. ii. 26.   John viii. 44.
[2] Isa. xlix. 24.   1 Pet. v. 8.   [b] See note B.

fluenced by holy principle; to be wholly under the power of evil; "sin reigning over their mortal body," while they "obey it by means of the desires of the body," and "yield their members to it as the instruments of unrighteousness." Such were some, such were all true Christians, previously to their conversion; but God be thanked, that they who were the servants of sin, have, by obeying from the heart the form of doctrine which has been delivered to them, been "made free from sin;" freemen in reference to sin, and have become the servants of righteousness;" no longer "yielding their members servants to uncleanness, and to iniquity unto iniquity, but yielding their members servants to righteousness unto holiness."[1]

By the faith of the truth they are so identified with Christ, as that his death, resurrection, and new life, are theirs. They are brought under their influence, both justifying and sanctifying; "so that as he died unto sin once, and being raised from the dead dieth no more, death having no more dominion over him, but liveth to God, they also reckon themselves dead indeed unto sin, but alive to God through Jesus Christ our Lord: and the consequence is, they no longer let sin reign in their mortal body, that they should obey it in the lusts thereof; neither do they yield their members to it as instruments of unrighteousness, but yield themselves unto God, as those that are alive from the dead, and their members as instruments of righteousness unto God. For sin no longer has dominion over them: for they are not under the law, but under grace." "Whoso is born of God doth not commit sin: for his seed remaineth in him: and he cannot sin, because he is born of God."[2] The new nature is a holy nature, and, so far as a man possesses this nature, he does not sin. And every man who possesses it at all, possesses it in such a degree as that he habitually hates and avoids sin. Not that any Christian in the present state is completely freed from the influence of depraved principle: "If we say that we have no sin, we deceive ourselves, and

1 John viii. 34. Rom. vi. 16-20.   2 Rom. vi. 9-14. 1 John iii. 9.

the truth is not in us." While we are in the present state, "there is a law in our members which wars against the law of the mind;" but the Christian "consents to the law that it is good," "delights in the law of God after the inner man;" and though, "with the flesh," *i. e.*, so far as he is unrenewed, "he serves the law of sin," yet with the spirit, *i. e.*, so far as he is renewed (and this constitutes his prevailing abiding character), "he serves the law of God;" and though often, when he loses sight of the truth, which sanctifies as well as comforts, constrained to sigh out, "wretched man, who will deliver me?" yet, habitually, he rejoices in the begun and advancing emancipation from the principles of evil, "thanking God through Jesus Christ," who hath delivered, who is delivering, and who will deliver; rejoicing that not only is "there no condemnation to him, being in Christ Jesus," but that "the law of the Spirit of life in Christ Jesus, has made him free from the law of sin and of death."[1]

§ 2.—*Christians are the servants of God.*

Having made these cursory remarks on the condition of Christians as free, free in reference to God, free in reference to man, free in reference to the powers and principles of evil; let us now, for a little, attend to the second view of their condition. While in one point of view they are free, in another, they are " servants, servants of God." These are by no means inconsistent representations. So far from this, it is only by becoming the servants of God that men can cease to be the slaves of Satan and sin. The only true liberty of which a dependent being like man is capable, is the free use of his faculties in the service of God. Independence, strictly speaking, belongs only to God. Man in seeking it, instead of obtaining, lost liberty. Seeking to be supreme lord of himself, refusing to be the servant of the best of beings, he necessarily became a slave of the worst. It is the very condition of our beings, as creatures, that we

---

[1] 1 John i. 8.   Rom. vii. 14; viii. 2.

serve; " we have not the liberty to choose whether we shall serve or not, all the liberty we have is to choose our master." [1]

Men in their natural state are not God's servants. They are " the children not of obedience," as Christians are; they are "the children of disobedience." In one sense, indeed, all men are God's servants. They are all bound to submit to his authority; they are all under his control; they are all employed by him in the execution of his purposes. But Christians are God's servants in a sense peculiar to themselves. They are his peculiar property; they have been formed by him to the character of his servants; they have voluntarily devoted themselves to his service; they habitually employ themselves in his service.

They are his servants, for they are his peculiar property. All men are God's property. "All that is in the heaven and in the earth is his." Men may renounce God's authority, but they cannot despoil him of any part of what belongs to him. But Christians are God's property in a peculiar sense. They are his " purchased possession." Justice had doomed them to death, and they were bought off, "not by such corruptible things as silver and gold, but by the precious blood of Christ, as of a lamb without blemish and without spot." " Jesus gave himself for them, that he might redeem them from all iniquity, and purify them as a peculiar people."

As God purchased them to be his servants, so by the influence of his good Spirit he has qualified them for his service. Well may he say to each of them, " Remember thou art my servant: I have formed thee; thou art my servant;" and of them all as a body, " This people have I formed for myself; that they may show forth my praise." He has " shed his love abroad in their hearts;" he has " put his fear in their hearts." He has " put his law in their inward parts, and written it in their hearts." He has " created them anew in Christ Jesus unto good works," and " transformed them, by the renewing of their minds:" and, under the influence

[1] Sanderson.

of his good Spirit, he has induced them gladly and gratefully to enter into his service, to assume his easy yoke, to
take up his light burden. He has made them see and feel
the irresistible force of his infinite excellence and kindness,
as a motive to obedience. He has manifested to them " the
great love wherewith he has loved them," and " blessed
them with all heavenly and spiritual blessings ; " so that they
have been constrained to say, " What shall we render to the
Lord for all his benefits? Truly, O Lord, we are thy servants; we are thy servants; thou hast loosed our bonds."
" Other lords have had dominion over us; henceforth we
will make mention only of thy name."[1]

Finally, they are his servants, for they habitually employ
themselves in his service. Christians, knowing that " they
are not their own, but bought with a price," glorify Him
who has bought them " with their souls, and with their
bodies, which are God's." Influenced by his mercies, they
present themselves to him as " living sacrifices, holy and acceptable, which is their rational worship." Delivered by him
from their former tyrants, " they serve him without fear, in
righteousness and holiness, all the days of their life." They
acknowledge that it is their duty, they know that it is their
prevailing desire, to be entirely conformed to the will of their
Lord : " Whether they eat, or drink, or whatsoever they do,
they" would " do all to his glory." " Whatsoever they do
in word or in deed, they would do it in the name of the Lord
Jesus, giving thanks to God the Father through him." Their
desire is, " to be in the world as Jehovah's elect servant was
in the world, always about their Master's, their Father's, business ; finding it their meat to do his will, and finish his work."[2]

It concerns us all seriously to inquire, if the condition
which has been described be ours. Are we experimentally
acquainted with this liberty of the children of God ; are we

[1] Isa. xliv. 21; xliii. 21. Rom. v. 5. Jer. xxxii. 40; xxxi. 33. Eph. ii. 10.
Rom. xii. 2. Eph. i. 2, 11, 4. Psal. cxvi. 12, 16. Isa. xxvi. 13.
[2] 1 Cor. vi. 19, 20. Rom. xii. 1. Luke i. 74, 75. 1 Cor. x. 31. Col. iii. 17.
1 John iv. 17. John iv. 34.

the servants of God? The question should not be a difficult one to answer. On this subject, I believe, there may be presumptuous confidence. Where there is not only no evidence for, but very much evidence against a favourable answer, there are men "who speak great swelling words of vanity" about their Christian liberty, while their whole character and conduct proclaim them "servants of corruption." The only permanent satisfactory evidence that we are God's freemen is, habitual gratitude for our emancipation, showing itself by our "serving him without fear, in righteousness and holiness," "walking before him in love." The only permanent satisfactory evidence that we are God's servants is, our doing his work.

Owing to a variety of causes, there may be hesitation and doubt, where there is such evidence as ought to lay the foundation of humble confidence. But there is something wrong here also. Doubt on such a subject is, in no case, a good symptom, and it is obviously equally a matter of duty and prudence to seek certainty on a point so vitally connected with our highest interests. If we are indeed "free," and "the servants of God," why, by remaining in doubt about it, deprive ourselves of the abundant consolation, the good hope, the varied and powerful motives to holiness, which a clear satisfactory persuasion of this truth would naturally produce? And if we are not "free," if we are not the servants of God, and if, continuing in this condition, our final perdition is absolutely certain, is it not at least equally important that we should be distinctly aware of it? We may, though now slaves, yet be emancipated; we may, though now the servants of sin, yet become the servants of God.

One cause why many men remain at ease in a state of unconversion is, the ill-founded hope that they have been converted, or, at any rate, the absence of a thorough conviction that they are yet unconverted. Let us honestly turn to account, for the purposes of self-inquiry, the plain truths brought forward in this discourse, and we must arrive at a conclusion respecting our true spiritual condition.

And should that conclusion prove an unfavourable one, as I am afraid would be the case with some now present, O, let them continue no longer in a state so degrading and dangerous ! Brethren, you need not remain slaves. The ransom has been paid; the Deliverer stands ready to unloose your fetters; and if you remain unemancipated, it is because you will not avail yourselves either of the atoning sacrifice, or the quickening Spirit of the Saviour. Think what the wages of your degrading servitude will be: "Death, the second death, everlasting destruction." "If ye live after the flesh, ye must die;" "if ye sow to the flesh, ye shall of the flesh reap corruption." Consider, too, if ye perish, ye perish not unwarned; ye have been told, most distinctly told, what must be the end of these things: "Thus saith the Lord God, Behold, my servants shall eat, but ye shall be hungry: behold, my servants shall drink, but ye shall be thirsty: behold, my servants shall rejoice, but ye shall be ashamed: behold, my servants shall sing for joy of heart, but ye shall cry for sorrow of heart, and shall howl for vexation of spirit."[1] "Choose *now* whom ye will serve." There is surely no room for hesitation here; slavery and freedom: the slavery of Satan, the liberty of the children of God; the burning lake and the bottomless pit, and fulness of joy, rivers of pleasure, for evermore: these are the alternatives. There is no time for delay. "To-day if ye will hearken to his voice;" to-morrow you may be beyond its reach.

Should the conclusion prove a favourable one, as I trust it will in some, in many instances, O, how strong the obligations to distinguishing grace; how loud the calls to grateful acknowledgment; how powerful the motives to progressive holiness! "The more we attain unto the faculty of serving him cheerfully and diligently, the more still will we find of this spiritual liberty, and have the more joy in it. Oh! that we could live as his servants, employing all our industry to do him service in the condition and place

[1] Isa. lxv. 13-15.

wherein he hath set us, whatsoever that is; and as faithful servants, more careful of his affairs than of our own, accounting it our main business to seek the advancement of his glory: 'Happy is the servant whom the Master, when he cometh, shall find so doing.'"[1]

II.—THE DUTY OF CHRISTIANS.

I proceed now to the consideration of the view that is given us of the Christian's duty. His duty is generally to act conformably with his condition; to behave himself at once like a freeman and a servant,[2] while he guards against the abuse of the liberty wherewith he has been made free. He is to act " as free," yet taking care not to make his " liberty a cloak of maliciousness;" and he is to act as the " servant of God;" he is to use his freedom; he is not to abuse it; and he is to exemplify his condition as the servant of God. Let us attend to these three general views of the Christian's duty in succession.

§ 1. *The Christian's duty to use his freedom; to act " as free."*

First, then, Christians are to act *as* free. Their conduct is to correspond with their condition as freemen, not slaves. The whole frame of their temper and behaviour is to correspond to that liberty which is well called Christian liberty, being purchased by the blood of Christ, that " blood of the covenant " by which " the prisoners of hope" are " sent forth out of the pit wherein is no water," revealed to us in the gospel of Christ, that "royal law," that " law of liberty," and conveyed to us, bestowed on us, by that " free Spirit" of Christ, who, wherever he comes, brings liberty along with him.[3] The best way of bringing out the truth on this sub-

---

[1] Leighton.

[2] Christianorum libertas est serva libertas, quia liberati sunt, ut Deo serviant; et libera servitus quia non coacté sed sponte Deo et Magistratui obediunt.— GERHARD.

[3] Zech. ix. 11. James i. 25, 11, 8. Psal. li. 12.

ject, in a way in which it can easily be turned to practical
purposes, will, I believe, be shortly to attend to the Christian's duty as to the maintenance and use of his freedom in
the three aspects in which we have already contemplated
it ; freedom in reference to God ; freedom in reference to
man ; freedom in reference to the powers and principles of
evil.

(1.) *"As free" in reference to God.*

The Christian is to act "as free" in reference to God.
When I say the Christian is to act as free, I refer to the actings, not only, nor principally, of the outer man, but of " the
inner man" of the mind and heart. What is fundamental
here is the maintenance of a firm faith of that Christian
truth, that truth as it is in Jesus, by which the Christian
was freed both from the condition and dispositions of a slave,
brought into the state and formed to the character of a freeman ; and the cherishing of that humble, yet confident assurance, that he is in a state of favour with God, which naturally
grows out of this faith, and its necessary effects on the character and conduct.

Many professors of Christianity seem to labour under a
serious mistake on this subject. Uncertainty, doubt, perplexity, fear, seem to be the elementary principles of their
religion ; they seem to think the better of themselves that
they have no " confidence towards God," no settled satisfaction respecting their highest interest ; they appear to consider anxiety and alarm as the best proofs of spiritual life, the
best motives to spiritual activity ; and that the securest way
of getting to heaven, is by no means to anticipate as certain,
or even very probable, the getting there at last, but to be
" all their lifetime subject to bondage through fear of
death," and what is to follow it. They seem to think that it
would be presumption in any man to entertain that " good
hope through grace" which the Apostles cherished, and
which they call on all Christians to cherish. This may
have, as the Apostle expresses it, " a show of humility ;" but

it exhibits a deplorable ignorance of the first principles of Christian truth, an entire unacquaintance with the genius of the gospel economy.

There are, as we have already hinted, two things which a Christian should earnestly seek to hold steadfastly when he has obtained them, in order to his acting as a freeman towards God,—" the assurance of faith," and " the assurance of hope." The first refers to the testimony of God respecting the Saviour and his salvation. The second refers to the expectation of the personal enjoyment of the Saviour and his salvation. No man is a Christian at all who has not both the faith and the hope of the gospel ; and the measure of the holiness and the happiness of any individual Christian, is just the degree of this faith and hope, which are always proportioned to each other.

Surely there can be nothing good, there must be all that is evil, in doubting the testimony of God, that is, in treating the God of truth as if he were a liar. This is, properly speaking, unbelief : that which makes men slaves, and keeps them so ; that which prevents men from coming to God, and leads them to depart from him. It is the truth which makes us free. It is only as believed that it can do so ; it is only in the degree that it is believed that it can do so. Doubt with regard to the saving truth can never be right in any man ; in a Christian it is doubly folly and sin, and is indeed, as it were, spiritual suicide.

Doubt with respect to the safety of our own state, which is a very different matter from doubt of the saving truth, though the two things have intimate and interesting relations to each other, is in no case a desirable or even a proper state of mind. There may be but too much ground for it, both on the part of the unconverted and of the converted man ; but still it is a state which ought not to exist. As to the unconverted man, he ought not to be in *doubt* about his spiritual state ; he ought to *know* his state to be one of deep guilt and imminent danger. While he only doubts that all is not right, he is not in the way of being saved. He must know that all is wrong. He must be brought to see himself lost, else he never will come to the Saviour; and, if he were not wilfully blind, he could not help seeing that there is no room for doubt in his case. He is " condemned already, and the wrath of God is abiding on him." And there needs be no doubt about the matter; it is just as certain as the plain declaration of the God of truth can make it.

There may be ground for doubt as to the safety of his state in the case even of a converted man. Not that we believe that any really converted man will not be saved. We are fully persuaded of that declaration of the faithful and true witness : " I give unto my sheep eternal life ; and they shall never perish, neither shall any pluck them out of my hands. My Father, who gave them me, is greater than all, and none can pluck them out of my Father's hand."[1] But if a converted man lose sight of the truth, which is the great source in one view, in another the only channel, of true holiness and comfort in the human heart, and losing sight of that truth, falls under the power of worldly lusts, and " lust having conceived, bringeth forth sin,"[2] then doubts about the safety of his spiritual state, if he is not sunk into utter stupidity or strong delusion, must prevail. But this is plainly a state into which the Christian ought not to have brought himself; and it is as plainly a state, out of which the sooner he gets so much the better. Till he is, he can neither enjoy comfort nor make progress in holiness; and he can be brought out of it in no other way than by the truth which first made him free, again, through being anew apprehended in its meaning and evidence, exerting its natural influence, and thus, both directly and indirectly, furnishing the mind with satisfactory evidence that it is in a state of spiritual freedom.

This, then, is the first way, Christian brethren, in which you are to act as free towards God. Hold fast the faith of " the truth as it is in Jesus." Continue to count it " a

---

[1] John x. 28, 29.　　　[2] James i. 15.

faithful saying, and worthy of all acceptation, that Christ came to save sinners, even the chief." Reckon the divine testimony, that " God is in Christ, reconciling the world to himself, not imputing to men their trespasses; seeing he hath made Him who knew no sin, to be sin for us, that we might be made the righteousness of God in him,"[1] the very truth most sure. Seek the full assurance of faith respecting the Saviour's person and work, the fulness and freedom of his salvation. Keep always before your mind, as the great reality, God as holy love. And then, in the second place, hold fast the hope of the gospel; cherish an undoubting expectation of " the salvation that is in Christ, with eternal glory." Never doubt but that God will do to you all that he has said. " Hold fast the confidence and the rejoicing of the hope," founded on the faith of the gospel, " steadfast to the end." " Hold fast the beginning of your confidence," your first confidence, as sinners deserving hell, and never capable of deserving any thing else, yet hoping for eternal life, as the gift of God through Jesus Christ our Lord. " Give all diligence to the full assurance of this hope to the end."[2]

Then, under the influence of this faith and hope, engage with humble, joyful confidence in all the duties, both of interior and exterior religion. " In the full assurance of faith" that " we have a great High Priest, who for us hath entered into the heavens, Jesus the Son of God," go " boldly to the throne of grace." " Trust in the Lord; pour out your heart before him." Make him your refuge; knowing his name, put your confidence in him, and say, " My expectation is from him. He is my rock and my salvation; he is my defence; I shall not be moved. For God is my salvation and my glory; the rock of my strength, and my refuge, is in God." " Be careful," anxious, " for nothing; but in every thing by prayer and supplication, with thanksgiving, make

[1] 1 Tim. i. 15.   2 Cor. v. 19, 21.
[2] Heb. ii. 6, 14; vi. 11.   Psal. lxii. 1, 2, 7, 8.   Phil. iv. 6, 7, 19.   Heb. x. 14-23.

your requests known to God," in the assured expectation, that he will "supply your need according to his glorious riches," and make his "peace keep your heart and mind through Christ Jesus." And "having confidence, full persuasion, respecting the entrance of Jesus, even the entrance of his flesh into the holiest, by blood, by which he has consecrated for us a new and living way into the holiest, draw near with a *true* heart, in full assurance of faith, having your hearts sprinkled from an evil conscience, and having your bodies washed with pure water : hold fast your profession." Pray to him, and "ask in faith, nothing wavering;" believing that, "if we, being evil, know how to give good gifts to our children, much more will he give good things to them who ask him." "Come before his presence with thanksgiving, and make a joyful noise to him with psalms. Serve him with gladness ; come before his presence with singing. Enter his gates with thanksgiving, and into his courts with praise ; be thankful to him, and bless his name." In the same spirit perform all the duties enjoined on you. Walk at liberty, keeping his commandments. Make it evident that you account his yoke an easy yoke, his burden a light burden. "Run in the way of his commandments," thus making it evident that he has "enlarged your hearts." And "count it all joy when you are brought into manifold trials." Do not suffer as one who must suffer, but as one who would suffer, since such is the will of God. "Be patient," "be joyful in tribulations," knowing they are not the punishment of the slave, but the chastisement of the child ; and in fine, act as free in reference to God, by manifesting habitually a self-possessed, happy, contented mind. Let your whole demeanour speak the satisfaction you have in your privileges and hopes as freemen, the denizens of the New Jerusalem, "Jerusalem from above, which is free." Let your mien and gait be those of the children of a king. "Rejoice in the Lord always ; and again I say, Rejoice."

Oh ! how holy, how happy, would Christians be, were they thus to rise above the influence of the spirit of bondage, the spirit of fear, and to yield themselves to the full influence of the spirit of adoption, teaching them habitually to say, " Abba, Father !" How easy would be the most laborious duties, how light the heaviest affliction, if, in obedience to the merciful injunction in the text, we would but think, and feel, and act, as freemen in reference to God![1]

(2.) " As free " in reference to man.

I proceed to remark, that the Christian should act " as free " in reference to man. He should allow the truth, respecting his freedom from human dominion in reference to faith and duty, to produce its proper effect, both in preventing him from subjecting his own mind and conscience to human authority, and from attempting to subject the mind and conscience of others to his authority, or to the authority of others to whom he may have incautiously yielded an undue deference.

The command of our Lord, in reference to the former of these manifestations of freedom is very explicit. " Be not ye the servants of men." " Stand fast in the liberty wherewith Christ hath made you free, and be not entangled in any yoke of bondage." " Let no man spoil you."[2] The Christian does not act in character if he receive any doctrine, observe any ordinance, perform any duty, on any ground, except that he has seen with his own eyes, in what he knows to be a Divine revelation, that Christ has revealed the doctrine, appointed the institution, enjoined the duty. Christians obviously act at variance with their high calling, which is to liberty, when, in deference to human authority, they receive doctrines which Christ has not revealed, observe ordinances which he has not instituted, and perform as a duty what he never made one, or what, it may be, he has forbidden as a sin. When a Christian is tempted to do any

---

[1] Heb. iv. 14, 16; x. 22. Psal. lxii. 1 2, 7, 8. Phil. iv. 6, 7, 19. Heb. x. 19-23. James i. 6. Matt. vii. 7. Psal. c. James i. 3. Rom. xii. 12. 2 Cor. vii. 4. Phil. iii. 1; iv. 4.

[2] 1 Cor. vii. 23. Gal. v. i. Col. ii. 8.

of these things, he is distinctly to say to those who would
bring him into bondage, Who gave you authority over
my conscience? Who authorized you to add to, to alter,
or to repeal, any of Christ's ordinances? I have a Lord
of the conscience, but it is not you; if I were your servant,
I could not be His. "Whether it be right in the sight of
God to obey men rather than God, judge ye."[1]

But Christians must not only refuse to submit to receive
doctrines, institutions, and precepts from men, different from
those authorized by Christ; but they must take care to
receive Christ's doctrines, institutions, and laws on his own
authority, and not on that of other men. A man's creed may
be in accordance with Christian truth : he may observe no
ordinance but what Christ has appointed, and yet he may
be a slave to human authority; for he receives the one and
observes the other, not because he has, in the free exercise of
his own mind, seen that they bear the stamp of Christ's authority, but because he has been taught them by his parents,
or has found them in the writings of authors to whom he
has been accustomed to yield great deference. Such a man,
instead of being free from man, not only serves man, but
worships him. He puts him in the place of God or his Son,
of the one Father or the one Master. It has been admirably
said by one of the greatest ornaments of our denomination,
"To yield up our judgment in religious matters to any individual, or to any church, is to invest that individual or that
church with the attribute of infallibility; and consequently,
while we retain the character of protestants, practically to
adopt one of the worst errors of popery. You can have no
certainty that any doctrine which you hold is true, unless
you have seen it with your own eyes in the Scriptures. The
faith, therefore, of those who submit to be guided by the
sentiments of others, however learned, and wise, and holy,
is downright presumption; a venture in the most important
of all concerns upon the diligence, the impartiality, and the

[1] Acts iv. 19.

capacity of others, of which they can never be fully assured.
Let them seriously consider, that although their creed may
happen to be right, its orthodoxy will not recommend them
to God; who perceives, in their undue respect for human
authority, a criminal indifference to truth, and a virtual rejection of his authority, as the only foundation of faith."[1]

Or, to use the words of Bishop Sanderson,[2] one of the ablest
divines of the English church of a former age: "Is it not
blameworthy in us, and a proof of our carnality, to give up
our judgments to be guided by the writings of Luther, or
Calvin, or any other mortal man whatsoever? Worthy
instruments they were, both of them, of God's glory, and
such as did excellent service to the church in these times,
whereof we yet find the benefit; and we are unthankful if
we do not bless God for it: and, therefore, it is an unsavoury
thing for any man to gird at their names, whose memories
should be precious. But yet, were they not men? Had
they received the Spirit in the fulness of it, and not by
measure? Knew they otherwise than in part, or prophesied otherwise than in part? Might they not in many
things, and did they not in some things, mistake and err?
Howsoever, the Apostle's interrogatories are unanswerable.
What saith he? 'Was Paul crucified for you; or were ye
baptized in the name of Paul?' Even so, was either Luther
or Calvin crucified for you? Or were ye baptized into the
name of Luther, or Calvin, or any other man, that any
one of you should say, I am of Luther; or any other, I am
of Calvin; and I of him, and I of him? What is Calvin, or
Luther, but 'ministers by whom ye believed;' that is to
say, instruments, but not lords, of your belief?"[2]

It is an important part, both of Christian prudence and
Christian duty, to avoid all unnecessary dependence on, or

---

[1] Dr Dick.

[2] I gratefully confess myself indebted to the elaborate discourse from which
this quotation is made for many good thoughts and pithy expressions; which
are, however, so mixed up with my own thoughts and composition, as not to
admit of particular acknowledgment.

obligation to, our fellow men, as calculated to endanger our Christian independence of mind and spirit. There may be entire inward freedom from man, amidst deep external dependence. But dependence is not of itself desirable, in reference to the higher objects of the Christian life. Even to Christian slaves the Apostle says : "If thou mayest be free, use it rather." Christians should act on the ennobling principles and precepts of their Lord: "It is more blessed to give than to receive:" "Owe no man any thing, but to love one another:" "Be not the servants of men."

But Christians should act as free, not only in refusing to submit to human authority in religion themselves, but also in carefully abstaining from imposing the yoke of human authority on others. Their freedom should be manifested, not only in maintaining their own privileges as free, but in respecting the privileges of others. It is a curious inconsistency that not unfrequently occurs in human character, that men clamorous for, or jealous of, their own liberties, as they understand them, should yet be constantly invading the liberties of others. Unfond of being ruled, they are very fond of ruling. Wherever this is the case, the genuine spirit of liberty is wanting. Nowhere does this incongruity appear more monstrous than among professing Christians. An enlightened Christian distinctly perceives that his freedom from human authority is no peculiar privilege; he sees that it belongs equally to all Christians; nay, that it belongs equally to all men; and that, for religious opinions and usages, man is answerable to God only. He sees, that on this subject the privileges, the duty, and the responsibility of all men are substantially the same; and he acts on the principle, "Whatsoever ye would that men should do to you, do ye even so to them."[1] Holding, as he does, that man can confer no favour on man higher than the communication of just views of religious truth and duty, he is ready, by statement and argument, to endeavour to bring men to believe what

[1] Matt. vii. 12.

he believes, because he accounts it truth; and to do what he does, because he accounts it duty; but he does not use any other means. He dares not use force; he dares not use bribes; he dares not use any influence but the influence of truth.

Where the difference of opinion involves, in his estimation, the essence of Christian truth and duty, he of course must decline acknowledging the individual who thus differs from him as a Christian: but even here, though he may, though he must, think that that individual has not wisely, nor rightly, exercised his undoubted right of judging for himself, he never thinks of denying that he has that right; endeavours to think as favourably of him as circumstances will admit; recollects that he is not his judge; and rests satisfied, that He who is the final Judge, will, in this case as in all others, do what is right.

Where the difference of opinion does not affect the essence of Christianity, he not only does not attempt to impose his opinion on his brother, but he does not allow the difference of opinion at all to influence his conduct to him as a Christian brother. If he has evidence that Christ has received him, he receives him, and gives him all the liberty he himself claims; and does this, not as if he were granting him a boon, but merely as respecting that common Christian liberty which Christ has given to all his disciples.

We have a beautiful instance of this mode of acting "as free," in the case of the Apostle and the weak brethren, who made a distinction of meats and days. He would not allow them to impose their views on him. To any such attempt he gave the most strenuous opposition. He would not submit to it; "no, not for an hour." But, though he knew they were in a mistake, he does not seek to impose his views on them. He was persuaded that they, as well as he, reverenced the authority of their common Lord; that they, who observed the day, observed it to the Lord, just as he to the Lord did not observe it. He recollected, that in every such case "every man should be fully persuaded in his own mind," and that "whatsoever is not of faith is sin," and that "every one must give an account of HIMSELF to God;" and recognising, in the common subjection of mind to the seen authority of Christ, a bond of union stronger than any cause of alienation or separation, in honest differences, as to what is the mind of the Lord on certain minor points, he received these weak brethren as Christ had received them; and while desirous to enlighten them, till they were enlightened, he was better pleased that they should act according to their own conscientious views, though limited and incorrect, than according to his conscientious views, though wide and accurate. And he exhorted the two parties, which were then, as still, to be found in every Christian society, the strong as well as the weak, to allow one another to walk at liberty; forbidding the weak to condemn the strong, which they were apt to do, and the strong to despise the weak, which they were just as apt to do; cautioning them both against hindering or "destroying the work of God" by their mutual contentions; forbidding them "to judge one another" in such cases, but "to judge this rather, that no one put a stumbling-block in his brother's way;" putting them in mind of the impropriety of "judging another man's servant;" suggesting the solemn thought, "every man must give an account of HIMSELF," not of his brother, "to God;" forbidding them to separate on such grounds, to dissolve the bonds either of Christian love or church fellowship; and commanding them, "so far as they have already attained, to walk by the same rule, and to mind the same thing;" assured, that this is the way to come to a closer agreement on subjects on which they conscientiously differed.[1] How happy would it have been for the church had Christians always acted thus, "as free;" treating each other as the Lord's freemen; not attempting to lord it over one another's consciences! And how often would

---

[1] Rom. xiv. *passim*

the reader of ecclesiastical history have been spared the painful necessity of observing, in how many instances our Lord's saying has been verified, "Wo to the world because of offences!"

(3.) *" As free " in reference to the powers and principles of evil.*

It is now time that I remark, in the third place, that Christians should act "as free" in reference to the powers and principles of evil.   In their contests with their spiritual enemies, whether they are the spirits of darkness, the influences of the present evil world, or the remaining sinful propensities of their fallen and but imperfectly renewed nature, they should think, and feel, and act, as freemen, and not as slaves. When an unconverted man, aroused by whatever means to a sense of his danger from these quarters, attempts something like opposition, he is as a man fighting in chains; his resistance is short, fitful, and feeble; the victory of his enemies certain, speedy, and complete.   The issue of all such conflicts is confirmed slavery.   And even the Christian, if he enter on the combat with these enemies under the influence of "the spirit of bondage," makes little head against them. But if, when assailed by his great enemy, he know and believe that the Captain of salvation has vanquished him and his legions, and have entire confidence in the promise, that "Satan shall be bruised under his feet shortly,"[1] then like a freeman, who, though once the prey of the mighty, has been rescued out of his grasp ; who, though once his captive, now walks at liberty ; he takes to him the shield of faith, the breastplate of righteousness, the helmet of salvation, the sword of the Spirit, which is the word of God.   This is the whole armour of God.   Clothed in this panoply, and wielding these weapons, he resists the devil, so that he flees from him.   It is thus that he is able to quench all his fiery darts, and to turn to flight the armies of the alien.   Conscious of

---

[1] Rom. xvi. 20.

the value of freedom, carefully guarding himself from being entangled in Satan's snares, or led captive of him at his will, and acquitting himself like a good soldier of Christ Jesus,

> " ———— There's not a chain
> That hellish foes, confed'rate for his harm,
> Can wind around him, but he casts it off
> With as much ease as Samson his green wyths." [1]

In reference to the evil influences of the present world, things seen and temporal, let the Christian act as free, and show that he has been delivered from the present evil world by Christ giving himself for him; that by the cross of Christ, the world, which once, as a mighty monarch, swayed resistless power over him, is now crucified to him, a powerless, contemptible, accursed thing. Let him show that he feels that he is become *free* of the universe, and for eternity, by becoming the child of the Lord of the universe, who liveth for ever and ever; and that the vain, unreal, shadowy hopes and fears of this narrow, shortlived scene, are no longer to be the great moving principles of his conduct. Let him act as if the world, instead of being his master, is a part of his property. So far as it is fitted to promote his welfare, he is not the world's, the world is his; he is an inheritor of the world; and considered, as it often is in Scripture, as an enemy, let him show that " this is the victory that overcometh the world, even our faith." [2]

As to the propensities of his fallen and imperfectly renewed nature, so far as they are depraved, let him treat them as vanquished enemies, despoiled of their dominion, concerning whom the sentence has gone forth, " Sin shall not have dominion over you." Let him consider them as, like the Canaanites of old, doomed to utter destruction; " let not his eye pity, nor his hand spare." Let him " mortify his members that are on the earth," crucify the flesh with its affections and lusts, " resolutely cut off the offending right

---

[1] Cowper. [2] 1 John v. 4.

hand, pluck out the offending right eye," and cast them from him as an abominable thing. And so far as they are an original part of his nature, not to be extirpated but improved, let him remember that now he is not their servant; they are his; and let him use them as the efficient instruments of promoting the glory of his great deliverer. The best illustration of this part of the subject that is any where to be met with, is to be found in the 6th chapter of the Epistle to the Romans : " Reckon ye yourselves to be dead indeed unto sin, but alive unto God through Jesus Christ our Lord. Let not sin therefore reign in your mortal body, that ye should obey it in the lusts thereof: neither yield ye your members unto sin as instruments of unrighteousness ; but yield yourselves to God, as those who are alive from the dead, and your members to God as instruments of righteousness. For sin shall not have dominion over you : for ye are not under the law, but under grace. What then ? shall we sin, because we are not under the law, but under grace. God forbid. Know ye not, that to whom ye yield yourselves servants to obey, his servants ye are to whom ye obey ; whether of sin unto death, or of obedience unto righteousness ? But God be thanked, ye were the servants of sin ; but ye have obeyed from the heart the form of doctrine which has been delivered to you. Being then made free from sin, ye became the servants of righteousness. As then ye have yielded your members servants to uncleanness, and to iniquity unto iniquity ; even so now yield your members servants to righteousness unto holiness. For when ye were the servants of sin, ye were free from righteousness. What fruit had ye then in those things whereof ye are now ashamed ? for the end of those things is death. But now, being made free from sin, and become servants of God, ye have your fruit unto holiness, and the end everlasting life. For the wages of sin is death ; but the gift of God is eternal life through Jesus Christ our Lord." [1]

---

[1] Rom. vi. 11-23.

So much for the illustration of the first part of the general view of the Christian's duty. He ought to act in a correspondence to his state of liberty, "as free" in reference to God, in reference to men, in reference to the powers and principles of evil.

Many of the inducements which should influence the Christian to act as free, to maintain and assert his Christian liberty, have come before our minds in the course of our illustration of this duty. It may serve a good purpose, however, to glance at a few more before concluding this part of the discussion.

You cannot, my Christian brethren, neglect compliance with this injunction, 'Be "as free;" act in accordance with your condition as a condition of liberty,'—without obvious injustice to Him whom you acknowledge as your only Lord. You are HIS. He has brought you from slavery to liberty. When you act as free, you use his property in the way he wishes it to be used. But when you act otherwise, when you serve men, or the devil, or the world, or the flesh, you abuse his property; you dishonestly employ it for a purpose different from, opposite to, that for which he intended, to which he had destined it. " Ye are not your own, ye are bought with a price." " Be not then the servants of men :" Be not the servants of Satan : Be not the servants of divers lusts and pleasures.

But not only will you do injustice to Christ, you will do foul dishonour to God, if you do not act "as free." You will allow something else to occupy his place. He must be dishonoured, whoever or whatever is put in his room. But when you serve Mammon, serve your own belly, serve Satan, the worst of all beings, when you ought to "worship the Lord your God, and serve only HIM," O how deeply do you dishonour him !

Nor do you only dishonour God, you dishonour yourselves. You do not "walk worthy" of the privileges which have been conferred on you. " Ye know," or at least ye ought to know, " your calling, brethren." It is " a high and holy one." " You have been called into liberty." If ye are servants, ye are servants only of Him, whom to serve is the greatest honour which the most exalted creature can enjoy. It is immeasurable degradation for you to become the servants of men or devils, or worldly lusts and sinful passions.

Nor is there only degradation in it; there is fatiguing, profitless labour. Christ's yoke is an easy yoke; Christ's burden is a light burden. " His commandments are not grievous."[1] O how much is it otherwise with the yoke, and burdens, and commandments of his rivals! "They who follow lying vanities, forsake their own mercies." Every Christian who has made the experiment, and, alas! every Christian has made the experiment but too often, knows, like the Israelites of old, " the difference between Jehovah's service and the service of the kingdoms of the countries."[2] As you would not then rob the Lord who bought you, as you would not dishonour God, and disgrace yourselves, and wear yourselves out with fruitless fatigues and thankless labour, " walk at liberty, keeping his precepts;" " stand fast in the liberty wherewith Christ has made you free, and be not entangled with any yoke of bondage."

Well may Christians triumph in, and be jealous of, this glorious liberty; for as Luther, with his usual power, says— " Christ's truth maketh us free, not civilly, nor carnally, but divinely. We are made free in such sort, that our conscience is free and quiet, not fearing the wrath of God to come. This is the true and inestimable liberty, to the excellency and majesty of which, if we compare the other, they are but as one drop of water in respect of the ocean. For who is able to express what a thing it is, when a man is assured in his heart that God neither is, nor ever will be, angry with him, but will be for ever a merciful and loving Father to him for Christ's sake! This is, indeed, a marvellous and incomprehensible liberty, to have the Most High Sovereign Majesty so favourable to us, that he doth not only defend,

---

[1] 1 John v. 3.　　[2] 2 Chron. xii. 8.

maintain, and succour us, in this life; but also, as touching our bodies, will so deliver us, as that, though sown in corruption, dishonour, and infirmity, they shall rise again in incorruption, and glory, and power. This is an inestimable liberty, that we are made free from the wrath of God for ever; and is greater, more valuable, than heaven and earth, and the created universe. ' Blessed is the man who is in such a case ; yea, blessed is the man whose God is the Lord.' "

§ 2. *The Christian's duty, to guard against the abuse of his freedom.*

I proceed now to the consideration of the second department of the Christian's duty, as here delineated. He is to guard against misapprehending and misimproving his condition as free. He is to be careful, while using, not to abuse his liberty. He is not to use his liberty " as a cloak of maliciousness;" or, as the Apostle Paul has it in his Epistle to the Galatians, " he is not to use his liberty for an occasion to the flesh."[1] The first thing to be done here, is distinctly to apprehend the meaning of the terms in which this department of Christian duty is described. What are we to understand by " maliciousness?" what by " a cloak of maliciousness?" and what by "using our liberty as a cloak of maliciousness? "

The Greek word translated maliciousness[2] here, and malice in the first verse of this chapter, like the English words by which it is rendered, is often, when used along with other words descriptive of particular vices, such as anger, envy, covetousness, employed to describe that special vicious temper, and its manifestations, which is directly opposed to brotherly love and charity, so as to be equivalent to ill-will, malignity ; but when standing by itself, as in the case before us, it seems ordinarily employed as a general name for sinful dispositions and actions, as equivalent to sin or wickedness. Thus, when Simon Magus is called on to repent of his pro-

---

[1] Gal. v. 13.   [2] Κακία.

fane and wicked proposal, to purchase miraculous power by money, he is called on to "repent of his wickedness,"[1] that is, his sin; and Christians are called on to be "in malice," rather "in wickedness," in sinful disposition and habit in all their forms, children, while they are "in understanding, men."[2] Maliciousness is here just equivalent to sin, of whatever kind; and the injunction seems quite parallel with that from the Epistle to the Galatians, just quoted, "Use not liberty as an occasion to the flesh;" a general name for the depraved principles of fallen humanity, or for human nature as depraved.

But what are we to understand by "a cloak of wickedness?" The word rendered cloak,[3] which occurs nowhere else in the New Testament, signifies a covering of any kind. It is the word employed in the Greek version of the Old Testament to denote the covering of badgers' skins which was spread over the tabernacle.[4] It is here obviously used figuratively. A cloak of wickedness is something by which we attempt to conceal, from ourselves or others, the true character of some vicious disposition or action; an excuse, a pretext, an apology for wickedness. To cloak sin is to disguise wickedness. Our Lord says, that the Jews, who had heard his discourses and seen his miracles, had "no cloak" (not the same word as here, but a word of similar import); that is, were deprived of every pretext, excuse, or apology "for their sin," in rejecting him.[5] Josephus says, Joab had a plausible pretext for killing Abner, but he had no such cloak for the murder of Amasa. Men often attempt to conceal from others, and even from themselves, the true character of favourite vicious propensities and profitable sinful practices. Saul disobeyed God in not entirely destroying the property of the Amalekites; and he attempted to cloak his disobedience under the pretext of his being desirous of presenting a fit sacrifice to Jehovah.[6] Jezebel

[1] Acts viii. 22.   [2] 1 Cor. xiv. 20.   [3] Επικαλυμμα.

[4] Exod. xxvi. 14.   [5] Προφασιν.—John xv. 22.   [6] 1 Sam. xv. 15.

cloaked her murderous revenge against Naboth, under the pretext of zeal against blasphemy.[1] Economy is made the cloak of avarice; generosity, of extravagance; caution, of indolence; religious zeal, of personal resentment. And here the Apostle cautions Christians against cloaking wickedness under the pretext of liberty, against indulging any sinful temper, engaging in any sinful pursuit, under the mistaken impression, or the hypocritical pretence, that these were but the exercise of that liberty wherewith Christ had made them free. The general meaning, then, of the injunction, " use not your liberty as a cloak of wickedness," is thus sufficiently apparent. It may serve, however, a good purpose, to show how we ought to guard against such an abuse of our Christian liberty, in the three different aspects in which we have been led to contemplate it; our liberty in reference to God; our liberty in reference to men; our liberty in reference to the powers and principles of evil.

(1.) *Cautions respecting abuses of liberty in reference to God.*

First, Christians must not use their liberty with respect to God as a cloak of wickedness. Those men do so, who, under the pretext that they are free in reference to God, consider themselves as released from any obligation to make his law the rule of their conduct. The doctrine of the gospel undoubtedly is, that Christians are not subject to the Mosaic law; that nothing is obligatory on a Christian's conscience merely because it is contained in the law of Moses; and that the system of Divine administration, under which they are placed in consequence of their connexion with Christ, is not a system of strict law under which the rule is, " Do and live:" " He that doth them, shall live in them." And no provision is made for the pardon of any offence; but a system of grace, under which, not only is a full and free pardon bestowed on every believer, and eternal

---

[1] 1 Kings xxi. 10.

life promised as a free gift through Jesus Christ our Lord; but
" if any man," after believing, "sin, we have an advocate with
the Father, Jesus Christ the righteous, whose blood cleanseth
from all sin;" and if any man who has sinned, availing
himself of this Divine arrangement, " confess his sins, God
is faithful and just to forgive him his sins, and to cleanse him
from all unrighteousness." [1] The apostolic statements embodying these principles, such as, that Christians are " dead
to the law by the body of Christ;" that they are " delivered
from the law, that being dead wherein they were held;"
that " there is no condemnation to them;" that " Christ is
the end of the law to every one that believeth;" that they
are " not under the law, but grace;" that " Christ has
redeemed them from the curse of the law, having become a
curse for them;" that they " through the law are dead to
the law;" that " they who are led by the Spirit are not
under the law;" [2]—were liable to misapprehension and abuse,
and have, in all ages, been misapprehended and abused.

The enemies of apostolical Christianity grounded on these
statements one of their strongest objections against it,—that
it was a system that sapped the foundation of all religious
and moral obligation; and not a few who professed to embrace the gospel, while they did not understand it, actually
turned the grace of God into lasciviousness, and the liberty
which is in Christ into profane licentiousness; saying, and
acting out the impious saying, let us " continue in sin, because grace does abound." [3] And this we may remark, by
the way, is one of the proofs which we have, that what we
call evangelical Christianity, is indeed substantially apostolical Christianity; that we find the same objection urged
against its principles by its opposers, and the same abuse
made of them by men of corrupt minds who profess to embrace them. The system which many men would impose on
us as Christianity, giving no occasion for such misrepresenta-

1 John i. 9.
2 Rom. vii. 4, 6; viii. 1; x. 4; vi. 15.   Gal. iii. 13; ii. 19; v. 18.
3 Rom. vi. 1.

tion and abuse, distinctly thus disproves its identity with the Christianity of the New Testament.

This abuse has assumed various forms. Sometimes it has taken the form of this assertion : We are free from the law; "where there is no law, there is no transgression." What may be sin to other men is no sin to us. " There is no condemnation to us." God sees no sin in us. At other times it has embodied itself in the assertion : " The Spirit dwells in us." We walk according to the Spirit. They who want the Spirit may need the law; but we are a law to ourselves. We need only to follow the Spirit, and we are sure all will be right. The law is not for righteous men like us. We do not require the law as a guide to our conduct. But, whatever form it assumes, this is its general character ; it is using Christian liberty as a cloak for wickedness.

It requires very little consideration to perceive that this is a gross abuse of the doctrine of Christian liberty. We have seen that the Christian's liberty, in reference to God, consists chiefly in two things—deliverance from the condemning sentence of the law, which we have violated, and the curse which we have incurred; and deliverance from a slavish temper in reference to God and his law. No human ingenuity will ever be able to show that either, or both of these, imply a release from an obligation to conform ourselves to the will of God, as made known to us in his law. Both are necessary, in order to our yielding an enlightened, cheerful, and therefore acceptable, obedience to that law. Both are intended to produce this blessed result ; and in every case where these two species of liberty are really enjoyed, they actually do produce it in the degree in which they are enjoyed.

Indeed, a release from obligation to obey the Divine law is, in the nature of things, impossible, except on one or other of the following suppositions,—that God ceases to be what he is, an absolutely perfect being ; or that man ceases to be what he is, a rational being : for the law is nothing else but an expression of the duties which rise out of the relations which subsist between God as the absolutely perfect being, and man as his rational creature. Were God to become unwise, unholy, unjust, unmerciful, his law might, must, change: were man to sink into the state of an idiot or a brute, he would cease to be the subject of the Divine law:—on no other supposition can man's obligation to the Divine law be altered or destroyed.

Were the thing possible, it would be the most dreadful calamity which could befall him in reference to whom it took place; for the law of God is just the statement of the direct and only way to improvement and happiness. The person released from an obligation to regulate himself by it, is just a person at liberty to make himself and others as miserable as the caprices of his humour may suggest, or the extent of his power permit. And what sort of a world would it be if all men, or any large portion of men, were as fully relieved from responsibility, and the sense of responsibility, as idiots or madmen are; were selfishness, unchecked by remorse or religious fear, permitted to guide and direct the activities of men possessed of reason?[c]

The truth on this subject has been so well stated by an old divine, that I make no apology for making a considerable citation from his writings:—"Not to wade far into a controversy, in which many have drowned their reason and their faith, it shall suffice to propound one distinction, which, if well heeded and rightly applied, will clear the whole point concerning the abrogation and obligation of the moral law under the New Testament, and cut off many needless curiosities which lead men into error. The law, then, may be considered either as a rule or as a covenant. Christ hath freed all believers from the rigour and curse of the law considered as a covenant, but he hath not freed them from obedience to the law considered as a rule; and all those Scriptures that speak of the law as if it were abrogated or annulled, speak of it considered as a covenant. Those again

* See note C.

that speak of the law as if it were still in force, take it considered as a rule. The law as a covenant is rigorous, and under that rigour we are not if we be in Christ; but the law as a rule is equal, and under that equity we still are though we be in Christ. The law as a rule only showeth us what is good and evil, what we are to do, and what we are not to do ('He hath showed thee, O man, what is good, and what the Lord requireth of thee'), without any condition annexed, either of reward if we observe it, or of punishment if we transgress it. But the law as a covenant exacteth perfect, punctual, and personal performance of every thing that is contained therein, with a condition annexed of God's acceptance and blessing if we perform it to the full, but of his wrath and curse on us if we fail in any thing. Such was the law under which man was originally placed. But 'by reason of transgression, we having all broken that covenant, the law hath its work upon us;' it worketh wrath, it produceth punishment, and involveth us all in the curse; so that by the covenant of the law 'no flesh living can be justified.' Then cometh in Christ, who, subjecting himself for our sakes to the covenant of the law, first fulfilleth it in his own person, but in our behalf, as our surety, and then disannulleth it; and instead thereof establisheth a better covenant, even the covenant of grace; so that now as many as believe are free from the covenant of the law, and from the curse of the law, and set under a covenant of grace, and under promises of grace. There is a translation, then, of the covenant; but what is all this to the rule? That still is where it was; even as the nature of good and evil is still the same it was. And the law considered as a rule, can no more be abolished or changed than can the nature of good and evil be abolished or changed. It is our singular comfort, then, and the happiest part of our Christian liberty, that we are freed by Christ, and through faith in him, from the covenant and the curse of the law; but we must know that it is our privilege to remain subject to the law as a rule." God grants his law gra-

ciously; and " our duty, notwithstanding the liberty we
have in Christ, is to frame our lives and conversation according to the rule of the law, which, if we shall neglect under
the pretence of our Christian liberty, we must answer for
both—both for neglect of our duty, and abusing our liberty." [1]
We Christians are " not without law to God;" we are
" under the law to Christ."

No man who really enjoys the liberty of the children of
God can abuse it as a cloak for wickedness; for, in his mind,
freedom from the yoke of sin is indissolubly connected with
submission to the authority of God. But in every age of
the church there have been bold, bad men, who have indulged unholy, Antinomian speculations; and, given up to
strong delusions, have supposed themselves free while the
slaves of sin—

> " That bawl for freedom in their senseless mood,
> And still revolt when truth would set them free;—
> License they mean when they cry liberty." [2]

Of them does the Apostle speak in his second Epistle, as
" speaking great swelling words of vanity, and alluring
through the lusts of the flesh, through much wantonness,
those who were clean escaped from them who live in error.
While they promise them liberty, they themselves are the
servants of corruption: for of whom a man is overcome, of
the same is he brought into bondage." [3] Such men, too, were
those of whom Luther complains, " Men who would be
accounted good Christians merely because they rejected the
authority of the Pope; who will do nothing that either the
magistrate or God would have them to do; remaining in
their old, disorderly nature, however much they may make
their boast of the gospel;" and who, as Calvin says,
" reckoned it a great part of Christian liberty that they
may eat flesh on Fridays."

There have been men, too, of a better sort, who, from a
fondness of paradox and singularity, have adopted Anti-

---

[1] Sanderson.   [2] Milton.   [1] 2 Pet. ii. 18, 19.

nomian language, while the saving truth, which is sanctifying truth, substantially held by them, preserved them in a great measure from corresponding conduct. It is, however, of high importance, that on this, and indeed on every subject, we should learn to " speak the things that become sound doctrine," that we employ " sound speech that cannot be condemned."[1] And though happily in this country Antinomian tenets are in a great measure unknown, let every Christian remember that there are Antinomian tendencies in every human heart, so far as it is unrenewed; and let him set himself to watch, to check, to mortify all such tendencies in his own heart; and when the thought occurs, " may we not continue in sin, that grace may abound?" let him meet it with the apostle's strong disclaimer, " God forbid! how shall we, who are dead to sin, live any longer therein?"[2] Or by the plain common sense reflection, it were a strange way for a man to prove himself a freeman by voluntarily becoming a slave to his worst enemy.

(2.) *Cautions respecting the abuse of their liberty in reference to man.*

I remark, in the second place, that Christians must not use their liberty with respect to man as a cloak of wickedness. Christians may do this principally in two ways;—by an unsober and an uncharitable use of Christian liberty; and by neglecting what is duty, and committing what is sin, under mistaken apprehensions of, or false pretences in reference to, Christian liberty.

Every thing that is lawful in itself is not always expedient or proper in the circumstances in which we are placed. When it becomes inexpedient in my circumstances, it becomes unlawful for me. The Christian, who acts on the principle that every thing that is lawful in itself may be done at all times, and in all circumstances, will often make his liberty a cloak of wickedness. My doing what, considered in itself,

---

[1] Tit. ii. 1, 8.   [2] Rom. vi. 2.

my conscience—it may be well informed—would not prevent me from doing, but by no means requires me to do; my doing this in circumstances in which I have reason to believe that it may prove a snare to myself, or that it will give offence in the New Testament sense of the word, that is, throw a stumbling-block in the way of a worse-informed brother, is a violation of the injunction which we are now considering. A Christian must never do what is unlawful, but it may sometimes be his duty to refrain from doing what is lawful. It has been justly remarked, that "scarce is there any one thing wherein the devil putteth a slur upon us more frequently, yea and more dangerously too (because unsuspected by us), than in making us take the uttermost of our freedom in indifferent things. It, therefore, concerneth us so much the more to keep a sober watch over ourselves and our souls in the use of God's good creatures, lest, even under the fair title and habit of Christian liberty, we yield ourselves up to a carnal licentiousness, or to a criminal uncharitableness."[1]

There never was a Christian more fully conscious of his liberty than the Apostle Paul, more sensible of its value, and more determined in maintaining it. Yet observe what he says on this subject: "Let no man put a stumbling-block, or an occasion to fall, in his brother's way. I know, and am persuaded of the Lord Jesus, that there is nothing unclean of itself: but to him that esteemeth any thing to be unclean, to him it is unclean. But if thy brother be grieved with thy meat, now walkest thou not charitably. Destroy not him with thy meat for whom Christ died. Let not then your good be evil spoken of. The kingdom of God is not meat and drink. For meat destroy not the work of God. All things indeed are pure; but it is evil to that man who eateth with offence. It is good neither to eat flesh, nor to drink wine, nor any thing whereby thy brother stumbleth, or is offended, or is made weak. Hast thou faith? have it to thyself before

[1] Sanderson.

God. Happy is he who condemneth not himself in that thing which he alloweth. And he that doubteth is damned if he eat, because he eateth not of faith : for whatsoever is not of faith is sin. We then who are strong ought to bear the infirmities of the weak, and not to please ourselves. Let every one of us please his neighbour for good to edification. Take heed lest by any means this liberty of yours become a stumbling-block to them who are weak."[1] The rule in reference to matters which conscience permits, but does not enjoin, is, " Give none offence, neither to the Jews, nor to the Gentiles, nor to the church of God. Please all men in all things, seeking not your own profit, but the profit of many, that they may be saved." [2]

Happy is the Christian who, like Paul, knowing and feeling that he is free from all, and who will not be brought under the power of any, yet, like him, thus becomes the servant of all, that by all means he may save some. It was an excellent saying of Luther's : " Be free in every thing by faith. Be a servant in every thing by charity." We should know and be fully persuaded with the persuasion of faith, that all things are lawful; and yet we should purpose, and be fully resolved, for charity's sake, to forbear the use of many things, if we find them inexpedient. He that will have his own way in every thing, in itself indifferent, whosoever may take offence at it, makes his liberty but a cloak of wickedness by using it uncharitably.

But there is still a worse mode of using our liberty in reference to man as a cloak of wickedness. Christian liberty has not unfrequently been made a cloak of wickedness, by being pleaded as a reason for transgressing the laws, neglecting the duties, and disturbing the order of civil and domestic society. No man is the less, but rather the more, bound, in consequence of his being a Christian, to observe all the laws that regulate his civil and domestic relations, that are not inconsistent with the law of God. Nay, he

---

[1] Rom. xiv. 13; xv. 1.   [2] 1 Cor. x. 32, 33.

whose free servant the Christian is, has commanded him to serve HIM in serving those who, by the arrangements of his providence, are his superiors. In every thing that is not inconsistent with my duty to God, I, as a Christian, am bound to be "subject to the powers that be;" to "obey magistrates;" to "submit to every human institution for the punishment of evil-doers, and the praise of them that do well;" for this is the law of my Master in heaven. With the same exception, a Christian wife is bound to be "subject to her own husband; a Christian child to his parents; a Christian servant to his master; though in all these cases the civil or domestic superior should not be a Christian. My liberty as a Christian does not in the slightest degree relax the obligation of my civil or domestic obligations; and therefore, whenever the latter are violated under a pretence of the former, liberty is used as a cloak of wickedness. Christians should manifest their liberty in this matter, not by neglecting or violating civil and domestic duties, but by the cheerfulness with which they perform them, showing that here, as in every other department of Christian duty, 'they serve God without fear,' they 'walk at liberty, keeping his commandments.'" The honour of Christianity is very much concerned in Christians avoiding every approach to thus making their liberty a cloak of wickedness. This is very obvious from the language of the Apostle : "Let as many servants as are under the yoke," that is, as are slaves, "count their own masters worthy of all honour, that the name of God and his doctrine be not blasphemed. And they that have believing masters, let them not despise them, because they are brethren (because, as Christians, the servant and the master are on the same level); but rather do them service, because they are faithful and beloved, partakers of the benefit. If any teach otherwise, and consent not to wholesome words, even the words of the Lord Jesus Christ, and to the doctrine according to godliness; he is proud, knowing nothing, but doting about questions and strifes of words, whereof cometh envy, strife, railings, evil surmises, perverse disputings of men of corrupt minds : from such withdraw thyself." " Exhort servants to be obedient to their own masters, and to please them well in all things ; that ye may adorn the doctrine of God our Saviour in all things."[1]   Our text, viewed in its connexion, seems plainly to have a peculiar reference to the abuse of Christian liberty as an excuse for disobedience to civil rulers, exercising a malignant influence on the character and cause of Christianity.   " Submit yourselves to every human institution for the punishment of evil-doers, and the praise of them that do well ; for *so*" in this way " it is the will of God, that ye with well-doing put to silence the ignorance of foolish men : as free, and not using your liberty as a cloak of wickedness."

(3.)—*Cautions respecting the abuse of their liberty, in reference to the powers and principles of evil.*

It only remains, on this part of the subject, that I remark, in the third place, that Christians must not use their liberty in reference to the powers and principles of evil as a cloak of wickedness.   Christians must not say, because we are delivered from the wicked one, therefore we may, without sin or danger, put ourselves in the way of his temptations. There is no need that we watch against his wiles, or resist his attacks.   This were to use their liberty as a cloak of wickedness.   On the contrary, they are carefully to avoid whatever may naturally lead to a partial recovery of their enemy's power, and a corresponding loss of their freedom.   When they find that any thing, however innocent in itself, through his craft and their remaining depravity, becomes a temptation to sin, they ought to abandon it.   " Better it is by voluntary abstinence to part with some of our liberty as to God's creatures, than by voluntary transgression to become the devil's captives."[2]   Their duty is distinctly stated by the Apostle in these striking words, " Put on the whole armour of God, that ye may be able to stand against the wiles of the

---

[1] 1 Tim. vi. 1-5.   Tit. ii. 9, 10.   [2] Sanderson.

devil. For we wrestle not against flesh and blood, but against principalities, against powers, against the rulers of the darkness of this world, against spiritual wickedness in high places. Wherefore take to yourselves the whole armour of God, that ye may be able to withstand in the evil day, and having done all, to stand. Stand therefore, having your loins girt about with truth, and having on the breastplate of righteousness; and your feet shod with the preparation of the gospel of peace; above all, taking the shield of faith, wherewith ye shall be able to quench all the fiery darts of the wicked. And take the helmet of salvation, and the sword of the Spirit, which is the word of God : praying always with all prayer and supplication in the Spirit, and watching thereunto with all perseverance and supplication for all saints." " Be sober, be vigilant; because your enemy the devil, as a roaring lion, walketh about, seeking whom he may devour: whom resist stedfast in the faith." [1]

Christians must not say, because we have obtained emancipation from sin that dwells in us, because we know, and are sure, that this enemy shall not have dominion over us; for we are not under law, but under grace; therefore we need not be constantly engaged in an active warfare with conquered foes. This is an obvious abuse of Christian liberty. The true use of Christian liberty in this respect is pointed out by the Apostle in such passages as the following, which, though already quoted, we think it well to repeat: " Reckon ye yourselves dead indeed unto sin, and alive unto God through Jesus Christ," *i. e.*, reckon yourselves spiritually free. What then? have ye nothing to do but to sit down and enjoy your freedom? No. " Let not sin therefore reign in your mortal body, that ye should obey it in the lusts thereof. Neither yield ye your members as instruments of unrighteousness to sin : but yield yourselves unto God, as those who are alive from the dead, and your members as instruments of righteousness unto God. For sin shall not have dominion over

<hr>

[1] Eph. vi. 11-18. 1 Pet. v. 8, 9.

you: for you are not under the law, but under grace."[1] " We are risen with Christ," says the Apostle. That is another figurative view of our spiritual freedom. Well, then, have we nothing to do but to congratulate ourselves on our felicity, and indolently enjoy it? Ah! no. " Since ye are risen with Christ, set your affections on things above, not on things on the earth. Seek the things that are above, and heavenly. Mortify your members which are on the earth. Put off the old man with his deeds, and put on the new man with his deeds."[2] The grace of God towards his people, whom he has made free, is not expressèd by placing them in a condition where no enemy can assail them; but in enabling them to make such a use of the liberty and power he has given them, as that, feeble though they be in themselves, they become " more than conquerors through him who loved them." If we would " stand fast in the liberty wherewith Christ has made us free," we must be constantly on the alert against " those who would again bring us into bondage." It is a good saying of the judicious Hooker : " It was not the meaning of our Lord and Saviour, in saying, ' Father, keep them in thy name,' that we should be careless in keeping ourselves. To our own safety our own sedulity is required." And we must never bring into antagonism God's promises and his commands, our privileges and our duties. His promise enforces, not repeals, his law. Our privileges encourage and strengthen for duty : but by no means annul the obligation, or diminish the importance of obedience.

§ 3.—*The Christian's duty to act out his character " as the servant of God."*

We proceed now to the consideration of the third view of the Christian's duty, as corresponding to his condition. As in accordance to his condition as a condition of liberty, he is to act as free ; so in accordance with his condition as a condition of subjection, he is to act " as a servant of God."

---

[1] Rom. vi. 11-14.   [2] Col. iii. 1-5.

Obedience, active and passive subjection to the will of God, as made known in his word, and in his providential dispensations, forms the comprehensive duty of the Christian, as the servant of God. What lies at the foundation here, is a just apprehension, and a habitual contemplation of those truths in reference to the character of God, and to our relation to him, which form the ground of our obligation to serve him, and a perception of which is necessary to our feeling this obligation. He who would act as a servant of God, must keep before his mind the infinite wisdom and righteousness of God, which make it absolutely impossible that either in the injunctions of his law, or in the dispensations of his providence, there should be any thing unwise or unjust; the infinite benignity of God, which secures that "in keeping," and for keeping, "his commandments there will be a great reward!" that "all his paths, to them who keep his covenant, shall be mercy," as well as truth, and that "all things shall work together for good to them who love him;" the infinite power of God, by which he is able to carry forth into effect all the promises, however exceeding great and precious, which he has made to obedience, and all the threatenings, however dreadful, which he has uttered against disobedience; the infinite faithfulness of God, which makes it impossible that he should deny himself, and secures that, "though heaven and earth should pass away, not one iota or tittle shall pass," either from his promises or his threatenings, "till all be fulfilled."[1]

The Christian must not only keep habitually before his mind those perfections of his Divine Master which are displayed in his word and providence, but also the relations he bears to this infinitely great, and excellent, and benignant being. He must remember that he is HIS creature, and his NEW creature; that all that he is that is good, is the work of his hand; that all that he has that is valuable, is the gift of his common bounty, or of his sovereign grace; that both himself

---

[1] Psal. xix. 11; xxv. 10. Rom. viii. 28. Matt. v. 18.

and all that he possesses is His property, in a far higher sense than any thing can be the property of any creature; and that to alienate them from the purpose for which he designed them, to employ them in a way different from, opposite to that in which he has commanded them to be employed, is a crime, of which the basest frauds which can be committed by one fellow creature on another, in whatever mutual relation they may stand, is but an imperfect shadow. It is this setting and keeping the Lord always before us in his essential excellencies, and in his revealed relations, that forms the mind to those sentiments of supreme veneration, esteem, confidence, and love towards God, to that habitual sense of entire dependence on him, and of infinite obligation to him, which are necessary to lead us to " serve him acceptably, with reverence and godly fear;" and, at the same time, to serve him without " the fear that has torment," " in righteousness and holiness, all the days of our lives."

Next in importance to our thus cultivating the principle of obedience, is our making ourselves acquainted with the rule of obedience. He who would act as the servant of God, must " not be unwise, but understand what the will of the Lord is." And in order to this, he must study the word of God, he must observe the providence of God, and he must seek the guidance of the Spirit of God. He must make himself well acquainted with those " scriptures given by inspiration of God, which are profitable for doctrine, and for reproof, for correction, and instruction in righteousness, and by which the servant of God may be made perfect, thoroughly furnished to every good work." He must let this word " dwell in him richly, in all wisdom," that in all the variety of circumstances in which he may be placed, he may know what God would have him to do. He must make the Divine precepts the men of his counsel, and take them as " a lamp to his feet, and a light to his path."[1] There is no doing a master's will without knowing it.

---

[1] Eph. v. 17.   2 Tim. iii. 16.   Col. iii. 16.   Psal. cxix. 105.

In order to know our Divine Master's will, we must consider the operation of his hand, as well as attend to the declarations of his mouth ; we must study the Divine providence, in order to enable us wisely to apply the instructions of the Divine word ; we must learn to "hear the *rod*" as well as the *word :* and under a deep sense of our spiritual blindness, our tendency to overlook, and misapprehend, very plain intimations of the Divine will both in his word and in his providence, and of our indisposition to comply with his will, even when we cannot help perceiving it ; we must seek the good Spirit, who is promised to enlighten our darkness, and to rectify our obliquities.   Believing that if any man lack wisdom, the knowledge of God's will, he should ask it of God, who giveth liberally, and upbraids not, we should in faith, nothing doubting, in the full assurance of faith, present these prayers : " Open mine eyes, that I may behold wonders out of thy law. Put thy Spirit within me.   Write thy law on my heart ; put it in my inward part.   Hide not thy commandments from me. Teach me the way of thy statutes.   Make me to understand the way of thy precepts.   Order my steps in thy word."

Thus cultivating the principle of obedience, and studying the rule of obedience, Christians are to act as the servants of God, by exercising the principle, and applying the rule in actual obedience, both active and passive.   They are to regulate the whole outer and inner man, according to the Divine will.   They are to "serve him in their bodies and in their spirits, which are his."

They are to "serve him with their spirits," believing, willing, loving, choosing, fearing, hoping, *according to his word*.   Those high things within, which no human, no created power can control, must be entirely subjected to the Divine authority.   When a Christian is acting in character as a servant of God, the answer to the question, Why do you account that true ? is, God has said so ; Why do you account that false ? God has said so ; Why do you will this ? God has said it is right ; Why do you choose that ? God has said that it is good ; Why do you fear that ? God has interposed a prohibition or uttered a threatening respecting it; Why do you hope for that? God has promised it.

This internal obedience must be manifested in external obedience. The language of our conduct must be, "The Lord our God we will serve, and his voice we will obey:" we must "deny ungodliness and worldly lusts, and live soberly, righteously, and godly." We must serve him in the various appointed institutions of secret and public religion: "entering into our closets, shutting our doors on us, praying to our Father, who seeth in secret." "Not forsaking the assembling of ourselves together," but "walking in all the ordinances of the Lord blameless;" and such of us as have families, saying with Joshua, "As for me and my house, we will serve the Lord." But we must not suppose that it is only when we engage in strictly religious services that we are to act as the servants of God. His law of justice, truth, and love, is to regulate all our transactions with our fellow men, and in performing our various relative duties, as superior, inferior, or equals, we are to do all "as to the Lord."

Our obedience to God as his servants, is to be passive as well as active. It has been justly said, that obedience consists in the subjecting of a man's own will to the will of another. If that subjection be in something to be done, it is active obedience: if it be in something to be suffered, it is passive obedience. Now, as God's servants, we must not only do, but suffer his will. And we must show our passive obedience, by being contented with his allotments, and by being submissive to his chastisements. It is meet that the servant of so great, and wise, and good a Master, should be satisfied with the place in the family he assigns him, with the kind and degree of work he allots him, with the kind and measures of food, support, and wages he gives him. We are not acting like the servants of God, when we grudge and murmur at his appointments, and envy those to whom he may have assigned a higher place, and more abundant accommodations. We should say in such a case, "Should it be altogether according to my mind?" Has he not a

right to do what he wills with his own? It is not for God's
servant to choose out the lot of his inheritance. It is in
better hands. We must never say, never think, that he is
a hard Master. "Having food and raiment," however
scanty and coarse, we should "be content;" "content with
present things." We should learn of that old and experienced servant of God, the Apostle Paul, what the good
Spirit had taught him; in whatsoever state we are, there-
with to be content." Our passive obedience as God's servants is to be shown in our patience as well as in our con-
tentment. What servant is there whom the great Master
does not require to chasten? "He does not afflict willingly."
It is always for our fault. Such is his justice, and such is
his goodness, it is always for our profit. We certainly do
not act like well-informed and well-dispositioned servants, if
we do not take patiently, cheerfully, thankfully, those afflictions which we deserve, which we need, and which the great
Master not only means for our good, but will make effectual
for the purpose for which he intends them, the making us
"partakers of his holiness." Such is a hasty sketch of that
obedience which, as servants of God, Christians owe to their
Divine Master.

It may serve a good purpose to notice some of the characteristic marks by which the obedience of Christians, as
servants of God, ought to be, and indeed is, distinguished
from what is not unfrequently mistaken for it.[1] There are
particularly four characteristics to which I wish to turn
your attention. In order to act as the servant of God, the
Christian's obedience must be implicit, impartial, cheerful,
and persevering. Let me say a word or two in illustration
of each of these. If we would act as the servants of God,
our obedience must be implicit. We must do what God
bids us do, because God bids us do it. There are many
who do many things which God commands, who never obey

---

[1] These characteristics are noticed Disc. v. P. i. § 1, p. 103; but, as the illustration here would be imperfect without a reference to them, I have, at the risk
of appearing "actum agere," introduced them again.

God. The doing what God commands may be agreeable to my inclination, or conducive to my interest; and if on these grounds I do it, I serve myself, not God. What God commands may be commanded by those whose authority I acknowledge, and whose favour I wish to secure; if I do it on these grounds, I am man's servant, not God's servant. I only serve God when I do what he bids me, because he bids me. Every thing he bids me do is right, and ought to be done for its own sake. Every thing he bids me do is fitted to promote my happiness, and ought to be done on this account; but it is only so far as I do it for the Lord's sake that it is obedience. God is the only being in the universe that deserves to be implicitly obeyed. I act like a fool when I believe what the wisest and best man in the world tells me, when I do what the wisest and best man in the world bids me do, if he do not give me a satisfactory reason for it; but I act like a wise man when I believe what God tells me, and do what God bids me, though I have no other reason but that he tells me, and that he bids me; for there can be no stronger proof of the truth of a proposition than that the omniscient and infinitely-faithful One utters it; no stronger proof that an action is right, than that the infinitely wise and righteous Governor of the world has commanded it. The temper of the servant of God is expressed in these words, " Speak, Lord, thy servant heareth:" he listens; he listens to under-stand, and to understand that he may obey. " I will hear," listen to, believe, obey, " what God the Lord will speak."

If we would act as the servants of God, our obedience must be impartial as well as implicit. It will be impartial if it be implicit. There are too many who profess to be Christians who are partial in the law of the Lord. To use a familiar but expressive phrase, they " pick and choose " among his commandments. They do this, but they leave that which is commanded with equal explicitness undone. In every case of this kind it is plain that the soul of true obedience is wanting. If I do any thing just because God commands it (and if I do not do this, I do not obey God at all), I will do whatever he commands me. Instead of thinking, as some seem to do, that their strictness with regard to certain portions of commanded duty, will be sustained as an excuse for their neglect or violation of other parts of commanded duty, I will account God's commandments concerning all things to be right, and I will abhor every wicked way. "Ye are my friends," says our Lord; ye are my servants, says his Father—our Father, his God—our God, "if ye do," not some things that I command you, not many things that I command you, but "whatsoever I command you."

If we would act as the servants of God, our obedience must be cheerful. It must be obedience from the heart. "God is a Spirit," and he who would serve him must serve him with his spirit. Mere bodily service profits nothing. And not only must there be spirit in the service, there must be a free spirit; not the spirit of bondage, but the spirit of adoption. It must not be the spirit of fear, but of love. There are men who do many things from the fear of punishment. The external service of God (and with them there is, there can be, nothing but external service), is very irksome; but then they hope by submitting to this penance to escape the still more painful sufferings of a future state. It is otherwise with the Christian. His language is, "Truly, O Lord! I am thy servant, thou hast loosed my bonds. I walk at liberty, keeping thy commandments. Thy commandments are not grievous. In keeping thy commandments there is great reward. I will be thy servant for ever."

This leads me to remark, that if we would act as the servants of God, our obedience must be persevering. God's servants are not hired servants, engaged for a term of years. They are bought with the blood of his Son; and they are not only to serve him on earth, but even in the better world they are to serve him day and night in his temple, and to go no more out. The promise is, "He that endureth to the end shall be saved." The command with promise is, "Be faithful to death, and I will give you the crown of life." The perfections of the Divine character, and the relations he bears to us, out of which grow our condition as his sons, never change. He always continues our Lord, we must always continue his servants.

There is still another important view of the Christian's duty suggested by his being required to be " as a servant of God," to which I wish shortly to call your attention before leaving this part of the subject. Every Christian should consider himself as engaged in a work committed to him by God, to the right management of which all his time, talents, property, and influence are to be devoted, and a work to be carried on as under God's eye, and of which an account must be given before his tribunal. " No Christian liveth to himself, no Christian dieth to himself. Whether he live, he lives to the Lord; and whether he die, he dies to the Lord: living and dying he is the Lord's."[1] When a man becomes a Christian, he is called into the vineyard of the Lord, and his work is assigned him; or, to vary the figure, he is entrusted with so many talents, and required to occupy them till the Lord come.[2] He is not here to obtain pleasure, honour, or wealth for himself. His business is to " seek the kingdom of God and his righteousness ;" to promote in himself and around him that kingdom which is not of this world, " which is not meat and drink, but righteousness, and peace, and joy in the Holy Ghost."[3] Like his Lord, then, whose meat it was to do the will of his Father who is in heaven, and to finish his work, he should continually be about his Master's business, " as ever in the great Taskmaster's eye," remembering that yet a little while he will call his stewards to give an account of their stewardship, and " every man shall receive his own reward according to his own labour." The Christian should always act as if these words were sounding in his ears: " Every man's work must be made manifest. The day shall declare it. It shall be revealed by fire. The fire shall try every man's

[1] Rom. xiv. 7, 8.   [2] Luke xix. 13.   [3] Matt. vi. 33.   Rom. xiv. 17.

work."[1]   Happy is that man whose work shall stand the trial, and abide ! He shall receive a great reward.

So much for the illustration of that view of the Christian's duty which corresponds to his condition considered as one of subjection. It is to act " as the servant of God."

The motives which urge Christians to the performance of his duty are numerous and powerful. The service of God is in the highest degree reasonable, pleasant, honourable, and advantageous.

It is a most reasonable thing that Christians should act as the servants of God. It is most reasonable that all men should serve God. A disobedient creature is a moral monster. Can any thing be more reasonable than that the will of the all-wise and thrice holy and infinitely benignant Jehovah, should be the rule of the conduct of his creatures ? All that men are and have is the gift of God. He gives them their existence, and all their faculties of reason, and action, and enjoyment. " In him they live, and move, and have their being." It is his sun which warms them ; his air which they breathe ; his flax and wool which clothe them ; his corn, and wine, and oil, which support them. It is his Spirit which gives them understanding. He gives them life and favour, and his visitation preserves their souls; and far, infinitely far, above these manifestations of kindness, he has, for the great love wherewith he loved our fallen race, given his Son, " that whosoever believeth on him might not perish, but have everlasting life ;" and is ready with him to bestow on the guiltiest of the guilty believing on him, all heavenly and spiritual blessings. Surely, if it be reasonable to be just, if it be reasonable to be grateful, all men should serve God. But, besides these powerful reasons why all men should serve God, very strong additional ones urge Christians to this duty. They have been put in possession of the blessings of the Christian salvation. " In Christ they have redemption through his blood, the forgiveness of sins, according to the riches of divine grace." The very design of this redemption is, "that they may serve God." "Christ gave himself for them, that he might redeem them from all iniquity, and purify them unto himself a peculiar people, zealous of good works."[1] Is it reasonable that the great design of the death of the Son of God should be obstructed? They have had the Holy Spirit in his enlightening, sanctifying, and consoling influences bestowed on them. God has given them "one heart," and put "a new spirit within them; and has taken the stony heart out of their flesh, and has given them a heart of flesh." For what end? "That they may walk in his statutes, and keep his ordinances, and do them."[2] And is it not reasonable that the great design of the gift of the Spirit should be accomplished? It is surely right that the great object of their deliverance from the hands of their enemies should be attained; and that is, that they may "serve God in holiness and righteousness before him all the days of their lives." Still farther, they have, in the free exercise of their own choice, devoted themselves to God's service. They have said each of them, "I am the Lord's; I am thy servant; thou hast loosed my bonds. I will pay my vows to the Lord in the presence of all his people."[3] And is it not reasonable that these obligations, so freely incurred, so solemnly acknowledged, should be discharged?

But, in the second place, the service of God is in the highest degree pleasant. "His yoke is easy, and his burden is light." "Wisdom's ways are pleasantness, her paths are peace." "In keeping God's commandments there is great reward." "His commandments are not grievous."[4] It is difficult to convince an unconverted man of this. Indeed, he must become a converted man before he can have personal experimental evidence of these truths. But every con-

---

[1] Tit. ii. 14..   [2] Ezek. xi. 19, 20.
[3] Isa. xliv. 5.   Psal. cxvi. 16, 18.
[4] Matt. xi. 30.   Psal. xix. 11.   1 John v. 3.

verted man knows that it is so. The following is a true as
well as a beautiful picture: " Behold that servant of the
Lord; he is just rising from his knees, where he has been
saying to his heavenly Master, ' Thou hast dealt well with
thy servant, according to thy word. Thou art good, and
dost good; teach me thy statutes.'[1] Take him aside, and
converse with him. Ask him if the service of God is not a
delightful one? his answer is, ' I love his commandments
above gold, yea, above fine gold; and I delight myself in
his commandments, which I love.'[2] But you are often in
heaviness? ' Yes; but my sorrow shall be turned into joy.
The tears of penitential regret and patient suffering are
sweet: and I am never happier than when, with a broken and
contrite heart, ' I turn my feet unto his testimonies.'[3] But
the world frowns on you? ' What then, God smiles on
me; he lifts up the light of his countenance on me. I have
peace—peace which the world cannot give, and cannot take
away. Heaven is my home; death is my friend. Providence
manages all my affairs. My Master in heaven cares for me,
and I am " anxious for nothing."' But your happiness is all
in prospect? ' O, no! I have " the earnest of the inheritance;" I have a " peace that passeth all understanding;" he
is faithful who says, " Great peace have they who love my
law." I " joy in God;" I find it good to draw near to him.
" His statutes are my song in the house of my pilgrimage."
It was once otherwise; I once thought, that to be God's
servant was to be a slave; what I then thought freedom
I now see to be most debasing slavery, and I find that his
service is true freedom.' ' O taste and see that the Lord
is good: blessed is the man that trusteth in him.' "[4]

In the third place, the service of God is highly honourable. Men count it an honour to serve kings and princes.
But what is the honour of being prime minister to the

---

[1] Psal. cxix. 65.　　　[2] Psal. cxix. 47.　　　[3] Psal. cxix. 59.
[4] Eph. i. 14. Psal. cxix. 165, 54; xxxiv. 8. The picture here sketched is
more fully delineated by Mr Jay, in his sermon entitled " Neutrality in Religion Exposed."—Sermons, vol. ii. pp. 337, 8.

greatest of earthly monarchs, compared with the honour of being the servants of the Most High God, the King of kings, and the Lord of lords? It is well said by an apocryphal writer, 'It is a great glory to follow the Lord.'[1] The highest angel in heaven counts this *his* highest honour. The office is honourable, and the discharge of its duties secures honour from him who is the fountain of all honour, —obtains the approbation of him whose good opinion is of infinitely more value than the applause of the whole universe of created intelligent beings. "Them who honour me," says Jehovah, "I will honour." "If any man serve me," says our Lord, "him will my Father honour." How far elevated above all earthly honour will the servant of the Lord stand on that day, "when the King shall say to him, Come to me, thou blessed one; well done, good and faithful servant, enter thou into the joy of thy Lord!"[2]

Finally, the service of God is in the highest degree advantageous. Our service of God can never merit any thing from him. It is always imperfect and faulty ; and, even though it were not so, we should still be unprofitable servants, for we would do only what is our duty to do. We cannot be "profitable to God, as he who is wise is profitable to himself."[3] We can lay him under no obligation. But he has laid himself under obligations. He has promised that affectionate, sincere, persevering service, shall not lose its reward. His command and promise to his servants is: "Be strong, and let not your hands be weak; for your work shall be rewarded."[4] In illustrating the pleasantness of the service of God, we have seen that it brings its reward to a considerable degree along with it; but there remains "the recompense of reward" to be bestowed when the work is finished. Of that reward we can form but very inadequate ideas. "It does not yet appear what we shall be." We may fairly conclude, however, from the language of Scripture, that "the reward of the inheritance" is incomparably

---

[1] Wisd. xxiii. 28.

[3] Job xxii. 2.

[2] John xii. 26.   Matt. xxv. 21.

[4] 2 Chron. xv. 7.

superior not only to all we can enjoy, but to all we can conceive in the present state. It is "a crown of glory and of life;" an "enduring substance;" an "inheritance incorruptible, undefiled, unfading;" an "eternal weight of glory," "fulness of joy, rivers of pleasure for evermore."[1] And this reward is not more valuable than secure, to all who act as the servants of God. "To them who, by a patient continuance in well-doing, seek for glory, honour, and immortality, he will render," as their gracious reward, "eternal life." "Faithful is he that hath promised, who also will do it." "God is not a man, that he should lie; nor the son of man, that he should repent: hath he said it, and will he not do it? Hath he spoken it, and will he not make it good?"[2] Surely, then, Christians ought to act as the servants of God. Constrained by the mercies of God, they should present themselves to him " a living sacrifice, holy and acceptable, which is rational worship;" they should be "steadfast and unmoveable, always abounding in the service of God, knowing that their labours shall not be in vain in the Lord."[3]

These motives are directly addressed to those who are engaged in the service of God; their force will be perceived and acknowledged by them, and I trust under their influence they will become more diligent in the discharge of their honourable and delightful duties than ever. But what shall we say to those who are not free, or if free, are what the Apostle terms "free from righteousness;" who are not the servants of God, but the slaves of his and their great enemy? We could say much of their degradation, and criminality, and wretchedness; but we prefer " proclaiming liberty to these captives, and the opening of the prison to those who are thus bound."[4] Fellow sinners, we call your attention to the truth, "the word of the truth of the gospel."

[1] Heb. xi. 26.   Col. iii. 24.   1 John iii. 1.   1 Pet. v. 4.   James i. 12.   Heb. x. 34.   1 Pet. i. 4.   2 Cor. iv. 17.   Psal. xvi. 11.

[2] Heb. x. 23.   1 Thess. v. 24.   Numb. xxiii. 19.   [3] 1 Cor. xv. 58.

[4] Isa. lxi. 1.

That truth, understood and believed, will make you free, free indeed; and that very truth which will loose the fetters of guilt and depravity, of Satan and sin, will bind on you the easy yoke, lay on you the light burden of the Divine service. Remaining in your present state, which you well know is far from a happy one, you will become more and more miserable throughout eternity. Unless you are released from the chains of condemnation and depravity, you must erelong, bound hand and foot, be cast into the prison of hell, whose adamantine gates open only inward. He whom you have chosen as your master, shall then be constituted your jailer and tormentor. He opens not the house of his prisoners. The prey of the mighty shall not then be taken away, nor the captives of the terrible one be delivered. To his prisoners the gladsome sound, Go forth, will never come. Poor prisoners of hope! It comes to you now. It has come to you often, but you have lent a deaf ear to it. It comes to you once more, it may be only once more. May it not come in vain!

Note A.

This verse is obviously not a complete sentence, and must be considered as connected either with what goes before, or with what follows, or with both. Its meaning and design cannot well be distinctly apprehended, unless this question respecting its construction be satisfactorily resolved. If it be considered as connected with what precedes it, then the words are descriptive of the manner in which the duty of submission, for the Lord's sake, to every human institution " for the punishment of evil-doers, and for the praise of them who do well, whether to the king or emperor, as supreme ; or to governors, as to them sent by him"— *i. e.* to the institute of civil government, whatever its form may be—ought to be performed by Christians. It ought to be performed in a manner suitable to their condition, as at once a condition of freedom and of subjection ; in a way becoming at once the glorious liberty wherewith Christ had made them free, and that entire subjection to the mind and will of God which befits those who are HIS servants. It intimates that, " being set at liberty by Christ, they are not to enthral themselves to any creature, however elevated, nor to submit to any human institution as slaves, as if the ordinance or institution itself, as a human ordinance and institution, did by any inherent power bind the conscience ; but that, as the Lord's freemen, in a manner becoming so exalted a character, they should yield a cheerful subjection to the power of civil magistrates, and a ready obedience to their lawful commands, from a regard to the authority of Christ, the sole Lord of their conscience, requiring them so to do,—taking heed ' not to use their liberty for an occasion to the flesh,' not making that a cloak or excuse for disrespect or disobedience to their civil superiors : for though, in the highest sense of the term, they be not the servants of men, but of God, and therefore are not bound to obey any human command without a reference to the authority of God requiring them to do so ; yet, on the ground of his command to be subject to the higher powers, they are bound to yield to them such honour and obedience as does not interfere with the supreme reverence and obedience which they owe to Him as the only Lord of the conscience." [1] This, from the punctuation adopted by our translators, seems to have been their view of the reference and meaning of the words. The whole passage, from the beginning of the 13th verse to the

[1] Sanderson

end of the first clause of the 17th, may be viewed as one sentence; in which case, the words of the 16th verse stand connected both with what goes before and with what follows. Thus, "Submit yourselves for the Lord's sake to every ordinance of man for punishing evil-doers and rewarding those who do well, whether to the king as supreme, or to governors as to them who are sent by him (for so is the will of God, that with well-doing ye put to silence the ignorance of foolish men): as free, and not using your liberty as a cloak of maliciousness, but as the servants of God, honour them all—all civil magistrates, whether supreme or subordinate." To the first mode of connecting the 16th verse it is an objection, that it seems an unnatural mode of concluding a sentence, and gives a very disjointed aspect to the whole period; and to the second, that the four injunctions in the 17th verse are so closely connected, that it seems improper to separate one of them from the rest. We are disposed, therefore, to consider the 16th verse as the commencement of a new sentence, which closes with the 17th.

Note B.

The passage referred to, Rom. vi. 20, has received another interpretation. It has been supposed that ελευθεροι here is used as if it were the participle ελευθερωθεντες, as it seems to be, ch. vii. 3, where ελευθερα is obviously equivalent to κατηργηται in verse 2. In this case τη δικαιοσυνη must be rendered, "by righteousness;" and the words, ελευθεροι ητε τη δικαιοσυνη, are the statement of the fact, the consequences of which are stated in verse 22. This secures to δικαιοσυνη its ordinary meaning in the Epistle; and the use of απο in verse 22 seems to intimate, that another idea is meant to be conveyed there, than by the use of the dative without a preposition, in verse 20.

Note C.

"When he was to do for us the part of a Redeemer, he was to redeem us from the curse of the law, not from the command of it; to save us from the wrath of God, not from his government. Had it been otherwise, so firm and indissoluble is the connexion between our duty and our felicity, that the Sovereign Ruler had been eternally injured, and we not advantaged. Were we to have been set free from the preceptive obligation of God's holy law; then, most of all, from that most fundamental precept, 'Thou shalt love the Lord, thy God, with all thine heart, soul, might, and mind.' Had this been redemption, which supposes only what is evil and hurtful as that we are to be redeemed from? This were a strange sort of self-repugnant redemption, not from sin and misery, but from our duty and felicity. This were so to be redeemed as to be still lost, and every way lost, both to God and to ourselves, for ever. Redeemed from loving God! What a monstrous thought! Redeemed from what is the great, active, and fruitive principle—the source of obedience and blessedness—the eternal spring, even in the heavenly state of adoration and fruition. This had been to legitimate everlasting enmity and rebellion against the blessed God, and to redeem us into an eternal hell of horror and misery to ourselves. This had been to cut off from the Supreme Ruler of the world for ever, so considerable a limb of his most rightful dominion; and to leave us as miserable, as everlasting separation from the fountain of life and blessedness could make us."—Howe. "None can be exempted from this law, unless he will be banished from his own essence, and be excommunicated from human nature."—Culverwel.

EXPOSITORY DISCOURSES.

DISCOURSE XII.

A FOURFOLD VIEW OF THE DUTY OF CHRISTIANS AS FREE, YET THE SERVANTS OF GOD.

1 Pet. ii. 17.—Honour all men. Love the brotherhood. Fear God. Honour the king.

In our last discourse, our attention was turned to the view which the preceding verse gives us of the condition and character of true Christians. Their *condition* is one both of liberty and of subjection : they are " free," yet " the servants of God." They are " free ;" free in reference to God, both as to state and disposition ; free in reference to man ; free in reference to the powers and principles of evil : they are " the servants of God," redeemed by the blood of his Son ; formed by his Spirit to the character of servants, being made acquainted with his will, and disposed to do it ; devoted by their own most free choice to his service ; and actually engaged in that service, obeying his law, and promoting his cause. Their *duty*, when viewed generally, consists in acting in a manner suited to their condition, as equally a condition of freedom and subjection. They are to act " as free" in all the varied senses in which they enjoy the privilege of liberty, guarding against abusing that privilege in any of its forms, "as a cloak," pretext, apology, or excuse for sin ; and they are to act " as the servants of God," to cultivate the principle of obedience, habitually keeping in view those perfections of the Divine character, and those relations which they bear to God, in which the obligation to serve God originates, and the belief of which is the grand means which the Holy Spirit employs to fit and dispose us to recognise and discharge that obligation ; to make themselves acquainted with the rule of obedience, carefully studying the word of God, observing the providence of God, and seeking the guidance of the Spirit of God ; and to exercise this principle, and apply this rule in actual obedience, both inward and outward, both active and passive.

To this general view of the Christian's duty, as an acting in conformity to his condition, the Apostle adds a somewhat more detailed and particular account, for the purpose of illustration. In the words before us, he specifies four different ways in which Christians are to conduct themselves " as free," and yet "as the servants of God." They are to " honour all men," they are to " love the brotherhood," they are to " fear God," they are to " honour the king." Let us now proceed to inquire into the meaning of these Divine injunctions, and into the motives which urge to a cheerful compliance with them. And while we do so, may God give us the understanding mind and the obedient heart ! May He " open our understandings," to understand this portion of " Scripture given by inspiration of God," that we may become wiser; and open our hearts to love it, that it may be the effectual means of making us better as well as wiser; giving us clearer views of what is our duty, and a deeper impression of our obligations to discharge it !

" Here," as the good Archbishop remarks, " are no dark sentences to puzzle the understanding, nor large discourses, and long periods, to burden the memory.   As the Divine Wisdom says of her instructions in the book of Proverbs, These precepts are all 'plain ;' there is nothing 'froward or perverse,' nothing 'wreathed,' as it is in the margin, involved, distorted, perplexed, difficult, in them. And this gives check to a double folly among men, contrary the one to the other, but both agreeing in mistaking and wronging the word of God. The one is, of those who despise the word, and that doctrine and preaching which is according to it, for its plainness and simplicity; the other, of those who complain of its difficulty and darkness. As for the first, they certainly do not apprehend the true end for which the word is designed, that is, to be the law of our life; and that it is mainly requisite in laws that they be both brief and clear. It is our guide to light and happiness; and, if that which ought to be our light were darkness, how great would that darkness be! It is true that there be dark and deep passages in Scripture for the exercise, yea for the humbling, yea for the amazing and astonishing, of the sharpest-sighted readers. But it argues much the pride and vanity of men's minds, when they busy themselves only in these, and throw aside altogether the most necessary, which are therefore the easiest and plainest truths in it, evidencing that they had rather be learned than holy, ' wise than good,' and have still more mind to 'the tree of knowledge' than to 'the tree of life.' In hearing the word, too many are still gaping after new notions, something to add to the stock of their speculative and discoursing knowledge, loathing the daily manna of such profitable exhortations, and 'requiring meat for their lust.' There is an intemperance of the mind as well as of the mouth. You would think it, and may be not spare to call it, a poor cold sermon, that was made up of such plain precepts as these : ' Honour all men : love the brotherhood : fear God : honour the king :' and yet this is the language of God. It is his way, this foolish despicable way, by which he ' guides and brings to heaven them that believe.' "

As to those who complain of the difficulties of Scripture, let them but believe and do what is perfectly level to the apprehension of the simplest mind, and they will thus take the most probable means of arriving at just views of what is obscure ; for he is faithful who has promised. " If any man will do—that is, be willing to do—the will of my Father in heaven, he shall know of the doctrine, whether it be of God;"[1] and, at all events, he will soon and certainly find his way to that region where all difficulties are removed, all mysteries are unveiled, all obscurities are explained. There, in God's light, he shall see light; no longer seeing as through a glass darkly, but face to face; no longer knowing in part only, but knowing even as he is known. But to return to the illustration of the Apostle's four comprehensive precepts.

I.—CHRISTIANS ARE TO " HONOUR ALL MEN."

The first particular duty which he calls on Christians to perform " as free, and yet as the servants of God," is the honouring of all men. " Honour all men." To bring out the true and the full meaning of this important and very comprehensive precept of the Christian law, it is necessary to remark, that "all men" is here used in contrast with some men, and to inquire who are these some men referred to. In looking into the immediate context, we find two classes of men mentioned, to either, or to both of whom, the apostle may be considered as referring. These are " the brotherhood"—that is, true Christians, " the chosen generation, the kingdom of priests, the holy nation, the peculiar people, the dwellers in light, the people of God." If the reference is to them, the sentiment contained in the words before us is : While " the saints, the excellent ones of the earth," ought to be the objects of your highest respect and honour, as well as affection, yet you are not warranted to regard unbelieving men with contempt because they do not belong to the Holy Society, are not " partakers of the benefit ;" but, on the contrary, wherever from civil or natural relation, or from intellectual endowments, or moral dispositions, they are the proper objects of respect, you are bound to render honour to whom honour is due.

[1] John vii. 17.

The brotherhood is not, however, the only class of men mentioned in the context. There are also " the men ordained for the punishment of evil-doers, and for the praise of them that do well : the king as supreme, and the governors who are sent by him." These are to be honoured, all of them honoured, by being obeyed and submitted to. If the reference is to them, then the sentiment conveyed is : While magistrates are to be honoured in a manner suited to the nature and design of the office which they fill, no human being is to be despised. There is a respect due to every man, just because he is a man ; there is an honour due to the king, but there is also an honour due to all men. As the language of the Apostle, without using undue violence, may be considered as suggesting both these important and closely connected sentiments, I shall endeavour briefly to illustrate and enforce them in their order.

§ 1. *Honour not to be confined to the brotherhood, but rendered to all to whom it is due.*

The first principle which we consider, as suggested by the Apostle's words, is, that the respectful regards of Christians are not to be confined " to the brotherhood," but are to be extended to unbelieving men, according to the claims which, from civil or natural relation, from intellectual endowments or moral dispositions, they may have on them. Honour is to be yielded to all to whom honour is due, though " aliens from the commonwealth of spiritual Israel, and strangers to the covenant of promise."

The injunction viewed in this light, like the strikingly similar one, " Use not your liberty as a cloak of wickedness," seems, from the peculiar circumstances and previous habits of thought of many of the primitive Christians, to have been far from unnecessary. It seems plain that a very large proportion, at least of those to whom this epistle was addressed, consisted of Jewish converts. The Jews were accustomed to consider their own nation as the chosen people of Jehovah, and on this account as worthy of the highest honour ; while they

regarded the Gentiles, the nations as they termed them, all
the rest of mankind, with a malignant contempt, which its
objects, in most instances, repaid with liberal interest. They
very generally considered all authority exercised by Gentiles over Jews as impious usurpation; and if they submitted to it, they did so " for wrath sake," not " for conscience sake ;" not because obedience was in their estimation
right, but because disobedience was found in their experience unsafe ; not from a sense of duty, but from a fear
of punishment. There was some hazard that these habits
of thought and feeling, modified by their new circumstances
and relations, might influence the Jewish converts ; that
they might regard the spiritual nation, of which they had
become a part, by believing with sentiments similar to those
with which they used to contemplate " Israel according to
the flesh ;" and unbelievers, whether Jews or heathens, in a
light corresponding to that in which they looked on the
Gentiles in the days of their Judaism ; and indeed, from
various passages in the apostolic writings, it seems, to say
the least, highly probable that this hazard was, to some extent, realized.

It was of importance, then, for the apostles distinctly to
assert, that the new religious relations and duties of Christians by no means unhinged their existing natural and civil
relations, or interfered with the duties rising out of them,
except by furnishing clearer directions for, and stronger motives to, their performance. Christian subjects are bound to
honour heathen or Jewish magistrates. The command,
when there were no magistrates even professing Christianity,
was, " Let every soul be subject to the higher powers. The
powers that be are ordained by God." " Submit to every
human institution for the punishment of evil-doers, and the
praise of them who do well."[1] Christian servants were to
regard with the honour which finds its expression in cheerful, conscientious, uncomplaining obedience, their heathen

---

[1] Rom. xiii. 1.

masters. "Servants," says the Apostle in the next verse, "be subject to your masters with all fear; not only to the good and gentle, but also to the froward." And the Apostle Paul, speaking of masters not believing, says, "Let as many servants as are under the yoke count their own masters worthy of all honour, that the name of God and his doctrine be not blasphemed."[1] Christian wives were bound to honour their heathen husbands. The relation was not dissolved, nor its duties changed. "If the woman hath a husband that believeth not, and if he be pleased to dwell with her, let her not leave him;"[2] and it is plainly to Christian wives in these circumstances, that the commandment in the beginning of the 3d chapter of this Epistle is addressed: "Likewise, ye wives, be in subjection to your own husbands; that, if any obey not the word, they also may without the word be won by the conversation of the wives; while they behold your chaste conversation coupled with fear." Christian children were bound to honour heathen parents by providing for their support when necessary, and by "obeying them in the Lord"—that is, so far as their commands did not interfere with those of their Master in heaven.

On the same principle, wherever a Christian met with distinguished intellectual endowment or acquirement, extensive knowledge, remarkable wisdom, or with manifestations of integrity, public spirit, patriotism, benevolence, in unbelieving Jews or heathens, he was not to shut his mind against the admission that such intellectual and moral excellencies did exist, nor his heart against the feeling of respect and honour which they are naturally fitted to awaken, because their owners did not belong to the Christian community. In such cases, though so far as the display of moral qualities was concerned, they were, we believe, of very rare occurrence in the primitive age, Christians were to do full justice, and "render honour to whom honour was due." In yielding honour to heathens, corresponding to the natural

---

[1] 1 Pet. ii. 18.   1 Tim. vi. 1.   [2] 1 Cor. vii. 13.

and civil relations of society, they did honour to Him who established these relations; and in yielding honour to heathens corresponding to their intellectual and moral endowments, they did honour to Him who conferred these gifts.

The principle we have been illustrating is of universal application, and the precept grounded on it of permanent obligation. Christians of the present age are equally bound, with those of the primitive age, to "honour all men" in the sense in which we have explained these words. The circumstance that individuals, who from their natural or civil relation, or from their intellectual or moral qualities, have a claim on respect, are not Christians in the only proper sense of the term, though necessarily giving to that respect a different character from what it would naturally assume if they were Christians, ought to be felt by true Christians as a reason why they should be particularly careful in answering such a claim. They should act on the principle, recommended to Christian wives by the Apostle, to guide them in their conduct to their heathen husbands. In that readiness to acknowledge what deserves to be honoured wherever it is found, they may do much to remove prejudice, and to recommend Christianity to a favourable consideration; and win them without the word, to whom there might be no opportunity of presenting the word; or who, if it were presented to them, would not listen to it.

Few things have injured the cause of genuine Christianity more, than a bigoted blindness on the part of some of its professors to the unquestionable claims to respect of various kinds of men, who, unhappily for themselves as well as the world, have neglected or resisted the evidence of the truth as it is in Jesus. Such men are deeply to be pitied; they are, in many cases, greatly to be blamed; in no case are they blameless: but still their fault, their fatal fault, if persisted in, ought not to prevent us from honouring them for that which, in their station, or attainments, or character, or conduct, is really honourable. Those men who please themselves with the thought, that in despising these men they are showing their enlightened zeal for Christianity, are greatly mistaken. They are manifesting their own ignorant, ill-judging mind, and their wayward, ill-regulated temper. Their zeal is, " a cloak of maliciousness." In the name of the religion of love, they are gratifying low and malignant feelings ; and, if they are true Christians, they plainly in this case " know not what spirit they are of."

And surely if the law of Christ expressly requires honour to be given to men according to their rank, and endowments, and attainments, and character, though they are not Christians at all, its spirit must be very hostile to that petty, selfish, malignant temper, which, availing itself of the unnaturally divided state of Christ's church, leads those possessed by it to withhold honour from men the most distinguished for their talents, their worth, and their usefulness, and, it may be, to cherish towards them sentiments of bitter contempt ; merely because they belong to a different section of the great body bearing the name of our common Lord, separated by barriers which exist only in their prejudiced minds from that to which they happen to be attached. Alas ! how much has there been among Christian denominations of "biting and devouring" one another, and "smiting fellow-servants," who ought to have been " esteemed very highly in love for their work's sake !" How different from, how opposite to, the spirit of the injunction before us, " Honour all men," is this ! Surely, if we are to honour all men who deserve honour, much more are we to honour all Christian men who deserve honour, though they follow not with us.

§ 2. *Honour not to be confined to classes, but extended to all men.*

But we apprehend the Apostle's words not only suggest the principle, that the respectful regards of Christians are not to be confined to the brotherhood, but are to be extended to unbelieving men, according to the claims which, from natural or civil relation, or from intellectual endowments or moral dispositions, they may have on them : They appear to us to intimate another very important principle, that there is a respect due to every human being, and that it is a Christian duty to cherish that respect, and to act accordingly.

There is an honour which we owe to men, just because they are men; an honour of course due to all men, without exception and without distinction. That honour is not the honour of moral esteem. There are individuals, many individuals, that deserve to be approved and admired for their moral qualities. Man, as God made him, deserved thus to be honoured; but the moral qualities which universally characterise mankind as a race, in their present state, are not those which are the proper objects of approbation, but of disapprobation. What is the testimony of Him who knows what is in man? "Every imagination of the thoughts of his heart is only evil continually. The heart is deceitful above all things, and desperately wicked." In man, that is, "in his flesh," *i. e.*, as man in his present fallen state, "there dwelleth no good thing." Fools, they say in their heart, there is no God; "they are corrupt, they have done abominable works, there is none that doeth good. The Lord looked down from heaven upon the children of men, to see if there were any that did understand and seek God. They are all gone aside, they are altogether become filthy; there is none that doeth good, no not one. Their throat is an open sepulchre: with their tongues have they used deceit: the poison of asps is under their lips: whose mouth is full of cursing and bitterness: their feet are swift to shed blood: destruction and misery are in their ways: and the way of peace they have not known: there is no fear of God before their eyes."[1] This is what man is, what man has made himself, the very reverse indeed of what God made him; yet what he is, and what he must continue to be, till God newmake him, "create him anew in Christ Jesus to good works."

The foundation of the claim for honour to all men, as

---

[1] Gen. vi. 5.   Psal. xiv. 1.   Rom. iii. 10-18.

men, does not then consist in their moral state as exempli-
fied in their conduct; that, in a rightly constituted mind,
must call forth the sentiment of strong disapprobation, not
unmingled with contempt, disapprobation for wickedness,
contempt for folly, both of which are plainly immeasurable :
it lies in their possession of a spiritual, rational, responsible,
immortal nature. Every human being is, from the very
constitution of his nature, of far more importance and dignity than a whole universe of inanimate matter, or even of
irrational animate beings. Every human being has the
capacity of apprehending truth and its evidence, of distinguishing what is true from what is false, and what is
good from what is evil ; every man has the faculty of knowing, loving, praising, serving, and enjoying God ; every man
is destined to an immortality of being. An eternity of ever-
growing knowledge, and holiness, and happiness, or of ever-
augmenting depravity, and degradation, and misery, is before
every individual of our race. These faculties form the
native nobility of every human being ; and to think, and
feel, and act towards every human being, as possessed of
this nobility, is to honour all men, and to perform the duty
enjoined in the text. And surely to despise the possessor
of that for the loss of which the gain of the whole world
could not compensate, however humble his rank, however
low the degree of his civilisation, however limited his knowledge, ay, however depraved his character, is obviously
at once irrational and immoral. The feeling such endowments should excite in their possessor is mingled gratitude
and fear. The feeling they should excite in others, that of
solemn interest.

The cultivation of an habitual reverence for man, as man,
the noblest of the works of God in this region of his universe, and, though fallen from his high estate, capable of,
destined to, restoration to more than his pristine glory, is
obviously of the greatest importance. It affords constant
motive, and gives right direction to our benevolent feelings
and exertions in reference to our fellow-men. It impresses us

with the strong thought, how much good, and how much good
of the very highest kind may be done, when such a being
as *man* is the object of our benevolence.   It leads us chiefly
to think of, and provide for, and relieve, those wants and
miseries which belong to him as the object of our reverence;
his wants as an intelligent, responsible, religious, immortal
being; and it at the same time guides us in the use of the
means fitted to gain the desired end in reference to such a
being, leading us to remember what, even by some persons
not destitute of benevolence, seems often overlooked or forgotten, that in endeavouring to reclaim and relieve him, we
must deal with him as a being who has reason, and conscience, and feeling, as well as ourselves; who may be
reasoned or persuaded into a better mind, but cannot be
scolded, or beaten, or bribed into it, and who must "give
an account of himself to God."

The want of this feeling has contributed in no limited
degree to the production and permanence of some of the
greatest social evils which prevail in the world.   Had man
had reverence for man, slavery with all its horrors could
never have existed.   Every feeling like honouring our common nature must be extinct, before man can make property
of his brother, can treat him as if he was not a person at all,
but a thing, a portion of his goods and chattels.   Had this
sentiment prevailed, there would have been no murder; far
less would there have been those wholesale legalized murders
which civilized nations commit under the name of war.
The notorious disgraceful fact never could have existed, that
it was no uncommon thing for men not only outwardly to
express, but inwardly to feel, more regard to some dog or
horse they love, than to poor distressed partakers of
their own nature; thus "reflecting," as Archbishop Leighton says, "at once dishonour on themselves and on mankind."   It has been justly remarked, that "respect is the
parent of kindness.   From contempt to injury the transition
is short and easy.   He that despises human nature, wants
only the opportunity to oppress man.   The pride of man

leads him to treat the sensitive nature that is beneath him,
as if it were so much inanimate matter. It is the feeling
that they are so far beneath him, that induces him to be
so careless of the sufferings of the lower creation, and just
the more careless as they are inferior to his level. He
scarcely thinks of moving in the slightest degree out of his
way to save the reptile from pain, or mutilation, or death.
And it is on the same principle that much, very much, of
the oppression exercised, and the injury inflicted by one
class of men on another, is to be accounted for. Would
so many rich men have oppressed their poorer brethren,
ground their faces, and despised their cause; would so
many rulers have wrested judgment, and crushed those
whom they should have protected ; would so many princes
have spilt as in sport the blood of thousands, and made the
murder of mankind a game; would so many tyrants have
trampled on the neck of nations, and treated millions as
made for one, had they honoured man, had they considered
that every human creature, whatever may be the meanness
of his birth, the contractedness of his education, the depth
of his destitution, is an image of God, an heir of immortality,
a being containing in him capacities of illimitable improvement; a wonderful creature, who in its chrysalis state, under a humble form, conceals within his bosom wings which,
if expanded, may carry him upward and onward in the pursuit of glory, honour, and immortality, for ever."[1]   It is
because man does not honour man, that there is so much
reason for the complaint—

> " The natural bond
> Of brotherhood is sever'd as the flax,
> That falls asunder at the touch of fire.
> He finds his fellow guilty of a skin
> Not colour'd like his own ; and, having power
> To enforce the wrong, for such a worthy cause
> Dooms and devotes him as his lawful prey,—
> Chains him, and tasks him, and exacts his sweat
> With stripes, that mercy, with a bleeding heart,
> Weeps when she sees inflicted on a beast."[2]

[1] Joseph Fawcett.   [2] Cowper.

The prevalence of infidel opinions among the great body of our people is deeply to be deprecated, for many causes; and, among these causes, its tendency to destroy man's reverence for man is by no means the least important. This has been put in a very striking point of view by Robert Hall, and I make no apology for laying the substance of his illustration before you: 'The supposition that man is a moral and accountable being, destined to survive the stroke of death, and to live in a future world in a never-ending state of happiness or misery, makes him a creature of incomparably greater consequence than the opposite supposition. When we consider him as placed here by the Almighty Ruler in a state of probation, and that the present life is his period of trial, the first link in a vast and interminable chain which stretches into eternity, he assumes a dignified character in our eyes. Every thing that relates to him becomes interesting; and to trifle with his happiness is felt to be the most unpardonable levity. On the opposite supposition, he is a contemptible creature, whose existence and happiness are insignificant. He is nothing more than an animal, distinguished from other animals merely by the vividness and multiplicity of his perceptions. He is entirely of the earth earthy, and his spirit, like those of his fellows, goes down to the earth. From these principles it is a fair inference, that to extinguish human life by the hand of violence, must be quite a different thing in the eyes of a sceptic from what it is in those of a Christian. With the sceptic it is merely the diverting the course of a little red fluid called blood; it is merely lessening by one the number of many millions of fugitive contemptible creatures. The Christian sees in the same event an accountable being cut off from a state of probation, and hurried, perhaps unprepared, into the presence of his Judge, to hear that final, that irrevocable sentence, which is to fix him for ever in an unalterable condition of felicity or of woe.'[1]

Reverence for man is the great security both for property,

---

[1] Modern Infidelity Considered. Works, i. p. 41-47.

liberty, and life; and just views of man, as a responsible and immortal being, are the foundation of this reverence. Most justly, as well as forcibly, has the distinguished author referred to remarked, that "the speculations of atheistical philosophy matured, gave birth to a ferocity which converted the most polished people in Europe into a horde of assassins. Having been taught by them to consider mankind as little better than a nest of insects, in the fierce conflicts of party they trampled on them without pity, and extinguished them without remorse."

Besides the obvious connexion which the principle enjoined in the text has with the security and promotion of all the more important interests of society, there are other and most powerful motives which urge us to cultivate and exemplify it. To the question, Why should we honour all men? we have already given the reply, Because all men, viewed as rational, responsible, and immortal, deserve to be honoured; and because the honouring of men is necessary, in order to the attainment and security of the greatest amount of social happiness. We now add: we should honour all men; for God, the fountain of true honour, the best judge of what is to be honoured, honours man, honours all men. He has honoured them, in making them honourable in the possession of those capacities to which we have already referred. The eighth Psalm, whether descriptive of man in the primitive, or man in the millennial state, is a striking proof that God honours man. And in the place he has assigned them among his creatures on this earth, and in the arrangements of his providence, he takes kind notice of the whole race. He makes his sun to shine, and his rain to descend on all. " Have we not all one Father," and is he not a kind Father to us all? " Behold God is mighty, yet he despiseth not any." He is " mindful" of our race, he " visits" man.[1]

For reasons known only to himself, but necessarily most sufficient, he shows a respect to men which he did not show to angels. When men ruined themselves, he did not act as

---

[1] Psal. viii. 5-8; comp. Heb. ii. 6, &c. Matt. v. 45. Mal. ii. 10. Job. xxxvi. 5.

if their perdition would be a slight matter, an easily repa-
rable loss. He was gracious to them, and said, "Deliver
them from going down to the pit : I have found a ransom."
And their deliverer sent by him was not an angel, not the
highest of angels, but his own Son ; and that deliverance was
obtained by nothing short of the sacrifice of the life of that
Son. What an apparatus of means has he called into
being for bringing this deliverance home to individual men,
in the revelation of his word, the ordinances of his worship,
the influence of his Spirit! And these amazing dispensations are the result of love to the race, love to the world, the
love of man ; and the deliverance is not a deliverance for
men of particular nations, or particular ranks, but for men
of every rank, every nation, Jew and Gentile, Greek and
Barbarian, male and female, bond and free.[1]

In his dealings with man he honours him, acting to him
in a way corresponding to his nature. He does not act towards him as if he was a piece of inanimate matter, or a
brute animal. He seeks to enlighten and convince his
mind, and to engage his affections. He says, " Come now,
let us reason together." He employs " cords of a man, bands
of love;" arguments and motives fitted to his reason, and
conscience, and heart, to his service.[2]

Jesus Christ, the only begotten of God, honours man.
He has taken into union with his divinity *man's* nature. He
never so honoured angels : they count it an honour to call
him Lord ; but man may, without presumption, call him
brother. "The word of life," the living one who was "in the
beginning with God, who was, and is God became 'flesh."
" Inasmuch as the children are partakers of flesh and blood,
he also took part of the same ;" and in human nature he
died for men, " the just in the room of the unjust," giving
himself a " ransom for all," and bringing in an everlasting
salvation—a salvation suited to all, needed by all, and to
which all are invited, with an assurance that " whosoever

---

[1] Job. xxxiii. 24. Col. iii. 11.   [2] Isa. i. 18. Hos. xi. 4.

believeth shall not perish, but have everlasting life." His
command is, " Go ye into all the world, and preach the gospel
to every creature." It is his will that his salvation should
be brought near " to every creature under heaven."[1] Farther, he carried human nature to heaven with him. A *man*
sits on the throne of the universe ; one who is not ashamed
to call men brethren, and whom the most abject of the
human race may call brother. This is the true dignity of
human nature. " Human nature," as an old divine forcibly
remarks, " has become adorable as the true Shekinah, the
everlasting palace of the supreme Majesty, wherein the
fulness of the Godhead dwelleth bodily ; the most holy
shrine of the divinity, the orb of inaccessible light, as this,
and more than all this, if more could be expressed, or, if we
could explain that text, ' The word was made flesh, and
dwelt among us.' "[2]

It is obvious, then, that we cannot treat disrespectfully or
contumeliously any human being without dishonouring God
and his Son. " When a piece even of base metal is coined
with the king's stamp," to use Bishop Sanderson's illustration, " and made current by his edict, no man may henceforth
presume either to refuse it in payment, or to abate the value
of it ; so God, having stamped his own image upon every
man, and withal signified his blessed pleasure, how precious
he would have him to be in our eyes and esteem, by express
edict proclaiming, ' At the hand of every man's brother will
I require the life of man : I require every man to be his
brother's keeper ; for in the image of God made he man ;'[3]
we must look to answer it as a high contempt of that sacred
Majesty, if we set any man at nought, or make less account
of him than God would have us. The contumelious use of
the image is in common construction even understood as a
dishonour meant to the prototype. The Romans, when
they meant to set a mark of public disgrace or dishonour on

---

[1] 1 Pet. iii. 18.　1 Tim. ii. 6.　John iii. 16.　Mark xvi. 15.　Col. i. 23.　Heb.
ii. 11.

[2] Barrow.　　　　　　　　　　　　　　　　　　　[3] Gen. ix. 5.

any eminent person, did manifest their intention by throwing down, breaking, trampling upon, or doing some other like disgrace to their statues or pictures. And Solomon, in sundry places, interpreteth all acts of oppressing, mocking, or otherwise despising our neighbours, not without a strong reflection upon God himself; as leading to the contempt and dishonour of their Maker. ' He that oppresseth the poor reproacheth his Maker : but he that honoureth HIM hath mercy on the poor.' ' Whoso mocketh the poor reproacheth his Maker ; ' and surely there is much force in this interrogation, ' Why settest thou at nought, not only thine own brother, but the brother of the Lord of glory ? ' Why despiseth thou him for whom Christ died ? [1] "

There is indeed something revoltingly unnatural, something inconceivably mean and base, something grotesquely absurd, in a human being regarding with contempt any other human being. Surely, the man who treats any man as a mean contemptible creature, should in a double sense be ashamed of *himself*, for what is HE but a *man*? How insignificant the distinction which elevates one man above another, in comparison of the distinction which elevates all men above the brutal tribes ? How little does wealth, or rank, or even human learning, bulk in the eye of angels ? How highly do they estimate reason, conscience, affection, capacity for being like God, immortality ? The man who contemns any man, shows that he does not so much value himself because he is a man, but rather, whatever respect he has for human nature, flows from his being a partaker of it. How mean, how absurd, how thoroughly contemptible, is pride ! Surely, " pride was not made for man, nor haughtiness of heart for him who is born of a woman."

The sentiment of honour for man, as man, which we have been illustrating and recommending, should manifest itself in the whole of our conduct to our fellow men, especially to those who in any respect may be our inferiors, whether in intellect, or talent, or acquirement, or moral worth, or rank, or wealth, leading us to " condescend to them that are of low estate:" but it takes its best form, when it leads us to use all the means in our power to raise our fellow men in the scale of true honour and excellence ; to rescue them from the influence of ignorance, and error, and superstition ; to put down slavery, oppression, war, and misgovernment, in all its endlessly varied forms ; to make men free, intelligent, industrious, moral, religious, and happy, to the greatest attainable degree on earth ; to save them from the shame and everlasting contempt which awaits unimproved advantages and unanswered responsibilities in eternity; and to secure to them that " glory, honour, and immortality," which, while " the gift of God through Jesus Christ," is to be sought for and obtained " in a constant continuance in well-doing."[1]

Few things are better fitted at once to stimulate and to guide in such noble enterprises, than enlightened, impressive views of the true grandeur of human nature. While humbled to the very dust with the overwhelming evidence, without us and within us, of the fearful degradation of human nature by sin, let us never forget what it was when God made it, what it is still capable of, what it still is when God makes it anew on earth, what it will be when he completes the work of transformation in heaven. Human nature was a stately beautiful fabric as God reared it. It is majestic even in ruins, exciting in every right constituted mind awe as well as sorrow.[a] As its desolations are repaired by the plastic powers of the Divine Spirit, symmetry and beauty are seen developing themselves ; and when, in the heaven of heavens, man stands forth, nearest of all created beings to Him who sits on the right hand of the Divine Majesty, bearing the image of the Second Adam, the Lord from heaven, then will it be felt by all intelligent beings, that

[1] Rom. vi. 23 11, 7.   [a] See Note A.

human nature is indeed one of the most wonderful results
of Divine wisdom, and power, and love.

Right views, equally of man's meanness and his greatness,
are to be obtained only by studying the representations which
are contained in the Divine word, an impressive abstract of
which is contained in the following plain but striking stanzas :

> " Lord! what is man? extremes how wide
>   In his mysterious nature join:—
> The flesh to worms and dust allied;
>   The soul immortal and divine.
> Divine at first—a holy flame,
>   Kindled by the Almighty's breath—
> Till, stain'd by sin, it soon became
>   The seat of darkness, strife, and death.
>
> " But Jesus—Oh! amazing love!—
>   Assumed our nature as his own;
> Obey'd and suffer'd in our place,
>   Then took it with him to his throne.
> Now what is man, when grace reveals
>   The virtue of a Saviour's blood?
> Again a life divine he feels,
>   Despises earth, and walks with God.
>
> " And what, in yonder realms above,
>   Is ransom'd man ordain'd to be?
> With honour, holiness, and love,
>   No seraph more adorn'd than he.
> Nearest the throne, and first in song,
>   Man shall his hallelujahs raise;
> While wond'ring angels round him throng,
>   And swell the chorus of his praise." [1]

He who believes this, he alone who believes this, will
" honour all men."

II.—CHRISTIANS ARE TO " LOVE THE BROTHERHOOD."

THE " BROTHERHOOD," and OUR DUTY AS CHRISTIANS
TOWARDS THE BROTHERHOOD : these are the two interesting
topics to which our attention is now to be successively
directed.

[1] Olney Hymn.

§ 1.—*Of " the brotherhood."*

A brotherhood is an association of brothers. Now, who are the brethren that are here referred to, and what is that association of them which is termed "the brotherhood?" It is scarcely necessary to say, that the language is not here used in its strictly literal signification: the signification in which John was the brother of James, and Andrew of Peter. In its analogical or figurative employment, which is manifold, it entirely overlooks the distinction of sex, and far overleaps the boundaries of families. "There is neither Jew nor Greek, Barbarian, Scythian, bond nor free, male nor female," here. It is usual in Scripture to speak of all the descendants of Jacob as brethren, and it is no uncommon thing to represent all human beings as brethren. The reason of this is obvious. With regard to their animal frames, they are all the descendants of the original pair; for "God has made of one blood all the nations of men for to dwell on the face of the earth;" and, with regard to their immortal minds, they are all "the offspring of God." He is "the Father of spirits." "In him we live, and move, and have our being." "We have one Father, one God hath created us."[1] From our common human, and our common Divine paternity, we are all members of the same family; we are all brethren.

On the footing of this common relation, mankind form a great variety of associations for a corresponding variety of objects, all of which, from what lies at their foundation, may be called brotherhoods. A nation is a great brotherhood. Municipal bodies, societies for promoting science, for diffusing knowledge, for relieving distress; all these are so many minor brotherhoods. To all mankind, as brethren, we owe a duty, and that duty is love; and to all the brotherhoods, all the associations, of our human brethren, to which we belong, we likewise owe a duty, the fulfilment of which also is ex-

[1] Gal. iii. 28. Col. iii. 11. Acts xvii. 26, 28. Mal. ii. 10.

pressed in that all-comprehensive word love ; and the manner in which this principle of love should manifest itself towards all our brethren of mankind individually, and towards all the particular brotherhoods with which we may be connected, and the motives which urge to the cultivation and exercise of this principle in all these various ways, would afford abundant materials for interesting and useful discussion.

But it cannot be reasonably doubted, that "the brotherhood" spoken of in our text, is an association of men, not as men, but as Christians. "The brotherhood" to be loved, is placed in contrast with the "all men" who are to be honoured ; and therefore our appropriate employment, in this part of our discourse, is to inquire in what peculiar sense Christians are brethren, and what we are to understand by that brotherhood, that association of brethren, which ought to be the object of the love of all individual Christians.

It is obvious, from the Acts of the Apostles and the Apostolical Epistles, that "brethren" was the first name used to express the mutual relation of Christians to each other, as "disciples" was that employed to express their common relation to their Lord. It was indeed the name given them by their Lord: "One," said he, "is your Master, and all ye are brethren."[1]

The giving of this figurative appellation to Christians, rests on a wide and varied foundation. They are spiritual brethren, for they have all a common origin. They are all "the children of God, by faith in Christ Jesus." They have all "received the adoption of sons ;" they have entered into the kingdom of God, by being "born again, born of the Spirit, born, not of blood, nor of the will of the flesh, nor of the will of men, but of God ;" born, "not of corruptible seed, but of incorruptible, by the word of God, which liveth and abideth for ever." They have all Abraham for their father. "Being Christ's, they are Abraham's seed, and

[1] Matt. xxiii. 8.

heirs according to the promise;" and, as they are Abraham's spiritual children, they are also the offspring of mystical Sarah; the patriarchal church under the covenant of promise; "the children, not of the bond woman, but of the free." Ancient Jerusalem, "Jerusalem above," both as to time and place, "is the mother of them all."[1]

They are all spiritual brethren, for they have a common character. They all, though in different degrees, resemble their Father in heaven, and their great Elder Brother. They are "renewed after the image of him that creates them," "in knowledge, righteousness, and true holiness." They "are conformed to the image of God's Son." They already bear the spiritual, as they will by and by bear the outward image of "the Second Man, the Lord from heaven." They have "the mind in them that was in him;" they are "in the world as he was in the world;" his animated images, his "living epistles, known and read of all men."[2]

They are spiritual brethren, for they have a common education. They are all nourished by the "sincere milk of the word." In a higher sense than the Israelitish brethren, who were their prototypes, "they all eat the same spiritual meat, and they all drink the same spiritual drink:" "the flesh of the Son of Man, which is meat indeed, the blood of the Son of Man, which is drink indeed." They are all taught by the same Spirit; taught materially the same truths, so that the differences on vital subjects among true Christians are always rather apparent than real—differences rather about the meaning of words than the truth of principles; and they are all disciplined by the same paternal Providence, for "what son is he whom the Father chasteneth not?"[3]

They are spiritual brethren, for they have a common residence. They dwell together in that spiritual "better country," of which Canaan was an emblem, a state of favour

[1] Gal. iii. 26; iv. 5.   John iii. 5, 6; i. 13.   1 Pet. i. 23.   Gal. iii. 29; iv. 26.
[2] Col. iii. 10.   Rom. viii. 29.   Phil. ii. 5.   1 John iv. 17.   2 Cor. iii. 2.
[3] 1 Pet. ii. 1.   1 Cor. x. 3, 4.   John vi. 55.   Heb. xii. 7.

and fellowship with God; and in that spiritual house of which the temple was a type, "the church of the living God." They are "not strangers and foreigners" to one another; they are "fellow citizens," they belong to the one "household of God;" and they shall all dwell for ever in their Father's house of many mansions above; "the house not made with hands, eternal in the heavens."[1]

Finally, they are spiritual brethren, for they have all a common inheritance. "If children, then heirs; heirs of God, and joint-heirs with Christ Jesus." They are "begotten again to a living hope, to an inheritance incorruptible, undefiled, and that fadeth not away, reserved in heaven for them."[2]

Such are the brethren who are here referred to. Men brought out of their natural condition of guilt and condemnation, into a state of forgiveness and acceptance; men "transformed" in their characters, "by the renewing of their minds" in the exercise of the same Divine grace, by the operation of the same Divine influence; and thus, by these changes of state and character which are common to them all, materially the same in each, placed in a most intimate endearing relation to each other, with common views and affections, common likings and dislikings, common hopes and fears, common joys and sorrows, a common interest, common friends, common enemies, they are brothers indeed.

Relation and duty are correlate ideas, and the weight of obligation corresponds with the closeness of the connexion. Those who are connected together as brethren, must be bound to feel towards one another, and to act towards one another, as brethren. The whole of the duty which one Christian brother owes to another Christian brother, to all other Christian brethren, is that which is here enjoined towards the brotherhood—Love. This duty is clearly described, and powerfully enforced, in the following Apostolic injunction: "Seeing ye have purified your souls in obeying the truth through the Spirit unto unfeigned love of the brethren, see that ye love one another with a pure heart fervently: being born again, not of corruptible seed, but of incorruptible, by the word of God, which liveth and abideth for ever."[1]   Christians are bound to love all men with a love of benevolence; but the love of esteem and complacency which a Christian ought to cherish towards a Christian, is a sentiment very different from this general benevolence; a sentiment of which none but a Christian can be either the object or the subject.   This affection originates in the possession of a peculiar mode of thinking and feeling, produced in the mind by the Holy Spirit, through the knowledge and belief of Christian truth, which naturally leads those who are thus distinguished to a sympathy of mind and heart, of thought and affection, with all who, under the same influence, have been led to entertain the same views and cherish the same dispositions.   It has for its end the highest good, the spiritual improvement and final well-being of its objects, consisting in entire conformity to the mind and will of God, the unclouded sense of the Divine favour, the uninterrupted enjoyment of the Divine fellowship, the being with and like the ever-blessed Holy, Holy, Holy One.

This subject, the duty of the brethren to the brethren, individually considered, is a very interesting and important one; but the subject to which our attention is now to be turned, though nearly allied to it, is still a different one, the love of the brethren to the brotherhood as a body.

The "brotherhood" is the brethren in an associated form, in a social capacity; and it is plainly necessary, in order to our distinctly apprehending the nature and extent of the duty here enjoined, that we clearly perceive what is its object. It is the more necessary that this be attended to, that mistaken apprehension as to what this brotherhood, or, in other words, what the Church of Christ is, has led into very important practical mistakes, and induced men, under the impression that they were loving and honouring the brotherhood, to hate and persecute the brethren. Men have often thought they were showing their regard to the church by maltreating its true members.

It is impossible to read the New Testament carefully, without perceiving that it is the intention of Jesus Christ, not only to render his followers individually holy and happy, as so many distinct children of God; but, in subordination to this end, to form them into a happy, holy fellowship, the bond of which should be the faith and love of the same truth, and the objects of which should be the united worship of their common God and Father, the united promotion of the honours and interests of their common Lord and Saviour, and their mutual improvement in the knowledge of Christian truth, the cultivation of Christian dispositions, the performance of Christian duty, and the enjoyment and diffusion of Christian happiness. This society, founded on Christ's institution, subject to his authority, regulated by his law, animated by his Spirit, devoted to his honour, and blessed by his presence, is the Christian church. This is the brotherhood. None ought to be admitted into, or retained in this society, but those who, by an intelligent consistent profession of the faith of the gospel, give evidence that they are brethren; and all who are brethren should readily join themselves to, and be readily welcomed by, the brotherhood.

This society, though one in its principles and objects, was necessarily from the beginning divided into separate associations, composed by the brethren residing in the same immediate vicinity, meeting together for the common observance of the Christian ordinances. These associations considered themselves each as a component part of the great brotherhood, "the Holy Catholic Church," "all who in every place call on the name of the Lord Jesus." The members of one of these brotherhoods were viewed as members, of course, of the great brotherhood, and were recognised as such by being readily admitted into fellowship in all the offices of religion, by other Christian societies in other localities, on producing a satisfactory letter of attestation from the society with which they were more immediately connected.[1]

Nor was this all. In joining the Christian brotherhood they connected themselves not only with the whole of the brethren on earth, but also with those who had finished their course, and had been admitted into the mansions of celestial purity and rest. They joined the great " family in heaven and in earth called by the one name;" they " sat down with Abraham, and Isaac, and Jacob, in the kingdom of their Father;" they came to "an innumerable company of angels, the general assembly, to the church of the first-born, whose names are written in heaven, and to the spirits of the just made perfect."[2]

There are various important truths respecting the church of Christ, suggested by its being termed a brotherhood, especially the two following, which I shall merely notice in passing. First, none but brethren ought to be admitted to be its members. An ungodly man is fully as much out of his place in a Christian church, as Satan was when he presented himself among the sons of God; and, secondly, there must be no tyrannical rule in the church of Christ. "The kings of the Gentiles exercise lordship over them; but ye shall not be so. Be not ye called Rabbi; for one is your master, even Christ, and all ye are brethren."[3]

This goodly fellowship, this noble brotherhood, was not only in its elements, but in its social capacity, its organized form, the fit object of the respectful ardent attachment of each of its members ; and this respectful affectionate attachment was to be manifested in a corresponding course of conduct. Every Christian had a duty to discharge, the sum of which was, love to the Christian brotherhood with which he

---

[1] Rom. xvi. 1.   3 John 8, 9.
[2] Eph. iii. 15.   Matt. viii. 11.   Heb. xii. 22, 23.
[3] Luke xxii. 25.

was connected, and to the whole Christian brotherhood both on earth and in heaven; and it is to this, we apprehend, that the Apostle refers, when, in the motto of our address, he calls on Christians to love the brotherhood.

The Christian church does not now, alas! exhibit, as it did in the primitive age, the appearance of one unbroken brotherhood. There are many societies who call themselves churches, and who sometimes take to themselves the name, as, if not their exclusive property, at least belonging to them with some peculiar emphasis of meaning, in whom we can trace scarcely the slightest identifying marks of the ancient Christian brotherhoods; though even among the adherents of these, we find not a few whom we gladly recognise as "faithful and beloved brethren in Christ Jesus;" brethren, but not a brotherhood. In other cases, we find both brethren and a brotherhood; but then, in too many instances, we find additional bonds added to the simple silken ties of primitive fellowship, which, by attempting to carry union in opinion, and uniformity of usage farther than the great Master warrants, hazard the continuance of union within, and prevent the recognition of other Christian brethren and other Christian brotherhoods, who are determined to "stand fast in the liberty wherewith Christ hath made them free," and count all terms of fellowship not of his establishing, but various forms of "the yoke of bondage."[1]

Still, however, there are, under a very considerable variety of external form, many religious societies which, with all their defects and faults, and none of them want these, are, in their elementary principles, indeed Christian brotherhoods; and these Christian brotherhoods, substantially united, though in many respects different from, and in some even opposed to one another, along with those individual Christian brethren who are, in too great numbers, to be found in connexion with societies which are secular and anti-Christian in their

[1] Gal. v. 1.

constitution, form the whole Christian brotherhood now on earth.

§ 2. *Of the Christian's duty to the brotherhood.*

Now, in this department of the discourse, my object is briefly to inquire what is the duty of the individual Christian brother to this brotherhood, both towards that one of its minor divisions with which he comes to be more immediately connected, and towards the whole brotherhood, the whole collection of Christian churches and Christian individuals whom he can recognise as forming the visible holy family, the children of God, the brethren of Jesus Christ, " the Holy Catholic Church."

Let it not be forgotten, that it is the duty of a brother towards the brotherhood that I am inquiring into. It is the duty of every one who is not a brother to become a brother, of every man who is not a Christian to become a Christian ; but, till he does so, he had better let the brotherhood alone. It is a happy thing for all parties concerned, when " believers are added to the church, multitudes both of men and women," and when " of the rest," the unbelieving remainder, " none dares to join himself to them."[1]

The first way in which a Christian brother is to show his love for the brotherhood, as an institution or society, is by joining himself to it; and, in order to do this, he must connect himself with some particular Christian brotherhood. It is in this way he forms a visible connexion with the whole visible brotherhood. There are some good men who seem to be fond of being Christians at large, connected with the whole society invisibly, but visibly with no individual society. The sectarianism and impurity which are to be found, more or less, in all existing Christian churches, afford but too plausible an excuse, but they afford no sufficient reason, for this course. Of the great ends to be gained by connexion with the Christian brotherhood, some cannot

[1] Acts v. 13, 14.

be gained at all, none of them gained in a high degree, without joining the fellowship of some particular church ; and it is plain that, if all Christians were taking the same liberty as these privileged persons, there would be no such thing as a visible church on earth. As soon as Saul came to Jerusalem, " he assayed to join himself to the disciples." Both his eagerness and their caution are full of instructive example. They were backward to receive him, because " they doubted whether he was a disciple." And not less worthy of imitation are the conduct of Barnabas, who "took him and brought him to the Apostles," and their ready reception of him on Barnabas' testimony, so that " he was with them coming in and going out at Jerusalem."[1]

Having shown his love to the brotherhood, by joining himself to it, the Christian brother is to give further proof of his love to it after he has become one of its members. He is to be regular in attending on all its meetings for the observance of ordinances. He is not to " forsake the assembling together, as the manner of some is ;" he is to " continue steadfastly in the apostolic doctrine and fellowship, and in breaking of bread, and in prayer." Every member of the brotherhood is to show his love, by performing the duties belonging to the place he holds in the society. He is cheerfully to contribute of his time, and labour, and property, for gaining the great objects of the brotherhood, both within and without its pale ; the overseers, by " watching for souls as those who must give account;" the members, by " obeying them that have the rule over them ;" " the younger," by obedience to the elder ; and the whole body, by " submitting to each other in the fear of God." " He that ministers, must wait on his ministering ; he that teacheth, on teaching ; he that exhorteth, on exhortation ; he that giveth, must do it with simplicity ; he that ruleth, with diligence ; he that showeth mercy, with cheerfulness." " He who is taught the Word is to communicate to them who

---

[1] Acts ix. 26, 27.

teach in all good things." The statute "which the Lord has ordained" must be observed, "that they who preach the gospel, should live on the gospel;" and they who, "for Christ's sake, go forth, asking nothing of the Gentiles," ought, by the other members of the society, to be "brought forward of their journey after a godly sort." Love to the brotherhood is thus to be shown by contributing to the maintenance of those ordinances, by which the highest interest of the society are promoted, and by which it is enabled to perform one of its principal duties, in "holding forth the word of life" to a world perishing for lack of knowledge.[1]

Another way in which the Christian brother is to show his love to the brotherhood, is, by endeavouring to preserve its purity. The introduction of corrupt members into the Church of Christ, is not only great cruelty to the individuals immediately concerned, but it is inflicting a most severe injury on the brotherhood. It is in reference to this crime, for it is no less, that the Apostle says, "If any man defile the temple of God, him will God destroy." An unchristian man can do no good, he must do mischief in a Christian church. "A little leaven leavens the whole lump."[2]

It is peculiarly the duty of official Christians, elders, and pastors, to show their love to the brotherhood by a careful attention to this matter. To them the command is given, "Let every man take heed how he buildeth" on the foundation. A Christian brotherhood will serve its peculiar purposes, both internal and external, just in proportion to its purity. A small Christian society, composed of right materials, will be far more powerful in doing good, than a large Christian society where the materials are of an inferior kind. It should, then, be the constant care of the rulers of every Christian brotherhood to admit none but those who appear to be Christians, and to retain none after they have proved themselves not to be Christians. But this will be,

---

[1] Heb. x. 25. Acts ii. 42. Heb. xiii. 17. 1 Pet. v. 5. Eph. v. 21. Rom. xii. 7, 8. Gal. vi. 6. 1 Cor. ix. 14. 3 John 7.
[2] 1 Cor. iii. 17; v. 6.

this can be, but very imperfectly done, if the members of the society generally do not give their assistance to the overseers or bishops, by watching for one another's souls, "looking diligently lest any man fail of the grace of God, lest any root of bitterness spring up and trouble the brotherhood, and thereby many be defiled." That man does not love the brotherhood, who does not conscientiously attend to our Lord's directions in the 18th chapter of the gospel by Matthew, for the removal of offences.[1]

Still further, the brother is to show his love of the brotherhood by seeking its peace. No society can well gain its object whose members are at variance with one another: and, when the nature and designs of the Christian brotherhood are considered, it must be plain, that to *its* prosperity peace is of peculiar importance. The things which make for peace are the things which edify the brotherhood. He who loves the brotherhood intelligently, will study "to be quiet, and to do his own business." The way to secure peace in any society is for every member to do his own business; and there is not a more certain likelihood of producing discord than for men to neglect their own business, and become "busy bodies in other men's matters." He will not, like Diotrephes, " love," and seek to have "the pre-eminence ;" but " by love serve his brethren." He will " avoid foolish questions, which gender strife rather than godly edifying." He will " leave off contention before it be meddled with;" and he will " mark those who cause divisions and offences contrary to the doctrine which he has learned, and avoid them." He will be found a steadfast upholder of the three great laws of the brotherhood, on which its peace so much depends. " Let all things be done in charity," " let all things be done to edifying," " let all things be done decently and in order."[2]

In the next place, the brother is to show his love of the

---

[1] 1 Cor. iii. 10.   Matt. xviii. 15-20.
[2] 1 Thess. iv. 11.   1 Pet. iv. 15.   3 John 9.   Gal. v. 13.   2 Tim. ii. 23.   Tit. iii. 9.   Prov. xvii. 14.   Rom. xvi. 17.   1 Cor. xiv. 16, 26, 40.

brotherhood by seeking its increase. Brethren die; but the brotherhood is immortal. It is the part of a good church member to exert himself to have the breaches made by death and otherwise repaired, and to prepare for the blank which his own removal is soon to make. This is not to be done by robbing other churches, by seeking to thin the ranks of some other brotherhood. There is something very unseemly in the proselytizing spirit which distinguishes too many Christian sects, and which marks them as sects indeed. If a member of one Christian brotherhood seek admission into another, bringing satisfactory evidence that he is a brother, he is not to be refused; nor is Christian liberty even to seem to be trenched on by inquisitorial investigation into the reasons which, he says, are satisfactory to his own conscience for the change, either on the part of the church left or the church joined; but it is not the natural order of things to gather churches out of churches. Little is gained, and often much is lost, in this way.

Churches should be kept up by conversion rather than by proselytism; and the love of the brotherhood is a principle which operates in entire harmony with the love of souls, in seeking to turn men from the error of their ways, that it may be said of them, " Ye were as sheep going astray; but ye are returned to the Shepherd and Bishop of souls." Every converted man should endeavour to bring as many of the prodigal children home to his Father's house as possible, that there may be joy in the brotherhood on earth as in heaven, that " those who were dead have become alive again, and those who were lost are found."[1] The member of a Christian church who, in this way, is the means of adding even one member of the right kind to its communion, is a real and great benefactor both to the individual and to the community, both to the brother and to the brotherhood.

Finally, the Christian brother is to show his love to the brotherhood he is immediately connected with, by making

---

[1] 1 Pet. iii. 25.   Luke xv. 32.

its welfare, in all the extent of meaning belonging to that word, the subject of his frequent and fervent prayers. This was one of the ways in which the Apostle Paul, who had a great deal of the love of the brethren, as well as of love to all men, expressed his affection for the brotherhoods with which he was peculiarly connected. "Without ceasing he made mention of them always in his prayers, for the grace of God to them, that they might in every thing be enriched by him, and come behind in no gift; and that they might be perfectly joined together in the same mind and judgment." We, my brethren, should imitate his example, and, like him, when we "bow our knees to the Father of our Lord Jesus Christ, of whom the whole family in heaven and earth is named," we should bear on our hearts the brotherhood; and pray that it may be made and preserved free, and pure, and peaceful, and active, and prosperous, and that "the whole body fitly joined together and compacted by that which every joint supplieth, according to the effectual working in the measure of every part, may make increase of the body, unto the edifying of itself in love."[1]   It is thus that the Christian brother is to love the brotherhood, of which he forms a member.

But he is never to forget that that brotherhood, ay, that that class of brotherhoods, however numerous, with which it may be connected in ecclesiastical arrangement, is but a very small portion of the great Christian brotherhood, consisting as it does of all the associations which, whatever be their differences and faults, deserve the name of Christian churches, being collections of men honestly associated from a regard to Christ's authority, founded on the faith of his gospel, to observe his ordinances; and of all true believers, though they may not be in Christian fellowship, properly so called, whether standing aloof from all the sections of Christian churches, or connected with societies which we cannot recognise as Christian churches: and with regard to

---

[1] 1 Cor. i. 4, &c.   Eph. ii. 14; iv. 16.

all these portions of " the household of faith," he is to love them, and " do good to them as he has opportunity." [1]

One of the best ways of showing love to the whole brotherhood, is by a careful discharge of our duty to the particular brotherhood we are connected with. We will do more, I believe, towards having our neighbours' vineyards well kept, by keeping our own well, by making it quite a pattern vineyard for order, and freedom from weeds, and fruitfulness, than by leaving our own vineyard untended, and occupying our time in pointing out their neglects and faults; thus ultroneously assuming the office of " keepers of other men's vineyards." It is impossible to say how extensively beneficial might be the influence of a single congregation, however small, all the members of which set themselves to do all that lies in their power, according to the stations they bear in it, that, in the quiet working of Christ's simple machinery, their brotherhood should do all the good possible within and without its pale. This, however, is by no means to interfere—it will not—with every legitimate means of obtaining freedom and purity, both as to doctrine and communion and order for the whole brotherhood, and for breaking down " middle walls of partition," and hastening onward the fulfilment of the Saviour's prayer, in that visible union of his genuine followers, which will come on the world with the force of a demonstration that the Father hath sent his Son.[2]

The duty of every brother to the whole brotherhood on earth, cannot be more succinctly and accurately stated than in the well-considered words of the Westminster Assembly: " All saints that are united to Jesus Christ their Head, by his spirit and by his faith, are united to one another in love, have communion in each other's gifts and graces, and are obliged to the performance of such duties, public and private, as do conduce to their mutual good, both in the inward and outward man. Saints by profession are bound to main-

---

[1] Gal. vi. 10.   [2] John xvii. 23.

tain a holy fellowship and communion in the worship of
God; and in performing such spiritual services as tend to
their mutual edification, as also in relieving each other in
outward things, according to their several abilities and necessities, which communion, as God offereth opportunity, is
to be extended to all those who in every place call on the
name of the Lord Jesus."[1]

It is plain that the Westminster divines never contemplated any thing similar to what has long existed in this
country; different bodies of Christian churches holding
the same doctrines, observing the same ordinances, and following the same order, occupying the same territorial region, yet living as distinct, so far as ecclesiastical communion is concerned, as if their creeds were contradictory,
their institutions different, and their modes of government
incompatible. Such an unnatural state of things does not
seem to have entered into their minds. Their remarks refer
to sister churches situated in different countries, or organized
on different platforms, or to individual members of such
sister churches. But *a fortiori*, on the principles so well
stated in the paragraph just quoted, churches in the circumstances described are bound not only to occasional communion and friendly co-operation, but to entire union, to ecclesiastical incorporation.[b]

With regard to the duties of Christian brethren and
Christian brotherhoods to other Christian brotherhoods, with
whom circumstances may prevent complete union, I beg
briefly to observe, that it is the obvious duty of every Christian brother to love not only his own brotherhood, or rather
his corner of the one great brotherhood; but, without being
blind to defects and faults, to cherish affectionate respectful
sentiments to all Christian churches who hold the Head, and
habitually to express these sentiments in fervent supplication to our One—common Father, in the name of our One—
common Mediator, and under the influence of the One

---

[1] Westminst. Conf. ch. xxvi. § 2.   b See note B.

Spirit, and, as occasion offers, gladly to embrace opportunities of promoting their internal improvement and outward prosperity ; and what is true of Christian brethren is equally true of Christian brotherhoods. Especially should we use every means in our power towards the realization of that wide enlargement of the brotherhood, which prophecy leads us to anticipate as drawing near in these later ages of the world, when " all the ends of the earth are to remember, and turn to the Lord, and the kindreds of the people worship before him;" when " the little one shall become a thousand, and the small one a strong nation;" when " the handful of corn sown on the top of the mountains shall shake like Lebanon;" when the mother of us all shall " enlarge the place of her tent, and stretch forth the curtain of her habitation : when she shall not spare, but lengthen her cords, and strengthen her stakes; for she shall break forth on the right hand and the left; and her seed shall inherit the Gentiles, and make the desolate cities to be inhabited;" when " the kingdoms of this world shall become the kingdom of our Lord and his Christ; and he shall reign for ever and ever." Every lover of the brotherhood should express his love by adopting this resolution and acting it out : " For Zion's sake I will not hold my peace, and for Jerusalem's sake I will not rest, till the righteousness thereof go forth as brightness, and the salvation thereof as a lamp that burneth." " Peace be within thy walls, prosperity be within thy palaces. Lord be merciful to us; and bless and cause thy face to shine on us. That thy way may be known on the earth, and thy saving health to all nations. Let the people praise thee; let all the people praise thee." [1]

It only remains, on this part of the subject, that I say a word or two as to the love which we should cherish towards that part of the great brotherhood who are not on earth,

[1] Psal. xxii. 27.   Isa. lx. 22.   Psal. lxxii. 16.   Isa. liv. 2.   Rev. xi. 15.   Isa. lxii. 1.   Psal. cxxii. 6, 7 ; lxvii. 1-3.

but in heaven, and the manner in which we should express it :—

> " One family we dwell in him,
>   One church above, beneath,
>   Though now divided by the stream,
>   The narrow stream of death." [1]

The stroke of mortality has broken many a strong and
tender band; but it has not broken, it could not break,
the band which binds Christian brother to Christian brother.   We have no reason to think our brethren on high
have forgotten us, or ceased to love us.   We know we have
not forgotten them, nor ceased to love them.   They stand
in no need of our offices of kindness; they are beyond the
reach of imperfection, and want, and suffering; but they
are the proper objects of a very tender and ardent affection—
an affection which has more of the purity of heaven, and
the permanence of eternity, than any other affection which
has a fellow-creature for its object.   That affection is surely
not one that must live in the heart without ever finding appropriate expression in this world.   Our love to our brethren
in heaven, is to be shown in our giving thanks to Him who
loved them and us, for making them " more than conquerors;" in keeping steadily in our mind's eye all that was
excellent in their character and conduct, both for model and
for motive; in giving " all diligence, to the full assurance
of hope; that we may not be slothful, but followers of them
who through faith and patience are inheriting the promises ;"
in maintaining steadfastly that good cause which was dearer
to them than life when here, and which we know is dearer to
them now than ever; and in often practising the first notes
of the ever new anthem, which, as sung by them, and to be
sung by us, shall " everlastingly echo in heaven :" " Unto
Him that loved us, and washed us from our sins in his blood.
Salvation to our God and the Lamb for ever and ever." [2]

These remarks have been entirely addressed to the brethren.   They alone could relish them ; they alone, indeed,

----

[1] Ch. Wesley.   [2] Heb. vi. 11, 12. Rev. i. 5, 6.

could fully understand them. But is there any one here uninterested in them? Not one. " Strangers, foreigners, aliens, from the commonwealth of Israel," from " the household of faith," there may be here; but every one of these must become " brethren," else they are undone for ever, for there is no salvation but by union to the Saviour—" the first-born among the many brethren." We dare not say to such persons, make a profession of brotherhood. No; in your present circumstances this were but to accumulate guilt, to increase danger, to aggravate damnation. But we do say, become brothers. The brethren with one voice of invitation say, " We were once like you, ' far off;' " but we have been " brought nigh." You, too, may be brought nigh by that all-attractive blood of Jesus' cross. Are you very guilty, very depraved, very wretched? So were some of us; ay, so were all of us, but " we have been washed, we have been sanctified, we have been justified, in the name of our Lord Jesus, and by the Spirit of our God." His blood is as efficacious, his Spirit as free as ever. Oh, come to him, and then come to us! Give yourselves to him, and then give yourselves to us by his will. Come to him; he will put you among the brethren; he will not be ashamed to call you brethren; he will give you the brother's inheritance, the goodly land. Come to us, we will do you good; we will love you as brethren, and you will love us as brethren; we will strengthen one another's hands, and comfort one another's hearts; and move onwards and upwards, till we, one by one, join the goodly fellowship above. And when God has filled up the number of his chosen ones, a number which no man can number, then will the completed holy brotherhood be presented by their Elder Brother, " a glorious church, without spot or wrinkle, or any such thing," to his Father and their Father, his God and their God, " with exceeding joy," to dwell for ever in " his presence, where there is fulness of joy, and rivers of pleasure for evermore." There will be no need, then, to press the exhortation, " Love the brotherhood." They will all

of them be thoroughly " taught of God to love one another." " Come with us, and we will do you good; for the
Lord hath spoken good concerning Israel."[1]

III. CHRISTIANS ARE TO FEAR GOD.

Let us now, in the third place, turn our attention to the
account here given us of our duty to God—we are to FEAR
him: that is, in other words, we are to cherish an awful
sense of his infinite grandeur and excellence, corresponding
to the revelation he has made of these in his works and
word, inducing a conviction that his favour is the greatest
of all blessings, and his disapprobation the greatest of all
evils, and manifesting itself in leading us practically to seek
his favour as the chief good we can enjoy, and avoid his disapprobation as the most tremendous evil we can be subjected
to. Such is the fear which the Christian man ought to
cherish and manifest towards God.

The foundation of this fear of God is in God himself.
The only way in which we can apprehend what this fear is,
and why we should cherish it, is by turning our minds to
the contemplation of the venerable excellencies of the Divine
character; and if we do distinctly perceive the truth and its
evidence on this subject, not only will there be lodged in our
understandings and consciences a conviction that we ought
to fear God; that this is the first and highest requirement
of reason as well as of revelation; but the sentiment will lay
hold of our heart, and obtain a place in our affections, corresponding to our apprehensions of the truth and its evidence.

Every thing about God is fitted to fill the mind with awe,
and it would seem as if nothing short of insanity could prevent any being possessed of reason and affection from habitually feeling the sentiment of supreme veneration. He is
the inexhausted, inexhaustible fountain, of all the being, all
the life, all the intelligence, all the power, all the activity,

---

[1] Numb. x. 29-32.

all the excellence, all the happiness in the universe.　He is
" the first and the last, and the living One ;" " from everlasting to everlasting ;" immense, " filling heaven and earth
with his presence," " a God at hand, a God afar off;" unchanged, unchangeable, " without variableness or shadow
of turning ;" " the same yesterday, to-day, and for ever."
Infinite in power, having called into existence myriads of
worlds, capable of calling into existence myriads more ; up-
holding all these worlds, himself upheld by none ; controlling all things, himself uncontrolled ; " doing according to
his will in the armies of heaven, and among the inhabitants
of the earth." Infinite in knowledge ; " known to him are
all his works from the beginning of the world."ᶜ " Every
creature is manifest in his sight :" " all things are naked
and open in his eyes." " Hell itself is naked before him,
and destruction has no covering." Infinite in wisdom,
" wonderful in counsel," as well as " excellent in working,"
" wise in heart," as well as " mighty in strength ;" his judgments are unsearchable, his ways past finding out." Infinite
in holiness, " of purer eyes than to behold iniquity, and he
cannot look on sin ;" the " Holy, Holy, Holy" One. Infinite in righteousness, " he is the Rock, his work is perfect ;
all his ways are judgment : a God of truth, and without iniquity ; just and right is he." " Far be it from him, that he
should do wickedness; and from the Almighty, that he
should do iniquity. For the work of a man shall he render to
him, and cause him to receive according to his ways. Yea,
surely God will not do wickedly, neither will the Almighty
pervert judgment."¹ The benignity of the Divine Being
may seem a quality fitted to excite love rather than fear, yet
are there two qualities of it ; its immeasurable extent, and
its immaculately holy character, which are well fitted to
deepen the impression of awe produced by the eternal, infi-

ᶜ See note C.

¹ Rev. i. 17, 18. Psal. xc. 2. Jer. xxiii. 24. James i. 17. Dan. iv. 35. Acts
xv. 13. Heb. iv. 13. Job. xxvi. 6. Isa. xxviii. 29. Job ix. 4. Rom. xi. 33.
Hab. i. 13. Isa. vi. 3. Deut. xxxii. 4. Job xxxiv. 10.

nite, immutable power, and wisdom, and rectitude. There
is mercy with him and plenteous redemption ; but the mercy
that is with *him*, is mercy which leads men to fear him.[1]
Such is the truth, stated in the plainest, most unadorned
language, respecting God. But "how small a portion is
heard," or can be heard "of him!" "Who can by searching find out God? who can find out the Almighty unto perfection? It is higher than heaven; what can we do? deeper
than hell; what can we know? The measure thereof is
longer than the earth, and broader than the sea."[2] When
we have strained our faculties to the utmost, in conceiving
of grandeur and excellence, we are still at an immeasurable
distance from the grandeur and the excellence which has
made his infinite nature their eternal dwelling-place.

His is the greatness; and the most exalted of his creatures,
his whole creation, is before him less than a drop to the
ocean, than an atom to the universe of matter, less than nothing and vanity. His is the power; and all created might
is in his hand, to be exerted, directed, restrained, and re-
sumed, at his pleasure. His is the glory; and all created
splendour, in his presence, fades into obscurity, and vanishes
into nothing. His is the victory; in all his purposes he ever
is the overcomer; and all victories gained by his creatures
are won by power derived from him. His is the majesty;
and all the potentates of the earth before him are contemptible worms, and their loftiest thrones are not worthy to
be his footstool. All that is in the heavens and the earth is
his; he is the maker, preserver, governor, supreme and sole
proprietor of the universe, of whom, and through whom, are
all things. His is the kingdom; unbounded dominion
belongs to him; his reign stretches throughout immensity;
and eternity, and all powers and authorities, in all worlds,
are under his feet. And all this physical and intellectual
greatness, this infinity of power, and wisdom, and dominion,
is heightened by corresponding moral grandeur. His is a

---

[1] Psal. cxxx. 4, 7.   [2] Job xi. 7.

purity before which the holiness of angels waxes dim : His a righteousness, of the stability of which the everlasting mountains is a faint figure : His a benignity, of which all the kindness in the hearts of men and angels is but a shadow.

Surely this being is worthy to be feared ; surely he is the meet object of the supreme esteem, and reverence, and love of all intelligent beings ; surely, to be the objects of his approbation, and love, and care, is the highest honour and happiness of such creatures ; to be the objects of his disapprobation, is the deepest disgrace and misery that can befall them ; and of course, to seek his approbation, in conformity of mind and will to him, is their highest wisdom and duty.

Such are the convictions and feelings of the unfallen and restored, the angelic and human, inhabitants of the celestial world. Their unceasing hymn is, " Holy, Holy, Holy, Lord God Almighty, great and marvellous are thy works, just and true are thy ways ; who shall not fear thee, and glorify thy name ? Thou, Thou only, art holy." And this enlightened, affectionate sense of the infinite grandeur and excellence of God, is in their minds a principle of supreme allegiance to his holy government, rendering it morally impossible that they should disregard his authority, or seek their happiness in any thing but in union of mind and will and enjoyment with him.

Had sin never been introduced into the universe, this would have been the only kind of fear of God that ever would have existed. It would have been a fear without torment. The same excellencies which produced awe would have produced confidence and love. All would have feared God ; none would have been afraid of him. Indeed, fear, in the sense of the anticipation of evil, would have had no being ; it would have had no object ; for evil was an impossibility under his government while his intelligent creatures retained their allegiance.

But sin has been introduced into the world, and, from the very excellence of the Divine character, God appears as the hater of sin and the punisher of sinners, and, of course, an object of fear or terror to them, as even imagination cannot grasp the miseries which may be expected from infinite wisdom and power employed as the agents of incensed justice. He has inflicted severe and numerous evils both on sinning men and angels; and he has threatened to inflict still more dreadful evils on them. He has " cast the angels who kept not their first abode, down out of heaven into hell," and " reserved them under chains of darkness to the judgment of the great day," when they shall be doomed to everlasting punishment in the lake that burneth with fire unquenchable, prepared for them. He has visited the sin of man with many and varied tokens of his displeasure. Death has entered into the world, and passed over all men ; and the declarations of his faithful word are, " The wages of sin is death. The soul that sinneth shall die. God will turn the wicked into hell. There is no peace to the wicked. God is jealous, and the Lord revengeth ; the Lord revengeth and is furious : the Lord will take vengeance on his adversaries, and he reserveth wrath for his enemies. The Lord will not at all acquit the wicked. Who can stand before his indignation, and who can abide in the fierceness of his anger ? His fury is poured out like fire, and the rocks are thrown down by him. In the day of wrath and revelation of the righteous judgments of God, he will render to every man according to his deeds ; to them that are contentious, and do not obey the truth, but obey unrighteousness, indignation and wrath, tribulation and anguish, upon every soul of man that doeth evil." Who can hear these faithful sayings without exclaiming, " Thou, even thou, art He who is to be feared; and who can stand before thee when once thou art angry ?" " It is a fearful thing to fall into the hands of the living God." [1]

It is obvious, then, that God, to sinful intelligent creatures, has become the object of fear in a sense altogether different from that in which he would have for ever continued to have been an object of fear to them had they remained in

[1] 2 Pet. ii. 4. Jude 6. Rom. vi. 23. Ezek. xviii. 4. Psal. ix. 17. Isa. lvii. 21. Nahum i. 2, 3. Rom. ii. 6, 8, 9. Psal. lxxvi. 7. Heb. x. 31.

innocence. To the sinning angels, for whom no salvation has been provided, and who know that no salvation is provided for them, every one of those perfections which, in their own nature, are fitted to produce holy awe, is to them a source of unmixed terror, as all of them go to enhance the security, the severity, and the duration of their misery. They have nothing to expect from God but " a certain fearful looking for of judgment," and then " everlasting destruction from his presence, and from the glory of his power ;" and but for the sovereign mercy of God, he must have been to all sinning men, equally as to all sinning angels, thus an object of this fear that has torment.

But God, who is rich in mercy, for the great love wherewith he has loved man, has formed and executed a plan of deliverance from the tremendous evils to which he has exposed himself by sin ; and he has done this in a way which places in a stronger point of light his hatred of sin, than the infliction of eternal punishment on the whole sinning race would have done. He has made to meet on his incarnate Son the iniquities of us all. Exaction has been made, and he has answered it. He has been wounded for our transgressions, bruised for our iniquities, and has undergone the chastisement of our peace. He has borne our sins in his own body on the tree ; he has given himself for us, the just in the room of the unjust. God, in the word of the truth of the gospel, has set Him forth a propitiation in his blood, declaring his righteousness in the remission of sins that are past through his forbearance, declaring his righteousness that he is just, and the justifier of him who believeth in Jesus ; and he has committed to men the ministry of reconciliation, sending them forth to proclaim " God is in Christ, reconciling the world to himself, not imputing to men their trespasses ; seeing he has made him who knew no sin, to be sin for us ; that we might be made the righteousness of God in him. As Moses lifted up the serpent in the wilderness, so is the Son of man lifted up ; that whosoever believeth in him may not perish, but have everlasting life. God so loved the world, that he gave his only begotten Son, that whosoever believeth on him may not perish, but have eternal life. For God sent not his Son to condemn the world, but to save the world."[1] Every human being who credits this faithful saying, worthy of all acceptation, obtains a personal interest in the Christian salvation, and is secured of all its blessings.

While the sinner continues unbelieving, he is exposed to all the evils denounced against sin ; and in the degree in which he becomes aware of his situation, previously to his embracing the gospel, must be the subject of that fear of God, that dread of his righteous vengeance, which is the habitual sentiment of devils.   This emotion, which is just a consciousness of having merited the displeasure of God, a realization of the danger of suffering from his hand the punishment of their sins, plainly possesses no moral excellence, though to a certain extent it may check open sin, and is overruled by the good Spirit for urging men to look around for deliverance, and to flee for refuge to the hope set before them in the gospel.   It is as plainly a sentiment which the faith of the gospel, in the degree in which it prevails, banishes from the heart.   "Faith worketh by love ;" and the love which faith works " casts out" *this* " fear."

But while the faith of the gospel casts out this fear, it produces that fear which is enjoined in the text, and which is one of the leading principles of Christian obedience.   The grandeur of the Divine character is more strikingly manifested in these Divine dispensations, the incarnation and sacrifice of the Only-Begotten, by which the salvation of sinners is made consistent with, and illustrative of, the Divine holiness and righteousness, and a statement of which form the gospel message, than in all the other works of God. Nothing is so well fitted to put the fear of God, which will preserve men from offending him, into the heart, as an enlightened view of the cross of Christ.   There shine spotless holiness, inflexible justice, incomprehensible wisdom, omnipotent power, holy love. None of these excellencies darken or eclipse the other, but every one of them rather gives a lustre to the rest. They mingle their beams, and shine with united eternal splendour: the just Judge, the merciful Father, the wise Governor. Nowhere does justice appear so awful, mercy so amiable, or wisdom so profound.[1]

These views of the Divine character naturally and necessarily produce an awful sense of his infinite excellence, and a holy fear of offending him. They lodge deep in the heart the conviction, that it is "an evil thing and a bitter to sin against him." It appears to the mind, under the influence of this principle, absolute madness to do what is opposed to the will of him who is infinitely wise, and righteous, and good; and thus to lose the sense of his approbation, and to expose ourselves to his rebukes and chastisements, in order to obtain any good which man can bestow, or to avoid any evil which man can inflict.

This fear of God, which is to be obtained by contemplating these displays of the Divine character, is to be manifested in carefully avoiding whatever is opposed to his will, whether in the way of neglecting to do what he has commanded, or doing what he has forbidden, and in keeping out of the way of temptation, and abstaining even from the appearance of evil. This fear of God ought to be the habitual disposition of our hearts. We should be in the fear of the Lord all the day long; and we should never forget, that the only satisfactory proof that God has put his fear in our heart, is to be found in our not departing from him. The best evidence we can afford that we fear the Lord, is our delighting greatly in his commandments; by our perfecting holiness, in cleansing ourselves from all filthiness of the flesh and the spirit by the fear of God. Such is the Christian's duty to his Supreme Ruler; to fear him; to act as if we considered his authority to be supreme; no blessing to be compared with his approbation; no evil to be

[1] Maclaurin.

compared with his displeasure. Thus will we find, that "the fear of the Lord is a fountain of life, to depart from the snares of death." [d]

Nothing can be more reasonable, more worthy of a rational being, than compliance with this command; nothing more unreasonable than neglect or violation of it. Well may we say with Nehemiah, "Ought ye not to walk in the fear of our God?" or with Jeremiah, "Fear ye not me? saith the Lord : O foolish people, and without understanding. Will ye not tremble at my presence, which have placed the sand for the bound of the sea, by a perpetual decree that it cannot pass it; and though the waves thereof toss themselves, yet can they not prevail; though they roar, yet can they not pass over it? Who would not fear thee, O King of nations? for as much as there is none like unto thee, O Lord; thou art great, and thy name is great in might." Or, in the words of our Master who is in heaven, "Be not afraid of them who can kill the body, and after that have no more that they can do. But I will forewarn you whom you shall fear: Fear Him, who after he hath killed, hath power to destroy both soul and body in hell; yea, I say unto you, Fear him." Or, in the words of his angel, "Fear God, and give glory to him; for the hour of his judgment is coming." Let us then habitually fear "that great and dreadful name, the Lord our God;" let us " feel the force of his almightiness;" [1] let us fear, that so we may not come short of the rest and promise of entering into what has been left us; " let us have grace, to worship God acceptably with reverence and godly fear: for our God is a consuming fire." [2]

IV.—CHRISTIANS ARE TO " HONOUR THE KING."

Let us proceed to make a few remarks on our duty as Christians to our subordinate ruler, the civil magistrate.

[d] See note D.   [1] Jeremy Taylor.
[2] Neh. v. 9. Jer. x. 7. Luke xii. 4, 5. Rev. xiv. 7. Heb. xii. 28.

While we "fear God," we are to "honour the king." "The king" is here to be considered as an expression just equivalent to the civil magistrate. The command is, pay a proper respect to every person who is invested with civil authority, especially to those who are at the head of the government. The honour here referred to, is that which is due to the office, whatever may be the personal character of him who fills it; the respect due to the magistrate when acting as a magistrate. When the magistrate is personally possessed of those qualities which are the proper objects of respect; when he is a man distinguished for his wisdom, piety, prudence, justice, and benevolence—he is to be honoured for these, and honoured the more because he is a magistrate, as high station abounds with temptation, and he who in such trying circumstances acquits himself well, is worthy of peculiar respect; but whatever be his personal character, though he may be an irreligious and immoral man in his private capacity, which is always to be regretted, especially as it is apt to bring the magistracy into contempt, we are to respect him in his official capacity, and to honour him while he performs the functions of public ruler. Christians must keep far away from the behaviour of those whom the Apostle in his second Epistle describes as "presumptuous and self-willed, who despise governments, and are not afraid of speaking evil of dignities."

The honour which we are to cherish for the magistrate is to be manifested chiefly in our conscientious and cheerful obedience to all his lawful commands. We are bound to disobey him if he commands us to do any thing which is forbidden by the law of God; and we are not bound to obey him if he lays on us commands unwarranted by the constitution and laws of the country; but, with these exceptions, we are to be "subject to the higher powers." We are not to think, that if we are obedient in some points we may venture to be disobedient in others. We are to obey all lawful commands; for all rest on the same authority. Whosoever keepeth the whole law, with the exception of offending in one point, is guilty of all; guilty of despising the authority of the whole law, guilty of failing in his duty as a good subject. It is the less necessary that I dwell on this subject, as not long ago I had an opportunity of discussing it at full length when illustrating the 13th and 14th verses of this chapter: " Submit yourselves, for the Lord's sake, to every human ordinance for the punishment of evil-doers, and the praise of them who do well; whether it be to the king, as supreme; or to governors, as to them who are sent by him."

It will be proper before concluding, that I in a few words point out the connexion between the two precepts, Fear God; Honour the king. The connexion is twofold. The first precept is at once the foundation and the limit of the second.

It is its foundation. The loyalty of a Christian man rests on a regard to the Divine authority. He honours the king because he fears God. There are many who, in their obedience to civil authority, are influenced entirely by reasons of expediency. They are "subject, not for conscience but for wrath's sake." They obey, because otherwise they would be punished; and they show this by violating law without scruple, when they think this can be done with advantage and impunity. There are others who obey because they consider it right to obey: but in their notion of what is right, they have little or no reference to a recognition of Divine authority. Their obedience has nothing of the character of a religious duty: they obey the magistrate as they pay their debts: they think both right; but in both cases " God is not in all their thoughts."

The enlightened consistent Christian recognises civil government as a Divine ordinance. He believes the doctrine laid down by the Apostle, that " there is no power but of God, that the powers that be are ordained of God, and that whosoever resisteth the power resisteth the ordinance of God." He believes that the magistrate is " a minister of God to him for good," and acts accordingly, being " subject for conscience sake." He recognises the authority of God in these commands, " Fear the Lord and the King. Render to Cæsar the things which are Cæsar's. Let every soul be subject to the higher powers. Be subject to principalities and powers. Obey magistrates; submit to every human institution for the punishment of evil-doers, and for the praise of them who do well, for the Lord's sake." Obedience with him is not a matter of human arrangement, of expediency, of interest, or even of mere moral right; it is a religious duty.

This secures a uniformity of obedience which nothing else can, and therefore there is no class of subjects whose loyalty may be so securely counted on as enlightened Christians. They obey the magistrates because God commands them to do so, and perform their civil duties as " doing service to the Lord." What Nehemiah says of himself, in reference to certain practices of his predecessors in the government, a Christian man may say of himself, in reference to the practices of eluding civil duties and evading civil taxes, in which many who, it may be, pride themselves on their loyalty, do not scruple to indulge when they can do it safely : " so did not I, because of the fear of God."

But as the precept, "fear God," is with a Christian the foundation of his civil obedience, so it is also its limit. A Christian should honour the king so far, and only so far, as this is consistent with fearing God. Should the civil magistrate require us to do any thing that is inconsistent with the Divine law; should he require us to neglect what God has commanded, or to do what God has forbidden—we must fear God, and not honour the king, if such obedience is to be accounted honour. The principle on which we are to act in such cases is a very plain one : " We ought to obey God rather than man ;" and, whatever the consequences may be, it must be acted on; and he who really fears God will rise above the fear of man. Fearing God, he will know no other fear.

Shadrach, Meshach, and Abednego, honoured the king by

a faithful discharge of their duties as superintendents of the province of Babylon ; but when he commanded them to worship the colossal image he had erected in the plain of Dura, with the assurance that, if they did not, they should be cast into a burning fiery furnace ; fearing God, they were " not afraid of the king's commandment ;" but respectfully, yet determinedly, said, " Be it known to thee, O king, we will not serve thy gods, nor worship the golden image which thou hast set up." Daniel, on being prohibited to pray by a royal edict, by a monarch whom he most faithfully served, disregarded the edict, and took good care that this should be no secret. " When he knew that the writing was signed, he went to his house; and his windows being open in his chamber toward Jerusalem, he kneeled on his knees, and prayed, and gave thanks before his God, as he did aforetime." The very Apostle who says, " Be subject, for the Lord's sake, to every ordinance of man," when the Jewish magistrates commanded him and John " to speak no more in the name of Jesus," replied, " Whether it be right in the sight of God to hearken unto you rather than to God, judge ye :" and when called to account for acting out this principle, his answer was, " We ought to obey God rather than man."

It seems a common notion that I am bound to obey the law just because it is the law; and if what the law requires is a wrong thing, the magistrate, not I, must be answerable for it. But neither Scripture nor reason sanctions such a transfer of moral responsibility. " Every man must give account of HIMSELF to God." Most certainly I am bound to obey the law of the land because it is the law of the land ; but only so far as obedience to that law does not necessarily imply disobedience to the law of God : no farther. " Honour the king " must always be subordinate to " fear God :"

> " Let Cæsar's dues be ever paid
> To Cæsar and his throne ;
> But consciences and souls were made
> To be the Lord's alone."[1]

---

[1] Watts. " Sic honorandus Rex, ne contra Deum peccemus."—CHRYSOSTOM, in Matt. Hom. lxxi.

I have thus finished the illustration of the Apostle's account of the condition and duty of Christians. It may serve a good purpose, before taking leave of the subject, to present you with a general outline of the statements which have been made.

The condition of Christians is, at once, one of perfect liberty and entire subjection. They are " free," and they are " the servants of God." They are free in reference to God, both as being delivered from a condemned state and a slavish character; free in reference to their fellow men ; free in reference to the powers and principles of evil. They are the servants of God, bought by the blood of his Son, formed to habits of obedience by his Spirit, voluntarily devoted to and actually engaged in his service.

Their duty is generally to act according to their condition ; to act as freemen in reference to God, men, and the powers and principles of evil, guarding against abusing their freedom in any of these forms ; and to act as the servants of God, cultivating the principles of obedience, habitually keeping in view those perfections of the Divine character, and those relations in which they stand to God, in which the obligation to serve God originates, and the belief of which is the grand means which the Holy Scriptures employ to fit and dispose us to recognise and discharge that obligation ; making themselves acquainted with the rule of obedience, carefully studying the word of God, observing the providence of God, and seeking the guidance of the Spirit of God; and exercising this principle, and applying this rule in actual obedience, both inward and outward, both active and passive,—obedience characterised by implicitness, impartiality, cheerfulness, and permanence.

More particularly their duty is to " honour all men," to cherish respect for all who from their station, endowments, or character, deserve respect, though they are not Christians ; and to cherish and express in their conduct respect for every human being, as a rational, responsible, immortal being ; to

" love the brotherhood," to cultivate and manifest an affectionate regard to the Christian society by joining a Christian church; being regular in attending its assemblies, contributing time, labour, substance to its objects, seeking its purity, peace, and increase; and by cherishing, and in every becoming manner expressing, an affectionate regard to the whole household of faith, both in earth and heaven, the one family called by the worthy name; " to fear God," cherishing such an awful sense of his infinite grandeur and excellence, as will make us practically consider his approbation as the highest of blessings, his disapprobation as the greatest of evils; and, finally, " to honour the king," to yield a cheerful conscientious obedience to the laws, an obedience founded on and limited by the command to fear God.

All that remains now is the practical application. But this must be attended to, not here, but elsewhere. " If ye know these things, happy are ye if ye do them." May our improved character and conduct in all the various relations of life, show that we understand how practically to apply the instructions we have received, and that we have learned, " as free, not using our liberty as a cloak of wickedness, but as the servants of God, to honour all men; to love the brotherhood; to fear God; and to honour the king." "Wherefore, my beloved brethren, laying apart all filthiness, and superfluity of naughtiness, let us show that we have received with meekness the ingrafted word, which is able to save our souls: but be ye doers of the word, and not hearers only, deceiving your own selves," not God; not your brethren even generally, only your own selves. " For if any be a hearer of the word, and not a doer, he is like unto a man beholding his natural face in a glass: for he beholdeth himself, and goeth his way, and straightway forgetteth what manner of man he was. But whoso looketh into the perfect law of liberty, and continueth therein, he being not a forgetful hearer, but a doer of the work, this man shall be blessed in his deed."

NOTE A.

" Man was God's own creature, raised out of nothing by his mighty and most arbitrary hand : it was in his power and choice, whether he ever should have a being; any or none; another, or this, of so noble an order and kind. The designation was most apt of so excellent a creature, to be immediately sacred to himself and his own converse, his temple and habitation, the mansion and residence of his presence and indwelling glory. There was nothing whereto he was herein designed, whereof his nature was not capable. His soul was, after the required manner, receptive of a Deity. Its powers were competent to their appointed work and employment. It could entertain God by knowledge and contemplation of his glorious excellencies, by reverence and love, by adoration and praise. This was the highest kind of dignity whereto created nature could be raised, the most honourable state. How high and quick an advance! This moment nothing; the next, a being capable and full of God."

*   *   *   *   *   *

" The stately ruins (of human nature) are visible to every eye, that bear in their front, yet extant, this doleful inscription,— HERE GOD ONCE DWELT. Enough appears of the admirable frame and structure of the soul of man, to show the Divine presence did some time reside in it; more than enough of vicious deformity, to proclaim that he is now retired and gone. The lamps are extinct; the altar overturned: the light and love are now vanished, which did the one shine with so heavenly brightness, the other burn with such pious fervour. The golden candlestick is displaced, and thrown away as a useless thing, to make way for the throne of the prince of darkness; the sacred incense, which sent rolling up in clouds its rich perfumes, is exchanged for a poisonous hellish vapour. The comely order of this house is turned all into confusion; the beauties of holiness into noxious impurities; the house of prayer into a den of thieves. The noble powers, which were designed and dedicated to Divine contemplation and delight, are alienated to the service of the most despicable idols, and employed into vilest intuitions and embraces: to behold and admire lying vanities; to indulge and cherish lust and wickedness. * * * Look upon the fragments of that curious sculpture, which once adorned this palace of that great King: the relics of common notions; the lively prints of some undefaced truth; the fair ideas of things; the yet legible precepts that relate to practice. Behold with what accuracy the broken pieces show them to have been engraven by the finger of God; and how they now lie torn and scattered, one in this dark corner and another in that, buried in heaps of dust and rubbish! There is not now a system, an entire table of coherent truths to be found, or a frame of holiness; but some shivered parcels. And if any, with great skill and labour, apply themselves to draw out here one piece, and there another, and set them together, they serve rather to show how exquisite the Divine workmanship was in the original composition, than for present use to the excellent purposes for which the whole was first designed. * * * You come amid all this confusion as into the ruined palace of some great prince; in which you see here the fragments of a noble pillar, there the shattered pieces of some curious imagery, and all lying, neglected and useless, among heaps of dust. * * * The faded glory, the darkness, the disorder, the impurity, the decayed state in all respects of the temple, too plainly show THE GREAT INHABITANT IS GONE."—HOWE. Living Temple, Part ii. ch. iv.

"Homo est animal rationale, et ex hoc, cunctis terrenis animantibus excellentius atque præstantius, sed in qualibet minutissima muscula bene consideranti stuporem mentis ingerat, laudemque pariat creatoris. Ipse itaque animæ humanæ mentem dedit, ubi ratio et intelligentia in infante sopita est quodammodo, quasi nulla sit, excitanda scilicet atque exercenda ætatis accessu, qua sit scientiæ capax atque doctrinæ, et habilis perceptioni veritatis et amori boni. Qua capacitate hauriat sapientiam virtutibusque sit prædita, quibus prudenter, fortiter, temperater et juste adversus errores et cætera ingenerata vitia dimicet, eaque nullius rei desiderio nisi boni illius summi atque incommutabilis vincat. Quod etsi non faciat ipsa talium bonorum capacitas in natura rationali divinitus instituta, quantum sit boni, quam mirabile opus omnipotentis, quis competenter effatur, aut cogitat? Præter enim artes bene vivendi, et ad immortalem perveniendi felicitatem quæ virtutes vocantur, et sola Dei gratia quæ in Christo est, filiis promissionis regnique donantur, nonne humano ingenio tot tantæ que artes sunt inventæ et exercitæ partim necessariæ, partim voluntariæ, ut tam excellens vis mentis atque rationis in his etiam rebus, quas superfluas, imo et periculosas perniciosasque appetit quantum bonum habeat in natura, unde ista potuit vel invenire, vel discere, vel exercere testetur? Vestimentorum et ædificiorum ad opera quam mirabilia, quam stupenda industria humana pervenerit, quo in agricultura, quo in navigatione profecerit : quæ in fabricatione quorumque vasorum, vel etiam statuarum et picturarum varietate excogitaverit et impleverit : quæ in theatris mirabilia spectantibus, audientibus incredibilia facienda et exhibenda molita sit : in capiendis, occidendis, domadis irrationalibus animantibus, quæ et quanta repererit : adversus ipsos homines, tot genera venenorum, tot armorum, tot machinamentorum, et pro salute mortali tuenda atque reparanda, quot medicamenta atque adjumenta comprehenderit : pro voluptate faucium, quot condimenta et gulæ incitamenta repererit : ad indicandas et suadendas cogitationes, multitudinem varietatemque signorum, ubi præcipuum locum verba et literæ tenent : ad delectandos animos, quos elocutionis ornatus, quam diversorum carminum copiam : ad mulcendas aures, quot organa musica, quot cantilenæ modos excogitaverit : quantam peritiam dimensionum atque numerorum : meatusque et ordines sideru quanta sagacitate comprehenderit, quam multa rerum mudanarum cognitione se impleverit, quis possit eloqui, maxime si velimus non acervatim cuncta cogerere, sed in singulis immorari ? In ipsis postremo erroribus et falsitatibus defendendis, quam magna claruerint ingenia philosophorum atque hæreticorum, quis existimare sufficiat ? "

＊　　　＊　　　＊　　　＊　　　＊　　　＊

" Apostolus de ipsis in illud regnum prædestinatis loquens : Qui proprio, inquit, filio non pepercit, sed pro nobis omnibus tradidit eum, quomodo non etiam cum illo omnia nobis donavit ? Cum hæc promissio complebitur, quid erimus ? quales erimus ? quæ bona in illo regno accepturi sumus, quandoquidem Christo moriente pro nobis tale iam pignus accepimus ? qualis erit spiritus hominis, nullum omnino habens vitium, nec sub quo jaceat : nec cui cedat : nec contra quod saltem laudabiliter dimicet, pacatissima virtute perfectus ? Rerum ibi omnium quanta, quam speciosa, quam certa scientia sine errore aliquo, vel labore, ubi Dei sapientia de ipso suo fonte potabitur, cum summa felicitate, sine ulla difficultate ? Quale erit corpus, quod omnimodo spiritui subditum, et eo sufficienter vivificatum nullis alimoniis indigebit ? Non enim animale, sed spirituale erit, habens quidem carnis, sed sine ulla carnali corruptione, substantiam."—AUGUSTINUS. De Civitate Dei, Lib. xxii. cap. xxiv.

NOTE B.

The sentences which follow formed part of the discourse, when delivered as an address to a joint meeting of the United Secession and Relief Presbyteries of Edinburgh. The union anticipated has been consummated under the happiest auspices. Esto perpetua.

" These two bodies[1] are, in reality, more united than any one large ecclesiastical body that I am acquainted with; and it would be much easier to prove that most of those bodies should become two or more distinct societies, than that our two distinct societies should not become one. I will not speak of the great Antichristian confederacy, which boasts of union as one of its characteristics ; but in which almost every variety of opinion, every degree of belief, and unbelief, and misbelief, may be found, under the cloak of ' exoteric faith in the bond of ignorance, fear, and hypocrisy.'[2] Nor will I speak of the established churches, those ' cities of the nations,' daughters of ' Great Babylon,' which, in this respect, have generally a strong likeness to their mystic mother; but I run no hazard of being confuted when I say, that there is far less extent of agreement of sentiment, and much greater diversity of opinion, among the Congregationalists, or the Baptists, or the Methodists, in Britain, who are generally regarded as each forming but one body, or in either of the great bodies of Presbyterians in America, than in the two churches which are represented here this evening. I do not think that it would be easy to prove that these churches should ever have been separate, I should not like to try it, though their separate existence may easily be accounted for, on principles which throw no discredit on the conscientiousness of either body ; but I am quite sure it would be very difficult to prove that they ought not now to be one. I know no argument which would prove that I should not unite with the Relief Church, which, if fairly followed out, would not compel me to abandon the communion of the United Secession Church. It has been my conviction for a considerable period, that if these churches are not ripe for union, they ought to be so ; and, while utterly indisposed to push an incorporation of the two bodies at the hazard of mutilating either, or of pressing brethren to take a step regarding which they are not ' fully persuaded in their own minds,' I am more and more convinced, that if those ministers and people in both bodies, who see their way clear, would act out their principles to the full extent that the decisions of the two supreme courts warrant, the period could not be distant when the feeling of wonder why, being one, we should still continue divided ; and the experience of the sacred delights and solid advantages of such occasional intercourse would call forth,

[1] The United Secession and the Relief Churches.   [2] Jortin.

on the part of the Christian people, an expression of desire for complete union, which the two Synods would not only feel warranted to respond to, but would feel it impossible to refuse to gratify. The Lord hasten it in his time."

Note C.

There is something very pleasing in the following ascription of praise to God, by a bishop of the 12th century, clothed though it be in monkish rhymes, which Archbishop Usher designates "Rhythmos *Elegantissimos;*" an epithet which makes us somewhat doubtful if his Grace's taste was at all proportionate to his piety and learning:—

> " Super cuncta, subter cunctus,
> Extra cuncta, intra cunctus,
> Subter cuncta, nec subtractus,
> Super cuncta, nec elatus,
> Inter cuncta, nec inclusus,
> Extra cuncta, nec exclusus,
> Intra, nusquam coarctaris,
> Extra, nusquam delataris,
> Subter, nullo fatigaris,
> Super, nullo sustentaris."
>
> HILDEBERTUS. Rhythm. de Trin.

Note D.

The following account of the fear of God which Christians should cherish, by Archbishop Leighton, presents a noble specimen of the most of the characteristic excellencies of that most saintly man, sound divine, and elegant scholar:—

" This fear hath chiefly these things:—1. A reverend esteem of the majesty of God, which is a main fundamental thing in religion, and that moulds the heart most powerfully to the obedience of his will. 2. A firm belief of the purity of God, and of his power and justice; that he loves holiness and hates all sin, and can and will punish it. 3. A right apprehension of the bitterness of his wrath and the sweetness of his love: that his incensed anger is the most terrible and intolerable thing in the world, absolutely the fearfullest of all evils; and, on the other side, his love, of all good things the best, the most blessed and delightful, yea, only blessedness. Life is the name of the sweetest good we know; and yet this ' loving-kindness is better

than life,' says David. 4. It supposes likewise sovereign love
to God, for his own infinite excellency and goodness. 5. From
all these things spring a most earnest desire to please him, and
in all things, and unwillingness to offend him in the least; and
because of our danger through the multitude and strength of
tentations, and our own weakness, a continual self-suspicion, a
holy fear lest we should sin, and a care and watchfulness that
we sin not, and deep sorrow and speedy returning, and humbling
before him, when we have sinned.

" There is, indeed, a base kind of fear, that, in the usual distinction, they call servile fear; but to account all fear of the
judgments and wrath of God a servile fear (or, not to stand upon
words), to account such a fear improper to the children of God,
I conceive, is a wide mistake. Indeed, to fear the punishment
of sin, without regard to God and his justice as the inflicter of
them, or to forbear to sin only because of those punishments, so
as if a man can be secured from those, he hath no other respect
to God that would make him fear to offend, this is the character
of a slavish and base mind.

" Again, for a man so to apprehend wrath in relation to himself as to be still under the horror of it in that notion, and not
to apprehend redemption and deliverance by Jesus Christ, is to
be under that spirit of bondage which the Apostle speaks of,
Rom. viii. And such fear, though a child of God may for a
time be under it, yet the lively actings of faith and persuasion
of God's love, and the feeling of reflex love to him in the soul,
doth cast it out; according to that of the Apostle, 1 John iv. 18,
' True love casteth out fear.' But to apprehend the punishments the Lord threatens against sin as certain and true, and to
consider the greatness and fearfulness of them, but especially the
terror of the Lord's anger and hot displeasure above all punishments, and (though not only, no, nor chiefly for these) yet, in
contemplation of those, as very great and weighty, to be afraid
to offend that God who hath threatened such things as the just
reward of sin; this, I say, is not incongruous with the estate of
the sons of God, yea, it is their duty and their property even
thus to fear.

" 1. This is the very end for which God hath published these
intimations of his justice, and hath threatened to punish men if
they transgress, to. the end they may fear and not transgress;
so that not to look upon them thus, and to be affected with them
answerably to their intendment, were a very grievous sin, a
slight and disregard put upon the words of the great God.

" 2. Of all others, the children of God have the rightest and clearest knowledge of God, and the deepest belief of his word; and therefore they cannot choose but be afraid, and more afraid than all others, to fall under the stroke of his hand. They know more of the greatness, and truth, and justice of God than others, and therefore they fear when he threatens. ' My flesh trembleth for fear of thee (says David), and I am afraid of thy judgments;' yea, they tremble when they hear the sentence against others, or see the execution on them, it minds them when they see public executions; and ' knowing the terror of the Lord, we persuade men,' says St Paul; they cry out with Moses, Psal. xc., ' Who knows the power of thine anger? even according to thy fear so is thy wrath.' It is not an imagination nor invention that makes men fear more than they need; His wrath is as terrible as any that fears it most can apprehend, and beyond. So that this doth not only consist with the estate of the saints, but is their very character, to tremble at the word of their Lord: the rest neglect what he says, till death and judgment seize on them; but the godly know and believe that ' it is a fearful thing to fall into the hands of the living God.'

" And though they have firm promises, and a kingdom that cannot be shaken, yet they have still this grace by which they serve God acceptably with reverence and godly fear, even in this consideration, that our God, even he that is ours by peculiar covenant, is a ' consuming fire,' Heb. xii. 28, 29.

" But indeed, together with this, yea, more than with these, they are persuaded to fear the Lord by the sense of his great love to them, and the power of that love that works in them towards him, and is wrought in them by his. ' They shall fear the Lord and his goodness in the latter days,' Hos. iii. 5. In those days his goodness shall manifest itself more than before; the beams of his love shall break forth more abundantly in the days of the gospel, and shall beat more direct and hotter on the hearts of men; and then they shall fear him more, because they shall love him more.

" This fear agrees well both with faith and love; yea, they work it: compare Psal. xxxi. 23, with Psal. xxxiv. 9; and that same Psal. xxxiv. 8, with 9, and Psal. cxii. 1, with 7. The heart, touched with the loadstone of Divine love, trembles still with this godly fear, and yet looks fixedly by faith to that star of Jacob, Jesus Christ, who guides it to the haven of happiness.

" The looking upon God in the face of Jesus Christ takes off that terror of his countenance that drives men from him; and in the smiles of his love that appear through Christ, there is such a power as unites their hearts to him, but unites them so as to fear his name, as the Psalmist's prayer is. He puts such a fear in their hearts as will not cause them depart from, yea, causes that they ' shall not depart from him.'

" And this is the purest and highest kind of godly fear that springs from love ; and though it excludes not the consideration of wrath, as terrible in itself, and some fear of it, yet it may surmount it ; and doubtless, where much of that love possesses the heart, it will sometimes drown the other consideration, that it shall scarcely be sensible at all, and will constantly set it aside, and persuade a man purely for the goodness and loveliness of God to fear to offend him, though there were no interest at all in it of a man's own personal misery or happiness."

DISCOURSE XIII.

THE DUTIES OF CHRISTIAN SERVANTS ENJOINED AND ENFORCED.

1 Pet. ii. 18-25.—Servants, be subject to your masters with all fear; not only to the good and gentle, but also to the froward. For this is thank-worthy, if a man for conscience toward God endure grief, suffering wrongfully. For what glory is it, if, when ye be buffeted for your faults, ye shall take it patiently? but if, when ye do well, and suffer for it, ye take it patiently, this is acceptable with God. For even hereunto were ye called: because Christ also suffered for us, leaving us an example, that ye should follow his steps: who did no sin, neither was guile found in his mouth: who, when he was reviled, reviled not again; when he suffered, he threatened not; but committed himself to him that judgeth righteously: Who his own self bare our sins in his own body on the tree, that we, being dead to sins, should live unto righteousness; by whose stripes ye were healed. For ye were as sheep going astray; but are now re-turned unto the Shepherd and Bishop of your souls.

In these words we have a further illustration of the general injunction laid on Christians by the Apostle at the 12th verse of this chapter, to "have their conversation honest among the Gentiles;" that is, so to conduct themselves as that even their heathen neighbours should be constrained to approve them. That injunction is, as it were, the text of a considerably long paragraph which immediately follows. The manner in which that command was to be obeyed, was by a careful performance of relative duties, especially such as they owed to their heathen connexions. Of the excellence of such a course of conduct they were qualified judges, which they were not of duties of a more strictly religious and Christian character. All Christians were, therefore, to yield a loyal subjection to civil authority, as lodged both in

its supreme and subordinate administrators; to cherish and
display a becoming respect for all who on whatever ground
had a claim on respect; to cultivate and manifest that peculiar regard to the Christian society, which in Christians
even heathens could not help considering as becoming and
proper; and to show a reverence for the supreme civil power,
based on, and only limited by, the reverence due to Him
who is " King of kings, and Lord of lords." The natural
tendency of such " good works," habitually and perseveringly
maintained, was to overcome the prejudice of their heathen
neighbours, and constrain those " who spoke against them as
evil-doers, to glorify God in the day of visitation."

Another way in which the same desirable object was to be
sought is that specified in our text: such Christians as stood
in the relation of servants, especially to heathen masters, faithfully discharging the duties, and patiently submitting to the
hardships connected with the situation in which they were
placed. The passage contains an account first of the duties
of Christian servants generally, and of the manner in which
they should be performed; they are to be " subject to their
masters," and they are to be so " in all fear." And then
of the duty of a particular class of servants; they who have
not good and gentle, but froward masters, and of the motives
which urge to its performance. Though their service may
be harder, and their treatment more severe than those of
their more favoured brethren, they are to be equally obedient and submissive; and they are to act in this way,
because such conduct is peculiarly well-pleasing to God,
and because it is a part of that holiness, that conformity to
Christ, to which as Christians they were called. Let us
turn our attention to these important and interesting topics
in their order.

§ 1. *The foundation and nature of the relation between
Servant and Master.*

Servants, at the period when, and in the country where,
the Christians, to whom the Apostle's Epistle was directed,

lived, were divided into two classes, the bond and the free; the first, slaves, persons who had been taken in war, or had been born in a state of slavery, or had, for certain considerations, sold their freedom; the second, hired servants, persons who, as in this and other free countries, voluntarily sell their time and labour, during a specified time, for a certain price, under the name of sustenance and wages. The injunction of the Apostle is intended for both these classes; for, however a person may be brought into the condition of a servant, the duties of that condition are substantially the same. Before entering on the consideration of these duties, it may not be without its use to unfold, in a few sentences, the nature and foundation of that relation in which these duties originate.

All men, viewed merely as men, are equal. They have all the same nature, and there are rights and duties common to all. They all belong to the same order of God's creatures, "God has made of one blood all the nations of men for to dwell on the face of the earth."[1] Their bodies have the same members, their minds the same faculties. They are all rational, responsible, immortal beings, and every man is equally bound to treat every other man according to the laws of truth, justice, and humanity.

But while, in reference to nature, men are equal, in reference to condition they are endlessly diversified. In bodily qualities, such as beauty, strength, and agility; in mental faculties, such as judgment, imagination, and memory; in external circumstances, from the rudest state of barbarism to the highest state of refinement, from the most abject poverty to the most abundant wealth, the greatest differences prevail among the possessors of our common nature. And these differences, to a great extent, are the necessary effect of the operations of the God of nature and of providence.

In consequence of this diversity of condition, individuals are not sufficient for their own comfortable support, and stand in need of one another's assistance; and the happiness of

---

[1] Acts xvii. 26.

society depends on mutually giving and receiving: giving what they can spare, receiving what they need. Out of these facts grow all social arrangements, and, among the rest, the relation of master and servant.

A person possessed of property finds it inconvenient or impossible for him to do personally many things which he finds it desirable should be done, and he parts with a portion of his property to induce another person, fit for accomplishing the objects in view, who has time, and skill, and capacity of labour to dispose of, to do for him what he cannot do, or is not inclined to do for himself. The master has no natural authority over the servant. He has no more right to demand the labours of the servant, than the servant has to demand his property.

The relation, when legitimately formed, originates in a bargain or agreement between two independent individuals; the one having property, the other labour, to dispose of. The master stipulates that the servant shall perform certain services for certain wages; and the servant stipulates that the master shall pay him certain wages for certain services. The result of the bargain is, that the master has authority to demand the stipulated service, and the servant has a right, which he may call on their common superior to enforce, to receive his wages.[1]

§ 2.—*The duties of Christian servants in general.*

Having thus stated, as shortly and plainly as I could, the nature and foundation of the relation of the servant to the master, let us now attend to his duties. These are all summed up in one very comprehensive word in the passage before us: "Subjection." "Servants, be subject to your masters:" that is, let your will be regulated by their will. In other words, be obedient to their commands; be submissive to their arrangements.

---

[1] In this and the succeeding part of the discourse, the author has availed himself of the useful labours of Bishop Fleetwood, in his "Sermons on Relative Duties," and of Dr Stennet, in his "Discourses on Domestic Duties."

(1.) Servants are to be obedient to the command of their master; that is, they are to do what their master bids them, in the way in which he requires it to be done, to the best of their ability. A servant cannot reasonably expect to be his own master; to be allowed to choose how he shall employ his time; what he shall do, or even in what manner the service required shall be executed. He has taken a price for his time and his capacity of labour, and it is but just that he who has bought them should dispose of them. They are no more his than his wages are his master's. He is a person under authority, who, when bid come, must come; when bid go, must go; and when bid do this, must do it.

The servant's obligation to obey, however, is by no means unlimited. It has bounds corresponding with the master's right. No master has, or can have, a right to command any thing that is inconsistent with the Divine law; and of course no servant can be under an obligation to comply with such a command. The rule is plain and absolute, when the will of an earthly master is opposed to the will of our Master in heaven, "We ought to obey God rather than man."[1] Should a master require his servant to speak falsely, to act fraudulently, or to violate any Divine command, such a command should meet with a respectful, but peremptory refusal. And it is for the servant to judge whether a particular command is or is not consistent with the Divine law: for "every one of us shall give an account of *himself* to God."[2] It will not be sustained as an excuse at the Divine tribunal, for a servant doing what was wrong, that his master commanded him to do it. Servants ought, however, to take care not to withhold obedience to a just command, from a pretended regard to conscience, when the true cause of their non-compliance is their sloth or self-indulgence. In such a case there is a double guilt contracted. The human master is disobeyed, and the Divine Master is insulted. There is a shocking union of dishonesty and impiety.

---

[1] Acts v. 29.　　　　[2] Rom. xiv. 12.

A master has, can have, no right, to command what is impracticable, what is not in the servant's power; and therefore, in such cases, the servant is under no obligation to obedience. The Israelites were not to blame when they did not obey Pharaoh, commanding them to make bricks, when he withheld from them straw. There is nothing wrong in a servant refusing to attempt what he knows to be an impossibility, or what he is aware cannot be done, or attempted to be done, without materially injuring him. It is quite possible, indeed, that a servant may pretend incapacity for a particular piece of service, when what is wanting is not power but will; but no Christian servant will ever act in this way, and masters ought to be careful not to impose any unreasonable burdens; acting always on that rule of our Lord, which, if carefully attended to, would keep every thing in social life right: "Whatsoever ye would that men should do to you, do ye even so to them."[1]

Masters have no right to demand obedience in matters that do not fall within the limits of the agreement entered into with the servant; and of course servants are under no obligation to yield obedience in such cases. At the same time, servants of a right disposition will not, where the comfort of the family is obviously concerned, be very nice in measuring the precise limits of the appropriate sphere of service, and will conscientiously guard against making their freedom from obligation in this matter a cloak of sloth and ill temper.

With these exceptions, servants are bound to obey their masters in all things. A servant must not trifle with, or disobey a command, because *he* thinks it refers to a matter of but little moment. That is a subject in which he is not at all called to judge; and what he thinks of little importance, may be in his master's estimation, and in reality, a matter of the greatest importance; nor is difference of

[1] Matt. vii. 12.

opinion, though the servant may be right, nor disinclination to the service required, to be considered as affording any reason for disobedience. A servant may give his opinion, if he do it respectfully, to his master, without any violation of duty; but he is never to forget, that it is not his judgment, but his master's, that is ultimately to determine the matter; and this even although his master assigns no satisfactory reason, or no reason at all.

This obedience, which is due by servants to their masters, ought to be characterised by respectfulness, faithfulness, diligence, and cheerfulness. A rude, forward, assuming behaviour, is exceedingly unbecoming in servants. The Divine command is, that Christian servants, even in the case of their masters being heathens, "count them worthy of all honour, not answering again:" "And if they are believers, that they do not despise them, because they are brethren."[1] Faithfulness must also characterise the Christian servant. Both with regard to the time, and the property, and the reputation of his master, he must be faithful. He must guard these as if they were his own. There must be "no purloining, but a showing all-good fidelity." Diligence is a third character which should distinguish the obedience of the Christian servant. All trifling, sauntering, and loitering should be avoided; and they should not be eye-servants, as men-pleasers, but diligent in business, as the servants of God. And, finally, they should be cheerful in their obedience. Few things are more unworthy of a Christian servant than that mulish surly obstinacy, which Solomon so graphically describes when he says: "He is not to be corrected by words; for though he understand, yet will he not answer." The Apostle Paul enjoins Christian servants, with good-will to do service, as to the Lord, and not to man. This forms the most important part of the Christian servant's duty, to obey the commands of his master.

---

[1] Tit. ii, 9. 1 Tim. vi. 1, 2.

(2.) Under the general head subjection, however, is also
included submission to the appointments of his master.
The economy of the household is to be directed by the
master; and where these arrangements in no degree interfere with Divine appointments, and are not precluded by
express stipulation, the servant must submit to them, though
they may be in many respects disagreeable to him. The
hours of rising and retiring to rest; the quality, and to a
certain extent the quantity of sustenance, and a vast variety
of other arrangements, must to a great extent depend on the
will of the master; and it is an important, though sometimes not a very easy part of the Christian servant's duty, to
submit to these without murmuring, and not permit them to
fret the temper, so as to unfit for the cheerful and principled
obedience which the law of Christ requires.

The manner in which the duty of subjection should be
performed, the temper in which obedience and submission
are to be yielded, comes now to be considered. "Servants,
be subject to your masters in all fear." It has been common
to consider these words as descriptive of that respectful feeling which servants should cherish towards their own masters,
and to which we have already alluded. I apprehend, however, that the fear here referred to is not the fear of man in
any of its forms, but the fear of God. The phrase "all
fear," according to the idiom of the New Testament, signifies a high, or the highest degree of fear; as "all acceptation" is the highest degree of acceptation, "all wisdom"
every kind and degree of wisdom; and it is not according
to the genius of Christianity, or indeed of revelation generally, to inculcate any high degree of fear of man. On
the contrary, a leading object which they contemplate, is to
elevate the mind above the fear of man, and, by leading man
to fear God, to free him from all other fear. "Who art
thou," says the Prophet, "that thou shouldest be afraid of a
man that shall die, and of the son of man that shall be as
the grass?" "Be not afraid of them," says our Lord, "who
kill the body, and after that have no more that they can

do:" "Be not afraid of their terror," says the Apostle; "neither be ye troubled." The Prophet says, "Sanctify the Lord in your heart, and let Him be your fear and your dread:" and our Lord says, "Fear Him, who after he has killed the body, can cast both soul and body into hell-fire; yea, I say unto you, Fear him." And his Apostle repeats the injunction of the Prophet, "Sanctify the Lord in your heart."[1]

The fear of God is the temper in which Christians are to perform all their duties. They are "to cleanse themselves from all filthiness of the flesh and the spirit, and to perfect holiness in the fear of God." They are to "submit themselves to one another in the fear of God."[2]

The word "fear," without the adjunct "of the Lord," is certainly used in the New Testament to signify religious fear; fear which has God for its object. That is plainly its meaning when it is said, that "Noah, moved with fear, prepared an ark;" and when it is said, "Pass the time of your sojourning here in fear." That seems its meaning, when the Corinthians are said to have received Titus, "with fear and trembling;" and when Christians are commanded to "work out their own salvation," or rather, as we are disposed to think, to labour for one another's salvation, "with fear and trembling: for it is God who worketh in them, both to will and to do of his good pleasure."[3] In the parallel passage in Eph. vi. 5, the "fear and trembling" with which servants are to perform their duties, is strictly connected with, "in singleness of your heart, as to Christ; not with eye-service, as men-pleasers; but as the servants of Christ, doing the will of God from the heart." And in Col. iii. 22, what in the passage just quoted is called "fear and trembling," is explained by the phrase "fearing God."

[1] Isa. li. 12.   Luke xii. 4.   Isa. viii. 13.   Luke xii. 5.   1 Pet. iii. 14, 15.
[2] 2 Cor. vii. 1.   Eph. v. 21.
[3] Heb. xi. 7.   1 Pet. i. 17.   2 Cor. vii. 15.   Phil. ii. 12.   On the last of these passages—a difficult one, and generally, I think, misunderstood—Pierce's Note deserves to be consulted.

Comparing all these passages together, I can scarcely doubt, that " with all fear," in the passage before us, is equivalent to, with a deeply pious temper; and that this, too, is its meaning at the second verse of the next chapter—where " chaste conversation mingled with fear," is, I apprehend, just, chaste pious behaviour, purity obviously rising from piety.

Christian servants then, in performing their duties, are to do them from a regard to the Divine authority, depending on the Divine assistance, looking forward to the Divine tribunal, desirous, above all things, of the Divine approbation ; fearing lest in any thing the Divine disapprobation should be incurred.   This is just one of the many instances in which we find Christianity converting every thing into religion, teaching men " to set the Lord always before them ;" and in the most ordinary offices of life, " whether they eat, or drink, or whatsoever they do, to do all to the glory of God."[1]

§ 3.—*The duties of a particular class of Christian servants.*

Let us now turn our attention for a little, to the view which the Apostle gives us of the duty of a particular class of Christian servants, and of the motives which he employs to urge them to its performance.   The servants he refers to are those who have not " good," kind, " and gentle masters," but " froward," perverse, unreasonable, rough, unkind masters.   Now what is *their* duty ?   It is still to be subject, just as if they were good and gentle.

It is no part of a Christian's duty to enter into the service of a froward master, if he can possibly make a better of it ; nor to remain in his service any longer than engagement requires, or other circumstances admit ; and it is not wrong for a Christian servant to avail himself of all the means which the law of his country furnishes him with, to protect himself from injury and ill-usage from a froward master.

[1] Psal. xvi. 8.   1 Cor. x. 31.

But the Apostle supposes the Christian servant, or slave, in the providence of God, placed under a froward master. Even in countries where the interests of servants are much better cared for by law than in the age and country referred to by the Apostle, servants who have froward masters have often a great deal of suffering to submit to from unreasonable commands, and arrangements, and unkind overbearing tempers, that no law can protect them from ; and this was the case to an immeasurably greater degree among those to whom this Epistle was directed.

Now, what was their duty ?   Was there any relaxation in the precept, " Be subject ?" None in the least. The unkind irritating behaviour of the master, is not to be sustained as an excuse for evading or disobeying his commands, or even for yielding a grudging obedience : the hardships of the situation are to be patiently submitted to while they continue ; and there is to be no attempt to lessen or remove them by neglecting or violating relative duty. This makes us see how necessary it is for the Christian servant to do his duty " with all fear," in a pious spirit, from a regard to God's authority ; feeling that though the commands of his master are in themselves harsh and unreasonable, it is a wise and good command that requires him, in his circumstances, to be subject to his master within the limits already described ; that though the yoke of the earthly master is oppressive, the yoke of the Master in heaven is reasonable.

§ 4. *Motives to the discharge of these duties.*

(1.) *Patient endurance of undeserved wrong enforced, by the consideration that it is " acceptable to God."*

This duty of cheerful patient obedience to harsh and unreasonable masters, is a very difficult one, and therefore the Apostle enforces it by very powerful motives. They are two ; first, patient endurance of undeserved suffering, is of high estimation in the sight of God ; and, secondly, it is a part of that conformity to the image of God's Son, to secure which was one great design of the sacrifice of God's Son, to which Christians are called. Let us look at these two motives in their order.

The first is stated in these words, "For this is thank-worthy, if a man for conscience toward God endure grief, suffering wrongfully: for what glory is it, if ye be buffeted for your faults, ye shall take it patiently? but if, when ye do well, and suffer for it, ye take it patiently, this is acceptable with God." The Christian servant under a froward master is described as "suffering wrongfully." He does his duty faithfully and cheerfully, yet he does not receive the kind treatment his conduct merits; he may not be treated *illegally*, so as that his master lays himself open to punishment, but he may be made to endure a great deal of severe suffering within these limits. That may take place, often does take place even now, and in this country, where the rights of servants are better understood, and more effectually pro-tected, than in most countries; and must have taken place to a much greater degree in ages and countries where heathenism and slavery prevailed, and where even the civil rights of hired servants were much more limited than they are with us.

When the Christian servant acted in character, though suffering wrongfully, he "endured grief;" that is, not merely felt the uneasiness his master's treatment of him naturally produced, but bore it meekly and patiently. The word "endure," is employed in the same sense as when it is said, "Moses endured, as seeing him who is invisible." "We count them happy that endure." "Blessed is the man that endureth temptation," that is, trial.[1] There is neither merit nor demerit in merely suffering. It is the manner in which we suffer that deserves praise or blame.

Now, says the Apostle, a Christian servant conscientiously doing his duty to a froward master, bears patiently the un-kind and injurious treatment he receives from him, "for

[1] Heb. xi. 27.   James v. 2; i. 12.

conscience towards God." Some have supposed, that that means, that the bad treatment of the froward master was persecution because the servant was a Christian. That this might be, often was, the case, we cannot doubt; but that is not the idea conveyed by the words. He does not suffer wrongfully for conscience towards God; but for conscience towards God he "endures," patiently suffers grief. He submits patiently to suffering from an enlightened regard to the character and will of God. He believes that he is in his present circumstances by the providence of God; he knows God requires him to bear the evils he is subject to with fortitude and patience; he believes that God will support him under them, in due time deliver him from them, and make them work for his good; and therefore he "endures" them. "Such a servant's obedience is not pinned to the goodness and equity of his master, but when that fails will subsist upon its own inward ground. This is the thing that makes sure and constant walking. It makes a man step even in the ways of God."[1]

Now, says the Apostle, a Christian servant acting in this way is an object of the complacent approbation of God. "This is thank-worthy," this is "acceptable with God;" there is glory in this. It is the same word that is rendered "thank-worthy" and "acceptable," and no good end is gained by varying the rendering. God regards with complacency the Christian servant who, from a regard to his will, from a trust in his character, quietly and patiently bears unprovoked wrong, and does not allow his master's unworthy behaviour to influence his discharge of his duty to him. And to every Christian, the assurance that God looks with complacency on a particular course of conduct, is one of the most powerful motives which can be suggested for following it. Men may count you mean-spirited in submitting to such usage. God, who is infinitely wise, and whose approbation is of more importance than that of the whole universe of created beings, ap-

[1] Leighton.

proves your conduct, counts your meekness true glory, and regards you with affectionate complacency. His eye rests benignantly on you. That far more than counterbalances the sour looks, and the harsh language, and the unkind treatment of the froward master.

That such conduct, the patient endurance of undeserved suffering, is a proper object of complacent regard, the Apostle shows, by contrasting it with the patient endurance of deserved suffering: " For what glory is it, when ye are buffeted for your faults, ye shall take it patiently? but if, when ye do well, and suffer ('for it,' is a supplement, and should not have been inserted; for there is no reason to think the servants suffered *for* doing well, but only notwithstanding their doing well), ye take it patiently, this is acceptable with God."

In these words the Apostle meets the very natural thought: It is very hard to suffer when we deserve reward; we could receive merited chastisement without complaint; we should feel that in that case complaint was unreasonable; but to endure undeserved, unprovoked, grief; to meet with insult and outrage, instead of the kind treatment our dutiful conduct entitles us to, this is hard indeed. The Apostle does not deny this: but he says, you are placed in circumstances in which you have an opportunity of drawing down upon yourselves a larger measure of the approbation of God, than had you been placed in what you might have thought better circumstances. Neither God nor man could have regarded, with approbation, your conduct in meriting chastisement. If, after meriting chastisement, you had submitted to it patiently, both God and man would have approved of your conduct as what was fitting in the circumstances; but they would not have considered it as deserving of praise; the opposite kind of conduct, murmuring under chastisement incurred by fault, would have appeared most unreasonable and blameable. But God, and all good men who think along with God, will regard you with a high degree of affectionate complacency, if, under strong temptations to

murmur, you "possess your souls in patience," and instead
of, in any degree, "rendering evil for evil," endeavour to
" overcome evil with good."[1]

The reason why such conduct is peculiarly acceptable to God is, that all undeserved suffering, endured
patiently from religious motives, shows the submission of
the mind and will to God. It is an embodiment of the
soul of true religion, "Not my will, but thine be done.
The cup which my Father giveth me to drink, shall I not
drink it?"[2]

It may be worth observing, in passing, that from the language used, it is plain that masters had then the power of
corporeal chastisement, and that they were not slack in using
it : "If ye be buffeted for your faults." All ranks of men,
and especially the subordinate ones, have great cause to be
thankful to Christianity, which not only changes the hearts
of individuals, but mitigates and mellows the manners of
communities. No master in our land can buffet a servant
but at his peril.

This, then, is the first motive which the Apostle urges on
Christian servants to patient endurance of unmerited suffering from froward masters.

And is it not a powerful one? What the Christian
would be at is the praise of God. If he can secure that, is
it not enough? As Archbishop Leighton says, "If men commend him not, he accounts it no loss, and little gain if they
do. He is bound to a country where that coin goes not,
and whither he cannot carry it; and therefore he gathers it
not. That which he seeks in all is, that he may be approved
and accepted of God, whose thanks to the least of those
whom he accepts is no less than a crown of unfading glory.
Not a poor servant that fears his name, and is obedient and
patient for his sake, but will be thus rewarded. Not any
cross that is taken, what way so ever, it comes as out of his
hand, and carried patiently, yea, and welcomed and em-

[1] Luke xxi. 19. Rom. xii. 17, 21.　　　[2] John xviii. 11. Luke xxii. 43.

2

braced for his sake, but he observes our so entertaining it. Not an injury which the meanest servant bears Christianly, but goes upon account with him, and he sets them so as that they bear much value through his esteem and way of reckoning them, though in themselves they are all less than nothing, as a worthless counter stands for hundreds or thousands, according to the place you set it in. Happy they who have to deal with such a Lord; and be they servants or masters, are avowed servants to Him. When he comes his reward will be with him."

The great principle which the Apostle requires Christian servants to act from, in cheerfully doing the duties and enduring the hardships of their condition, is "conscience towards God." Submission to the Divine will, respect to the Divine authority, desire of the Divine approbation should be, and if we are Christians will be, the ruling principle of our conduct in all our actings and sufferings in life. To borrow the striking words of him whom in these discourses I so often quote, "Let us all, whether servants or not, set the Lord always before us, and study, with Paul, to have a conscience void of offence towards God and towards man. Let us apply constantly to our actions and to our inward thoughts the command of God. Let us walk by that rule abroad and at home, in our houses and in the several ways of our calling, as an exact workman, who is ever and anon applying his rule to his work, and squaring it. Let us, from conscience towards God, do and suffer his will cheerfully in every thing, being content that he should choose our condition and trials for us; only desirous to be assured that he has chosen us for his own, set us apart for himself, and secured for us the glorious liberty of the children of God, and the full redemption of the purchased possession." Let us seek as our great object, that whether we sleep or wake we may be accepted of him, and obtain at last the inheritance, as those who serve the Lord Christ. Let us steadily walk in the way that leads to this inheritance, overlooking this momentary scene and all things in it, accounting it a very indifferent matter what our outward state here be in this moment, provided we may be happy in eternity. Whether we be high or low here, bond or free, imports but little, seeing all these differences will so quickly be at an end, and no traces of them found for ever. It is so with individual man in the grave : you may distinguish the greater from the less, the monarch from the slave, by their tombs, but not by their dust ; and yet a little while in the reckoning of the Eternal, and all these external distinctions will pass away; the palace and the cottage equally disappearing, while " the elements melt in fervent heat, and the earth and all the works that are therein are burnt up." Yet, then shall the " righteous shine forth in the kingdom of their Father," and their lustre shall be proportioned to their right-eousness ; when all earthly splendour has vanished in dark-ness, patient endurance of suffering for conscience sake shall be found unto glory inextinguishable ; and the slave who for conscience to God, in circumstances of peculiar trial endu-ring great suffering wrongfully, proved that the mind of Christ was in him, and that he had learned to walk in the steps of the example he has left behind him, shall receive tokens of a degree of Divine approbation, which may be withheld from many who, placed in what men reckoned far more enviable circumstances, have not attained to the same measure of conformity to him who is the brightness of glory, the excellency of beauty, the " first-born among many brethren."

(2.)—*Patient endurance of undeserved suffering enforced from a consideration of Christ's sufferings.*

I go on now to turn your attention to the second mo-tive by which the Apostle enforces the duty of Christian ser-vants patiently enduring undeserved suffering. That motive is stated in the following words :—" For even hereunto were ye called: because Christ also suffered for us, leaving us an example, that ye should follow his steps : who did no sin, neither was guile found in his mouth : who, when he was reviled, reviled not again; when he suffered, he threatened not; but committed himself to him who judgeth righteously: who his own self bare our sins in his own body on the tree, that we, being dead to sin, should live to righteousness: by whose stripes ye are healed. For ye were as sheep going astray; but ye have returned unto the Shepherd and Bishop of souls." The motive is derived from the sufferings of Christ, and may be considered as so far a simple one; but as these sufferings are plainly, in different parts of the text, viewed in different aspects, first as exemplary, and then as expiatory, it must also, if we would feel its full force, be considered as a complex one. " Hereunto are ye called " Patient, undeserved suffering is a portion of that conformity to Christ, to which, as Christians, ye are called: " Hereunto are ye called." Patient, undeserved suffering is a part of that universal holiness to which ye are called, and to secure which, so far as man is concerned, was the great ultimate object of our Lord's expiatory sufferings. The motive is presented in the first of these aspects in the 21st, 22d, and 23d verses, and in the second of them in the 24th and 25th. Let us attend to them in their order.

1.—*Christians called to patient suffering as a part of conformity to Christ.*

" Hereunto were ye called," or to this were ye called. The first question that requires to be answered here is, to what does the Apostle refer in these words? What is it that he represents these Christian servants whom he is addressing as called to? Some have supposed that it is suffering for the cause of Christ—suffering on account of being Christians, that he refers to; and that the force of what he says may be thus stated, " Ye are called to suffer for Christ, and it is very reasonable that ye should be so called, for HE suffered for you." There can be no doubt that the Christians of that age were generally called to suffer for Christ, and in a remarkable manner; there can be as little doubt that it is a very good reason why Christians of every age should suffer for Christ, that HE suffered for them ; but a little attention will make it evident that it is not suffering merely for the cause of Christ, but patient, undeserved suffering, whatever might be the occasion that is here referred to; and that the motive is not the general statement, Christ suffered for us, but Christ has set us an example of the patient endurance of undeserved suffering.

The substance of the apostle's argument may be thus stated : To this are ye called as Christians, even to the patient endurance of sufferings wrongfully inflicted, from a regard to the will of God. And how does it appear, that as Christians, they are *called* to this ? They were called to be " conformed to the image of God's Son," and in particular they were called to " the fellowship of his sufferings," to suffer with him, like him, " in order to their being glorified together with him." [1]   " He left them an example that they should follow his steps."   He suffered ; his sufferings were undeserved sufferings ; he suffered for *them*, not for himself; and he sustained these undeserved sufferings most patiently, and from regard to the will of God.   " When reviled, he reviled not again; when he suffered, he threatened not, but committed himself to him who judgeth righteously."   Admitting these premises, it follows that Christian servants, exposed to undeserved sufferings, should not allow these sufferings to interfere with the discharge of their duties, but should bear them without murmuring, in submission to the divine will.   Let us look a little more closely at the facts here stated, the general principles here laid down, and the bearing which the two in connexion have on the duty of Christian servants exposed to unmerited suffering from froward masters, and of all Christians exposed to unmerited suffering from whatever cause.

And first, Of the facts here stated.   The first of these is, " Christ suffered." [2]   Our Lord, on assuming human nature,

---

[1] Rom. viii. 29.   1 Cor. i. 9.   Phil. iii. 10.

[2] Petrus non exprimit *quod* Christus passus sit, sed simpliciter dicit Χριστος σταθεν ut innuat, omne passionis genus Christum pro nobis tolerasse.—Jo. Hus.

became capable of suffering; and having become a man born of woman, his days were few, and full of trouble. The sufferings which he endured were in number, variety, and severity, such as no human being ever experienced. He was " a man of sorrows and acquainted with grief." His countenance was more marred than that of any man, and his form than that of the sons of men."[1] The language which the Prophet Jeremiah puts in the mouth of desolated Jerusalem might have been most appropriately used by him : " Is it nothing to all you who pass by : behold and see if there be any sorrow like unto my sorrow ?" The Captain of our salvation was made " perfect through suffering."[2]

These sufferings were all unmerited—unmerited by him. They were richly merited by those for whom, on whose account, for whose benefit, in whose room, they were endured, but they were utterly undeserved by him. His desert was the highest degree of enjoyment, of which his assumed nature was capable. When he suffered, he suffered for others, not for himself. Viewed in whatever light you please, his sufferings were undeserved from men. Viewed apart from the relation, which in glad compliance with the will of his Father he stood to ill-deserving, hell-deserving sinners of the human race, they were undeserved from his Father.

The idea, which is certainly intended to be suggested by the expression, " Christ suffered FOR us," is more fully brought out in the words that follow, " who did no sin, neither was guile found in his mouth." In this clause the words of the Prophet Isaiah, in the two chapters of his prophecy, are certainly alluded to, if not directly quoted : " Who did no violence, neither was guile found in his mouth." It is scarcely possible to doubt that in these words there is a reference to the two charges which were brought against our Lord, and for which he was tried before the supreme, civil

[1] Job xiv. 1.   Isa. liii. 3; lii. 14.   [2] Lam. i. 12.   Heb. ii. 10.

and ecclesiastical courts of his country.　Before the Roman
government he was accused of " violence," of " perverting
the nation and forbidding to give tribute to Cæsar, stirring up
all the people throughout all Jewry from Galilee to Jerusalem,"[1] and before the high priest and Sanhedrim he was
accused of " guile," of false doctrine in calling himself the
Son of God, " making himself equal with God."　The first
charge his enemies so completely failed in substantiating,
that the Roman governor, peculiarly sensitive on such a
subject, and likely to have his suspicions easily roused and not
easily allayed, after the closest examination, declared " I find
no fault in this man,"[2] that is, nothing even approximating
to the charge brought against him had been proved.　And as
to the second, there needed no proof that he made such
claims; he readily admitted this : but he accompanied his
claims with abundant evidence, that in making them there
was " no guile in his mouth ;" he spoke nothing but the
truth.　All the sufferings, then, which were inflicted on him,
as if he had been a perpetrator of crime, a teacher of falsehood, were undeserved sufferings.

But while this seems the direct reference of the words,
they are without doubt intended to convey the idea of the
perfect innocence, the absolute excellence of our Lord.
Actions and words are the expression of thoughts and feelings; and he who neither in deed nor in word offends may
well be presumed to be a perfect man.　It has been truly and
beautifully said, that " all Christ's words and actions flowed
from a pure spring that had nothing defiled in it ; other men
may seem clean as long as they are unstirred, but move and
trouble them, and the mud arises.　But in his case, though
stirred and agitated to the utmost, the deep fountain of his
mind and heart remained, though troubled, perfectly pure,
and sent forth nothing but the most pellucid streams."　Men
tried him, devils tried him, God tried him, and the result
always was, " he did no sin, no guile was found in his

---

[1] Luke xxiii. 5, 14.　　　　[2] John v. 18.　Luke xxii. 70; xxiii. 4.

mouth." Nothing could convict him of sin. There was no fault in him. He was, indeed, such a high priest as became us, " Holy, harmless, undefiled, and separate from sinners." " He was all fair; there was no spot in him."[1]

The third fact is, He endured all these undeserved sufferings with the utmost patience. " When reviled, he did not revile again ; when he suffered, he threatened not." He patiently " endured" the " so great contradiction of sinners against himself," to which he was exposed. In many cases he maintained a meek silence, at other times he replied to their upbraidings and reproaches with calm reasonings, affectionate expostulations, and benignant prayers. When called a Sabbath breaker, he replies by telling them that his Father, as well as himself, worked on the Sabbath-day, asking them whether it was lawful to do good or evil on that day; putting them in mind, that " the Sabbath was made for man, and not man for the Sabbath ;" and bidding them " go and learn what that means, I will have mercy, and not sacrifice." When charged with casting out devils by the power of Beelzebub, the prince of devils, he merely rebuts the shocking imputation by showing its absurdity. When upbraided as a companion of the dissolute and worthless, he justifies the conduct on which they grounded the foul imputation, by saying, "they that are whole need not the physician, but they that are sick. I came not to call the righteous, but sinners to repentance." When charged with blasphemy for saying to the man sick of the palsy, " Thy sins be forgiven thee," he merely directs their attention to the effect of his words, as containing a sufficient vindication of them. When they calumniate him as an impostor and seducer of the people, he makes no sharp answer, but appeals to the work which he had done among them, as abundant evidence of the truth of all he said, as proving that he had not come of himself, but been sent of his Father, God. When they took up stones to throw at him, all that he says is, " Many good works I have showed you of my Father; for which of these works do ye stone me?" When he was rudely addressed, inhumanly treated by a menial while at the bar of the San-hedrim, his reply was, "If I have spoken evil, bear witness of the evil; but if well, why smitest thou me?" And when in the extremity of his suffering, the high priests, the soldiers, and the populace vied with each other who should most em-bitter his dying agonies, by scornful taunts and bitter revilings, they could draw forth from him neither re-proach nor threatening. With a heart full of pity, he turned from them to his Father, and urged the only palliat-ing circumstance, in their crime, as an argument for their pardon, " Father, forgive them, for they know not what they do."[1]

Well does Archbishop Leighton say: "None ever did so little deserve revilings: none ever could have said so much in his own just defence, and to the just reproach of his ene-mies, and yet in both he preferred silence; none could ever threaten so heavy things as he could against his enemies, and have made good all that he threatened, and yet no such thing was ever heard of him. The heavens and the earth, as it were, spoke their resentment of the dishonour done to him who made them. The darkened sun, the shaking earth, the rending rocks, uttered rebuke, and denounced vengeance; but He held his peace. He was silent; or, if he spoke, it was to show how far he was from revilings and threatenings."

The only other fact mentioned is, that when Christ pa-tiently endured unmerited sufferings, he did so, from a regard to the will of his Father. It was not stupidity, it was not stoicism, it was enlightened, affectionate piety which produced this patient, unresisting, uncomplaining suffering. " He committed himself to him who judgeth righteously."

He looked above all second causes to the Great First Cause.

---

[1] John v. 17. Mark ii. 27. Matt. xii. 26. Luke v. 23, 31. John x. 32; xviii. 23. Luke xxiii. 34.

He saw all coming forth from Him who is "wonderful in counsel, and excellent in working." He saw in the events which occurred to him the manifestation of his will; and fully confident of his wisdom, and righteousness, and faithfulness, and benignity, he meekly submitted to them, persuaded that He would do all things well. "The cup which my Father giveth me to drink, shall I not drink it?" "Shall I say, Father, save me from this hour: for this purpose came I to this hour. Father, glorify thine own name; not my will, but thine be done."[1] He was persuaded that both HE and his righteous cause, the cause of the divine glory, and the salvation of man, were safe, perfectly safe, in the hands of "him who judges righteously." He believed and he did not make haste. His own deliverance and glorious exaltation, the salvation of the millions for whom he was pouring out his soul unto death, and the merited punishment of the obstinate opposers of truth and righteousness, he was persuaded were as certain as if they had already taken place. They would all take place at the time, and in the manner, that seemed best to infinite wisdom, and holiness, and benignity; and he was willing to suffer as severely and as long as was requisite, according to the arrangements of Him who alone has wisdom, to the gaining these grand objects. His temper is strikingly described in the words of one of his servants, who had much of the mind that was in him: "Lord, what thou wilt: when thou wilt: how thou wilt."[2] These are the facts, then, which regard to our Lord stated in the text: He suffered; his sufferings were undeserved; these undeserved sufferings were borne with patience: this patience originated in submission to the will of God.

Let us now turn our attention a little to the general principles here laid down. These are two. In thus patiently enduring undeserved suffering from a regard to the divine will, our Lord set an example to his people; and to the imitation of this example Christians are expressly called.

---

[1] John xviii. 11; xii. 27, 28.   [2] Baxter.

The first of these principles is stated in these words :
" Christ *also* suffered for us, leaving us an example that we
should follow his steps." ' Ye servants, who have froward
masters, are suffering; but remember ye are not the only suf-
ferers, Christ also suffered ; suffered undeservedly, suffered
patiently, suffered piously, leaving you an example that ye
should follow in his steps : he did all this with the intention
of showing you what you might expect, and how you should
behave.'

It is quite plain, that within certain clearly defin-
able limits, our Lord's character and conduct is the great
exemplar after which his followers are to fashion theirs.
They are commanded to have the mind in them that was in
him.   They are to think as he thought : they are to feel as
he felt : they are to " walk as he also walked." They are to
be " in the world as he was in the world. " To follow him,"
is the comprehensive term which describes all the varied
duties of discipleship. In running the Christian race, we
are constantly to " look to him" as the " exemplar as well as
the rewarder." [1]

Whatever was peculiar to him as a person invested with
an office altogether peculiar, that of Mediator between God
and man, the Saviour of sinners, and possessed of supernatural powers, fitting him to accomplish the great ends for
which he was invested with that office, is obviously not to be
considered as exemplary. Within that circle none must
attempt to walk but he. It would be folly and impiety to attempt to expiate sin, either our own or other men's; or, without
a divine commission, to work miracles, or to do what, when
done by our Lord, obviously went on the supposition of his
possessing a species of authority and knowledge which do
not, which can not, belong to his followers, forgive sins, or
pronounce on the spiritual state and eternal destiny of individual men.

But in the great leading principles of our Lord's conduct,

---

[1] Phil. ii. 5.   1 John ii. 6; iv. 17.   John xii. 26.   Heb. xii. 2.

supreme love to God, disinterested love to man, there can be no doubt that he is our exemplar ; and, supposing him placed in our circumstances, we are always to think, and feel, and act, as he would have thought, and felt, and acted. There may be some difficulty in certain cases, though they are of rare occurrence, in saying, whether a particular action of our Lord, recorded in the evangelical history, is to be to the letter imitated by us : but there can be no difficulty in the case before us ; for the mode of conduct referred to is just the natural expression of those great principles of love to God, and love to man, by which, in common with Christ, all Christians should be animated and guided ; and we have the express declaration of an inspired writer, that in submitting to undeserved suffering, and in enduring it patiently and piously, it was the intention of our Lord to exhibit to his people a picture of the trials which they might expect to meet with, and a pattern of the manner in which they ought to sustain these trials. This fact of itself sufficiently shows that Christians, then, are bound not only to admire, but to imitate, their Lord, in meekly and piously submitting to undeserved suffering.

This is made still more evident by the second general principle laid down in the text. To this meek, pious submission to suffering, in imitation to Christ, Christians are expressly called. To this "hereunto are ye called," that is, when you were called to be Christians, you were distinctly told that you would meet with suffering, with undeserved suffering, and that you would be expected to bear it in a meek, pious spirit. What says our Lord ? "If any man will be my disciple, let him deny himself, take up his cross, and follow me." "If the world hate you, ye know that it hated me before it hated you. If ye were of the world, the world would love its own ; but because ye are not of the world, but I have chosen you out of the world, therefore the world hateth you. Remember the word which I said unto you, the servant is not greater than his Lord ; if they have persecuted me, they will persecute you : if they have kept my saying,

they will keep yours also. In the world ye shall have tribulation. These things have I spoken to you, that ye should
not be offended," stumbled when they come to pass:
thinking it strange, as if some strange thing had happened
to you. " Behold I tell you before." [1] And what say the
Apostles ? They assure Christians that it is " through much
tribulation that they are to enter into the kingdom ;" and that
" all who will," who are determined to, " live godly in this
world, must suffer persecution." They bid them " count it
all joy when they are brought into manifold trials ;" tell
them that it is needful that they " for a season be in heaviness through these manifold trials ;" caution them against
counting fiery trials strange things, and exhort them when
they meet with them to " rejoice that they are partakers of Christ's sufferings." And as to the manner in which
these afflictions are to be borne, this is their calling : " Let
patience have its perfect work." " Humble yourselves under
the mighty hand of God." " Be patient, stablish your
hearts, for the coming of the Lord draweth nigh." [2]

Having thus shortly illustrated, the facts stated, Christ
suffered, he suffered undeservedly, he suffered patiently, he
suffered piously ; and the general principles stated, In thus
meekly and piously enduring, undeserved suffering, Christ
has set an example to his followers which they should
imitate ; and, To this imitation of Christ's example in meek,
pious, endurance of undeserved suffering, they are expressly
called ; we proceed to show the bearing that the two,
taken in connexion, have on the enforcement of the duty
which the Apostle is here enjoining on Christian servants in
peculiar circumstances. As there is nothing either in the
duty enjoined, or in the motives enforcing it, peculiar to the
situation of servants, as both are equally applicable to all
Christians when exposed to undeserved suffering from their
fellow men, it may serve a good purpose, in the succeeding
observations, to treat the subject in this more extended view.

[1] John xv. 18-20 ; xvii. 33.
[2] Acts xiv. 22. 2 Tim. iii. 12. 1 Pet. i. 6 ; iv. 12, 13. James i. 4. 1 Pet. v. 6.

It clearly follows, from the facts stated, and the principles laid down, that Christians need not wonder, and ought not to be discouraged, when they meet with undeserved suffering from the world; that they should be careful that all the sufferings they are exposed to from the world be indeed undeserved sufferings; and that they ought to submit to these undeserved sufferings in a spirit of meek forgiveness towards those who inflict them, and of humble, hopeful resignation to HIM by whose appointment they are subjected to them.

I observe, then, in the first place, that Christians need not wonder, and ought not to be discouraged, when they meet with undeserved sufferings from the world. Christ suffered—suffered without deserving suffering—suffered from those from whom kindness, not injury, was deserved. If Christ thus suffered, is it strange that Christians should thus suffer? So far as they deserve the name, they are like Christ; they have his Spirit; they speak like him; they act like him. The world in the midst of which they live is substantially the same as the world in the midst of which he lived. How can they expect, then, to be otherwise treated in it, or by it, than he was? Can they deserve ill usage less than he did? Can they deserve kindness more than he did? What is the unreasonableness and unkindness implied in treating even the best of them ill, compared with that implied in treating him ill? This ill treatment by the world, without a good reason, is one of the proofs that we belong to Christ. If the world love us out and out, it is a proof that we are its own; for the world thus loves none but its own. " Can the Christian choose but to have the same common friends and enemies with his Lord? Could he be gratified with the friendship of that world which hated and murdered his Master, and, if he was here, would hate and murder him over again? Would he have nothing but kindness and ease, where Christ had nothing but enmity and trouble? Would he not rather refuse and disdain to be so unlike the Lord?"

" There is a family on earth
    Whose Father fills a throne;
But, though a seed of heavenly birth,
    On earth they 're little known.
Where'er they meet the public eye,
    They feel the public scorn;
For men their fairest claims deny,
    And count them basely born.

" But 'tis the King who reigns above
    That claims them for his own,—
The favour'd objects of his love,
    And destin'd to a throne.
Were honours evident to sense
    Their portion here below,
The world would do them reverence,
    And all their claims allow.

" But, when the King himself was here,
    His claims were set at nought;—
Would they another lot prefer?
    Rejected be the thought.
No; they will tread, while here below,
    The path their Master trod—
Content all honour to forego
    But that which comes from God." [1]

I remark, in the second place, that Christians should be careful that all the sufferings they are exposed to from the world be indeed undeserved sufferings. Christ suffered for us, not for himself: " He did no sin, no guile was found in his mouth." His sufferings were in the sense we have already explained, undeserved sufferings; and in thus suffering, he set us an example, that we should follow his steps. Every sufferer has not fellowship with Christ in his sufferings. He who brings suffering on himself by his folly and sin, manifests not likeness, but unlikeness to the Saviour. He does not follow in his steps. He travels in a different, in an opposite, path from that in which he travels. A Christian has fellowship with Christ in his sufferings, "fills up what is behind of the sufferings of the Lord Jesus," [2]

---

[1] Kelly.   [2] Col. i. 24.

only when his sufferings are like Christ's, "sufferings for righteousness sake," or at any rate sufferings unprovoked, undeserved. All suffering as coming from God is deserved. The holiest man on earth, though he should be the most afflicted, is punished less than his iniquities deserve. But Christians must take care that, so far as men are concerned, their sufferings are undeserved snfferings. Christian servants, who have froward masters, are to take care that if buffetted, they be not buffetted for their faults. Christians must take care that however much evil their enemies may do them, they may have no evil thing to say truly of them. They must so conduct themselves as that their enemies, like Daniel's, shall not be able to find any thing against them, "except concerning the law of their God."[1] None of them must "suffer as a murderer, or a thief, or an evil doer, or even as a busy body in other men's matters." When they suffer, let it be as Christians, innocently, undeservedly. Then will they have no cause to be ashamed, but rather to "glorify God on this behalf." Being "partakers of Christ's sufferings they may well rejoice, for when his glory is revealed, they shall be glad also with exceeding joy."[2]

I observe, in the third place, that Christians should submit to the undeserved sufferings to which they are exposed in a meek, patient, forgiving spirit. When Christ suffered, not on his own account, when he suffered undeservedly, having done no sin, no guile having been found in his mouth, "when reviled, he did not revile again, when he suffered, he threatened not," and in this he hath "set us an example, that we should follow his steps." We do not act like Christians, for we do not act like Christ, when we make the fact that our sufferings are undeserved an excuse for impatience under them, or revengeful thoughts and wishes in reference to their authors. Christians only then can be said to have fellowship with Christ in their undeserved suf-

---

[1] Dan. vi. 5.   [2] 1 Pet. iv. 13.

ferings, when they endure them, as he endured his, and requires them to endure theirs. When they "love their enemies, do good to them that hate them, bless them that curse them, and pray for them who persecute them and despitefully use them;" when they do not seek to avenge themselves, when they are not "overcome of evil, but overcome evil with good;"[1] such is the course Christians should follow, for such is the law, such the example of their Lord. And there is an additional reason, very touchingly urged by the Apostle, in his Epistle to Titus, why they should thus be "gentle, showing all meekness to all men," even those who are most unreasonably unjust and wicked to them, "for they themselves were sometime foolish, disobedient, deceived, serving divers lusts and pleasures, living in malice and envy, hateful, and hating one another."[2]

I observe, in the last place, Christians should patiently endure the unmerited sufferings to which they are exposed, in a spirit of pious resignation. Christ, when he personally submitted to undeserved sufferings, "committed himself to Him who judgeth righteously," and in this too he hath "set us an example that we should follow his steps." In his sufferings he saw the appointment of his Father. However unjust these sufferings were as coming from man, they were just as coming from him. They were the expression of holy displeasure at the sins of men, whose place he, by his own most voluntary consent, occupied. In number and severity they were just what He willed them to be; he believed He would sustain him under them, deliver him from them, and make them the means of fully accomplishing him as the Captain of Salvation, and he committed himself unreservedly into HIS hands, persuaded that He would do all things well.

In like manner Christians are to see in the men of the world who treat them unjustly and unkindly, "the hand," "the staff," "the rod" of Jehovah; and of all the afflictions produced by their instrumentality to say, "This cometh

---

[1] Matt. v. 44. Rom. xii. 21.　　　　　[2] Tit. iii. 2.

forth from the Lord of Hosts, wonderful in counsel, excellent in working." They are to recollect that though they have not deserved this, though they may have deserved the very reverse from those who maltreat them, they deserve this, far more than this, at the hand of God : " It is of his mercies that they are not consumed." They are to remember that both as creatures and redeemed creatures, he has an undoubted right entirely to manage their affairs. They are to believe that he orders all things well and wisely; that he " will not suffer them to be tried above what they are able to bear ; " that he will sustain them under their afflictions ; that he will make them work together for their good ; work out for them " a far more exceeding and an eternal weight of glory." And under the influence of these convictions, they, when suffering according to the will of God, like their Lord who, when suffering according to the will of God, " committed himself to Him who judgeth righteously," are to " commit the keeping of their souls to God in well-doing, as unto a faithful Creator." [1] Thus have I endeavoured to bring out the force of the motive to patient endurance of undeserved suffering on the part of Christians, grounded on that example of our Lord, to the imitation of which they are called in their high and holy calling.

2. *Christians called to patient suffering, as a constituent part of that holiness, to secure which was a great end of Christ's expiatory sufferings.*

But the Apostle represents our Lord's sufferings not only as exemplary, but also as expiatory ; and he represents them in the latter, as well as the former aspect, as affording powerful motives to the performance of the duties which he is enjoining. He not only says, perform the duty of patient pious endurance of undeserved suffering, " for hereunto were ye called, because Christ also suffered for you, leaving us an example, that we should follow his steps ; " but also, perform

---

[1] Isa. viii. 5.   Psal. xvii. 14.   1 Cor. x. 13.   2 Cor. iv. 17.   1 Pet. iv. 19.

this duty, " for hereunto were ye called, because Christ also suffered for you, bearing himself your sins in his own body on the tree." " That Jesus Christ is in doing and suffering our supreme and matchless example, and that he came to be so, is a truth; but that he is nothing further, and came for no other end, is a high point of falsehood : for how should man be enabled to learn and follow that example, unless there was more in Christ; and what would become of that great reckoning of disobedience that man stands guilty of? No, these are too narrow. He came to bear our sins in his own body on the tree ; a body prepared for him, and given to him to bear this burden, to do this as the will of the Father, to stand for us in the room of all offerings and sacrifices. And by that will, says the Apostle, we are sanctified, by the offering of the body of Christ once for all." [1]

To explain the statement made by the Apostle respecting the sufferings of Christ, viewed as expiatory, and to show its force as a motive to the discharge of the duties which he is enjoining, are the objects I have in view in the remaining part of this discourse.

The statement made by the Apostle naturally divides itself into three parts : When Christ suffered for us he himself bore our sins in his own body on the tree; when he thus suffered, it was, that we being dead to sin, should live unto righteousness; and the effect of this is that we are healed by his stripes : we, who were like sheep going astray, are thus brought back to the Shepherd and Bishop of souls. The first part of the statement describes the nature ; the second, the design ; the third, the consequences, of our Lord's sufferings for us. Let us attend to these important topics in their order.

And, first, let us attend to the account which the text gives us of the NATURE of our Lord's sufferings. When he suffered for us, " he himself bare our sins in his own body on

---

[1] Leighton.

the tree." These words plainly intimate that the sufferings of our Lord were *penal*, that is, they were the manifestation of the displeasure of God against sin : when he suffered, " he bare sin ;" that they were *vicarious*, that is, they were the manifestation of the displeasure of God against the sin, not of the sufferer, but of men in whose place he stood, for he had no sin ; " he bare our sins :" and that they were *expiatory ;* that is, they were intended for, and effectual for, the purpose of expiating, or making atonement for the sins on account of which they were inflicted, laying a foundation for the pardon of their sins in a way consistent with the perfections of the Divine character and the principles of the Divine government. He bare them that he might bear them away.

I need not say that " the tree" here means the cross, the accursed tree, just as we call the gibbet, the fatal tree. I am not sure that our version of these words, " he bare our sins on the tree," fully and exactly brings out the Apostle's idea. The thought which the English words naturally suggest is this, Christ bare our sins *on* the cross. He suffered the penalty of our sins, and made expiation for them when he was crucified, and by being crucified. Now crucifixion, and the sufferings endured during crucifixion, were no doubt a part of the penalty of our sins, a part of the price of our salvation, but they were only a part of it. The inward agony of Gethsemane, equally with the pain and the shame of Calvary, was the payment of the ransom of man. The whole of our Lord's sufferings, from the moment he became capable of suffering, till the moment he became incapable of suffering, when on the cross he gave up the ghost, were that adequate expression of the Divine displeasure against sin, which reconciles the exercise of mercy with the claims of justice ; and he as really, though not so obviously, bare our sins when he lay a helpless infant, in the manger in Bethlehem, as when he hung, an agonized man, on the accursed tree. The words admit, perhaps require, certainly have received, from some of the ablest scholars and the soundest divines, a slightly different rendering, which brings out this important truth :

"He himself bare our sins in his own body *to* the tree."[1]
It is the same word that in the verse before us is rendered
on, that in the following verse is rendered *to*, "Ye are returned *to* the Shepherd and Bishop of souls." This, then,
we apprehend, is the Apostle's statement, "He himself bare
our sins in his own body *to* the tree."

There are two questions which must be answered in order
to our fully apprehending the meaning of these words:
What are we to understand by our Lord, when he suffered
for us, "bearing our sins to the tree? and what is the
import of the phrase "He himself in his own body" bare
our sins to the tree?

Let us then enquire, what we are to understand by our
Lord's bearing our sins to the cross. Our sins are represented here as a burden which had been laid on our Lord,
and which he bore to the cross, where he got rid of the
burden. Now, what are we to understand by "our sins?"
What by their being laid on our Lord? What by his
bearing them, bearing them to the cross?

"Our sins" here are our liabilities to punishment on account of our violations of the Divine law, and the necessary
consequences of these liabilities; in other words, guilt in the
sense of binding over to punishment, and punishment itself.
"Our sins," meaning by that phrase our acts of violation of
the Divine law, cannot by any power, not even that of God,
be transferred from us and laid on another. It must always
be true that we committed them. It never can be true that
another committed them. Neither can our sinfulness, our
culpability, our blameworthiness, in committing those acts
be removed from us or transferred to another. It must
always be true that *we*, we alone, were to blame for our
violation of the Divine law. It never can be true that in
this sense our guilt can be transferred to another; but liability to punishment, and the punishment to which we are

---

Επι το ξυλον.   *Vide* Robinson on Επι. iii. 6. (α) and (β).   Mat. iii. 13; xii. 28;
xxii. 34.   Acts. iv. 26.   Luke iii. 2.   2 Thess. i. 10.   1 Pet. iii. 12.   Answering
to the Heb. אל. Psal. xxxiv. 16. Sep.

liable, may be transferred from us, and laid on another, and the statement in the text obviously goes on the supposition that "our sins," in this sense, were laid on our Lord Jesus Christ.

Now what do we mean when we say that our sins in this sense were laid on Christ? We mean, that by a Divine appointment, Jesus Christ, the incarnate Son, the God-man, was, with his own most free consent, subjected to the liabilities to punishment which man's sins had incurred; and to the punishment, that is, to the evils manifestative of the Divine displeasure at the sin of man, which necessarily rose out of these liabilities. This is the truth which is taught us when it is said, that when "we all like lost sheep had gone astray, and had turned every one to his own way," God made to meet on his righteous servant "the iniquities," the ill deserts, the liabilities to punishment, "of us all." And the consequence was, "exaction was made." *He* not *we* became answerable; and "it pleased the Lord to bruise *him*," and "he was wounded for our transgressions, and bruised for our iniquities." The same truth is stated, when it is said, "God sent forth his Son, made of a woman, made under the law;" and when it is said "God made him who knew no sin, to be sin for us;" *sin* there meaning, a guilty person not in the sense of a culpable person, but a person, by a Divine appointment, liable to evils manifesting the Divine displeasure against sin, just as *righteousness* in the antithetical clause means a righteous person, a person standing clear of all claims for punishment at the hand of the Divine law, and enjoying the acceptance of the Supreme Lawgiver. It is still the same idea, when it is said, "Christ became a curse," that is, accursed, doomed to endure evils which the law denounces against transgressors, "for us," in our room, who were "a curse," accursed, doomed to punishment. Laying our sins on our Lord, is the same thing as what is ordinarily expressed by imputing our sins to him.[1]

---

[1] Isa. liii. 4-7.   2 Cor. v. 21.   Gal. iii. 13.   It is an acute remark of CAMERO:—" Si quis dicat ' Christum pro nobis factum esse peccatum et maledictum' idem certo dicitur formaliter, sed significandi modus et considerandi

Now, if we distinctly apprehend what is meant by laying our sins on Jesus Christ, we can have no difficulty in understanding what is meant by his bearing or carrying these sins. It means that as he, by Divine appointment, stood in our room, he incurred our liabilities, he was exposed to, and actually endured evils which we had deserved, and which were the expression of the Divine displeasure against our evil deserts ; and that all the multiplied and multifarious evils that he was exposed to, were the consequence of his, by Divine appointment, occupying this place, and being charged with these liabilities.

This fearful load of responsibility and of suffering our Lord " bare to the cross." The cross was the term of his humbled life and of his vicarious endurance. The words before us, are substantially equivalent to, " he became obedient unto death, even the death of the cross."[1] He continued obedient, till he had exhausted all the demands of the law on him, as the victim of human transgression, in offering up to God his completed sacrifice. He " carried our sins " during the whole of his humbled state; and still laden with them, he submitted to be nailed to the cross, in its shame, and agonies, and unknown conflicts, consummating the great work of expiation; and in his dead body hanging on it, intimating, according to the statute of the Mosaic law, " cursed is every one that hangeth on a tree," that he had been liable to the vengeance of public justice, and that he had now fully paid the debt with which he had been charged, " restored that which he had not taken away."

He carried our " liabilities to the tree :" they were there crucified with him : they expired with him : they were buried with him. He rose again, but they did not : they are buried for ever in his grave. " It is finished," said the Saviour; and the Supreme Ruler nailed the bond, which

---

diversus est; nam cum Christus dicitur factus esse pro nobis *peccatum* notatur relatio et σχεσις pœnæ ad culpam, cum vero dicitur *maledictum* notatur pœna simpliciter."—Opera, p. 518.

[1] Phil. ii. 8. Μεχρι θανατου, θανατου δε σταυρου.

had been fully paid, to the cross. " The handwriting which had been against us was blotted out for ever." He thus finished the work which the Father gave him to do. He completely did his will, in " the offering of his body once for all." He " finished transgression, made an end of sin, and put away sin by the sacrifice of himself."[1] So much for the import of the expression, Christ has borne our sins to the cross.

Let us now, in a sentence or two, unfold the import of the somewhat peculiar phraseology : " He, *his own self,* bare our sins *in his own body* to the tree." There is here, I apprehend, a tacit contrast between our Lord and the Levitical priesthood. Aaron and his sons are said to bear the iniquity of the congregation, to make atonement for them before the Lord :[2] but this they did, not by presenting themselves victims, but by presenting, as the representatives of the people, the sacrifices on which the sins of the congregation had been laid: they did not lay themselves, but these sacrifices, on the altar. But Jesus " Christ being come, a High Priest of good things to come, not by the blood of bulls or of goats, but by his own blood, obtained eternal redemption for us : He purged our sins by himself." He carried them in his own person to the altar of justice ; and by his own sufferings and death, made expiation for them. " He offered *himself,* without spot, to God."[3] It was this which gave efficacy to his sacrifice. It was because it was " He himself," the Only-Begotten of God, " in his own body ;" in a human nature, infinitely dignified by connexion with the Divine, prepared for him for this very purpose, to suffer, and die in our room, that he was able to carry our sins, even to the cross ; and by bearing them there, to bear them away completely and for ever. The meaning of the whole passage may be summed up in these words : Jesus Christ, being the Son of God, has, by his vicarious sufferings and death, fully expiated the sins of men.

[1] John xix. 30.   Col. ii. 14.   Dan. ix. 24.   Heb. x. 9, 10; ix. 26.
[2] Lev. x. 17.   [3] Heb. ix. 11, 12, 14.

Let us now turn our mind a little, to the account here given us, of the DESIGN of our Lord's expiatory sufferings. " Christ bare our sins in his own body on the tree, that we, being dead to sins, might live unto righteousness." It has been usual to consider these words as meaning, that Christ expiated our sins, that we, through the influence of his Spirit (a channel for the communication of which is opened up by the atonement), " having died to sin," that is, having been delivered from the love of sin, having had our sinful propensities mortified, may live a holy life, such a life as is consistent with righteousness, such a life as the righteous law of God demands. The passage has been considered as exactly parallel with the declaration, that " Christ gave himself for us, that he might redeem us from all iniquity, and purify unto himself a peculiar people, zealous of good works."[1] A closer examination of the passage will persuade us, that the Apostle's meaning is somewhat different from this.

There can be no reasonable doubt, that the " sins" to which Christians are represented as dead, through the expiatory sufferings of Christ, are the very same " sins" which, in these expiatory sufferings, He bare and bare away. Now, we have seen, those " sins" are liabilities to punishment. The direct reference, then, is not to the depraving power, but to the condemning power, of sin, which is the source, the foundation, of its depraving power. To be " dead to sins," is to be delivered from the condemning power of sin ; or, in other words, from the condemning sentence of the law, under which, if a man lies, he cannot be holy ; and from which, if a man is delivered, his holiness is absolutely secured. " To live unto righteousnes," is plainly just the positive view of that, of which " to be dead to sins" is the negative view. ' Righteousness,' when opposed to ' sin,' in the sense of guilt or liability to punishment, as it very often is in the writings of the Apostle Paul, is descriptive of a state of justification. A state of guilt is a state of condem-

---

[1] Tit. ii. 14.

nation by God; a state of righteousness is a state of acceptance with God. To live unto righteousness, is in this case to
live under the influence of a justified state, a state of acceptance with God; and the Apostle's statement is: Christ
Jesus, by his sufferings unto death, completely answered
the demands of the law on us, by bearing, and bearing away
our sins, that we, believing in him, and thereby being united
to him, might be as completely freed from our liabilities to
punishment, as if we, in our own person, not he himself, in
his own body, had undergone them; and that we might as
really be brought into a state of righteousness, justification,
acceptance with God, as if we, not he, in his obedience to
death, had magnified the law, and made it honourable; and
that thus delivered from the demoralizing influence of a
state of guilt and condemnation, and subjected to the sanctifying influence of a state of justification and acceptance,
we might " serve God, not in the oldness of the letter, but in
the newness of the Spirit;" "Serving him without fear;"
" Walking at liberty, keeping his commandments."

The sentiment of the Apostle is the same as that which
his " beloved brother Paul, according to the wisdom given
him," states and illustrates more fully in the first part of
the sixth chapter of the Epistle to the Romans; where he
shows us, that Christians are by faith united to Christ, as
dying, dead, raised again; and that the moral transformation
of their character, is the natural and necessary result of
their being, as it were, united to Christ in his dying, and in
his rising, and in his new life.[1]

The ultimate design of the atonement, in reference to
man, is to form him to a holy character; but its direct
design, with a reference to this, is to bring him out of a state
of guilt and condemnation, into a state of pardon and
acceptance. Had not Christ died, men could not have been
pardoned; and man remaining unpardoned, must have
remained unsanctified. Since Christ has died, the man who

[1] Rom. vi. 1-14.

by faith is interested in the expiatory efficacy of his sufferings and death, is restored to the Divine favour; and if
restored to the Divine favour, must, in the enjoyment of the
influence of the Holy Spirit, the communication of which is
the great proof of the Divine favour, be conformed to the
Divine image. The tendency of the expiatory sufferings of
Christ to gain their design, must be obvious to every one,
who reflects, that they removed otherwise insurmountable
obstacles in the way of man's holiness; that they opened up
a way for the communication of that influence, which is at
once necessary and sufficient to make men holy; and that,
as a display of the Divine character, and the subject of a
plain, well-accredited revelation, they furnish the fit instrumentality for the Holy Spirit to employ, in making men
holy. These are but hints on a subject, which would
require a volume to do justice to; but if followed out, they
will be found to give important lights in the investigation
of the principles of Christian doctrine, and in the guidance
of the exercises of Christian experience.

Let us now attend to the account here given of the
EFFECTS of the expiatory sufferings of our Lord. "By his
stripes ye are healed;" and though "ye were as sheep going
astray, ye are returned to the Shepherd and Bishop of your
souls." The effects of the atonement on those who, by
faith, are interested in its saving efficacy, are described by
two instructive figures: the healing of diseased persons, and
the reclaiming of lost sheep; both of them borrowed from
the liii. chapter of the Prophecy of Isaiah, to which also the
Apostle refers, when speaking of our Lord bearing our sins.

"By His stripes ye are healed." Sin is often represented
in Scripture as a disease. It makes men miserable in themselves, useless, sometimes loathsome, often dangerous to
others; and its natural and certain termination, if allowed
to run its course, is death, the second death, eternal death.
Various, endlessly-various methods, have been invented for
curing this disease. The best of them are mere palliatives.
The only effectual cure is that here mentioned: "the

stripes" of the righteous servant of God. This is a cure
which it never could have entered into the mind of man to
conceive; and even when made known, it seems foolishness
to the wisdom of this world: the disease of one man healed
by the stripes of another! the death of Jesus on a cross,
the means of making men holy and happy! Yet so it is:
"The foolishness of God is wiser than men; and the weakness of God stronger than men."[1]

Man's disease is a very deep-rooted one. It arises out of
the circumstances in which he is placed. It has affected
the inmost springs of life, and it discovers itself by an endless variety of external symptoms. The "stripes" of the
Great Physician answers all these peculiarities. The expiatory sufferings of Christ, when the sinner believes, change
his state. They take him out of the pestilential region of
the Divine curse, and translate him into the health-breath-
ing region of Divine favour. In the Divine influences, for
which they open the way, is given a powerful principle of
health, which penetrates into the very first springs of
thought, and feeling, and action; and in the views which
these sufferings give us of the holy benignant character of
God, the malignity of sin, the vanity of the world, the importance of eternity, there are furnished, as it were, remedies
fitted to meet and remove all the various external symptoms
of this worst of diseases.

This was not a matter of speculation, but of experience,
with those to whom Peter was writing. " By his stripes ye
are healed." You were once depraved and miserable; you are
now comparatively holy and happy: and you know how the
change was effected. It was by the expiatory sufferings of
Jesus Christ: His stripes have healed you.

The same truth is brought before the mind under another
figure, in the words that follow: " Ye were as sheep going
astray: but ye are returned to the Shepherd and Bishop of
your souls." The natural state of mankind is like that of

strayed sheep. It is a state of error, of want, of perplexity,
of dissatisfaction, of danger. It is a state that gives no
promise of improvement. The strayed sheep, if left to itself,
will wander farther and farther from the fold, till it perish
of hunger, fall over the precipice, or be devoured by the
wild beast. Such is the state of all men by nature; but
all true Christians have, like those to whom the Apostle was
writing, "returned to the Shepherd and Bishop,"[1] that is,
overseer " of your souls." They have been reclaimed from
their wanderings, and have found peace and security, the
green pasture of heavenly truth, the still waters of heavenly
consolation, under the care of Him who is the good Shepherd, the kind, faithful Overseer of souls.

And how were they brought back? It was by the expiatory sufferings of their Saviour. "The good Shepherd
laid down his life for the sheep."[2] Without this, they could
not have been reclaimed. It is the voice of his blood; the
blood "that speaketh better things than that of Abel;"[3]
that penetrates their hearts and leads them to return. It is
his love and his Father's, manifested in these sufferings,
when apprehended and believed, that brings them near him,
and keeps them near him. Every Christian knows this.

It is an excellent use which one of the greatest of the
fathers[4] would have us to make of this statement : " We
were as sheep going astray : but are returned to the Shepherd and Bishop of souls." " Let us not despair of those who
yet wander, but rather, earnestly pray for them. We once
wandered as well as they ; the grace which brought us back
can bring them back. The numbers of the saints are to be
increased from among the unholy. Those who to-day are
goats may be sheep to-morrow ; and the tares of to-day may

---

[1] The use of the word Bishop, appropriated, as it now is in the English language, to a particular ecclesiastical officer, of whom the New Testament knows
nothing—the Diocesan Hierarch of the Papal and Anglican churches—is here
obviously improper ; and were not our ears familiar to it, would be even
ludicrous.

[2] John x. 11.   [3] Heb. xii. 24.   [4] Augustine.

to-morrow be good grain. With God, through Christ, nothing is impossible."

Having thus very cursorily considered the Apostle's statement respecting the nature, design, and effects of our Lord's sufferings, viewed as expiatory, let us now still more cursorily show the force of this statement considered as a motive to those duties which in this paragraph he is enjoining. Did Jesus Christ, God's Son, bare our sins? Was he treated, both by God and man, as if he had sinned? Did he bear our sins in his body to the cross, patiently enduring all that was necessary to their expiation? Is it not, then, reasonable and right that we should devote ourselves *to* him who devoted himself *for* us? Should we not patiently do and suffer whatever he calls us to do and suffer? If he, to expiate our sins, voluntarily took upon himself "the form of a servant," and in that form submitted to such toil and suffering, should not his people who, in the course of providence, are placed in the situation of servants, from a regard to Him, cheerfully do the duties and submit to the hardships to which they may be exposed? Did he expiate our sins, "that we, being dead to sin, might live unto righteousness?" that we might be freed from the irritating, demoralising influence of a state of condemnation, and be subjected to the tranquillising, sanctifying influences of a state of pardon and acceptance with God? Should not we, then, who profess to believe in him, and through that faith to be interested in these saving effects of his atoning sacrifice, in our cheerfully doing and suffering all the will of God, show that in our case the expiatory sufferings of Christ have, indeed, served their purpose, that we are dead to sin, that we are alive to righteousness? Have the great ends of the atonement been in some degree answered in our experience? Have we obtained some measure of spiritual health and welfare by virtue of the stripes which he received from God and men for our sakes? Surely, then, we should not take in ill part the shame and suffering we may be exposed to, especially that which we meet with on his account, for bearing his name, sustaining his cause.

It is well said by an old Scotch divine : " None can with patience and cheerfulness suffer wrongs for Christ, but they who do by faith apply the virtue of his sufferings for them to their own souls, for the pardoning and subduing of sin, quickening of their hearts in holiness, and healing of their spiritual distempers : which effects of his death are so sweet to them that partake of them, that they cannot but cheerfully endure the worst that men can do against them, rather than do the least thing that may be offensive to him."[1]

Have we, in consequence of the good Shepherd laying down his life for us, been reclaimed from our wanderings, joined to his flock, and blessed with his pastoral care? Should we not, then, entirely resign ourselves to his guidance, and follow him fearlessly and readily through paths, however rugged and thorny, while he is conducting us to his heavenly fold? Should we not have perfect confidence in his love and power, manifested in dying for us, and in reclaiming us from our wanderings, and therefore readily do whatever he commands, because he commands it; cheerfully submit to whatever he appoints, because he appoints it?

Thus have I endeavoured to bring out the meaning and force of the Apostle's statement respecting the nature, design, and effects of the sufferings of Christ, viewed as expiatory, as a motive to Christian duty generally, and especially to the patient endurance of such undeserved suffering as Christians may be exposed to. The practical effect of those powerful motives on our minds and conduct will be proportioned to the degree in which we understand and believe the great fundamental principles of the doctrine of Christian faith on which they are founded; and neglect of, or carelessness in duty, and impatience under affliction, are to be traced to want or weakness of faith in these principles.

Let us, then, not cease to pray, each for himself, and all of us for each other, and " desire that we may be filled with the knowledge of his will in all wisdom and spiritual under-

---

[1] Nisbet.

standing, that we may walk worthy of the Lord unto all pleasing, being fruitful in every good work, and abounding in the knowledge of God : strengthened with all might, according to his glorious power, unto all patience and long-suffering with joyfulness, giving thanks to the Father, who hath made us meet to be partakers of the inheritance of the saints in light : who hath delivered us from the power of darkness, and hath translated us into the kingdom of his dear Son ; in whom we have redemption through his blood, even the forgiveness of sins."[1]

[1] Col. i. 11-14.

DISCOURSE XIV.

THE CONJUGAL DUTIES OF CHRISTIANS ILLUSTRATED AND ENFORCED.

1 Pet. iii. 1-7.—Likewise, ye wives, be in subjection to your own husbands: that, if any obey not the word, they also may without the word be won by the conversation of the wives; while they behold your chaste conversation coupled with fear. Whose adorning, let it not be that outward adorning of plaiting the hair, and of wearing of gold, or of putting on of apparel; but let it be the hidden man of the heart, in that which is not corruptible, even the ornament of a meek and quiet spirit, which is in the sight of God of great price. For after this manner in the old time the holy women also, who trusted in God, adorned themselves, being in subjection unto their own husbands: even as Sarah obeyed Abraham, calling him lord: whose daughters ye are as long as ye do well, and are not afraid with any amazement. Likewise, ye husbands, dwell with them according to knowledge, giving honour unto the wife, as unto the weaker vessel, and as being heirs together of the grace of life; that your prayers be not hindered.

Divine revelation has often been compared to the sun; and it were easy to trace out many striking, pleasing, instructive analogies between these two glorious works of God. To one of these analogies, suggested by that portion of Scripture which now lies before us, I would, for a moment, solicit your attention. The sun, from his high throne in the heavens, diffuses light and heat and genial influence over all the earth, smiling benignantly on the lofty mountain and the humble vale, the populous city and the obscure village, the fertile field and the wilderness, the noble's mansion, with its richly cultivated demesne, and the peasant's cottage, with its surrounding barren waste. "His going forth is from the end of heaven, and his circuit unto the ends of it, and there is nothing hid from the heat thereof."[1]   The sun is a common good.   It is for the world, for all the world.

It is thus, also, with divine truth enshrined in the Bible. It pours forth direction, and motive, and warning, and comfort suited to all men, to men of all countries, all ages, all conditions ; to the young, to the middle aged, and to the old ; to the rich and to the poor, and to those to whom neither poverty nor riches have been given ; to the prosperous and to the afflicted ; to the happy and to the miserable ; to man in the lowest and in the highest station in society and state of civilization ; to the savage and to the sage; to the monarch and to the slave.   It is the moral sun of the world of humanity, shedding pure light, holy influence over the whole of its diversified surface.   No class of men is overlooked ; every individual, however circumstanced, may find suitable instruction here.

In the verses immediately preceding our text, we see the light of inspired truth shining most benignantly on the humble dwelling of the Christian slave, and guiding and sustaining, and cheering him, amid his unmerited sufferings and ill-rewarded toils.   And in the text itself, the sun of righteousness sheds beams full of healing on the very sources of society, in those directions, by complying with which, families might be made the abodes of a tranquil enjoyment and holy happiness, which would lead the mind backward to Eden, and forward to heaven.

The words that lie before us, are a farther illustration of the general injunction given to Christians, to "have their conversation honest among the Gentiles," that is, so to conduct themselves as that even their heathen neighbours should be constrained to approve and respect them.   The manner in which this injunction was to be obeyed, was by a careful performance of relative duties, especially such as they owed to their heathen connexions.   Of the excellence of such a

---

[1] Psal. xix. 6.

course of conduct they were qualified judges, which they were not of the principles of their holy faith, nor of duties of a more strictly religious and Christian character.   All Christians, therefore, were to yield a cheerful, loyal subjection to civil authority, as lodged both in its supreme and subordinate administrators; to cherish and display a becoming respect for all who, on whatever ground, had a claim on their respect; to cultivate and manifest that peculiar regard to the Christian society, which, in Christians, even heathens could not help perceiving to be becoming and proper; and to show a reverence for the supreme civil power, based on, and limited only by, the reverence due to Him who is " King of kings, and Lord of lords."   Such Christians as stood in the relation of servants, especially to heathen masters, were carefully to discharge the duties and submit to the hardships connected with the situation in which they were placed. The natural tendency of such conduct, such " good works," habitually and perseveringly maintained, was to overcome the prejudices of their heathen neighbours, to convince them that they had misapprehended the true character both of their religion, and of themselves; and to constrain those " who spoke against them as evil-doers, to glorify God in the day of visitation."

Another way in which the same desirable object was to be sought, was by those who stood in the relation of husbands and wives, conscientiously discharging the duties which grew out of their union.   And when we reflect on the manner in which the duties of the conjugal relation were neglected and violated among heathens; how much there was of the harshness of the tyrant in the character of the heathen husband, and of the baseness of the slave in the character of the heathen wife; how much pollution and cruelty prevailed, in what should be the sanctuary of purity and love—we cannot help seeing, that few things were more calculated to strike, and to strike favourably, heathen observers, than the exemplification of the genius and power of Christianity, in softening the character of the husband, and elevating, at once, the condition and character of the wife; and in thus giving an order, and purity, and endearment, and enjoyment to the domestic circle, not only beyond what heathen philosophy had accomplished, but beyond what it had ever dreamed of.

Such is the connexion, we apprehend, in which the interesting passage I have read, is introduced; and it contains a brief statement, and a powerful enforcement, of the conjugal duties; first, of the duties of the wife, and then, of the duties of the husband.

The whole of the conjugal duties, like, indeed, all duties, may be and are "summed up in one word, love;" "husbands," says the Apostle Paul, " love your wives;" and the same Apostle commands Titus, to take care "that the aged women teach the young women to love their husbands."[1] But the appropriate form of love, in any particular case, when embodied in action, depends on the relation in which the party who loves stands to the party beloved. Parents are to " love their children," and show that they do so by "bringing them up in the nurture and admonition of the Lord." Children are to "love their parents," and they are to show that they do so, by " being obedient to them in the Lord." Masters are to love their servants, and they are to show this by being kind and considerate in their requisitions and arrangements; and servants are to love their masters, and show that they do so, by being obedient and submissive, diligent and faithful.[2] In the like manner, husbands and wives are to " love one another, with a pure heart fervently;" and they are to manifest that love by a careful performance of the duties which rise out of, and are suited to, the relation in which they respectively stand to each other. What these are, we are told by the Apostle, in the passage before us. The duties of the wives are, subjection, chaste conversation coupled with fear, and an adorning of themselves; which is described, first, negatively, and then posi-

---

[1] Eph. v. 25. Tit. ii. 4.   [2] Eph. vi. 4, 1, 9, 5.

tively; and the motives urging to the performance of these duties are two, first, that thus they might, probably, be the means of converting their heathen husbands; and, secondly, that thus they would follow the example of holy women in former ages. The duties of the husbands are, dwelling with their wives according to knowledge, and giving honour to them; and the motive urging to the performance of these duties are three: first, that the wife is 'the weaker vessel;' secondly, that their wives, as Christians, are, equally with themselves, heirs of the grace of life; and thirdly, that an opposite mode of conduct would hinder their prayers. Let us attend, then, in their order, to these statements and enforcements of the conjugal duties.

PART I.

I. THE DUTIES OF CHRISTIAN WIVES.

And first, of the duties of wives. Their duty is thus stated and enforced, in the first six verses. " Likewise ye wives, be in subjection to your own husbands; that, if any obey not the word, they also may without the word be won by the conversation of the wives; when they behold your chaste conversation coupled with fear: whose adorning, let it not be that outward adorning of plaiting the hair, and of wearing of gold, or of putting on of apparel; but let it be the hidden man of the heart, in that which is not corruptible, even the ornament of a meek and quiet spirit, which is in the sight of God of great price. For after this manner in the old time the holy women also, who trusted in God, adorned themselves, being in subjection to their own husbands: even as Sarah obeyed Abraham, calling him Lord : whose daughters ye are as long as ye do well, and are not afraid with any amazement."

§ 1. *Subjection.*

The first duty of Christian wives, mentioned by the Apostle, is SUBJECTION. " Be in subjection to your own husbands." The Apostle Paul enjoins the same duty in similar terms : " Wives submit yourselves to your own husbands, as to the Lord : Wives submit yourselves unto your own husbands, as is fit in the Lord ;" and he commands Titus, in " speaking the things that become sound doctrine," to exhort " that the aged women teach the young women to be obedient to their own husbands."[1] I believe, that in the conjugal relation, matters are best managed when there is little display, or assertion of superiority, or rule, on the part of the husband, but where the spouses " submit themselves one to another, in the fear of God."[2] There can, however, be no doubt, that God, both as the God of nature, and the God of revelation, has distinctly indicated that the rule of the domestic society is vested in the husband. Hear the declarations of Scripture : " Adam was first formed, and then Eve. The man is not of the woman, but the woman of the man. The man was not created for the woman, but the woman for the man. The Lord said, it is not good for man to be alone, I will make him a helpmeet for him. The man is the image and glory of God, but the woman is the glory of the man." Even in a state of innocence the husband had rule ; and after the introduction of sin, of which the Apostle gives this account, " Adam was not deceived, but the woman being deceived, was in the transgression," the Divine will was then declared : " And to the woman he said, Thy desire shall be to thy husband, and he shall rule over thee."[3]

This appointment is in entire concurrence with sound reason and true expediency. " In all communities, if there is to be order and peace, there must be rule. There can be no happiness without peace, no peace without order, no order without subordination, no subordination without subjection. Perpetual strife would arise from equality, or contested superiority."[4] To secure the advantages of society in all its forms, authority must be established, and submission

---

[1] Eph. v. 22. Col. iii. 18. Tit. ii. 5.　　　　　　　[2] Eph. v. 21.
[3] 1 Tim. ii. 13. 1 Cor. xi. 7-9. Gen. ii. 23. Tim. ii. 14. Gen. iii. 16.
[4] Jay.

enjoined.   The only question in such a case is, where should
the authority be lodged?   And in the case of the domestic
society it would seem that the question admitted only of one
answer.

The subjection of the wife is extensive, but by no means
unlimited.   It is subjection " in the Lord ;" such a subjection as becomes a Christian woman who feels her own
responsibilities to the One Master in heaven.   " His authority is primitive, and binds fast ;" as Leighton says, " All
Christians have their patents and privileges from him.   He
therefore is supremely and absolutely to be obeyed by all."
Besides, " it is not the submission of slaves to their master, or
of subjects to their sovereign, or of children to their father.   It
is a subjection that has more of equality in it, accords with
the idea of a helper, a companion and a friend ; springs originally from choice, and is acquiesced in for the sake of propriety and advantage."[1]   It has been very justly remarked,
" Whatever bitterness there is in this subjection arises from
the corruption of nature in both parties : in the wife a perverse desire rather to command, or at least a repining disinclination to obey ; and this increased by the disorder and im-
prudence and harshness of the husband in the use of his authority.   But in a Christian woman, the conscience of
divine authority, will carry it, and weigh down all difficulties, for the wife considers her station.   She is set in it ;
it is the rank the Lord's hand has placed her in, and
therefore she will not break it.   Out of respect and love to
him, she can digest much frowardness of a husband, and
make her patient subjection an offering to God.   ' Lord I
offer this to thee.   For thy sake I humbly bear it.' "[2]

It is a happy thing when the personal excellence of a
husband makes submission a compliance with inclination ;
but a Christian woman, even when her husband is not so
wise or reasonable in his requisitions and arrangements as
she could wish, yet, because by God's providence, he is her

---

[1] Jay.   [2] Leighton.

own husband, and God's command is to be subject to her own husband, she is subject to the marital authority, not only "for wrath, but for conscience sake." Such conduct is acceptable to God, and generally draws down tokens of his approbation. By following this course, many a woman has spent a life of respectability and usefulness, who, by acting otherwise, would neither have been respectable nor useful; and many a family has been a scene of order and peace, where otherwise there would have been nothing but confusion and every evil work. Besides, it is the submissive wife who generally gets most of her own will.[1]

§ 2.—" *Chaste conversation coupled with fear.*"

The second duty of Christian wives, mentioned by the Apostle, is "chaste conversation coupled with fear." Conversation here, and uniformly in the Scriptures, does not signify mutual talk, colloquial intercourse, familiar discourse, but habitual conduct, manner of life. Chaste conversation means much more than abstinence from gross vice, direct violation of the seventh commandment; actual infraction of the marriage covenant. Indeed such things were not even to be named among Christians. The reference is rather to an avoidance of every thing that has even the appearance of an approximation, to the indulgence or display of sentiments and feelings, inconsistent with that purity of mind, that chastity of heart, which the Christian law requires. There is, as has been justly observed, an audacity of countenance, a boldness of look, a levity of discourse, a freedom of manners, a forwardness of behaviour, a challenging, obtrusive, advancing air, very unbecoming the sacred decorum which should mark the character of Christian females. Their conduct must be such as to awe the licentious and keep them at a distance; and their language must be free of all foolish talking and jesting, which is not convenient, does not suit with their character and profession, as holy women. " Diffi-

---

[1] Casta ad virum matrona parendo imperat.—PUBLIUS SYRUS.

dence, the blushings of reserve, the tremulous retiring of modesty ; the sensation that comes from the union of innocence and danger ; the prudence which keeps far from the limits of permission ; the instructive vigilance which discerns danger afar off; the caution which never allows the enemy to approach near enough, even to reconnoitre,"[1]—all this, which virtuous women understand far better than any man can describe it to them, is included in chaste conversation.

This " chaste conversation" is to be " coupled with fear." Some suppose that fear here is respect to their husbands ; others that it is that timidity which I have just noticed. I rather think that here, as at the 18th verse of the preceding chapter, "fear" is the fear of God, reverence for the divine authority, fear of the divine displeasure. Their chastity, like all their virtues, was to have a religious character, to be based on faith, and sustained and nourished by those principles which naturally spring from faith of the truth respecting the divine character. Genuine religion is the grand security of all the virtues ; and it was of importance that these Christian wives of heathen husbands should make it plain that their chaste behaviour, which their husbands could not but appreciate, was the result of that religion which they neglected or opposed.

§ 3. *The adorning themselves with inward ornaments.*

The third duty enjoined on Christian wives refers to the manner in which they were to adorn themselves : " Whose adorning let it not be that outward adorning of plaiting the hair, and of wearing of gold, or of putting on of apparel ;[2] but let it be the hidden man of the heart, in that which is not corruptible, even the ornament of a meek and quiet spirit, which is in the sight of God of great price." The love of ornament belongs to the species ; but it is a prin-

---

[1] Jay.

[2] Ενδυσις ἱματιων. Lyra gives an odd reason for the use of the plural here :—
"Solent enim feminæ TOT induere vestes, TOTQUE tunicis, peplis, palliis, iisque sericis, byssinis, preciosis et sumptuosis se ornare ut unius ornatus, multis feminis sufficere possit."

ciple peculiarly strong in the female part of it. That a
maid should forget her ornaments, or a bride her attire,
is spoken of by the inspired writer as a very unlikely thing.[1]
There is nothing wrong in this principle in itself. It serves
important purposes. Its want is felt as a serious draw-
back. A sloven is disagreeable, a slattern intolerable;
Christianity makes no war with any thing in any of man's
natural principles but their abuse. Its object is not to ex-
tirpate them, but to prune them, to train them, to make
them yield good fruit. Thus it is with the love of ornament, which is natural to the female mind. The Apostle
gives directions as to the guidance and regulation of this
principle. These are both negative and positive. Let us
look at them in succession.

The negative direction is, " Let not the adorning" of
Christian wives—and the remark is applicable to Christian
women generally—" let not their adorning" be that outward
adorning of plaiting the hair, and of wearing of gold, and of
putting on of apparel. Some have considered these words,
and the corresponding words in the First Epistle to Timothy,
" In like manner that women adorn themselves in modest
apparel, with shame-facedness and sobriety; not with broi-
dered hair, or gold, or pearls, or costly array,"[2] as an absolute prohibition of Christian women, artificially to dress their
hair, to wear ornaments composed of gold, silver, and precious stones, or to clothe themselves in any garment but
what is plain and unadorned. I think Christian women
may very easily fall into more dangerous misinterpretations
of the Scripture than this; yet I have no doubt it is a misinterpretation. The words before us do not contain a
positive prohibition of all ornamental dress; but they are a
statement that these ornaments were not for a moment to be
compared to ornaments of a higher kind. " I will have
mercy and not sacrifice," means I prefer mercy to sacrifice.
And the passage before us means, pay more, far more, atten-

---

[1] Jer. ii. 32.   [2] 1 Tim. ii. 9.

tion to the adorning of your minds and hearts with Christian graces and virtues, than of your bodies with jewels and splendid apparel.

At the same time, I have no doubt that these words were intended to suggest some very important hints as to the principles on which Christian women should regulate their dress. Christian women should carefully avoid every thing which has the appearance of immodesty or levity in dress. Abandoned women were, in the apostle's time, distinguished by their very great attention to external ornament. Christian women, on the contrary, must adorn themselves in modest apparel. It is most unbecoming that a woman, professing godliness, should wear the attire of a mere woman of the world, much more the attire of a harlot. No fashion can sanction such a mode of dress.

Christian women should also avoid undue expense in their mode of dress. It cometh of evil when Christian females aspire to, and indulge in, a richness of apparel and ornament, which is unsuitable to their rank in life, and which curtails their means of Christian beneficence, especially in clothing the poor. " Such excessive costliness," says the good archbishop, " both argues and feeds the pride of the heart, and defrauds, if not others of their dues, yet the poor of their charity, which in God's sight is a due debt, too ; and far more comfort shalt thou have on thy death-bed to remember that at such a time, instead of putting lace on my own clothes, I helped a naked back to clothing; I abated somewhat of my former superfluities to supply the poor with necessities ; far sweeter will this be than to remember that I could needlessly cast out many pounds to serve my pride, while I grudged a penny to relieve the poor."

There is still another hint which this negative injunction is intended and fitted to give. That dress should not occupy an undue share of the attention and time of Christian wives. The apostle intimates that it is a very subordinate thing. No Christian woman will suffer the adorning of her body to be either her business or her delight. She will

not render herself responsible at the bar of God for the
work of hours, days, weeks, months, in a long life of years,
which might, which ought to, have been otherwise and
more worthily employed, in a way more becoming rational,
responsible, immortal beings.   Listen to the good archbishop again : " To have the mind taken and pleased with
such things is so foolish and childish a thing, that if most
might not find it in themselves, they would wonder at many
others of years and common wit, not twice children, but always ; and yet truly it is a disease that few escape.   It is
strange upon what poor things men and women will be vain
and think themselves somebody ; not only upon some comeli-
ness in their form or features, which, though poor enough, is
yet a part of themselves, but of things merely without
them ; that they are well apparelled, either richly or well
in fashion.   Light, empty minds are as bladders, blown up
with any thing ; and they that perceive not this in themselves are most deluded ; but such as have found it out,
and abhor their own follies, are still hunting and following
them to beat them out of their hearts, and to shame themselves out of such fopperies.   The soul fallen from God hath
lost its true worth and beauty, and therefore it basely de-
scends to these mean things, to serve and dress the body,
and to take share with it of its unworthy borrowed ornaments, while it hath lost and forgotten God, and seeks not
after him, knows not that he alone is the beauty and ornament of the soul, and his Spirit and his graces its rich attire."

This naturally leads to the apostle's positive injunction
regarding ornaments.   It is in these words : " But let it be
the hidden man of the heart, in that which is not corruptible ; even the ornament of a meek and quiet spirit, which
is in the sight of God, of great price."   The general meaning here is plain enough.   There is some difficulty, however,
in fixing the construction of the passage, which is obviously,
to some extent, elliptical.   The precise meaning, of course,
varies according as the words are construed.   Some would

construe them thus: " Let your adorning not be that outward adorning of plaiting the hair, and of wearing of gold,
or of putting on of apparel; but let it be the hidden man
of the heart," the new creature, ' the inner man,' the holy
character, which springs out of the faith of the truth, " in
that which is incorruptible," which is, not like gold and jewels
put on thy corruptible body, but which inheres in the incorruptible mind, " the ornament of a meek and quiet spirit,
which in the sight of God is of great price." Others would
construe them thus: " Let the hidden man of the heart, in
contrast to the outward man of the body, be adorned with
the incorruptible ornament of a meek and quiet spirit, in
contrast with the corruptible ornaments of gold and apparel—an ornament, which in the sight of God is of great
price, in contrast with the estimation in which men hold
external ornaments." The latter construction seems to me
to bring out most exactly the Apostle's thought, which let
us now endeavour shortly to illustrate.

" The inner man of the heart" is just the heart, which is
the inner man. The heart in its ordinary figurative sense
is the mind of man considered both as the seat of intellect
and of affection, the soul. Christian women, indeed all
Christians, whether men or women, should be most solicitous
about the welfare and the ornament, not of the outer man,
the body, but of this inner man, the soul. And the ornaments with which it is to be adorned must be suitable to
its nature; they must be incorruptible. The soul is indestructible and immortal; and so should its ornaments be.
The appropriate ornaments of the soul are truth and holiness, knowledge, faith, hope, love, joy, humility, and all the
other gifts and graces of the Spirit, wisdom, prudence,
fortitude, gentleness; these are the jewels with which the
inner man should be adorned. The outward man is corruptible. Dust it is, and unto the dust must it return.
However stately and strong, and graceful and beautiful, it
must, ere long, be a mass of putrefaction, a ghastly skeleton,
a heap of bones, a heap of dust, indistinguishable from the

dust by which it is surrounded. And all its ornaments are, like itself, destructible. Moth and worm destroy the richest garments; silver and gold are perishable things. Gold, though tried with the fire, perishes. But neither time nor eternity can destroy either the soul or its appropriate ornaments. The soul is immortal; these ornaments are not put on it; they are essential qualities of itself, and while it endures, they must endure.

There is particular notice taken of one of these imperishable ornaments, of which it was the duty of the Christian wives to see that that they were possessed, " the ornament of a meek and quiet spirit." Nothing is more ornamental to a Christian wife than a meek and quiet spirit. No deformity is more unsightly than its reverse; a discontented, fretful, peevish, domineering spirit. Hateful every where; it is no where more hateful than in woman; in no woman so hateful as in a wife. Hear the declaration of the inspired Israelitish sage: " A continual dropping in a very rainy day, and a contentious woman, are alike. It is better to dwell in the corner of a housetop alone than with a brawling woman in a wide house. It is better to dwell in the wilderness than with a contentious and angry woman. Whoso hideth her hideth the wind, and the ointment of the right hand, which bewrayeth itself."[1] How beautiful, on the other hand, is the Christian woman who, amid the endlessly perplexing details of domestic management, maintains an unruffled temper, and in Christian patience possesses her soul. It is a lovely picture which has been drawn of a Christian wife, as " one who can feel neglects and unkindnesses, and yet retain her composure; who can calmly remonstrate and meekly reprove; who can yield and accommodate; who is not ' easily provoked,' and is ' easily entreated;' who would endure rather than complain, and would rather suffer in secret than disturb others with her grief."[2]

This ornament, and the whole class it belongs to, is " in the

---

[1] Prov. xxvii. 15; xxv. 24; xxi. 19.   [2] Jay.

sight of God of great price." One of the reasons why many
females are so fond of fine clothes and rich ornaments is,
that these are admired by others. But by whom are they
admired? By men, and most admired by the least wise
and worthy of the species, men whose opinion is little
worth. But this ornament of the hidden man of the heart
is " in the sight of God of great price." He who alone
has wisdom admires it. Yes, " he looks to, he dwells with,
the meek, the humble, the lowly heart." And his approbation is of more value than that of all the other beings in the
universe. " Not she who commendeth herself, not she
whom men commend, is approved, but she whom God commendeth." The meek and quiet spirit, like faith, will " be
found to glory and honour and praise at the coming of our
Lord Jesus." [1] In that day, the man who for his genius,
learning, or successful ambition, excited the wonder of
nations, and whose praises were celebrated from age to age,
and through widely distant countries, but who never obtained, because he never sought, the honour that cometh
down from above, shall be filled with shame, covered with contempt; while the woman of a meek and quiet spirit, who in
the retirement of very lowly domestic life, performed conscientiously the laborious duties, and sustained patiently the varied
trials of her humble sphere, from regard to the authority of
God, and under the constraining influence of the love of his
Son, shall be seen to be " glorious within," one whom the King
of kings delights to honour, and to whom he will say, in the
presence of assembled men and angels, " Well done, good
and faithful servant; enter thou into the joy of thy Lord."

" Men think it poor and mean to be meek. Nothing is
more exposed to contempt than the spirit of meekness. It
is mere folly with men: but that is no matter: this over-
weighs all their disesteem: 'It is with God of great price.'
And these are indeed as he values them, and no otherwise.
Though it be not the country's fashion, yet it is the fashion

---

[1] Isa. lxvi. 2.   2 Cor. x. 18.

at court, yea, it is the king's own fashion : Learn of me, says he, for I am meek and lowly in heart. 'And when he girds on his sword, and rides forth prosperously, it is for meekness, and truth, and righteousness. Some that are court-bred, will send for the prevailing fashions there, though they live not at court : and though the peasants think them strange dresses, yet they regard not that; but use them as finest and best. Care not what the world say; you are not to stay long with them. Desire to have both your fashions and your stuffs from heaven. The robe of humility, the garment of meekness, will be sent you.' Wear them, for his sake who sends them you. He will be pleased to see you in them; and is this not enough? 'It is never right in any thing with us till we attain to this; to tread on the opinion of men, and eye nothing but God's approbation.'"[1]

It may perhaps be worth while noticing, before closing this part of the discourse, that the greatest of all the Grecian philosophers, Plato, has a passage which strikingly resembles that which we have been illustrating : " Behaviour, and not gold, is the ornament of a woman. To courtezans, these things, jewels and ornaments, are advantageous to their catching more admirers; but for a woman who wishes to enjoy the favour of one man, good behaviour is the proper ornament, and not dresses. And you should have the blush upon your countenance, which is the sign of modesty, instead of paint; and worth and sobriety, instead of gold and emeralds."[2] It is impossible not to notice the similarity; but it is as impossible not at the same time to notice the superiority. The philosopher is entirely of the earth, earthy. The Apostle brings the authority of God, and the power of the unseen world, distinctly into view. While Plato leads wives to seek exclusively the honour which comes from men, Peter teaches them to seek the honour that cometh down from God ; the true judge of excellence, the great fountain of honour.

[1] Leighton.   [2] Plato de Repub.

II.—MOTIVES ADDRESSED TO CHRISTIAN WIVES TO THE PERFORMANCE OF THEIR DUTIES.

§ 1. *The probability of Converting their Husbands.*

Let us proceed now to the consideration of the motives by which the discharge of these duties is recommended. The first of these motives is drawn from the probability that, by following the course enjoined, the Christian wife might be the means of converting to the faith and obedience of Christ, her heathen or Jewish husband. Christian wives are to be in subjection to their husbands ; they are to have a chaste conversation, mingled with fear. They are to adorn themselves, not so much outwardly, by having the body ornamented, plaiting of hair, wearing of gold, or putting on of apparel ; as inwardly, by having the mind adorned with the ornament of a meek and quiet spirit, in order that such husbands as have not been converted by the word, may be won to the faith of Christ by "the conversation ;" that is, the character and conversation of their wives.

The Apostle here obviously goes on the supposition, that a Christian woman may have for her husband a man who is not a Christian. Then, as now, the wife might be an heir of glory, and the husband a son of perdition. The closest natural alliance might be associated with the most complete spiritual disunion ; and between persons who are so intimately connected, as to be no longer twain, but one flesh, in reference to spiritual character, privilege, and hope, there might be a great gulf fixed. They who have civilly all things common, spiritually may have nothing common : no common principles, no common feelings, no common hopes or fears, joys or sorrows.

This is very far from being a desirable state of things. On the part of the converted person, it must be the source of constant and most fearful anxiety and temptation ; and this just in proportion to the degree of his or her piety, and of the love cherished to the unconverted partner. It is a state of things into which a very rare peculiarity of circumstances can make it even innocent for a Christian to enter. Some Christian moralists have held that there is no combination of circumstances which can do this; but that in every case, for a Christian to contract marriage with an unbeliever, is a direct violation of the law of Christ. To this opinion I was myself at one time an adherent; but on further reflection I must say, that this appears to me to be taking higher ground than the Scripture warrants. The two passages of Scripture commonly quoted in support of this sentiment, when carefully examined, will be found incapable of answering the purpose. The first of these passages: "Be not unequally yoked together with unbelievers,"[1] obviously refers to church fellowship, and not to the marriage relation, as must be obvious to every person, who reads it in its connexion. The second of them, where the Christian widow is said to be at liberty to marry whom she will, "only in the Lord,"[2] does not mean that she must marry a Christian man, or remain unmarried; but that, in using her liberty, she ought to act as a person "in the Lord," in a manner becoming a saint: just as when Christian children are required to obey their parents in the Lord, the meaning is, not that they obey their parents if they be Christians, but that they obey their parents as Christians are bound to do.

It is quite a possible case, that it may be a Christian's duty to marry, where it may be impossible for him to obtain a Christian partner; and it is to be recollected, that marriage is a secular, not a religious relation. At the same time, these cases are of very rare occurrence; and generally speaking, the Christian who does not marry a Christian, does not act like a Christian. In all ordinary circumstances, for a Christian to marry a person, with the distinct understanding that that person is not a Christian, or indeed without satisfactory evidence that he or she is a Christian, is equally criminal and unwise. The principles and the his-

[1] 2 Cor. vi. 14.   [2] 1 Cor. vii. 39.

tory of Scripture are equally opposed to such connexions; and I believe that there are few violations of Christian duty that are more frequently, indeed all but uniformly, and severely punished than this. The consideration which, in some such cases, has blinded the eyes of individuals to the impropriety and folly of such conduct; the hope of becoming useful, in the highest sense of the word, to an object of affection, by becoming the means of conversion, is plainly most fallacious. We must not do evil that good may come: and it should be remembered, that if there may be conversion on the one side, there may be perversion on the other. And in the whole circumstances of the case, the latter may be the more probable of the two events. The sad result of the marriages of the anti-religious sons of God with the daughters of men, is recorded in Scripture, as a beacon, to warn all succeeding generations against such unnatural and unhallowed connexions.

But a Christian woman may, without fault on her part, find herself the wife of an unconverted man. It is a possible thing that she may have been deceived in her estimate of the character of him whom she has chosen for her companion through life. The mask of religion is often assumed to serve a purpose; and sometimes it has so much the appearance of reality, that it is not wonderful that mistakes, sad mistakes, are committed by the inexperienced; or, what is of much more frequent occurrence, and to which, in all probability, the Apostle refers, both were in a state of unconversion when the marriage relation was formed, but a change in the wife has taken place subsequently. She, under Divine influence, has been led to embrace a vital Christianity, while her husband remains destitute of, or opposed to it; "dead in trespasses and in sins." She becomes a subject of Jesus Christ, while he continues a rebel. What probably would have prevented, what, in ordinary circumstances, ought to have prevented, marriage, does not dissolve it. The Christian wife is not warranted to withdraw from her unconverted husband on that ground. She

must continue with him, and perform to him all the duties
of an affectionate and respectful wife. She must be in
subjection to her own husband, probably more in subjection
than ever, for her conversion will likely have greatly widened
her view of conjugal duty, and deepened her sense of its
obligation.

The situation referred to is a very trying one, and the
Apostle proposes a very powerful and encouraging motive to
a discharge of its difficult duties. He holds out the hope of
the Christian wife becoming the means of the salvation of
her husband. He supposes a very bad case : he supposes
that the husband has not " obeyed the word," that is, " the
word of the truth of the gospel ;" he has resisted its claims
on his attention, faith, and obedience. The Christian wife,
no doubt, has endeavoured to bring him within the reach of
the Christian preacher's voice : it may be, he refused to come ;
or he came, but departed unimpressed, unbelieving : it may
be scoffing and blaspheming. The Christian wife, if she
acts in character, will use more private means to bring her
husband under the influence of the word, by reading the
Scriptures and other good books, if she can get him to listen
to them ; and by wisely and affectionately, with her own living voice, endeavouring to convey to him the saving truth ;
but all may be in vain, all often has been in vain, apparently
worse than in vain ; so that all direct attempts to effect a
change have to be abandoned, as likely to do mischief rather
than good, hardening prejudice, provoking resistance.

Still the Christian wife must not despair ; especially she
must not be weary in the well-doing of a conscientious performance of her conjugal duties ; and the motive, the all-
powerful, the sweetly constraining motive, so full of power
over the principles of the Christian, and the affections of the
wife, is : and " what knowest thou, O woman, whether thou
shalt save thy husband ?" Even without the word, which he
will not obey, he may be gained by thy chaste conversation,
obviously based on and sustained by Christian piety. It has
been said justly, that " men who are prejudiced observe

actions a great deal more than words."[1] The cheerful,
affectionate, constant performance of all conjugal duties,
especially when it is made quite plain that this is the result
of Christian principle, is fitted to make impression even on
unthinking and insensible men. The difference which conversion has made to the better on the relative conduct of the
wife, almost necessarily leads the husband's mind to what
has produced it, and gives birth to the thought, ' that cannot
be a bad thing which produces such good effects.' His prejudices are gradually weakened. By and by he, it may be,
voluntarily commences to talk on a subject on which formerly he had angrily forbidden all conversation, accompa-
nies his wife to the Christian assembly, and ultimately listens
to, believes, and obeys the word which he had formerly
rejected. " A life of undissembled holiness, and heavenliness,
and self-denial, and meekness, and love, and mortification,
is a powerful sermon, which, if you be constantly preaching
before those who are near you, will hardly miss of a good
effect. Works are more palpably significant than words
alone."[2] This is the natural tendency of a quiet, cheerful,
persevering performance of conjugal duty to unconverted
husbands; not only to those who are good and gentle, but even
to those who are froward; and by the accompanying blessing
of the good Spirit, this has not unfrequently been its blessed
effect.

There is something very beautiful in the phraseology in
which the conversion of the Jewish or heathen husband is
described. He is said to be " won." He was lost; lost to
true happiness; lost, continuing in his present state, for eternity; but when he is brought to the knowledge of the truth,
he is won, gained, gained to himself, gained to the Saviour,
" added," as Leighton says, " to His treasury, who thought
not his own precious blood too dear to lay out for this gain."

The motive here presented to a truly Christian woman is
certainly a very cogent one. Its force has been finely

---

[1] Αφωνον εργον κρεισσον ατρακτου λογου.—ŒCUMENIUS.   [2] Baxter.

brought out by a great living preacher : " The salvation of
a soul ! the salvation of a husband's soul ! O seek that ye
lose not him who is so dear to you, ' in the valley of the
shadow of death.' See that the parting at death be not a
final parting. Let your friendship survive the desolations of
time, and be renewed to infinite advantage beyond the
grave. To the tie that nothing but death can sever, seek
to add one which defies even his power to cut asunder.
Think, O wife, of the happiness which will result from the
success of your endeavours. What pleasure will attend the
remainder of your days, now of one heart and of one mind.
How sweet will be the counsel you can now take together.
How delightful to go to the house of God in company. How
enlivening to add the *our* Father of the family altar to the
my Father of the closet, which witnessed your wrestling with
God, that he whom you loved might also be led to say *my*
Father. And what will be your joy and crown of rejoicing
in that day when, before assembled men and angels, he will
say : ' Blessed be the providence which attached us in
yonder world, and has still more united us in this. " The
woman thou gavest me to be with me," led me not to " the
tree of knowledge of good and evil ;" but to the tree of life
which is in the midst of the paradise of God." '[1] The practical effect which the pressing of this motive should have on
the Christian wife is excellently expressed by one of the fathers of the church : " Let a prudent woman first of all
endeavour to persuade her husband to become partaker with
her in those things which lead to blessedness ; but if he
prove impracticable, let her still apply with all diligence to
a virtuous life, in every thing yielding obedience to her husband, and doing nothing contrary to his will, except in such
things as are reckoned essential to virtue and salvation."[2]

§ 2. *The example of holy women in former ages.*

The second motive presented by the Apostle to Christian

---

[1] Jay.   [2] Clem. Alex.

wives to stimulate and encourage them in the performance
of their conjugal duties is, that in doing so they would follow the example of holy women in former ages : " For after
this manner, in the old time, the holy women also, who
trusted in God, adorned themselves. Even as Sarah obeyed
Abraham, calling him lord, whose daughters ye are as long
as ye do well, and are not afraid with any amazement."
There is a natural tendency in the human mind to regard
with veneration the characters of those distinguished for
sanctity who lived in distant ages ; and it is an additional
recommendation to any course of conduct urged on us, that
it was followed by those to whom we have been accustomed
to look up as models. The good women whose names are
recorded in the book of God, such as Sarah and Hannah,
were with the pious Hebrews objects of affectionate admira-
tion. They deserved to be so. Their sanctity and purity
of manners, for they were " holy," joined to their piety, for
they " trusted in God," made them objects of the love, fit
models for the imitation of their descendants. They were
in subjection to their own husbands, had a chaste conversation, coupled with fear. They adorned less the seen man
of the body than the hidden man of the heart ; and their ornaments were not so much golden jewels or costly apparel,
as the meek and humble spirit, which is, in the sight of God,
of great price. No one who is not thus characterised can
share the honour which belongs to these illustrious females.
Every one who is thus characterised does share their honour.
However inferior in her talents, however obscure in her
situation, however poor in her circumstances ; every such
woman, every such wife, is recognised as a daughter of
Sarah, a sister of Hannah, and the other holy women who
" built the house of Jacob, and did worthily in the families of
Israel."[1]

Sarah is particularly noticed as having obeyed Abraham,
and as having shown her respect for him, by calling him

[1] Ruth iv. 11.

lord. The particular instances in which Sarah obeyed
Abraham are not distinctly specified by the Apostle. It has
been supposed that the reference may be to her obeying
Abraham's voice, when he obeyed Jehovah in leaving the
land of their nativity, where they had many relations and
probably abundant possessions, to go forth into a land of
which they knew no more than that Jehovah should afterwards tell them of it; and to her yielding up Isaac, her only
son, the son of the promise, the son of her old age, to the
disposal of his father, when he received the strange command to take him and offer him up for a burnt-offering. If
in these two trying cases Sarah did yield a ready obedience
to her husband's expressed will, she well deserves to be represented as a model to wives in succeeding ages. The reference,
however, does not seem so much to particular instances as
to the habit of obedience. Indeed, in one instance at least,
she seems to have carried her disposition to obey her husband to an extreme; for when he instructed her to equivo-
cate in Egypt, and represent herself as his sister, she would
have done well respectfully to have replied "I must obey
God rather than my husband." Her exemplary character
as a wife was manifested also in the manner in which she
was accustomed to address her husband; she called him
lord. Though of the same rank with her husband, a
member of the same family, and distinguished by peculiar
honours as the mother of the son of the promise, she never
thought herself above the humblest duties of her station,
but habitually reverenced her husband.

It deserves notice as a proof how ready God is to approve
of, and to testify his approbation of what is good in the conduct of his people, that the speech of which this compellation
was a part, was in substance an expression of unbelief respecting the promise of God, for which at the time she was
severely reprimanded; yet here, after the lapse of so many
ages, she is spoken honourably of for the only good thing in
that unhappy speech, a becoming expression of respectful
regard for her husband. How readily does God pardon the

sins of the upright in heart! And how highly does he estimate, how graciously does he accept, their poorest services!
He does " not forget" them.[1]

Sarah was highly honoured among the pious Jews as the
wife of Abraham, the father of the faithful; and the mother
of Isaac, the son of the promise. A daughter of Sarah was
to the Jewish women an appellation of similar desirable-
ness and dignity, as to a Jewish man, a son of Abraham.
All truly Christian women were daughters of Sarah, as all
truly Christian men were sons of Abraham : " Children, according to the promise; not of the bondwoman, but of the
free." [2]

There is more true honour connected with this spiritual
lineage than springs from deriving our birth

> " From loins enthron'd, or sovereigns of the earth." [3]

Now this honour belongs to all Christian wives " so long as
they do well." While they discharge the duties of their station
from proper motives, and in a proper manner, they will be
reckoned the heirs of her faith, sharers in her honours; they
will be blessed with obedient Sarah and faithful Abraham.
The Apostle's declaration goes on the same principle as our
Lord's, " If ye were the children of Abraham, ye would do
the works of Abraham." [4] Doing the works of Sarah, ye
prove yourselves to be her daughters.

The Apostle adds, " And are not afraid with any amazement." There is some difficulty in fixing the precise meaning and reference of these words. I shall state to you in a
very few words what I consider as the most probable interpretation that has been given them. The best principles
may be carried to extremes. The duties we owe to superiors
are not likely to be performed with propriety and regularity,
if we have not a respect for their persons and a fear of their
displeasure; but this may easily become excessive. This fear
of man in all its forms brings a snare. It was the duty of

---

[1] Gen. xviii. 12. Heb. vi. 10.   [2] Gal. iii. 29; iv. 31.
[3] Cowper.   [4] John viii. 39.

the Christian wives of heathen husbands to respect and fear them; and to show this by a ready obedience to their lawful commands, a ready compliance with their lawful appointments; but they must not allow their fear of their husbands to lead them to neglect their duty as Christians, or to violate the law of their Lord and Master. This was a strong temptation, for heathen husbands were often very arbitrary; and the existing laws as well as customs, put the happiness of their wives in their power to a degree of which, from the state of things which the progress of religion, and civilisation, and law has produced in this country, we happily can form but an inadequate conception. So long as the will of their husbands did not run counter to the will of their Lord, they could scarcely be too submissive; but when they forbade what he commanded, or commanded what he forbade, then the reply must be ready to be respectfully made and steadily acted out, " We must obey God rather than man." " I am under strong obligations to you, but I am under infinitely stronger obligations to him. I would not willingly incur your displeasure, but I dare not subject myself to his indignation."

And so it must be still. Every Christian wife must remember that she has higher duties than those she owes to her husband, even those she owes to her God and Saviour; and whenever these come, as they sometimes do, into competition, she must not be " afraid with any amazement," but calmly say, I would willingly do and suffer very much for my nearest and dearest earthly relation, but I will not sin for him. His lordship does not extend to my mind and conscience; as to these, I have one Lord, the Lord who bought me; my Master is in heaven. In this case, as in every other of a similar kind, it is proper that the individual should carefully guard against mistaking humour for principle; be very sure that the compliance with a husband's will is indeed incompatible with obedience to a Saviour's, before such a course is adopted; but when this is made clearly out to the conscience, there must be no hesitation;

we must deny ourselves, our best, most useful, human affections, and follow him. If in this sense a child do not hate his father, a brother his sister, a wife her husband, they are not fit for being Christ's disciples. In matters of conscience all Christians, whether men or women, whatever relation in domestic or civil society they may occupy, must be principled, decided, resolute, firm. All Christians of whatever sex, and in whatever station, must " add to their faith knowledge," to enable them to discern their various duties, to understand their various obligations and their comparative strength; " and to faith" and " knowledge," or enlightened faith, he must add " virtue," that is, fortitude to enable them at all hazards to perform the one and discharge the other.[1] They must learn not to be afraid of man's terror, neither be troubled, but sanctify the Lord God in their heart, and make him their fear and their dread; and fearing him they will know no other fear. An enlightened fear of God will equally lead a Christian wife to yield all due respect and obedience to her husband, and to refuse that species and degree of respect and obedience which are due only to God.

This superiority to fear in matters of duty, seems spoken of as a point of resemblance to Sarah. It is plain from the slight hints we have in Genesis, that she was not deficient in firmness of character, which sprung out of the faith ascribed to her in the 11th chapter of the Epistle to the Hebrews; and the hope in God by which she, in common with the other holy women, was characterised.

It may not be improper to state that a somewhat different view has been entertained of the reference and design of this concluding clause. In the very passage where Sarah's respect for her husband, manifested in her calling him lord, is recorded, she is represented as, under the influence of fear, denying the truth: " Then Sarah," it is said, " denied, for she was afraid."[2] To this, it has been supposed, that the

---

[1] 2 Pet. i. 5.   [2] Gen. xviii. 15.

Apostle refers, as if he said, ' Imitate Sarah in what was good, but avoid her failings. Honour your husband, but guard against such fear as would lead you, like Sarah, acting incongruously with her character as a holy woman trusting in God, to deny the truth.'

Such is the Apostle's view of the duties of Christian wives, and of the motives which ought to stimulate them to the habitual performance of them. As might be expected there is a peculiar reference to the circumstances in which Christian females were placed at the period in which the Epistle was written, among the nations amid whom those Christians dwelt, to whom it was addressed; but in all its essential principles it is equally applicable to all ages and to all countries. The individual who realizes the force of these motives, and exemplifies these precepts, habitually in heart, temper, and behaviour, whatever station she occupies, is a blessing to society, an ornament to the Church of God. Happy is the man who has such a wife. He who has found such a wife has found a good thing, and has obtained favour of the Lord. Happy are the children who have such a mother, happy the family who have such a mistress, happy the congregation which has many such members. " Such a gracious woman retaineth honour." " Her children rise up and call her blessed; her husband also, and he praiseth her. Favour is deceitful, and beauty is vain; but a woman that feareth the Lord, she shall be praised. Give her of the fruit of her hands, and let her own works praise her in the gates."[1]

PART II.

Out of all the relations in which human beings can be placed to each other, whether as superiors, or inferiors, or equals, grow mutual obligations, and reciprocal duties. In no case is the one party free and the other bound. Each has his peculiar right, and each his peculiar duties. The

[1] Prov. xxxi. 30, 31.

child has rights, as well as the parent; the servant has rights, as well as the master; the subject has rights, as well as the magistrate; and, as a necessary consequence of this, the parent has duties as well as the child; the master as well as the servant, the magistrate as well as the subject. In none of the relations of human society, can the one party with truth say to the other, you are my debtor, but I owe you nothing. The debt of love is a debt which, though we should constantly be paying to all, we never can discharge to any. We must all ever owe love to all; and the particular form in which the various instalments of this inextinguishable debt is to be paid by one individual to another, depends on the relation which subsists between them, and is indeed just the appropriate duty of that relation. We find the Apostle Peter applying this principle, in his statements of the duties of the fundamental and primary relation, of domestic life, that of husband and wife. He has stated and enforced the duties of the wife; he has taught the Christian wife what she owes to her husband, even to her unconverted husband, and why she should be conscientious in discharging this debt. He has explained her duty, and the motives by which it is enforced. He now proceeds to show Christian husbands that they have duties as well as rights; and that while they have important claims on their wives, their wives have important claims on them; claims, certainly, not the less sacred and cogent, that they to whom they belong have, in comparatively rare instances, the means of authoritatively enforcing them.

I. THE DUTIES OF CHRISTIAN HUSBANDS.

The view of the duty of the husband to the wife, given by the Apostle, is like that given by him of the duty of the wife to the husband, accompanied with a statement of some of the motives, which urge to its performance. My object, in the remaining part of this discourse, is to unfold the meaning of the Apostle's injunctions, and to point out the appropriateness and force of the considerations which he adduces in support of these injunctions.

You will observe, that my object is not to give you a full account of the duties of husbands, and of the motives enforcing them. Had that been my design I should have taken for my subject the whole of the Christian law, as laid down in the following passages of Scripture, passages which I hope every husband in this assembly has engraved on the tablet, not only of his memory, but of his heart. " Husbands, love your wives, even as Christ also loved the Church, and gave himself for it, that he might sanctify and cleanse it with the washing of water by the word; that he might present it to himself a glorious Church, not having spot, or wrinkle, or any such thing, but that it should be holy, and without blemish. So ought men to love their wives as their own bodies, for he who loveth his wife loveth himself: for no man ever yet hated his own flesh, but nourisheth and cherisheth it, even as the Lord the Church : for we are members of his body, of his flesh, and of his bones. For this cause shall a man leave his father and mother, and shall be joined to his wife, and they two shall be one flesh. This is a great mystery : but I speak concerning Christ and the Church. Nevertheless, let every one of you, in particular, so love his wife even as himself. Husbands love your wives, and be not bitter against them."[1]

My object is a much more limited one. Taking for granted, with the Apostle, that the husbands addressed, were possessed of that peculiar affection, without the possession of the elements of which the marriage relation ought never to be formed, and without the careful cultivation and steady development of which, the duties of that relation cannot be performed, nor its comforts enjoyed, I mean to confine myself to those manifestations of this principle, and those motives urging to these manifestations, to which the Apostle's object naturally led him particularly to advert, in

---

[1] Eph. v. 25-33. Col. iii. 19.

showing the Christians to whom he was writing, living in the midst of heathens ignorant of their religion, how to " have their conversation honest among the Gentiles, that so with well-doing they might put to silence the ignorance of foolish men." For this purpose he exhorts Christian subjects and Christian servants to be particularly attentive to their civil and domestic duties ; for this purpose he exhorts Christian wives to be exemplary in all their conjugal duties ; and for this purpose he, in our text, exhorts Christian husbands to " dwell with their wives according to knowledge, giving honour unto the wife as to the weaker vessel, and as being heirs of the grace of life, that their prayers be not hindered."

A certain degree of obscurity is cast over this passage, by the manner in which it is construed in our version. I should think few intelligent persons have ever read the passage without feeling as if the first reason given for honouring the wife, were a somewhat paradoxical one. It seems very plain, that the Christian husband should honour the Christian wife, because she is equally with himself an " heir of the grace of life ;" but it seems odd, that her being the weaker vessel should be assigned as a reason why she should be *honoured*. It is a very good, a very persuasive reason, to sympathize with her, to help her, to be kind to her; but it does not seem to have much cogency in it as a reason for honouring her. On looking into the text, as it came from the Apostle's pen, there appears no trace of this apparent incongruity. The words translated, " to the wife, as to the weaker vessel,"[1] and which might, with equal propriety, be rendered, " with the wife as with the weaker vessel," immediately follow the words, " dwell according to knowledge," and precede, instead of following, as we would naturally suppose from our version, the words, " giving honour." They are plainly intended to qualify the first clause, just as the words, " as being heirs of the grace of life," are intended to qualify the second. The wife being the weaker vessel is

---

[1] ʽΩς ασθινιστιρω σχιυιι τω γυναιχιιω.

the reason why the husband should " dwell with her according to knowledge ;" just as her being a fellow heir of the grace
of life, is the reason why he should honour her ;[1] and the
importance of presenting any hindrance to their prayers, is
a motive equally bearing on both of the duties enjoined.
The method, then, which seems best fitted to bring out the
meaning and force of the text is, first, to explain the first injunction, " Dwell with the wife according to knowledge,"
and its appropriate motive : " She is the weaker vessel ;"
then the second injunction, and its appropriate motive:
" Honour her, as she is a joint heir of the grace of life ;"
and, finally, the concluding consideration, which is equally
fitted for giving force to both these injunctions.

§ 1.—*To " dwell with the wife according to knowledge, as
being the weaker vessel."*

Let us now proceed to the illustration of the first injunction, and its appropriate motive ; " likewise ye husbands
dwell according to knowledge, with the wife, that is, each with
his own wife, as being the weaker vessel." Let the husband
dwell with his wife. Let him dwell with her according to
knowledge. What is the meaning of these expressions ?
The expression, let the husband dwell with his wife, seems
naturally to suggest the idea that, in the Apostle's estimation, each family should have a separate habitation ; that
they should not only dwell in the same house, but that as
every man should have his own wife, and every woman her
own husband, every man and wife should have their own house.
The son when he becomes a husband, should " leave his
father and mother, and cleave to his wife."[2] This is the
arrangement dictated by nature and reason, an arrangement
seldom disregarded without uncomfortable consequences.
Different households should have in all ordinary circumstances different houses. Many dishonourable things

---

[1] Ὃς bis hic ponitur : priore loco pertinet ad γνωσιν, alter ad τιμην. Γνωσι
poscit *infirmitas vasis* : Τιμην *co-hereditas* injungit. BENGEL.
[2] Gen. ii. 24.

among the Gentiles, originated in the neglect of this arrangement.

But this, though apparently included in the injunction, does not exhaust its meaning. It plainly implies, that not only should the husband and wife have the same and a separate house, but that the husband as well as the wife should ordinarily, habitually, dwell in that house. Wives are, no doubt, peculiarly bound to be " keepers at home." That is their principal and all but exclusive scene of duty and usefulness; but husbands, too, are bound, in all ordinary circumstances, to make their house their home. " It is absurd," as has been justly said, " for those who have no prospect of dwelling together, to enter into the marriage state ; and they who are already in it, should not be unnecessarily abroad." Circumstances may occur which may make absence from home, even for a considerable time, a duty on the part of the husband, but these are exceptions from the general rule. There is much force in the inspired apothegm, " as a bird that wandereth from her nest, so is a man that wandereth from his place." [1] " Those persons," says Baxter, " live contrary to the nature of this relation, who live a great part of their lives asunder as many do, for worldly respects ; when they have several houses, possessions, or trades, and the husband must live at one, and the wife at the other, for their commodity sake, and only come together once in a week, or in many weeks. Where this is done without great necessity, it is a constant violation of their duties. And so it is for men to go to trade or live beyond sea, or in another land, and leave their wives behind them ; yea, though they have their wives' consent, it is an unlawful course, except in a case of mere necessity or public service, or where they are able to say that the benefits are likely to be greater to the soul and body than the loss. The offices which husbands and wives are bound to perform for one another, are such as for the most part suppose them dwelling under

[1] Prov. xxvii. 8.

the same roof, like the offices of the members of the body for each other, which they cannot perform if they are dismembered and divided." How can a man from home discharge his duties to his household? family devotion, family instruction, family discipline, must all, so far as he is concerned, be neglected.

There are husbands who are seldom from home in the sense now explained, who yet are very deficient in the duty here enjoined, dwelling with their wives. Though never from home in one way, they are but seldom at home in another. Their leisure hours are spent abroad. They seem fonder almost of any society than the society of their wives. It is a shrewd remark, which observation but too fully confirms, "when a married man, a husband, a father, is fond of spending his evenings abroad; it implies something bad, and predicts something worse."[1] To dwell with the wife is to associate with her as the husband's chosen companion and confidential friend. There are some husbands who never consult their wives, and even leave them to learn from a third person matters in which they are deeply concerned. This is not as it should be. He who enters into the spirit of the Apostle's advice, will, amid the occupations of the day, please himself with the thought of enjoying her society in the evening, as the best refreshment after his toils. Her presence will make his own mansion, however humble, far more agreeable to him than any other which he may occasionally visit. The anxieties and cares attendant on her maternal and domestic character he will endeavour to soothe and relieve. When she is happy he will be happy : when she is afflicted he will be afflicted. He will rejoice with her when she rejoices, and weep with her when she weeps. His heart will safely trust in her, and, by a constant interchange of kind offices, he will increase both in her and in himself that entire confidential esteem and love, which makes all relative duties easy and pleasant.[2] This is for the husband to dwell with the wife.

[1] Jay.   [2] Stennett.

But what are we to understand by dwelling with her "according to knowledge?" These words may mean, let the Christian husband, in his intimate and habitual intercourse with his wife, conduct himself like a well instructed Christian man, who knows the law of Jesus Christ, and the powerful motives by which it is enforced. We rather think, however, that the meaning is, let him conduct himself intelligently, wisely, prudently. There is no prescribing particular rules in a case of this kind. " Wisdom is profitable to direct ;" and as it is profitable, so is it necessary. In every department of relative duty, wise consideration, prudent tact, is necessary ; in none more than in the conjugal department. The peace of the family, the comfort, and even the spiritual improvement both of the wife and of the husband, depend on this holy discretion. This knowledge, or wisdom, will enable them to form a just estimate of his wife's character, of her talents, her acquirements, her temper, her foibles, and will lead him to act accordingly. Christian husbands should act circumspectly, not as fools, but as wise. It is the more necessary that such wisdom be exercised, from the difficulty of guarding equally against a foolish fondness, which suffers sin on the object of affection, and a forbidding harshness of demeanour, which disheartens and discourages. The wife is not a servant who can be dismissed; not an ordinary friend, who, if found unsuitable, can be quietly parted with. She is joined to thee by a bond which, in ordinary cases, nothing but death can dissolve. She is the mother of thy children ; regard to her, regard to them, regard to thyself, all require thee to dwell with her according to knowledge. Act wisely, and the results will be unspeakably advantageous. Act foolishly, and there is no saying what the consequences of this, even in one instance, may be. Beware of in any way injuring her; beware of in any way being injured by her. Seek to bless her, and to make her a blessing to you, to your children, to all with whom you are connected.

The Apostle notices particularly one reason why the husband should dwell according to knowledge with the wife. She is " the weaker vessel." The word translated " vessel" seems here to mean framework or fabric. Both man and woman are the framework or fabric of God. Both are weak; but the woman is the weaker. Both in body and mind some women are stronger than some men; but, in ordinary cases, the female, in the human as in other species of living creatures, is weaker than the male. In delicacy of apprehension, both intellectual and moral, and in capacity of passive endurance, the woman's mind is, I apprehend, far superior to the man's. But, generally speaking, the woman is the weaker fabric. She has a feebler corporeal frame; and her mental constitution, especially the sensitive part of it, is such as to require cautious, kind, even tender treatment from those about her. Therefore it is meet that her husband should sustain her weakness, and bear with her infirmities.

It is folly, and is productive of mischief, to treat wives as if they were children. It degrades them in their own estimation, and prevents their improvement; but it is wisdom, and is productive of the best consequences, to treat them as what they are, women, beings of keener sensibilities and feebler frames than ours; and to have a wise, kind consideration for their peculiar privations and sufferings, their wearisome days and sleepless nights, their anxieties and sorrows, their watchings over our sick and dying children, and their angel-like ministrations to ourselves in the season of affliction. The feebleness of their frame should keep husbands in mind of the insecure tenure by which they possess them, and lead them to dwell with them, as they will wish they had done, when they must dwell with them no longer.

The Apostle does not suppose a Christian husband can be intentionally unkind to his wife; but he supposes that from want of consideration, he may do injury in a degree he little thinks, to one whom he loves; and therefore he puts him in mind that his wife is the weaker vessel, and

that it is his duty to dwell with her " according to knowledge." Very worthy men, not at all deficient in good sense
or in good feeling either, but not distinguished by a nice
sensibility, need the hint ; and a great deal of suffering, not
the less severe that it is not designed, and cannot be com-
plained of, might be saved if it were but attended to.

> " It is well to mark how a passing word—
> Too lightly said, and too deeply heard—
> Or a harsh reproof, or a look unkind,
> May spoil the peace of the sensitive mind." [1]

§ 2. " *To honour the wife as a fellow-heir of the grace of
life.*"

The second injunction to Christian husbands is, "Give honour to the wives as being heirs together," or joint-heirs " of
the grace of life." Here, again, we have first the precept, and
then the motive. The Christian husband is to honour his
wife. Some interpreters have supposed that the honour
here spoken of is an honourable maintenance. There can
be no doubt that the word " honour " is repeatedly used with
this signification in the New Testament ; [2] and there is as
little doubt that it is the duty of a husband to give to his
wife all the comforts which his circumstances in life can
afford, and provide for her both while he lives, and, in all
practicable cases, after his death ; but we cannot look at the
close of the sentence without perceiving that it is not to this
that the Apostle refers. It is such honour as properly belongs to the wife as " an heir of the grace of life." It is
quite plain that the Christian husband is supposed to have
a Christian wife ; and he is not to treat her as the heathen
treated their wives, or even as the Jews treated theirs.
He is to view her as spiritually standing on the same level
with himself, being in Christ Jesus, " where there is neither
male nor female," any more than Jew or Greek, bond or
free. He is to esteem her as " a child of God," " a daughter

---

[1] C. Fry.   [2] Matt. xv. 6. 1 Tim. v. 17.   Acts. xxviii. 10.   Τιμαις.

of the Lord God Almighty," "an heir of God, a joint-heir
with Christ Jesus." He is to love her, because Christ loves
her, and because she loves Christ. He is to respect her
as a living image of the Redeemer, having received out of
his fulness grace for grace.

The Apostle particularly notices, that the wives are to be
honoured as equally with their husbands heirs of the grace
of life. "The grace of life." Grace is here favour, the favour of God; not in the sense of the principle in the Divine
mind, but of some signal effect and manifestation of it. The
grace or favour of life is that Divine grace or favour which
consists in life. The "life" referred to is that eternal life
which is "the grace to be brought to us at the coming of
our Lord Jesus," "the gift of God through Jesus Christ
our Lord," "the salvation that is in him, with eternal glory."
"Life is," as Leighton says, "a sweet word, but sweetest of
all in this sense. That life above is indeed only worthy the
name. This we have here, in comparison, let it not be
called life but a continual dying: an incessant journey towards the grave. If you reckon years, it is but a short
moment to him who attains the fullest old age: but reckon
miseries and sorrows, it is long to him who dies young."
This life is the fruit of the Divine favour. It is the GRACE
of life. "If we consider but a little," to quote the good
Archbishop again, "what it is, what we are, that this is the
grace of life, will quickly be out of question with us, and we
shall be most gladly content to hold it thus, by deed of gift,
and shall admire and extol that grace that bestows it."

Christian husbands and Christian wives are equally heirs
of this grace of life; and no consideration is so much fitted
to lead a Christian husband to honour his wife as this. It
has been finely said : "This is that which most strongly
binds these duties on the hearts of husbands and wives, and
indeed most strongly binds their hearts together, and makes
them one. If each be reconciled to God in Christ, and so
heirs of the grace of life, and one with God, then are they
truly one in God, each with other, and that is the surest

and sweetest union that can be. Natural love hath risen very high in some husbands and wives, but the highest of it falls very far short of that which holds in God. Hearts concentrating on him are most excellently one. That love which is cemented by youth and beauty, when these moulder and decay, as they do soon, it fades too. That is somewhat purer, and so more lasting, that holds in a natural or moral harmony of minds; yet these likewise may alter and change by some great accident. But the most refined, most spiritual, and most indissoluble is, that which is knit with the highest and purest spirit. And the ignorance or disregard of this is the true cause of so much bitterness, or so little true sweetness, in the life of most married persons, because God is left out; because they meet not as one in Him. Loth will they be to despise one another that are both bought with the precious blood of one Redeemer, and loth to grieve one another. Being in him brought into peace with God, they will entertain true peace between themselves, and not suffer any thing to disturb it. They have hopes to meet one day, where there is nothing but perfect concord and peace. They will therefore live as heirs of that life here, and make their present state as like to heaven as they can, and so a pledge and evidence of their title to that inheritance of peace which is there laid up for them. And they will not fail to put one another often in mind of these hopes and that inheritance, and to advance and further each other towards it. Where this is not minded, it is to little purpose to speak of other rules. Where neither party aspires to this heirship, live they otherwise as they will, there is one common inheritance [abiding them, one inheritance of everlasting flames; and, as they increase the sin and guiltiness of each other by their irreligious conversation, so that which some of them do wickedly here on no great cause, they shall have full cause for doing there—curse the time of their coming together; and that shall be a piece of their exercise for ever. But happy those persons, in any society of marriage or friendship, who converse so together here as those that shall live so eternally together in glory."[1] The Christian husband, when he realizes these truths, cannot but honour his Christian partner; cannot but treat her with cordial respect, as one, equally with himself, redeemed by the precious blood of Christ; already blessed with many invaluable heavenly and spiritual blessings in Christ, standing in a most dignified relation to the great God our Saviour; already animated by his Spirit and adorned by his image, and destined to be one day perfectly like him, their common life, when he appears in his glory; when she becomes an inheritor of that blessed world where they "do not marry nor are given in marriage, but are as the angels of God."[2]

It is obvious this is a motive, which in its full force can be felt only by a Christian husband, in reference to his duty to a Christian wife. But it suggests strong reason to the Christian husband to do his duty, even in reference to an unconverted wife. She belongs to the race of which Christ is the Saviour. She is capable of becoming an heir of the grace of life; and her husband's discharge of conjugal duties, under the influence of the faith of the gospel, is well calculated to remove prejudice against vital Christianity; and in connexion with other means for her conversion, which Christian principle and conjugal love will induce him to employ, may very probably be blessed, to the joining them together in a union more intimate and sacred than even that of marriage; a union over which the severing stroke of death has no power. "How knowest thou, O man, whether thou shalt save thy wife?"[3]

II.—MOTIVE ADDRESSED TO CHRISTIAN HUSBANDS TO THE DISCHARGE OF THESE DUTIES: "THAT THEIR PRAYERS BE NOT HINDERED."

Having thus shortly illustrated the two injunctions, with the appropriate motives by which they are respectively en-

---

[1] Leighton.   [2] Matt. xxii. 30.   [3] 1 Cor. vii. 16.

forced, let us, ere we close, shortly attend to the general consideration which bears equally on both these injunctions. Christian husbands are to dwell with their wives according to knowledge, and to give honour to them, that their prayers be not hindered. It is plainly taken for granted here, that Christians habitually engage in prayer. "The heirs of life," as Leighton says, "cannot live without prayer: none of them is dumb; they all speak." They all seek intercourse with their heavenly Father. Having the spirit of adoption, they cry, Abba, Father. They pray in secret; and when two of these heirs are brought together in the closest of human relations, they pray together, and a great deal of their improvement and happiness depends on these prayers together and apart. Any thing which hinders the latter materially interferes with the former. Now it is quite plain, that the neglect of conjugal duty on the part of the husband to the wife, is fitted to hinder both his own prayers and the prayers of his wife, and their common prayers. The temper that leads him to neglect his duty to his wife, unfits him for his duty to his God; and though human unkindness, even from our best human friend, should but lead us to go with greater alacrity to Him who is a Friend at all times, yet the jars and contentions of husband and wife, are in their own nature calculated so to embitter the spirit of both, as to unfit for prayer, which should always be presented with holy hands, and must be offered without wrath if it is to be offered without doubting.

There seems a direct reference to family prayers. How can they be attended to at all, if the husband do not dwell with his wife? how can they be usefully attended to, if they dwell not together in unity? How are they likely to come to that agreement in reference to things which they ask, and the temper and disposition in which they ask them, which is so necessary to prayer serving its purpose either on their own minds, or as an appointed means of having our need supplied according to God's glorious fulness? If family prayers are hindered, what hope of family prosperity, in the best sense of the words? and if conjugal duty is neglected, how can they but be hindered? They are in danger of being neglected, or disturbed, or discontinued. Let, then, Christian husbands, and wives too, guard against every thing which may hinder family prayer. Let their whole conduct toward each other look back and forward to the family altar. Let it be consistent with devotion, preparatory to it, indicative of its influence. Avoid whatever makes an introduction into the Divine presence less easy or less delightful. Keep open a passage wide enough to advance together to the throne of grace: go hand in hand. Agree touching the things which ye shall ask, and it shall be done for you of your Father in heaven.[1]

The passage before us is merely a particular application of a great general principle: the connexion between holy conduct and devotional exercises. They act and react on one another. The more conscientiously we perform our various duties, the more will we be disposed, for the more enjoyment will we find in, and the more advantages will we derive from our devotional exercises; and the more we engage in devotional exercises in a right spirit, the more will we be inclined and enabled, in all holy conversation and godliness, to adorn the doctrine of God our Saviour in all things. Calling on the name of the Lord and departing from iniquity are closely conjoined. To secure frequency, constancy, comfort in prayer, we must live holily; and, to secure our living holily, we must be "constant in prayer:" "praying always, with all prayer and supplication, in the Spirit, and watching thereunto with all perseverance."

Thus have I finished my illustrations of the Apostle's exposition and enforcement of conjugal duties. I conclude in the words of an honoured elder brother (Mr Jay), whom I have more than once referred to in the course of this discourse, and whose works generally I most cordially recom-

---

[1] Jay.

mend as a family book : " Let all who stand in the marriage relation be willing to know and practise the duties which spring from it. Enter, my brethren and sisters, the temple of revelation, and bow before the Divine oracle. Say, Lord, what wilt thou have me to do? Speak, Lord, for thy servant heareth. Extract from the Scripture the mind of God concerning yourselves individually. Take home the words I have been explaining. Do not, ye husbands, take away the duties of the wife, nor, ye wives, the duties of the husband, but both of you respectively your own, and say—' O that my feet were directed to keep thy statutes : I have chosen the way of truth; thy judgments have I laid before me : Through thy precepts I get understanding, therefore I hate every false way : I have sworn, and I will perform it, that I will keep thy righteous judgments.' "